D1598420

Reform and Revolution

Raymond Robins, wearing his American Red Cross uniform, overcoat, and hat, taken in a Moscow photographic studio in 1917. (Courtesy of the Elizabeth Robins Papers, Fales Library, New York University.)

Reform and Revolution

*The Life and Times
of Raymond Robins*

Neil V. Salzman

THE KENT STATE UNIVERSITY PRESS
Kent, Ohio, and London, England

© 1991 by The Kent State University Press, Kent, Ohio 44242
All rights reserved
Library of Congress Catalog Card Number 90-5358
ISBN 0-87338-426-1
Manufactured in the United States of America

Library of Congress Cataloging-in-Publication Data

Salzman, Neil V.
   Reform and revolution : the life and times of Raymond Robins.
      p.   cm.
   Includes bibliographical references (p.   ) and index.
   ISBN 0-87338-426-1 (cloth : alk.) ∞
   1. Robins, Raymond, 1873–1954.   2. Diplomats—United States—
Biography.   3. Social reformers—United States—Biography.
4. Soviet Union—History—Revolution, 1917–1921.   5. United States—
Foreign relations—Soviet Union.   6. Soviet Union—Foreign
relations—United States.   7. United States—Foreign
relations—1913–1921.   I. Title.
E748.R657S25   1991
327.2'092—dc20   90-5358
[B]

British Library Cataloging-in-Publication data are available.

To the memory of my father,
Sidney Salzman,
who first shared with me the importance
of many of the themes of this book

Contents

Illustrations

Acknowledgments

The author's work in the preparation of this book has been aided by numerous individuals, without whose suggestions, encouragement, and help it may not have been carried through.

Lisa von Borowsky not only gave the author permission to use the Robins Papers at the State Historical Society of Wisconsin, Madison, and the hitherto "closed" collection of Raymond Robins's letters at the Library of the University of Florida at Gainesville, she also shared her valuable recollections. Ms. von Borowsky's kind hospitality provided the author the opportunity to see Robins's boyhood environment and Chinsegut, the Robins estate. It was during this visit to Florida that some of the earliest papers of Robins were brought to light. (These papers are discussed extensively in the bibliography.) Ms. von Borowsky's insights, as close friend and "daughter" in the Robins household for more than thirty years, have been of inestimable value.

After the publication of his acclaimed *American Russian Relations: 1781–1947* in 1952, Prof. William Appleman Williams began work on a full biography of Robins, being instrumental in having the Robins Papers deposited at the State Historical Society of Wisconsin. Before committing myself to this study I wrote to Professor Williams at Oregon State University. His warm and considerate encouragement was a most important factor in my determination to write this biography. His recent passing is a loss to us all.

Mr. John C. Dreier, Robins's nephew, kindly shared his memories and offered many suggestions. Josephine L. Harper, manuscript curator at the State Historical Society of Wisconsin and Kay Thompson, her assistant, were particularly helpful during my stay at the reading room. Their assistance made the long hours of research comfortable and fruitful. Archie Motley, at the Chicago Historical Society, provided valuable research suggestions based on his unique knowledge of the sources available in that city.

Louise Gates Eddy of Jacksonville, Illinois, was most helpful in permitting me to examine the Robins folder in the papers of her late husband, Sherwood Eddy, and continued to inform me of the appearance of any additional material of value to my study.

Laura V. Monti, special collections chairperson at the University of Florida Libraries in Gainesville, has been most helpful in her correspondence with me and in the great care that has been given to the organization of the Robins Collection.

Frank Walker, curator of Fales Library of New York University, and his assistant, Russell James, were valuable guides through the rich materials of the Elizabeth Robins Collection in their expert care.

Prof. Joanne Elizabeth Gates, whose biography, "'Sometimes Suppressed and Sometimes Embroidered': The Life and Writing of Elizabeth Robins, 1862–1952," will soon be published, has been of great help in sharing her insights into the Robins family history and the relationship between Raymond and Elizabeth. Her edited transcription, with Victoria Joan Moessner, of Elizabeth's Alaskan diary of 1900 has been of great value in treating Raymond's three-year Alaskan adventure.

Dr. Ruth D. Bruune and Dr. Lawrence Sharpe, psychiatrists, and neurologist Dr. Bertel Bruune have given of their time and expertise in helping me to suggest a diagnosis for Robins's unusual childhood illness and his adult depression and amnesia. Dr. Sharpe's interest and generous commitment of time were particularly helpful and deeply appreciated.

Catherine Hartnett, Rose Kudurshian, Victoria Petrofsky, and Mary Warner were indefatigable through the arduous task of typing the earlier drafts of the manuscript.

Fairleigh Dickinson University lent assistance by providing a diminished schedule of teaching and a grant in the final stages of research. Ruth Boetcker, Michael Adams, Robert Kelly, and Mark Horan, reference librarians at the Friendship Library of Fairleigh Dickinson, were a constant help in obtaining research materials. Neal Sturm, director of the Academic Computer Center, went well beyond the call of duty to tame and reconcile computer software and hardware. Karen McMahon, Social Science and History Department secretary, has given capable and cheerful help throughout.

Nancy Rogers, of the Public Library at Millbrook, New York, has been untiring in providing help with secondary sources through interlibrary loan.

I would like to thank the many individuals who have read drafts of various chapters and shared their valuable thoughts and suggestions. My dear friend Robert Ubell lent not only his excitement, interest, and support for my work, but also his expertise as an editor and his keen understanding of the complexities of the issues raised here. John Schoener, Alex Jackinson, Celine Hertzman, Susan Jedren, Robert Montera, Ruth Boetcker, Morris U. Schappes, Max Rosenfeld, Carol Jochnowitz, Al Salzman, Aram Salzman, Noah Salzman, and Jean Connor read major portions of the manuscript and their comments led to significant improvements.

Professors William L. O'Neill, William Appleman Williams, James K. Libbey, and William Dannenberg read and commented on major portions of early drafts and provided valuable suggestions. Prof. Bernard Weisberger was kind enough to bring to my attention materials on Robins in the papers of Robert M. La Follette at the Library of Congress. Prof. John Hubbell, at Kent State University Press, has been a valued and perceptive critic, whose interest and insights have been a boon. Julia Morton, Flo Cunningham, and Linda Cuckovich, also at the press, have provided thoughtful help throughout. Robin Flam-Salzman and Prof. Edward M. Bennett provided critical readings of the entire manuscript and made numerous suggestions that have improved the book considerably. Obviously, however, for all judgments, evaluations of evidence, and writing here I bear full responsibility.

Finally, I thank my sons Aram and Noah, who now fully appreciate the writer's challenge, Gabriel, who is just learning the joys of speaking, and my wife Robin, who, through her careful reading of the manuscript and her warm understanding, has helped make the writing of this book a deeply satisfying challenge.

Abbreviations

ABP	Arthur Bullard Papers, Library of Princeton University, Princeton, New Jersey
AGP	Alexander Gumberg Papers, State Historical Society of Wisconsin, Madison
APP	Amos Pinchot Papers, Library of Congress, Washington, D.C.
AWO	Allen Wardwell, Oral History Research Office, transcript of recorded reminiscences, Butler Library, Columbia University, New York
AWP	Allen Wardwell Papers, Bakhmeteff Archive, Butler Library, Columbia University, New York
BLP	Robert M. La Follette Papers, Library of Congress, Washington, D.C.
CCP	Chicago Commons Papers, Chicago Historical Society
CMP	Charles McCarthy Papers, State Historical Society of Wisconsin, Madison
CRCP	Charles R. Crane Papers, Bakhmeteff Archive, Butler Library, Columbia University, New York
CTP	Chicago Teachers Federation Papers, Chicago Historical Society
DPO	DeWitt Clinton Poole, Oral History Research Office, transcript of recorded reminiscences, Butler Library, Columbia University, New York
DPP	DeWitt Clinton Poole Papers, State Historical Society of Wisconsin, Madison
ERP	Elizabeth Robins Papers, Fales Library, New York University, New York
GCP	George B. Creel Papers, Library of Congress, Washington, D.C.
GGP	George Gibbs Papers, State Historical Society of Wisconsin, Madison
HIP	Harold Ickes Papers, Library of Congress, Washington, D.C.
MBP	Anita McCormick Blaine Papers, State Historical Society of Wisconsin, Madison
MRP	Margaret Dreier Robins Papers, Library of the University of Florida, Gainesville
RLP	Robert Lansing Papers, Library of Congress, Washington, D.C.
RP	Raymond Robins Papers, State Historical Society of Wisconsin, Madison
RPC	Raymond Robins Papers, Chinsegut Hill Sanctuary, Brooksville, Florida
RPG	Raymond Robins Papers, Library of the University of Florida, Gainesville
SEP	Sherwood Eddy Papers, property of Louise Gates Eddy, Jacksonville, Illinois
SHP	Samuel Harper Papers, Libraries of the University of Chicago, Chicago
SLP	Salmon O. Levinson Papers, Libraries of the University of Chicago, Chicago
TPC	Thomas D. Thacher Papers, Bakhmeteff Archive, Butler Library, Columbia University, New York

TPN   Thomas D. Thacher Papers, New York Public Library, New York
TPY   Thomas D. Thacher Papers, Yale University Library, New Haven
TRP   Theodore Roosevelt Papers, Library of Congress, Washington, D.C.
WBP   William E. Borah Papers, Library of Congress, Washington, D.C.
WJP   William V. Judson Papers, Newberry Library, Chicago
WPC   Woodrow Wilson Papers, Library of Congress, Washington, D.C.
WTP   William Boyce Thompson–Herman Hagedorn Papers, Library of
         Congress, Washington, D.C.
WTUP   Records of the National Women's Trade Union League, Library of
         Congress, Washington, D.C.

Introduction

The biography of [Raymond] Robins remains to be written; and if the pen that writes it is in any way worthy of the subject, it will be a fascinating story.
—George F. Kennan, in *Russia and the West Under Lenin and Stalin*

In the early 1980s the relationship between the United States and the Soviet Union deteriorated seriously. In the United States, those in positions of power reversed the policy of détente, finding in it weakness, disadvantage, and lack of resolve rather than security and peace. The Soviet Union was perceived as expansionist, committed to Third-World destabilization, and the driving force behind the arms race. Until the fifth year of the Reagan administration, the United States acted in accord with its perception that it is wiser to defend itself against, rather than engage in dialogues with, those who present "Communist threats."

The Bolshevik regime was far from its present superpower status in the winter of 1917–18, when most observers in Petrograd and Moscow expected the Lenin government to topple any day. Yet it is to this precarious moment that we can trace the origins of America's resistance to the Soviet Union. Within weeks of the Bolshevik Revolution, the State Department began to consider plans that finally resulted in Allied military intervention in Archangel, Murmansk, and Vladivostok, casting the template for future antagonistic relations.

But at the same moment, an alternative, minority view of revolutionary Communist Russia was being formulated by a handful of Allied observers stationed in Russia that winter. In contrast to the dominant opinion, these mavericks believed that the new regime was sustained by vast support, responding to the needs of workers and peasants. These observers believed that it deserved Allied recognition and cooperation.

Beginning in Petrograd in 1917, Raymond Robins was one of the most notable to voice this minority view of the Russian Revolution—a perspective stifled by the official State Department approach, which thoroughly dominated American foreign policy toward the Soviet Union from its inception. However, since 1987 we have witnessed a dramatic transformation in U.S.-Soviet relations, culminating in the ratification and implementation of the

1

Intermediate Nuclear Forces Treaty and the apparent end to the Cold War. This new direction in U.S.-Soviet relations is characterized by precisely the kind of dialogue and cooperation that Robins had recommended from 1917 on. Thus, in this light, it is timely to look more closely at Robins's minority perspective.

Raymond Robins (1873–1954) reflected many currents in the Progressive movement and American life in the first decades of this century. First, he believed that the settlement house provided a key instrument for solving many grave city problems—problems which had to be solved if genuine democracy were to be achieved in America. What's more, he was an activist and leader in the struggle for women's suffrage, child labor laws, the eight-hour work day, the right of labor to organize, prohibition, and renewed Christian faith in the context of a social gospel. He fought political corruption and embraced a body of reform measures that finally materialized in 1914 as the Progressive party platform, which he helped formulate as the Progressive party candidate from Illinois for the U.S. Senate.

Robins's life is remarkable for the diversity of his experience. Following his early days as a miner and, later, as a young attorney, he entered Democratic party politics in San Francisco, only to escape to the goldfields of the Klondike. For three years, first as a prospector, and then as a Congregationalist minister, he challenged the dangers of the Arctic winter and the lawlessness of Nome in the throes of gold fever. Returning from Alaska, Robins immersed himself in Christian evangelism. At a settlement house in the slums of Chicago, he engaged relentlessly in struggles for social justice, while at the same time confronting and resolving the most profound personal problems. For twenty-three years, he and his wife, Margaret Dreier Robins, made their home in a tenement that became the center of their social work, union organizing, women's suffrage, and political activity. Margaret was president of the National Women's Trade Union League for many years, and she was a leading figure in the suffrage and labor movements.

Robins quickly became enmeshed in the politics of the notoriously corrupt Seventeenth Ward. This led to his involvement in Chicago municipal elections, candidacy for statewide office, and eventually to his central role in founding the Progressive party.

But Robins's most significant achievement occurred thousands of miles from the turmoil of American social reform. In June of 1917, five months after the fall of the Romanov dynasty, he arrived in Petrograd in the midst of revolutionary upheaval. He came to Russia as a member of the American Red Cross Commission, a post suggested by Theodore Roosevelt. Composed of a diverse group of individuals with few clearly defined objectives, the commission was sent to assist with domestic emergencies, freeing Russian forces to support the Allied position on the eastern front in the First World War.

Robins, who had always felt committed to righting the wrongs in the world around him, had a new personal mission. Until called to serve voluntarily in the war, he crusaded for American reform; but his presence in the ferment of the Russian Revolution gave new dimension to his zeal and purpose. At first he worked in support of the Provisional Government, headed by Alexander Kerensky, but soon came to appreciate its weaknesses. After the November Bolshevik Revolution, William Boyce Thompson, head of the Red Cross Commission, left Russia and was succeeded by Robins.

With the aid of the Russian-born, naturalized American translator and guide Alexander Gumberg, Robins—without official U.S. sanction—immediately entered into negotiations on the role of the American Red Cross with the Bolshevik leaders, including Trotsky and Lenin. In fact, Robins may have been the first American to have stepped into Trotsky's private office at revolutionary headquarters at Smolny. With the same fervor that led him to risk death in Alaska and physical and emotional breakdown from overwork in Chicago, he tried to convince the Bolsheviks of the wisdom of Soviet-American cooperation. Far more difficult, however, was his attempt to persuade Washington that Lenin and Trotsky were not criminal agents in the pay of the German enemy. Robins's aim was to demonstrate that Russian-American cooperation was critical, not only for long-range American self-interest, but for the immediate war effort as well.

During his entire Russian adventure, Robins campaigned for Bolshevik-American rapprochement. He believed that the lives of thousands of Allied soldiers on the western front depended on his efforts. The Bolsheviks, who had come to power under the slogan of "Peace, Land, and Bread," were committed to immediate negotiations with Germany for an end to the war. The Allies feared that a divided German and Austro-Hungarian army, fighting on both the eastern and western fronts, would emerge united in the West if a Russian-German peace were signed. The stalemated war of attrition would then take a major turn in favor of the German enemy. The withdrawal of Russia from combat meant that the United States and its allies might lose the war.

Although Robins succeeded in convincing William Boyce Thompson, Wall Street copper magnate and conservative, of the wisdom of Bolshevik-American cooperation, he failed to persuade the American ambassador, David Francis, and Secretary of State Robert Lansing. Nor was he able to convince Woodrow Wilson.

In Moscow and Petrograd, members of Allied missions had already stereotyped the Marxist Russian Revolution as fanatic and temporary. According to Robins, their myopic and paranoid hostility toward the Bolsheviks resulted from an "indoor opinion," an opinion created by those who had never left their offices, drawing rooms, or restaurants. Robins felt that they were unable to gauge Bolshevik support from factory workers, soldiers, and peasants. Unlike his privileged colleagues, Robins had spent years "outdoors," among Americans in labor and social struggles. Employing the same approach in Russia, with the assistance of his able translator, Alexander Gumberg, he attended mass meetings of factory workers and deliberations of the soviets and met with men and women of all social classes. Within days of the Bolshevik Revolution, he concluded that, in contrast to the rootlessness of Alexander Kerensky's Provisional Government, the Bolsheviks were powerfully organized, and most important, they had succeeded in securing mass support. In sharp contrast, Washington expected the imminent overthrow of the Bolshevik regime and feared that any sign of friendly contact would seriously prejudice a new regime that might emerge.

In spite of Robins's initiatives, the United States remained aloof from Soviet Russia. The Soviets signed a separate peace treaty with Germany at Brest-Litovsk, and but for fortunate military developments on the western front with American participation, Russia's withdrawal as a combatant might well have led to a German victory in the war.

Robins's support for an alternative policy toward Soviet Russia was not on ideological grounds. Actually, he opposed bolshevism, communism, and socialism. He believed that these systems denied freedom, individuality, and an opportunity to realize human potentialities. Despite his sober appraisal, however, he understood the depth of the Russian people's support for the revolution and so he urged the United States to recognize the Bolshevik government and to develop economic cooperation.

It took another fifteen years from the time of his departure from Russia, and many Soviet and international developments, for Robins's view to penetrate American policy. Throughout those years, his friends Senators William Borah, Hiram Johnson, and Medill McCormick pressed for a change in U.S. policy toward Russia. In 1933 Franklin D. Roosevelt's administration finally recognized the Union of Soviet Socialist Republics and exchanged ambassadors. Still, Robins's perception of the Soviet Union never occupied a central position in the State Department. American policy toward the Soviets has largely remained hostile.

In 1917—as today—the critical question for American foreign policy toward Russia or, for that matter, toward any nation undergoing revolutionary upheaval is whether the United States has accurately appraised the power, mass support, and depth of the revolutionary movement. This is especially important in those countries that have overthrown authoritarian governments allied with the United States.

Robins's seemingly disparate experiences underscore how his work in America helped prepare him to understand the Soviet system, the appeal it had for ordinary Russian workers and peasants, and its ultimate domination by the Bolshevik party. Robins was a unique individual who dug into the grass roots of the Russian Revolution. He stripped away blind opposition in order to assess realistically what would best serve American interests in dealing with the Bolshevik government. He championed this realism at a critical moment in Soviet-American relations, and had his recommendations prevailed, the American-Soviet relationship could have been far different, with more positive results for both countries and the world. Robins's role and outlook shed light on how a different road could have been followed, and they fortify the present U.S.-Soviet negotiations and cooperation.

Part One

The First Search

1

Childhood

Well—its a boy. A fair specimen apparently—black wig—color of eyes and
weight will be given as soon as ascertained. His name I judge will be Raymond
Robins—subject to advice and revision—but likely to stand.
—Charles E. Robins, writing to
his mother, 17 September 1873

No one could have predicted Raymond Robins's role in history based on his
conservative, Protestant ancestry. His father, Charles Ephraim Robins, born
in Ohio in 1832, was a direct descendant of Obedience Robbins, who came
to America from England in 1621 and went with Parson Hooker into the
wilderness of Connecticut to found Hartford. Raymond's grandfather, and
Charles's father, Ephraim, founded the Western Baptist Education Society in
1835. It was later chartered by the state of Kentucky as the Western Baptist
Theological Institute. Ephraim Robins was an insurance executive and one
of the originators of the agency insurance system, which decentralized and
facilitated the writing of policies, revolutionizing the insurance industry in
the United States in the decades before the Civil War. Charles's mother,
Jane Hussey Robins, third wife of Ephraim and twenty-two years younger,
lived until 1885, forty years after the death of her husband, and played an
important role in raising Raymond and his siblings.[1]

Raymond's mother, Hannah Maria Crow, was born in 1836, in Louisville,
Kentucky, with ancestry that traced back to colonial Maryland and Virginia.
The Robins and Crow families were related by blood; both claimed high
breeding and social position.[2]

Charles Robins's first marriage was to Sarah Young Sullivan of Zanes-
ville, Ohio. They had a son, Eugene, in 1856 and the marriage ended in di-
vorce in 1860. During those years Charles worked as a cashier in the Franklin Bank in Louisville and suffered from poor health. Charles recovered and
in 1862 married Hannah Crow, the daughter of his mother's sister. In the
same year, Hannah bore their first child, Elizabeth. During the early years
of his second marriage, Charles was involved in a banking partnership in
Louisville, but in the throes of the widespread financial crisis in the South
during the Civil War, this partnership dissolved. Most of the family fortune
of Hannah Robins was lost, and before the war was over, with slightly more
than $30,000, Charles, Hannah, and Elizabeth moved to New York. Charles

9

Hannah Maria Crow Robins and Charles Ephraim Robins, Raymond's mother and father. (Courtesy of the Elizabeth Robins Papers, Fales Library, New York University.)

hoped to restore the family prosperity in Manhattan, but settled on Staten Island in an attempt to avoid an urban life. He dreamed of a big house with plentiful orchards and fine gardens and developed his business activities on Broadway and Wall Street. Each day he returned to the earth, planting and pruning on the land near Eltingville, Staten Island.

Charles was meticulous and conscientious, preoccupied with the accurate detail of his business activities. In fact, on the basis of his diaries and correspondence, there is hardly anything that distinguishes his affect in his business affairs from that of his personal life, with the possible exception of occasional acerbic wit in the latter. He was an ambitious man, but his business failure in Kentucky, followed by his "loss of [his wife's] thirty thousand dollars on Wall Street," disillusioned him with the business world. He had a college education, but after his business failures felt it had been a waste. He resolved that his children would not make a similar mistake. He intended to transform his idealized and stolen hours in the orchard and garden into a way of life and hoped that his children would secure their livelihood as scientific farmers.[3]

Charles Robins was concerned with social and humanitarian problems. He was interested in Robert Owen and "the experiment in community work and community control of produce." The name, writing, and ideas of Owen were familiar and often quoted in the Robins household. Utopian socialist communities were still growing and new ones were being founded in the last decades of the nineteenth century. Worker ownership, management, and governing of "Owenite" communities often had shown success in terms of productivity, profitability, and the quality of life of members of the community. In the United States and England in the 1860s and 1870s, well before the rising tide of revolutionary Marxist influence, the ideas of Owen, Charles Fourier (the early nineteenth-century French utopian), and other socialist theorists received considerable attention and support among the educated middle class. Owen's cooperative ethic appealed to Charles Robins, especially in the face of his failure at competitive capitalism.[4]

Hannah Robins bore seven children in the eleven years between 1862 and 1873, the year of Raymond's birth. Two of the seven, a boy and a girl, died in the first year of infancy. The second Robins daughter, Eunice, was born in 1866 and, always in poor health, died at twenty. Saxton, the eldest surviving son, was born in 1869 and Vernon, three years later.

In 1872, a few months after Vernon's birth and just one month before Raymond was conceived, Eugene, Charles's son from his first marriage, died at the age of sixteen. The father could not be consoled. Charles mourned for Eugene as if he were his one and only child. It was one of the rare instances of any expression of emotion from Charles. Even then, when writing about it, he chose his words with literary propriety.

> Eugene is—gone, mine no longer: *any* love and yearning will go hungry to my grave. When alone, & undisturbed I call him all the time,—Eugene . . Eugene—my son, my love—come to me—speak to me: tell me in some way that —you *are*.
> No voice or sign.[5]

Hannah Robins also was burdened heavily by Eugene's death and particularly by the events that surrounded it. She had to contend with Charles's destructive response and the death that year of their third daughter, Amy, one year old. Yet another pregnancy, in 1873, surely unwanted, was added to the trials of caring for the infant, Vernon, and three-year-old Saxton. And there was the total financial disaster of Charles's Wall Street loss of Hannah's inheritance of $30,000. All this, within the same year, overwhelmed Hannah Robins. Raymond was born on 17 September 1873 and six weeks later was stricken with dysentery. At first, he was not expected to survive. Soon after he was out of danger, Hannah suffered a serious depression. Following the practice of the time, the five surviving children were placed in the care of an adult female, in this case, their paternal grandmother, Jane Hussey Robins, in Putnam, Ohio. Hannah's condition improved and she joined Jane Robins, who was both her aunt and mother-in-law, in raising the three small boys in the family Old Stone House. But the strains on Hannah remained great; her mental health always at risk.

Soon after the family gave up their Staten Island home, Charles left to carry out a series of mining and farming ventures in the hope of salvaging the family's financial future. By 1879 Charles Robins had established himself as the treasurer of a gold-mining company with interests high in the mountains of Rio Grande County, Colorado. He worked hard, doing much of the assaying himself, and he brought Elizabeth there to spend her seventeenth summer to share the great outdoors. Later, when Elizabeth was in her twenties, she used experiences from this visit to Colorado and similar adventures to write several novels and short stories.

During his first years of life, with his father absent and his mother suffering from depression, Raymond turned to Elizabeth, eleven years older. She was not merely a surrogate parent, but a playmate and focus of adoration.[6] Raymond's earliest memories were of the Old Stone House and Grandmother Jane Robins, with whom he spent his first five years. His attachment to Elizabeth, who felt that "he had been like my little son when I was myself a schoolgirl," was extraordinarily intense.[7] His emotional involvements with his two brothers, only a few years older, and his sister Eunice were unusually limited, and with only a few dramatic exceptions, these relationships remained of little importance during Robins's life. So it was particularly painful when, at five years of age, with his grandmother too old to care for him and his two brothers, he was separated from Elizabeth and sent off to Louisville, to live in the household of his mother's brother-in-law, Dr. James Morrison Bodine, dean of the Faculty of Medicine at the University of Louisville. There he and his two brothers were looked after by his mother, when she was well enough to manage, and by his married cousin, Elizabeth Bodine McKay—"Mother" McKay. Raymond's beloved sister Elizabeth, at fifteen, left for boarding school, and Eunice remained with her grandmother in Putnam. These years after Elizabeth's departure were the most painful in Raymond's troubled childhood.

Elizabeth recounted some details of Raymond's infancy and early years in her two autobiographical works, but her absence for most of his later childhood denies us her novelist's insights. The few morsels she does record, of the time when she served as "mother," are touching and revealing.

> I loved going back to the early winter evenings, sitting with the three little boys by the dining-room fire, eating red apples and shell-bark hickory nuts, while the stories were told. Not too near the boys' bedtime, Israel Putnam [the legendary general of the American Revolution, after whom Putnam, Ohio, was named] would be going with his torch into the dark mouth of the cave to meet the wolf. There was a touch too much of realism about this true pioneer story for the little Putnamites. Fortunately some thoughtful person had given one of us a book of Greek Heroes for the young. But my brothers cared less to be read to than to be "told." So we had the Trojan War, the Voyage of the Argonauts, the search for the Golden Fleece and all the rest by word of mouth, with no doubt highly unclassical additions. But Raymond never forgot those stories. I have heard him use them in middle life for symbols and illustrations, with a glance at me, as one quoting a common friend.[8]

"People think Raymond the brightest boy they ever met," Hannah wrote to Elizabeth in 1881, when Raymond was eight years old and living in a boarding house with his brothers and mother in Louisville. "I look at the beautiful child with tears in my eyes," she continued. "He inherits the fateful gift of genius. I tremble for his future, I have never known it to bring happiness to its possessor."[9]

Seven months later, while Hannah and the three boys were still living in the single room on Second and Chestnut Streets in Louisville, Raymond suffered the first of many violent convulsive seizures. For two years the family lived with the fear that at any moment he could be stricken with the wild uncontrolled behavior. "When the paroxysms came on," Grandmother Jane Robins wrote to Elizabeth, "only a strong man can hold and control him . . . he struggles violently . . . talking strangely. When he opens his eyes and comes to himself he says he has been asleep and knows nothing of what he has been doing—there is no suffering connected with the paroxysms." All of the symptoms suggest that Raymond suffered from some form of psychic epilepsy.[10]

Dr. Bodine made every effort to make a diagnosis and treat the condition. At first, santonin was administered, on the assumption that Raymond was suffering from the effects of a parasitic worm. Following standard medical practice of the time, small doses of arsenic were given as a sedative. A heavy diet of meat was prescribed, and following the advice of his father, to help him "*forget* his turbulence in sleep, his mind must be turned to other matters . . . his trouble is *pure* neurosis." Raymond was sent to work with Saxton as a "cash boy" in a Louisville store, carrying payments and change back and forth. But in spite of all these efforts, Raymond suffered more than fifteen attacks in the following year.[11]

"Raymond has had no recurrence of the awful visitation," Hannah could finally write to Elizabeth in June 1883, "looks the picture of robust health and a stranger would never believe anything wrong."[12] The malady seemed to disappear as quickly and mysteriously as it had come.

Raymond's recollections of Louisville were always tainted by the bleakness of the boarding house, his troubled mother, and "the terror" of his seizures, whereas he treasured the sweet earlier years spent with his caring sister and grandmother. Sent from his grandmother's household at the same moment he was separated from Elizabeth, he felt rejected and hopeless, despite the fact that he was in the care of his mother and a kind and favorite uncle. It was in Louisville, in the face of a lasting feeling of betrayal, that he began a struggle to assert his independence. A week after his mother had reported his improved health to Elizabeth, he ran away from home, hiring himself out as a water boy in a brickyard at Frankfort, Kentucky. A little short for his age and already bearing the black penetrating eyes, prominent nose, and straight, jet-black hair that as an adult won him the nickname "Panther," he worked for $1.25 a week, from six A.M. to six P.M., including Saturdays.

14

Raymond (at left) and his brother Vernon, 7 May 1881. (Courtesy of the Elizabeth Robins Papers, Fales Library, New York University.)

Raymond slept in the bed of the night watchman while he made his rounds, and Raymond gave it up to him with the coming of morning. When Raymond was finally found, the Bodine family held him in disgrace: he had carried water for black workers.[13]

In late fall 1883, after Raymond reached ten years of age, his father and uncle, Dr. Bodine, decided it would be best if Raymond joined his married cousin Elizabeth Bodine McKay, her husband, Zachary McKay, and their four-year-old daughter, Mary, in their move from Louisville to Florida. In November Raymond had *"light* recurrences of former troubles. A change was necessary." Charles decided that it was important that Raymond be away from his sick mother and Saxton, who was deeply affected by the illnesses of both his mother and brother. A tract of land had been bought by Dr. Bodine near Brooksville, a choice influenced by Charles, who convinced Dr. Bodine of the physical and psychic wisdom of a life on the land. Dr. Bodine gave the land to his daughter and son-in-law to begin an orange grove. "Mother" McKay warmly accepted the role of foster mother to Raymond in the new life on Bodine Grove, and from the first moment he thrived in the outdoor life. Never again did Raymond experience the seizures that plagued his eighth and ninth years.[14]

When Saxton and Vernon were old enough to be actively involved in work, Charles took his savings from Colorado and bought land in southern Florida. It was not long after Raymond had been settled at Bodine Grove, some two hundred miles to the north. Finally fulfilling his dream of farming, Charles built Nama, a small house near the Caloosahatchee River on the Gulf coast and bought additional parcels of land and registered them in the names of his children. With Nama, Charles felt that he had regained control over his life and could begin to unite his grown children under his wing. Charles took his two older sons, Saxton and Vernon, with him, but Raymond was not brought along at that time because he was ten (still "too young"), a part of the Bodine household by then, and because for Charles caring for two boys of eleven and thirteen was hard enough. Elizabeth wrote: "I saw the plan in practice; saw the beauty of the setting, felt the hopelessness of its end—given my father's age and circumstances." Charles was only forty-eight in 1884 when he began his Nama dream, but the time between the first planting of a citrus grove and its profitable fruit-bearing years would have made him an old man before he could make a profit. Furthermore, his financial resources were limited, as were his physical strength and experience. After only a few years, Nama failed.

Raymond, years later, recalled:

> OUR FATHER lives for me in a half dozen pictured-events, . . . the massive brow deep lined with suffering; the gray brown eyes with that same light of unimpeachable integrity in their steady glance, all wreathed with that wondrous smile that played with the furrows of care like the last clear rays of an Indian summer's sun on a winter's day. . . .

> The deepest memory I have of OUR FATHER is his lying in a hammock on the upper porch at Nama, seemingly an old man as I urged his selling Nama, . . . As we talked I suggested that later on he would have another more beautiful HOME, his eyes flashed and he said "this is my last HOME, I will never have another" and then he put his arm around me and his eyes were filled with tears. And so there has seemed behind me a heritage of sorrow and *defeat*—from which I must needs flee to have any possible chance for escape.[15]

In 1885, after years of deterioration, Hannah was finally diagnosed as schizophrenic and institutionalized at Oaklawn Sanitarium in Jacksonville, Illinois. After leaving Louisville for Florida, Raymond never saw his mother again, although she lived until 1901. Elizabeth did see her occasionally, but seldom shared her impressions and feelings with Raymond, either in person or in their letters. Elizabeth decided when Raymond was a child, and later they agreed, that since his mother's condition had caused him so much suffering, and since he could not even remember what she looked like, there would be no point in talking about her. Nevertheless, his childhood trauma and the knowledge of his mother's life in an asylum had enormous impact on Raymond for the rest of his life. "Most vivid of all" his memories of his mother was her recitation of a poem: "If I should die tonight,/My Friends would look upon my quiet face,/Before they laid it in its resting place," and her singing of Stephen Foster's "The Old Folks at Home" as she accompanied herself on the piano. Both memories, so full of sadness, touched him deeply.

> *my* eyes are filled with tears, and that MOTHER who for some strange reason I scarce remember and whose face I do not recall at all, LIVES a sorrowing soul in my inner heart. Was she as sad and broken hearted as these two pictures hung on the walls of my memory seem to portray? Always I have been a sort of "sobersides," looking out upon a shadowed scene—*anticipating failure*. Was my time of gestation one of sorrow for OUR MOTHER, was I *unwanted*—for so I have always felt a hidden sense, even in the high moments of my checkered days? And it has been this sense of fleeing from an impending pre-determined DOOM, that has led me to put as far behind me as I could the folks and memories of my earlier years.[16]

Eventually other Louisville cousins came south to work and live at Bodine Grove, with high hopes of making it a successful venture. Frank Bodine, Elizabeth McKay's brother, came with his family and soon was in charge. Unlike "Mother" McKay, Frank felt put upon by the burden of caring for Raymond, and his relationship with the sensitive boy was strained. In retrospect, Robins felt that he was tolerated by Frank Bodine for two reasons only: he was strong and worked hard. Raymond's dislike for Frank developed into a competitive drive and a desire by Raymond to prove his superiority. Early in his stay at Bodine Grove, Raymond elaborated on his dream of buying land and building a tropical haven for himself and his sister Elizabeth. Raymond had his eye on nearby Snow Hill, a grand old plantation, where his success would best reflect on the failure of Frank.[17]

In contrast to Raymond, Elizabeth was a strikingly beautiful young woman, with curly blond hair—always pinned up—piercing green eyes, and a very shapely figure. While still in her teens, she demonstrated her talent as a writer and then went on to a successful acting career, beginning with the Boston Museum Theatre. There she met George Richmond Parkes, a fellow actor, with whom she eloped when she was twenty-three. She was not ready for the marriage, but after Parkes's many pleas agreed, and as a concession to her family affiliation, the marriage was held in an Episcopal church. "Well, dear," she wrote to her father, informing him of the marriage, "in Salem, the place where maids aforetime were bewitched and paid their penalty, I a week ago paid mine."[18]

While Parkes loved Elizabeth passionately, their two years of marriage were bitterly unhappy for him and led to a drinking problem. Dressed in full medieval armor, he leapt to his death in the Charles River at the stroke of midnight, leaving a histrionic suicide note proclaiming that he could no longer bear her rejection. For Elizabeth, it was a painful and ironic portent, for she was at the point of fulfilling his wish that she give up her acting career and "really be his wife."[19]

Raymond was twelve, heady with the dream of making a home for himself and his sister, when he learned of Elizabeth's marriage. His sorrow seemed unbearable. "He has told me," Elizabeth wrote in her autobiography,

> when news came that I was married he went away and hid in the hay loft. He heard them calling, calling, but he was safe, crying behind the hay—till evening and hunger drove him indoors. I could not understand his feeling so acutely, for we had not at that time been together for several years. But he explained long after, that in marrying, I had betrayed his trust. As far back as he could remember it had been our plan, my solemn promise, that when he grew up we would have a farm, with a fishpond, and live together "forever and ever, Amen."[20]

Raymond's boyhood sadness subsided slowly, but some years later the dream was revived, as it was revived time and time again in adulthood.

The other family circumstance during this period that intensified Raymond's feelings of exclusion and betrayal was the fact that his father and brothers were living together, without him, at Nama. Through these emotional crises "Mother" McKay was kind and affectionate. She was truly a loving mother, easing Raymond's sadness through his adolescence—his years of exploration in the fields, groves, and byways around Brooksville. Even when Raymond, in his mid-teens, finally joined his father and brothers, Elizabeth Bodine McKay remained his emotional anchor.[21]

Robins's intelligence and intensity attracted people to him even as a boy, and this helped nurture his confidence and faith that he could be loved. At the moment when each traumatic emotional blow could have destroyed him, someone was there to cushion the impact and help him find the resilience to move on. His sister, his grandmother, and "Mother" McKay, each at a different time, came forward to offer comfort. But one of his most important relationships was outside the family, with Fielder Harris, a black man who worked on Bodine Grove. Harris was a man of gentle and understanding temperament, with a deep sense of awe and appreciation for the wonders and mysteries of nature. "He was the interpreter to an eager hearted lad of 13, of earth and sky, of forest and river, of animals and plants and all the magic of the outdoor world."[22]

Although Robins owed many debts to the ideas of famous men, Fielder Harris was the individual who made the most profound impression. Beyond their mutual respect and friendship—which transcended the rampant racism of the time—Harris nurtured in "my boy" a passionate involvement and acuteness of interest in nature. Later in life Robins's correspondence and public speaking, often with spellbinding power, wove in his striking impressions of the forest and stream. He identified intimately with the wilderness, just as Harris had done. In fact, Robins was filled with a special reverence for Harris.

> Uncle Fielder had the unbound confidence of my foster mother and he was during those impressionable years my closest associate. Unable to either read or write, his mind was filled with the immemorial wisdom of the field and farm, forest and stream. A wise fisherman and a mighty hunter . . . he fished by the moon's phases; planted crops and trees and killed hogs and hunted deer and bear by the same high wisdom. He believed unfalteringly in the efficacy of the left hind foot of a graveyard rabbit captured at midnight in a cemetery in the dark of the moon. He carried one for years and may do so still. He was the best axman, oarsman, runner, wrestler and jumper in the county. He was a master of horsemanship; broke the wildest of mules, tamed range cattle and was altogether my ideal for those seven years.
>
> As in the way with arrogant youth I would now and again expatiate upon my splendid and prosperous future—I was a poor relation on a sandhill farm—and promised him among other glories that after I had made a fortune and built a home I would surely take him to New York.[23]

In spite of Robins's patronizing references to Harris—his superstition, his "darky" ways—the two shared an undeniable love for one another. "Dear Boy," Harris dictated in a letter to Raymond, "I want to say this to you. The day you and I were sitting in the sitting room I taken a close observation [of] you, whither you knew it or not, and such eyes I've never beheld in a man before, pure, clear and bright. If you[r] heart (which I certainly believe it is) is as pure as your eyes depict, you are heaven bound."[24] At the time of Fielder's death in 1924, Robins wrote of their relationship to his close friend and fellow peace crusader Salmon O. Levinson. "In his passing the oldest link of intimate fellowship of my youth and this present time is broken."[25]

Raymond's luck in finding warmth and concern outside the family circle included another man who was a teacher and father to him. "William A. Fulton," Robins wrote of the well-to-do and most highly respected citizen of Brooksville, "was possibly the greatest single influence in my intellectual life

Fielder Harris, close friend of Raymond Robins, pictured here in 1914 with his little son Raymond. Raymond Harris was Robins's godson, and Margaret Harris was Margaret Dreier Robins's goddaughter. (Courtesy of the Elizabeth Robins Papers, Fales Library, New York University.)

during the building years from twelve to sixteen."[26] But Raymond's luck was more than matched by his remarkable accomplishments, which drew men like Fulton to him. "Raymond says he will be sure to go to Congress from this part of Florida," Charles wrote proudly to Elizabeth before

Raymond had yet reached his fourteenth birthday, "and everybody says the same who knows him. Brooksville people say he is the smartest boy they ever saw. He has declaimed from the stump several times. He consumes the papers and every book that comes in his way and hears no call when reading. He says politics is lovely, and he likes to know all about them—as well in Europe as in America."[27]

Raymond's first formal schooling in Florida was limited to three months a year at the neighboring Rock Hill School. But during the third winter at Bodine Grove, when Raymond was thirteen, Fulton realized the potential in Raymond and agreed to tutor him. Here again, a warm relationship was established between the appreciative boy and a responsive man—a friendship that extended into Raymond's adult life. Fulton, who was the most successful businessman in Brooksville (according to Robins), introduced Raymond to the world of ideas and history as an integral part of life. Fulton also had a hand in redirecting the energies and ambitions of his teenage pupil from farming to prospecting and business.[28]

In a letter written to his sister while still a teenager and while in partnership with Fulton, Raymond described his control of some kaolin clay deposits. "As a result of all this," he concluded, "I am now *somebody*."[29]

By the age of fifteen, the serious traumas were behind Raymond. He was endowed with remarkable intelligence, sensitivity, fierce determination, good health, and loving friends and family. He was ready for the steep road to adulthood and the plantation house atop Snow Hill.

2

"Success," 1890–1897

Though you were here only four months, the estimate formed of your up-
rightness and ability by all those without exception who came to know you is
something very remarkable in the case of a boy of seventeen.
                                        —Charles E. Robins to his son Raymond,
                                        Alva, Florida, 31 August 1891

RAYMOND, by age thirteen, had already developed an intense drive to succeed. His childhood perception of abandonment by his mother, betrayal by
his sister, and real abandonment by his father seemed to him to demonstrate his shortcomings and worthlessness. His relationships with foster parents "Mother" McKay, Fielder Harris, and William Fulton gave him strength
and warmth; but could not free him from the pall of these rejections.
Only hard-fought struggle to achieve some purpose, which dominated every
aspect of his life, could uplift him, give him some peace of mind, even if only
temporarily.

From his mid-teens to his twenties Raymond was consumed by a desire
for wealth. His lust for money and the challenge to get it was sparked, at
least in part, by his desire to beat Frank Bodine at his own game of becoming a citrus king. In addition, Raymond's mother and her ancestors had been
landed gentry in the antebellum South, and his father's side was marked by
accomplishment and wealth in the insurance business. "I would have you
know," Raymond wrote of his Crow and Robins forebears, "that behind me
are generations of gentlefolk, ancestors and kinsmen of fidelity and power."
But there he was an adolescent, raised as a "poor relation on a sandhill
farm," the family name and fortune at its nadir. Raymond dreamed of saving the Robins family. He was caught up in the great mystique of success.
Perhaps it was the influence of William Fulton, who became Robins's kaolin-
prospecting partner. From 1891, at eighteen, to 1901 Robins was preoccupied by his search for money. And if we are to accept the testimony of
Elizabeth, he had the energy and genius to succeed.

During his sixteenth and seventeenth years Robins considered Bodine
Grove in Hernando County his home, yet he remained unsettled and moved
around a great deal, taking one job, then another. He worked along the
lower west coast of Florida driving cattle, where at Punta Gorda the herds
were shipped to Cuba. He also worked for a short time around Alva, near

his father's orange grove, and many years later he recalled: "A cowboy from my 13th to my 17th year, twice a year driving cattle . . . around the little village of Fort Myers . . . paid in Spanish Dubloons worth $15.50 at the bank. Better than half a century gone, I hunted alligators in Okechobee, shot them under the flash of Bull's Eye lanterns, drew them into the boat with grappling hooks keeping a wary eye out for the swing of a tail that would knock you ten feet into the lake."[1]

At seventeen, after many attempts at asserting his economic independence (he even started his own small orange grove), Robins finally left Brooksville. On his own, his first job was at Dunellen, Florida. He earned fifteen dollars a month, plus board, as manager of a commissary store at a phosphate mine. Shortly after starting the job, he came down with malaria and he recalled later that his drive for life and taking his "weight in calomel and quinine" pulled him through.[2] Following his recovery from malaria, Robins told of coming upon an advertisement seeking coal miners at Coal Creek, Anderson County, Tennessee.

I believe that Robins's mining experiences at Coal Creek and Leadville, as narrated in the following pages, are apocryphal mosaics based on contemporary newspaper and personal accounts of others that Robins came across during his prospecting trip at about this time. Beginning around 1905, Robins shared these autobiographical accounts of the year 1891–92. He used these tales to establish himself more firmly as "a working man," as a member of the brotherhood of "union men," so that in his union and strike campaigns he could speak not only for union men, but as one of them.[3]

Feeling that thirty dollars a month (instead of fifteen) was worth the trip and the hard work, Robins made the move to Tennessee. In his tale, Robins wanted to trace his roots not only to the soil, but to one of the most hazardous and exploited brotherhoods of industrial America. He claimed it as a period of active union organization and struggle, charged with new ideas about exploitation, class consciousness, and the power of collective action.

Robins later told of working a twelve-hour day, seven days a week for a dollar a day at No. 3 mine, Coal Creek. He ate his lunch together with the mules at the lower level of the mine and did not see the sun for weeks at a time. The mine was located in an area of "faulty" geologic formation. Extensive timbering and shoring of the shafts made the operation expensive for the owners. Casting safety aside, the owners chose to economize at the expense of safety. Robins told of noting the danger of a cave-in and telling the straw boss, who dismissed him with, "If you don't like this mine, get the hell out of here."

Sixty years later, Robins told William Appleman Williams that soon thereafter there was a cave-in. Robins said he could never forget the shift boss shouting: "Dig men Dig! You've got three minutes to dig and the rest of your lives to think about it."

Despite that close call, with no one even hurt, Robins related that conditions in the mine remained just as bad. There seemed to be no solution to the danger, the inhuman living conditions, and the twelve-hour day, seven-day week. Then one day, a few weeks after the cave-in, Robins told of a new man hired who electrified the No. 3 mine barracks at Coal Creek and made a special mark on Robins. He was just another miner who also slept on a straw pallet in one of the six-tiered bunk beds, but he happened to be given a place above Robins. During their discussions about poor working conditions, the stranger related tales about organized labor and unionism. "He told me about Leadville, Colorado," Robins explained, never revealing the name of the influential stranger, "where he worked eight hours a day, got $3.50 a day, and didn't have to work Sunday. It sounded to me like the New Jerusalem. I was not quite sure it was true, but I wanted to talk with him about it."[4]

After working his twelve-hour shifts, Robins explained that he could hardly keep awake as the stranger spoke through the night and into the morning hours. But the newcomer's foul-smelling pipe and the pan of cold water in which Robins kept his feet, allowed Robins to stay awake long enough to learn all of labor's problems and receive unionism's complete creed.

The miners of Coal Creek and all of eastern Tennessee faced an additional serious challenge: the convict labor system. By 1891 most states had already outlawed the contracting of prison labor to private corporations. However, in Tennessee, Georgia, Alabama, and a number of other southern states, the practice, which usually victimized blacks, was still common. Free union and unorganized miners had to compete constantly with convict labor, and any dispute or strike meant the threat of convict scabs. The Coal Creek Rebellion against the convict labor system began in April 1891, with the effort of the Tennessee Coal and Mining Company to replace its miners with convicts. In those mines already organized by the Knights of Labor, the company waited for the expiration of the union contract before bringing in convict labor. For four years, in one of the most extraordinary sequences of confrontation between armed miners and the Tennessee State Militia, under orders of Gov. John P. Buchanan, the drama was played out. Convict barracks, behind barricades near the mines, were taken by armies of miners, and in one case the prisoners were given civilian clothing, put aboard trains, and sent back to Knoxville or Chattanooga. Larger state militia forces arrived to enforce the law and the commands of the governor. Again the miners responded, only to be overpowered by the militia.[5]

In the early months of the rebellion, Robins became a union evangelist at No. 3 mine and helped spread the union gospel to the miners. More than eighty-five percent of the men at Coal Creek were eventually enrolled in the union. Robins told of his role as one of the spokesmen of a committee that presented a list of "requests" to the boss.

He had a swivel chair and was leaning back in it, and his clerk had said we might go in.

He said, "I understand you are a committee?"

We said we were.

He said, "Spit it out."

My knees were knocking together and I was frightened, but the other fellows looked at me. So I tried to tell him what we wanted. I didn't say "demands." We didn't have any. We said what we thought was right, that we should get $1.10 a day and that we should work eleven and a half hours a day instead of twelve. We thought we had to say something about hours. And we asked for one half day a week. We didn't ask for Sunday. We had to make a good case for that half day and so we said we wanted to wash our clothes.

He looked at us and said, "Well, is that all?" And we said, "Yes." And he said, "Well, you're fired. Get out of here."[6]

Robins related that his fellow union committee members waited for the whistles to blow at the end of the shift. When the men emerged from the mine, a strike was announced. Only those who manned the water pumps remained at work to keep the mine from flooding. In retaliation, the mine operator contracted convict scabs, mostly blacks, but the union drove the scabs out, after giving "a pretty good account" of themselves.[7]

When the state militia arrived, Robins recounted, the strikers were meeting in a neighboring field—one that did not belong to the mine owner—yet the miners were ordered to disperse. The workers stood their ground and the militia opened fire.

"Some got killed and some got wounded and some ran away. I was fleet of foot and I ran and lived with some farmers up in the hills until the strike was broken." Afterwards, Robins tried to get work in other mines in Anderson County, but he learned the effectiveness of the blacklist, which named him as an "agitator and trouble-maker."[8]

Although contract convict labor had been lawful in Tennessee since 1871, the tide of union and public opinion opposition grew during the four succeeding years of the Coal Creek Rebellion and finally achieved success in 1896 with the decision of the state legislature of Tennessee not to renew its monopoly convict labor contract with the Tennessee Coal, Iron and Railway Company.[9]

The Coal Creek experience, as Robins integrated it into his life's story, was the first in which he, at eighteen, used the power of his personality and public-speaking talents in what he would later call a "campaign." The Coal Creek drama was intended to reveal Robins's intense drive for justice for those who had been denied fair treatment. It suggested his first opportunity to fight the good fight for the good cause, and most important, it allowed him to claim himself a member of the rank and file of the group for which he fought. His later tongue-in-cheek allusions to himself in his most personal correspondence as "An Industrial Knight Errant, Sir Raymond of Hernando," was not altogether in jest.[10] From his teens, the "battle" fired his imagination, charged him with energy and purpose, but also complicated and threatened his ambitions to get rich and salvage the family name and social position. Although it took many years and much anguish, Robins did manage to resolve this conflict.

Robins explained that in 1892, after escaping the search following the failed strike, he decided to "beat [his] way" to the "New Jerusalem" of union mines in Leadville, Colorado, so temptingly described by his pipe-smoking bunkmate. The railroad connections from Tennessee and Alabama west and north to Colorado were best made by heading south to New Orleans. He hopped a freight train on the Louisville and Nashville Railroad to Mobile and then went on to Louisiana's great cosmopolitan port, where he hoped to stay a while in his first big city. Arriving without any money, he survived by eating bananas dropped by stevedores unloading ships from Central America. He continued on his way by freight car to Leadville, where he arrived hungry and anxious, not knowing whether Leadville was the New Jerusalem he had imagined. He had also been warned about the danger of being marked as a vagrant, which made him all the more tense about finding work. Finally, at a saloon, in exchange for sweeping the floors and cleaning the spittoons, he was given a free lunch. He "hit it pretty hard," he recalled, in his dramatic telling of the story.[11]

By coincidence, the local union office was just above the saloon; but Robins failed to be accepted as a member at first. "We don't give cards to hoboes anyway." The saloon-keeper suggested he seek the help of Davis Williams, the check boss (the union representative assuring a closed shop) at the mine. Williams looked Robins over and asked to see his hands "to see whether [they] had corns on [them], to see whether [he] was a soft handed bum or a worker." Although Williams approved, Robins's membership had to come before the rank and file of the union. At a meeting that night, he was accepted, but not without debate and not without skepticism, especially since he had worked in unorganized mines. Robins argued that in most of the mines of Tennessee there were no trade unions and that he had helped organize the miners at Coal Creek. He promised that he would work hard and obey union rules. Ten years later, in a speech, "Why I Believe in Organized Labor," which Robins gave in dozens of towns and cities across the country, he described what his union membership at Leadville had meant. Apart from the immediate rewards of membership—an eight-hour work day, Sundays off, and $3.50 a day:

> I learned democracy. I learned the power of the group. In the trade union meeting, after the main business that is before us, we talk and we have the hour "for good and welfare of the union" when we can make motions and learn how to make them, learn something about parliamentary law.
> You begin to feel that you were part of the community, that you with the other workingmen, amounted to something; that you had some importance, that you were not just one individual in a big mine.[12]

This conviction, that the dignity and self-respect of the individual can be won through identity and solidarity with a group or movement, makes many of Robins's activities understandable. Coupled with his drive for leadership in "campaigns" (and the right of labor to organize was one of many), he thrived on drawing citizens into the movement, swelling its ranks to win democratically the struggle for the just cause. Self-sacrifice and unlimited energy were the hallmark of his activism, but in June of 1892, at eighteen, Robins explained that he left the Leadville mines, still in search of fortune. Coal Creek and Leadville sharpened his understanding of labor's struggle, and while he knew the justice of that struggle in the depths of his heart, he could not imagine a life for himself as a miner; he was not a manual laborer —not a "commoner." Robins was a descendant of "gentlefolk" of breeding and means and he meant to return to that position, to that social status. Only from such a place would he feel at peace to continue to struggle for social justice in America.

Later, when he was twenty years old, with a new self-confidence and awareness of the power of his personality, Robins wrote to his sister Elizabeth:

> As to the "Amenities" or "Arts of Life" I know little, and at present care less. I am rough, awkward, and ugly and have sense enough to know it. You may doubtless judge that my acquirements are equal to my aspirations and capabilities, and you may be right.
>
> There is a deep widespread dissatisfaction among the commoners of America, especially in the West and South. This feeling will have expression in large and general manner, no matter what its form, before the first quarter of the 20th Century shall have passed away, and in that hour *my* education will count more than white hands, polished manners or the most extensive knowledge of the "Amenities and Arts of Life."[13]

From Leadville, Robins headed back to Florida to accept a job offer. There, he worked as a clerk for E. W. Agnew and Company of Ocala, "the largest general store this side of Jacksonville." After only a few months on the job, Robins knew that this was no way to get rich. On 9 January 1893, he took a new position with S. W. Teague and Company, "the largest real estate firm in Florida . . . pioneers in the development of the phosphate industry which . . . represent[ed] a cash value of twenty million dollars in this state."[14] Now Robins found himself on the other side of the mining business, working as a prospector and dealing with ruthless businessmen. Instructed to buy up all available land and use any means "to make it impossible for anyone to come in and mine profitably," he did as he was told, effectively monopolizing phosphate-mining operations in the region for his employers.[15]

Robins also prospected independently and successfully for kaolin clay deposits. He acquired land options worth at least $10,000, but he could not finance the mining operations through local capital. Robins sought the help of his uncle, Lloyd Tevis, of San Francisco, who had made a fortune in California real estate and had often helped his sister Elizabeth in the early days of her acting career. With a letter of introduction from Tevis, Robins went to New York for the financing he needed.

Robins was appalled by the extremes of wealth and poverty that he saw in New York. From his perspective of small-town Ohio, Kentucky, and Florida, New York was a hell. "If the social conditions here are the best fruits of this boasted civilization," he wrote to Elizabeth from a small businessman's hotel on West Broadway, "then glad indeed am I that my earlier years were spent among barbarous influences."

At the Wall Street offices of H. B. Hollins, Robins met with wealthy investors, and after his first session with them, he felt in control, confident he could get the backing. Never having had the opportunity of a college education, Robins was especially sensitive to the presence of the junior partners of the firm, all introduced as graduates of the best schools. Robins was disdainful of their ability, all of them privileged sons of senior partners. The following day, James R. Whitaker, the firm's lawyer, led Robins "over every step of the ground and made him prove up on every assertion." At the end of their negotiations, it was Whitaker who was in control; Robins had been "taken" by the skilled legal mind. An honest demand of $10,000 for Robins's interest in the deposits was whittled down to only $3,000. The New York lawyer had not been dishonest or even unscrupulous; Robins understood that he had simply used his knowledge, experience, and legal skills to best advantage. Robins brooded over this experience. Against the advice of his co-workers at S. W. Teague, Robins decided to leave the business world and study law.[16]

Meanwhile, Elizabeth was making a great name for herself on the London stage as a master interpreter of Ibsen. Her play *Alan's Wife* (1893) and novel *George Mandeville's Husband* (1894) were published. In spite of debilitating headaches, she won high praise from the demanding drama critics of London's West End and secured a place among the British literati. On 30 November 1894, after a kaolin-prospecting expedition to Texas and through much of the South, Raymond wrote to his sister: "You will understand that a great lawyer with me does not mean only success or fame; it means a dominant force in reforms of the coming crisis when the poverty and misery of this western world rise in their blind might to test the endurance of the social fabric fashioned by the fathers a little over a hundred years ago. And the *constitution will stand;* but the abuse of its provisions will be rendered impossible in the old way."[17]

Robins never had a high school or college education. He attended the Rock Hill School near Bodine Grove, and from thirteen to sixteen, he studied with William Fulton. Robins's childhood letters and a sermon he wrote at the age of fifteen demonstrate both his mastery of English and his precocious mind. Thus the objections of his co-workers to his study of law were based not on any concern that he would fail, but rather on the abandonment of his successful career in prospecting and real estate. Following the practice of the time, Robins "read law and clerked" under the guidance of an attorney, O. T. Green of Ocala, Florida, and within a year stood for his oral examination. Judge Richard S. Hocker, of the Marion County Court qualified Robins for the bar, but suggested that he continue his studies at the University of Virginia. Robins decided instead to study at Columbian University (now George Washington University) because two U.S. Supreme Court justices, David J. Brewer and John M. Harlan, were on the faculty there. Although Brewer was a defender of property rights, he had a reputation as a reformer in Kansas. Harlan was a strong supporter of the Thirteenth and Fourteenth Amendments to the Constitution and supported federal action to safeguard the civil rights of blacks.

"I met in debate . . . graduates of Yale, Harvard, and Princeton. . . . After six months of sparring with this class, I was willing to enter battle in the hottest competition in the fastest city in America. I had felt and weighed this bogey the 'college-bred man.'" Robins completed the prescribed three-year LL.B. requirements in a single year, receiving his degree on 7 June 1896 at twenty-two years of age—a feat he accomplished at a cost of "$700.50 (for living and educational expenses) and 14 lbs. of flesh."[18] His stay in Washington had many advantages. The Supreme Court Library, with resources unobtainable elsewhere, helped in his studies immensely. He observed the different courts—from coroner's inquest to Supreme Court—and made regular visits to both houses of Congress. There, he carefully observed the spectrum of debate and public speaking, which honed his own noteworthy skills.

> I spared neither time nor money that would enable me to feel and understand those sides of life that I knew least of. Every play or opera . . . I saw, every important lecture I heard . . . no man of notoriety there that I did not study, and quite a few of them I personally met. I made a circuit of the churches of the city, heard Talmage, Herron, Keane, McKay-Smith . . . every phase of religious thought . . . to Alexander Kent hurling defiance at dogmatic creeds, citing Spencer not Moses as the true expounder of the moral law.[19]

Robins resolved that San Francisco would be the best place to open his law office. He had seen many parts of the United States, but concluded that "California is the richest gem in Americas's crown. The productions of her soil embrace the possibilities of every Zone, and every product is the highest quality of the species."[20] On his journey west, he stopped in Denver to see his brother Saxton.[21] For the first eight years of Raymond's life, he had lived sporadically in the same household with Saxton, four years older, but the brothers were never close. During their adolescence, only the most tentative and infrequent correspondence was maintained and little more can be said of their communication with their "middle" brother, Vernon, who had married his first cousin and remained in Louisville, where he went on to practice medicine. Only Elizabeth, the oldest of the Robins children, tried to sustain close family ties. The second Robins daughter, Eunice, ill much of her life, had died in 1886.

Whereas Raymond had managed to survive through the years of separation from his mother and rejection by his father, Saxton was emotionally crippled. He was three years old at the time of his mother's breakdown and from an early age was troubled and "unfit." But, Raymond reasoned, since their sister Elizabeth was a woman of extraordinary accomplishment, their brother Vernon was in a Chicago medical school, and he himself was a lawyer, why could not Saxton make something of himself? Success was within the grasp of the Robins children, yet Saxton was on the brink of skid row.

Two years before their meeting in Denver, Raymond had visited Saxton in Cincinnati and found he "had done nothing of value, had taken no grasp on life . . . had gone steadily down." Raymond had shared his misgivings about Saxton with Elizabeth, but she rejected this harsh judgment. Raymond later wrote to Elizabeth that, after sending him ten dollars a month for six months, "I found Saxton on my arrival at Denver, ragged, dirty and hungry, almost a physical wreck, an inveterate cigarette smoker, engaged at that time in the best position he had held for six months, viz, night clerk at a low lodging house where thieves, street jugglers, and the submerged and dissolute of all classes in a mining city congregate; receiving a miserable pittance and salary and the right to sleep among 'toughs and thugs' during the daylight hours." Raymond resolved that only he could save his fallen brother, so he entered into a "formal legally binding contract" in which Saxton agreed that Raymond would oversee his moral, physical, and intellectual rebirth while they lived together in San Francisco. "I have frequently observed myself," Raymond wrote to Elizabeth, "and others have often remarked upon, the power I seem to exert over all that come into the circle of my influence, I am giving this quality a rather severe test."[22] Sure enough, six months later, after Raymond had put up his shingle at 318 Golden Gate Avenue, Saxton joined him in San Francisco to live an upright life. Saxton agreed to continue the study of law, which he was supposed to have been doing during the previous year.

There was a dimension of Raymond's concern for his brother beyond his pompous pronouncements. He knew that Saxton needed constant reassurance and that "with someone near him every day that understands him, and is willing to pay the price of constant vigilance, and frequent disguised support," he could stand on his own feet and make a life for himself.[23]

This sketch of Raymond's interaction with his brother suggests some of the complications and contradictions in Raymond's own personality, his judgmental arrogance veiling serious self-doubt. He did not simply pass through stages of weakness and overbearing strength; he exhibited weakness and strength, doubt and assuredness, nearly simultaneously—and his enormous energy seemed, at least in part, to be generated by the conflict of the two within him. Writing about himself six years later, at the age of twenty-nine, after many hardships in the long Alaska adventure and the painful dissolution of plans to live with his sister, Robins began to see for himself some of the contradictions in his personality. "I sometimes wonder if ever there lived such another queer fellow as I am. I surprise myself constantly by the strange and impossible drifts that appear from time to time in my feelings. What a mystery we all are!"[24]

San Francisco in 1896 was a boomtown and the financial, commercial, and social center of the West. During the previous decade, real estate values soared, the population mushroomed, the city spread, new construction appeared everywhere, and great fortunes were made. Although prosperity was interrupted by a burst real estate bubble in the summer of 1887, a stock market panic in 1893, and the Pullman strike in 1894, the city rebounded quickly. As a railroad center, agriculture, oil, gold mining, banking, insurance, and the lucrative oriental trade of the port city were the sound base of its economy. The serious threat to San Francisco's preeminence—Los Angeles and the sunny south—was only in its infancy before the turn of the century. In 1900 San Francisco had a population of 342,000, the ninth largest community in the United States, but its level of municipal corruption put it much higher on that list of American cities. There were strong voices of reform in Fremont Older, editor of the San Francisco *Bulletin,* and sugar millionaire Rudolph Spreckels, who provided financial backing to carry out an investigation of the new political machine of Abraham Ruef, "the virtual dictator of city politics" and heir to Boss Sam Rainey. However, the wealth and pervasive power of the four railroad magnates—Collis P. Huntington, Charles Crocker, Mark Hopkins, and Leland Stanford (who later offered Robins a position with the Southern Pacific Railroad)—"influenced the development of San Francisco and the west and permeated every feature of life from politics and justice to architecture and social custom."[25]

Soon after starting his San Francisco law practice, Robins joined the influential Democratic Iroquois Club. In just a matter of weeks, after contributing to and stumping for the state Democratic slate, he assumed leadership positions in the club.[26] He supported William Jennings Bryan through the thick and thin of the 1896 presidential race, and with the resignation of John P. Irish, who left the Democratic ranks to support William McKinley, Robins took his place as the chairman of the city and county organization committee. Robins's speaking ability was an asset to the party and he was sent stumping for Judge James G. McGuire in the California gubernatorial race. Robins experienced the rise of his political star at just this time. A bright future seemed further assured following the returns of the presidential election of November, when San Francisco made an unexpectedly strong stand for Bryan while Robins was election organizer. "I was just young enough to think I'd done it."[27]

In March of 1897, after many months of trying to build up his practice by arguing criminal cases, Robins joined forces with Max Popper, a well-known San Francisco politician. They worked together to halt machine corruption in the politics of both parties, which were making an all-out effort to sew up control of the police and fire departments of the city. Boss Rainey of the Democratic machine, in cooperation with the leaders of the Republican party, managed to get two important laws passed by the state legislature. The laws' provisions raised the fire and police department payroll budget by approximately $60,000, and since Rainey controlled the hiring and salary distribution of the municipal payroll, he could reward allies with raises and punish opponents by withholding them. These additional funds assured his unchallenged power in San Francisco.[28]

Popper tried in vain to block this move by lobbying against the budget in the state legislature in Sacramento, but once it had become law he had no recourse but to turn to the courts to argue its unconstitutionality. He asked Robins to represent the interests of the people of San Francisco in the case. "I am sole counsel of the plaintiffs (the taxpayers of San Francisco)," Robins proudly wrote to his sister, at a time when she was becoming the theatrical sensation of the London stage, "and will have opposed to me the ablest attorneys on this coast."[29]

Popper and Robins lost the first phase of the legal battle in the Superior Court of the City and County of San Francisco, since Judge Emmet Seawell of that court was a close associate of the Rainey machine. Robins's letter to Elizabeth refers to the appeal that was immediately filed with the state supreme court. That appeal hinged on the fact that the charter under which San Francisco had been incorporated as a city was private and not under the same state constitutional budget guidelines as those cities whose charters were public. The Rainey legislation, which sought to make certain budget changes in the charter through the state legislature, was therefore unlawful. On 24 April Robins wrote to Elizabeth again, this time describing the battle in detail.

> Yesterday in the Supreme Court of San Francisco I did some measure of justice to the name I bear. . . . In argument that lasted from half past ten A.M. to nearly five o'clock in the afternoon, I met and withstood—single-handed and alone—in a great Constitutional debate, the repeated assaults of the two ablest lawyers of California, one Judge John Garber, the acknowledged head of the San Francisco bar, and leader of the legal profession on the Pacific Coast.
>
> It was the grandest day of my life. Not that I did not meet with reverse, not that I did not make mistakes, not that I do not now see things that I should have done, and that I did things that were better left undone, but, because the character of my argument and the effect of it demonstrated that I possess the measure and mold of a great lawyer. Young, obscure, insignificant in appearance, and in the court practically unknown, opposed by these legal giants, it was a sorry outlook for my client when I began the argument of his cause. After I had spoken for about one hour, a change was manifest in the attention of the Court and onlookers, and at the conclusion of my opening argument which lasted nearly three hours, I had passed from the category of the obscure and untried into the ranks of those members of the profession of acknowledged ability and power.[30]

Robins wrote this account before he had learned the favorable decision of the court, and as he later went on to say, the final decision was of little consequence. He had seen the electric impact of his arguments in the tense silence of the courtroom. He felt the power of his words and was thrilled by his personal magnetism—and for the cause of good and right. He gloried in the fact that he really was "somebody."

Robins's success was followed by offers from leaders of both the Democratic and Republican parties ("big-wigs" of the "little thieves" and the "big thieves," in Robins's terms). He was also offered a retainer of $4,000 to serve as attorney for the Southern Pacific Railroad.

This flush of success meant that he could finally revive his passionate dream of reuniting with his sister. "How I wish darling that you were here tonight," Raymond wrote, in the same letter in which he described his supreme court triumph, "that I might sit at your feet and tell you all my heart would speak of joy, and hope and the golden harvests that the coming years will yield." He suggested in the third person that "Bessie" come back to her native land and live with her brother. "Neither will marry," and "each will join hands to help the other in whatever each may prefer." He held out the excitement and hope of the growing city of San Francisco as the site for their work together.[31]

Raymond's profound disappointment at Elizabeth's letter of refusal can only be suggested, for his response was entirely irrational. Elizabeth decided to remain in London, and as she tried to explain in her autobiographical book, *Raymond and I*, he did not understand the degree to which she had found a life for herself in the creative world of London. Raymond had the misguided notion that if he were to amass a large enough fortune, he would be able to induce the one person he really loved to come to his side. And since the San Francisco Supreme Court victory had not brought him the companionship he desperately wanted, he was ready to try some other means of winning his sister to his side, even if it meant years of struggle, danger, and sacrifice.[32]

3

Alaska, 1897–1900

Like the bark of the hounds on the ear of the hunter, like the scent of burning powder in the nostrils of the war-horse, is this call that bids me enter this mad rush for the Yellow God. Back of the material advantage, beneath the cold calculations of cent per cent, burns an unquenchable love in my Soul for the battle, the quarterless conflict of men desperate with desire and urged to supreme effort by tremendous possibilities, this is the glory and the shame that intoxicates me with an irresistible charm. I live only in action.
—Raymond Robins to Elizabeth Robins, 25 July 1897

IN 1897 Saxton and Raymond Robins caught the "gold fever" and decided to leave San Francisco for the Klondike. Raymond had demonstrated his skill as a lawyer, particularly in his victory before the state supreme court, "Yet," he wrote to Elizabeth, "I am very poor in dollars and cents. . . . Lack of clothes, lack of books, lack of means to pay the legitimate costs of the 'game' I am competent and desirous of playing—these handicaps meet me at every turn. Still before me stretch five possibly ten years of waiting for the fruits of my toil."[1]

To the amazement and disbelief of all who knew him, Raymond's new impulse ignored all the effort, intense study, and accomplishment of the previous two years. His achievements at the Columbian University had been to no avail. All his talent, dynamism, and power to convince people had not worked with the one person who mattered, Elizabeth.

As a child, Elizabeth was his surrogate mother. As an adolescent he continued the fantasy of that relationship, and as a man at the age of twenty-four, he seized the possibility of finally gaining the warmth, affection, and love he had been denied. He may have chosen his sister because she had already proven that she could care for him. His self-consciousness about his appearance and a lingering sense of inferiority led to a painful shyness that made other relationships with women almost impossible. Robins's joining the gold rush can only be explained by Elizabeth's refusal to live with him in San Francisco. Had she accepted, he would in all likelihood not have gone. Her refusal was a denial of his success.

Three months before making the decision to go to Alaska, while exulting in his supreme court victory and the dream of himself and Elizabeth together in San Francisco, he wrote to her, proposing that they build a life there together. His yearning was great, yet it was matched by an equal and knowing fear that she would refuse. Just in case, assuming that she would not come, "this is what I propose to do. . . . I shall prepare to marry. I am not in love and do not expect to become so in anything like the popular sense of the term. I will use the best judgment I possess, find the woman that seems to me the best fitted for what I believe to be the probable measure of my life, and then set about to win her with the same determination that I would a law suit."[2]

Elizabeth did refuse, and Raymond gave up his plans for an immediate and expedient marriage and, with Saxton in tow, decided instead to gamble on the slim odds of the Alaska gold rush. He hoped to change her mind by striking it rich. "I shall not expect to make money mining, I have played that game and know its delusions fairly well. But there is a premium in such a place for the cool head and the steady hand in many ways." In the same letter, dramatically announcing his manly intentions in the "ice bound Clondyke" and ignoring her refusal, he reasserted his plans for the two of them. "And if I win, we will build a house in the Santa Cruz mountains near this city, I shall continue my professional career free from the pall of poverty, you shall do the things that are more excellent and reign as Queen over my possessions—the inspiration and guide of my life. If I lose, bah, it is unthinkable."[3] Years later, in 1934, in connection with this letter, Elizabeth wrote, "I could not fail to know that if I instead of producing the latest Ibsen in London, had been sharing his life in San Francisco, Raymond would not have joined the Klondike rush of '97."[4]

Word of the Bonanza Creek "strike" near Dawson, reached the outside world after the spring thaw of 1897, when the steamer *Excelsior* sailed south from Alaska to San Francisco with $700,000 in nuggets and gold dust. The epidemic of "gold fever" began to spread in the United States at the very time of Raymond's disappointment. And being in San Francisco gave him the opportunity to look through the guarded, plate-glass display cases in the bank with gold dust and nuggets heaped on black velvet, challenging his first resolve not to make money mining. Who was more qualified than he to undertake the hardships and dangers of the "magnetic north"? He had been a miner as well as a prospector. His father had been involved in gold-mining ventures in Colorado. If he and his brother Saxton worked together, couldn't they manage to hit "paydirt"?[5]

On Saturday, 7 August 1897, a chilly overcast day, Raymond and Saxton Robins boarded the "steam schooner" *National City* at the Folsom Street wharf at San Francisco, bound for Saint Michael, Alaska. In Raymond's diary for that day he wrote: "The Klondike excitement has brought down to the wharf fully 1500 people, friends of passengers and citizens. Nothing like it has occurred in the history of Frisco. It probably stands alone in the records of the ravages of the gold fever." The blast of the steam whistle sounded and the ship set out into the bay. In a dark woolen sailor's hat and heavy coat,

Raymond climbed the forward rigging to find a good vantage point for the sights along the harbor; as they passed through the Golden Gate "the lights broke brilliantly from the city."[6]

The brothers had agreed that Saxton should assume the alias "Harry Earle," while Raymond retained his own name. Throughout Raymond's Alaskan diary and even among closest friends, Saxton was referred to by this pseudonym; the fact that they were brothers remained a secret. This arrangement eliminated the possibility that others would judge one by the actions of the other. The Alaskan venture was a test of Saxton's strength of character and independence. He met courageously the challenges of physical danger and privation, but his underlying feelings of worthlessness and hopelessness were a constant struggle for him.[7]

Passage and baggage on board the *National City,* including one ton of tools and supplies, was $225. The destination was Saint Michael, near the mouth of the Yukon River. The Robins brothers and others on board planned to take the river steamer up the 1,500-mile course of the Yukon to Dawson and the Klondike. They had chosen this all-water route as safest, least arduous, and most economical, but complications arose even on the first days of the voyage. The "grub" on board the ship was terrible, and Raymond complained to the captain. The steward later confronted Raymond and accused him of being the ringleader of malcontents whose complaints were unjustified. "He became nasty, I angry, jump at him, force him into corner and hammer his nose with my fist. Crowd collects and I leave heartily ashamed of myself." But Raymond was hardly ashamed, as he continued in his diary, "It will increase my popularity as nearly all despised the man I thrashed."[8]

Raymond met and talked over the coming adventure with many men on board ship, and in his diary he sized them up in terms of whether or not they had the stuff to make it through the ordeal. There was a young lawyer from Oakland—Irish, impulsive, loyal, and six feet tall—Albert F. Shulte, who remained in contact with Robins for many years. R. B. Todd was an experienced miner, and "William H. Matheson, 33, 5'7"," the same height as the Robins brothers, was "a bachelor, a Scotsman, a Presbyterian in faith, of Prince Edward Island, tough school, carpenter by trade and handy with tools. And finally there was Stewart A. Prescott, Matheson's partner, 40, 6'2", tall, well proportioned, blue eyes, blond hair, a typical Viking of Norse legends— uneducated in books and learning of schools, wise in woodcraft and the frontier life . . . U.S. army, 5 years Indian Service, great manner, dead shot and proud of it."[9] It was not long before the easily made shipboard friendships of the Robins brothers and these four men evolved into a prospecting partnership, which was tested by their fight against death on the frozen Yukon River.

The *National City* docked at Saint Michael on 22 August, after fifteen days at sea. Within a few hours the beach nearby had become a city of tents and the prospecting partners shared their first labors together. They built a roof over their leaking and overloaded storage barge and then put up a large tent to house everyone. The initial days and nights, surrounded by hundreds of prospectors, were pervaded by a "general suspicion and bad faith." The partners took turns as watchmen "all night with our rifles across our laps." After taking on passengers that had just come down the Yukon from Dawson, on the boats of the Alaskan Commercial Company, the *National City* set out on its return voyage to San Francisco. Raymond and his companions tried to book passage for the trip up to Dawson, but the number of passengers was limited on the boats of the Alaskan Commercial Company and the North American Transportation and Trading Company, and "not a single pound of provisions" was permitted on board. "They want thousands of hungry men so they can sell them provisions at fabulous prices," Raymond noted in his diary.10

The partners listened to the advice of those who had just returned from the goldfields. "They would not start up river without enough provisions to last all winter." They could not rely on the steamships; they had to find some other means. They talked with Father Barnum, the resident head of the Roman Catholic missions in Alaska, who told them of the early days when small boats rigged with sails went as far as 600 miles up the river. The men yearned to believe in the possibility. The alternative was a winter immobilized and wasted at Saint Michael without even the timber to build a cabin for themselves or wood for fire.

It was no surprise to find that the only boats available were those in the hands of the Alaskan Commercial Company, in very poor shape, and at prices five times their value. Raymond, Saxton, and their partners tried and failed to engage tugboat captains to haul their barge upstream, and they finally resolved to buy a small eighteen-foot sailboat with oars and make a try on their own.11

The Robins brothers and their partners caulked and prepared their boat, selling some of the excess provisions that would not fit on board. They christened her the *Sophia T.* and at 2:25 P.M. on 1 September, along with two other boats manned by others who had made the same desperate decision, they "pulled out into the bay." Two days later, after some progress and always trying to keep land and the other two boats in sight, they came upon an Indian village where they were able to trade tea and tobacco for ducks and geese. The day following, just as they sighted Point Romanoff, marking half the distance to the mouth of the Yukon, they finally met with the high seas they feared. One of the other boats, the *Tulare*, got caught in the breakers and was drawn to the rocky shore. The men on the *Sophia T.* made it to the Yukon delta late the next morning, 7 September. Reaching the Yukon, however, was no relief. Reduced winds limited the tacking possibilities on the river. After meeting the other two boats on 12 September and recounting the "hair breadth escape" of the *Tulare*, the crew of the *Sophia T.* rowed from sunrise till sunset for three days straight, crusts of ice growing on the oars with each stroke. They made it to Russian Mission by 24 September, and to Raymond's surprise, the strange sight of the "rude wooden cross" on the adjoining hillside "in this wilderness of the north" made a deep impression. Raymond was a self-professed Deist or liberal Unitarian, embarking on a life-and-death adventure. Amid the hostile emptiness he reflected on "the native, alien in language, race, habits of life, [who] bows his head at the name of Jesus Christ. This is a fact full of deepest meaning if one stops to consider."[12]

They pushed on for six more days and finally, after losing some supplies while nearly capsizing and experiencing the increasing danger of collision with ice floes, the six men managed to pull their boat to the right bank of the river and drag their remaining supplies ashore. They searched out a good location, began digging out a foundation for a fireplace, and started cutting logs. It was 30 September, and they quickly had to create conditions to survive a nine-month hibernation.

They built a cabin on the leveled ground by stacking cottonwood logs till the wall was six feet high. "A gable of split logs for roof—over these straw and boughs then one foot earth—cracks closed with mud—rough stone fire place built in end and doors just large enough to admit a man—window—four Mason fruit jars built into side of cabin." They called it Big Chimney Camp.

> Our cabin forty miles above Russian Mission, half way to Holy Cross mission. Four hundred miles from St. Michaels, eighty from Anvik, Six hundred from gold fields, ten to nearest Indian Village, Forty to nearest White person, two thousand five hundred to telegraph and Railway. Eight months time from civilized world on right bank of Yukon on the side of a bald mountain sixty feet above the river. Yukon two miles broad here. Our cabin sixteen by eighteen feet, walls five and half feet high. Our "library" contains three Bibles, two law books, Byron's poems, a book on mining and *Theory of Human Progress* by Wordsworth.[13]

The story of those nine months is a fascinating one, as full of suspense and human perseverance as is any tale or novel by Jack London.[14] In fact, the story has been told by Elizabeth Robins with the skill of London. After visiting Raymond at Nome, Alaska, in 1900, and with the help of his diary and that of Albert Shulte, Elizabeth wrote *The Magnetic North* (1904). It begins with the first days on the Yukon and ends with the coming of the great spring "breakup" of the ice in June 1898. At Raymond's request his name is not used in the novel, nor are those of his five companions, although there is no careful attempt to disguise the real identities of the fictionalized characters.

After Big Chimney was completed and the supply of firewood was adequate, the men settled down to the more difficult task of passing idle time. Raymond started discussion meetings to consider aspects of the Bible and

Big Chimney Cabin on the bank of the Yukon River during the winter of 1897 with its six inhabitants. In the front row, left to right, are Saxton and Raymond. (Courtesy of the Elizabeth Robins Papers, Fales Library, New York University.)

other questions. This Yukon Symposium made for some excitement, but the underlying tenseness and anxiety grew with the realization that the carefully rationed bacon, beans, and flour might not be enough to last the winter. The question remained beneath the surface long after the Yukon had frozen solid and the winter storms had begun. "Each meal . . . had come to mean a silent struggle in each man's soul not to let his stomach get the better of his head and heart."[15]

Further impact of those months of denial in the cabin is reflected in this conversation from *The Magnetic North:*

"I came out here a Communist," said the boy [Raymond] one day to the Colonel [Shulte].

"And an agnostic," smiled the older man.

"Oh, I'm an agnostic all right, now and forever. But this winter has cured my faith in Communism."[16]

In February 1898, months after the last travelers passed Big Chimney Camp, two successful prospectors appeared from upriver by dog sled. They had traveled from Big Minook Creek near Rampart following the trail of the Yukon ice on their way to Saint Michael. The new guests had nuggets and gold dust and many tales of rich strikes just 500 miles to the north. With this new knowledge and rather than waiting for the food to dwindle along with the last vestiges of humanity, Raymond and Shulte (Col. George Warren, in *The Magnetic North*) decided to push ahead in the direction of the goldfields, regardless of the midwinter dangers. Nowhere do we learn why Saxton did not head on with Raymond; either Saxton was unwilling or, given Saxton's limitations, Raymond decided against it.[17]

The two left for Big Minook Creek and Rampart with one sled loaded with supplies, alternating with the pushing and the pulling. Their first destination and possible haven in case of emergency was the Holy Cross Mission, about forty miles above their cabin. They hoped to make it to this Jesuit outpost in two days with one night spent on the trail. They planned these days as a test of their strength and navigation along the snow-covered river. They arrived at the mission on schedule on 12 March, determined to continue on, the full danger now apparent.

As I look back upon my first winter in Alaska, its hardship and suffering are appalling. There were times when I coveted death. And on the icebound snow-covered tundras with the North wind howling, miles from any human habitation, starvation possible, death imminent, my self-confident pride of intellect and sceptical philosophy was tried in the balance and found wanting.

Do not misunderstand me, I am not easily alarmed and I have not been frightened into the Kingdom of God. As an agnostic I could have died fearlessly and been glad that the struggle was over. But to live an agnostic among such surroundings and be human, this was impossible. The deathlike stillness of the long Arctic night, the cold mocking sunshine of the quickly passing daytime, the constant presence of the Ice King eager to touch you into dreamless sleep, starvation staring at you with hollow eyes and sunken cheeks, so environed, you must either drug the senses into dullness with tobacco or whiskey, or realize that without faith in something not ourselves, we shall either turn demon or go mad.

In the midst of this never-to-be-forgotten journey over the ice and snow, we stopped for a night and a day at a Jesuit Mission on the Yukon. Here were four Priests of the Order, five Sisters of St. Ann and two Brothers, teaching the Indians not only religion but the three R's and habits of domestic cleanliness and order; quietly and gladly wearing out their lives serving others, doing good without money and without price.[18]

At Holy Cross, Robins again met Father Barnum, who had first suggested the use of a small boat back at Saint Michael. The impression made by this priest can be likened only to that made by Fielder Harris and William Fulton in Robins's boyhood. Father Barnum came from a family of wealth and position; he had a Johns Hopkins education; he had traveled widely and was a "man of the world," and in Robins's words, "He had married the woman of his choice; she had died in childbirth, the babe stillborn."

That winter evening "by the flickering candle light" the priest related to Robins the only source of consolation he was able to find. And the impact of the "miracle of Eternal Life" that was so strongly felt was in some way shared, "yet not here, nor for many months to come, was I to understand the power of the Christian faith and the marvel of the life in Christ. While not convinced, I was deeply moved by the love and service of this consecrated Priest. My difficulty was an intellectual one and no amount of personal testimony nor example could have converted me from the error of my ways."[19]

Father Barnum pleaded with Robins and Shulte to remain at the mission, especially since they were without a dog team. Barnum's offers of dogs were refused, since it was obvious that they were badly needed to help supply the mission. With only a new cover for the sled made by one of the sisters, and a little more bacon in addition to the supplies they arrived with, the partners headed north toward Anvik, following the big bend in the Yukon River just beyond Holy Cross. After a few days, in a very sparsely inhabited region, Robins had another profound experience.

> In one of the darkest hours of our long journey we camped by the side of a gulch in the mountains, and prepared to rest for the night. It was bitterly cold. Not a breath of air stirred the loose snow in the gulch. The stillness was so oppressive I could not sleep. Rising, I drew on my parka, mitts and moccasins, and slipping on my snowshoes went a short distance up the gulch. The night was terrible yet superb. As far as the eye could reach stretched the spotless coverlet of snow. . . . the gorgeous streamers of the Aurora, shot from horizon to zenith, gleamed in all the colors of the rainbow, then flickered, rose again, faded and died away. Over all brooded the inexpressible silence of the Arctic night, full of awful menace, yet sublime. As I walked slowly along the edge of the mountain I saw in the distance a snow white cross. I thought I was going mad, turned and started for the camp. After walking a few rods I looked back. There stood the white cross, solitary, on the mountain side. I started towards it, expecting each moment it would fade away, but on getting nearer, I saw the end of a rude fence reaching above the snow and knew I was standing by an Indian grave. The cross was rudely fashioned from a birch sapling, and so covered with frost crystals as to appear to rise phantom-like from the surrounding snow. I stood there looking at this symbol of the Church militant and triumphant, over a hundred miles from any human habitation, alone amid the boundless expanse of snow and ice. And I thought of the simple carpenter's son, that was born in the village of Nazareth amid the hills of Galilee,

nearly nineteen hundred years ago. I saw him dressed in simple robes, teaching the multitudes on the Mount, as never man taught before.

And I said in my heart, Jesus of Nazareth was more than an ethical teacher, the Bible is more than a historical moral code. That cross is more than the symbol of human superstition and vanity, more than the evidence of "morality touched with human emotion."[20]

In that hostile environment, Robins imbued that lonely cross, so distant from himself, with all the hope and affirmation of life that he very desperately needed; another man might have seen this desolate sign of death as an omen of his impending fate. In Robins's later evangelical work, this became the most often told tale of the many personal life adventures with which he spiced his speeches and sermons. His search for self depended on this kind of drama and led to his ultimate conversion, which came many months after the incident of the "snow white cross." He always looked back on it as his singular prophetic sign.

The most fearsome stretch of the trip was between Anvik and Kaltag. Robins fell over a precipice, lost his snow shoes, and was entirely dependent upon his partner to rescue him. He hung for hours on a narrow ledge until Shulte found him and threw him a line. Later, during a blinding snowstorm, Robins was up front pulling the sled along, conscious only of the struggle to go forward. After a long stretch he was shaken from his somnambulism when he realized how heavy the sled had grown. When he turned around, Shulte was gone. Desperately, Robins went off to try to find him in the swirling snow. After what seemed an interminable search, he finally came upon a dark heap nearly covered by falling snow. For the next days, until they reached Kaltag, Robins had to guide his snow-blinded friend and place his two hands in position to be able to push the sled from behind.

At Kaltag they were finally able to rest and trade for a small dog team, the one possible chance to complete the trip. Just beyond Nulato, near the small village of Koyukuk, they staked out a new trading post, but on their way back down the Koyukuk River they lost the trail and wandered away from the Yukon. Trusting to intuition and the instinct of their dogs, they traveled generally eastward for about one hundred miles before they finally picked up the trail again. On 9 May 1898, with their supplies almost gone and in a terribly weakened condition, they arrived at their destination, Rampart, at the junction of Big Minook Creek and the Yukon.

Like most mining towns in Alaska during the gold rush, Rampart was a sea of tents and shacks with the largest permanent buildings belonging to the trading companies along the dockside. Robins and Shulte set up their tent and, with their grubstake quickly running out, began to try their luck at prospecting, remembering the good luck of the two prospectors who had passed through Big Chimney Camp. But the partners were latecomers and the pickings that remained were poor. They managed day by day, stranded in

Rampart until the great spring breakup. Until that cataclysmic end of winter, of thundering ice and raging water heading for Norton Sound and the Bering Sea, Robins eked out an existence by taking odd jobs, even if payment only came in the form of a meal. He put aside just enough money to buy passage on the first riverboat heading up to Dawson and the Klondike.

Robins waited more than a month, but nearly half the population of Rampart had been waiting since the great freeze had put a stop to river traffic in September. Disillusionment at Big Minook Creek only intensified the hope of a big strike at Bonanza Creek, upriver in the Klondike. When the first steamer finally arrived in mid-June, its passengers included the four men who Raymond and Shulte had left behind at Big Chimney. The reunion was joyous, as they were amazed that they all had survived.[21]

This reunion at Rampart marks the end of the story recounted in *The Magnetic North*. Raymond left there in June, but though it seems probable, there is only secondhand evidence that he continued on to Dawson. Shortly thereafter he returned to San Francisco to refinance his prospecting and went back to Alaska in August 1898, but again there is no hard evidence of his itinerary. Dated documents place him in Juneau during the winter of 1898–99, and in the Klondike during the summer of 1899, followed by a journey by river steamer down to Saint Michael at the end of August. From that point on he was in Nome, and Elizabeth's Alaskan diary and book *Raymond and I* tell that story based on her visit to him there in the spring of 1900. The story of the publication of *Raymond and I* is both interesting and pertinent here. It appears in the foreword and was written by Elizabeth's close friend Leonard Woolf, husband of Virginia Woolf.

> Elizabeth Robins wrote this book over 20 years ago. In 1934 she brought the MS to my wife and myself and asked us whether we would publish it. We agreed at once, but then difficulties arose. She gave the book to her brother, Colonel Raymond Robins, to read and he objected to its being published during his lifetime. Eventually he agreed to its being published after his death, and she gave the MS to us and left us all rights in it under her will. I undertook not to publish it while Colonel Robins was alive. Elizabeth died in 1952 and Raymond in 1955 [*sic,* 1954], and it has therefore become possible to fulfil her wish and publish the book. I have to thank Miss Lisa von Borowsky for permission to quote from Colonel Robins' letters.

> Elizabeth and Raymond are a remarkable brother and sister. She was a great actress, the first and, almost certainly, the best actress of Ibsen in English. She wrote a best selling novel, *The Magnetic North*. She was also, as this book shows, a great character. So too was her brother Raymond, in his time a colonel, an unofficial ambassador to Soviet Russia, and a modern—somewhat quixotic—crusader on behalf of any peoples or person who he thought to be despised, downtrodden or persecuted.[22]

Loyal Lincoln Wirt, who first met Raymond at Juneau, told Elizabeth that her brother had "reached Dawson in the spring of '98 to find all the good claims gone." He had to take "hard work, any work, one could be thankful for." After only a few weeks at Dawson, Raymond managed to book passage for a return trip to San Francisco, where he hoped to get solid financial backing based on his year's experience and continue his prospecting in earnest. Raymond wrote to Elizabeth from San Francisco on 1 August 1898:

> For a few days I am in the land of the civilized once more. It is not possible . . . to write to you fully of my campaign in Alaska. This is the most important fact—Saxton is on his feet and doing finely. What I have lost I shall regain in time. My interests in the Yukon are of uncertain value. . . .
>
> Saxton is engaged in the service of the North American Transportation and Trading Company. . . . He is industrious and steadily forging ahead. Considering his past this is worth all the sufferings and hardship of our Alaskan experience.
>
> All through my journey on the trail, in the mines, everywhere, I had the picture I have carried of your dear face for nearly eight years. I have kept the faith.[23]

While Raymond returned to San Francisco, Saxton settled down in a job at the trading post in Anvik, on the Yukon River. A year and one-half later, on her way from Nome to Dawson, Elizabeth made contact with Saxton at Anvik. She was a passenger on the river steamer *Susie,* on the last leg of her Alaskan journey to rescue Raymond. Elizabeth and Saxton spent three hours together, filled with the urgency of their lost relationship that both feared would never be found. To spend the time with his sister, Saxton had to bring a canoe on board the steamer, come along the twenty-three miles to Greyling, and then paddle back. "I see before me," Elizabeth wrote in her diary, "a thin, haggard, and yet not sickly-looking man of 31, long face, stubby moustache, dark red-brown almost black in some lights, unshaven for the rest, and I think unwashed. . . . He wears a black cut-away waistcoat, a fancy lawn shirt and silk tie—brown corduroy trousers—a soft cap—a clean handkerchief, a gold watch and chain, a red cross badge. His beautiful teeth are tobacco stained and filled with gold. His hands are not clean; and tremble." Saxton recounted all of the adventures of the winter in Big Chimney Camp, the attempts at prospecting, and his resolve never to go back to the life he had left in San Francisco. "I suddenly feel with a sinking of the heart," Elizabeth continued, "that I have no more to say to this poor brother of mine, whom fate has used so hardly—I am full of sorrow for him—but I feel helpless—at a . . . life that always just 'misses it.'"

Late in the spring of the following year, 1901, while still in Alaska, Saxton committed suicide. The particular circumstances that led to his death are not documented and are further obscured by a family myth that "he was killed by Indians." Raymond, Elizabeth, and Vernon resolved to keep Saxton's suicide a secret. Given the first-cousin relationship of their parents, sensitivity to the emotional problems of their mother and Raymond, and the suicide of

Elizabeth's husband, the pact was sealed. Another terrible irony in this connection is Elizabeth's novel, *The Open Question,* which deals with the suicide of married cousins. Published under her penname, C. E. Raimond, just three years earlier, it explores suicide carried out in the face of hereditary disease. Only one extant letter, written by Raymond to Elizabeth on 29 June 1942, reveals the truth—that Saxton took his own life.[24]

Raymond left San Francisco early in August 1898, just one year after his first trip north. His plans for the next half year are unclear, but he did spend many months in Juneau where he "haunted" the library of the Protestant mission of the minister Loyal Wirt. His long ledger notebooks, with their orderly entries, suggest some of his activity. He took notes on ancient history, world literature, and commentaries on the Bible; but most of these entries are undated and without indication where they were written. One complex metaphysical diagram suggests a rambling disconnection from reality.[25]

It appears that Raymond went north to Juneau to go over Chilkoot Pass and take the overland route to the Klondike, but for some reason he remained in Juneau. Wirt recounted to Elizabeth that "He was like a man waiting for something, but quietly, with assurance that it would come. I used to say: 'Why don't you set up a law office?' 'No, I left all that behind in San Francisco,' he would say and he would sit and read in our Juneau Library." After a while they prevailed upon him to lend a hand to the Self Improvement Society for the miners. "'He used to give us brilliant talks. When we were alone we would argue about the big questions. He could always floor me in an argument—but, Silbert [Elizabeth's pseudonym for Wirt] smiled, 'I had my moorings.'"[26]

Raymond was able to raise some money in San Francisco, but the experience of the long winter march from Big Chimney Camp to Rampart stood in the way of his immediate return to "the service of Mammon," the quest for gold. He reached Juneau in a state of confusion, unable to determine what he really wanted out of life. He even abandoned his only source of love and compassion, his sister, to whom he did not write for nearly a year. She later wrote:

> But though I would not believe he was dead, I found it hard to believe he was alive and yet made no sign. In the past, whether he wrote anyone else or not, he wrote to me—if not for two or three months, then a glorious great screed filling up the gap in a way that kept me abreast of his life.
>
> Now, when for over a year no letter of any sort had come, the problem of his silence pressed hard, pressed intolerably.[27]

Elizabeth's rejection and the hardships of the Alaskan winter, which left him nothing, were very hard to bear. But despite the powerful impression made on him by Father Barnum and the eerie spiritual vision of the snow white cross, Raymond held fast to his agnosticism and despair.

After a month of trying to find himself, he took hold and resolved to search out answers and purpose in "universal history and literature." This was the beginning of his first reading in these areas since his teenage studies with William Fulton. Committing himself to the mastery of *General History* by Phillip V. N. Myers, Raymond once again had a goal. His notes show concern for every detail, and there are many lengthy passages that he copied from the text. Among them are his first and only extant notes on Russian history.[28]

"On the 17th of February [1899]," he wrote to Elizabeth of the "crisis of my life,"

> by merest chance, I began to read *Natural Law in the Spiritual World* by Professor [Henry] Drummond [1892]. Late in the night I finished the book. My hour had come. This book took possession of me. Day and night I thought of this wonderful revelation of the teaching of Jesus, and the life of the Spiritual World. Wherever I looked I saw the words "Except ye be born again ye cannot enter the Kingdom of God." "I am the way, the truth and the life." "And as many as received him to them gave he power to become the sons of God." Here at last was an expression of the fundamental doctrines of the Christian faith, in the terms of the rest of our knowledge. Here at last was Christian dogma developed, explained and proven, by the scientific method.
>
> At last the scales fell from my eyes. But the light was blinding. Since then until a few days ago I have been much like one in a dream. Slowly have I drawn away from my worldly interests until when I reached Dawson I found I was in debt. Then, for a time, a little regret seized me. At times I thought I was losing my mind. But the night passed away. Through the glorious dawning of a new life, I see the radiant face of the blessed Master, Jesus the Christ Son of God, and Redeemer of Mankind.[29]

This transformation was also observed by Wirt, who in turn shared the experience with Elizabeth:

> When Mr. Robins came to Juneau he was an agnostic. One day in the library he caught sight of Drummond's *Natural Law in the Spiritual World* and laughed at the title, but he took the book down and stood with it in his hand. An hour he stood there reading. He took the book home. . . . One day he came and said he was conscious of a great change at work in him. He was helping us more and more in the Mission—but no matter how much he did, he refused to be paid anything. We were always trying to get him to cast in his lot with our work for good and all. But he wasn't ready yet. He left us and went to Dawson. He was going to see about some claims. In the summer—last summer that was—I found Mr. Robins in Dawson carpenting for a living.[30]

During the remainder of the spring and early summer of 1899, Raymond remained "in a dream." His time, thoughts, and energy seem to have been completely overwhelmed by the new spiritual-emotional challenge. Just managing his material needs by day labor, he turned from history and literature to Bible study and analysis. His notebooks marked this change and became filled with problems in Christianity along with his own sermons. He prepared complex diagrams of the classification of the universe into the "Spiritual, Vital—Flesh is Flesh, and material" subdivisions.

Nowhere in Raymond's diaries, personal papers, or letters does he raise the question of his own sexuality. In two letters to Elizabeth, written three decades later, he does discuss sex, admitting his utter ignorance and the false notions that formed the basis of both his own anguish and his preaching before tens of thousands of young men and women throughout his evangelical career.

> I wrote to you something about sex, I have read more about it and talked with two of the wisest physicians possible in this land on that theme and I am shocked and startled and surprised beyond words, as to what I have thought in the past and what now appears to be the truth. Why folks have not written the truth, and why those that know the truth do not proclaim it from the housetops and the prisons if necessary is more than I can understand. I am profoundly interested in what seems to have been the false education on this matter we have had and that I myself have been guilty of in the colleges and universities of this country and Canada and Australia and South Africa and China and Japan and Russia. What a matter of deep damnation ignorance really is![31]

At the age of seventy-four Robins tape-recorded his recollections of his early life and spoke more frankly about his sexuality than any previous evidence revealed. John C. Dreier, Robins's nephew and editor, suggested that "the experiences on which they were based, were, like classic myths, less important for their factual component than for the glimpses of inner reality." "When I'd ask questions," Robins explained about Fielder Harris's openness,

> he gave me the answers. One time, when I was just getting to the age where I would feel my prick, I told Fielder that it was stiff. He said, "Well, that's a hard-on. That's all right, don't bother about it; it will pass away. Your'e getting big enough now, where you'll be thinking about that, and that's what makes babies. Only it takes two: a male and a female. But, you mustn't trifle with it, because Raymond, 'There ain't no conscience in a stiff prick!'" And he was everlastingly right—if you yield to it, and that isn't what you want to do. You want to be decent and right.

Nevertheless, forty pages later in the edited transcript of the tape recordings, Robins boasts of his life in Alaska: "My continued poverty and my hard, vigorous life had kept me from loose living with women, but I had had sexual relations with women who were not supposed to be whores."[32]

In this time of loneliness, at the age of twenty-six, he was deeply bewildered about sex. He permits himself the abstraction of "Flesh is Flesh," but cannot, even in his deepest personal writing, consider what that means to him personally. In one letter, in 1905, to his fiancée, Margaret Dreier, he refers to the "evil power of temptation" in him. In Juneau he spent his time

immersed deeper and deeper into the foggy confusions of too many theological problems. He disconnected himself from the pain of his personal problems to find relief and comfort in a new spiritual life and Christian service.
From August 1898 to July 1899 he never wrote to Elizabeth; he had replaced
her with Jesus.[33]

Although his feelings, motives, and spirit remained in turmoil during this
time in Juneau, his activities began to take on orderly and constructive di-
mensions. In the spring he began to work in earnest for the Christian missions in Juneau, speaking, teaching, and proselytizing among the miners and
workers. He began giving sermons and had great appeal to churchgoers and
skeptics alike. Nevertheless, in the late spring he set out for Dawson and the
Klondike to settle his affairs as a prospector. With little money, he could not
get hold of the supplies needed for another attempt with the pick and pan.
Instead he took a job as a carpenter, earning from four to ten dollars a day
"butchering wood." Wirt, who passed through Dawson, begged Raymond to
give up carpenting and join him in mission work, but Raymond refused. At
last he was able to deal with one of his problems—his relationship with his
sister. He had to confront his failure as a prospector and admit it to her, the
person for whom he had endured so much. His first letter to her after his
year of confusion, divided commitments, and anguish was written from the
Klondike on 26 July 1899. Christian service had given him the solid ground-
ing he had been missing.

> My two years' race with fortune is over and I have lost. I am about one
> thousand dollars in debt and have no assets of any immediate value. This is the
> exact condition of my affairs. Now do not be concerned about my future. I
> have made my bed and am content to lie on it. My first duty is to pay my
> debts, and this I shall endeavor to accomplish by January 1, 1900. I shall suffer
> in nothing except pride and the personal esteem of some fair weather friends.
> My health was never better and I am confident of being independent before I
> leave this place.
>
> I do not now expect to make a fortune, am not in truth especially concerned
> about this matter of a fortune anymore. This may be "sour grapes" but the il-
> lusion is very real to your dollar-eager brother of a short time since. I have
> seen another vision and shall endeavor not to be disobedient to its warning.
> While I have lost the dollar race I seem to see with clearness certain incompar-
> able gains as a result of my experience in Alaska and the Northwest. We shall
> speak of this at some later time.[34]

Early that summer the Methodist Episcopal church superintendent of Alaska
missions gave Raymond Robins authority to represent the church in Alaska's
interior and to "preach the gospel wherever its authority extends." On 14
July he received a second written authorization from the Quarterly Conference of Juneau Alaska Missions.[35] Finally, he decided to join L. L. Wirt at
Saint Michael, where a typhoid epidemic had broken out. While on board ship
heading down the Yukon, he wrote to Elizabeth of his new commitment.

My desire now, as well as my duty, is no longer wealth, nor fame, but simply to serve. If as the result of my living here, I can add to the sum of sweetness and light in this world, I shall not go empty handed into the next. Like a worthy laborer, I would meet my Master in the harvest time, bringing in my sheaves. And having, by the mercy of God, been permitted to save my own soul alive, though buried in selfishness and vain ambitions, should I not turn to the many that know not God, and seek to discover to some at least the glory of the risen Lord and the mystery of eternal Life? So, laying aside every weight that can be put away in honor, with serene and confident faith I have entered upon the work of a disciple of Him of Nazareth.[36]

Father Barnum, the snow white cross, and Drummond's *Natural Law in the Spiritual World*—in Robins's mind, these were the three forces that led him to his decision. He thus saw only his positive motivations; he did not allow himself to be overwhelmed by the failure, loneliness, and emptiness of his life at that moment. He pushed deeper into his unconscious his pervasive fear of hereditary madness. Instead, in a surge of determination that was characteristic of so much of his life, he brushed the failure aside, minimized its significance, and plunged into the enormous challenge of missionary work.

Robins reached Saint Michael during the first week of September 1899, but when he arrived Loyal Wirt, who had pleaded with him to come, had left for Nome, 200 miles further up the coast. Conditions there were even worse than those at Saint Michael. Robins settled down and resolved to work with the sick and troubled in the town that exactly two years earlier he had risked his life to leave. Wirt had been to San Francisco to hire nurses and buy hospital supplies for the mission at Nome, and on his way back his ship put in at Saint Michael because of bad weather. Wirt met Robins and convinced him to come with him, since "by all signs, next summer Nome will be the Dump Heap of the north."

At Nome the conditions matched the worst descriptions. The tundra water was being used carelessly and typhoid was rampant. Because of the discovery of gold along the beaches of Nome earlier in 1899, "boom" conditions overwhelmed the town's limited facilities. Once again, as at Rampart, Dawson, and other gold-strike towns, the tents sprang up for miles around and until the winter freeze, with the mud often knee deep. In addition to the huge mounds of supplies along the beach as far as the eye could see, there was every description of contraption being used to dig the beach sands. Grains of gold dust had been churned up by the great onrush of waters from the interior to the sea since the end of the great ice age. As much as twenty dollars in gold could be panned in a day, and because the beach was public domain, no permanent claims could be made. Each storm swept away all signs of ownership, leaving a smooth expanse where the gouged surface had been, ready for the next onslaught of feverish miners anxious to reestablish themselves on "their" section of beach. The unusual transience of the beach claims made Nome alluring, because everyone could get some gold. Twenty dollars a day from a beach claim meant as many as sixteen hours of backbreaking work with a pan or one of the more efficient "machines." This situation, unique in Alaska, along with Nome's remoteness and minimal government, made conditions ripe for corruption and outlawry, in addition to the rest of the misery.

The church in Nome, the Hospice of Saint Bernard, was a short distance from the beach, back on the tundra, and Robins lived "up the little dark stairs [in] the narrow loft above the church. There wasn't much light from the solitary window, but there was a stove and a fire burning. Behind the cotton curtains on one side were his bed and primitive toilet things. In front of the window stood his rude writing-table; nail racks for pencils; all his business papers, envelopes and docketed-ledger etc., all left open."[37] This was his study, where he continued his writing and commentary begun at Juneau in the long, narrow ledgers. Now these ruminations were incorporated into his "straight talks" (he initially disliked calling them sermons), in which he pulled no punches. Robins's reputation as a preacher spread, even reaching San Francisco by midsummer. An old friend there wrote of the strange news that Robins had become a minister.

> I wrote you an urgent letter to drop that country and come back to civilization. I then took the position that nothing but muscle-headed change, that brains were a useless encumbrance, but it appears that I was wrong and that brains, yours at any rate, are bound to make their influence felt even among the ice floes of Nome. I can assure you that it was a surprise to learn that you had taken charge of a Congregational church as pastor. I supposed myself fairly familiar with your views, even on religious subjects but your latest convinces me that I was a poor reader or you did not know yourself how fate plays with us.
>
> . . . [Y]our sermons I learn are most effective and vigorous, I would be willing to make any sacrifices to sit in the front pew Sunday morning drop in unexpectedly and hear you haul the dark characters over the coals. I hear you hit straight from the shoulder. Well old man I don't know exactly how to write you since you have become a follower of the gentle Nazarene. An inherent respect for the cloth makes me feel that I should not be as familiar and outspoken as in the old days and yet I cannot imagine you being anything but the same old Robins.[38]

Many people began asking that he take charge of the church, but Robins was reluctant. Finally he accepted, making a number of stipulations: there were to be no collections, and no professional actors were to participate in church entertainments. He was told that he would receive $1,200 a year. He refused that sum and demanded that he be paid only fifteen dollars a month. The ensuing debate and the resultant friction nearly caused an end to the plan, but agreement was finally reached and he accepted fifty dollars a month.

Ten days of soul-searching followed, and Robins resolved to remain for the winter "in the most northerly mining camp in the world." He wrote that he would be "assistant to the Superintendent of Alaska Missions for the Congregational Church of America, preaching the Gospel of Christ and

Front Street, Nome, Alaska, 1900, at the height of the gold rush fever. Elizabeth confided to her diary that "the most exciting thing in Nome was Raymond." (Courtesy of the Elizabeth Robins Papers, Fales Library, New York University.)

tending the sick." This letter, dated 2 November 1899, reached Elizabeth long after Raymond's outpouring of religious faith, which upset her deeply, for she felt sure that Father Barnum had won her brother to Catholicism. Her fear, following the long months without word from him, persuaded her to go to Alaska to rescue him. For two and one-half months, ignoring the warnings and pleading of friends, and especially of her brother Vernon, she planned her trip, setting her sights on leaving England in the early spring. She felt responsible for her brother's desperate situation and the even more desperate solution he had chosen. His Nome letter of 2 November both jarred Elizabeth and at the same time eased her fear of his conversion to "Romanism." She was still in England when William Stead published an article she had written on Cape Nome, and on the basis of its good reception, she got an assignment to travel through the Yukon and to write a series of articles on the Alaskan gold rush. Although relieved that Raymond had not converted, she pursued her plans to be with him.[39]

Comforted with the knowledge that Elizabeth would be at his side, Robins turned to his new work. On 7 January 1900, the day before leaving Nome,

Bird's-eye view of the shoreline tent city early in the Nome gold rush. (Courtesy of the Elizabeth Robins Papers, Fales Library, New York University.)

Loyal Wirt, as missionary superintendent, licensed Robins "to preach the Gospel for the period of one year; to administer the Sacrament, officiate at Marriages, administer Baptism and perform such other functions as usually pertain to the office of Clergyman, for the same length of time, or until full ordination."[40] Wirt had to leave to arrange for the shipment of supplies from Seattle and to travel to the hospice's sponsoring church in Boston to raise funds—"the most wealthy and conservative Church in New England."[41] Wirt met Elizabeth in Boston while she was on her way to Nome. He shared with her all he knew of Raymond, from their first meeting in Juneau to their parting words. The first pages of Elizabeth's Alaskan diary are charged with her joy and excitement at learning that her brother, "my boy," was well.

During Wirt's absence Robins took on most of his responsibilities. After Coal Creek, the Leadville mines, and the corruption-ridden machine politics of San Francisco, Robins felt that he could make some impact on the chaotic and lawless conditions that plagued the hard-working prospectors of Nome.

Soon after the "beach strike" at Nome, a grand conspiracy was hatched by Alexander McKenzie, a wealthy Dakota political boss, who formed the Alaska Gold Mining Company. After "contributing" stock in the company to influential friends and U.S. senators, McKenzie attempted to have the U.S. Congress enact legislation (the Hansbrough amendment to the new Alaska Code of 1899) that would authorize the company seizure of mining claims "at any time owned . . . by aliens residing in Alaska, including even claims bought from aliens in good faith by United States citizens." Congress never passed this amendment, but McKenzie managed to get Pres. William McKinley to appoint his coconspirator, Arthur H. Noyes, a Minneapolis lawyer, to the newly created federal court at Nome. Within days of his arrival in Nome, Noyes used the court to drive miners off their claims and arrest those who

52

Nome, 1900. Minister Raymond Robins, age 27, wearing suit, bow tie, and Stetson, with unidentified Nome neighbors. Photo taken by Elizabeth during her visit to Nome. (Courtesy of the Elizabeth Robins Papers, Fales Library, New York University.)

resisted. The Alaska Gold Mining Company "received" the claims and began immediately the intensive operation of the easily worked properties, while irate miners seeking legal redress had no choice but to travel 3,000 miles to the nearest U.S. circuit court in San Francisco. During the two months' wait for the return of the miners' representatives with a circuit court order, McKenzie "sewed up the town," forcing the lawyers to join his camp or "he would see to it that their cases never reached a hearing."[42]

The problem Robins faced was not unlike union organizing; there were dangers from the bosses as well as difficulties in convincing the masses of men that through a united front they could gain the upper hand, could check the corrupt court and town officials. With his earlier experience in mind, Robins began using the pulpit of the Hospice of Saint Bernard as the rallying point for the "campaign" to clean up Nome—its neglected water supply, sanitary conditions, health facilities, law enforcement, and corrupt federal court.

During the winter of 1899–1900, according to Robins, the big money interests "kept the Nome law enforcement and judicial system in its pocket." And when the Nome chief of police did act independently, it was in his own personal interest. He ran his office "on the fines exacted from prostitutes, gamblers, and criminals, and he pays his police out of his own pocket. He can afford to. The City Hall is turned into offices and the rents go into the pocket of the Chief." Most lucrative for the police was complicity in "lot jumping." In addition to being put off his claim by Judge Noyes's orders, the owner of a legal claim would be arrested on some trumped up charge and kept in jail awaiting trial, his "house" and supplies would be moved from his permanent claim above the beach and the lot taken over by the chief's stooge. "It isn't alone the shelterless who are uneasy these nights in Nome. . . . No man knows how soon his house or his tent, may be picked up and thrown into the road."[43]

Disregard for law and private property also threatened the sanctity of life. Robins recalled a Norwegian miner named Olsen, a newcomer, who asked for advice to resist "the gang" who sought to squeeze him out of his claim. Robins recommended that he "stand pat." Olsen was murdered a few days later and Robins was called to fetch his body for a burial service. Enraged, and convinced of his responsibility for this innocent man's death, Robins devoted his Sunday night sermon to a challenge to the Nome gang, the thievery, and corruption. His supporters called for a mass meeting. The agents of the Alaska Gold Mining Company and the Alaska Commercial Company tried to intimidate Robins, but when that failed they tried a different tactic. They engaged Dick McArthur, a staunch supporter of the status quo, who feared that the reform movement would jeopardize his legal and established mining interests. He was assigned the task of "putting the infernal preacher out of action." Elizabeth wrote, "In the middle of the winter night entrance would be effected through a window into the room where Raymond slept, and he was not to come out alive."[44]

The murder plot was never attempted; instead, the gang tried to pack the mass meeting with its own supporters and claques. Robins arrived late and moved to a side wall to "protect his rear." The gang's speaker was persuasive and seemed to be winning the support of the uncommitted. He attacked Robins and the forces that sought to disrupt the "orderly and peaceful" process of the established government. But then, as recorded in the minutes of the Brown's Hall mass meeting, this young lawyer of the vested interests turned his attack to the motives and selfish aims of Robins, labeling him a hypocrite. However, no one who had been in Nome for any length of time was unaware of Robins's work for the sick and destitute. It was possible that Robins was misguided, but few doubted his sincerity. The attack discredited the speaker in the eyes of the angry audience in Brown's Hall, the largest in Nome, and when some of his followers spotted Robins back in the crowd "they passed him over their heads to the stage." Robins, "the intellect and the driving force of the opposition," responded to every charge and then made his own. His allegations were not the vague generalities of the lawyer; he detailed specific cases of usurpation and corruption, particularly those of Key Pittman, the leader of the self-proclaimed "reform government" of Nome. Pittman later went on to the Senate of the United States, representing the state of Nevada, but his days of power in Nome were cut short after that night in Brown's Hall. "Never saw a better fight," recalled Ralph Rogers, a witness to the mass meeting, some months later to Elizabeth Robins.

> Don't believe a more brilliant thing was ever done in the Halls of Congress than [the] speech that night in Nome. He called those fellers down! His sanitary measure has saved thousands of lives this summer. Oh, the people appreciate him. He can do what he likes. They'll build his church because *he* says a church is a good thing. Even the saloon-keepers—the better sort will help build Robins's church—and the rest will just keep a respectful distance—they're afraid of him. He'll be the corner-stone in this great new empire up here. He'll be Governor or anything he likes. . . . Why, I tell you, there's men alive and prospering today who would a died—suicides last winter—if it hadn't been for your brother. His reading room and his talks—his friendly ways, no nonsense, just straight forward sense and goodness made people feel there was something worth living for. . . .
>
> I ain't given to worshippin' mere men. I don't think there's anybody the world can't get on without—but—well, I'm inclined to make an exception of your brother.[45]

In stark contrast to this eyewitness account is that of Bernard Schwarz, who was critical of Robins for not demanding the immediate takeover of municipal government by the partisans of his cause. The more radical element that demanded takeover felt that Robins had "sold-out" and "later on when your application for membership in the Miners Union came up for consideration, they turned you down and so you were dethroned!"[46] Any such takeover would have flown in the face of what duly constituted law there was in Nome and that was the order of the United States commissioner who vested power in the Chamber of Commerce until the spring, when elections could be held. The episode is a telling one, since Robins had to make a judgment on the legitimacy of a revolutionary overthrow of a "seated" government. Only one year after receiving this angry letter, the details of which are not corroborated, Robins had to make the same kind of judgment—this time on the epic scale of the Russian Revolution.

Pittman was forced to resign as municipal judge and relinquish his authority to the Chamber of Commerce, which was charged with the responsibility for governing the town under the order of United States commissioner, Judge Alonso Rawson. McKenzie and, a year later, Noyes were found guilty of contempt of court by the San Francisco Circuit Court. Noyes's punishment was a $1,000 fine; McKenzie was sentenced to a year in jail, but on grounds of illness, President McKinley pardoned him. With the major culprits out of the picture, the reformers hoped that the power of law enforcement in Nome would be transferred to the small detachment of the United States Army, stationed at Nome under Lt. Wallace M. Craigie, but to no avail.[47]

The ousting of the gang was a great accomplishment, but Robins's hope to clean up Nome was not affected by the change in the political picture.[48] The brothels and gambling joints remained and the lawlessness went on as usual, although without official sanction.

The problems Robins encountered in his church work were just as exasperating as those in the rough and tumble of Nome and its surrounding mining districts. Hardly a week went by without some "cheechalker" (newcomer) laying claim to the lot that was the construction site of the hospice's new church. Each new claim involved another confrontation, often requiring a show of force. In the end, one enterprising mining company made a claim and took the hospice to court and won, pending appeal.[49]

The most serious hospice problem was the debt of close to $18,000 that had been amassed by Loyal Wirt. The evidence available indicates that Wirt had mismanaged the finances. He had taken along to Nome not only his wife and sister-in-law, but about half a dozen hangers-on, who performed few if any services for the hospice. Given the costs of food, fuel, and lodging under the pressing scarcities of Nome, the hospice lost a small fortune on their upkeep alone. Added to this was Wirt's mismanagement and misappropriation of funds and supplies, although apparently not with criminal intent. Because nearly all the trading companies in Nome were impatient creditors, any newly arrived medical or construction supplies bound for the hospice were impounded in lieu of payment.[50]

All this came to light while Wirt was back in Boston trying to cover the debt with contributions from the sponsoring church. Robins had become convinced of Wirt's irresponsibility, which he believed bordered on the criminal, and he resolved that Wirt had to be relieved of his position if the hospice were to survive. The debts raised doubts about the hospice's mission and honesty, and Robins felt it his obligation to restore its reputation. The spiritual and humanitarian force Robins wanted to build, such as that of the Holy Cross Mission, required the devoted services of several men like Father Barnum—not for one or two winters, but rather for a lifetime. As the spring drew on into June, Robins knew that he had to make a major decision.

On Thursday, 14 June 1900, after nearly two weeks out of Seattle, the steamship *Tacoma*, with Elizabeth on board, came within sight of Nome and promptly ran aground on a sandbar. Elizabeth anticipated the completion of the last portion of her 7,000-mile mission: "I come on deck in the morning to find the welcome of glorious weather, a light breeze blowing and the sunshine whitening all the thousand tents of Nome. There are frame buildings, too, but the general impression is tents, tents, up the beach and down the beach and away to the tundra. Half a dozen steamships are anchored in the bright water and the two miles between us and Nome are dotted, here and there, with row boats, dories and an occasional steam launch." Time passed slowly as the *Tacoma* rode peacefully at anchor two miles off Nome, the passengers awaiting arrangements for the trip ashore. There, news reached her of the *Aberdeen*, aground and ready to go to pieces against the ice; the *Robert Dollar*, which had to go back to Seattle for repairs; the *Santa Ana*, "burned to within two inches of the water"; the *Garonne*, damaged by some disaster; and the *Ohio*, flying the "dismal yellow flag" signaling smallpox on board and the quarantining of the ship. While anxiously waiting she tried to take in her good fortune. Then, she recounted, "For some reason, I don't know why, I turn and see a pair of shining eyes set in a fine dark face. The slender young man, wearing a soft black hat and a mackintosh, is coming towards me. 'Raymond,' I say, and he, with a show of milk-white teeth, 'Sister.'"[51]

The question in both their minds was whether or not he would devote his life to the hospice. If not, there was another concern, one that was to remain unresolved for years thereafter: would they build a life together?

During his year in Nome Raymond had made a full life. He was dedicated to his work at the hospice and to the reform of Nome. He saw clearly the forces against which to fight, to campaign. He had made many enemies during the winter, but from his point of view they were the pawns and dupes of the manipulators and the corrupt. On the other hand, he had won many devoted friends and admirers who were willing to put their lives on the line in his behalf. Even Dick McArthur, who had plotted his assassination, eventually became "one of my best friends." Nome had given him a new sense of self-assurance, and an awareness of the force of his personality and leadership.

"No one could walk the waterfront at Raymond's side, or the 'streets' of the tent and timber town," Elizabeth wrote in her diary with pride and wonder, and not realize the magnet he was to the eyes and minds of the Nome inhabitants. Their look hung on him: they turned when he had passed. One saw in their faces something more than curiosity. Just what, I couldn't have said. Whatever it was, vaguely it pleased me. It brought me slightly mystified happiness. And over and over I had seen that excitement quicken in some faces. At what? One of the Old Guard had caught sight of Raymond. It will be set down to my preoccupation with my brother, but the truth is: the clear impression of older inhabitants made on me was that the most exciting thing about Nome was Raymond.[52]

Throughout the dark, lonely, and harsh months, every individual had to struggle for his own sanity and survival. And there was Robins, untiringly ministering to the sick, burying the dead, comforting the troubled, and preaching a gospel of hope and brotherhood. At Nome he inspired the awe in others that he had felt for Father Barnum at Holy Cross. Although it meant sacrifice and suffering, Raymond thrived on it and yearned for more.

His vision of a life of service and self-denial in Nome was sweetened and further intensified by his thoughts of marriage. Miss Rosa Lamont (Elizabeth's weakly disguised pseudonym for her in *Raymond and I* is Clare McCalmont) had the official title of Church Visitor at Saint Bernard, with many duties. Robins thought of her as steadfast, honorable, and devoted. "She is not clever, she is not beautiful, but she is good, good, good, and she is healthy and strong—and she loves me."[53]

Rosa was not like other young women Robins met in Nome, "hanging about his study and making excuses from a sense of propriety"; she allowed only the most subtle indications of her devotion to Robins. They talked only rarely and then never about their relationship. Raymond revealed to Elizabeth that the marriage he envisioned, but had not yet proposed, could in no way be compared to their relationship. He wanted his wife to be the maker of his home, the bearer of his children, the devoted and unquestioning support, the source of warmth and comfort. Painfully setting aside his first dream of a life of comradeship with his sister, he reconciled himself to and even favored the idea that his wife would not be a source of intellectual stimulation or even passion, but rather a tender friend, a haven of repose.

Elizabeth arrived at the moment of decision about his future, his role at the hospice, the forcing of Wirt's resignation, his proposed marriage, and Nome as his permanent home. Elizabeth saw the Alaskan adventure as Raymond's act of desperation. She felt she was most responsible; she had to bring him back.

A week after her arrival, Loyal Wirt returned, and Robins resolved to confront him with his misdeeds. He demanded and received Wirt's verbal and "written promise to Raymond Robins that I will on his demand not earlier than sixty days and not later than six months resign from, the superintendency of the Alaska missions . . . and this is done for the good of the

Congregational Missions of Alaska."[54] According to Elizabeth, almost everyone in the hospice felt the necessity of reestablishing a clean slate by remov-
ing Wirt, but most were aware of Elizabeth's purpose in coming to Nome
and feared that she would be successful and take her brother away. What
would the hospice do then? Who could provide the leadership to avoid bankruptcy and failure? Raymond was torn by the dilemma. Each side constantly
placed its case before him, at one moment subtly, at another passionately,
pleading with him to stay and, in Elizabeth's case, to come away.

Elizabeth's thoughts and feelings are preserved in a letter, which she did
not give to Raymond for some time, hoping that he would decide to leave on
his own; but when all else failed, she handed it to him.

> My dearest Brother: I have tried to disguise from you my realization of the
> extreme danger you are in here, and though my withholding of the truth was
> prompted by tenderness for you, it was wrong and harmful. It is not tobacco
> and coffee alone that break down fibre; tobacco and coffee cannot even do it so
> effectually as living under the tension you live under. My dear boy, we can't
> treat Sevres china as we can treat your granite ware. Robins folk aren't meant
> for the awful grind that is crushing the beautiful life out of you.
>
> One man here who has observed you, said to me with pitiless candor: "Mr.
> Robins will not listen to reason—*one day he will snap!*" I hated the man for saying
> it, but I know he was only saying what others think. You have spoken, my
> dear one, of "the conditions of power." Believe me they are not the conditions
> of Nome. If once you could get away you would see it as clearly as I do and
> you'd save yourself in time.
>
> Oh, my dear, my dear, I am crying as I write this. I came all these leagues to
> see my young, young brother—feeling old myself and tired—ready to rejoice
> in your youth and strength. When I turned round that day on the *Teresa [Tacoma]*
> and saw your careworn face I could have wept aloud for the betrayal—how
> you were squandering these precious days when the sober and *lasting* founda-
> tions should be laid—not in fear and fanaticism and blind sacrifice but in well-
> directed, well-ordered work—work that *holds up* the house of life, not under-
> mines and shatters it.
>
> Dear, I must say to you with all the earnestness that's in me—all the love—
> all the faith in your genius—Come out of this while it is yet day. You are
> young—and yet don't be deluded. 26 isn't far from 30 and then youth is be-
> hind instead of before. If I didn't love you so much—so much—I wouldn't risk
> this letter—but I dare not go away leaving this unsaid.
>
> And the truth is that if you care for the good that we are born to do in the
> world, get away from this place before the life here drags you down.[55]

It was true—at twenty-six years of age it is remarkable that so heavy a
responsibility could have fallen on Raymond. And Elizabeth's fears did not
address all the dangers. Five weeks later, the decision was made. Raymond
quit Alaska before the end of summer, but for the next thirty years, in all
his wide-ranging activities, he kept to the same pace and intensity of activity

that caused Elizabeth so much concern. And as the observer in Nome predicted to Elizabeth's horror, Raymond did "snap," several times, each requiring long periods of recuperation. He ignored all warnings, and once involved in his work, he failed to consider any physical or mental limitations.

Elizabeth believed that the unique circumstances and responsibilities of Nome had a particularly destructive effect, and she was convinced that Nome was not worth the sacrifice. In the end, it was this latter idea, rather than concern about strain, that led to his decision to leave. Raymond would have tried to meet Elizabeth's challenge that "Robins folk aren't meant for the awful grind." More than anything, Raymond wanted to demonstrate with his life that he *was* made of "granite ware."

Elizabeth also warned Raymond about his intention to marry Rosa. "Wait, even if this marriage should be the best thing in the end. 'You aren't absolutely certain it is the best, or you wouldn't be asking me.' I offer to take him abroad. After a total change of scene and opening-out of life, then come back, and if Clare McCalmont is still *the* woman—why, then that is what she is."[56]

Elizabeth saw Raymond's marital plans as one more manifestation of his desperation and withdrawal from the real world and his failure at striking it rich. And she knew too well that that desperate gamble for gold was undertaken for her—to win her to his side for the rest of his life. She saw the marriage as part of his escape into the God-forsaken world of Nome, where these failures would be submerged beneath the daily crises of the boomtown. During the weeks of her stay she recorded his changing moods on the question of the marriage and whether or not he would leave or remain. She had to leave and hoped that he would make the trip up the Yukon with her and then leave Alaska for good. Always with a tortured ambivalence, they shared the dream of building a life together and sharing a home. "He was evidently still afraid of my possible remarriage and loss to him a second time," Elizabeth wrote. But she too was afraid of the depth of her attachment to her brother. "I stand at the window feeling suddenly lonely—and I think how strong this brother-bond bids fair to become when I am hurt that he wants to leave me for a few minutes before bedtime to see a nice good girl . . . how much trouble I might be laying up for myself if I linked my life closely to the existence of this dear free-lance. Other men I might hold fast—a brother was free at any moment to cut himself adrift." Only in the last days before her departure did he finally promise her that "I shall not marry anybody in Alaska, and I shall not marry."[57]

By the time Elizabeth left Nome on 26 July, Raymond had agreed to remain a short time longer and to meet her in Seattle in late September. He felt free to make this decision only after he had been informed that three qualified churchmen were being sent to work at the hospice in Nome by the Congregational Churches of America. Although Robins had doubts about these ordained and "qualified" men and their ability to cope with Nome, he could no longer justify his remaining as essential to the survival of the hospice. He could return to the fantasies and dreams with Elizabeth. Their new home was to be called "The Road House," since they planned a life of travel and intense activity.[58]

As Robins's commitment to a life of self-sacrifice dwindled and the model of Father Barnum seemed to pale, he began to reconsider his initial reason for coming to Alaska. With Elizabeth at his side, he again concerned himself with money. He wanted to be able to provide without limit for both their needs. So, although she had achieved some financial success through her writing and acting and had amassed more than $6,000 in savings, he resolved to make one more try in the goldfields.

Elizabeth sailed across Norton Sound for Saint Michael and then by river steamer up the Yukon to the Klondike. Raymond's activities for the next weeks, however, are clouded in mystery, with many differing accounts of where he was and what he did. According to an 8 August letter to Elizabeth, he had little money and was planning some kind of mining venture with D. J. Elliott of the hospice. It is important to note that Elizabeth made no mention of the success or failure of such a venture, but it was during the few weeks following her departure that Robins, years later, claimed he found gold. According to William A. Williams, who closely followed Robins's account given in an interview conducted in 1949, "he started east toward the Eldorado area. Finding the river areas staked solid with claims, he began to work along the old creek beds up in the hills. Ignoring the jibes of those who had no use for such 'bench claims', he worried through until his spade turned out the pocket of a long-gone river, Robins cleared over a quarter of a million dollars in raw gold."[59]

He did not find a fortune in gold in Alaska, nor did he claim that he had until more than five years after he left Alaska. During his first years in Chicago, from 1901 to 1904, he was hard pressed financially and often had to borrow money from his sister.[60] There is no mention of any gold whatsoever. The complex reasons for his creation of the myth of independent wealth of Alaskan gold is best explained in a later chapter, in connection with his settlement house work and his marriage to Margaret Dreier.

On 21 August 1900 Robins planned to leave for Seattle, but the widespread typhoid epidemic had finally reached him. Elizabeth, who by this time had arrived in Dawson, also came down with the fever, and both brother and sister recovered only after a long convalescence. It was not until early October, in a Seattle hospital, that Raymond approached Elizabeth's bed. "After I had lain there nearly eight weeks, late one afternoon, a man came into my room, quiet, intensely pale, his close black curling beard making more startling the pallor of the waxen face. At first sight I think he looks like Christ. The grave eyes are shining; he comes forward, drops into a chair by my bed, and lays his head down beside me without a word."[61]

Robins's three full years in Alaska following the "mad rush for the Yellow God" and, then, the equally compelling commitment to the simple teacher of Nazareth, although filled with purpose and personal sacrifice, did not fulfill his innermost yearning for the love and comfort of his sister. The contradictions within his complex personality left him still torn by the dilemma of "the glory and the shame" of his divided life. Alaska had provided no resolution. At the moment of reunion with his sister, he had no idea where he would turn.

Part Two

Chicago—A New Life

4

The Settlement Worker

The demands on R. are increasing: judges, lawyers, editors, politicians, business men, "best citizens," plain men,—every kind of a man up and down the scale of human development—want him, daily & hourly and want him badly! Proposals of importance in law, finance, political life, and philanthropic work are made to him daily, & though he accepts none of these he is guiding and counselling in great enterprises. I feel as if Chicago were the world's ship of state with R. at the helm & with it is the feeling equally strong that if C. can go *right* other cities & other lands will take heart of courage & follow.
—Margaret Dreier Robins to Elizabeth Robins, September 1905

Robins left Alaska on the last boat out before the winter freeze, at the end of September 1900. He went directly to the hospital bedside of his sister Elizabeth in Seattle, Washington, where he too was admitted to continue a slow recovery from typhoid fever.

Elizabeth set out for her home in London as soon as she was well, and after overcoming a relapse, Robins followed her there. For three months he traveled in the circle of her friends and acquaintances, meeting many of the notables of London's intelligentsia—H. G. Wells, George Bernard Shaw, and Gilbert Chesterton. Although these months were rich in so many ways, the emotional turmoil that pervaded the Alaskan experience was neither eased by his return to Seattle nor by this visit. He slowly and painfully reconciled himself to setting aside the dream of living with Elizabeth.

Despite the emotional letdown, Robins discovered an unexpected niche for himself. He developed a great camaraderie with Keir Hardie, who was founder of the Independent Labour party and the first man elected to Parliament as an independent workers' representative. Hardie too had begun his involvement with unionism as a coal miner and had entered the political arena to help the working man. Unlike Robins, Hardie built an alliance of socialist and trade union forces.[1] Robins visited Toynbee Hall, in London, where Canon Samuel A. Barnett had established the prototype of the settlement house. Robins was deeply impressed by the commitment of the men and women who served the slum dwellers of the East End, as had been Jane Addams, the founder of Chicago's Hull House settlement, thirteen years before. The workers' dedication and selflessness reminded Robins of Father Barnum and the brothers and sisters of Holy Cross Mission.[2] Thus Raymond chose to make a life for himself, a life without Elizabeth, in America—in Chicago.

In April 1901, shortly after his return from England, he explained to Elizabeth that "Chicago is the centre of the American position. New York is to be the financial mistress of our country, but Chicago is *the* industrial centre of the New World. To industry not wealth to men not money belongs the future." At 140 North Union Street, in the building that first housed the Chicago Commons settlement house, in the slums of the "deadly 17th Ward," Robins took a small apartment. It was as Spartan as his quarters at the Saint Bernard mission.[3]

Unlike established and corrupt Boston or Philadelphia, Chicago was a relatively new boomtown when Robins settled there. In 1850 its population was barely 30,000. Its population doubled between 1880 and 1890, and it swelled to 1,698,500 with the tide of eastern and southern European immigrants by 1900. Major parts of the central city still suffered from unpaved streets, an inadequate sewer system, and the pervasive stench of the stockyards. Nevertheless, in Lincoln Steffens' words Chicago was "an example of reform." In his *The Shame of the Cities* (1905), Steffens suggests a simple theory that explains why Chicago was able to avoid the worst excesses of municipal corruption, which Steffens so ably exposed. Unlike his associates on the staff of *McClure's Magazine,* who attributed the corruption and mismanagement of American cities to the "growing pains" of our young republic, Steffens believed that the older, established cities had had the time to build corrupt party machines. Chicago, according to Steffens, was too young; it had not. Its youth was its saving grace. Vigilance, however, was imperative.[4]

The reform success of the Chicago Civic Federation and the Municipal Voters' League, exemplified by the civil service law, charged Robins with enthusiasm upon his arrival in Chicago. He joined the Municipal Voters' League, made contact with social and charitable agencies concerned with the Seventeenth Ward, where the Chicago Commons was located, and studied the problems and needs of the district. After a few months of adjustment, Robins decided to "serve" at the Chicago Commons, founded and headed by Graham E. Taylor. "The experience of my past years conditions me against any hard and fast plans as to the means and localities of service," he wrote to Elizabeth. "Nevertheless I feel a sense of permanency in my present surroundings that I have not enjoyed before." During his time in San Francisco, he did not send for his books and belongings, stored in Florida. Now, with this new sense of commitment, he did, since he felt he could "strike such roots into the religious and civic life of this city as is given to me to send forth."[5]

By 1901 there were thirteen active settlement houses in Chicago. Jane Addams's Hull House, the first, was established in 1889. The University of Chicago Settlement and the Chicago Commons, both founded in 1894, were the fourth and fifth, and by 1910 there were thirty-three. A similar pattern of growth in the settlement movement can be seen nationwide, with 74 in

1897, 103 in 1900, 204 in 1905, and 413 by 1911. Robins was one of thousands of American men and women, mostly middle-class or well-to-do college graduates in their twenties and thirties, who, during the first decades of the twentieth century, had made the same commitment. Few, however, arrived with his extraordinary range of experiences.

Many historians have tried to explain the motivation for this widespread commitment to the settlement movement. Some have seen it as the ineffective guilt response of a bloated urban middle class in the face of immigrant suffering. Others see the guilt leading to a genuine humanitarian response. Still others view the guilt only within the confines of the biographic details and subconscious of the individual settlement workers. Robins's motivation fits within none of these. Whereas his parents may have fit the mold of the guilt-ridden middle-class volunteer, the financial deprivation of Robins's childhood and adolescence disqualifies him.

Robins was a man painfully alone who needed camaraderie; a man who felt deeply inadequate and wanted to prove his worth to himself and others. He succeeded often with the latter, but seldom with the former. Robins felt his life meaningless without serving others, for he was smitten by the example of Christ. This self-abnegation was a widely shared experience in the settlement movement. Robins was thrilled by the influence and power he could bring to bear on others and yearned to exercise that power to rally them to a good cause. Throughout the Chicago years, his settlement work was a form of struggle against extreme mental depression, which on a number of occasions overwhelmed him and required medical treatment and hospitalization. His outpouring of letters to his sister chronicles both his settlement work and the emotional challenge.[6]

As part of his energetic approach to his new responsibilities, Robins formulated a grand ideal of "threefold service," in which he resolved to devote one-third of his time and energy to improving social and economic conditions, one-third to reforming political institutions, and one-third to human spiritual and moral needs. During these first months in Chicago he studied the field of settlement work, learning all he could about the movement, its history, philosophy, and purpose. He turned to his old ledger notebook, which he had used during the desperate days of spiritual search in Juneau. Under the heading "Notes on Settlement Studies," he entered these principles, taken from C. R. Henderson's *Social Settlements:*

> Political liberty is a mere picture, the reality is economic freedom (p. 13).
>
> There are two ways of improving a nation's state, the first is by altering the institutions of the country the other is by the regeneration of the peoples' character (p. 17).
>
> But it is his undeniable right to be permitted to develop all the power God gave. The workingmen must help themselves if they are to be helped (p. 17).
>
> The settlement movement is, in actual historical origin in incentive scope and impulse, a University movement outward upon the world (p. 81).

All is positive and creative rather than destructive and polemical (p. 158).

Progress will never be organic until the religious spirit breathes through every act and institution (p. 91).

The laissez faire principle in society is full of unsuspected peril (p. 158).

Local government can do more and is every day doing more, to improve social conditions than is done by all the churches missionaries and societies put together (p. 57).[7]

"Social Economic Legislation, Labor Programmes, Child Labor," Robins continued in his notes, examining more concrete questions of concern for the settlement worker, "Woman Labor, Training in Social Citizenship, Study of Foods, Child Saving Agencies, Cooperation, Housing of the Poor, Popular Recreation, Public Baths." These were Henderson's suggested concerns for the settlement worker; Robins accepted them as mandated obligations, and added education, public health, prison reform and prisoner rehabilitation, housing for the homeless, and job placement for the unemployed.

For the next twenty-five years, each of these concerns was woven into the fabric of his work life. As a settlement worker, he found, along with Jane Addams, Graham Taylor, and others, that harsh conditions of housing, education, health, and sanitation could not be ameliorated without local government action, and thus the settlement worker was forced into the arena of ward and city politics. The underlying economic plight of the working classes, which Robins had experienced personally from childhood and now witnessed in both the city and the nation, planted the seeds of his commitment to the cause of organized labor and unionism. As a result of a pragmatic interaction of ideas and experiences he formulated a social Christian activist philosophy that was the basis for his settlement work and, sixteen years later, for his judgment of the Bolsheviks and the Russian Revolution.

Robins's first year of settlement work at the Chicago Commons began with his involvement in the urgent need for parks and playgrounds in the Seventeenth Ward. He wrote to the Chicago Bureau of Charities and a response came from Robert Hunter, who at the same time was serving as superintendent of the Chicago Municipal Lodging House.[8] Hunter asked for a detailed map of the ward and the suggested sites of the parks and playgrounds. Robins complied, the sights were deemed appropriate, but nothing came of this first effort; however, it was not forgotten. Several years later, through the pressure of the City Homes Association and the Bureau of Charities—Robins serving on the boards of both organizations—several parks were constructed. When Robins could muster the organizational and political power to carry out a needed reform, he returned to the problem and renewed the fight. This same sequence of events characterized dozens of "campaigns" on as many issues throughout his twenty-five years in Chicago.

Robins's first contact with the Municipal Lodging House (MLH) may well have been this correspondence with Robert Hunter, a fellow settlement resident. Hunter, who headed the MLH during its first year, 1901, resigned the superintendency in February 1902, and Robins was offered the position. It was his first opportunity since Nome to make and carry out policies on his own initiative, and he became immersed in the task immediately. On 22 February 1902 Robins wrote to Elizabeth:

> I am now pressed by a number of very important people in the civic life of Chicago, to take the superintendency of the Chicago Municipal Lodging House. I am sought to make a systematic study of the tramp and vagrant problem, and men of large means will help carry out my conclusions, if I can make them appeal to their judgment. You will understand why this field attracts me with a peculiar force. If I can get this opportunity to do some original laboratory work in sociology, without being limited by considerations of political and financial obligation, I shall accept this task. It will cover all the large cities in this country, and will take many months.[9]

The nature and purpose of the MLH drew Robins into a field of activity that differed considerably from that of the Chicago Commons. Nevertheless, he did not relinquish his involvement in settlement work. If anything, it intensified and led to his simultaneous superintendency of the MLH and head residency of the Northwest University Settlement a year and one-half later.

The purpose of the MLH was stated plainly on a free ticket that was distributed widely throughout Chicago. The face of the card reads: "Good For/ Lodging, Food and Bath/at the/Chicago Municipal Lodging House/12 N. Union Street." The reverse side reads:

> The City of Chicago has established a Municipal Lodging House for the benefit of all homeless and indigent men and boys in this City. Lodging, a bath and food are provided free for every applicant for one night, and longer if he is honestly seeking employment. The crippled, old, or infirm are sent each morning to hospitals, dispensaries or homes. Each lodger receives personal investigation, and his case is disposed of upon the facts alone. Employment is found for the industrious and able-bodied. The citizens and housewives of Chicago are requested therefore to refuse alms, and to refer all applicants to the Municipal Lodging House by means of this ticket.[10]

The card indicates nowhere that the MLH was under the jurisdiction of the Chicago Police Department,[11] which had established it as a police measure against vagrants, indigents, and tramps. Among the strongest supporters of the MLH were the conservative business and financial forces in Chicago, who saw the vagrant and tramp problem as a threat not only to the social order, but to their interests as well. Like most workers in the settlement and social service movements, Robins seldom hesitated to curry financial and political support for the MLH from those whose only concern was the control of the undesirables. Often, and with sardonic self-awareness, Robins found himself seeking the support of those powerful and wealthy individuals who, in Robins's judgment, were themselves significantly responsible for unemployment and homelessness.

Robins had been penniless and without a job in New Orleans as a young man and understood the MLH as a humane rather than penal solution to the growing problem of vagrancy. He believed that if each man who entered the door were treated with respect and consideration, that man could leave ready to return to society as a productive asset. Both Robins and James Mullenbach, assistant superintendent, interviewed the men who came to the MLH. They were confronted by an endless army of drifting men and boys, unemployed, their health destroyed as a result of unsafe and inhuman working conditions, venereal disease, and alcoholism. A humane personal approach included counseling, an active job search, and at least a temporary home outside the lodging house. Robins fought to remove the onus of the police detention center, poorhouse, or workhouse from the reputation of the MLH and worked to establish it instead as a social rehabilitation institution to which men could freely turn without fear or stigma.

Robins acted on the belief that this transformation could best be achieved by job placement. He got the cooperation of the Civil Service Commission and private industry, and his major commitment of time to the MLH was devoted to finding employment for the residents. His success is demonstrated by the fact "that within five months over 7,500 men had passed through the institution and that of these over forty per-cent had found permanent and remunerative work." But for the budget-minded City Council of Chicago and the establishment business interests, the success of the MLH was not measured necessarily by its humane approach and employment record; rather, it was lauded because of its economies. In Robins's first and second annual reports to Francis O'Neill, general superintendent, Department of Police, Robins pointed to "the most conspicuous effect" of the MLH:

> During 1900 and 1901 (the two years previous to the opening of the municipal lodging house) the total number of lodgings given homeless men and boys in the police stations of Chicago was 218,605.
> During 1902 and 1903 the total number of lodgings given at the police stations and the municipal lodging house combined was only 32,555.
> Decrease in the total number of lodgings required by homeless men and boys at the expense of the city . . . 186,050.[12]

Despite these numbers, the question of where these thousands found shelter remains an open one. While Robins does not address it, we have good reason to assume that although some were helped by various charitable organizations and many avoided the city, the majority went without lodging. Robins was working for a structured and humane MLH in a police system that treated transients and homeless individuals as vagrants and criminals and sought a sharp cut in their number. Robins had to prove the fiscal effectiveness of the "Chicago System," as it came to be known nationwide, in its first years. The improved quality of the service rendered was limited to the facilities available at the new building at 12 North Union

Street, which opened in 1903. But by 1914 the enlarged MLH system of Chicago provided 452,361 lodgings, and instead of "chasing drifters from Chicago, the institution seemed to be attracting them."

In the first years of the MLH, Robins corresponded with Caroll D. Wright of the Department of Commerce and Labor, in Pres. Theodore Roosevelt's administration, with the hope of creating a National Commission on Municipal Lodging Houses. To make this agency effective in combating vagrancy and unemployment, Robins saw the need for a coordinated network of municipal lodging houses throughout the country.

After deciding on this plan and the viability of the MLH as a new vehicle for the solution of many of America's social ills, Robins was engaged by "men of large means" to undertake a nationwide speaking tour to promote the idea. This was the first of dozens of such national campaigns. The tour culminated in Robins's participation in the National Conference of Charities and Corrections in Boston in June of 1904. Upon returning to Chicago, he was swamped with inquiries from public officials interested in his work and methods.[13]

Soon after beginning his involvement in the settlement life of Chicago, Robins returned to the same staggering schedule he had at the Saint Bernard mission in Nome. Despite Elizabeth's reminding him of his human limitations and her repeated warnings in response to his elaborate descriptions of his crushing schedule of work, he did not for a moment consider modifying the pace, intensity, or extent of his commitments. "What could be more extraordinary than such a day as this," he wrote to Elizabeth, full of pride and excitement:

Rise at 4:30 go to the M.L.H. in the lodging house district of the slums; stand at the head of a line of 170 homeless men and boys of all classes and conditions, talk one to two minutes with each, dissect his condition and need by simple direct, revealing questions, then send or direct him to such relief as our so-called civilization has provided. From this line sift five professional vagabonds or thieves arrest them call the patrol wagon and send them to the police station. Breakfast at 8:30. Police court at nine o'clock, prosecute the malefactors then back to the M.L.H. and go into the peculiar facts of special cases reserved, as runaway boys, spent men, etc. etc. Back to the Settlement, attend to the mail, meet such neighborhood persons or demands as are listed for attention. Change clothes and go to the north side taking lunch with Mrs. [Emmons] Blaine [i.e., Anita McCormick] and discussing some C.H.A. [City Homes Association] plans. Take the 2:00 train for Evanston and speak to a group of students at the Northwestern University. Back to the Settlement for the public hour from 4 to 5. Settlement dinner with almost always some guests often 10 or 12. Rush from dinner and don evening clothes, down to a banquet at the Auditorium of the Fields and Workshops Society, sit through a long dinner and tiresome speeches by Henry C. Lytton merchant prince, Mrs. Margaret Springer daffy society woman eager for notoriety, and Frank O.

Lowden republican machine candidate for governor of Illinois. Then I make a speech and in ten minutes have caught these idlers up into the stream of intensest human interest and sympathy, and they are cheering wildly the most radical sentiments—they know not why. Slipping quickly away to avoid the foolish congratulations across the city to the M.L.H. to see that all is well with that night's quota of hungry, homeless, hopeless human waste and wreckage. Then back to the Settlement and to bed as the clock is striking 1 A.M.[14]

After less than a year as head of the Chicago MLH and the campaign to expand and reform its operation, Robins delegated responsibility for its day-to-day operations to O. DeWitt Wescott, the new acting assistant superintendent. Robins's schedule of public speaking, which first focused on the extension of the MLH idea, then began to include a number of other questions of social reform. Wescott, who was also involved in work at Hull House during 1903, kept Robins informed on all developments at the MLH.[15]

Robins's effectiveness as a speaker and his initiatives at the MLH brought him to the attention of the Board of Directors of the Northwest University Settlement (NUS) Association. On 25 July 1903 Robins agreed to their offer to head the NUS, also in the Seventeenth Ward and only a mile from the Chicago Commons. Robins continued as titular superintendent of the MLH for another year after joining the Northwest University Settlement and remained head worker there until 1905.[16]

While still involved in both agencies, Robins became active in the City Homes Association (CHA), which served as a coordinating body for social reform institutions seeking improvement of housing, health conditions, sanitation, parks, playgrounds, and the housing of transients and the homeless. Through the effort of Robins as superintendent of the MLH and secretary of the executive committee of the City Homes Association, the new MLH building was constructed in 1903 to serve its expanded activities.

In the winter of 1903, three City Homes Association members—Robins, Jane Addams, and reform activist and philanthropist Mrs. Emmons Blaine (heiress to the millions of her father, inventor and industrialist Cyrus McCormick)—joined forces to fight for the appointment of a qualified chief sanitary inspector for the city of Chicago. Major positions in the Sanitation Department were held by political appointees, and incompetence and corruption prevailed. The deadly typhoid epidemic of 1902 made the bad situation all the more disastrous. Working under the leadership of Jane Addams, the three brought the scandal before the press and public and forced an investigation by the Civil Service Commission.

Three months of testimony resulted in a report that "suspended the Chief Sanitary Inspector, the Assistant Chief and eleven sub-inspectors, which was followed by their immediate indictment by the grand jury of Cook County." But the struggle for a qualified chief inspector had only just begun. Using the stationery of the NUS Association, Addams, Blaine, and Robins solicited qualified candidates from as far away as Scotland. Charles B. Ball, a highly qualified candidate, was identified by the City Homes Association in New York City—so urgent was the need that the CHA even paid the cost of his transportation to Chicago to take a civil service examination for the post. Ball scored highest by eight points among twenty-eight competitors, but barrier after barrier was placed in the way of his appointment by the city administration.

First, he was rejected because he was not a Chicago resident. Second, following provisions in the law, the city administration chose to give precedence to another candidate (tenth on the list) because he was a Civil War veteran. This last ploy brought the entire social settlement community to join in the outcry. After a lengthy court battle that involved a final appeals court decision, the appointment of Charles Ball was won.[17]

By the end of 1904 Robins had joined many more reform organizations: the Referendum League, the Peoples' Veto Committee, and the Citizens League of Chicago "for the suppression of the sale of liquors to minors and drunkards." He was appointed to the Board of Inspectors of the Juvenile Home by the Board of Directors of the Juvenile Criminal Court Committee. In mid-1902, shortly after taking on the superintendency of the MLH, he joined the executive committee of the Public Ownership League, an organization that sought public ownership of utilities and municipal transportation facilities as well as voter initiation of legislation, the use of the referendum, an equitable system of taxation, and the direct nomination of candidates through primaries.[18]

As a result of his speaking tours on the tramp problem and its solution through the MLH, Robins became involved in the movement for the reform of America's penal institutions. He joined the National Committee on Prison Labor and the National Conference on Charities and Correction and served on the executive committees of both. He carried on correspondence not only with fellow reformers and committee members, but also with wardens at various prisons, most notably Winston Salisbury of the state penitentiary at Lansing, Michigan.[19] As late as 1916 Robins was further involving himself in prison reform by joining the Humanitarians, an organization specifically created to stop the brutalization of prisoners.

During the first years in Chicago Robins considered himself a "social service worker." In that role, he joined his settlement and CHA colleagues in a diligent effort to prohibit "alcove rooms" (a room constructed without any source of light or ventilation) in the tenements of Chicago. In 1906 their efforts paid off; Chicago outlawed such unhealthy tenement construction, as did many municipalities throughout the country.[20] A major and effective area of his settlement activity was the preparation of studies and reports, which became the basis of reform legislation. Robins undertook research and made recommendations on street cleaning and sewage disposal. As a member of the Building and Grounds Committee of the Board of Education, his study of vocational training led to the establishment of a new school for trades and crafts. Upset over unfulfilled requests for adequate toilet facilities for six schools in the poorer districts, he forced the preparation of a report by the Board of Education on the sanitary and toilet conditions throughout the city. The report resulted in the necessary renovation and construction to remedy the situation.

Again in his role as "social service worker," and this time as a member of the City Club of Chicago, Robins joined the Smoke Abatement Control Committee to prevent industrial pollution. The most pressing problem faced by this group was financial, so Robins gave money as well as his skill as a public speaker.[21]

As a result of his work at the MLH and the NUS, Robins gained first-hand insight into the serious social, emotional, and health problems of prostitution and venereal disease. He won a reputation as an expert on the problems and their prevention and control. In 1906 he spoke on several occasions on "The Increasing Prevalence of Sexual Vice and Venereal Disease Among the Submerged" before distinguished audiences of doctors and social hygiene specialists. Given prevalent attitudes in that era, his message was enlightened—he stressed the social and economic circumstances that led to the problem, rather than any inherent moral defects of the poor.[22]

The concerns of the aged also drew Robins's attention. He studied the plight of the countless people in the charity homes of Chicago who had lived productive and responsible lives; he spoke out for the principle of guaranteed pensions, a principle only realized thirty years later with the enactment of Social Security. "The man is not improvident who has spent his money caring for his wife, and educating his sons and daughters to become useful, intelligent members of society," Robins asserted. "He has done a service to the state. He has earned the right to share in some of its wealth. He should be guaranteed a pension for life."[23] The proposal for a guaranteed pension and others like it demonstrate that although Robins was not a socialist, he did not hesitate to espouse unpopular or radical ideas.

Robins's work consumed his days, and only in his correspondence with Elizabeth did he share his excruciating depressions. His colleagues in the settlement and reform movements were told that he was "ill" only when he could no longer function and was remanded to rest and treatment on doctors' orders. Robins was also plagued by a piercing loneliness and an ambivalence about fulfillment—settlement work vied with a dream of an idealized life with his sister. From his first days in Chicago until his marriage in 1905, he was sustained by these two passionate drives—service and love for his sister. They were not harmonious, or even mutually attainable.

For fifty-two years, from their reunion in Nome in 1900 until Elizabeth's death in 1952, brother and sister struggled with the dilemma of their yearning to "make a life together" and their fear and knowledge that it could not work. They never actually made the attempt, and yet for five decades, the dream, and the ecstatic hopes and crushing disappointments surrounding it, animated their lives on opposite sides of the Atlantic. Robins's first years in Chicago were punctuated with love letters to Elizabeth, some extolling her virtues, some putting forth their deeply painful dilemma, some filled with longing and yearning. The language of these letters often gives pause as to Raymond's ability to separate fantasy from reality, in terms of the likelihood and purity of the consummation of the dream.

> It ill becomes my knowledge of myself to listen to the thought, that I am the corner-stone of your plan for a home. No more impossible person for a home's foundation ever lived than Raymond Robins. For the remainder of my life I shall be known as a strange madman chasing shadows, led on by a far glory that saner mortals do not see. Again, it [is] not probable that I shall endure many years. Not that I am ill nor that I fear disease, but that the surges of the spirit will lead me into strains that will break this thread of mortal life, while I am yet young in years. This I believe.[24]

One week later, he wrote:

> You are very close to me this afternoon darling. All that divides us is overwhelmed by a strange consciousness of your nearness and love. I long for you with a great hunger—yet I would not have you here. Neither would I be with you. What a paradox life is! O Bessie a fierce longing fills my heart. Why are you so incomparable! Your spiritual presence was the heart of the yesterdays, and your love and acceptance gave the crowning glory to the North land story. I have you in my arms, and I kiss your lips—and I love you with my whole Soul. God help me.[25]

"My love cries out from the depths of a boundless love such greeting as only you can understand," he wrote nine months later, in expectation of a visit from Elizabeth:

> I feel that catch in the throat that thrilling joy from a great gladness that makes the blood tingle, and gives one the sensation of walking on air.
> It is wonderful! The ugliest libel on God's image that "hangs" around the brothels of these river wards touches me to pathetic tenderness—this 17th ward is Paradise. I want to hug my friends and kiss the dirty faced children that I meet on the streets.
> This exaltation from the thought of your nearness half terrifies me. My sleep is broken with dreams of Sister Bessie, and I am counting the hours until I have you in my arms.[26]

In January 1903, abandoning all caution and his numerous warnings, carrying expectations to the most dizzying heights, Raymond wrote to Elizabeth of the fulfillment of the dream.

We will do this thing you plan. We will go together in the springtime to the woods and mountains and find a home. And it will be our home yours and mine until the end of earth.

It had been well for each of us to have had this wide experience, and this service in separation, through the long years. Think of it darling twenty-one years since we were together under our own roof. And in all that time neither of us has had a home.

And what a home we will build. And it will speak to us of the best in the memories of the Old Stone House, and Bayside and Nama, of Kentucky and England, and Mexico and Alaska. And it will be HOME for Elizabeth and Raymond. This shall be done. We of one blood, bound together by the invisible fabric of a great love woven by the loom of time from the changing day threads of thirty years—we will do this thing. I pledge you in the name of the Everlasting Father.[27]

On 14 August of the following summer, 1903, one month after his appointment to head the Northwest University Settlement, Robins had a serious nervous breakdown. He refers to the specific day of the breakdown several times, and "Luray" as the place where it occurred, but there is no indication of what the particular crisis was. The plans for finding a home with Elizabeth had failed, his staggering work schedule in the Seventeenth Ward did not abate, and he was plagued by a deep sense of guilt—"the corroding bitterness of unrepentant sin"—concerning his sexuality.[28] A year earlier he had written to Elizabeth:

I do know that the warfare with the flesh has been none too successful, and that the cost of fighting this losing battle has been high.

"O wretched man that I am who shall deliver me from the body of this death! I thank God through Jesus Christ our Lord." Darkness and a blind struggling with conflicting purposes—Powers of Evil and Spirits of Light. For many months a half unconscious surrender to the wicked One.[29]

Exactly to what Raymond refers is not clear. Probably his sexual drives finally forced him to either illicit sex or masturbation. Whether fantasy of Elizabeth played a role in this sexual release is also unknown—perhaps the purity of the dream had been defiled and Raymond could not withstand the guilt, disappointment, and confusion. Perhaps the sexual release was in and of itself, regardless of Elizabeth's fantasy role, guilt provoking enough to cause Raymond psychological damage. His recuperation lasted many months, and there is no record of the nature of his treatment, nor by whom he was treated. When he did return to his responsibilities in the fall, he was dissatisfied with his work and still suffered. "There are times when I hold my breath and my temples throb as the shadow of the great terror creeps upon me," he wrote to Elizabeth, in December, in his first letter in many months.

Days pass and no word quickens the long night of waiting, tho each morning I say—today I shall hear!

Why have *I* not written? My spirit is overwhelmed. Despite some seeming fine gains I know I have lost steadily in the threefold life since August 14th. An inexplicable bitterness corrodes the days. Some unknown canker is eating out the heart of life. A vague terror haunts me wakens me from sleep four, three, two o'clock sometimes and drives me wearily around the endless circle of fruitless thought.

My work is thought to be good, it is in reality miserable for the most part. I seem constantly breaking faith. At times memory fails me—the wheels of the brain seem to catch 'n hang—slowly twist loose again—I am often befogged by a heavy dullness that enfeebles body and mind.

Still I fight on. No cure can help me. Sometimes gleams of glorious light break through—I may go down into the everlasting darkness but I know God reigns.[30]

Only at the end of February, after a medical crisis caused by tonsillitis, did the depression lift, allowing Robins once again to feel hope and some joy in his life and work. He explained to Elizabeth that "two lingering glimmering lights—a half paralyzed faith in God, a wholly dumb love for you" had saved him. "I have loved you more than sister, more than mother, more than wife, more than all combined." And with the return of well-being came the rekindling of the dream of Elizabeth joining him, a problematic sign of mental health.[31]

On a hot July afternoon in 1903, Robins walked into Spauldings Department Store in Chicago and set eyes on Anita McCormick Blaine. Mrs. Blaine who had been widowed and left with a young son, was an active worker in numerous committees and organizations in the reform movement of Chicago. She served on the boards of directors of many settlement and charity organizations and was also one of the most generous contributors. She served on the executive committee of the City Homes Association and worked with Robins and Jane Addams for the appointment of a qualified chief health inspector. It was that renewed contact in December of 1903 and again in the spring of 1904 that led to Robins's falling in love with Mrs. Blaine.

"Through the long difficult years since early childhood I have walked alone," he wrote to her, in the spring of his love. "At times the heart hunger has seemed unbearable and hard-pressed by the strange cross currents of life I have wished for the end. But with the dawn came the blessing of labor and the service of humanity has taken the bitterness from the wine of life."[32] He wrote a deluge of letters, seeking to win her by pouring out his heart. And since he had just found himself after the long depression, there was special poignancy in his pleas. All his openness, personal revelations, and declarations of love had come to naught. His love was not returned, nor did his proposals of marriage ever receive a hint of acceptance.

In mid-April, Robins once again fell ill under the emotional strains of this rejection and his work schedule, often allowing himself no more than three or four hours of sleep. He took a short leave of absence from both the MLH and the NUS. Several of the letters wishing him a swift recovery tell of the worry that "you would sooner or later break down under the terrible strain that you have been working under for some time."[33] After his rest, consuming involvement soon filled his days again. However, "the several revivals of spirit of which I have written have all gone out in deepening gloom," he wrote to Elizabeth in midsummer. "Absolutely no one knows yet that I am dying at the heart, no one but you and I. I greatly doubt if what is left is worth saving . . . but I know that in another year of this condition the end will have come." He pleaded, "If you came now you might save me from the slow destruction which proceeds from the utter desolation of spirit."[34]

Raymond's hopes soared in expectation of a visit from Elizabeth, but then his only direct response to news that she would not come was "To say that I am disappointed is to speak mildly." The rest of his response took the form of a list of plans to complete responsibly his unfinished business for the "purpose of retiring from . . . public work." He then told Elizabeth that to leave "me out of consideration of any permanent plan for yourself is not only justified but possibly inevitable. . . . It is quite possible that the whole matter will be adjusted on a permanent basis so far as I am concerned by the kindly intervention of 'the long sleep.'" Raymond ended his desperate letter with an agonized ambivalence: "If you can make permanent arrangements that are satisfactory and safe for a home in England I should most earnestly urge you to do so. We can each live alone, we do not know that we can live together."[35]

For the next two months Raymond lost himself in work, his unfinished business—the rebirth and renewal of urban America. Nevertheless, pressured by his doctor, friends, and colleagues, and under protest, he set off for a two-week rest in Florida—to visit his boyhood friends and home, which he had not seen for fourteen years. Although the salvation of urban America was delayed, the visit to Florida resulted in an extraordinary rebirth and renewal for Robins. The dramatic transformation was obvious to all his friends and acquaintances upon his return to Chicago, "many say looking ten years younger." "I have found the blessed waters for which Ponce de Leon sought. I am as if born again," he began his joyous account to Elizabeth.

> Not since the great Nome days have I been and felt so splendidly well. All the aching weariness has gone from body and brain. My spirit is refreshed and unconsciously my lips sing and my heart beats rapidly to the quickened music of life. Two weeks in the Florida Pine Woods about the hallowed paths of boyhood in old Hernando—two weeks of utter rest, contrast, stock-taking, and spiritual readjustment have brought me again to the mount of Vision. It is as if a great weight had rolled from me taking away the oppression of body mind and spirit.[36]

For two unhurried weeks, Raymond visited his old friends and the familiar haunts of Hernando County. William Fulton, mentor and surrogate father of his adolescence, spent hours with him in sweet reminiscence. The pressures of the never-ending army of homeless in the cold gloom of Chicago's December was replaced by "days in the woods for the most part stretched out on the sweet beds of pine needles looking up in utter peace through the waving tops of the mighty pines at the fleecy clouds on into the everlasting blue. The warm sweet air filled my lungs a great drowsy joy filled my heart and I slept hour after hour—all night and most of the day. Slowly the vision returned, slowly, light, hope and power filled my soul and a great rejoicing rolled in upon my life."[37]

Raymond rekindled his deep love for the Florida paradise, its cypress swamps, live oaks, Spanish moss, and shining long-needle pines. He returned to Snow Hill, "ten miles from the Gulf of Mexico . . . fanned by sea winds tempered and sweetened . . . through the pine forests and is I believe as healthful and kindly a spot as is to be found in the world." The abandoned plantation house on the crest still commanded forty-mile views to the horizon in every direction. "Slowly before me rose the vision of our HOME," he wrote to Elizabeth, "and in the silence of that glorious desolation my lips uttered—CHINSEGUT."[38] This Innuit Eskimo word, the spirit of things lost and regained, replaced "The Road House" as the symbolic name of the home Raymond hoped to build with Elizabeth. For the first time the wheels were put in motion for the purchase of lands and the building of that home.

Until the great frost of 1895, Hernando County had had among the most productive citrus lands in Florida, but the frost devastation had bankrupted many growers and had driven land values to unprecedented lows for more than a decade. In elaborate detail, Raymond suggested to Elizabeth the financial wisdom of buying up the Snow Hill lands and having the glories of the tropical flora and fauna share their homesite. In less than a year, with Fulton as his agent and $5,000 borrowed from Elizabeth, Raymond bought sixty acres on the crest of Snow Hill, 120 surrounding acres, and contracted for the reconstruction of the house.

The work of the winter months that followed his return to Chicago was as demanding as ever, and while the strain was great, the terror of depression did not return. The surge of energy and reaffirmation of the Florida time was still with him. "I have made three or four really great speeches lately," he wrote, and concluded, "Never has the power of life and faith and truth seemed so manifest. Today I am very tired and hungry for some one to love."[39] Raymond turned to Anita McCormick Blaine once again, more to express his sadness and yearning, than in expectation of her fulfilling his dream.[40]

Six weeks later, Robins spoke before the parishioners of Plymouth Church in Brooklyn and met Margaret Dreier. His subject that evening was the social gospel of Jesus, one of his favorites. There followed a dinner, which he and Margaret attended, and they had an opportunity to talk about their mutual interests and problems. Margaret, who had become active in the

Women's Trade Union League, was concerned with the problem of making the league an effective force in bettering the conditions of working women in New York City.

Raymond and Margaret discovered in one another the same resolve: a dedication to a life of service in the cause of humanity. They also shared a commitment to the social gospel of Jesus and were drawn to one another by their mutual mission. Robins's experiences as one of the toiling masses impressed Margaret—he did not speak from a pulpit floating in the clouds of abstraction and intellectualization. His ideas on the organization of labor were tempered by the harsh realities of personal experience and suffering. Robins's education in law and his ordeal in Alaska gave depth to his experience and made him all the more attractive to Margaret. He was intuitive in his discussions with Margaret, even anticipating questions that had arisen in her mind regarding the work of the Women's Trade Union League (WTUL) and its goals for the future.

Margaret was thirty-seven and Raymond thirty-two years old at the time of their meeting. She was a heavyset woman, about five feet two, with curly brown hair, a determined jaw, intense eyes, and a not unattractive face. Like Raymond, she was an unswerving and dedicated worker for the causes she espoused. On occasion she even surpassed his remarkable achievement as a public speaker.

She was born in Brooklyn, New York, in 1868, the daughter of German-born parents who had come to the United States in the 1860s and had achieved great financial success. Her older brother had already married and Margaret headed the Dreier household (herself and three sisters), in fashionable Brooklyn Heights. In her early twenties, Margaret had become active in philanthropic and social work in New York. Just a few months before meeting Raymond she became the founding president of the New York Women's Trade Union League. She was also president of the New York Committee of Household Research.

Paralleling Raymond's MLH concerns, Margaret was a supporter of Emma M. Whittemore's mission and home for wayward women in New York. From volunteer work in Brooklyn Hospital's nurses' training school between 1890-94, she went on to the State Charities Aid Association and Long Island State Hospital. She organized the Woman's Municipal League in Brooklyn Heights and was its secretary for many years. There, between 1903-4, she led the successful fight for state regulation of employment agencies, an effort that won her a place in the public eye and reform ranks. At the same time, Margaret volunteered at Asacog (settlement) House and University Settlement House, on New York's Lower East Side. She experienced the commitment and camaraderie with the residents that she soon shared with Raymond.[41]

"Dear Margaret Drier," Raymond wrote in his very first letter, misspelling her name,

I am sending you by today's mail the third annual report of the Municipal Lodging House and some other printed matter related to our work in Chicago. I find that I am more concerned with your understanding and sympathy in all these things than for that of any other person I know. I have no explanation for this fact and probably need none. We are very busy in the attempts for settlement of the industrial war now raging in this country. I have just been called to the City Hall and must not please myself in saying more at this time. Please send my kindest regards to all members of your family.[42]

After only weeks of courtship, Raymond and Margaret declared their love for one another. In a letter to Margaret soon thereafter, Raymond revealed his past love for Anita Blaine and his deep love for his sister. "I am sending you today by express," he continued,

a picture of Bessie (who is Elizabeth) that I have carried for thirteen years. It has never left me and has comforted my heart in every great hour since I began my struggle with the powers of darkness in the inner and the outer worlds. I have carried it through the tangled fastness of the cypress swamps of Florida and it was with me when I met the Master on that terrible glorious night in the ice bound mountains of the North. I can part with it now for I have your image graven on my heart. This I thought. Bessie was my great light until I found my own beloved one.[43]

With the relinquishment of Elizabeth's photograph to Margaret, there began a most painful struggle between Elizabeth and Margaret for the first loyalties of Raymond. While Raymond managed with great difficulty to navigate a course that was truthful to both loves and loyalties, the two women disliked one another almost immediately. It soon became obvious that the three could share no common ground. The focal point of the conflict was Chinsegut, which was to have been the home of Elizabeth and Raymond. In spite of the five years of tortured ambivalence in their relationship and the unresolved, or unresolvable, question of their living together, Elizabeth experienced Raymond's marriage as a betrayal, mirroring his childhood experience of her marriage. Elizabeth's loan of the money to buy Chinsegut, which became Margaret's home with Raymond, was a most bitter irony—one that disturbed Elizabeth for the rest of her life.

But for the first time in his life, Raymond found a love and devotion uncomplicated by painful ambiguities. For the first time he was free of dependency on Elizabeth, and instead he tried to share his relationship with his sister with his bride-to-be. In his letters to Margaret he conveyed the feeling and novelty of finding fulfillment rather than rejection. "Your blessed letter has flooded my heart with gladness," he wrote to Margaret on the eve of the announcement of their engagement,

and made this whole dreary world of grimy tenements and muddy rain beaten streets glorious with divine light of love.

Elizabeth Robins, 1891, as she appeared in the leading role in Henry James's *The American*, the longest running of James's plays. This was Raymond's favorite photo of his sister. He carried it with him throughout Alaska and finally gave it to Margaret as a token of love. (Courtesy of the Elizabeth Robins Papers, Fales Library, New York University.)

Never before did any written word so grip my heartstrings and bring my whole being into such joyous response of loyalty and devotion. I am half frightened darling by the sweeping power of this great awakening within my spirit. Surely I have never lived before!

My darling I am wholly yours. For the first moment since my great hour in Alaska I realize a power greater than my passion for justice, stronger than my love for human freedom, mightier than my sense of duty. Devotion for you Margaret has become an enthralling power in the hidden depths of my heart—in the innermost chambers of my soul. Pray for us both my blessed wife that we may be led of God—that we fall not under temptation through this great joy this beautiful communion of our spirits in Love.[44]

Their engagement was announced on 12 June, and although they had attended conferences and other public gatherings together throughout May, their intention to marry came as a surprise to their friends and family. Both had spoken of their intention not to marry, but to devote time and energy to their respective reform responsibilities. However, "his challenge had aroused her more than anything she had heard. Almost at once they fell in love. He wooed her as ardently as he did everything he undertook," and they married only a few months later.[45]

The marriage was performed in Margaret's home at No. 6 Montague Terrace on 21 June. Guests included Elizabeth, who had come from England for the occasion, their brother Vernon, Raymond's friend and co-worker at the Chicago MLH James Mullenbach, many of the Robinses' Louisville relatives, and Mrs. Anita McCormick Blaine.

The Chicago newspapers suggested that the match was a misalliance and compared the marriage to two similar "settlement marriages." J. G. Phelps Stokes, heir to his father's millions, had married Rose Harriett Pastor, "a Russian Jewish girl of the Ghetto of New York who had been working for $12 a week in a cigar store." Stokes's sister married a settlement worker, Robert Hunter, "a former Chicagoan, who had gone to do settlement work on the East Side in New York," and who had been a resident of Hull House and had preceded Robins as head of the MLH.[46]

It is still a matter of conjecture, but it appears that Raymond's hypersensitivity to the innuendos of the press led to his invention of his gold strike in Alaska. A quarter of a million dollar fortune of his own, putting him on an equal financial footing with Margaret, would silence those who looked at their marriage with suspicion. A confirmation that he had no such fortune was his need to borrow $5,000 from Elizabeth to buy Snow Hill.[47]

Chicago was to be their home, and at 372 West Ohio Street, and later at 1437 West Ohio Street, in the heart of the Seventeenth Ward, they rented a tenement walk-up apartment. "#372 is a perfect workshop and fortress," Raymond wrote to Elizabeth two years later.

It is now so well organized and equipped that the machinery runs without friction. We each have an office typewriter etc. with telephone connection on our desks. We have about 800 volumes of working library and it is all that we need. We can be as alone as if we lived in different flats, and we can bring the one to the other by touching a bell-button. This establishment runs well inside of $2,500 yearly cost. More and more the advantage and beauty of our living appeals to Margaret. Its simplicity has so increased her effectiveness and released so much time and energy for her real work that she wonders how at

84

Raymond and Margaret Dreier Robins seated together, soon after their marriage in 1905. Standing: (behind Raymond) Katherine Dreier and Mary Dreier to her right. Unidentified woman below. Taken in the Dreier country home in Stonington, Connecticut. (Courtesy of the Elizabeth Robins Papers, Fales Library, New York University.)

Robins at 32, in 1905, the year of his marriage to Margaret Dreier. (Courtesy of the Elizabeth Robins Papers, Fales Library, New York University.)

6 Montague Terrace she ever did anything. Our manner of living also frees us from social obligations of the kind we don't want. It also releases several thousand dollars a year from the living expense account for effective social and industrial service. The year has been full of awakenings and change. M and I have grown together and away from other old points of view. The rapid movement almost startles us at times. Life is very full, very wonderful and very blessed.[48]

In the decades-old tradition of the social settlement movement, they chose to live among the people with whom and for whom they were devoting their life's work. "This modest apartment was the center from which they launched their crusades for democracy, peace and social justice."[49] It was not simply motives of Puritan self-denial that brought them to the tenement, but rather the conscious understanding that one of the most critical struggles for the affirmation of humanity and life in the modern world was in the slums of the cities.

5

Organized Labor

We faced a mob of some five hundred steel trust thugs and held them at bay
for four hours last Sunday night in the Kiski Valley in western Pennsylvania.
This is the real struggle of our generation and I thank God that I am free to
fight with the workers against the industrial despotism of the Steel Trust.
—Raymond Robins to Elizabeth Robins, 5 August 1909

The dollar must give way to the home; dividends must be second to childhood
and womanhood; all industry must conform to this standard; both the state
and the church must sit in judgment; unfair working conditions and dishonest
competition must be condemned and outlawed.
—Raymond Robins, in *Public*, 12 September 1907

AT the turn of the century the tide of public opinion in the United States was
rising in favor of labor unionism. The great numbers of unemployed and
impoverished resulting from the depression of the 1890s gave pause to the
middle class, which had accepted labor radicalism stereotypes and rejected
unions out of hand. Between 1897 and 1904 union membership in the United
States quadrupled, from 447,000 to 2,072,700, and from 1898 to 1908 the
Erdman Act made it a federal offense to discriminate against workers because
of union membership. In 1896 the Tennessee State Legislature ended convict
labor contracting under public opinion and union pressure.[1]

Employers did not sit idle in the struggle. With well-financed campaigns
of speech making and advertising, they called for the retention of the "open
shop," or in more recent antiunion language, the "right to work" (eliminating the requirement of union membership to work at any job). Intransigent
employers, such as Henry Clay Frick, devoted considerable resources to discrediting the union movement at the very time that it was becoming a significant social and economic force.

Within a year of her arrival at 327 West Ohio Street, Margaret Dreier
Robins had become the leading woman in the Chicago labor union movement. She served on the executive boards of the Chicago Federation of Labor, the Illinois State Federation of Labor, and the American Federation of
Labor. Soon after arrival she made her first speech before the state convention of the Illinois Federation of Woman's Clubs and joined the Women's
Trade Union League of Chicago. In 1906 she took on the vice-presidency of

both the Chicago and the National Women's Trade Union League (NWTUL). Margaret held the presidency of the Chicago league until 1913, at which time, under her influence, a rank-and-file "trade union woman" was elected to that important post. As president of the national league from 1907 until 1922, Margaret gave priority to the cause of labor above all other commitments, and as a result, Raymond was drawn more deeply into union work. Margaret relied on Raymond's assistance as a speaker, legal advisor, legislative organizer, and catalyst for attracting influential support. They both became convinced of the need "for social welfare legislation," but always maintained that labor organization was more important. Raymond fought for the right to strike, picket, boycott, and engage in collective bargaining, and he served on several important arbitration commissions. Although "settlement worker" was Raymond's public image, and speech announcements throughout the Chicago years referred to him respectfully as a "social service expert," his labor movement work was of equal significance. "I suppose most of the struggle in the universe is a struggle for power, on the part of the employers, of labor and of different groups everywhere," Robins concluded, recounting his union struggles as a miner. "But . . . as a group you amounted to something, whereas alone you were rather helpless. If one man . . . lays down his tools . . . it doesn't make any difference; there are plenty more. But when 300 men lay down their tools something happens. You began to learn the group power, you began to learn that the brotherhood of labor was a better thing."[2]

One of Raymond's first union-related activities after moving to Chicago was as spokesman for the United Mine Workers Union in the anthracite coal strike of 1902. Robins already had a reputation as a gifted speaker with strong prolabor leanings—and he still carried his union card from Leadville. In October the coming of winter brought a crisis in the six-month-old strike, since the hard anthracite coal was the only fuel that could be used in many industries and homes. Intense negotiations were conducted for more than a year before the strike was called in May 1902, and talks intensified thereafter. John Mitchell, president of the United Mine Workers Union, called on Robins in October to join a delegation that was to meet with Pres. Theodore Roosevelt. The conflict in the strike involved hours and wages, but the irreconcilable issue was recognition of the union as the legitimate negotiating representative of the workers. It was the immovable position of the mine owners on this question that led Roosevelt to threaten federal takeover of the mines, the first time any such threat had ever been used by a president of the United States.[3]

Robins spoke for the union delegation and its request to force arbitration on the mine owners and operators: "Mr. President, we contend that those who ask the protection of civilization should use the methods of civilization. A long strike due to arrogant management or arrogant labor leaders is economic war. Therefore we ask of you arbitration."[4]

After meeting with the union representatives, Roosevelt asked Robins if he could remain in Washington to repeat the union's position before the mine owners and operators. Before agreeing, Robins felt he had to get permission from the officials of the United Mine Workers Union. The question of his acceptability was raised, but with the support of Mitchell, he was accredited to speak for the union. But circumstances did not permit Robins to repeat the union demands before the mine owners and operators. Under the pressure of Roosevelt's threat of federal takeover and through the influence of J. P. Morgan, both sides of the dispute accepted the appointment of a presidential commission and promised to abide by its recommendations. The entire solution was precedent-setting—never before had the White House been used in such a manner to solve a labor dispute.[5] Many of the hour and salary questions were settled in favor of the union, but it was not until thirteen years of additional struggle that the United Mine Workers Union finally won formal recognition as the bargaining agent for its members. For Robins, this episode had long-term significance. Not least important was his meeting Roosevelt, with whom mutual respect and admiration developed, often bringing them together in the years that followed.[6]

In 1907 at the National Conference of Charities and Correction, Robins's controversial speech, entitled "The One Main Thing," asserted that the first responsibility of the national conference was "to aid the workingmen in their struggle for fair wages, shorter hours and security of employment."[7] He called for the improvement of working conditions and the securing of labor's right to organize. This speech represents a complete statement of the practical objectives of mainstream labor organization in the United States, often called "business unionism." Other labor organizations in nineteenth- and twentieth-century America, such as the Knights of Labor, the Industrial Workers of the World, and Socialist and Communist labor parties, adopted broader agendas of social and political struggle. While Margaret and Raymond worked tirelessly for ambitious programs of social and political reform, these efforts were carried out through organizations and activities separate from their union responsibilities, which focused entirely on "the evils and problems arising in the place of employment."[8]

In keeping with this reality, Robins combined his labor focus with his settlement work. Much of this activity was centered on the education, health, housing, and recreation needs of children. Taking his cue from one of his favorite biblical passages, "But the earth hath he given to the Children of men," Robins became deeply involved in the Industrial Committee of the International Federation of Women's Charities in an effort to secure an adequate child-labor law. The work of Robins, Jane Addams, and many others in the settlement and reform movements of Illinois resulted in "one of the most advanced pieces of protective legislation for children," the Child Labor Law of 1903, which replaced the inadequate law of 1897. The new law strictly regulated minimum age limits for factory employment at fourteen and carefully stipulated maximum hours as well as eliminated night work in most cases. It also eliminated various categories of dangerous jobs for workers under sixteen years of age. While in Springfield, Illinois, lobbying for the bill, Robins was awed by the power of his co-worker Jane Addams—"simple as a child, with a heart of oak and a brain like a Damascus Blade, looking out from quiet steadfast gray eyes with reaching honesty and unfaltering constancy."[9]

The following year, Robins and Addams joined forces to try "to awaken an understanding interest in the industrial problems of America among the influential women's clubs of Illinois." The clubs were federated into a representative state organization that met annually and represented the "ability and influence of the great middle class." But Addams and her co-workers in the settlement and labor movements were not able to convince the Illinois Federation of Women's Clubs to admit "trades union women" into the organization, nor to deliberate seriously the "conditions of the working class" in the state. On 19 October 1904 Robins gave a speech at the state convention of the federation. He was charged with the responsibility of "heating to the welding point the sympathies of the members . . . in behalf of the working women and children of Illinois." He succeeded. For the first time, trade union delegates secured admission to the federation, and the headlines read: "Raymond Robins Causes a Sensation Before Women's Federation."[10]

Supporting trade unionism in the first decade of the twentieth century was often complicated by the problem of racketeering and corruption. To champion honestly the cause of labor organization meant a dangerous commitment to cleaning one's own house of crooks and opportunists. Serious corruption existed among many Chicago unions, but the most obvious and difficult case for the reformers was the Chicago Federation of Labor (CFL) under the control of Martin B. ("Skinny") Madden, who had been a Chicago building materials dealer before his notorious involvement in the Building Trades Council and the CFL.

In the early days of the federation, before the successful reform efforts of Robins, T. P. Quinn, John Fitzpatrick, and Ed Knockles, the CFL was controlled by "the burglars: a group of politicians who served the Democratic organization in the City and the Republican organization in the country . . . [who] were immune from police interference." The corruption was brazen and violent. Anton Johansen, a long-time member of the reform wing of the federation, recalled that at a CFL election, "on Sunday morning, in walked five or six ruffians who destroyed the ballots and nearly murdered Mike Donnelly, who at that time was head of the Amalgamated Meat Cutters and Butcher Workmen's Union." In response to this attack on both individuals and the democratic process, thirty men met and organized a plan to expose the corruption. Because the daily papers were controlled partly by fear but mostly by favor, the reformers decided to produce a publication of their own. Robins contributed $1,000 to pay the printing costs of the paper, and in it was an editorial by T. P. Quinn with the headline: "Skinny Madden and his

Banditti." The editorial was a bill of particulars, which gave the time, place, industry, and the specific bribes received by Madden for selling out to employers at the expense of labor union men and women. In the following days, the newspapers quoted from this article and, of course, credited Quinn for the exposure. The revelations and resultant scandal galvanized the reform community and soon led to the election of labor reformer John Fitzpatrick to the presidency of the Chicago Federation of Labor.[11]

Robins's major contribution to "cleaning labor's house" and supporting trade unions was his hundreds of public addresses, spanning thirty-five years and delivered in nearly every state. The problems of labor corruption and antiunion public opinion, the latter shaped by the controlled press and funded by business interests, required a massive campaign of reform and reeducation. "You ask, why the 'Unions do not repudiate their dishonest leaders?' They do repudiate them," Robins began one of his popular labor speeches and, with great rhetorical effect, continued: "The great employers ask 'why are not labor men more honest,' and then they offer them a fortune to betray their fellows." Robins enumerated many cases of rank-and-file reform initiative within unions, concluding with the example of the ouster of Skinny Madden. Robins quoted another, often-made charge: "The unions are brutal and violate the law and are frequently led by unprincipled men," and then responded:

> Yes, many times this is true. But the union men haven't any monopoly of these characteristics. The packers and mine owners and railroad magnates are brutal and lawless and unprincipled enough to deserve some of our condemnation. Further, it should never be forgotten that these men are tempted only by boundless greed and lust for power, while the workers fight for their homes and bread. We don't seem to mind how the labor laws are violated and the workers are deliberately poisoned and crippled and killed in smelter and mine and factory, yet when in the blind helpless resistance of infuriated masses of men someone is killed, then we are very much outraged and demand the troops to protect human life and enforce the law lest the foundations of the State crumble.

Continuing, Robins described the barbarisms of strikebreakers and company thugs, of the patronizing attempts of companies to provide "amusements" for their workers while ignoring their basic needs. He defended the democratic nature of the union, providing leadership from the rank and file, in contrast to the dynastic process that determined most of the aristocracy of American wealth. To win his audiences to his point of view, Robins argued his prounion position on constitutional as well as moral and humanitarian grounds. He expressed indignation at the injustice of denying working men and women their democratic right to assemble peaceably and to act in their collective interest.

Another often-heard charge against unions was that their leaders and supporters were socialists and anarchists. Robins denied the charge and while disregarding anarchism, he felt it necessary to explain carefully his personal opposition to socialism, giving the reasoning and analysis that he used all his life.

> You ask "are we not socialists?" We are not. As we understand economic socialism, it is not unscientific and immoral. While we believe that it is a bad system that permits the strong to exploit the weak, we are certain that it is a worse system that would require the weak to exploit the strong. We believe that there are two kinds of wealth. One kind that is individual, produced by human brain and hand under dominion of a human will and this wealth belongs to him who will produce it. The other kind is produced by the community and is social or common as distinguished from individual wealth. This latter wealth belongs to the whole people, is a proper common heritage regardless of individual merits and should be taken for the whole people in the form of taxes and used for their benefit in municpal, state and national undertakings for the common good. We believe that there are two proper kinds of industry, public and private. We believe that private industry (business) should be carried on by private individuals, firms or corporations under free competition for private profit. We believe that public industry (business) should be carried on by officers of the people for the benefit of the community.
>
> We are confident that this distinction rests upon a sound economy and will ultimately be the established policy of this country and the world.
>
> We do not believe in the philosophy of the class struggle as an interpretation of past social history nor as the method of future development in civilization. We believe that the whole progress of social order has been toward individual freedom, rather than toward collective domination. We think that we note this principle in the breakdown of the Roman Catholic system of spiritual control on the one hand, and in the universal failure of autocratic, aristocratic, or socialistic political control on the other. We see no reason for believing that the culmination of the struggle for industrial control shall be different. Industrial despotism whether through a few trust officials or through a majority of the electorate is alike reprehensible to our ideas of fundamental natural rights and the historic movement of civilization toward individual freedom.
>
> We are disposed to stand against its surrender to self-appointed captains of industry or to those selected by the accidents of popular election, with the same ardor that we would resist the spiritual domination of Rome or the political despotism of Russia. We do not believe that freedom for the individual human spirit and the individual human body has been won only to be surrendered to collective tyranny over the human hand.[12]

Within Robins's ideological framework, working persons would receive full, fair compensation for their labor, determined through negotiation and the collective bargaining process. Marx's concepts of surplus value of labor—the necessary exploitation of labor as the basis of profit—and the inevitable drive for maximization of profit as the central force within the capitalist system were rejected along with the idea of class struggle. Robins envisioned a society of individual initiative, incentive, hard work, and creativity, all equitably rewarded. He saw only two conditions that would require restriction of that reward: (1) when there was inadequate compensation and inappropriate working conditions for those employed by the individual or "private business" initiator, and (2) when that private or individual business became monopolistic, infringed on the free initiative of others, or was in fact a "public business" or industry. And "public business," for Robins and his reform allies, included all public services and utilities—water supply, gas, sanitation and sewage system, and mass transportation facilities. Thus the public interest could be served without unleashing the tyranny of the majority; and the freedom of the individual could be preserved while protecting the public interest. That Robins predicted a system of public and private business division "will ultimately be the established policy of this country and the world" is one of many examples of his prescience.

Circumstantial evidence suggests that Robins never made a systematic study of Marx, Marxism, or any other socialist theorist.[13] However, beginning in San Francisco, Robins did study Henry George's *Progress and Poverty* (1880). He joined a host of young lawyers, socially conscious "university men and women," and reformers, including the reform mayor of Cleveland Tom L. Johnson and the renowned lawyer and author Clarence Darrow, who embraced the George commitment "to abolish all taxes save one single tax levied on the value of land, irrespective of the value of improvements on it." George presented his plan persuasively as a solution for the ills of land monopoly, land speculation, franchise monopolies, monopolies dependent on protective tariffs, agrarian impoverishment, and the excesses of the business establishment that caused both rural and urban poverty. The single tax plan held out the hope for the reestablishment of liberty and economic opportunity in the context of a just, free enterprise individualism, denying the necessity of Marxist socialism.

Robins's conviction about the applicability of the single tax idea to the real world was given powerful confirmation by the beach gold strike at Nome. That unique phenomenon, which demonstrated the central role of land value as the foundation of the economy, involved twenty dollars a day (a substantial sum in 1900), which any able-bodied person could earn who was willing to put in sixteen hours a day panning the free beach sand for gold. Thus the scale of wages in Nome for all jobs began at twenty dollars for a sixteen-hour work day. This led to the complete reversal of the unemployment and surplus labor situation in Nome; this was proof positive for Robins that the single tax system of Henry George was on the mark.[14]

From 1904 to 1908, still introduced as a social service expert, Robins toured the nation on behalf of the Henry George Lecture Association. He often held forth in different cities on fourteen successive days and sometimes as many as two or three times a day. From 1904 to 1915 he was a subscribing member of the Joseph Fels Fund, which sought as its major aim the institution of the single tax system. His commitment to the ideas of Henry George, like that of so many socially and ethically conscious settlement workers and reformers of the period, was stimulated by the hope for a panacea to the complex and enormous labor, social, and economic problems facing the American people. But Robins was not satisfied with relying on the single tax idea alone; there were too many other possibilities for reform.

Public and private industry, public and private property, and the sacredness of the fruit of an individual's labor—Robins worked out a reconciliation of some of the opposing forces operating in America. He was active in the Henry George Lecture Association and the Joseph Fels Fund, both concerned with social or common wealth, which "should be taken for the whole people in the form of taxes and used for their benefit." This same distinction is the basis for Robins's long struggle against the "traction interests" who privately owned the municipal transportation system of Chicago and operated it not as a public trust, but rather as a private enterprise for the benefit of stockholders who were concerned only with profits. The Municipal Ownership League—Robins was among its most active members—sought public ownership of the public transportation system, a "public industry."

Since Robins denied both the syndicalist position of organized labor achieving state power and the socialist position of labor owning and operating the means of production, he had to adopt the only remaining possibility that could solve the problems of the working man in America—the creation of strong unions along traditional "business union" lines, accepted under the law as the representative bargaining agent of the workers. Robins's ideological testament is sharply drawn, but the realities of social, labor, and political reform presented him with developments that did not permit a dogmatic adherence to this antisocialist position. The *Chicago Daily Socialist*—"A Paper Without a Muzzle"—was often one of the few newspapers willing to champion the causes for which Robins fought, and as a result, he was a constant source of financial and moral support. A. M. Simons of the editorial board wrote to Robins on this very question of ideological compromise.

> Thanks for the check, and for the many times that you have helped us with our struggles. If you are an opponent, I wish we had more of the same sort.
> I certainly want to see a unity of the labor force of America, but I want to see them united for Labor and not as tools of capitalism. I want to see the workers of this country united politically for the defense of their own interest and I will never knowingly let devotion to sectarianism or partisanship stand in the road. Socialism, or the emancipation of Labor would smell just as sweet to me under one name as another. But I want to be sure that I am not getting a gold brick.[15]

Occasions arose during the Chicago years when Robins's opposition to Socialist party candidates led to serious threats to his goals in all areas of reform. This occurred especially in those parts of the country where the reform forces were able to develop an effective political alliance under the Socialist party banner. This occurred in several cities in Wisconsin, and especially in Milwaukee. Even the normally conservative Social Service Committee of the Men and Religion Forward Movement of Milwaukee voted overwhelmingly in favor of the Socialist ticket because of its clear social reform position, and Robins was occasionally embarrassed by these radicals because he chaired the National Social Service Committee. These Socialist settlement workers and reformers, who were also committed to Christian revival in the social gospel of Jesus, complained to Robins of the harm he was doing. "Practically all the leading Protestant Preachers are with the Socialists here *locally* and your words *(as reported)* and the Men and Religion Movement are being used against us. If you were here I'm sure you would fight with us."[16]

In this case, as with the *Chicago Daily Socialist*, Robins resolved the conflict along pragmatic rather than ideological lines. He never denied alliances nor withheld support from individuals or causes because of such differences. The final criteria were always the purpose of the alliance, the character and goals of the individual, and the justice of the cause. Robins's efforts in behalf of Eugene Victor Debs, who personified American democratic socialism at its best, are a clear example of this consistent fairness. Most American Socialists and pacifists, like Jane Addams, condemned the First World War, opposed American participation, and spoke out against the draft. However, Debs's speech of 18 June 1918 at Canton, Ohio, was ruled by the federal courts to have given aid and comfort to draft evasion, and he was sentenced to ten years in federal prison. According to Sherwood Eddy, Robins went to President Harding in the winter of 1921 and "begged Harding to bring Debs from his prison cell in Atlanta and hear him for himself. Harding did so, and to his credit, and that of Robins as well, Harding released Debs from prison on Christmas Day, December 25, 1921."[17]

Justice for democratic socialism was, however, far less central to Robins's work than his commitment to labor union recognition and collective bargaining. On 3 February 1908 the Supreme Court ruled on the suit of *Loewe v. Lawlor*, better known as the Danbury Hatters case. D. E. Loewe and Company was awarded triple damages amounting to $222,000 against leaders of the hatters union because the union initiated a national boycott to win a closed shop. The short- and long-term implications of the ruling was a blow to organized labor and the condemnation of the decision was spontaneous and nationwide. The methods of demonstrating opposition to the ruling were as varied as the groups that lent support to the trade union movement. Newspaper editorials, political cartoons, and speakers platforms were used by the friends of labor to denounce the decision.[18] The trade union movement of Chicago, under the auspices of the CFL, joined many other cities across the country in holding a National Protest Meeting. Robins was asked to be the major speaker at the Chicago meeting, which was held on Easter Sunday, 19 April 1908, at Federation Hall.

"Darling Blessed Holy Wife," Robins wrote to Margaret that morning, before going off to speak,

All the earth is bathed in sunshine, the temple bells are ringing joyously and all the world and his wife are passing by gaily garbed in white and flaming colors on their way to celebrate the Resurrection Morning.

I worked until the late night finishing my talk for this afternoon. It is done. The best that I can say in this great hour is arranged and I await—the hour and the judgment.

Somehow my heart is heavy. I feel spent and the sense of age like "the hungry generation" treads me down. I am only 34 yet I seem very old. These last days I seem to have passed through the age long struggle of the Group of Toil; the conflicts, success and defeats of LABOR through the centuries, seem a part of my own experience. As soon as the meeting is over this afternoon I shall feel much better. This regardless of whether I do well or ill. My heart is too much wrapped up in this talk, I have thought and dreamed and sensed nothing else now for days.[19]

Robins began that afternoon with the warning that "the cause of organized labor and the rights of the group of toil, are more in jeopardy at this moment than at any other time within the last thirty years." He discussed the rights of workingmen to organize and improve their condition and, further, whether such improvement was "important to the welfare of the nation?" For his answers to these questions, he turned to a source he had used many times before, and always with striking results—Abraham Lincoln. Two of his favorite quotations from Lincoln were woven into his speech that afternoon:

I quote him as he spoke in the city of New Haven on the 6th of March, 1860: "I am glad to see that a system of labor prevails in New England under which laborers can strike when they want to. . . . Labor is prior to and independent of capital. Capital [wealth] is only the fruit of labor and could never have existed if labor had not first existed. Labor is the superior of capital and deserves much more consideration."

This is Abraham Lincoln, not an Anarchist, who tells us this great truth of the right and dignity of labor in the civilization of mankind.[20]

Robins discussed the improvement in the national economy and welfare that result from improved working conditions, and higher salaries. He spoke of the economic wisdom of a more widespread distribution of the national wealth, of the "social consequences" of a humane eight-hour day. He pulled no punches. He spoke as harshly of the "men of God" as he did of the "group of plunder."

If this room was full of preachers instead of workingmen, I would like to say to them: "Gentlemen, if you will make a demand for shorter hours and better wages for the group of toil and stand by it, then they may have some time and interest enough to come into your churches." Then the clergymen would understand why their churches are empty of working men and they would know why working people have small faith in the religion of those who say on Sunday, "Now be good and you will be happy," while they help exploit these same working people the other six days in the week.[21]

Robins spoke of the true source of America's wealth, strength, and productivity as well as "moral power and progress" in the hands of the common man, because he is "not implicated in the steal" that characterizes so much of the business world. In words that are surpassed only by those of Walt Whitman, Robins created a powerful affirmation of the "group of toil" and exposed the forces at work in American life that sought to deny it.

"Does labor enjoy that superior consideration in the halls of legislation and the decisions of the courts that Lincoln said it deserved?" And in case after case, judicial, legislative, and executive, Robins demonstrated that the reality in America was the opposite.

"Where then does the workingman turn? To the Trades Unions—the Only Friend of Labor." Robins spoke briefly of the accomplishments and potentialities of the movement for overcoming the great handicaps of labor. But what of the challenge posed to unionism by the Supreme Court decision in the Danbury Hatters case? Robins again turned to Lincoln and the precedent of the Lincoln administration's opposition to the Dred Scott decision of the Supreme Court. "'Somebody has to reverse that decision,'" Robins quoted Lincoln, "'since it is made, and we mean to reverse it, and we mean to do it peaceably.' And organized labor in this country means to reverse the decision in the Danbury Hatters' Case, and we mean to do it peaceably."22

Robins spoke of the "Conspiracy to Make Trades Unions Illegal" and maintained that the only way to stop that conspiracy as well as reverse the court decision was through "intelligent political action." He voiced concern about the underlying conflict in American society, and while never using the words "class struggle," he did develop the "Property Idea of Labor vs. Citizenship Idea of Labor." Here, in contemporary language, he juxtaposed the two sides of the eighteenth- and nineteenth-century debate—Locke's primacy of property rights versus Rousseau's primacy of human rights.

From Robins's point of view, the property idea of labor was a continuation of the mentality that led to the Dred Scott decision, namely that an employer had no obligation to the worker other than his contractual obligation to pay the agreed-upon sum for the agreed-upon work. The "Property Idea of Labor" maintained that an employer could treat a worker as he pleased so long as the pay-for-labor contract was fulfilled. If displeased, either party was free to end the contract. Robins maintained that this attitude was the root cause of most of the social and economic ills of the country. He concluded by examining the inevitable conflict between the forces behind the property idea of labor and the unions, which stood behind the citizenship idea.

> We are now engaged in the third great struggle in the life of this nation, the struggle for industrial freedom. We have more resources and more power of action this afternoon than was ever before held by the group of toil in all the history of the world. We are able if we are but willing, to realize that old dream of the race, not the dream of great men nor of great classes; but the

dream of a great people, from the man who digs the ditch, up to the last exalted expression of intellect or genius; strong free men and women entering into the labor and festival of life on fair terms, and bringing forth a heritage of useful service with untainted honor. And I believe with all reverence that when the group of plunder read this decision in the Hatters' Case they said in their hearts: "This is the death of organized labor," but I say to you, meeting as we are today in every city in the land, the earnest minded and lion-hearted workers of this country know that this decision, instead of being the death of organized labor, marks the resurrection of organized labor.[23]

Later that afternoon Robins returned home and wrote once again to Margaret.

> Easter Day 1908
> The Resurrection of Organized
> Labor in this country.
>
> Darling blessed sweetheart wife—
> The meeting is over, I was blessed with power from the Father—I made a really great speech. Some of the points created a tremendous sensation. It has been a great hour in the cause of the Group of Toil.
> I spoke for one hour and 45 minutes and the group were under the spell as one man.[24]

Robins was not alone in this appraisal of the speech. Louis Post also discussed the important parallelism between the Dred Scott decision, which sanctioned slavery, and the Danbury Hatters case, which sanctioned the destruction of unionism. "His speech," Post affirmed, "both in form and substance, was one of the kind that become historical landmarks of political revolution. And his audience rose to the supreme importance of the situation."[25]

The National Protest speech led to an intensification of Robins's trade union work. As a result of that speech, which was widely reported and reprinted in an authorized edition of 5,000 copies, many more leaders and labor movement rank and file turned to Robins for help and leadership. One such call came from the Nebraska State Federation of Labor in June of 1909; Robins's experience helped when this federation was in its first stages of organization.

In November 1908 Robins attended a convention of the American Federation of Labor at Denver. He was deeply moved by the solidarity and hope created by delegates from all parts of the country and exhilarated by the role he and Margaret were playing.[26] Two days later, while on his way to speaking engagements in Minneapolis, he wrote to Margaret again: "We have stood together in that high peak of the ancient Rockies like two Eagles of the Group of Toil preparing for a swoop down upon the . . . ranks of the Group of Plunder."[27]

In 1910, after many years of campaigning, the Chicago and Illinois trade union and reform movements managed to get a ten-hour-day work law for women passed by the state legislature in Springfield. R. C. Ritchie and Company, a large laundry concern that employed women primarily, challenged the law before the Circuit Court of Cook County, and Judge Richard S. Tuthill of that court granted the company an injunction on the grounds that the law was an unconstitutional abridgement of the right of contract. The lines of the struggle were drawn. This time, however, the unions were joined not only by the National Consumers League; Louis D. Brandeis, the prominent lawyer; and Professor Samuel N. Harper, noted historian at the University of Chicago, but also by William J. Calhoun, acting in his official capacity as the Illinois attorney general. In this case the state legislature was pitted against the lower court ruling, and the political implications for the elected representatives became as much a consideration as the issue of the legality of the ten-hour law.[28]

Robins, Josephine Goldmark of the National Consumers League, and Louis Brandeis prepared a 600-page brief. It was primarily a sociological study of the reasons and justification for limiting the working day of women. It cited cases and opinions of experts in related fields worldwide. Supporters of the law viewed the brief as critical ammunition in the fight. But because of carelessness or intent (it was never made clear), the brief was not filed with the state supreme court by the legal deadline. There was a furor, with accusations and recriminations on all sides.[29] When the case was finally brought to trial the material in the brief was allowed in evidence and Brandeis pleaded the case successfully before the court, which upheld the law in its entirety on 21 April 1910.

Robins's activities always involved the preparation of speeches and the accumulation of evidence to support his position before audiences and sometimes the courts, but he loved the confrontation, the challenge in the face of violence—if it was for the good cause. "You may say what you like," Elizabeth quoted her brother, "a fight is a fine thing." In describing Robins in Nome after driving off claim jumpers with a pistol in his pocket, Elizabeth provides insight into his fiery disposition when he fought his battles for labor: "I know his hot young blood has been full of the joy of battle and that, as some men are lured by the shine of gold, he is lured by the bright face of danger."[30]

No situation better exemplifies Robins's thirst than the speech he gave at the little town of Apollo in Kiskimenatas Valley, Pennsylvania, during the strike of the Amalgamated Association of Iron, Steel and Tin Workers of America (AAISTWA) in August 1909. The union, which fared badly in its first strike in 1901, was forced into calling another in June 1909, when the management of the American Sheet and Tin Plate Company, a division of the United States Steel Corporation, announced "that all its plants after June 30, 1909, will be operated as 'open' plants." If carried out, the plan meant an end to the hiring of union labor and the destruction of the union itself.[31]

For two weeks, Robins explained, he had been "going through the mill towns of Pennsylvania, Ohio, West Virginia and Indiana, giving such aid and comfort as I may to the Union men now on strike against the great Steel Trust and the U.S. Steel Corporation. It has been a moving and warlike time. I have been ordered out of town at times and at times have remained and spoken under armed guards of union men." The town of Apollo was completely controlled by the mill owners and no store owner or proprietor would cooperate in any way with the workers.

> The printers refuse to print the posters of dodgers announcing the meetings— a hardware man refused to sell them a die with a number 6 on it to stamp a correction on some notices they had printed elsewhere—the hotel man was told his hotel would be burned to the ground if he kept Raymond and some other men over night, and the man who had rented them the open lot where the meeting was to be held begged to be let off, but finally was persuaded to let them hold their meeting in spite of the threats.[32]

Before Robins had a chance to begin, a man from the United States Steel Corporation, with several armed bodyguards, followed by a mob "partly under the influence of drink," approached and said, "it would be suicide to carry out the program." Robins ignored the man, turned around, and asked the chairman to introduce him. "I must admit," recalled an eyewitness, "that we feared for the worst but was willing to die for the cause. As pale as death he rose, fully determined to do or die, weak at first then finally with a voice likened to a Patrick Henry he went through his grand ordeal."[33]

That night, after the strike-breaking mob had been liquored up a bit more thoroughly, they were encouraged to attack the strikers and the hotel where Robins finally got accommodations. "All night long a dozen or more of the strikers stayed out on the balcony of the hotel ready to fire if necessary." But there were no incidents and on the days that followed Robins traveled to other parts of the state to speak in behalf of the union. Only at Consonant, where the lights were turned out in the hall in the middle of the speech, was there any other harassment. On that occasion, Robins continued in the dark and the audience stayed with him to the end.[34]

Again in August the striking workers of the Amalgamated Association of Iron Steel and Tin Workers of America, this time in Steubenville, Ohio, asked for Robins's help. He made three separate trips to this town to help in the drawn-out struggle. The strike lasted another full year after Robins's effort in Steubenville. It was not until 27 August 1910 that the union accepted defeat and called off the strike. Sympathetic students of American labor history maintain that this defeat "resulted in the complete elimination of the Amalgamated Association; thereafter the Steel Corporation . . . refused to deal with any union. For the decade following 1909 . . . the Steel Corporation arbitrarily determined hours, wages and working conditions."[35]

On 21 August 1910, seven days before the union "surrender," Robins evaluated the "collateral issues of that battle [that] have been won," knowing full well that the strike would soon be called off and a long struggle lay ahead. He would not consider the failed strike a defeat. The workers had won the abolition of Sunday work, and the twelve-hour day had been fiercely attacked and was "doomed." "The sanitary condition . . . had undergone a complete revolution. The government investigation that we forced has resulted in a clean up all over the United States. The Workingmen's Compensation Commission has about completed . . . a satisfactory law."[36]

In the fall of 1909, as the AAISTWA strike still wore on, Samuel Gompers, president, and Frank Morrison, secretary-treasurer of the American Federation of Labor, along with John Mitchell, were arrested for their part in a boycott against the nonunion Buck Stove and Range Company. The company lawyers used the decision in the Danbury Hatters case as precedent for the charges, this time against the national leadership of the American trade union movement. Throughout the country attention centered on what retaliatory action labor should take since the conviction of the three was a possible death blow to organized labor. Some of the tactics of retaliation suggested were radical, some were violent.

Robins was rarely confronted by plans of organized labor that he could not support. With the "G. M. and M." arrests Robins opposed the most radical tactics. His position in that situation provides insight into his approach to the general question of radical activity. "The General Strike is an impossibility," he wrote to his sister-in-law Mary Dreier, who was even more active than he was in union work. "Nothing would be so disastrous to the cause of organized labor in this country. As for our people to countenance a General Strike, it would be a foolish failure and discredit our whole undertaking." Instead, Robins suggested a series of protest meetings with a one-day strike of all organized labor not devoted to protection of life and health. He wanted to set the one-day strike "far enough in the future to admit a propaganda work," which he considered the critical ingredient if the demonstration was to be a success.

> An organized attack upon the present members of congress at the next congressional election waging a vigorous war against all those present members that opposed organized labor would be a helpful thing to do.
> I shall be glad to have G. M. and M. go to jail. I think that this fact would do more to cement the men of labor into an effective fighting force than anything that could happen.[37]

Robins opposed any measure that might lead to a widespread disruption of the social and economic order. He denied socialism as an ideology and socioeconomic system even if achieved democratically, since it would represent a tyranny of the "weak" majority over the "strong" few. Therefore, he also rejected revolution for America. In Russia of the Bolshevik Revolution, he would again be forced to confront the question of the justification for revolution; in that situation he affirmed its necessity. In the context of the American experience, however, he remained steadfastly a reformer, denying the necessity or justification for social revolution. The Chicago years involved struggle to bring about change, but always within the limits of the humanely and flexibly interpreted Constitution and established social and economic institutions of the United States.

Robins's counterproposal to the call for a general strike included protest meetings, a one-day nationwide strike or work stoppage for symbolic and propaganda purposes, political action at the polls, and finally, the great lesson of self-sacrifice of the union leaders going to jail for their principles— these were his arsenal for reform. Robins's thinking was inextricably related to his Christian convictions, his reading of the New Testament basic to his approach to reform. Commenting on the remarks of William Jennings Bryan, Robins explained his approach to the boycott: "'If eating meat make my brother to offend I will eat no meat while the world standeth.' Here again my thoughts wandered from his text to another and I thought of how well this could be used in defense of the industrial boycott of unfair products. There is a certain sense in which the boycott is the only effectual application of the brotherhood principle to modern conditions."[38] Robins's thinking on the boycott in the Buck Stove and Range dispute was sustained. The three-year-long battle, in which the company was backed by the American Manufacturers Association, was a union victory. The Buck works "are now union from the basement to the top story," Robins proudly wrote to Elizabeth.[39]

After 1910 Robins's political commitment and heavy speaking schedules for the Men and Religion Forward Movement precluded his stumping activities for troubled or striking unions around the country. He turned his attention to a different vehicle for his personal message and call for justice and social reform. Although he worked for the hope of Christian revival and an American rededication to the social gospel of Jesus, he never forgot labor's struggles.

In the fall of 1910 he was asked to arbitrate the dispute between the Philadelphia Rapid Transit Company and the trolleymen's union. There were two arbitrators stipulated in the agreement, one appointed by the union and the other by the company, and provision for a "third arbitrator (should he be required)." There had already been a strike by the trolleymen, as well as a settlement, in the spring of that year. The issue that nearly brought on another strike was seniority rights and the interpretation of parts of the settlement language that related to who were "loyal men." On 3 November, after long delays, the two sides presented their arguments before the arbitration commission of two. The presentation lasted until 9:30 at night and the arbitrators were deadlocked. Robins wanted to avoid the admission of a third arbitrator because he felt it could only hurt the cause of the union. Tension rose on both sides for six days while an attempt was made to find a formula for settlement. The more radical among the rank and file of the union were made impatient by what they believed to be delaying tactics of the company and the arbitration procedure itself.[40]

On 9 November Robins went to the mass meeting of the union at the Labor Lyceum, where the men were hoping to hear a favorable report on the arbitration. After making his way through the crowds to the podium, Robins learned of the abduction and assault of C. O. Pratt, the leader of the car men. Pratt had just been released when Robins reached the hall. "The men were wild with excitement and wanted to go on strike at once. Pratt asked me to make a speech to kill time until he could get the meeting in hand. This I did under very difficult circumstances."[41] Meetings went on at the Lyceum until 5 A.M., with Robins speaking again at 3 A.M. He called for calm and patience in that hour of justified anger. Shortly thereafter, the arbitration commission of two provided a workable settlement that was a victory for the union.[42]

Throughout these years of union struggles, settlement, and reform work, Raymond shared with Margaret the hills and pine forests of his childhood— the lands that he bought in Hernando County. Back in 1905, just after their wedding and before settling down to work in Chicago, he took her to see Snow Hill, which he "thought to be the highest hill in Florida. It was the hill which drew him when he felt alone. He used to ride there to look out upon the vast forest where one's soul could stretch toward the infinite." There, in the following year, they began rebuilding the old mansion house that became their haven from the slums of Chicago and the battle for reform.[43]

On the thirty-first of December 1908, at one of those times of reflection and repose, when Margaret and Raymond found nature, quiet, and seclusion at Chinsegut, their hilltop sanctuary, Raymond listed his year's accomplishments in his diary.

> Rudovitz and Buck.
> 161 talks, 62 cities, 19 states, 30 sermons, and eight demonstrations, 4 ministers meetings in universities, 3 state democratic conventions, one hall convention, one summit Pikes Peak, two state labor conventions, one national labor convention, 19 central labor assemblies, four local unions, one miners convention, one interstate convention of Woman's Trade Union League, 3 womens' clubs, one mother's club, 4 state ratification meetings, 6 settlements, 4 Y.M.C.A.s, Cooper Union, Faneuil Hall, out door talks upon labor policy, religion, education, social service, settlements, travel, public schools, transportation, law, single tax, five banquets of seven luncheons, 12 diners, 61 nights in Pullman cars, traveled 43,362 miles within the year. The busiest, hardest year.[44]

The tally for 1908 was no more extraordinary than that of any of the other twenty-five years they lived in Chicago. Margaret's stewardship of the Women's Trade Union League through all those years never left open to question that her first commitment was to the worker. As the tally so clearly demonstrates, Raymond served the cause of reform in many different ways. However, in 1908 more than in any other year, he joined with Margaret and the rank and file to fight the cause of organized labor.

6

The Mission
of the Social Gospel

We are ready to talk to you but if you keep your gospel in the shelter and in
the protected places, if you find it only in the shadowed isles in the comfortable homes, if Christian men keep their Christian consciences separate from industrial life and the political activities of our day, then we question the whole
business. We do not believe it is on the square and we would rather follow
Karl Marx than Jesus Christ. That is the challenge as it comes to me. That is
the strain in the great new social age when the old individualized control is
breaking down, when the new social control is not yet born. When the need of
all life is that the power and the passion of the master should meet life at the
places of strain.
　　　　　　　　—From Robins's speech, YMCA Cleveland Conference,
13 May 1916

FROM his earliest childhood Robins saw a sad and problem-filled world reflected
in his father's and mother's suffering. He searched for the answer—the good
news—and found it in religion. He felt compelled to convince others to follow
the same path.[1]

Unlike many of the causes for which he worked, his dedication to the Christian evangelical mission was constant. All subsequent commitments, movements, and activities were reconciled with his vision of Jesus and his message to
humankind. Robins's activities for social reform, trade unionism, and political
rejuvenation were steps in the attainment of human salvation in this earthly
life. He worked tirelessly and ceaselessly, his enthusiasm and dynamism fired
by the conviction that earthly woes were ameliorable through the efforts of
those who saw the way.[2]

Robins's crusades harnessed his greatest talent, public speaking, to preach
his personal vision of Christianity and service. In the days before electronic
mass media, the only method of putting such talent to work was through personal appearances over as widespread an area as possible. Because the railroad
was the fastest means of transportation, Robins spent a good part of those
years on trains traveling between speaking engagements. Although during the
first years in Chicago his speaking activity was centered in the city itself, by
1907 he turned more of his attention to broad, national questions and the podium became his workplace.

While in Nome, Robins had evolved a personal interpretation of the social gospel of Jesus and its essential corollary of service. When he first came to Chicago, he had his first experience with a journal of opinion as a tool for change. When John Palmer Gavit left his position as the founding editor of *The Commons, A Monthly Record Devoted to Aspects of Life and Labor from the Social Settlement Point of View*, Robins assumed some of his duties. Shortly thereafter, in January 1902, Robins's first article, "Politics and Labor," appeared in *The Commons*. But Robins had the temperament of a preacher-activist; he was far more comfortable on the podium. His writing was often moving and powerful, but it did not compare with the impact of his spoken words.[3]

During the ensuing years, and in the speeches he made during a 1907–8 tour, Jesus was the central concern. Human existence and fulfillment were measured by one's relationship to Christ and by how one served humanity, as Christ had commanded. Until 1910 Robins was willing to include this message as one among many that, taken together, addressed the pressing problems facing America. Beginning in 1910, he resolved to work for a new Christian social conscience.

This aspect of Robins's work was part of a general movement in American Protestantism that can be traced to the origins of the Reformation itself. The immediate impetus can be found in a new religious social consciousness that was reflected in two works which had an important influence on Robins: Washington Gladden's *Social Salvation* (1902), and Walter Rauschenbusch's *Christianity and the Social Crisis* (1911).[4] Robins's unique experience, outlook, and charisma allowed him to fashion a message of Christian social responsibility with a practical immediacy that was missing from most social gospel declarations at that time. Robins captivated his audiences.

In October 1907, under the management of Luther S. Dickey, Robins began the first of many lecture tours of the United States and Canada. The tour was sponsored by the Public Publishing Company, whose magazine, *The Public*, was edited by Louis F. Post. The magazine was dedicated to political and social reform and the single tax ideas of Henry George, whose unsuccessful 1886 Chicago mayoralty campaign was managed by Post. Robins hoped that through wide circulation *The Public* would be a national journal of reform and single tax advocacy.[5] But at the same time Robins was shaping his social gospel program and religious work. He saw no inconsistency with, nor contradiction between, these two fields, unlike many of his colleagues.

Under the enterprising managerial skill of L. S. Dickey, Robins sallied forth to win support for *The Public*. Less than one-third of the speeches were paid for by fees, which ranged from $3 to $75; more money was collected in contributions than in lecture fees. At the end of the tour, Dickey proudly reported the success of "Mr. Robins [who] made 82 addresses to audiences aggregating 35,000 people."[6]

Robins's speaking schedule was arduous, but meeting speaking commitments was not nearly as difficult as filling the hall. Public lectures were competitive, a source of entertainment. A speaker whose name was not widely known might face empty seats. Robins's 1907-8 tour was a year of initiation. Louis Post's biographical sketch of Robins, with the dozens of testimonials to his speaking prowess, was prepared specifically to introduce Robins to the committees that chose lecturers. Luther Dickey worked hard as an "advance agent," creating the preliminary publicity to assure a well-attended meeting.

****

Please Read and then Hand to a Friend!

An Address by

THEODORE ROOSEVELT

in Milwaukee

was duly announced in the newspapers and otherwise advertised. Although the weather was fine, less than forty persons were present to hear him, for he was very little known. That was nineteen years ago

---

If the people of Milwaukee generally knew the remarkable power as speaker possessed by

RAYMOND ROBINS

of Chicago

and the value of the message which he brings, there would not be standing room at the

CONGREGATIONAL CHURCH

GRAND AVENUE AND 22ND STREET. [etc.][7]

****

From October 1907 to June 1908 Robins spoke on diverse subjects before even more diverse audiences, making every effort to integrate the social gospel and single tax themes. Beginning in Brooklyn, speaking under the auspices of the Brooklyn Women's Single Tax League, he then spent more than a week in Jersey City, New Jersey, as the leading light in reform mayor Mark M. Fagan's bid for reelection. Fagan campaigned on a platform of public ownership of utilities and as a renegade from the corrupt Democratic party machine. Robins was hesitant to join a political battle so far from his usual constituency, but Fagan's victory proved to him and to many of his friends that his involvement in the campaign was the first step in his rise to a position as a "national figure" in the political reform movement.[8]

After New Jersey, Robins also spoke before groups of settlement workers in New York, and before the Pennsylvania Equal Suffrage Association, students at the University of Wisconsin, union groups, the National Single Tax Conference, local political clubs, teachers associations, and men's clubs; but nearly half of his engagements were before church groups.[9] A list of the subjects of Robins's lectures in 1908 includes nearly every reform concern of that era.[10] Robins was diplomatic and sensitive to the different social and political dispositions of his audiences, and the titles he chose for his lectures allowed great flexibility.[11] His advocacy of trade unionism is nowhere set forth point blank. Instead he championed the child, the woman, the homeless, and the relationship between the union and the home. The obvious evils of crime and corruption needed no such care in the choice of titles, nor did the positive values of democracy, good government, and the message of Christ. But he did affirm his commitment to the radical causes of women's suffrage and the single tax.

Robins made no claim of originality. A careful reading of his speeches confirms this. His genius was in his ability to apply information already known and create insights by approaching a problem from a new vantage point. This ability, along with his keen sense of drama and the personalization of subject matter, led to striking success.

On the day following his windup speech at a political rally for Fagan in Jersey City, Robins spoke on "Crime and Criminals" and "Side Lights on Graft and Grafters." The speech was widely advertised by flyers that introduced Robins as the "Noted Lecturer and People's Politician." The next day, an admirer wrote this letter to L. S. Dickey:

> Mr. Raymond Robins spoke last night in the pulpit of the First Presbyterian Church of South Orange, New Jersey. There are many people in the world who talk in public. Some of them know what they are talking about; Mr. Robins belongs to that class.
> Some of them talk from devoted hearts, with no effort to distinguish themselves; Mr. Robins belongs to that class.
> Some of them talk with such magnetic power as to make an address of seventy-five minutes seem but a few minutes long; Mr. Robins is in that class.
> Some of them so speak that those who hear them hear Jesus Christ, as He promised should be the case, and their hearts, consciences and wills are profoundly moved and they wish to hear him again; Mr. Robins is in that class. He should be heard, as far as possible, in every pulpit in the land.[12]

Robins's extraordinary speaking schedules for the winter and following spring, and especially his work for the Men and Religion Forward Movement three years later, nearly fulfilled this suggestion.

In the spring of 1908 Robins began speaking on behalf of William Jennings Bryan, the Democratic candidate for the presidency. Bryan was opposing William Howard Taft, Theodore Roosevelt's handpicked successor and an antilabor conservative. After Bryan's failure in November, Robins turned his attention to labor struggles. For the next two years, his concern for the trade union movement held a priority in time and interest. By 1910 the apportionment of his time and energy changed. In his "notes on Settlement Studies," Robins repeated: "There are two ways of improving a nation's state, the first is by altering the institutions of the country, the other is by the regeneration of peoples' character."[13] After nine years of work at the first method, Robins turned to the second—a spiritual and moral regeneration of the American people.

By 1911 Robins focused these new energies in a YMCA-sponsored, interdenominational protestant organization, the Men and Religion Forward Movement (MRFM), in which he headed the "social service department." The movement called for the creation of a new Christian man and woman in America, through the "crystallization of a new social conscience . . . [based on] a new statement of old scriptural truth and a new method in the Christian Service." The MRFM, and Robins in particular, called for a shift "from individual to collective," from the personal quest for salvation to a compassionate responsibility for all of humanity, particularly the poor and others afflicted by modern industrial society.

Robins planned concrete programs of health care, education, child care, job training, counseling, and housing as part of "a new unity of the Protestant men and women in community service." Taking the settlement house as his model and embracing the religious ecumenism of settlement workers, Robins hoped to see every church and synagogue in America carrying out the settlement house agenda of service. The MRFM again took the cue from the settlements, which used the social survey as a scientific technique for identifying the needs of a community, publicizing the facts, and implementing programs.[14]

The MRFM's roots were deep in the American tradition of revivalism and evangelical crusades. Robins attempted to apply a newly revived faith to social, industrial, and economic problems in the form of Christian service.

The first campaign lasted through the fall, winter, and spring of 1911–12, under the auspices of the International Committee of the YMCA of North America. A committee was to oversee the coordination of the tour and its organizational format, but for the most part, Robins had autonomy in his choice of speeches and the presentation of his personal vision of Christian service.

The MRFM tours were major undertakings compared to Robins's other speaking engagements. They involved several days of sequential prayer meetings, mass meetings, town district meetings, minister's conferences, institutes on social problems conducted by experts, and a culminating mass meeting. The local YMCA made elaborate preparations, raised funds, and conducted publicity campaigns to ensure a big turnout. Of the seventy-six cities visited in 1911–12, Worcester, Massachusetts, responded to the call in an exemplary fashion.

The town fathers established a Committee of One Hundred and prepared for an "Eight Day Campaign." "Not a Revival, Not a series of Religious Meetings in the Usual Sense, But a Program of Work," read the headlines on a half-page in the Worcester *Daily Telegram* on Saturday, 6 January 1912. The middle of the advertisement contained a photo of Robins and the announcement of the mass meeting at which he was to speak to open the campaign. The caption read: "If you want to know what the Men and Religion Forward Movement has to say in Social Service, on the application of the principles of religion to society, business, politics, hear Robins Sunday." Nearly half of the front page of the newspaper was devoted to the news story of the opening of the "Great Eight Days' Campaign" and the methods of disseminating information on it to the surrounding towns.

Robins was usually "star speaker at the mass meeting" that initiated and ended the work in a given town. Often he shared this important role with Fred B. Smith, the experienced and effective evangelist of the New York YMCA. The two men worked well as a team and while traveling the evangelical circuit together were close friends and associates. At the time of the Worcester campaign, Smith offered Robins the post of international head of a newly created Social Service Division of the YMCA, with an annual salary of $5,000. The salary and the position would have left Robins free to work full-time to orient Y activities toward his ideas of social service. Robins eventually rejected the offer because it would have meant moving to New York and severing ties with Chicago. Nevertheless, it is worth noting that the international committee of the YMCA, after a four-hour meeting, had resolved unanimously to create this new division specifically with Robins in mind as its first head.[15]

At the conclusion of the 1911–12 MRFM campaign, Robins submitted stenographic reports of his speeches to *The Survey* at the insistence of his friends in the movement. They were published under the title "Sermons on Social Service" and provide a meaningful insight into Robins's synthesis of social worker and evangelist. The list of some of his speeches included: Social Service and the Gospel; Democracy in Industry, the Problem of Our Day; To All Who Work; The Social Purpose in the Churches, Message to Ministers; The War on Poverty and Disease; and To Save the City We Must Save the Child.[16]

Robins used the MRFM and the YMCA as platforms from which he could call for social reform. Elizabeth and his sister-in-law, Mary Dreier, viewed both organizations as conservative stumbling blocks in the fight for social justice. Over the years Robins had to assure them that his evangelical work was a positive contribution to the cause of reform. Many of Robins's friends and associates found his involvement in the usually conservative and often reactionary revivalism mystifying, if not outright suspicious. "I have been receiving quite a number of letters," wrote Daniel Kiefer, his old associate and an active single taxer, "from parties inquiring how you come to be mixed up with the Men and Religion Forward Movement. To each I have replied that I did not know anything about it but felt pretty certain that you thought you had some opportunity there and were making the best of it."[17]

With reference to this very letter, C. H. Ingersoll, a co-worker in reform, wrote to Robins on his views: "Dan Kiefer is after your scalp, or more specifically, that part of it which covers your religious department and I have been defending your association with a lot of citizens whom he insists are dead wood religious people. . . . I think Dan is trying to get you mad enough to write him a letter of some sort. Go for him."[18]

Many reformers and labor organizers were not as willing to accept Robins's activity in the MRFM. On one occasion a number of years later, he was scheduled to speak before an audience of workers in Paris, Illinois. As he reached the podium, a moment before his first words, he was handed a note:

> The workingmen present tonight expect an answer to the following questions: 1. Are you connected with the Men and Religion Forward Movement? 2. Is J. P. Morgan a contributor to the Men and Religion Forward Movement funds? 3. Did you refuse to debate with Reverend Parson of Pittsburgh on the question of workingmen's relations with the Men and Religion Forward Movement? 4. Why did you shut up the ceremonies and force the garment workers back to work at Hart, Schaffner and Marx?[19]

There is neither a record of whether Robins answered these questions, nor whether he was responsible for the alleged deeds. The reference to the ceremonies and the strike at Hart, Schaffner and Marx is unclear. But Raymond and Margaret played a key role in organizing and carrying out that strike of men's clothing workers in 1910–11 and in achieving the landmark arbitration agreement that served as a model for years to come. Important here is that Raymond had to face allegations that he had sold out to the big money interests he had so often attacked.

What was Robins's relationship with the "interests" during the Chicago years? A number of contributors and activists in Chicago reform were millionaires; most noteworthy was Anita McCormick Blaine, heiress to the Cyrus McCormick fortune and Robins's close friend and co-worker. As early as 1907, Robins was instrumental in acquiring a donation of $6,500 from Andrew Carnegie for the purchase of a church organ. But far more interesting is Henry Clay Frick's communication with Robins, shortly after Robins began his active involvement in the MRFM:

> Dear Raymond:
> I still think the suggestion of Carnegie financing a great Conservative labor daily, by no means chimerical. Fix it so that you and I can see him, and then run the paper. Let me hear from you. If you desire it, I will write you a brief memo as to how the matter should be organized and operated, so as to avoid the danger and accomplish the good.[20]

This handwritten letter resulted in nothing. Robins did not shun contact with the rich; he prided himself on having and using such connections to support the causes for which he worked. But the record demonstrates that such contacts, most often developed through Robins's religious work, were limited if they did not involve the same commitment to reform. Robins's dedication to "the group of toil" made him feel somewhat uncomfortable amid upper-class respectability and "culture." His personal correspondence, especially to Mary Dreier and labor movement friends, is filled with his condemnation of the exploitation and immorality of the "moneybags . . . group of plunder." At the same time, he aspired to wealth, position, and power. The most obvious outward sign of such position could not, of course, be the home he and Margaret shared in the tenement walk-up flat in the slums of the Seventeenth Ward. That home was the monument to their reform work and sacrifice. Chinsegut, the beautiful and constantly enhanced "estate" they built in Florida, was the mark of such position and gentility.

Robins was always concerned about the suspicion caused by his evangelism. A further complication was his convincing attacks on socialism. In retaliation, his socialist adversaries attempted to undermine his credibility by pointing to his involvement in religious causes. Robins defended himself and his MRFM work as forward-looking and in the interest of social progress. "It is about the farthest removed from an emotional individualistic revival of any undertaking under religious auspices that could be imagined," he wrote to Elizabeth in England. "Nothing could be further from the spirit and method of the work I do in social service than the spirit and method of the usual religious revival."[21]

In the summer of 1911 Robins participated in the Conference of the Presbyterian Church of North America. He joined his fellow social reformers in an effort to win this important and conservative body of church governance to the Christian service position. But the delegates advocating "social responsibility" were in the minority and were labeled radical. The moderate Christian service program Robins advocated, including the right of labor to organize, legislation to limit hours and working conditions, especially for women and children, pure food and drug laws, and taxation to fund programs for the unemployed and indigent, had no chance of adoption, until he hit on the idea of giving "so radical a speech that they would pile all the condemnation of . . . radicalism upon my head . . . and let the 'radical' proposed program through." It worked.[22] If many on the left viewed Robins's religious work with suspicion, stereotyping all evangelism as conservative if not reactionary, many in the YMCA, the Congregationalist Church, and the Men and Religion Forward Movement distrusted him for his prolabor, reform, and "radical" politics. No less a friend than Fred B. Smith candidly revealed his early distrust of Robins privately and wrote of it publicly years later.

> I first began to hear about his work in Chicago in the years of 1905 to 1910. I had been trained in religious work in what might have been termed the intense evangelistic emphasis for the individual. Hearing of Robins' utterance and methods in social service, I was quite certain that he was unorthodox in theology and a dangerous radical in methods. I did not wish to quarrel with him and therefore quietly planned not to meet him.[23]

Smith was relatively open-minded and ready to reexamine his thinking. To those "in religious work" who were traditionalists, conservative, and dogmatic, Robins attempted to explain his Christianity:

The Men and Religion Forward Movement came at a time when materialistic socialism was vigorously advancing all along the line in the United States. Debs had made a coast to coast campaign in a special train and had polled for president about one million votes. There were socialist representatives in several state legislatures, some members of Congress and a number of mayors of the socialist faith. In the city of Minneapolis, in Pittsburgh, in San Francisco and in many other places I crossed swords with the socialist leaders during the Men and Religion Forward campaign. There has been a steady decline in the socialist vote and the class cleavage of materialist socialism in this country since the Men and Religion campaign. Under the drive of Men and Religion the workers, Progressives and Liberals found hope for the future inside the American system of law, economics and social order. This will be historically its most significant contribution to the social order of this country and the world.

Its second greatest contribution was the establishment of the social service program and vitalization of the social message of the Gospel of Christ in all religious groups in this country. It affected powerfully the Catholic and Jewish groups as well as the Protestant.[24]

These conflicts of interest suggest the embattled, unconventional positions Robins took. Throughout his life, this did not change; in at least one case, his advocacy of United States recognition of and cooperation with the Bolshevik leadership led to doubt of his loyalty to the United States and round-the-clock surveillance by federal authorities. Similarly, labor activists and single tax radicals could not explain his evangelism unless they attributed to him a conservative political agenda. Robins's public speaking was far more than an expression of thought, emotion, and concern. He referred to his talks as battles, struggles which had to be won if life were to have meaning.[25]

Robins was an excoriating self-critic when he felt he had failed, but when he sensed the impact of his charisma and energy in the faces and response of the audience, he forgot all modesty. Two weeks after the Worcester, Massachusetts, campaign ended, Robins spoke before a standing-room-only audience of more than four thousand at a MRFM mass meeting in Pittsburgh. It was considered one of the key cities in the nationwide campaign, and Robins was particularly anxious to make a great presentation. Although the Pittsburgh newspapers reviewed this speech favorably, Robins wrote to his wife:

> I made to this magnificent assemblage one of the feeblest talks of the campaign. It was simply rotten. My voice broke and I stammered and words died on my lips. There was no power of the spirit.
>
> If I could go to you and put my head in your lap and cry like a tired child I would be oh so glad. I do not know why I should have been so wretchedly feeble. I have never wanted to make [unclear text] good, and yet I have seldom made, in all my life a more complete failure.

Soon thereafter, Robins reported that the speech was probably not quite so bad, especially since he received many compliments and found it well received in the press. In the same letter reporting this "complete failure," he described his next speech: "Yesterday was a great field day for me here. The ministers meeting was the greatest in this town's history. But while I made a really great speech, I lost my head in answer to an especially vicious socialist question and skinned them alive and not in a wholly Christian manner."[26]

In the end, interpreting his Bible with care, Robins was the yea-sayer of the Book of Psalms rather than the nay-sayer of Ecclesiastes. He completed the 1911–12 MRFM tour with a deep sense of accomplishment and an even stronger commitment to the movement as a force that would transform society. After devoting most of his time and energy to Theodore Roosevelt and the Progressive ticket in the fall of 1912, he decided to join Fred B. Smith in an even more ambitious MRFM World Tour. The idea, organization, and methods were to be the same as those used in the national tour, but the itinerary included Hawaii, Japan, Korea, China, the Philippines, Australia, South Africa, and Great Britain.

The objective of the Smith-Robins World Tour was to link Christian workers in a World Gospel Conquest, to "increase power to Specialized Christian work for Men and Boys," and to revitalize the Protestant church in general. Once again Robins thrived on the evangelical experience, only this time his audience spanned much of the planet.[27]

His letters written during the tour provide a global comparative social commentary on living and working conditions. He visited factories and slums and found conditions far worse than in the United States. He was most upset by the child labor system in a Chinese cotton mill in which "little boys and girls of seven years of age working fourteen hours a day seven days in the week for six cents a day, with a cursed system of fines, and each worker, man, woman and child was searched as they leave the mill each night. Never have I . . . seen child slavery reduced to so exact a science." Robins went on to attack the "Chinese capitalism" and the consuls who "hold their jobs through the influence of shareholders in the homeland." He asked, "is this the capitalists heaven and the worker's hell on Earth?"

Typically, Robins wrote his analysis not only of the situation, but of the possibilities for solution. "Now I have a plan for helping the situation but I will not write it, but want to talk it over with you when we meet again. One caution, do not think they can be helped by organization or trade unionism. This will not be possible for a generation because of poverty, ignorance, and the mighty host willing to take their places."[28] Was Robins suggesting revolution to overthrow the "worker's hell"? We do not know the specific plan he had in mind. But we do learn later from his Russian experience that, under economic and social conditions such as those prevalent in China, he was not opposed to political and social revolution.

Always at the conclusion of a "campaign" or a year, Robins prepared a retrospective account of his accomplishments. "Homeward bound at last!" he wrote in a letter to his boyhood teacher and friend, William Fulton, "Nearly seven months by land and sea! This is my twelfth steamer, and when I reach port I will have been 91 days at sea since the 17th of January. When we reach New York I will have made 233 addresses to over 147,000 different people, and my words have been translated by interpreters into ten languages. I have visited 13 foreign lands in four continents, and the islands of the pacific." To the childlike enthusiasm for adding miles and speeches, there is added the harsh and self-critical judgment. "Out of all the hundreds of meetings all around the world," he continued to Fulton, "there are just three that I remember without a sense of failure and regret that I did not do better work."29

After his return to the United States and for the next four years, Robins divided his time between evangelical campaigns and his important role in Illinois and national Progressive party politics, including his U.S. Senate candidacy.

After the expected defeat at the polls in November 1914, Robins again returned to his social gospel evangelism. He was dissatisfied with the results of the Men and Religion Forward Movement in terms of actual numbers won to the cause of Christian service. To solve the problem, he decided on two courses of action. First, he would turn to a different audience—college students. Second, he would ask for a written commitment or decision from his listeners as a demonstration of their willingness to serve.

By focusing on college students Robins felt he could reach the source of America's future leadership. Further, he felt that the colleges and universities provided "a culture and contact with life that would lift them above special class prejudices. . . . Here men are trained to think in universal terms." Robins was speaking of the optimum—of what a college education should provide, or the goal to which higher education should aspire. He was really asking: if not in the colleges and universities, then where?

Freedom from class prejudice was not the only essential for lasting and creative leadership. An involvement with Christ was even more important.

> My experience . . . has demonstrated unquestionably that men without the passion for, and personal fellowship with Jesus Christ have not stayed with the problem of effective and necessary leadership.
>
> My desire is to interpret into the lives of these men the living permanent values of my life, for what they are worth, so that these men may begin where I have left off.
>
> A word about my method of work. No originality is claimed for it—neither that it is better than any other man's method. It is mine. It is all I have. My purpose is to take hold of any honest hook of human need to lead a soul back to the power and freedom of Jesus Christ. There is just one center to this work—that is Jesus Christ. There is just one Personality under heaven that can adequately help a man—that Person is Jesus Christ. My purpose in using what has been called the social approach to the spiritual need of men is because it is my own experience, it is scripture and it works.
>
> I am in this work because the world needs leaders. Potential leaders are in the colleges and universities. They cannot lead successfully and permanently

without the power of Jesus Christ to meet their own and the needs of other men. In fellowship with Him, what may not a generation of Christian leaders accomplish?[30]

Robins needed to personalize an idea or a cause for it to have real and lasting meaning to him. His generalization, that those who do not live with Jesus "have not stayed with the problem of effective and necessary leadership," is an expression of what he thought was the driving force of his own effort: energy and leadership. He felt that it was his spiritual relationship with Christ that allowed him to go on, in spite of setbacks, illness, and emotional breakdown. He tried to credit that relationship with the responsibility for his accomplishments.

In all of Robins's activities, the degree of his involvement was inextricably linked to his emotional and personal identification with the cause. When these elements were not present, his interest was minimal. When present, his energy and dedication knew no bounds. Because he identified so completely with his causes, success or failure in their behalf determined his sense of value as a human being. It was under such self-imposed pressure that he turned with deep feeling to his sources of solace: at times, when he felt she would not be crushed by the weight of the pain, to Margaret; when devastated and losing control, to Elizabeth; for reaffirmation, to his sister-in-law, Mary Dreier; and in facing the struggle of life, to God.

His 1915–16 tour was part of the National Christian Evangelistic Social Campaign and was similar in many ways to the MRFM tour of 1911–12. The difference lay in the use of the final mass meeting, at which the students and faculty were urged to sign "decision cards" as an unmistakable indication of their new or renewed commitment.

Grateful for the deeper revelation I have received of the power and meaning of the Gospel of Jesus Christ, and believing that Christian living is the only way for the complete redemption of the individual and social life, and desiring to do God's will and to have his power in my personal experience and life work—

I hereby make a decision to seek a daily life
of victory and fellowship in service
with Jesus Christ as Savior and Lord.

Name_____Address_____Church Preference_____[31]

Very early in the tour, the distribution of the cards, as well as the compulsory attendance at the inaugural mass meeting or convocation, led to conflict. Robins felt the need to press forward his cause. He sought the coercive power of the college administrators to assure attendance throughout the sequence of meetings. Once involved, the skeptical or disinterested member of the college community could be won over. "We are fully agreed as to the unwisdom of forcing attendance," Robins wrote to John Childs, the administrator and agent of the tour, "but it seems to me there ought to be some plan . . . that would operate . . . in the matter of attendance, culminating [in] the Decision Meeting." The conflict over mandatory attendance intensified and Robins finally stipulated that only the initial mass meeting required the attendance of the entire college community if he were to undertake a campaign at a given institution.[32]

After many months, traveling through twenty-six states and a province of Canada, holding campaigns at forty-two colleges and universities, the statistical tables of accomplishment were compiled, this time with a new column: "Decisions." The total there reads 8,274. Attendance: 57,141—men's meetings, 7,834—girls' meetings, 39,900—joint meetings, and 1,609—faculty meetings. Robins spoke on: College Men and Civic Leadership; College Men and Industrial Problems; Principles and Methods for Social Control; Mastery—The Secret Power; and The Strain and Challenge of a Changing Social Order. Presented with a great sense of urgency, Robins asserted that these issues required the attention and devotion of the new, dedicated generation.

Robins's success as an evangelist was remarkable, often resulting in lifelong impact on many who heard him. During a campaign directed toward college youth in Brooklyn in the spring of 1917, a Raymond Robins Service Club was established in the Brooklyn Central YMCA. Robins succeeded in winning adherents among the most diverse audiences—"conservative, radical, moral, religious or economic, [where] he seems to fill the human demand as no other lecturer does."[33] He appealed to universal values, using his personal experiences—presented with drama and passion—which came naturally from a message concerned with crisis and the urgent need for change. Since his method depended so much on this personal synthesis, one can better understand his harsh self-criticism at moments when he felt he had failed. On those occasions when the personal and universal were not in harmony, he was crushed and sometimes his listeners felt that he was egotistical.[34] When the two were developed successfully, the result was a deeply moving experience, with the audience attributing to him deep humility and sensitivity.

"Some evil spirit must have taken possession of me," Robins wrote to Mary Dreier, during the 1915–16 College Campaign. "I have done altogether the poorest and feeblest series of addresses that I have done in years . . . and now I am like a dried up spring from which the water has ceased to flow. . . . There is nothing to do except to wait the return of power. What a great opportunity has been lost." Then, just one day later, he wrote again to Mary. "Yesterday evening the power came back with a flooding richness and I have made one of the greatest speeches yet made by me. It was on the industrial problem and before the four hundred odd sons of privilege. I was able to tell the issues of the group of toil with compelling power. I am thankful beyond words."[35]

Late in the 1930s Robins wrote out a long list of his campaigns, spanning nearly his entire lifetime. The list, at first chronological and then as items came to mind, includes his political, labor, social service, Christian service, and foreign policy activities and reveals the diversity of his work and the many burning issues of his times.

1. Bryan (1896)
2. Suffrage Amendment to California Constitution (1896)
3. Nome (1900)
4. Dever [Reform aldermanic candidate, elected in 1902]
5. Harrison
6. Dever [Reform aldermanic candidate, reelected in 1906]
7. Harlan [Candidate for mayor of Chicago]
8. Dunne [Reform candidate for mayor of Chicago]
9. Merriam [Charles E., University of Chicago professor, reform candidate for alderman]
10. Dever [Reform candidate for mayor of Chicago]
11. Bryan [1908]
12. Progressive [1912?]
13. Progressive [Robins's bid for U.S. Senate in 1914?]
14. Men and Religion [Men and Religion Forward Movement, 1911-12]
15. Smith Robins [MRFM World Tour, 1912-13]
16. Colleges and Universities [Evangelical Campaign, 1915-16]
17. Hughes Campaign [for the presidency on the Republican ticket, 1916]
18. Harding Campaign [for the presidency on the Republican ticket, 1920]
19. Outlawry of War Campaign [with Salmon O. Levinson, throughout the 1920s]
20. Coolidge Campaign [for the presidency on the Republican ticket, 1924]
21. Law Observance and Enforcement Campaign [for observance and enforcement of the Prohibition amendment on moral and constitutional grounds]
22. Hoover Campaign [for the presidency on the Republican ticket, 1928]
23. Allied Forces for Prohibition Campaign (1931)
24. Roosevelt Memorial Campaign
25. Fagan for Mayor Campaign [reform candidate in Jersey City, New Jersey, 1907]
26. Danbury Hatters' Case Campaign
27. Russian Refugee Rudovitz Deportation Campaign [1908]
28. Woman's Ten Hour Law Campaign
29. Woman's Suffrage National Campaign
30. Hold the Eastern Front Russia Campaign
31. Beverage for Senator Primary Campaign
32. [Hiram] Johnson for President primary campaign
33. Growers cooperative control Citrus Campaign [in Hernando County, Florida]
34. Dever for States Attorney
35. Dever for Mayor [Reform candidate for Mayor of Chicago, elected in 1923]

36. Dever for Mayor
37. Anti-intervention in Russia
38. Municipal Lodging House Campaign
39. Social Settlement Campaign
40. Small Parks and Playgrounds Campaign[36]

Central to Robins in nearly all these campaigns was his role as evangelist and public speaker. He aimed at winning the hearts and minds of men and women of good will to the just cause, and he accepted no limitations in what might be accomplished by the power of the spoken word. Only in this light can his tireless activity be understood.

7

Chicago Politics

We are used to hard fights. This is largely a workingman's district. Our candidate stands for the best interests of the workingman. We are relying on an awakened public intelligence for success and believe our candidate will win.

—Raymond Robins, quoted in *The Record Herald*, Chicago, 19 November 1902, on the State Senate race of John J. McManaman

POLITICS in Chicago at the turn of the century was unique, making effective reform much easier there than in many other American cities. Chicago had its bosses, with many wards dominated by the local machine; but there were many situations in which the balance of power between the regular Democratic and Republican parties was in flux. In Philadelphia and Boston, by contrast, single-party machines controlled elections, leaving little chance for committed reformers to succeed in the political arena. As a direct result of Chicago's political arena, the settlement, charity, and reform workers involved themselves decisively in nominations and election processes;[1] likewise many Chicago social settlements were active in reform politics from the first days of their creation. (Some students of this period have suggested that such political involvement was a last resort.[2]) Such activism is epitomized in the 1894 founding of the Chicago Commons by Graham Taylor. In 1895 (according to Lincoln Steffens's muckraking classic, *Shame of the Cities*), Taylor was chosen as one of the "Nine" Chicago citizens to form a Municipal Voters' League for political reform. The league's first focus was the aldermanic elections in the spring of 1896. They identified the corrupt incumbents and candidates in both parties, published their records, and endorsed and campaigned in behalf of the nomination and election of honest men. Their success was remarkable. Sixteen of the twenty-six aldermen identified as corrupt were not renominated. Four of the rejected ten who did run for reelection were defeated. League recommendations were adopted in twenty-five wards.[3]

Robins took up the gauntlet of political activity as an integral part of his settlement work in the Seventeenth Ward soon after his arrival and was the "most effective reformer,"[4] "not even Graham Taylor exerted a greater influence on politics in the 17th Ward than did Raymond Robins."[5] "It was all incomprehensible," reported Lincoln Steffens, amazed by the power exercised by the Municipal Voters' League and the Chicago Commons reformers: "the Seventeenth Ward, a mixed and normally Democratic ward, in one year for a Republican by some 1300 plurality, the next year for a Democrat by some 1800, the third for a Republican again."[6]

Robins's first important contact with the established powers in Chicago city government did not relate to his reform work. It came in the wake of the assassination of Pres. William McKinley on 6 September 1901, only four months after Robins had begun work at the Chicago Commons. On 8 September Abraham Isaacs and his family were arrested and charged with complicity in the assassination. Isaacs was a "philosophical anarchist" and led a group of like-minded persuasion on the west side of Chicago. He published a periodical called *Free Society,* printed on a handpress in his tenement apartment, where he lived with his wife, son, and daughter.

Robins knew Isaacs through their participation in the Free Floor Forum, which was held in the basement of the building in which Robins lived at 140 North Union Street. The Commons sponsored these open meetings to serve the people of the district as an educational exchange of ideas on the social and economic problems of the day and also as a demonstration of the democratic right of free speech in America for the many immigrants who attended.

"All of Isaacs' discussions were marked by learning, patience, and a gentle and forgiving spirit," Robins explained, in an account of the injustice of the anarchist's arrest. Robins, who learned as much about radical thought as any other regular in the crowded hall each week, described the intense exchange of ideas, especially between the socialists and the philosophical anarchists, led by Isaacs. "He was a vegetarian," Robins continued, "a non-resistant of the Tolstoian school and took the extreme view of individualism. I had visited at his home and had urged upon him and his followers rational cooperation with the progressive forces of our American social and economic life."[7] Robins also was affected by the long suffering and persecution that the Isaacs family had experienced in czarist Russia, ultimately leading to their emigration and settlement in the United States.

The Isaacs case became relevant to reform and city politics just prior to the assassination of McKinley. An investigation of the Chicago Police Department had begun and special attention was given to the detective bureau. Robins noted that "they were in need of a scapegoat and there had been one or two interviews indicating that if the Chicago business people did not stand by the Police Department they might have another Haymarket riot to contend with."

After the attack on the president, members of the detective bureau arrived at the Isaacs home with a patrol wagon and proceeded to use the methods which Attorney General A. Mitchell Palmer was later to make infamous: in their "search" for weapons, bombs, and written evidence of the Isaacses' role in the plot, the police destroyed the handpress and type cases and confiscated books and writing materials. Isaacs and his son were imprisoned at different police stations, while his wife and daughter were "imprisoned with the women of the street."

On the following morning Robins and Jane Addams made several fruitless attempts to provide bail for Isaacs and his family, but the scapegoat mentality prevented all efforts at freeing the "harmless visionaries," as Robins called them. Finally, the two settlement leaders appealed to Mayor Carter Harrison to grant them an interview for purposes of putting the facts of the case before him. Robins demonstrated his political acuity by arguing that the handling of the entire affair was very much against the best interests of the police department and the administration of the "stand-pat" mayor. "These people had been permitted to live in Chicago for a number of years right under the eyes of the police: if they had been hatching up such a crime it was an indictment of the police and the administration." The mayor seems to have responded to this reasoning and permitted Addams and Robins to visit the prisoners.[8]

Several days later, the assurance of innocence was sustained by the court. In retrospect, it is clear that the influence and prestige of Jane Addams and not that of the unknown newcomer Robins was primarily responsible for the fair treatment of the Isaacs family. But the need for fortitude was not over. When "patriotic" mobs stoned Hull House and the Chicago Commons to repay Addams's and Robins's efforts, the two did not waver. It was the kind of confrontation that Robins loved best—in the name of the innocent— where the lines were clearly drawn between the good and the evil.[9] Robins even was moved to do battle using the printed word, which he had never done before. In his very first published work, which appeared in *The Commons*, he included a strong critique of Theodore Roosevelt, McKinley's newly sworn-in successor as president, for his support of "legislative persecution" against men like Isaacs. "For philosophic anarchy," Robins declared, "there is just one cure, a free government providing equity for all its citizens."[10]

Robins explained the political action of settlement workers and the toleration for speakers at the Free Floor Forum whose views were considered radical or "dangerous."

> I took the position that . . . it was necessary to defend these helpless peo-
> ple, quite as much on the grounds of ordinary justice and the right of free
> speech. . . . We took the position at the settlement that to allow these people
> to come and blow off their steam was a good deal better social policy than to
> persecute them and have them feel that they had a great cause for which if
> only a hearing was granted the whole world was eagerly waiting. The out-
> come fully justified our faith.[11]

Robins modified this faith in the case of Emma Goldman, "a thoroughly ill-balanced if not vicious woman," seeing in her "dangerous" iconoclastic so-cial criticism "cheap publicity and painless martyrdom." But with Robins in support of their freedom of expression, the publication of the "harmless" anarchist *Free Society* was resumed by Abraham Isaacs, continuing for a number of years thereafter.

Two important aspects of the Isaacs incident were defined by Robins. First, "The public had its excitement and the investigation of a rotten Detective Bureau was squelched."[12] Second, "In all this great city just one person of position and influence . . . fearless Jane Addams of Hull House has dared to stand with me against the popular outcry. . . . Graham Taylor . . . wavered and fell back but this little woman stood like a stone wall."[13]

Robins's initiation into the Chicago electoral arena came in the winter of 1901, when he decided to carry on the political reform work of his predecessor, James Walsh. In 1897 Walsh had studied the legislative problems of the district and was a reform candidate for alderman of the Seventeenth Ward. Following in his footsteps, Robins began to investigate and expose corruption in city government, especially that which directly affected the lives and well-being of the residents of the poorer districts of the city.

In the third week of March 1902, two weeks before the aldermanic elections, the campaign committee of the Democratic (reform) candidate William E. Dever, who had lost to the Republican Frank Oberndorf in 1900 by 1,257 votes, appointed Robins campaign manager for the "hopeless" last-ditch effort—"members of our own club laughed at the idea of electing Dever." Robins began his work by spending two days in the city clerk's office and from the 6,000 pages of the Chicago City Council records for the four previous years compiled "a record of infamy against Oberndorf." Robins orchestrated a packed-house campaign inauguration, huge mailings, twenty-six district meetings, four ward mass meetings and, on election day, "manned every one of the polling places with challengers, watchers and runners. . . . I met the gangsters with their own weapons," Robins boasted to Elizabeth, "organization with organization, and force with force, and in a free field I have never doubted the power of righteousness over wrong."[14]

Following Dever's election on 1 April 1902, many people were suggesting Raymond Robins for the Democratic nomination for the Twenty-first State Senatorial District. Robins's reputation had spread by word of mouth faster than had any written word by or about him. Henry Barrett Chamberlain, assistant secretary, and Walter L. Fisher, secretary of the Municipal Voters' League (aside from president George Cole, its most influential leader), pressed for Robins's nomination. Many in the forefront of Chicago reform politics were anxious to see Robins run for political office. "I had a talk last night with Dever," Chamberlain explained to Graham Taylor, "and Dever feels about Robbins [*sic*] just as I do—that he is a broad, clean-cut, powerful young man. . . . Dever feels that Robbins is too high class a man for the organization, but I told him that we have been bringing the people up to a higher standard, and I believe that the right sort of work would enable us to land Robbins."[15]

Disregarding the pressure to run, Robins decided to support the nomination and election of the best candidates in city and statewide elections. In the race for the Twenty-first State Senatorial District seat, Robins supported an independent candidate, John J. McManaman, a laborer who, like Robins, had struggled to get an education and finally a law degree. His strongly worded nomination speech for McManaman condemned "machine ridden conventions of both the old parties which have nominated men for high public office that upon their own boasting confessions should be in Joliet [the Illinois state penitentiary]." The Republican candidate, Frederick E. Erickson, was a deputy sheriff and protegé of former senator and political boss Edward "Eddie" Dwyer. The Democratic candidate, Benjamin M. "Benny" Mitchell, was well connected to Democratic boss Roger C. Sullivan. Both of these men were notorious for their involvement in underworld affairs and "boodle" (graft) in Chicago. Robins and his associates did not intend to start a real third party movement at that time, but given the alternatives offered by the regular parties, they were forced to work for the election of an independent candidate.

McManaman's campaign was a critical turning point in the role of the Chicago Commons in the Chicago political arena. Robins foresaw such a transition in his nomination speech: "Those of us that dare to trust our fellow men see in the future a time when the machine bosses will be driven to their holes and the corporation lobby whipped from the State House at Springfield. The rule of the 'gang' is nearly over in Illinois. We need a man worthy of our past and prophetic of our future."[16]

The entire settlement and reform community within the district participated in the campaign, and Robins managed to bring Clarence Darrow, the Legislative Voters League, the Public Ownership party, and the Seventeenth Ward Community Club into the fight as well. Nevertheless, the outlook was bleak. Fearing a voters' rebellion and condemnation of the major parties by election of the untried independent McManaman, the Chicago newspapers reported that enormous sums were spent, particularly in behalf of Mitchell, to buy votes. "Young feller, yer'r dead right," Robins recounted the response of a factory worker who explained that because the price of coal was so high, many were willing to accept several tons in exchange for their vote. "An I'll stand by yer in spite of hell, but most of the bye's say, 'Benny's got the stuff, and winter's coming on.'"

Robins replied to this in a letter to Elizabeth: "Up and down this District I have told hundreds of hard-handed men that the time serving doctrine 'a man has to live' is a cheap and cowardly lie. With all the power God has given me I have sought to have them feel that 'sometimes a *man* has gloriously and triumphantly to *die*.' By a power not my own I have awakened them from a slavish obedience to corrupt powers, into open rebellion toward . . . their old political masters."[17]

McManaman won, and as Robins noted years later on the typescript of his nomination speech, "This man won an independent fight against both party organizations—the first success of this nature in the history of this district." The victory was far more significant in its long-range importance than in its immediate in terms of one more reform voice in the Illinois State Senate. McManaman's election was a political catalyst for the reformers, for previously, in most cases, the reform activists tried to force the regular parties to nominate suitable reform candidates rather than to organize the election campaign of an independent.

The advantageous flux of the aldermanic and state senate elections in Chicago was illustrated by a realistic promise made by Republican Alderman John Smulski, to secure Robins's endorsement by the Republican party if Robins could manage to get the regular Democratic party nomination. In those districts where there was an even balance of power between the Democratic and Republican forces, such as in the Seventeenth Ward (a part of the Twenty-first State Senatorial District), the reformers were most successful. After their first electoral victories, the major parties could not cavalierly disregard the will of the people. These elections not only forced the regular parties to take note of the political power of the Commons and Northwest settlements, it also gave enthusiastic and dedicated settlement workers the vitality and encouragement needed to carry on their political activity. The result was a "Chicago Commons [which was able] to build a Ward organization that controlled the political balance of power for nearly two decades, . . . and in effect dictated the outcome of 14 consecutive alderman's elections in the Ward."[18]

Between 1902 and 1904 (the next important election year), Robins was involved primarily in work at the Municipal Lodging House and Northwest University Settlement. His political activity centered in the Municipal Voters' League and Public Ownership League, which carried on their continuous fight against the "traction interests" of the Chicago Street Railway, which constantly sought to increase its franchise. By early fall 1904, the reformers of the Seventeenth Ward had undertaken a more ambitious project: the election of an independent candidate, Walter Elphinstone, to the Illinois House of Representatives. Elphinstone was a former shoemaker, long-time stalwart of the Chicago Commons, and president of both the Seventeenth Ward Community Club and the local Shoemakers Union.

Again, all the reform forces were mustered for a difficult campaign, and although publicly expressing enthusiasm, Robins confided to Anita McCormick Blaine: "I am leading a forlorn hope on the political field." In spite of these inner doubts, Robins worked ceaselessly, speaking on almost every night of the week for more than a month. He felt obliged to do all he could to try to defeat the Republican candidate, Fred Erickson, who had been nominated by the Republican convention against all the protests of the delegates of the Seventeenth Ward. The reformers felt the necessity of putting up their own candidate and making a good showing, or of being ignored by the major parties.

By 1 November the campaign had become "red hot" and Robins and his co-workers were concerned about hooliganism and ballot-box stuffing; although they guarded the polls on election day, Elphinstone lost. He placed last in a field of four candidates for the three available seats from the Twenty-first District. Nevertheless, the reformers were not discouraged. In the municipal elections in the spring, Dever, unopposed, had been returned to his seat as alderman for the Seventeenth Ward. In the Fifteenth Ward, reform candidate Albert Bielfus was elected, as was R. R. McCormick, a reformer running on the Republican ticket and the first Republican in the Twenty-first Ward for many years.[19]

In the mayoral election of April 1905, Robins joined Allen T. Burns, a settlement worker, and Harold Ickes, in his last year of law school, in support of John Maynard Harlan, Jr. Harlan was the son of U.S. Supreme Court Justice J. M. Harlan, who had been one of Robins's law professors. Paradoxically, the young Harlan was the regular Republican candidate and Robins's endorsement was a cause of bewilderment and concern in the reform movement. Time showed this support for Harlan, a conservative, to be the first in a long series of similarly "unfathomable" positions taken by Robins in behalf of conservative candidates for major executive office.

In this case, as in future cases, while Robins lent support to a conservative, he pressed for every reform plank the traffic would bear in platform committees and campaign caucuses behind the scenes. Robins believed that there were times when graft and corruption required confrontation and even a show of physical force, but he was also convinced that if he could gain entry to the inner circle of powerful men such as Harlan, he could win them to his reform creed. He had won conversions from the podium before hundreds of listeners, how much easier in the small circle of the "back room." Robins was neither naive nor deluded in his estimation of his power, and at some of the most crucial moments in his career, he succeeded.[20]

Robins was drawn into the campaign when Harlan requested his help with the preparation of the mayoral platform. From noon to two, on 9 February 1905, they "thrashed over his [Harlan's] proposals" and Robins "cut them unmercifully." Robins was flattered by the request and even more so by Harlan's compliments: "You are a better politician than I am Robins, but what I can't understand is how you could know so much and not have been in Chicago but four years. . . . If I am elected I shall expect you to feel that you are a member of my 'kitchen cabinet.'"[21] As this apparently was neither a case of political seduction nor a lead-in to other promises or deals, Robins took his opportunity for an inside track to further his reform program.

"Your position has been the talk of the liberal element, not only at our single tax table but wherever I have gone," read one of the letters Robins received within days of his declaration of support.[22] Harlan was not involved in the fight for municipal ownership of utilities or mass transit, nor was he

by any stretch of the imagination a reform candidate. Amid the growing furor, Robins was quick to explain the reasons for his "renegade" position.[23] It
came in a published article entitled "Who Shall Be Mayor?—To the Independent Voters of Chicago," in the *Chicago Daily News,* and formed a public
response to the "kindly protests," as well as the "insulting assumptions."
Robins noted that Harlan had no "blind allegiance to the Machine" and
achieved the nomination "by sheer force of an independent personal popularity," something that could not be said of his opponent, Judge Edward Dunne.

On the question of municipal ownership, upon which Dunne had taken
a much stronger stand than Harlan, Robins resorted to some unconvinc-
ing casuistry. He maintained that the problem was far too complex to be
solved by the facile methods proposed by Dunne and voiced his confidence in its accomplishment by Harlan's conservative approach. Robins was
indeed making excuses for Harlan on a plank in his platform with which
Robins did not agree; however, he was genuinely concerned about the Democratic party hacks then joining the municipal ownership bandwagon. It
had become clear to the machine politicians of both parties that municipal ownership was popular, and they felt they had to pacify the rising cry for its implementation.

Robins feared that the strong Dunne position on municipal ownership
merely reflected the shenanigans of the Democratic party back room. On
the other hand, Robins saw Harlan's position as honest, in the face of a
temporary popularity among the fickle public. Harlan proposed "A genuine
referendum upon all important legislative acts regarding public utilities" as a
democratic safeguard of the people's rights. As a longtime supporter of the
referendum and recall, Robins was attracted to Harlan's alternative proposal.

"Here is the real shadow behind Chicago in this campaign," Robins explained. "Not the base lie of Morgan behind Harlan, but the certain fact of
the 'grafters' behind Dunne." Robins described a city riddled with corruption
and of the "palsied administrative arm" of government. He wrote of the
worldwide reputation of Chicago as a city of ill-repute, tolerant of the worst
crimes and criminals.[24] Despite the concern and warnings of his friends,
Robins persisted in his support for Harlan and in his belief that Harlan's
election would ameliorate Chicago's problems.[25]

To Robins's disappointment, Harlan lost, but in the months that followed,
Dunne began to carry out his campaign promises for municipal ownership
of public transportation and utilities. As a result Robins revised his opinion
of the new mayor. In May of 1905, after Dunne had been in office for five
months, violent demonstrations instigated by anarchist extremists shook
Chicago. Robins used this opportunity to bury the hatchet with Dunne and,
in an open letter to the mayor, expressed his solidarity with Dunne's stand
in behalf of the peaceful electoral process. Robins asked to be considered "a
volunteer in readiness for any demand within my power in helping preserve
order under the dominion of our constituted authorities." On the following

day, the mayor reciprocated in a kind and appreciative letter, and in the years thereafter, the two men forged a strong and close political alliance for reform in Chicago.[26]

Among the many posts held by Robins during the Dunne administration was his seat on the new Board of Education. He served with Jane Addams, Anita McCormick Blaine, Louis Post, and others. Some of Robins's activities in the public schools, such as the construction of improved bathroom facilities and playgrounds, have already been discussed in connection with his settlement work. More important were his accomplishments on the board which had important political repercussions. "Mr. Robins . . . reduc[ed] the number of seats to a room from 54 to 40," declared his fellow reformer and co-worker Margaret Haley, business representative of the Chicago Teachers Federation, and she added to the list of his accomplishments: "abolition of a one-man power administration; . . . official advisory representative teachers' councils; abolition of . . . secret marking of teachers and re-examination for salary promotion; raising and equalization of salaries for efficient teachers."[27]

Robins and his associates on the board had an excellent opportunity to carry out these reforms of the antiquated and custom-bound school system. In the case of school appointments and administration, the new board fought to withdraw the public schools from the political spoils system by instituting civil service examinations. A professional educator was appointed superintendent of schools with a long term of office and a salary sufficient to avoid the previous problems of transience, graft, and political pressure. Teacher appointment and advancement were regulated by a new system of examinations. All "special considerations" connected with contracts and supplies for the schools, particularly those for books and coal, were unearthed and stopped. Each measure, dictated by the rational goals of reform, created a more just and progressive educational system.[28]

However, a conflict soon arose over the provisions for teacher advancement and salary increments that the Teachers' Union felt were unfair, especially the retesting of experienced and tenured teachers. The issue could easily have been settled between the board and the union, especially since most of the members of the board, like Robins, were strong advocates of trade unionism and collective bargaining. The fly in the ointment was the provocations of the *Chicago Tribune,* the *Record Herald,* and the *Daily News.*

These newspapers occupied offices and plants built on land owned and leased to them by the Board of Education of Chicago. The ninety-nine-year lease had initially included a revaluation clause to adjust the land values for tax purposes. A previous board, not as circumspect as that appointed by Dunne, had eliminated the clause, "which means that the same rent is to continue no matter how greatly the value of the property increases," much to the pleasure of the newspaper owners. The influential newspapers were afraid of and angered by the new board and its reform agenda, which refused to endorse that dubious action of its predecessors.

In the board dispute with the Teachers' Union and with its reform policies in general, the *Tribune* attacked the board as a whole and the individual members, labeling them "freaks, cranks, monomaniacs and boodlers" (a contemporary but milder term for grafters).[29] "If the newspapers simply made editorial attacks," Raymond explained to Elizabeth, "it would not matter much, but every act of the Board is deliberately lied about . . . so that the public is kept in entire ignorance." From the start, the *Tribune* sought to use the teachers dispute and a change in contracts to eliminate cutbacks in supplying the schools as a means of discrediting the new board in the public eye. The *Tribune*'s influence was remarkable.

> Only those citizens who attend the meetings of the Board have any knowledge of what is being done for the education of the 250,000 children of the city. Ministers of every denomination have joined in the hue and cry of the press, and from the pulpits have thundered their denunciations and anathemas. Mass meetings are called by these reverend gentlemen "to consider the crisis in the public schools," and a petition has been signed by Mr. Gustavus Swift, packer, and others to be sent to the Charter Convention "to curb the power of the School Board."[30]

As negotiations between the board and the Teachers' Union progressed, a new issue was created by the "privileged interests"—the legitimacy of the board's recognition of the Teachers' Union as a bargaining agent. Although there were differences of opinion between the union and the board, there was a mutual respect and good faith. From Margaret Robins's point of view, as an interested observer, this was the issue that the newspapers managed to manipulate to create the furor against the board. "To many, this simply means that trade unionism won in this particular issue," she explained to her sister Mary, "and as there is a growing effort to stamp out trades unionism absolutely and entirely in Chicago, . . . to my mind it is distinctly a class struggle and of course the Teachers' Federation is a peg on which to hang other things."[31]

The opposition to the school board mounted to a feverish pitch, including the move to pass a "ripper" bill (a state law to supercede that of a city or county) in the state legislature to deprive the board of its powers, if not "to legislate the present school board out of existence." Nevertheless, measures enacted by the "radical" school board on which Robins served withstood the newspapers' attack. The reforms of teachers' councils, civil service, and supply contracts, including many of the just demands of the teachers, remained an integral part of the reformed school system.

Both Raymond and Margaret Robins became so deeply involved in the struggle for "a true Public School System" that they felt obliged to support Jane Addams's Hull House as the rallying point of support for the board. So strong had the outcry against the board grown as a result of the newspaper attack that the philanthropists who usually contributed to Hull House threatened withdrawal of support in the face of Jane Addams's radical role on the board. Margaret offered to subscribe up to $20,000 of her personal inheritance from her father in matching funds for any expenses or loss incurred by Hull House in its work on the school board issue. "I have told Raymond what I am doing and he is happy that I should wish to do it."[32] Margaret's offer was deeply appreciated by Addams and the workers at Hull House, but the need for its acceptance never came. Some significant gains had been made by the reform board, and while the controversy faded from front-page headlines, it reappeared a year later in even more divisive terms. That time Raymond Robins was at the center.

In addition to asking Robins to serve on the Board of Education, Mayor Dunne appointed him to the chairmanship of a specially created Committee on Candidates for Alderman of the Democratic Party, which screened the records of aldermanic hopefuls, especially on the issue of municipal ownership. Robins took on the responsibility of investigating the candidates and preparing reports on their qualifications with the stipulation that he have a free hand in his investigations and recommendations. Because Robins's committee had been mandated by the mayor, ostensibly the leader of the Democratic party in Chicago, the outcome of the committee report virtually determined the party nomination. Robins took on this task with a fervor and honesty that left many long-time political hacks anxious, if not enraged.

Shortly after noon on 18 February 1907, while walking only a short distance from his home, Robins was attacked by three men and beaten until unconscious. He suffered no serious physical injury and his recovery was swift. In addition to the three men indicted for the actual assault, James Carroll, brother of Edward F. Carroll, Democratic aldermanic candidate for the Thirty-first Ward, was also indicted as a coconspirator. The candidate himself was never directly implicated in the crime, and Robins eventually dropped the charges on the indicted men because he could not positively identify them and he feared that they had been framed by their opponents. It was clear to Robins, however, that it was the paid henchmen of Skinny Madden who were guilty. Madden, boss of the Building Trades Council and the Chicago Federation of Labor and a major force in Chicago back-room politics and corruption, summed up his approach to union leadership and city politics in saying: "Show me an honest man and I'll show you a goddamn fool." Robins's committee had reported that Ed Carroll, a Madden associate, "was utterly unfit" as an aldermanic candidate. Even the *Chicago Tribune* expressed indignation and outrage that the political contest in Chicago could have descended to such depths.[33]

Robins suffered an emotional relapse from the assault later that spring, and he remained with Margaret at her old home in Brooklyn Heights through June. In the summer he regained his strength, and he and Margaret returned to Chicago. But this was not the last time Robins faced violence as a result of his revelation of corruption in Chicago politics.

Three years later, in the summer of 1910, Robins had revealed the machinations of Benny Mitchell, machine candidate for the Twenty-first Senatorial District (which included the Seventeenth Ward). Robins's close friend John J. Sonsteby telephoned Robins on 30 July to warn him that Mitchell had threatened to shoot him. Two days later, by chance, Robins met Mitchell on the street and the confrontation nearly turned into a fistfight.

"Quite a crowd had now begun to gather," Robins recorded in a sworn affidavit, believing Mitchell's was not an idle threat. "I turned away as Mitchell said, 'You're on notice, open your damn mouth about me again and I'll get you.' I walked up La Salle Street without looking back, got on a Grand Street car at Lake Street and rode home."[34] Despite such threats Robins was not intimidated. "This is the hottest battle we have yet had in this State," he wrote to Elizabeth one week after the primaries that largely determined the result, "and there will be bloodshed before it is over." For the first time in his ten years in Chicago, Robins prepared his personal and business affairs, including a revised will, in expectation of the "'gang's getting [him].' Altogether I will do as much if not more in getting killed for free government in Illinois as by living for it [because] if I am 'put out of business' they will lose the legislature."[35]

The fall and winter of 1906–7 was a key period in the battle for municipal ownership of the Chicago trolley and street railways. Mayor Dunne had demonstrated to Robins's satisfaction that he intended to carry through his bold plans, and Robins became one of his first lieutenants in the fight against the "traction interests." Following the Henry George analysis advocated by Robins, the public transportation system of a great city was certainly one of the industries and services that had to be brought into the public sector of the economy. Private profit, enjoined the reformers, should not be the dominant factor determining the kind of service in the field of public transportation, where virtual monopoly conditions existed for the "traction interests" with the rich franchises.[36]

In October 1906, at the very height of the traction struggle in Chicago Raymond and Margaret faced and passed a difficult test of their public ownership commitment. Margaret learned of the bankruptcy of the Brooklyn Ferry Company of New York as a result of the competition from the publicly owned municipal ferries. The Dreier family had "held important interests" in the private ferry corporation for many years and Margaret lost twenty-five percent of her $300,000 estate. Margaret and Raymond resigned themselves to the financial loss and their steadfast work for municipal ownership never waned. "We are both pledged to this policy of municipalization," Raymond wrote shortly after learning of the bankruptcy, "and the change is absolutely in the interest of the public welfare."[37]

A central focus in the municipal ownership struggle involved an enormous petition drive and Robins spoke in its behalf at every opportunity.[38] Robins, his fellow settlement worker George E. Hooker, and Robins's friend and successor at the Municipal Lodging House James Mullenbach were put in charge of the delivery of the petition to the Board of Election Commissioners of Chicago. They arrived with "thirty-three separate packages" of petitions, containing approximately 184,000 names supporting an "ordinance reported to the City Council of January 15, 1907 authorizing the Chicago City Railway Co. and the Chicago Railway Company respectively to construct, maintain and operate street Railroads in said City, and providing for the purchase thereof of said City of its licensee."[39]

Although the petitions were finally validated, the "traction interests" managed to come out on top. In the next election, which included Mayor Dunne's bid for a second term, municipal ownership was a major issue between the Democratic incumbent and his Republican opponent, Fred Busse. This time Robins worked for the election of Democrat Dunne against Republican Busse, whom Robins considered "boss-controlled." It was also evident that the election of the Democratic ticket would have meant the achievement of the goals of the municipal ownership reformers.

According to Robins, "the people of Chicago fought the traction companies for ten years, and then were whipped by the passage of the ordinance involving what is known as the 'Chicago Plan.'" This plan, put forward by the private interests that controlled the public transportation franchises, allowed those interests to continue operating the streetcars under municipal "supervision and control." The ordinance, which had been presented to the people of Chicago as an election referendum, passed, and a later "audit of the [streetcar] companies' books showed that they had spent $400,000 in the election." Robins believed "the Chicago [plan] amounted . . . to an indeterminate surrender of the public interests to the private graft in street car operation in Chicago."[40]

The Chicago plan called for the creation of a "civil service commission." But Robins accused the commissioners of "betray[ing] . . . people, so that the thousands . . . might be exploited." As for the Chicago plan: "Certain it is that no more perfect scheme has yet been invented for watering the rich man's fields with the sweat of the poor man's brow . . . than the scheme of watered securities. . . . And the bleeding of the whole community in the name of a juggle is a method that has blinded the eyes of the community and is made a stock in trade whenever there is a public utility steal on foot."[41]

Another travesty was the Chicago Charter Convention, in which Robins held one of the most important positions as a delegate appointed by Mayor Dunne. Like a constitutional convention, this body was charged with revising or replacing the outmoded city charter and providing a new basic law more responsive to the needs of a modern metropolis. Robins and the reform movement in general had appealed for such a convention years earlier. As a delegate, Robins saw the unequalled opportunity of incorporating many of the reforms needed in Chicago into its basic legal code. He entered enthusiastically into the work of the subcommittee on municipal ownership of the Convention Committee on Utilities, and the report of this committee presented convincing arguments for the incorporation of a municipal owner-ship clause in the new charter.[42]

Soon after the convening, Robins found himself leading the progressive, reform wing of a predominantly conservative if not "enormously reaction-ary majority" in the convention. In addition to the issue of municipal re-form, Robins successfully championed adoption of his own measure for protection of tenement and slum dwellers. Considering the year, 1906, it was a remarkable provision, very similar to laws enacted years later in many cities throughout the United States. Robins's measure gave the city the power "to repair dangerous or unsanitary tenements if after due notice the landlord refuses to do so, and to collect the cost as a lien upon the building."[43]

For Robins, the charter convention was the vehicle for implementing yet another crucial reform—the vote for women. If the largest city in Illinois could pave the way, it was hoped that the state would soon follow. The re-formers felt that the aims of the women's suffrage movement would inevi-tably be achieved, but adequate impetus in that direction was lacking. The halls of the charter convention were an ideal forum and the new charter an ideal code of law for the furtherance of the suffrage cause.

Robins first became committed to women's suffrage through the influence of his sister Elizabeth, who was a leading suffrage and women's rights activ-ist in London. (Her play *Votes for Women* was a major sensation of the London stage in 1907.[44]) While still a law student, he attended a meeting of the National American Woman's Suffrage Association and joined their cause. The following year, while a novice attorney in San Francisco, he toured California, speaking in behalf of that state's women's suffrage amendment. In the election of 1895 the amendment lost by 24,000 votes, but in 1911, after a similar statewide campaign in which Robins figured prominently, it was fi-nally passed by the narrow margin of 6,000 votes in a total poll of 250,000.

California became the "first important state to adopt equal suffrage and it was a bitter and hard fought battle."[45] Robins was one of many reformers who saw the enfranchisement of women as a cure for America's ills. "I be-lieve that the solution of our social and economic problems . . . will be ex-pected only with the full enfranchisement of women. So believing that I am ready at any and all times to devote what time and money I may to the fur-therance of the equal suffrage cause."[46] Until the passage of the Nineteenth Amendment, Robins remained a suffrage activist. As the movement for ratifi-cation grew, so too did his involvement, with weeks at a time spent in cam-paigns across many states.

Although Robins appeared, from his support of women's suffrage, to be egalitarian, some of his reasons for placing so much faith in the voting power of women are naively discriminatory. The headlines reporting one of his broadsides against corruption and in favor of women's suffrage reveal the outlook of his times:

WOMAN RELIED ON TO REFORM CITIES MAN HAS DEFILED

RAYMOND ROBINS SAYS MUNICIPAL HOUSE CLEANINGS ARE UP TO
FAIR SEX

EXPECTED TO CLEAN UP AFTER "HIM," COLLECTIVELY AS WELL
AS INDIVIDUALLY

EQUAL SUFFRAGE IS THE ONLY HOPE OF CIVIC PRIDE,
SOCIOLOGIST ASSERTS

Following these headlines and under the heading "Raymond Robins' Epigrams" are solutions to corruption in the cities:

> Municipal misgovernment is largely a matter of bad housekeeping; men have always been notably bad housekeepers. Women are used to keeping house and can do it a lot better than men ever can.
> Men have always spent their time making dirt, and women in cleaning it up.
> I want women to have a chance to register a kick against bad municipal housekeeping.
> This city might not be so stupidly dull in its vulgarity and ugliness if women could vote; women have always brought beauty of color and form into men's lives.[47]

Obviously, Robins idealized women as more virtuous and less vulnerable to temptation and greed than were men. He wrote to Margaret that "the men dominate now and they are not as worthy of power as the women are. They, the women, do not suffer from the cause of liquor and licentiousness and they are less liable to be gross grafters as are the men."[48] It is understandable that Robins held such high hopes for the outcome of the enfranchisement of women—giving them the power to exercise these traits in the governing of the city. Once again, Robins had a critical message for which he could be the campaigner—the evangelical crusader. And once again success promised so very much that he felt no energy could be spared.

In 1908 Robins called for a women's "kick" at the job. However, this could not be called true foresight, for his speech was carefully limited to municipal government. He did not mention statewide or national office as appropriate for women, although it is possible he may have believed that they were.

Despite his efforts and those of Catherine Waugh McCulloch of the Illinois Equal Suffrage Association, Robins was unable to include the women's suffrage question in the proposed city charter of Chicago. Regardless of the little hope for its success, he had worked hard to marshall support for its adoption.[49] His failure was upsetting, but the fate of the proposed charter, which had been approved by the convention, was tragic. The state legislature at Springfield, dominated by the political bosses "either cut out or by adroit amendment nullified pretty much every benefit . . . approved under compromise by the convention." The unrecognizable, truncated vestige of the document Robins had struggled to put through could not receive the support of the Chicago reformers; in fact, it required their staunch opposition. Robins immediately joined the fight to defeat the unworthy charter sent back to Chicago for ratification through referendum. "The deformed Charter was overwhelmingly beaten," he declared to his sister.

> It was a crushing defeat for those interests and individuals [who altered the charter] that triumphed last April. We carried 31 wards out of a total 35, and most of these 31 by immense majorities. The papers had made me so conspicuous by their attacks that I have received quite undeservedly a large share of the credit and glory of the victory. My ward (the 17th) went 3 & 1/2 to 1 against the Charter. My political stock is worth 100% more than ever before in Chicago. I opened the campaign, wrote the only exhaustive attack upon the Charter and closed the fight the night before election at a great meeting on the southside.[50]

In addition to the defeat of municipal ownership and a reformed city charter, the reform movement in Chicago also had to face the 1908 defeat of Mayor Dunne, who had turned out to be a courageous leader in many common struggles. The new mayor, Fred Busse, had promised to remove the radicals and boodlers from the Board of Education, and upon his election tried to make good that promise. Disregarding the stipulation regarding tenure of office for appointees to the Board of Education, he demanded the resignation of twelve of the twenty-one board members.

Most of the twelve, and Robins was among them, were outspoken reformers who had been appointed by Mayor Dunne. Busse named their replacements, got the approval of this action from the City Council, and set 29 May 1907 as the date the replacements were to take office.[51] Knowing his allies in the courts, the mayor hoped to drag out the case through legal maneuvering until the expiration of their terms on the board. Eugene Garnett, the attorney for the ousted board members, along with Robins, who returned momentarily to his proven profession of law, sought an injunction against the mayor and the Chicago City Council.

All attempts at the injunction failed, as did the first attempts at *quo warranto* proceedings (a writ requiring a person to show by what authority he exercises a public office) with the state's attorney general, a close political associate of Busse. Finally the case came before the Illinois Supreme Court "which decided unanimously that the State's attorney was bound by law to institute *quo warranto* proceedings and that the removals had been utterly without even the color of legal right." After fighting their exclusion for eight months, the reformers reversed the action of Mayor Busse and resumed their positions, but by that time their tenures had nearly expired.[52]

Beginning as early as December 1907, while still deeply embroiled in the Charter Convention work, Robins joined yet another "campaign"; this one was for the nomination and election of William Jennings Bryan for the presidency. On Robins's retrospective list of forty campaigns, this was number eleven; however, the very first campaign he listed was the earlier Bryan bid for the presidency in 1896.[53] Bryan epitomized the popular democracy toward which Robins worked in the Seventeenth Ward and in citywide and state politics. While Robins mythologized Lincoln in one of his most popular public addresses, the only reason he refrained from doing the same for Bryan was that the man still lived. Robins shared with Bryan the great evangelical and oratorical talents that brought Bryan to a position of national leadership.

Robins began his speaking tour in New Haven, Connecticut, at Bryan's side, and in the course of the next eleven months leading up to election day 1908, he spoke in a dozen states from coast to coast.[54] Among Robins's most noteworthy appearances was one before the State Democratic Convention at Omaha, Nebraska, in March, again sharing the podium with Bryan. Robins's attack upon Taft left a lasting impression. During his stay in Omaha, he spoke before the Central Federated Union, the YMCA, and at least half a dozen different church groups. His theme was always the same—the pressing need for a populist Bryan presidency—but Robins presented his message with special emphases appropriate to each audience.[55] During his Omaha stay, Robins wrote a telling letter to Margaret that again revealed the sporadic nature of his oratorical inspiration. More important, it sadly confided his concern that Bryan, "the Great Commoner," was losing some of his power.

> The Lord was with me in great power. I have never spoken better in my life. I thank God Margaret!
>
> This morning I went with Mr. Bryan to Lincoln and out to his Fairview home for Dinner returning here at 6 P.M. The day has been very wonderful and Bryan looms large in heart and goodness and righteousness but his mental horizon seems misty at many points. He is a great and good man and his physical power and soundness is simply wonderful. He has the finest constitution I have known. His speech last night was very great and his method of presentation, simply magnificent. He spoke in the great convention hall to over five thousand people.
>
> My speech which preceded his was almost a complete failure. I have rarely spoken as poorly. It was a great opportunity and I simply was without power. Tonight, to two hundred men in the Central Labor Temple, I spoke with utter freedom and the mental and moral power of Jehovah. I think I know why I failed last night and I shall tell you of it when we meet again.[56]

The high point of Robins's involvement in the 1908 campaign came at the National Democratic Convention at Denver, on 9 July. His speech, portions of which were soon published in *The Public*, stressed the theme of the struggle of "the group of toil against the group of plunder," who had "wrung the special privilege of legislation, . . . cunning and greed." Robins turned his fire on Taft and recounted a confrontation between Taft and some questioners in one of his audiences. When asked what he would do to find jobs for the millions of unemployed, "God Knows," said Taft, according to Robins.[57] Bryan's cause and the workingman's cause—Robins declared them identical and he raised the issue of the Supreme Court attack against organized labor in the Danbury Hatters decision. Robins turned to the same arguments he used in his National Protest speech, and while fighting for Bryan's election, he simultaneously fought to have that decision overturned.[58]

Taft's victory at the polls as President Roosevelt's handpicked successor came as no surprise. Robins, freed from campaign obligations, devoted his time to organizing the Political Refugee Defense League to help fight the extradition of Christian Rudovitz to czarist Russia. Rudovitz had settled in the Seventeenth Ward after emigrating from Latvia, where he had participated in the Russian Revolution of 1905. In a lengthy leaflet, printed and distributed in part at Robins's expense (Jane Addams served as treasurer of the league), Robins described the circumstances surrounding the affair. Robins had some understanding of oppression in the Russian Empire as a result of his contact with Russian immigrants who attended the public forums at the Chicago Commons and later at Northwest Settlement. Once familiar with the injustice of the Czar's extradition application for Rudovitz, who had come to America to seek political asylum, Robins brought his influence to bear on all aspects of the case. He immediately petitioned the U.S. State Department through the Political Refugee Defense League, demanding that the czarist government's request not be granted.

> The Baltic provinces of Russia were in a state of revolution during the years 1905, '06 and '07. The revolutionists achieved here success attained nowhere else in the country. Oppression by the Tsar and the local barons—an oppression that was political, industrial and religious—had been so extreme that the people rose *en masse,* seized the towns and villages, turned out the bureaucrats, substituted their own officers and for several months enjoyed a complete provisional government of their own.[59]

Rudovitz was accused of involvement in a revolutionary tribunal's decision to punish informers in his district. Information that had been supplied to the tsarist army had led to the death of revolutionary leaders in the village of Benen. The Russian application for extradition alleged that the revolutionary tribunal of Benen appointed Rudovitz, along with "twelve or fifteen other men," to execute the informers. In addition to Rudovitz, one other immigrant to America was named under the provisions of the 1893 Treaty of Extradition between the United States and Russia. Article 3 of that treaty denied extradition, however, "If it be made to appear that extradition is sought with a view to try or punish the person demanded for an offense of a political character."[60]

Robins believed this was an obvious case of a man who, even if guilty of the charges against him, had committed "an offense of a political character" and deserved every benefit of American justice. The case was never brought before a court but was decided favorably for the Russian government application by a federal commissioner. It was after that decision and with the imminent extradition of Rudovitz at hand that Robins entered the case. More than any other step, Robins knew that public opinion would have to be marshalled on behalf of the defendant; otherwise the slow wheels of the federal bureaucracy would never have moved fast enough to reverse the commissioner's decision. Robins attacked not only the poor legal judgment of the commissioner, who had previously been a telegraph operator and government clerk, but the entire imperial tsarist government and its despotism. He depicted Rudovitz as a humble man who had fulfilled his Latvian patriotic obligation in his people's fight for freedom. The provisions of the extradition treaty as well as the essential values of American democracy dictated that Rudovitz be able to retain his refuge in the United States.

After the newspaper stories of the case had appeared in Chicago and elsewhere in the United States, Robins and his client waited anxiously for action from Washington.[61] Robins made one and then a second trip to the capital to present his case before the State Department officials whose jurisdiction included cases of extradition. Finally, after two months, Secretary of State Elihu Root officially refused the Russian application.[62]

The Rudovitz case was important for several reasons. Not only was it the first contact Robins had with the government of Russia, but it was his first education in Russian history and politics since the days in Juneau, Alaska, when he took notes on medieval Muscovy in his long ledger. It also again demonstrated the remarkable effectiveness with which he organized his campaigns. Robins recalled that this victory and the Buck Stove and Range Company boycott were his two most important accomplishments of 1908.

8

The Progressive Party

"Industrial Freedom" is the new war cry and its prophecy will be fulfilled if the Republic is to endure. Old party lines are being swept away, new forces gather— the old leaders are bewildered and led astray. It is a wonderful time—.
> —Raymond Robins to Elizabeth Robins, 26 October 1910, responding to Theodore Roosevelt's "New Nationalism" or Osawatomie speech

The whole purpose with which I entered the campaign has already been attained. All parties are now discussing the economic and social proposals of our platform and the debate is . . . upon how best to do these things rather than upon the merits of the propositions themselves.
> —Raymond to Elizabeth, 23 September 1912

It is the day after the greatest political battle fought in this country since the civil war. Wilson has been overwhelmingly elected but the Republican Party is wrecked and the Progressive Party after a ninety days campaign is the second party in the nation. It has been a glorious struggle and we are more ahead than I had thought possible.
> —Raymond to Elizabeth, 6 November 1912

THE Progressive movement was a wide-ranging response to the fast changing economic and industrial developments in America during the decades following the Civil War. It was a multifaceted and heterogeneous movement, varying in its emphases from region to region, from burgeoning city to country, from immigrant populations to second- and third-generation Americans, and from class to class. With all its diversity, it was a movement with a common goal—to regain moral control over government, business, and civil society from political bosses, corporate monopolists, and grafters who threatened the very foundations of the democratic tradition in the United States. The young generation of socially conscious politicians who entered the Progressive ranks were primarily from "well-established" middle-class families. The social gospel of Jesus—Christian social service—played a profound role in the thinking and dedication of those who joined the movement. Political activism among women, and particularly women's suffrage, was extolled as a cure for many of the evils for which men were responsible.

Nowhere in Richard Hofstadter's Pulitzer prize-winning work on the Progressive Era, *The Age of Reform,* does Raymond Robins's name appear. Yet all of his "distinguishing qualities" of progressivism are remarkably exemplified in the life and activities of Robins. Nor does Gabriel Kolko, another noted interpreter of the period, refer to Robins in his radical and popular reinterpretation of the Progressive Era, *The Triumph of Conservatism.* Kolko asserts that "business leaders, and not the reformers inspired the era's legislation regulating business," making the period from 1900 to 1916 years of preservation and conservation of the established social, economic, and political norms rather than an era of genuine reform. Robins's "radicalism," which was deeply concerned with the preservation of private interest and property along with the public interest, provides a valuable example of the very conservatism Kolko wished to depict, even though Robins would never have agreed with Kolko's thesis.[1]

The creation and dissolution of the Progressive party (1912–16) mark the culmination of the Progressive movement and the beginning of its fifteen-year decline. The Great Depression led to FDR's New Deal, which was in significant ways the rebirth of progressivism.

After McKinley's assassination in 1901, Theodore Roosevelt served out the presidential term; he was reelected in 1904. In 1908, in spite of excellent chances of election to a third term, Roosevelt stepped aside and named Taft as his successor rather than break his promise to abide by the "two consecutive terms" tradition of the presidency. By 1910 the Taft drift toward conservatism faced a strong popular current of reform. Coupled with his opposition to Taft and his rekindled presidential ambitions for 1912, Roosevelt dramatically embraced most of the reform principles for which Robins and his colleagues had been fighting for more than a decade.

Robins had worked unstintingly with his settlement, charity, and reformer allies, and although they had many accomplishments to their credit, they had only scratched the surface of the task before them. The limitations of attacking the great problems of the day from the restricted sphere of the social settlement, labor union, evangelical crusade, or even the arena of city and state politics had long since become apparent to Robins.

The results of the congressional and senatorial elections of 1910, a nonpresidential election year, validated the growing tide of reform. "The 'insurgent' movement has swept over the Republican party in the West," Robins exulted. "La Follette has developed a majority following in six states. . . . Taft has been a complete failure so far. Feeble and futile, his mind has been made up by the master pirates of his party." The conservatism of President Taft received a sharp rebuke with the defeat of many stand-pat Republicans and the victory of a surprising number of liberal and progressive Republicans. In state after state, the reform program was "kidnapped by the machines of both parties . . . and the miracle of the situation is that they will probably be forced to carry out their platform."[2]

In the state primaries before the Republican National Convention of 1912, Robins stumped a dozen states for reform candidates. He joined Robert M. La Follette in the West and wherever either of the two men spoke they "made lots of votes." Unfortunately, they had "too much territory for two men to cover," and as a result their candidates did not win in either Oregon or Nebraska. La Follette promised Robins that they could both "win California and [a] balance of power in the convention if you can come for ten days" and speak.[3]

When Taft was nominated over Roosevelt at the Republican National Convention in Chicago, the brazenness of the old-guard leadership set the stage for launching a third-party movement. "The Republicans committed suicide by the renomination of Mr. Taft," Robins observed, and concluded that he "will be the best beaten candidate that ever ran for President in either of the chief parties in the history of this country."[4]

Early in July, after the surprise Democratic nomination of Woodrow Wilson over Congressman Champ Clark (the machine-backed candidate), Robins was convinced that Wilson was "the best nomination for President since I have known public life. Woodrow Wilson will be the next President of the United States." At the same time, Robins believed that Roosevelt had made a critical contribution to the reform cause by exposing the conservative Republicans at their worst. The new Bull Moose (Progressive) party, Robins dispassionately observed, "will fail." However, Robins understood its important historic role—to unite the progressives of both parties, "drive the reactionaries and 'machines' of both parties together and develop a new alignment in the southern states, breaking up the solid south."[5]

A few days after penning these observations, Robins met with William F. McCombs, chairman of the National Democratic Committee and Wilson's campaign manager, to discuss Robins's possible role in supporting Wilson. A few days later, on 15 July, Robins received two telegrams, each from one of the founders of the Progressive party.

> Urge you very strongly . . . tremendous opportunity for you to infuse your message [of] social justice into progressive movement in same way you molded it into Men and Religion Forward Movement. . . . hope nothing will prevent your attending . . . conference would not commit you to Roosevelt in least but regard it as critical. . . . The framing of our program centers about you. . . . [Do] attend Oyster Bay luncheon next Thursday.[6]

Robins struggled with Roosevelt's motives and the threat of worship of "the man on horseback" rather than the sacredness of reform principles. Robins was thrilled that "the Plunderbund [the millionaire leadership of the Republican party] were panic stricken by the fear of his nomination." At the same time Robins was concerned about the man. "Roosevelt is superficial, is a cheerful liar, is a boundless egotist," he confided to Elizabeth, "and yet is personally honest, love[s] justice, is genuinely democratic in sympathies, and at this moment is serving the larger issues of the Republic more than any other public man."[7]

Robins's respectful declination of the invitation to meet with Roosevelt at his home was followed by five additional telegrams requesting that he reconsider. He did. On 18 July Robins met with Roosevelt, Paul Kellogg, Owen R. Lovejoy, and four other founding members of the party, and Roosevelt committed himself to the entire Progressive social and industrial program: "He agreed to stand for the *eight hour* day in all continuous industries, for the *minimum wage,* for supervision by the government of all casual trades, and for woman suffrage, for the I.R. and Recall [Initiative, Referendum, and Recall], for presidential primaries and the whole constructive radical program except the Single Tax."[8]

On the following day Robins returned to Oyster Bay and met with Roosevelt alone to discuss the party program. Robins received his pledge "to a straight out fight for the reforms of this New Economic and industrial age in which we live and to fight a necessarily losing battle in so far as his being reelected President is concerned. . . . I am still uncommitted to Roosevelt and his new party," Robins explained, "but if he takes all the steps I outlined I shall go to his support and devote myself to the greatest educational campaign in the history of this country with certain defeat ahead."[9]

When Herman Hagedorn was working on his biography of Theodore Roosevelt for the Roosevelt Memorial Committee, he prepared an account of these discussions between Robins and Roosevelt. Hagedorn sent the account to Robins along with an explanatory letter on 10 July 1930, asking for his verification.

> After the Republican Convention in June, 1912, and before the Progressive Convention in August, there were constant conferences at Sagamore Hill. Raymond Robins came to one of these conferences with eight Social Service planks. . . . Roosevelt agreed to them all and said that they should go in.
>
> "That's fine, Colonel," Robins answered, "but how can I be sure that they won't be cut out by the Resolutions Committee."
>
> Roosevelt answered that he would put him on the committee. . . . "I have already picked the man that I should like to see on that committee,—Merriam of Illinois." Roosevelt answered that he should be appointed. Robins said, "Suppose they out-vote Merriam?" Roosevelt answered, "Then tell him to come to me."
>
> Robins said, "Very good, I am going back to Chicago now to burn my bridges. I have always been associated with the Democratic Party. Now I shall go back and tell my Democratic friends and my Social Service friends that I am leaving them because . . . such trumpeting of these Social Service planks as you will give them will set this country forward as nothing else could."
>
> When the Progressive Convention met in Chicago in August, the Platform Committee played ducks and drakes with Robins['s] eight planks, finally cutting

them out entirely. . . . Robins went straight to Roosevelt's room. It was late
at night but the Colonel was still up. Perkins and Beveridge were with him,
telling him how ridiculous Robins' planks were.

"How can I raise money in New York," shouted Perkins, "with those planks
in the platform?"

Robins said, "How about it, Colonel?"

Roosevelt said decisively, "Those eight planks go in the platform or I am not
the candidate."

"There he was," said Robins afterwards, "with his doughbag on one side
and his wind-bag on the other." . . . but Roosevelt had only one reply—"Those
eight planks stay in or I am not the candidate."[10]

Although he had great respect and admiration for Roosevelt, dating back
to the 1902 anthracite coal strike, Robins's involvement in the new party
rested primarily on the hope that it would be the long-awaited force for reform in the United States. There is no record of Robins's specific verification
of Hagedorn's account in any of the Robins archives, but contemporary
documents and letters attest to its truth.

Following those meetings Robins recast his opinion of Roosevelt. He was
able to ignore Roosevelt's egotism, and in place of opportunism, Robins saw
self-sacrifice. He accepted Roosevelt as the champion of the growing movement for reform from the ranks of both the Republican and the Democratic
parties. But he was pressed continuously to account for his support of
Roosevelt and the new party. Robins articulated his view of the circumstances which necessitated that the reform-minded join the ranks of the
new party:

> For ten years men in all sections of our country, who have worked for pro-
> gressive legislation . . . have found the road blocked by powerful . . . ma-
> chines. This "machine" is unwittingly fostered by the division of the honest
> progressives of each community. . . . In the Democratic Party this "machine"
> rests upon the aristocratic and conservative political group in the South, who
> are under the influence of race prejudice and a servile labor policy, and in the
> North upon a compact group of paid plunderers, who enjoy special privileges in
> municipal contracts, gambling, prostitution, and other illegal occupations. In
> the Republican Party the "machine" rests, in the South upon a pay-roll brigade
> of Federal office holders, and in the North, upon a combination of big industrial
> plunderers, who use politics to maintain a special privilege in tariffs, credits,
> transportation and labor conditions. These two "machines" fight among them-
> selves for division of the spoils, but they unite against any genuine progressive
> legislation or effective administrative action in behalf of the whole people.[11]

Assuring his friends that Roosevelt had twice personally guaranteed that
he would stick to his promise of support for the reform and social service
planks of the party platform, Robins conveyed his contention "that he
[Roosevelt] will keep faith with the program, if elected." Robins, won over

as a result of personal contact, finally believed in Roosevelt's sincerity, but it was difficult to convince fellow reformers.[12]

Among the most difficult questions Robins had to confront concerned Gov. Woodrow Wilson, whose reform and progressive administration in New Jersey had brought him national attention and the support of many of the most earnest progressives. Reformers who supported Wilson believed that the Progressive party was unnecessary, but Robins maintained that "he will find his progressive policies ham-strung by the conservative Southern group . . . together with the 'pie hunters' of the North." In addition, Robins attacked the doctrine of narrow states rights, which "makes the Democratic Party an impossible instrument for the effective expression of the modern social and economic purpose of the people." Quite the opposite was to be found in the new concentration of federal power for social welfare at the heart of Roosevelt's New Nationalism.

Robins saw the old party subdivisions and the issues on which they had been divided as anachronistic, and he justified the new party on the grounds that it would help create two new realistic political alternatives in America along distinct conservative and progressive lines. In 1912 he chose the Progressive party because it held the promise of realizing the basic reforms for which he and his friends had worked so long. He believed that the Progressive party platform contained the "three elements indispensable for constructive social progress."[13]

> The first is a practical and effective method of popular control over the machinery of government, the initiative, referendum and recall, the direct primary, the direct election of federal senators, and an efficient corrupt practices act, together with rigid publicity of campaign expenses, make up a body of political machinery that would give effective expression to the will of the people.
>
> The second element is an economic and social program competent to meet the conditions of our complex modern industrial life. The Progressive Party outlines a policy of intelligent regulation of capital and the conditions of labor, while using the public power of taxation to prevent accumulation of social wealth in the hands of the few.
>
> The third element is suffrage for women. No political movement can be genuinely democratic and progressive that excludes the better half of the nation from sharing directly in the power and responsibility, as they share in the burden and labor of our national life.[14]

To the political realists who denied the possibility of success on election day, Robins replied: "Should we fail of election, we shall have broken up the old political crust all over the United States, shall have educated public opinion upon the most important points in an effective political and social program, and both of the old parties will be forced to accept many of the planks in the progressive platform." From this point of view the potentialities of the movement were unlimited. Minimally, it could stimulate a number of basic changes in the established political order; prophetically of course, it did, since within the next two decades, every plank of the Progressive party platform of 1912 had been enacted into law, either as a constitutional amendment or as an act of Congress.

For Robins, membership in the new party began yet another of his personal campaigns, which had as its purpose the education of the American people. "We have advanced a generation in political discussion within 60 days," Robins declared in late September, talking to great throngs and speaking for the initiative, referendum, recall, minimum wage, and woman suffrage, "shouting from the housetops what a year ago we were saying in small committees. . . . If the campaign stopped tomorrow and we were overwhelmingly defeated the value of the campaign would still be inestimable." At no time did he seriously consider the possibility of a Progressive victory in the presidential race. Just as Robins had worked the previous year for the spiritual and ethical revival of America in the Men and Religion Forward Movement, he saw the new party as the only real hope for initiating a political revival. "I am working as steadily and as happily in this campaign as in our mutual one of last winter. I have never before in politics felt that I was standing upon more than half truths, and advancing other than uncertain political fortunes. Now, I am sure that the whole result of this struggle shall be for the social welfare and the moral strength of the country."[15]

During the summer of 1912, while the lines of national battle were being drawn, Robins represented the Fifth and Eighth Congressional Districts in the Illinois State Central Committee of the Progressive party. Through the weeks preceding the Progressive National Convention, he was busy with his co-workers choosing reform planks to include in the platform—the "eight social service planks." Paul Kellogg, editor of *The Survey,* worked for the inclusion of extensive federal controls of industrial working conditions.[16] Benjamin C. March, an old single taxer associate of Robins, although mistrustful of Roosevelt and critical of Robins for retaining so high an opinion of him, urged Robins to explore possibilities for inclusion of some kind of land tax statement in the party platform.[17]

Staunch reformers in the Progressive party were concerned about the more conservative elements in the party. Because of Robins's acquaintance with Roosevelt, his early involvement in the movement, and his social service work, he was sought out by the radicals. These old friends and co-workers made suggestions and asked for assurances that the reform principles put forward by Roosevelt at Osawatomie, Kansas, and reaffirmed in the party platform of 1912, would not be abandoned. However, some in the reform movement could not reconcile themselves to Progressive party hero worship or the corrupt Democratic party alternative and turned instead to Eugene Victor Debs, the Socialist party candidate for president.

On 6 August, at the Progressive National Convention in Chicago, Roosevelt delivered his Confession of Faith speech. Before an audience delirious with enthusiasm, he made a clear and dramatic reaffirmation of his commitment to the reform program.[18] The *New York Times* appropriately described the fired participants at the convention as "crusaders"[19] and Robins, an "industrial knight errant," certainly belonged in that company.

Even before 7 August, when the actual nomination took place, Robins was advised that "the demand for you is going to be tremendous, and I would suggest that you accept no engagements after the 15th which are not made by the speakers bureau."[20] For the next three months, Robins's schedule was carefully planned to assure the greatest impact before the biggest crowds, particularly in swing districts. He spoke convincingly, but like the movement as a whole, he was constantly faced with a very hostile press.

Typical was an article in the *Illinois State Register* on 16 September which belittled the significance of the big turnout by assuring its readers that those in attendance were "Republicans, Democrats, prohibitionists, socialists and men and women of all parties." No mention was made of those who had come as adherents of the new party. Robins's speech was lampooned because he harped on the steamroller tactics used to nominate Taft and because of his "ridiculous" references to Roosevelt as "unselfish." Roosevelt himself was bitterly attacked for his insincerity, egotism, opportunism, and selfishness. Robins was treated tolerably because it was felt that he "has bolted into the third party merely because it gave him an opportunity to exploit his individual political program," but any favorable remarks he had made about Roosevelt were scathingly attacked.

The article echoed the prevalent theme that was heard throughout the campaign: "Governor Woodrow Wilson's nomination made the third party movement absolutely unnecessary. When the 'bull moose' speakers come to that wall of truth they expose their weakness." Robins did confront this "truth" by condemning the Democratic party machine, which, he maintained, would restrict any reforms Wilson sought in his New Freedom program. Nevertheless, Wilson's record and the expectations he elicited weakened the Bull Moose cause. In spite of such press coverage, Robins was one of the speakers most in demand for the Progressive cause, and if we take Robins's words at face value, he was campaigning not to elect Roosevelt—that failure was a foregone conclusion—but to carry the political dialogue to a higher level, to educate the American electorate. "There is no man in the state or national bureau that is called for as much . . . as Raymond Robins, and he will make more votes than any four men . . . that we have."[21]

The election results in November offered no surprises. Roosevelt's popularity gave him second place, leaving Taft far behind. Wilson had won easily. Debs's remarkable 897,000 votes of the 14,000,000 cast nationwide was the highest percentage of Socialist turnout in a presidential election in American history. While Debs, in jail, received more than double that number of votes as the 1920 Socialist candidate for president, his percentage of the popular vote dropped to half the 1912 level, a clear indication of just how high the tide of progressivism and unrest had reached in that fateful four-way race. Even President Taft saw the need to embrace some progessive positions in the campaign.[22]

The most perplexing postelection issue was the future of the Progressive party. Although Roosevelt had done well, the local and state slates of the party had not. If the party was to survive at all, much had to be done in the organization of local clubs and coordination of party activities on the county and statewide level throughout the country. This task, in Illinois primarily, was to demand the greatest part of Robins's time during the six months preceding the election of 1914.

Robins needed rest after the 1912 presidential campaign, but sooner than advisable, he returned to his breakneck schedule of evangelical meetings in the Men and Religion Forward Movement. Looking back on the two phases of his social service work in the evangelical MRFM and the politics of the Progressive party in 1914, he saw a common focus. "We have helped to crystallize into direct purposes and specific programs the more or less vague unrest and general protest against existing social wrongs among the leaders in both the church and the state. Within a twelve month [period] we have advanced a generation in our plans of social betterment and community service." Robins offered some hope that Wilson had the opportunity to free himself from the limits of his corrupt party: "Surely he will either mightily advance the social and economic freedom of our country or the Democratic Party will be divided and wrecked."[23]

Robins's postelection schedule included a 9 November visit with Roosevelt at Sagamore Hill, where the two talked through the election, its implications, and future plans. "Had he been elected it would have been a disaster for our Cause," Robins explained. "Defeated he is an immense asset for national progress. . . . This he seems to sense." Robins was harkening back to the theme that animated all his Progressive party work—that if the election of a third-party candidate was nearly impossible, the education of the electorate through the platform of a reform third party could bring about the desired political, social, and economic transformation. Had Roosevelt been elected, Robins believed it would have been for the wrong reasons—the adulation of the hero—and that would have eclipsed the reform agenda. With Wilson in the White House, Roosevelt, as leader of the movement, could continue the struggle for the Progressive platform.[24]

By December the elaborate plans for the evangelical Smith-Robins World Tour materialized. Robins was away from February to August 1913. In September he joined his fellow progressives in organizing the election campaign of the forthcoming year.

During the months following the Debs-Taft-Roosevelt-Wilson race, Robins reexamined his thinking about the new president. Even before Roosevelt had entered the contest, Robins was critical of Wilson after initially speaking in his behalf in the Illinois Democratic Primary. After a personal interview, Robins found Wilson too self-satisfied and close-minded for public office and refused many offers from high-ranking Democrats to enlist in the Wilson campaign.[25] Two months after the election, Robins reconsidered and felt that Wilson "is to do a man's work as president in a memorable way." Half a year later, after reading the text of Wilson's New Freedom speech, Robins's praise for Wilson grew even stronger. However, Robins's support of the Progressive party was in no way mitigated. Even with all the provisions for social reform contained in the New Freedom program, he was sure that the corruption in the Democratic party would negate these good intentions.

> I have read the New Freedom, and it is in the main, a splendid statement. I believe in Wilson personally rather more than any other public man, but I do not believe in the Democratic Party. I believe he shall fail just as I failed, just as I expect Governor Dunne [of Illinois] to fail for the same reason. His party is hopelessly corrupt and plutocratic, but Wilson is a shining light and will lend a great service to the cause of social justice in our land.[26]

When Robins returned to Chicago after nine months' absence, he was greeted with great relief by the warring factions in the Illinois State Central Committee of the Progressive party. From its very inception the party was divided on the question of approaches to "liberalism." There were those who fought to maintain the nineteenth-century notions of unhindered free-enterprise. This faction, headed in Chicago by Medill McCormick, one of the owners of the *Chicago Tribune,* succeeded in eliminating any references to the Sherman Anti-Trust Act from the Progressive party platform in the summer of 1912. The other faction, exemplified by Gifford Pinchot in Pennsylvania and Harold Ickes in Chicago, sought the limitation of monopoly and placed a much stronger emphasis on social legislation. Somehow, by the strength of his personality, his evangelical work, and his strong social service stand, Robins was able to mediate between these two camps.

On 8 October 1913, only a few weeks after his return, the party caucus met to discuss three issues: the $10,000 debt still outstanding from the 1912 race, raising additional campaign funds, and the election of a chairman for the State Central Committee. Robins was nominated for the post by the leaders of one faction and seconded by the leaders of the other and was elected to the post by unanimous vote.[27] Robins took his new commitment with striking seriousness. He mapped out a plan of activity for the months ahead, arranged organizational meetings throughout all 102 counties of the state, and linked the Illinois organization with the national service organization of the party in New York. In large measure he took upon himself the responsibility for the success or failure of the Progressive party in Illinois. "If I succeed here," he boasted to his sister, "I will represent the third state in the Union in the Progressive movement in this country. I shall make woman suffrage and the social and industrial demands of our platform the chief elements of education in the conduct of our campaign, and the promotion of our Party."[28]

His efforts, even during the first month on the job, did not go unnoticed. There began a series of suggestions, from many unrelated sources, that Robins serve the party not merely as a functionary and organizer, but as a candidate, and the one office in 1914 of enough importance and prestige to justify his commitment was that of U.S. senator from Illinois. One of the first such suggestions came from the noted journalist William Allen White, although it was soon followed by pleas from many of the party notables, finally including an urgent appeal from Roosevelt himself. Robins's unhesitating response to the initial suggestions was categorical refusal, and for excellent reasons.

> I have been in active public and political service for some 13 years and I have never been a candidate for any public office. I think that I was selected as Chairman of the State Central Committee . . . [because] the committee believed that I would be fair to all groups, that I would not take sides in any factional disputes and that I would myself be free of "personal ambition" for office. Under these circumstances I could not in good faith become a candidate for any office while I am chairman of the State Central Committee.[29]

The pressure mounted for his nomination. Publicly, Robins parried all these suggestions and successfully evaded the nomination. "They have a saying in the West," he confided to his sister, "that some men are 'ditch fillers' . . . when a herd stampedes if they sweep across a ditch or deep gully the lead bulls go down and are trampled to death, but the herd passes on safely over their bodies. My candidacy will be a ditch filling race, preparing the way for someone else in 1916."[30] Many were convinced, however, that the value of Robins's entry into the race was not as limited as this dire scenario. As pointed out by William Allen White, Robins's old and trusted progressive ally, his entry would at least split the Democratic vote and so with certainty stop Roger Sullivan, the corrupt Democratic machine boss, from entering the Senate.

The particular slate of candidates and the question of whether or not Robins would run were not the pivotal issues during the fall and winter of 1913. The Progressive party was more a name than a reality; the difficult organizational work had yet to be done. "We have to build from the bottom here," Robins explained to fellow Progressives nationwide, "and it will take practically all of my time for the next months to help form a vital organization from precinct workers up to and including the members of the state central committee. With patience, determination and keeping everlastingly at it I expect we shall work through these difficulties and form an organization that can win victories in the state within the next two years."[31] An essential part of this enormous task was the continuous flow of communications between Robins and hundreds of party stalwarts throughout the state. He warned constantly against the inclination to "fuse" with one of the old parties and emphasized the need "to put candidates in the field for every county and state office and to make a vigorous, vital campaign all along the line."[32]

By late winter, after months of work carried out from Chicago, he was able to begin the real work of building "from the bottom." In February, March, and April he arranged daily meetings in carefully chosen towns throughout Illinois. These meetings with Progressives were intended to gather the most able and committed citizens to carry on the local work of the party through the formation of permanent committees. These discussions lasted the entire day and usually achieved the desired results. Each evening, mass meetings were called in front of the local courthouse or town hall and were inevitably addressed by Robins, who turned them into Progressive party rallies. William Allen White was present at one of Robins's few organizing and speaking meetings outside of Illinois during this period. He described the occasion in this way: "That address of yours was more than an oration, it was a great event. Your conversion of Hy Allen [Henry J. Allen, Progressive candidate for governor of Kansas] was a wonderful thing. It was the laying on of hands if there ever was such a thing. I have never seen a more dramatic moment in Kansas history than that."[33] By March 1914 meetings and rallies had been held in thirty-seven counties; Robins's plans called for the completion of the tour through all 102 counties by 1 July.[34]

As early as 1 February, Robins complained to Mary Dreier and his sister Elizabeth of his lack of sleep, growing nervousness, and need for a long rest. But these symptoms had come at the beginning of the most demanding phase of his tenure as state chairman. "When I have finished this task if I have the strength," Robins wrote, only a thought away from sharing his concern about his health, "we will have the best organization that was ever put together in any political party in this State." For the next eleven weeks, in spite of his worsening condition, he spoke at least once daily, and on many occasions two and three times. By the second week in April his energies gave out and he suffered a nervous breakdown. Like the pioneer of the Progressive movement Robert "Fighting Bob" La Follette, "who worked so hard that he would annually collapse from nervous exhaustion," Robins knew what was coming.[35]

Margaret ushered him away from Chicago to Florida. Robins forwarded his resignation as chairman of the State Central Committee, but his colleagues did all they could to dissuade him. Harold Ickes, Robins's political confident, close friend, and business and legal advisor, wrote that his resignation would be "the most serious blow that has struck our party since it was organized." After learning the nature of the illness, Ickes wrote again, this time with more compassion.

I think I can appreciate the state you are in just now, probably as well as any one else. I am as confident as I can be of anything that sooner or later you will be back on the firing line. A man with your physique and fighting qualities does not go under easily. You are now reaping the accumulated reward of years of over-strain. You were bound to pay the price sooner or later in a depleted nervous system and I am glad, rather than dissatisfied, since the break had to come that it did come while your resistance is still as strong as it is. I think I know something about a nervous breakdown myself and I know how dark even a sunny sky may become at such a time. There is one lesson that I hope you have already learned, and that is, that you must no longer continue to burn your candle at both ends. You have no right to work day and night, the way you have been working, without change or relaxation and it is futile to believe that you get the same results that way as by spreading your work and influence over a longer period of years.[36]

Toward the end of his stay at Nome, Alaska, Robins had received a letter from Elizabeth that was remarkably similar to that from Ickes, warning Robins of the dangers of overwork. The two letters had some of the same language of caution and concern.[37] However, Robins merely awaited the renewal of strength that would enable him to return to the campaign with redoubled energy.

In the last week of May, while still recuperating, Robins received a personal plea from Roosevelt that he accept the Progressive nomination for the Senate, and since he had relinquished the state chairmanship to Medill McCormick, he no longer felt ethically bound to refuse the nomination. Certainly the urging of Roosevelt played some part in Robins's deliberations. Roosevelt, with uncharacteristic expression, wrote: "How I hope you will be our nominee for Senator. What a speech I could make for you. That speech would be a keen pleasure, not a talk like most speeches." The encouraging words from the widest spectrum of supporters was then supplemented by promises of major campaign funding. Toward the end of June, while Robins was still refusing the nomination, he received a telegram from La Verne W. Noyes, at one time the chairman of the Illinois Manufacturing Association "and bitter enemy of mine [Robins]," committing himself to financing Robins's Illinois Progressive party race for the Senate.[38]

Five days after receipt of the telegram of financial support, a delegation of the Illinois Progressive State Committee, including its new chairman, Medill McCormick, and committee member Harold Ickes, arrived by train from Chicago at Robins's Chinsegut estate. Although he was still recuperating, they came to draft him for the Senate race. "I have done my best to avoid this to me fatal step," he wrote to Mary, "but it cannot be avoided without dishonor."[39]

Robins's decision to accept the nomination was coupled with many far-reaching plans, including moving from the Chicago tenement apartment at 1437 West Ohio Street. He felt that one of the most important reasons for his influence was the fact that he had never run for elective office. He had been able to maintain his position as a principled and objective observer of the political scene. He firmly believed that his entry into a political contest as a candidate would bring that phase of his life to an end. "I have agreed to the great finale in Illinois this fall," he wrote sorrowfully to Mary Dreier, "My world has changed. I will now . . . give up my living in the old 17th Ward. . . . So long as I lived and served and asked for nothing I could be of real service to that crowded tenement community, but now I am just like all the other politicians. And to run and be a beaten politician is the final straw that will break the back of my influence in that mottled community." His public speeches would now be in his own behalf, and he had never done that before. The label "politician" would rob him of the trust Chicago had given him. "Will I ever see again in the upturned faces of the 'group of toil' the look of confidence and faith in my sincerity which has been so great a blessing in all these past fighting years."[40]

In the face of this brooding and ruminating and his real sense of desperation, Robins knew he had no alternative but to give his full commitment. "I have not forgotten the words of the Great Book, 'what thy hand findeth to do, do it with thy might.' I either had to lead or desert." Robins was not without bitterness at his being asked to make the sacrifice that this candidacy involved. "There are fifty worthy men in the leadership of our Party in Illinois who would be eager to make this 'sacrifice,'" he wrote to Elizabeth confidentially, and then scoffed at them since their reform efforts were carried out from the comforts of middle- or upper-class homes in privileged neighborhoods. "Not one of [them] would have lived the life I have lived for fourteen years for fourteen weeks."[41]

Although he looked upon the contest as "the first and the last" in which he would be a candidate (and this was so), and felt that in reality all he was doing was making "the best of my political funeral," he was determined that he would "do nothing and think of nothing but the struggle." While convinced of his impending loss, there were two gains that his candidacy was expected to achieve: first, a few more members of the legislature and state senate would be elected from the ranks of the reformers; second, the Illinois Supreme Court's ruling in behalf of the state's woman suffrage law would not be reversed by "the liquor and underworld interests . . . working night and day" to repeal the law. "At this late day I shall make no compromise for the sake of a few votes here and there," Robins wrote. "Already there have come to me these 'voices of a mean prudence' asking me to hedge on the liquor and labor questions. They are mistaken friends as well as cowards. I shall hedge on nothing essential."[42]

Another month and a half passed before Robins completed his convalescence. Thirty pounds lighter than when he arrived in Florida in April, he returned to Illinois to begin the new campaign. He made his first speeches in the coal-mining regions of the state, which had been either Republican or

Socialist. From his past reception, he had reason to believe that he would receive strong support from the rank-and-file miners and their leadership. And to his great relief, after his first speeches in his own behalf, he wrote: "I find that I can make my canvass with less personal shame than I had supposed. I did not relish . . . speaking for myself as a candidate. I forget all about my own candidacy in the advocacy of the Cause. So it will not be so terrible as it seemed."[43]

Robins spent the initial weeks of the campaign in downstate areas, making one-night stands in as many towns as possible. He returned to the Chicago area for the last two weeks before the Progressive State Convention at Urbana. There, in the small town in east-central Illinois, he gave the keynote address.

9

Campaign for the U.S. Senate

It was 18 September and Europe was at war. Robins began his keynote address as leader of the Illinois Progressive party by voicing the hope "that a peaceful Europe of the peoples may arise from this bloody struggle of the Europe of the kings." He praised President Wilson for his policy of neutrality and asked that the American people not move toward "hasty partisanship" because of ancestral connections. For many Americans the European war was a peripheral concern—the focus at hand was industrial, political, and urban conflicts and problems at home.

Robins compared the growing concentration of capital and industrial power with that of political power in the hands of the party bosses and the machine-run political process. He cited evidence to demonstrate that the two old parties did not represent divergent outlooks but even worked together to defeat the most urgently needed social legislation. It was under these conditions that the new party, under the leadership of "the most popular and the most constructive statesman of the age," was formed.[1]

Progressives demanded women's suffrage, which Robins declared "will do more to solve the problems of the modern city than all other measures combined." He pledged the party to the elimination of child labor, excessive working hours for women, unfair and unhealthy working conditions, and involuntary unemployment. Remembering the Coal Creek, Tennessee, experience with contract convict labor, Robins and the Illinois Progressive party opposed the transportation of prison-made goods across state boundaries. They promised "to improve the treatment of convicts, cut off the huge profits made by the social vultures who prey upon them and remove the unfair competition of prison-made goods with free labor."

The Payne-Aldrich protective tariff was "as unjust and stupid" as it was "corrupt and criminal." The Progressive party was committed to the creation of a tariff commission composed of independent experts and so designed as to be able to "take the tariff out of partisan politics" once and for all.

Before turning to a broadside against his opponents, Robins made a strong demand for the democratization of American political institutions through the enactment of the initiative, referendum, and recall. "We want the people to have the power to exercise this control not only at elections but during the three hundred and sixty-five days of the year." Robins reflected the faith held at the time that these provisions would assure a more representative and responsible body of officeholders. That faith, similar in its intensity to that given the enfranchisement of women, proved illusory. However, at the time these measures were vital and essential planks of the party platform.

Robins attacked his Republican opponent, Lawrence Sherman, for his lack of conviction and principle and the Democratic candidate, Roger Sullivan, for his corruption, strong-arm methods, and "experience in the arts of industrial and political piracy." Robins brought home the condemning fact that President Wilson endorsed Lawrence B. Stringer, Sullivan's "milk and water progressive democrat" primary opponent, but had not supported the machine boss Sullivan himself.

"Friends, we have a common purpose," Robins began his closing appeal,

> We may be Democrats, Republicans, Progressives, yet, we are citizens of the same State. . . . Our fathers did not follow Washington . . . nor answer the call of Lincoln . . . to the end that we should submit to be boss-ridden in our parties, machine controlled in our government. . . . They struggled and suffered and died that we might be a great, free people, brave and strong and true; . . . —from the man who digs the ditch and digs it on the square to be entitled to a decent wage and fair hours and just working conditions—up to the last exalted expression of intellect and genius bound together—yet free, working out the common destiny of the human race . . . [to] which all the nations of the earth shall come in God's appointed time.[2]

Robins's attack put both Sherman and Sullivan on the defensive. He pointed to Sherman's support of the Allen Law, which guaranteed monopoly control of the gas utilities in Chicago, and his support for the traction interests that monopolized public transportation franchises. As the *Chicago Tribune* pointed out: "Senator Sherman realizes the strategic importance of keeping his [Chicago] past from becoming entangled with his future." Even his record as a U.S. Senate incumbent provided ammunition for the Progressives. He had voted against the investigation of the scandal involving the New York, New Haven and Hartford Railroad; against grain inspectors in the interests of farmers; and against Parcel Post, supporting instead the interests of the private express companies.[3]

Sullivan's record required no investigation to reveal his deep involvement in corruption. His client, the Ogden Gas Company, not only overcharged and cheated the citizens of Chicago and achieved monopoly control through his efforts, but also provided to him an enormous personal fortune. In the August issue of *The Commoner*, William Jennings Bryan characterized the Progressive attitude toward Sullivan: "Every corruptionist in the Democratic party in that state will support Sullivan, and so will all whom the corruptionists can influence. There will be no division among the reactionaries, the veneered Republicans."[4]

At a Progressive rally in the Chicago Coliseum on 19 October, Theodore Roosevelt finally got the chance to make the promised speech for Robins.

In all the essentials of their actions Mr. Sherman and Mr. Sullivan stand together.

I may make my appeal in Illinois not merely to the Progressives, but to all honest Republicans and honest Democrats to repudiate both the Sullivan and Sherman machines. This they can do only by electing to the United States Senate as able and upright and genuine a popular representative as Illinois has ever sent to the body—namely, Raymond Robins.[5]

The registered Democrats who chose to reject the Sullivan corruption and adopt the Progressive reforms were brought together in the Raymond Robins Democratic League, which organized and expanded its ranks at every opportunity. The newspapers that supported Robins and the Progressive slate prominently publicized the names of important Democrats and Republicans who had come out for Robins, as well as the reasons for their change. *The Geneseo News* published a Raymond Robins supplement, giving the records of his opponents and a moving plea that "once again Illinois can have, and should have, a truly great man in the United States Senate."

On the national level, Robins received the support of Democratic Senators Robert L. Owen of Oklahoma and Thomas J. Walsh of Montana; Republican Senators George W. Norris of Nebraska and Moses E. Clapp of Minnesota; and Congressmen Robert Crosser, Democrat of Ohio, and James Manahan, Republican of Minnesota. Most were also members of the National Popular Government League, which actively supported Robins and repudiated his opponents for their nonprogressive and corrupt policies. In the words of the league: "Mr. Robins is the only man who can defeat in Illinois the forces of political reaction determined upon the destruction of popular government and represented by Mr. Sherman and Mr. Sullivan."[6]

After Robins had received the endorsement of so many notables, including Assistant Secretary of Agriculture Carl S. Vrooman, some Wilson cabinet members made public statements in support of Roger Sullivan. However, at no time in the campaign did President Wilson make a statement of support for Sullivan, although he did make many such statements for others seeking lesser offices in Illinois. The president wanted the additional Democratic vote in the Senate, but felt wary about besmirching his name by linking it with so unsavory a figure as Sullivan.[7]

Under this pressure the opposition retaliated by accusing Robins of being a "single taxer" and "land confiscator." The Sherman campaigners also publicized the very limited returns received in the Seventeenth Ward by Robins in the Progressive Party Primary, which was poorly announced and generally received minor attention throughout the state. In the hands of a sharp editorialist, these facts were used effectively against Robins.

In all the vast population of that ward, where Robins' managers claim he has done so much to endear himself to the workers, there were but twenty-six primary voters sufficiently interested in Raymond Robins to go to the polls and cast a vote for him on primary day.

Raymond Robins, 1914. This portrait was used in his campaign as Progressive party candidate for the U.S. Senate from the State of Illinois. (Courtesy of the Elizabeth Robins Papers, Fales Library, New York University.)

What's the answer? The answer would appear to be that the vociferous demand for the election of Raymond Robins as a special representative of the workingman is pure buncombe, . . .

When the Robins campaign is sifted down to hard facts the great prospects of a big vote claimed for him will be found to dwindle to the proportions of his primary vote in his home ward. He will be found contesting with the socialists for third place in the returns.[8]

Within days of the first accusations of single tax advocacy, Robins received warnings from many parts of the state: "unless this charge is answered in some way, it will cost Robins hundreds of votes."[9] Robins responded with a printed flyer that disclaimed any commitment to the confiscation of land and officeholding in the single tax Joseph Fels Fund, but he could not deny his membership in and support for its program. He even had to hedge the truth, since he was on the advisory board of the fund.

This was the only issue that worked against Robins. On occasion he was attacked for being overly righteous—for seeking a program too much committed to the precept "I am my brother's keeper." He was criticized for being a false idealist and therefore a hypocrite. The campaign was not above smear tactics and the agents of Sherman and Sullivan accused Robins of being a "radical" and a bigot. They claimed that he was an impractical reformer, one who would have no influence and would be able to achieve nothing for the benefit of the state in Washington.[10]

The election returns proved what William Allen White had predicted months before, that Robins's campaign would keep Roger Sullivan out of the Senate. Sherman won by only 17,258 votes, and although Robins had not been in the running, his 206,000 votes included more votes in many counties of Illinois than Roosevelt had gotten in the 1912 presidential race.[11] Robins ran about 80,000 votes ahead of the rest of the Progressive ticket in Illinois, but, he confided to Elizabeth, "I . . . was overwhelmingly beaten. The entire Progressive Party was wiped out. In only one state did we win any important office and that one was California where Hiram Johnson was re-elected Governor by a splendid majority."[12] When it was all over he was satisfied at having made a "sacrifice hit," as he called his role in getting Sherman elected.[13]

> I have nothing but a sense of satisfaction in looking back upon the late campaign. I made the best fight I knew how, and had the loyal and whole-hearted support of all the genuine Progressives of our state. We were submerged in a nationwide industrial depression and progressive principles will have to lay fallow until after the return of industrial prosperity.
>
> I am grateful for the defeat of Sullivan, and believe that the new result of the campaign is all that could be expected under the circumstances. The educational values of the struggles will endure long after its temporary results have passed away.
>
> Margaret is as happy as ever, neither of us have ever set any store upon success in a personal sense. We shall go on with each days work in the same old way.[14]

Only days after the election, Robins journeyed to Sagamore Hill to discuss the returns with Roosevelt. "He is great and full of fight as ever," Robins remarked in describing the visit. Robins also met with progressives Gifford Pinchot and E. A. Van Valkenburg, editor of the Philadelphia *North American*, and the progressive Democrats in Washington who had supported him. "I saw three members of the Cabinet at Washington and they have agreed to a program that will entitle Wilson to our support if it is carried out in the next Congress." A million and one-half voters in the Middle West voted the Progressive ticket in the 1914 election, and their votes would go far in determining the presidential election in 1916. Robins was a key leader in their ranks, and Secretary of State William Jennings Bryan and President Wilson wanted his support for that campaign.

After answering his postelection mail, Robins went south to Chinsegut. In the quiet of his hilltop retreat, so striking a contrast to Chicago and the madness of the campaign trail, he reflected on the race and his future. Rest and reflection was interrupted by a proposal from Harold Ickes, a grand plan to involve Robins in an advisory role in the Wilson administration.[15] Robins put this proposal aside and managed to continue a bit longer in the rare state of inactivity and rest.

"How I wish you were here," he wrote to Elizabeth soon after arriving at Chinsegut,

> and that we might have this blessed evening together by the great fire in the quiet of the Pine forest and under the sentinel stars.
>
> Sister Mine I have met "the enemy" dared him to [do] his worst and while I am defeated I am through with that old shadow forever. I shall do my work— what my hand finds to do—with my might, and take whatever comes in good heart. . . .
>
> The firelight glows and flickers, the voices of the starlit night hum a minor note of beneficent oncoming REST.
>
> Fielding has just brought in the last turn of wood. Pet has been cooking for me and has just left. The quiet is of the forest amid the everlasting hills.
>
> Lovingly your little brother, Raymond[16]

On 30 December 1914, while still at Chinsegut, Robins received a portentous telegram from the American League for the Limitation of Armaments asking him to "lead businessmen and social service people in fight to prevent our country from throwing away chance to lead world to new era." The league's eighteen founding members (the Henry Street Group, after the Henry Street Settlement House in New York) included major figures in the American reform and social justice movements—Jane Addams, Lillian Wald, Paul Kellogg, Emily Balch, John Haynes Holmes, Samuel McClure Lindsay, Owen Lovejoy, and Florence Kelley. The telegram stated that a $10,000 donation had been promised if Robins would head the campaign. The Henry Street Group also organized an "Anti-Preparedness Committee" as a countermeasure to Wilson's National Defense Bill and sought creation of a League of Neutral American Nations. (In 1916 this committee changed its name to the American Union Against Militarism and finally to the American Civil Liberties Union.)[17]

After seven weeks of rest, Robins could hardly resist so important a call to leadership. However, he knew very little about the problems and politics of international disarmament. Before giving the League an answer, he wrote to George Porter, assistant national treasurer of the Progressive National Committee, for advice. Porter suggested that Robins not get involved on the grounds that any meaningful progress toward disarmament would have to be initiated by the European powers involved in the conflict; an American initiative, Porter argued, might even hamper European efforts. The day after receiving this advice, Robins received a letter from Jane Addams, pleading with him to accept the offer. She assured him that the league's work was feasibile given competent and dedicated leadership and capable public speakers. Finding good leaders was the league's primary concern. To emphasize her point she complained about the recent leadership of the Chicago peace movement, one leader having resigned and the other, to their "horror," having joined the Navy League.[18]

At the outbreak of war, Robins had strong inclinations to be active in the peace movement. He had deep ties to both Germany and England; his sister Elizabeth was a British subject and Anglophile, while Margaret was of German descent and still corresponded in German with relatives in her hometown. At the same time, as a partisan of Roosevelt's militant foreign policy, Robins supported a national policy of preparedness. From the start, he saw the European conflict as autocracy standing in the way of a growing world democracy, but he could not reconcile himself to American entry into the war.

At the beginning of 1915 he had still not clarified his position on war and disarmament. Finally, Robins refused the league's offer of leadership and, following the *Lusitania* crisis, supported American entry into the First World War. (Eight years later, following his service in Russia and the peace settlement and especially as a result of the influence of Salmon O. Levinson, his close friend and peace activist, Robins became thoroughly versed in all the complexities and frustrations of international disarmament. He was a leader and spokesperson in the Outlawry of War Movement, which sought creation and ratification of an international treaty making war a crime among nations.)[19]

After refusing the league's offer, Robins turned his attention to the new Robins-Childs College Evangelical Campaign, which emphasized the acquisition of written pledges or "decisions for Christian service." It embodied Robins's hope for an ethical and Christian rejuvenation in America through the leadership and dedication of the young men and women at the colleges of the country. Robins was enlisting an army of his own. With each new "decision card," he felt that another soldier had entered the fight against social and economic injustice.

In 1915 Robins saw himself as "a man without a party" and felt that any genuine Progressive should remain uncommitted to either of the two major parties. He anticipated the Progressive party adoption of a prohibition plank and its unification with the small, religiously oriented Prohibition party. Such a coalition, he believed, could muster two million votes in the 1916 election and thereby take the election from a conservative candidate.

While Robins, like most settlement workers and social reformers, embraced the movement for prohibition of alcohol, he expressed privately his concern that it was rising to the forefront of the Progressive agenda at the expense of economic reform. "Our party would then become the public morals and church party of the country," he told Elizabeth in confidence, "and the economic issues would be submerged. . . . [W]e will have to pass through this period of division . . . involved in the alcoholic liquor traffic before we can get to the real economic cleavage in our political life. I have little joy in this program."[20] Robins resolved that "if our choice in 1916 is between a Republican reactionary and President Wilson, I shall support President Wilson to the full extent of my power."[21] Yet like many Progressives across the country, Robins still nurtured hopes that Teddy Roosevelt would run again in 1916 and this time would win and create the new democracy of the Progressive party platform.

Robins was too much a man of action to sit idly contemplating his dreams. On 3 May 1915 he sent off a letter to Roosevelt with his plans and ideas for the coming presidential race; the essential message was that the hero of San Juan Hill should run, and that he would win. "When this world conflict between militarism and democracy has been determined," Robins predicted,

> —in the only way that it can be determined—there will be just three nations with surplus men and money for active leadership in the world movement for the next thirty years. Japan with her oriental background, alien in race institutions and ideals to western civilization and dominated by Caesar's dream of world conquest, has already begun her great adventure. Russia with her simple peasant millions held in the superstition of the Greek Church, dominated by an Autocratic ideal backed by the black hundred, will break upon western Europe and the old east with the pent up fury of mighty waters long restrained. Against these two forces and their alien institutions and ideal of world dominion by force of arms will stand just one people and one power equal to their mastery, America—America with her ideals of democracy, of liberty under law of uncorrupted Christianity, and of social progress through peaceful industry education and commerce.
>
> Who can meet and master this tremendous challenge for domestic and international leadership of the true American Ideal? Theodore Roosevelt and Theodore Roosevelt alone.[22]

Robins's plan to win the Republican nomination for Roosevelt reflected a keen understanding of the needs and expectations of the American people. It exemplifies Robins's political insight at its best, but of course the entire plan rested upon Roosevelt's willingness to run.

Exactly one month later, on 3 June, Roosevelt responded. It was a fifteen-page typewritten letter from Oyster Bay, Long Island, with many handwritten interjections, the product of long and serious effort. "Your letter of May 3rd has touched and pleased me very much," Roosevelt wrote.

> As by this time you surely must know, you are one . . . of the half-dozen men with whom it has been a peculiar pleasure to be associated and whose

friendship I regard as an honor of which all my life I shall be proud. Indeed, I am tempted to say that of all the men with whom I have been associated in this movement you are the man with whom I have been in closest sympathy as regards what seems to me to be the most momentous issues among all the issues that we raised.

Therefore it is a matter of real pride to me that you should show for me the feeling you did in this letter of yours.[23]

It is common among men in public life who have had shared aims, goals, or commitment to exchange praise for one another so freely and often indiscriminately. However, an examination of the correspondence of both Robins and Roosevelt demonstrates that their mutual expressions of deep respect and admiration were unusual and sincere.

After agreeing with Robins's appraisal of the international situation, and strongly criticizing the American pacifists "headed to my great regret by Jane Addams," Roosevelt doubted the chances of another Roosevelt candidacy. He was no longer a popular figure or vote-getter and far too many "would accept my candidacy as a proof of greedy personal ambition." His support would hurt rather than help a cause to which he lent his name. The one hope was the creation of so enormous a public demonstration in favor of Roosevelt that his sense of duty would not allow him to refuse. "If it was a duty impossible to avoid, I would fight in the future as I have fought in the past," Roosevelt assured. "But I feel I have done my share; and what is infinitely more important, I do not feel that I can be of use in a leading position any more. I think the people have made up their mind that they have had all they want of me, and that my championship of a cause or an individual, save in exceptional cases, is a damage rather than a benefit." With this sad self-appraisal, Roosevelt concluded his long letter, and the question of his candidacy might have rested there. But for Robins such humility coupled with the touching expressions of warmth at the beginning of the letter encouraged an even greater sense of personal commitment to a Roosevelt candidacy.

Still it was a long time before the conventions, and perhaps as a result of Roosevelt's letter, Robins directed his energies toward other challenges. "I am afraid that I am not thinking about politics these days," he wrote to his friend Gifford Pinchot. "It has seemed to me that the work we had to do was more generally fundamental and elementary than some of us have supposed. . . . [We] have counted upon an intellectual propaganda when what was needed was a thorough-going spiritual revival."[24] Nevertheless, Robins had far from given up on political activity. Throughout the year, from the spring of 1915 to the spring of 1916, he worked in college after college on his "social service" evangelical tour—what he sometimes called "radical education in other than the political field."

On the very day that he expressed his disenchantment with politics to Pinchot, he wrote to his more radical friend George Record of the abandonment of progressive politics due to the war crisis. The diversion of the war, he believed, had led to the more conservative direction in domestic politics. Many stalwarts of the Progressive party were returning "to the fortress of the enemy," but he had resolved to fight on. "I believe that the 200,000 odd voters who supported me in the senatorial campaign are a sufficient nucleus on which to begin a fundamental, radical movement in this state, but the present war obsession will have to be overcome before we can make any real progress."[25]

The year that followed was for Robins a year of political observation rather than action; in terms of evangelical work in the college campaign, it was the opposite. Robins boasted to Elizabeth:

> I have traveled 45,766 miles and made 454 set addresses in 48 institutions of higher learning in the United States and Canada. The geographical range has been from Colorado in the west to the University of Toronto in the north and the University of South Carolina in the south and to Princeton University in the east. I have talked to over 60,000 students of men and women and 4,000 Protestant churchmen, being professors and tutors. Over 5,000 students have signed cards of discipleship for service.[26]

Through March and April, Robins kept up the pace. His work culminated in an international evangelical YMCA congress in Cleveland, Ohio, of more than 2,600 delegates from every major American city and more than ten countries. With the conclusion of that congress in mid-May he freed himself of his obligations to the YMCA and returned to an active role in politics.

The Progressive National Committee, meeting in January, had decided to hold a separate convention in Chicago at the same time that the Republicans were holding theirs. It was a move designed to maximize the influence of the Progressives as a separate party with its own slate of candidates or as a means of bargaining with the Republicans to assure the nomination of an acceptable candidate.[27] In his letter to Robins describing these developments, George Perkins's words sparkle with enthusiasm and great expectations. Perkins also informed Robins of his correspondence with Charles D. Hillis, chairman of the Republican National Committee, and of his plans to cooperate with him.

When the Progressive National Convention finally met on 7 June, Robins was temporary chairman and keynote speaker. Roosevelt did not come to Chicago still believing, and rightly so, that his motives would be misinterpreted. But his attention was centered completely on the events at both conventions. He wanted to bring his influence to bear as much as possible, including taking the nomination "if it was a duty impossible to avoid." Roosevelt's maneuvering in connection with the Republican nomination is a story unto itself. George E. Mowry depicts Roosevelt as an astute politician who somehow misjudged the situation in 1916, who thought he had a good chance to win the nomination by using the Progressive party as the lever. An argument can be made that Roosevelt believed that Wilson's neutrality endangered the very existence of the nation, and thus felt duty-bound to rescue America. Robins was enough of an idealist (among the "heroic," as Roosevelt referred to those with the courage to support him) to believe that the fate of the nation lay in Roosevelt's hands.

Roosevelt installed two direct telephone lines between his home at Oyster Bay and Chicago, one to the Progressive Convention and the other to the Republican Convention. He was a thousand miles away, listening on the phone, as Robins began his keynote speech:

> Times of stress and ferment bring tribulation to the weak and opportunity to the strong. The souls of timid men are vexed and the hearts of the valiant are uplifted. Four years ago brave deeds were done in Chicago. From every section of this country there gathered here men of leadership and character disregarding the ties and associations of a lifetime, even of generations, willing to sacrifice power and influence and friendship, the profits of lives of industry and honor in order that they might unite with their fellows in spirit to bring a new force a new impulse, a new hope into American politics. They enlisted for public service behind the bravest and wisest leader of the people in our time, behind the foremost private citizen in the world—Theodore Roosevelt.[28]

At this point, after describing himself and many others like him, Robins could not say another word. His mention of the name Theodore Roosevelt began ninety-three minutes of uninterrupted cheering. Roosevelt "Hears it at Oyster Bay," the headlines proclaimed. Ironically, the previous record for such a demonstration (eighty-nine minutes) was for Bryan at the Democratic National Convention in Denver in 1908. Robins held hopes just as great and with just as much sincerity then as he did in Chicago eight years later.

The cheering and tumult were orchestrated to demonstrate the enthusiasm with which the Progressives could once again fight for Roosevelt. But it was clear to those cheering as well as to those who sat through the entire hour and a half, "that no one . . . could have believed it spontaneous. Probably only one man hearing it caught the note of enthusiasm. That was Theodore Roosevelt himself." The difference between the drama and energy of the party convention in 1912, created to retaliate against the "crime" of the Republican party bosses, and the forced bravado of 1916 was sadly apparent. "When the Progressive Party was launched four years ago, the convention was intended as the beginning of a great crusade that would make Roosevelt President and reform the world. Today there was still unanimous devotion to Roosevelt. But the delegates had not the air of men beginning a great crusade, they were men waiting for the end of something."[29]

Robins's speech was drafted with a triple purpose: first, to develop unity in the party behind Roosevelt; second, to present the possibility of going ahead with progressive principles even if at the expense of "dear names"; and third, to prepare the convention for the possibility of backing a Republican candidate, provided he was committed to progressive principles. Following the outburst, Robins struggled to regain order. From all over the hall delegates were demanding the immediate nomination of Roosevelt by acclamation. Such a move would have defeated the plan of the Progressive National Committee, which sought to use its convention to force a Roosevelt nomination by the Republicans. That prospect was vetoed by the Republican National Committee. The one realistic hope remaining was to force the nomination of a Republican candidate with some progressive principles. Upon hearing the keynote speech, many at the convention believed that, with luck, they might fight for and win this last of the three aims.

The editorial in the *New York Times* on 8 June was to the point: "The Convention that holds its session in the Auditorium was called together not to nominate but to force a nomination upon the Republicans in the Coliseum. The prolonged uproar was part of a prearranged plan." It was the sad tale of "a convention without a party."[30]

For most of the next two days and nights, conference committees of both parties met, negotiated, and reported to their conventions. It soon became clear that the Progressives would have little say in the final choice of the Republican nominee. On Saturday, 9 June, the Republican Convention nominated Supreme Court Justice Charles Evans Hughes. The moment that news reached the Progressives at the Auditorium Theatre, Bainbridge Colby began a nominating speech for Roosevelt. George Perkins, still hoping for Progressive party support of the Republican nominee, tried to stop the hasty action, but within only a few minutes, Roosevelt was nominated unanimously.[31]

Roosevelt responded to the news with a telegram to the Progressive Convention stating that he could not accept the honor at that time. He hedged his refusal by stating that if the Progressive party agreed to support Hughes on the basis of his platform, he would make his refusal final. However, no alternative was provided by Roosevelt if Hughes's program proved unacceptable.[32]

The responses to Roosevelt's refusal were as diverse as the group that gathered for the Progressive Convention. Some who had fervently rallied to the call at Osawatomie felt that the cause of reform had been betrayed, that they had been wooed, jilted, and abandoned; no words were too vile to characterize their former hero. The opposite extreme was that of the "realists" who saw the political limits of the Progressive party and now welcomed the chance to reenter the Republican ranks with the hope of exercising influence. "This was a party of protest, and it served its purpose, perhaps too well," began an editorial in the *Detroit Journal* one month after the convention, when calm reflection put the episode in perspective. Entitled, "Progressives Become Obsolete," Robins singled it out as the best published expression of his viewpoint:

> If the Republican Party stood in need of chastisement, it got it. In a much chastened mood it will probably return to power.
> The rejuvenation and rehabilitation of the Republican Party is made possible by the almost complete conjunction of the two Chicago platforms and by

the nomination of a man who is no less for Americanization, preparedness and progress than Col. Roosevelt.

From a political point of view the ground has been taken completely from under Col. Roosevelt's feet. There is nothing left for him to do but to endorse the Hughes candidacy and to advise the Progressive Party to pool its resources with the parent organization. This is a bitter dose for the "lunatic fringe" of the Progressives, but such is the inevitable fate of those who build up a party upon a personality. . . . Those who hereafter aspire to form a third party in this country had better pin their faith to principles. . . .

. . . those who really were Republicans at heart and who took part in the split strictly on a political basis have an admirable opportunity now to return to the fold under auspices as good as could be hoped for. The Progressive Party as we have known it passes into history.[33]

The fate of the Progressive party would be decided at the meeting of the National Committee in Chicago on 26 June. In the weeks before that meeting, Robins remained undecided, awaiting an opportunity to meet with Hughes. It was a time of great confusion for many Progressives. "I find myself more in doubt over what to do in this campaign than at any other time in my political experience," Robins wrote to Mary McDowel of the University of Chicago Settlement. The party had "finished its course" and a choice had to be made between Wilson and Hughes. But Robins was distressed at having to make such a decision; "neither of the platforms are of great consequence. Neither of the party organizations are sincere."[34]

On the evening of 25 June, the day before the formal decision, a meeting was held in the Blackstone Hotel in Chicago. Robins was not a member of the National Committee but he was invited to give his views on whether or not the Progressives should support Hughes. Robins could provide no answer. He had interviewed Hughes, but the candidate had not yet indicated his position on women's suffrage. "As matters now stand," Robins wrote in uncharacteristic ambivalence, "I am for Wilson, but within ten days may declare for Hughes." As for the race in Illinois, Robins decided against supporting machine-chosen Democratic candidates. If there were a "decent" Republican, he promised to support him; if there were none, he was determined to stay out of the Illinois campaign altogether.[35]

The choice before Robins was not limited to the campaign of 1916. His credibility for steadfastness and commitment hung in the balance. His support for the Republican Hughes or the Democrat Wilson in 1916 would be a final determination of his party membership—"I shall choose my place of service for the rest of my active life in this campaign."[36] Because the decision was so momentous and the alternatives so unacceptable, Robins spent two months wandering from one contradictory position to another. It was a rare predicament for him.

After one of the interviews with Hughes in New York, following the Progressive Convention, Robins reported his impressions to key Progressives.

The issues: "woman suffrage, property rights vs. human life, conservation, the rights of labor, and the industrial and social reforms which form the creed of every true Progressive . . . I can find no fault with what Hughes said—." Robins was reported to have commented,

> his words were all that I could ask, but it was quite evident to me that he did not comprehend the fundamental truths from which these issues have their growth . . . and showed absolutely no appreciation nor understanding of the vital principles behind my questions. . . . [w]e all know that if a man reaches his age without reaching down into the roots of these problems, it is psychologically impossible for him ever to comprehend them fundamentally. Therefore, I regret to have to say his answers were not satisfactory to me and I cannot see my way to support him. My present intention is to work hard for Mr. Wilson's election, and to throw my whole heart into the work.[37]

After most Progressives had already committed themselves, Robins received a great deal of attention from the leaders of both parties. "I have never been . . . as popular personally as I am just now in a political sense," he confided to George Perkins.

> The governorship of Illinois and the nomination for president in 1920 is presented to me now daily, not only by my old friend, Roger C. Sullivan and his cohorts whom I have fought [and] denounced . . . but by representatives of the administration and independent citizens of substance and merit. I count it a great gain for our future plans that I am still as yet undeclared and quite frankly free to decide in favor of Mr. Wilson if I should finally so determine. As you may know offices and position are not the ultimate hope of my political activity.[38]

A week later Robins received advice from his old teacher, William Fulton, urging him to accept the offer of Sullivan for the Democratic nomination for governor of Illinois. Fulton argued that Robins could do a great deal from so important a seat of power. He also argued for Robins's support of Wilson. In his reply Robins noted that he had discussed his decision at great length with Justice Brandeis, Secretary of War Baker, and at long conferences with both President Wilson and Hughes. "While I could be nominated with Mr. Sullivan's support over Governor Dunne," Robins wrote, "and could then almost surely be elected over the Republican candidate, I would carry into office with me a Sullivan legislature and such an array of Sullivan officials in the State House as to largely ham-string my program of constructive legislation. I have no desire to be governor of Illinois simply for the uncertain honor of being governor."[39]

Later in July, Robins considered the broader question of which party offered the "mass voting control" that would move "most effectively for progressive principles." Since his decision was to affect his party affiliation permanently, he gave more thought to this concern than to the choice between

Wilson and Hughes.[40] Finally, Robins saw the Republican party as a more effective long-range force for progressive reform.

> Mr. Wilson was not the choice of the rank and file of the Democratic voters nor was he the choice of the Democratic convention four years ago. *He is distinctly an accident in Democratic leadership.* The Progressive menace on the outside and Mr. Bryan's magnificent leadership on the inside of the convention nominated Mr. Wilson over Mr. Clark who was the choice of the Democratic voters in the primary states and of the delegates on the floor of the convention.[41]

Robins was also convinced that Wilson was the superior candidate. However, using the same rationale he had used in the election of 1912, he felt that neither Wilson nor any other national Democratic officeholder could carry out basic reforms within the limits established by the boss- and Dixie-controlled party.

On 5 August Robins issued his public statement of support for Hughes and the Republican party. He exonerated Roosevelt for his abandonment of the Progressive party by arguing that his "declination to run as the Progressive candidate only, simply declared his acceptance of the verdict of the [Progressive] voters," three-quarters of whom had left the party in the primaries of 1916. Then Robins elaborated on the boss and Dixie control of the Democratic party. He contrasted it with the "voter mass control" of the Republican party, "conceived in moral revolt against human slavery; it was born, baptized and nurtured in the supreme national struggle to maintain the national heritage and fulfill the promise of equal opportunity to every citizen." In spite of the fact that "the Republican Party [was] often dominated by the masters of special privilege and made by them the instruments of vast exploitation," Robins declared himself a committed Republican and vowed "to reject [that] false or dishonest leadership."[42]

Robins cited the examples of California under Hiram Johnson and Wisconsin under Robert M. La Follette as evidence to justify his confidence in progressive "voter mass control" within the Republican party. He cited the failure of progressive Democrats, the "heartsick minority," in many other states, especially from his own sad experience in Illinois. He appealed to all progressives, whether Democrats or Republicans, to rally under the Republican banner and "help and be helped in our common struggle for social and industrial justice in city, state and nation." Robins concluded his nine-page statement with only one page devoted to his Hughes endorsement and one-third of that was a quotation from Robert M. La Follette.

"Hughes did rotten work in California," Robins wrote in confidence to Harold Ickes two weeks later, "I cannot find the strong clear headed man I talked with in the person that is being led around by the old Southern Pacific Gang, dining in scab hotels in the best organized union labor state in the union and helping the Standpat cause in the most Progressive commonwealth under the flag. If he keeps this lick up he will be blown out of the water and he will deserve it."[43]

Years before, in 1905, Robins had found himself in the position of having to support the Republican John Maynard Harlan, Jr., for mayor of Chicago. Then too Robins distrusted the Democratic party machine, which had nominated Edward Dunn, the more reform-minded candidate. Now in 1916, as in 1905 and as later in 1920, 1924, 1928, and 1932, Robins had to explain why he supported the more conservative candidate. Robins's personal correspondence reveals his many misgivings. He admitted that "the most vital reason for my personal support of his candidacy was Hughes' forthright position on womans' suffrage."[44] But Robins's frank admissions to George E. Lee, a Democrat, reveal his ambivalence. "If you folks win in the pending campaign I shall weep no tears. If our folks are successful I shall probably have the hardest four years of battle to make good my position that has yet come my way. Nevertheless we must remember that *if Wilson is successful my help will not be needed. If Hughes wins, I may be of some real service to the Progressive cause.*"[45]

To his fellow campaigner Gov. Hiram Johnson, Robins wrote: "I am enclosing with this a copy of my convention address and a copy of my statement in support of Hughes which has been termed my 'political obituary' by not a few of my radical friends."[46] Robins suspected the same, but he could never be sure, since his radical message in the Hughes campaign was so often positively received by the most conservative audiences. "Perhaps this is my greatest hearing," he wrote to Elizabeth, from Indiana.[47] Chester H. Rowell, California Progressive party state chairman, wrote to Perkins on 27 September 1916: "The One Eastern speaker who could do the most good would be Robins, since he could appeal both to the labor vote and to the Progressive vote, and as a former Democrat could be effective against the Wilson stampede among the independent voters."[48]

The year 1916 was the high point of Robins's political influence. His endorsement of Hughes was equated with betrayal of Wilson's progressivism. Later, Robins's unpopular position on U.S.-Bolshevik negotiations would be all the more weakened due to his alienation from Wilson.

Robins's old friends and fellow workers responded immediately to his alignment with Hughes and the Republicans. Their pointed analysis of his reasoning and contradictions had a sobering effect on Robins, especially coming from men and women with whom he shared mutual respect and admiration. As one colleague wrote to Robins:

> I lived in Kansas from 1887 to 1903 and received my political training in the Farmers Alliance and People's Party. The entire educational work of that organization was, as you remember, for not only social justice but for political freedom as well. This is why, although I detest Roosevelt's militarism, I endorsed with all my heart the program of the Progressives. I cannot understand your devotion to a man which seemed to obsess many of the progressives, but I could pass that by in order to secure the measures. I expected Roosevelt to do just what he did, but I did not expect it of Pinchot, nor of Everett Colby or a

Francis J. Henry or a William Allen White or a Victor Murdock, but the defection of none of these brave men would have shaken my faith half so much as to see your name on the list.[49]

From the avid readers and contributors to *The Public* came a flood of articles and letters attacking and supporting Robins. The emotional debate was carried out in every weekly issue for a month.[50]

But Robins stood firm and honored his public declaration. By 17 August he made arrangements with Ralph D. Cole, chairman of the Speakers Bureau of the Republican National Committee, for a nationwide speaking tour in behalf of Hughes. Beginning in Maine on 4 September, Robins spoke almost daily, traveling through Kansas, Indiana, Michigan, Connecticut, New Jersey, West Virginia, Missouri, Nebraska, Oklahoma, and Illinois. In his home state, he remained aloof from the Republican state candidates running for national and local office because in almost all cases they were the handpicked choices of the party machine he had fought against for so long.

While campaigning for Hughes he continuously stoked the fires of his limited enthusiasm.[51] Margaret was fully aware of his inner struggle and, parting with her sister Mary and many close friends and co-workers, painfully decided to support her husband by joining with equal energy in speaking for Hughes. She and several other prominent women in the Republican party organized the "first womens' political train in the history of the world. She will go clear out to California and back across the continent speaking for the right of women to vote and upon labor questions."[52] When Margaret was in Los Angeles and Raymond was in New York, both maintaining hectic schedules, Margaret telegraphed an account of an incident that reflects the tragic ambiguity of their position. "Anton Johansen's wife led a Wilson demonstration against us in San Francisco but when she saw me she made Scharrenberg hold her Wilson banner while I gave my Hughes banner to Mrs. Bancroft so that we might embrace to the utter amazement of both opposing forces."[53]

Raymond and Anton Johansen, a leader of the Chicago Federation of Labor, had worked side by side for industrial and urban reform for more than a decade. Margaret, as president of the National Women's Trade Union League had joined forces with the Chicago Federation to win many labor fights. They had all supported the Progressive party platform, along with so many other reformers, settlement workers, and union members. It embodied their hopes for a national movement of reform. The embrace of Margaret and Mrs. Johansen demonstrated that progressive goals were still far more important than party affiliations, even at the height of a campaign. However, after sixteen years of reform activity, Robins noted that the concern of the American public had undergone a serious change.

"I am convinced that the entire radical political, social and economic program will be submerged by questions of war and peace, preparedness and pacifism, international cooperation and isolationism." Still opposed to American entry in the war, Robins was very upset by this reorientation of national priorities. He saw the reform movement weakened and its plans and programs postponed to the postwar period, when, in fact, opponents were hoping to relegate reform to a permanent scrap heap.[54] Some planks of the Progressive platform were realized, the most notable being the Nineteenth Amendment to the Constitution, which guaranteed women's suffrage. However, in general this was a period of minimal progress for reform.

Although later Robins became a staunch supporter of the Allied war effort, risking his life on many occasions during the year in Russia, his appraisal of the impact of the war on domestic reform was prescient. As his priorities changed and he turned much of his time and energy to international peace and cooperation, his major focus for domestic social reform was the campaign for a constitutional amendment prohibiting the manufacture and sale of alcoholic beverages—the prohibition amendment. To Robins's dismay, reform principles were submerged through much of the 1920s. However, as a result of the Great Depression, they were revived and flourished during the New Deal, when Robins changed his political affiliation for the first time since 1916.

Part Three

The Mission in Russia

10

Origins of the Mission

Russia will speak. Russia may lose five million more of her youth and still out of that wonderful group of a hundred and sixty million have sufficient youth for the world's enterprise in days of peace. And Russia is just awakening. The war is transforming Russian life. Unused natural resources, the greatest of any nation in the modern world, vast forests, mighty mineral treasures in the hills, great fertile areas of soil. Russia will break, like waters long restrained, upon western civilization when the war is over. Russia, with her superstitious religious culture. Russia with her autocratic governmental institutions. Russia with her despotic political society backed by the Black Hundred of Cossack soldiers, Russia will speak.
> —From Robins's speech before the National Association of Life Underwriters, 20 September 1916

FROM the beginning of September to election day 1916, Raymond and Margaret Robins honored their decision to support the Republican party and stumped the trail for Hughes's presidential campaign. However, they were not surprised by the reelection of Wilson, nor, privately, were they disappointed.[1] What did concern Raymond was the election of a Republican majority to a House of Representatives hostile to Wilson and his progressive domestic program. As Robins put it, "The real decision of what the majority of the people of the United States wish in domestic and foreign policy has been postponed for four years."[2] Robins's speeches during the campaign focused on the question of the "mass voting control" of the Republican party, and for the first time, he devoted considerable attention to the war. Although Robins did not foresee the German industrial and military revival of the 1930s, he did see the end to Europe's monopoly in shaping world affairs. "When this war is over there will be just three voices speaking with assured and adventurous youth. . . . England, France, Germany and Italy may not speak for thirty years. I care not how much indemnity may come; I care not how the fortunes of the war may finally end; the actual waste, that irremediable loss of the splendid adventurous minds of those nations, has crippled them for thirty years, if not a hundred years of the world's enterprise."[3] The three nations to which Robins looked as the world's new leaders were the United States, Japan, and Russia.[4]

At the beginning of the war, Robins's strong attachment to Germany through Margaret's family and his sympathy for England through Elizabeth and her staunch Anglophilia led him to support a negotiated peace. But after nine months of bitter fighting and the sinking of the *Lusitania*, those prospects dimmed and he and Margaret became sharply divided in their loyalties. "If war is declared," Robins wrote in May 1915, "I shall join a troop that Roosevelt will command, and Margaret will go to Germany to serve in the hospital corps. We are in entire agreement upon the best action for each."[5]

By mid-July Raymond and Margaret were even more divided in their loyalties, although the possibility of her enlistment in a German hospital corps following an American declaration of war seemed doubtful. "If England is invaded," he wrote to his sister in London, "I think I should feel bound to enlist in her defense. I think if I were unmarried I should enlist with a Canadian regiment. I regard the success of the Allies as the most necessary issue of present day civilization." Margaret and Raymond managed an amicable and respectful acceptance of their differences. Raymond even defended Margaret's faith "both in the merit and ultimate success of the Teutonic kindred. She has made herself an able and informed advocate," he wrote to Elizabeth. But it is difficult to imagine the relationship between Raymond and Margaret surviving so fundamental a difference. For ten years Margaret and Elizabeth had struggled for control over Chinsegut and Raymond's first loyalties. At best the relationship between the two women was a state of truce. Tension and repressed anger pervaded their relationship, particularly during the first years of the war.[6]

During January 1917, when Germany resumed unrestricted submarine warfare, Robins's commitment to the Allied cause intensified. After the American declaration of War on 6 April, he volunteered in the "Theodore Roosevelt Division" and helped organize this division of the U.S. Army, which was to be sent to France under Roosevelt's command.

The three years of anguished ambivalence for Margaret were not over, although she decided to "give all her time . . . to war work. No daughter of Jamestown or Plymouth could be more vigorous or effective." Margaret's steadfast support for America's war effort made it no less bearable for her since she was constantly haunted by the thought of Raymond fighting in France against her German cousins.[7] Robins wrote enthusiastically, "I am now more concerned that we should have a fighting force under the American flag on the firing lines in France at the earliest possible moment than in any other one thing. The social, economic and religious reorganization after the war will become the first concern only when the war has been won by the Allies."[8] With heroic posture Robins wrote, "If the Roosevelt Division is sent to France I expect to be in its ranks." And to the coordinator of his college tour, Dr. William Irvine, Robins telegraphed: "Congressional action today makes order for mobilization of Roosevelt Division daily possibility. As one of its organizers my obligation to report immediately mandatory. Under circumstances believe you should arrange substitute."[9] He also wrote to Elizabeth: "To go into the trenches and face the ultimate issue once again will be like the old realities of the Alaskan trail, and the first years of the political and labor battle in this city. I long for it and will meet 'the enemy' with a certain deep gladness. I have been talking quite long enough."[10]

These charged expectations of immediate action on the western front were squelched. Neither Secretary of War Newton D. Baker nor President Wilson would consider Roosevelt's requests to serve even in a secondary position of command in such a proposed division. Roosevelt carried on a lengthy correspondence with Baker and swallowed his formidable pride even further by traveling to Washington to argue his case. No permission was forthcoming; the entire scheme was dropped, and Roosevelt's anger toward Wilson, which had been considerable because of Wilson's cautious war policy, was expressed from then on in an even more venomous stream of attacks.[11]

Robins was disappointed. The plan had whetted his old hunger for action, the exhilaration of the good fight, and the confrontation with danger. "Roosevelt could have taken 200,000 fighting men to France by August 1st," he complained to Elizabeth. "The most that can now be hoped for is 30,000 until after January 1918. His going would have aroused the fighting spirit of the whole American people. Who is Pershing? I am asked from every side." Robins returned to his speaking engagements, but two weeks later, on 10 June, he received the following telegram from Roosevelt: "Have urged H. P. Davison head of the Red Cross Association to send you with the Red Cross Committee to Russia. I regard this as a work of the utmost importance."[12]

Robins gave careful consideration to the invitation; he wanted to know what specific role he would play. His speech on Russia's postwar importance had already been reinforced by the overthrow of the Czar in the March Revolution, three months before. In a public address just weeks prior to learning of his appointment to the Red Cross Commission, Robins expressed his empathy with revolutionary developments in Russia.

> We rejoice in the dawn of freedom in Russia. After the supreme hour when the free men of France hurled back the invading hosts of autocracy at the battle of the Marne the most glorious moment in a hundred years was that hour when Catherine Breshkovsky was welcomed by a liberated people in the capital city of the Tsars. Heroic and suffering Mother of the Russian common life, saved from the living death of Siberian exile to behold the emancipation of one hundred and sixty million souls from the thraldom of centuries—beloved "Babushka" we rejoice with you this afternoon![13]

Robins hoped to make his service on the commission noteworthy and wanted definition of his responsibilities. He wrote to many friends, informing them proudly of his appointment. Some questioned the advisability of his devotion of energy to Red Cross work in Russia when his talents could be used better at home.[14] But Robins persisted in the conviction that he could make a unique contribution on the commission. He explored a number of possibilities, including serving in some special capacity for President Wilson.

While no one in authority gave any special mission to Robins in particular, Edward N. Hurley, a member of the War Council of the American Red Cross affirmed that the commission to Russia was given a far-reaching mandate.[15]

Robins's support of Hughes in the 1916 presidential race did not endear him to Wilson, nor to other members of his administration who made the foreign policy decisions. Nevertheless Robins persisted. "I shall enter upon this task with a special sense of responsibility to you," he wrote to Roosevelt, "and if the program of the Commission discussed in Washington is carried out, it will be a far reaching service to the Russian people and significant for the future of our international relations."

Robins never received a formal special assignment with the commission. The only documented request for the performance of a service by Robins was Secretary of War Newton D. Baker's suggestion that "his old friend Robins do what he could to break up the contraband ring headed by Pro-German Russians."[16] Robins was willful, determined, and his ego soared with his "special sense of responsibility." "It is a great moment in the life of every member of this party but bigger for me than for any other member," he wrote to Margaret. "This is because I mean to go the distance to help Russia to be free and I have an ideal for our work larger than my comrades."[17] Coming from most men this might be considered bombast; from Robins, it was an impassioned affirmation, deeply sincere, of his self-sacrifice; he wanted to risk his life if it would achieve the desired result—to help Russia to be free. But what did that mean in May 1917? At that moment, Robins had no way of knowing.

With his undefined special mission in mind, Robins requested letters of recommendation, or "credentials" as he called them, from the Chicago Federation of Labor and his old friend Louis F. Post, who was serving as assistant secretary of labor. Robins wanted to be sure that within the ranks of the revolutionary leadership of Russia he could prove that he had "long been identified with the organized labor movement" and that he "advocated the trade union cause in industrial conflicts in the United States and in other lands."[18] With the same end in mind and in the name of the National Women's Trade Union League, which was meeting in its biennial convention in Kansas City, Margaret sent two congratulatory cablegrams to Russia. The first was addressed to the "Committee of Workingmen and Soldiers' Deputies, Petrograd," and the second was sent directly to Catherine Breshkovsky, in care of the American ambassador to Russia, David R. Francis. Both were signed "The National Women's Trade Union League" and represented the will of the assembled delegates.[19] Raymond hoped that these expressions of common aims, in addition to Margaret's role as president of the NWTUL, would minimize suspicion by the revolutionary leadership in Russia and help lay a foundation of trust for his work on the commission.

The American Red Cross Commission to Russia cannot be understood without some knowledge of its personnel and the circumstances of its creation. William B. Thompson, a wealthy American copper magnate and financier, was convinced by the March Revolution (February in the Julian calendar) and by the downfall of the Czar that the most significant aim of the Allies in the World War at that moment was the maintenance of the eastern front. He believed that continued support of the new Russian government was the necessary means to achieve this end. Thompson assumed a personal responsibility for the fulfillment of that conviction. Herman Hagedorn, his biographer, points out that his contribution to the war effort was intended to match those of "his friends who were already deep in the war as field marshals and ambassadors."[20] Bernard M. Baruch, financial wizard, was on the Council for National Defense; Thomas W. Lamont, George Perkins's successor as director of the Morgan Trust Company, was playing an important role in inter-Allied finance; and Henry P. Davison headed the American Red Cross. All were friends of Thompson and they were all serving in critical positions.

With the help of Davison, Thompson developed a plan for a Red Cross commission. It was to be the instrument of America's support of Russia's continued participation in the war. The thirty members of the new body were to be uniformed and technically part of the armed forces, with appropriate ranks assigned to the doctors, sanitary engineers, inspectors, transportation experts, publicity men, secretaries, administrators, and cameramen.

Aside from the distribution of supplies, which could have been carried out by other American or Russian personnel on the scene, there were no clearly defined responsibilities for the commission. Neither the American ambassador nor a number of other official representatives on the scene felt that there was a need for the commission.[21] In addition, the entire project was organized and financed by Thompson, who carried the official title and responsibilities of business manager.[22] Thompson wanted to support the new Kerensky regime, sustain its army on the eastern front, and thereby force German armies to fight a two-front war. All other considerations were secondary.

The knotty question of who sanctioned such political activities was approached by Herman Hagedorn.

> How much of all this was reduced to definite instructions and how much remained a matter of hints and hopes: how much the Red Cross, the President, or the State Department were involved or only certain individuals who happened to be both Thompson's friends and executives of the Red Cross, no document revealed then or thereafter. But it was made clear to Thompson that as "representative of the United States," he would be expected "to undertake any work which," in his judgment, "was necessary or advisable in the effort to prevent the disintegration of the Russian forces."

In addition, it appears that a secret and confidential letter was written by President Wilson in which he further suggested the broader mandate under which the commission operated. Arthur Bullard, who served in the Russian office of the Committee on Public Information in Petrograd, reported to

George Creel: "Robins then showed me their letter from the President, which certainly was ample warrant for what they were trying to do." Robins, Thompson, and the other members of the Commission were committed to the cause of supporting the Russian forces in the war. However, Robins and Thompson shared little else as they embarked on the trip to Russia.[23]

According to Hagedorn, Robins was handed a list of commission members and responded, "'W. B. Thompson?' he gave a grunt of disapproval. 'What's that Wall Street reactionary doing on this mission?'"[24] And similarly, when Thompson realized that Raymond Robins was a member, he responded: "'Major Robins. That uplifter, that trouble maker, that Roosevelt shouter. What's he doing on this mission?'"[25]

As early as the Republican convention in 1912, Robins contended with the power of Thompson as an opponent of the Progressive wing of the Republican party. Again in 1916, when Robins was seeking support for a unified party with a strong reform commitment, Thompson stood in the way. But Robins's antipathy for Thompson was not going to stand in the way of his goal of service in Russia. "My object of getting the confidence and support of the other members of the mission has been fairly well achieved," he wrote to Margaret, "and today I think I have won the friendship and support of every important member."[26] Robins's judgment was well founded. Even Thompson revised his opinion of Robins and was won over, though cautiously, to his side. Thompson wrote to his wife en route to Russia that "Robbins [sic] . . . devote[s] his time now to the betterment of the laboring classes. . . . His doctrines are sound, for besides his efforts to secure a square deal for the working-man and his children he is fair and just in his attitude towards capital and the employer. . . . I know he is a man of high character, and he has great force of speech and adds much to the strength of the commission for he constitutes a connecting link between the laboring man of America and the laboring man of Russia."[27]

The members of the mission met at Chicago for the trip to Vancouver, and from there set out on the trans-Pacific and trans-Siberian journey to the Russian capital. Robins's diary and letters to Margaret during the months that followed are extraordinary, charged with excitement and rich in the detail of every aspect of the adventure.

> When the fog lifted we were in sight of the Russian Coast, old Asia that ancient hive from which our Aryan fathers swarmed over four thousand years ago. The sun came out gloriously and we steamed into Vladivostok harbor in the splendor of the morning.
> They are singing the Master Song of the Revolution the contribution of France to the spirit of liberty from oppression of all the peoples of the earth. A great red flag and a large black one are being waved by an enthusiast who is returning after twelve years in Siberia and four in America. He is a large viking . . . of a man, and has been called to run for the constitutional assembly by the zemstvos of his boyhood town.

We dock at Noon and are waited upon by a large delegation representing the Workingmen's and Soldiers Council, the zemstvos of the province, the local duma, the national and local Red Cross of Russia and some others including the American Consul and the English port guard.

We next leave for the Imperial Train the one that brought over Root and his party members of the American [Railway] Mission to Russia. It is the Czar's special train and contains the coach in which he wrote and delivered his ABDICATION! It is the most luxurious train I have ever seen. The gauge of the great Trans-Siberian Railway is five feet and this permits a car of greater width than we use in America. Our quarters are in the first coach marked CB [imperial initials] and we are placed in the center of the train.

Each room is finished in heavy polished mahogany, carved leather wainscoating, nickel-silver toilets, beautiful Russian leather seats, silk covered cushions, leather finished chair, writing table, clock, table lamp, thermometers, book rack, leather writing case, water caraffe, etc., etc.. The bedding is damask linen, the most elegant blankets I have yet seen, pillow cases of silk and all marked IP [imperial initials] with the double eagle and crest.

On the table in this car the Czar wrote his abdication and I am now writing you from this same table! In this dining car the Czar was standing when he handed his abdication to the representatives of the Duma on that eventful day in last March when the Romanov Dynasty came to its ignoble end.[28]

The trip west from Vladivostok was peaceful and without danger. However, incidents in towns along the way convinced Robins of the power of the local revolutionary soviets and the relative weakness of the representatives, if any, of the Provisional Government. On one occasion in Siberia, the imperial train was met by a "welcoming delegation" of local revolutionary militants whose suspicion of the aims of the commission was soon made evident. They were indifferent to the initial speech of "encouragement and congratulations" by Dr. Frank Billings, the official head of the commission, but the indifference soon turned to impatience and hostility. The crowd wanted "some evidence that the Americans understood what a revolution meant."

Shouts and threatening gestures soon followed. It seemed that the welcome would turn into a riot.

As the boldest of the crowd tentatively put his foot on the platform steps, the Commission's interpreter began to call for Raymond Robins. Moving quickly through the train, Robins appeared on the platform and was introduced. The crowd stopped, fell back, cheered and reformed as an audience. The interpreter hearing Robins' name being "noised through the crowd," and being "recalled as the active agent of the League which prevented the extradition of Christian Rudovitz . . ." had grabbed at a straw and caught a log.[29]

Robins won the crowd almost immediately. Not only did they forget their hostility toward the "American capitalists trying to keep Russia in the War against the will of the workers and peasants," but they cheered the man who spoke to them as a fellow worker and miner. Robins spoke of the common purpose shared by the Russian and American people in destroying

German militarism and autocracy and of the humanitarian aims of the commission. The train continued on its journey westward with wishes of peace and friendship from the "welcoming delegation."

Caught up in the war, the mission, and Russia's revolution, with childlike awe Robins looked from the windows of the Czars' train. "Flowers and flowers and again flowers," he wrote to Margaret from the desk of Nicholas Romanov II in the train's imperial study.

> The hills and plain and even the mountain sides glorious with countless blooms. I am permitted to ride on the front of the engine and I have enjoyed this more than I can say.
>
> Last night at eight o'clock the [Russian-Manchurian] frontier was closed and all the hundreds of returning refugees and others are held under the bayonet, at this little town until they shall be deported. Seldom will one witness such misery.
>
> The returning American Russians have been making great trouble and the government has at last resorted to this desperate measure. This is the bitter fruit of the I.W.W. ["Wobblies," or Industrial Workers of the World] and the wild men it has sent into Russia, all torn by the revolution and trying to find a way to live toward liberty! They will have much to answer for if Russian freedom fails.[30]

Long before reaching Petrograd, Robins experienced the conflicting expectations of the revolutionary situation—of the intense hope amid hopelessness and chaos.

> *Sunday, August 2, 1917*
> En Route Ekaterinburg on the 1st Class [text unclear] dirt and crowded with soldiers. . . . All day through fertile fields and peasant villages a wonderland of possible wealth.
>
> *3rd August, Siberia for the last day.*
> The troop trains are thrilling. The men are so young and gay and the women so old and sad eyed. The song is everywhere the great song of the revolution and the mighty call of France. A deep note runs through this Russian singing and it stirs one to tears. What a stark and mad world that will murder these fine fresh faced lads. Youth and old age, tears and laughter, music and sighs, the barren sorrow and the high adventure, all are here. There is something that moves me profoundly in this bleeding heart of the Russian peasant mother and wife, this toll of war from the best and bravest and youngest of the race.

On the following day, the imperial train crossed the divide in the Ural Mountains and entered European Russia. In Ekaterinburg (now Sverdlovsk), Robins visited a prisoner-of-war camp, and although the camp was only three days' journey from Petrograd, the beauty of the summer countryside made war seem far away. "Were it not for troop trains and prison camps," Robins reflected in his pocket diary, "it would not be possible to think of war."[31]

11

The Provisional Government

Think of it, we are to reach Petrograd on the 7th of August, just twenty years to a day since I sailed out of Golden Gate for the great adventure of the north. . . . I feel there is more than just a coincidence in this.
—Raymond to Margaret, 7 August 1917

Out of the Russian night I won a great friend. . . . [W]e met as enemies from battles on opposite sides of the barricades in the political and economic struggle [in America], and then under fire together and in the flaming light of the Russian Revolution saw into each others' souls and understood and became comrades in faith and work for the rest of the trail. Colonel William Boyce Thompson, Wall Street, New York.
—Raymond to Elizabeth, 1 October 1919

ROBINS was twenty-seven in 1900, when he returned to San Francisco from Alaska—"the great adventure of the north." For seventeen years thereafter he was in the thick of every major social struggle of the Progressive Era. At forty-four, although well-seasoned by those "Chicago years," he never had faced a challenge or danger equal to his Alaska experience. Revolutionary Russia was the match, and more.[1]

Writing from his car on board the Trans-Siberian Railway, nearing his destination after six weeks of travel, Robins reported on his new priorities—the military and political situation in Russia. Only hours before he had been immersed in the beauty of the foothills of the Urals and the wildflowers of the Russian steppe. Once in Petrograd, however, his singleness of purpose provided little room for admiration of nature's wonders. The realities of the revolutionary situation and the war were all-consuming.

On the very day the commission arrived in Petrograd a new Provisional Government took power under the premiership of Alexander Kerensky, a socialist, non-Marxist lawyer and deputy chairman of the Petrograd Soviet—the powerful revolutionary committee of workers, soldiers, and peasants. Kerensky had been a labor representative in the impotent Fourth Duma (parliament) under the Czar. Only days after the March Revolution toppled the monarchy, the Temporary Committee of the Duma dissolved itself and instituted the first Provisional Government, a conservative body in which notables from the aristocracy and upper classes predominated. It was headed by Prince Georgii Eugenevich Lvov, and Kerensky served as minister of justice. It lasted four months, forced to resign in the aftermath of mass demonstrations against its policies—the July Uprising. On 7 August it was replaced by the more representative Provisional Government headed by Kerensky.

Robins had to sort out these developments while trying to understand what the U.S. government had already done, was doing, and planned. He had learned about the disappointing results of the Root Mission, which had arrived in Russia just two months earlier to establish cooperative ties with the Provisional Government. President Wilson and Secretary of State Robert Lansing hoped that Elihu Root, a man of experience and reputation, a former secretary of state and secretary of war, as head of an American delegation would achieve such a purpose. But after a month of diplomatic and social engagements the mission returned to the United States with little accomplished. Robins was determined not to repeat such a failure. "A new ministry was organized yesterday," he wrote to Margaret,

> Kerensky had resigned because of the refusal of the army to fight. Now he is again premier with Korniloff in supreme command of the Army. They are in retreat all along the Russian front and 18,000 Russian troops have been shot by their own brothers. Great stores of grain and ammunition have been taken by the Austrians and the outlook is desperate. Many are leaving Petrograd. Bread lines, and milk lines everywhere.
>
> The long journey is over—forty days. Twelve days and nights on the same coach 5,500 miles in one direction and the longest possible railroad trip in the world. We are in a war held city. For breakfast this morning we had one slice of sour black bread, weak tea and nothing else. . . . Suffering is apparent on all sides. We shall be rationed in a few days. It is war and a sharp contrast to the great luxury of the past weeks. I am glad for it and we will be the better for some pinch of the world war that has made so many thousands suffer.
>
> All here is chaos! The government will last no one knows how long. It is a day to day affair. Buildings bear the marks of the revolution. Uncertainty is everywhere. Today we were received at the Embassy. Many leaving in anticipation of the bitter winter ahead. War relief seems about to give way to some civil relief for the poor of the larger cities. . . .
>
> We are here and the outlook is stormy in the extreme. The Root Commission did not get over with the Russian people. We will have to try and serve them well enough to make up for this failure.

"It was a curious thing," reported Alexander Gumberg, mission interpreter, "that Root—the politician, the diplomat, the statesman—saw nothing in Russia, and Thompson, the Wall Street promoter, who knew nothing of public or international affairs, saw the whole picture."[2]

On 18 August Robins reported on the crisis of the bread lines, which was the catalyst of the March Revolution that brought down the Czar.

> I have been giving attention to the bread, milk, meat and sugar lines. They last all day and far into the night. Some old women sit on the sidewalk and

Robins, Gumberg, and others in Petrograd in front of the Red Cross Pierce Arrow auto. In front row (left to right) are Robins, Jacob Peters (Cheka chief in Moscow), unknown Russian (George Kennan suggests Leo Karakhan, a Soviet foreign office official), the Russian boy mascot of the American Red Cross Commission, Alexander Gumberg (leather jacket), and Charles Stephenson Smith, AP correspondent. (Courtesy of the Thomas Thacher Papers, Bakhmetev Archive, Rare Book and Manuscript Library, Columbia University.) This photo also appears in Kennan's *Russia Leaves the War* and was provided to Kennan by Charles Stephenson Smith.

knit the long wait through. It is quite a place for discussion and debate and fine breeding ground for revolt. Not since the first great winter in the Yukon have I seen bread and food generally so much the centre of men's lives. What is fairly tolerable now will be impossible when the winter has come in earnest. As go these lines so goes the provisional government. If they shorten the government lives if they lengthen it will die.[3]

During the first days in Petrograd, Robins and members of the mission met with Kerensky, Catherine Breshkovsky, the Social-Revolutionary and "Grandmother of the Russian Revolution," Prince Peter Kropotkin, noted anarchist theorist, Paul Miliukov, first foreign minister in the Provisional Government, and countless other Russian public officials and American government and business representatives. In addition, they made the rounds of the American community in Petrograd. It was a hectic pace of introductions, luncheons, conferences, and dinners to discuss the Russian situation and the war effort in general. Robins met privately with many who knew the Russian situation firsthand in his attempt to understand the underlying problems and their possible consequences. On 10 August he had a luncheon engagement with Charles R. Crane, the plumbing magnate, whose interest in Russia and the East had spanned more than twenty years and whose visits to Russia eventually exceeded that number. Crane was also pessimistic about the future of Kerensky's Provisional Government and its capacity to fulfill Russia's commitments on the eastern front. While this government assumed responsibility for the czarist regime's commitments to the Allies, its liberal, centrist, and constitutional democratic program had only minor popular support. Kerensky's Provisional Government functioned in competition with and parallel to the grass-roots committees of workers, soldiers, and sailors—the soviets—whose influence grew each day. As a member of the Root Commission, Crane was finishing his task in Russia and soon returned to the United States. However, unlike Robins, Crane believed the hope for order in Russia rested in the hands of the czarist military commanders Alexei M. Kaledin, Aleksandr V. Kolchak, Anton I. Denikin, and Lavar G. Kornilov.[4]

On the evening of 9 August, Robins and other members of the commission as well as representatives of different official departments, met with Ambassador David R. Francis. Francis had assumed his post in 1916, at the age of sixty-five, after a career as the mayor of St. Louis, governor of Missouri, and secretary of the interior in the administration of President Cleveland. A little more than a year earlier, in response to Francis's request for advice, Crane encouraged Francis to accept President Wilson's offer of the American ambassadorship to Russia. Like Robins and most of the others on the Red Cross Commission, the ambassador had no previous diplomatic experience nor any significant knowledge of Russian history, foreign policy, culture, or language. "When confirmed," Francis wrote to Crane at the time of his nomination in February 1916, "I shall go to Washington for ten days or two weeks to familiarize myself with the relations between this country and Russia, and shall start for Petrograd as soon thereafter as possible."[5]

Robins managed an additional meeting with the second ranking representative of the United States in Russia, Brig. Gen. William V. Judson, military attaché to the ambassador as well as chief of the American Military Mission to Russia. These meetings with Judson were marked by special rapport and communication, which led the two eventually to join forces in the drive for Soviet-American rapprochement.[6]

Those first days in Petrograd were also devoted to the assessment of available Red Cross supplies and methods of distribution. Regardless of other activities and initiatives, the only unquestioned and officially sanctioned role for the Red Cross Commission was the distribution of relief supplies. However, to facilitate that process, the commission needed the cooperation of the political and military authorities. It was essential for the members of the commission to establish close lines of communication between their distribution agents and government officials. Without such communication, the humanitarian work could not have been carried out; transportation, the guarding of supplies, and the clearance required in wartime could not have been provided.[7]

But the head of the Red Cross Commission, William Boyce Thompson, arrived in Petrograd with plans and expectations far beyond this. He was intent "to go the distance to help Russia to be free," which meant much more than distributing supplies. Thompson plunged immediately into what he considered the most effective means of maintaining the Russian forces on the eastern front—staggering offers for the purchase of Russian government bonds and the distribution of millions of copies of President Wilson's War Message of 2 April 1917. Coming only three weeks after the March Revolution, Wilson expressed American commitment to the Russian people, offered congratulations for having finally thrown off the yoke of czarist autocracy, and welcomed a democratic Russia as an ally in the war against autocratic Germany and Austria-Hungary. In addition, Thompson hoped to subsidize the leading Social-Revolutionaries who were to aid in his anti-Bolshevik and prowar propaganda campaign.

The SRs, as they were called, were non-Marxist, populist revolutionaries who sought the empowerment of the peasant masses of Russia. They lent their support to Kerensky's Provisional Government as the left wing of a coalition that also included the Kadet, or Constitutional Democratic party, largely representing liberal and reform-minded middle-class interests. Both of these parties had a long-standing tradition of opposition to czarist autocracy, but their tactics varied considerably. The Kadets had remained within the law of czarist Russia; the SRs had spawned the full gamut of political action, including the first use of political terrorism in modern western history. In fact, they were the political faction with the largest base of mass support. They rejected the Marxist analysis of the Russian situation in general, and the Bolshevik approach in particular. Because of their mass appeal, their role in the Provisional Government, their willingness to sustain the war effort on the eastern front, and their opposition to Lenin, Robins and Thompson joined in their support.

Robins quickly became involved in these political activities (all paid for from Thompson's personal fortune), and within ten days of his arrival had prepared "Some Observations on the Present Conditions in Russia." His analysis supported the actions of Thompson and the commission in behalf of the Kerensky regime and demonstrated as well Robins's insights into the underlying forces and realities of the revolutionary situation. The revolution had struck a mortal blow to the elements that had provided the cohesion in Russian life for centuries—"the authority and power of the Russian state and Russian church, both personalized in the Tsar." The essential question

William B. Thompson (seated, center) and Robins (to his left) with junior members of the American Red Cross Commission and Russian associates, Petrograd, November 1917. (Courtesy of the Thomas Thatcher Papers, Bakhmetev Archive, Rare Book and Manuscript Library, Columbia University.)

that lay at the root of the chaos, confusion, and hopelessness was "What will furnish the new binder in Russian national life?" Robins's answer from that moment on remained: "The Ideals of the Revolution, 'Free Russia':—'Soldiers of the Revolution!'"[8] While not sure of what form the Revolution would take, what path, leadership, or ideology, Robins was convinced that a czarist restoration or aristocratic-militarist reaction would never succeed.

Robins, Thompson, and others were convinced that the success of the democratic revolution in Russia depended on the defeat of the Central Powers. The problem, however, was to convince the Russian workers, peasants, and soldiers that the Provisional Government of Alexander Kerensky was, or could be, the fulfillment of the revolutionary ideal.

Robins's position on the revolutionary situation necessitated a twofold attack. First, it was essential for the Allied governments to understand the depth of the commitment of Russia's people to the revolutionary ideal, regardless of the form it took. During those days of tumult and chaos many Russians, as well as representatives of Allied governments, were "remembering the old binder for authority in Russian life," Robins continued in his "Observations,"

> and believe that it can be reestablished and that even autocratic institutions with order and discipline in the army are desirable in the present crisis. There is no real need to discuss the question, for the fact is that it is absolutely impossible. Revolutions never go backward. The fact is, that a return of autocracy would also certainly mean a separate peace and civil war in Russia, a condition both for the Russian people and the interests of the Allies and Democracy throughout the world, vastly more injurious than the present chaos. Costly and discouraging as it is, we must work our way through and forward; not down and backward. There can be no effective prosecution of the war except by a revolutionary army. It may not be achieved by them; it certainly can not be achieved by any other.

The second point of attack was against the Bolshevik party, headed by Lenin, which called for an immediate end to Russia's participation in the "imperialists war" and identified the success of the revolution with such a peace.

By the summer of 1917 Russia was torn by many divisions in its social, military, political, and economic life. Farmers hoarded crops, manufactured goods were being sold at from four to as much as twelve times the normal price, and fear about the unknown future prevailed. Robins's solution to this situation consisted of the integration of his two points of attack, both of which, he argued, were mutually beneficial to Russia and the American war effort.

> To overcome this situation a new psychology is necessary. An appeal must be made to the people of Russia not in the name of the population of the cities, but in the name of the army,—the Revolutionary Army, Soldiers of Freedom,— the integrity of Russian homes, firesides and nationality. As conscription is almost universal, while the peasants will refuse to give their grain up for the people of the cities they will not refuse for the army, as the army had the content of their sons and brothers and fathers, for practically every village is represented at the front.
>
> The prosecution of the war to victory is synonymous with successful revolution and the support of the present Provisional Government, or such modified government as rests squarely upon the foundations of the revolutionary movement of last March.

Robins concluded his "Observations" with a tempting vision of peace and economic cooperation between the new Russia and America. It was a vision that he never forgot; it was a hope that he pursued after the Bolshevik seizure of power and long after the firm establishment of the Soviet Union.

Russia . . . presents the greatest possible field for commercial enterprise, the investment of capital and the consumption of manufactured products among the nations of the world. Her good will and sympathy, even though all investments for the time being seem to have been wasted and she conclude a separate peace with Germany, will constitute an investment that will pay in the next fifty years $100 for every dollar contributed. At the present time America is more popular with the Russian people than any other nation. The sordid attitude of the Englishmen and the frantic criticisms of the French, have alienated Russian sympathy. It is wholly possible for America to become the most favored foreign nation in the commercial and cultural sense, in Russia. I am confident that there are men enough in America with vision and understanding of this situation to insure that help and cooperation for Russia so necessary and so boundlessly fruitful for the better future of Russia, America and the world.[9]

Robins's sense of commitment to the Russian people and to the integrity of their revolutionary struggle were put aside in this final statement. He knew that the ultimate criterion that would determine whether or not the Provisional Government received strong support was American national interest. This statement was Robins's appeal to the powerful business interests in America, in the hope that it would provide the incentive to aid the Provisional Government and end the many fear-inspired stories of revolutionary fanaticism.

Robins wrote to Theodore Roosevelt,

a statement of what the present Russian situation means to me, and what I would like to see done for Russia in America, which was prepared more with you in mind than any other one person.

My present purpose is to remain here until I have done all that I can do, or Russia has declared a separate peace. This latter I do not believe will come to pass. There are dark days ahead for Russia. Many children may starve to death this winter, her armies may further mutiny and her economic and social life will be even more disorganized than at present. The aggression will remain.

You are too wise a man to make a mistake that some of our Americans are making and urge autocracy as the cure for the incompetence of democracy. It is good to think that you may be able to give the condition of Russia and the possibilities of her real aid consideration.[10]

Thompson and Robins began a coordinated propaganda campaign with Madame Breshkovsky, Nicholas Tschaikowsky, leader of the peasant cooperatives, and George Lazarov, Breshkovsky's good friend and loyal correspondent through the years of her exile in Siberia. Robins identified the latter as one "who had been the head of the underground station in Switzerland serving the Russian Revolution for many years." In addition there were two trusted members of Kerensky's own staff, General Neslouchovsky and David Soskice, Kerensky's private secretary. Under the chairmanship of Catherine Breshkovsky, this group constituted itself the Committee on Civic Education in Free Russia.[11]

To initiate the propaganda campaign, Thompson spent one million dollars to purchase newspapers, acquire printing facilities, and begin the production of a "vast quantity of pamphlet literature . . . with special relation to the minds sought to be influenced, written in the fashion of the workingman-peasant patois and revolutionary appeal." In addition, the Breshkovsky committee enlisted the assistance of capable propagandists and journalists whose loyalty to the task was unquestioned. The Kerensky regime cooperated with the effort by freeing men from military and political duties to serve on the staff of the newly formed committee.

"The situation here is desperate, and desperate remedies are justifiable," General Judson reported from Petrograd to his superiors at the War College Staff,

> The head of the Red Cross Commission here, Thompson, reports having contributed his own money to the extent of one million dollars for newspaper control and influence, hiring speakers, etc. This work similar to pre-election campaigns in the U.S. and similarly costly. . . . Thompson, assisted by Raymond Robins acts through a special Russian Committee of Conservative-Socialists, which may be expanded to include other elements to counteract the enormous propaganda from several sources hostile to the Allied interests. No U.S. agency has the direction of the Thompson movement, and perhaps that is for the best. Thompson needs privately subscribed funds if no Government funds are available, or must discontinue the work before more than well started.[12]

For Robins, the campaign was the kind of mission he had undertaken in Chicago as a settlement worker and labor spokesman. As in those campaigns, he saw the goals clearly, even though many remained unclear, undecided, or unsure. Once the Red Cross supplies had been unloaded and stored in warehouses under government protection, he developed those contacts necessary to carry out the even more important "political" work.

From the very first day in Petrograd he had characterized the Provisional Government as a "day to day affair." His appraisal of the Kerensky leadership one week later was not any more heartening. "We have met most all the officers and ministers of the supreme group here and among them are men of the highest quality, more men who are dreamers with responsibility and no capacity to bring their dream into being now that they have the power. Some are mediocre and a few sinister."[13]

The drama, romance, and historical significance of the revolutionary situation was constantly with Robins. The intensity in thought and feeling seemed to make him even more perceptive. "This morning I called on Madame Breshkovsky," Robins began his account of his first meeting with "Babushka."

> She was at her suite in the Winter Palace. It was a strange surge to pass through the guards and into this old heart of the autocracy and up to a ducal suite and there to find the old bent woman,—Babushka—who a few days ago was an exile for life in Siberia. . . . She is . . . a bit of wonderful human

scenery and with great influence as such to help Kerensky who she adores and supports to the last limit of her power. The old Grandmother fears famine and cold and the return of the autocracy. This is natural as these have been her fears all her long hard life. [Her office is] in the ducal suite in the Winter Palace of the Czars, surrounded by the soldiery that she has so long cursed, protected by them in all the pomp and heraldry of war, herself the foremost woman in spectacular influence in the Russian Empire—she who was yesterday the common convict in a Siberian prison!! As I left I kissed her old wrinkled hand and she drew near to me and kissed me on the cheek. Rare old spirit— too far gone in years to do more than be a moving and tragic and glorious figure in this wonderful hour for Russia and the world.[14]

One week later Robins shared with Margaret his impressions of Kerensky and the thin hope upon which all the effort hung.

Kerensky is 34 years old. He looks very much like a Hebrew although this is denied. He [is] strongly built with a face that shows power. His eyes are small and his skin is bad. He looks very tired, and seems nervous—but under control. His show of temper this morning was for effect upon Francis who had been bully-ragging him. I hope he will survive the present discouragement as he seems to me to present the only possibility of control this side of reaction or military dictator.

A workingman's lawyer a few months ago living in a little house and conspiring with the friends of the revolution. Now in the Czar's rooms in the Winter Palace with a battalion of soldiers ready to obey his orders and the Dictator of the greatest nation and largest land resource in this earth. It was a rare setting and the stage the greatest the world has ever known![15]

Three days later Robins witnessed the moving spectacle of two battalions being sent off to the front, one from the public square in front of the Winter Palace and the other from the training grounds along the Neva River. He was encouraged by this obvious demonstration of Kerensky's commitment to the Allied cause and "the Red Flag of the social democracy." But the second of the two was a women's battalion.

As they marched by saluting because of my uniform it was a moving sight. On their way to the carnage and death the terror and bitter strain of the flaming lines of steel—as they passed with steady step and clear eyes some of them wearing the emblem of the Battalion of Death the tears came unbidden to my eyes. What a sacrifice it is—this potential motherhood going to the shambles by the thousand and shaming in their fine courage all the feeble sneers of the [text illegible at this point] and the cowardice of the men that have fled the face of death on the fighting lines. Russia can never wholly fail with such a womanhood at the heart of her life.[16]

In late August Thompson sent Robins on a mission to Ekaterinaslov to make a firsthand report on the conditions that faced the hundreds of thousands of refugees there. On 1 September, while in Moscow on his way to

Ekaterinaslov, he attended the All-Russian Conference, which had been convened by the Provisional Government. "Fifteen hundred odd delegates, meeting in the great Theatre at Moscow, representing all the social orders in Russia, barons, landlords, great bankers, businessmen, peasants, soldiers, sailors, Provisional Government—practically the entire Russian people except the very small group of the Grand Dukes and the immediate Imperial family."[17] At this conference many of Robins's first impressions regarding the new source of political cohesion were confirmed. "On the main floor, seated in the center of the great hall," in an atmosphere of general disorder and confusion, he noted, "were some three hundred delegates who spoke a coherent note, knew what they wanted, and how they intended to get it. In this group were delegates from the Workmens', Soldiers' and Peasants' Soviets throughout Russia."[18]

The conference was marked by continuous conflict between the conservative old guard of cossacks, businessmen, and large landholders on one side and the socialists and radicals on the other. "Kerensky did some spectacular work as presiding officer, but he cannot stay through as the leader of the Russian people. Of this I am convinced."[19]

Robins had been in the vortex of events for three weeks when he made this appraisal. It suggests his appreciation for Kerensky's attributes as a speaker and leader, but it also demonstrates his uncompromising political acuity and realism. Kerensky's government was the only hope to carry out the Red Cross program; there was no choice but to support him, even with the probability of his imminent downfall. For five weeks, the tide of ambivalence rose and ebbed between hope and desperation.

Following the conference, Robins continued his journey south to Ekaterinaslov, where he was charged with the multiple responsibilities of determining the kind and quantity of relief supplies needed as well as ascertaining the morale of the army. He also had the fruitful experience of testing the actual power of the Provisional Government and seeing the interaction of other political forces vying for power. Again, he was impressed with the power of the local soviets and the fundamental democracy upon which that power rested. His conviction regarding the new revolutionary "binder" in Russian life was confirmed. As a result of his experiences in Ekaterinaslov and Moscow, he believed that he grasped the realities of the situation.[20]

Robins distinguished two major sources of opinion. One was in the urban areas among the middle and upper classes with generally little to gain by the social upheaval then in progress. To Robins, this was the "indoor," or "7%," opinion, the orientation so easily available to the Allied representatives and well-placed Russians whose experience of Russia was limited to the embassy chancelleries, conference rooms, restaurants, and hotels of Petrograd and Moscow. It was quite literally found indoors, since it was found amid the indoor warmth and comfort, rather than out in the countryside or in the factories.

The second source of Russian opinion could be found among the peasants, miners, factory workers, and soldiers, found only by enduring the difficulties of wartime travel to other parts of Russia. For this population, the revolution promised everything. That the needs of Russia lay with the revolution was to Robins the "outdoor" opinion and according to his estimation represented "93%" of Russia's population.

Robins was appalled that there were so many "indoor" men among the Allied missions to Russia. This limited view was both foolhardy and dangerous, in his opinion, both for the future of Russian-American relations and for the war effort. He did all he could to bring the "outdoor" view to the influential people in the Allied missions, but his success was sadly limited to only a few key people.

When Robins returned from Ekaterinaslov he urged Kerensky to appoint P. P. Batolin as coordinator and administrator of the relief food distribution. Batolin was a self-made millionaire "with some eight hundred agencies for the buying of grain in the Siberian and Ukrainian districts of Russia, several banks, and other facilities for assembling and distribution of grain." Thompson and Robins hoped that with such administrative initiative much of the critical food problem could be solved, leaving the new government free to act on its war commitments. But Kerensky delayed the appointment of the millionaire as he had in the days before the Moscow Conference.

Kerensky made a successful defense of the Provisional Government at the Moscow Conference on 1 September, and Robins, in spite of his pessimism, again resolved that at that moment Kerensky was the only Allied hope for a continued Russian war effort. With this in mind, Thompson "cabled to the American Government asking for an appropriation of one million dollars in ten days and three million dollars a month for three months" to ensure the success of the propaganda work that he had begun with his own million. The situation demanded immediate action, especially since authoritative sources estimated that the Germans were spending "not less than $10,000,000 per month" on propaganda in Russia.[21]

Robins held high hopes of carrying out the propaganda plan, even if Kerensky would or could not take the proper domestic steps to free his hand for the war effort. "The hour has struck!" Robins wrote in excitement to Margaret,

> The combination I had hoped for has been made by Colonel Thompson and we are now on the inside and I am in daily counsel with the inner group. You will understand why I cannot be more definite but you will know that the utmost that I have hoped for of opportunity has come to my door. It may be too late and the delay of three weeks fatal to the general plans, but it is great to get a chance and we now have that chance. Colonel Thompson is a wonder and we will play the game in just the manner I wished for.[22]

But events were to prove Robins's enthusiasm unjustified. In spite of the urging of Thompson allies in Washington, including noted journalist and

Root Mission member Charles Edward Russell, Wilson did not respond to Thompson's urgent request. Russell had pleaded for an understanding of Russian war-weariness and assured the president that "$5,000,000 expended now on this education campaign may obviate the expenditure of billions hereafter." Robins recalled that the State Department had informed Thompson that Edgar Sisson of the Committee on Public Information (COMPUB) "had been dispatched who would investigate this undertaking and determine whether it should be supported or no." Thompson concluded that he was not going to receive the necessary support and withdrew his financial backing from the project. "When the representative sent by the American Government for the purpose of this investigation, Mr. Edgar G. Sisson, arrived in Petrograd," Robins related the "indoor" handling of the crisis: "The Provisional Government had been overthrown and for more than two weeks the Bolsheviki had been in complete command of the Russian situation."[23]

The first serious threat to the regime began only two days after Robins returned from Ekaterinaslov—the Kornilov Uprising—which attempted to overthrow the Provisional Government and replace it with a military dictatorship. Robins recorded the phases of the action in letters to Margaret.

Petrograd, 9th September 1917

Back again and the struggle for control of internal Russia is on. Yesterday we were told that there would be trouble, and last night General in Chief Korniloff declared his dictatorship and has started for Petrograd with troops. Kerensky has removed Korniloff from the command of the army and arrested a number of his followers. Korniloff responds by arresting the commissioners of the civil authorities and the delegates of the soldiers in the workman's and soldiers councils. The big internal struggle has come.

Here we are comparatively safe. The front is engaged in civil war and the rear is ready for the same enterprise. It is freely prophesied that Petrograd will run red with blood and that Moscow will be in a state of siege within the next days. . . . Korniloff or Kerensky will be dictator within a few days. The dream of the revolution and government by irresponsible councils is over. The socialist Republic has been thoroughly discredited and the reaction is in full sweep. Kerensky shows courage and the ability to act. He has arrested Le Vov [*sic,* V. N. Lvov, a coup participant] and will have a great number of the aristocracy in irons by nightfall. All is on the jump and the air is tense with the uncertainties of the hour.[24]

Petrograd, 10th September 1917

The storm beats all over Russia. Civil war is at hand unless either Korniloff or Kerensky yields. The city is under martial law, all ordered off the streets by nine o:clock in the evening. Korniloff and his loyal Cossack troops are said to be only fifty versts from the city. Kerensky is reported to be abandoned and to be contemplating suicide. The air is full of rumors—it is a wild time.

Petrograd, 11th September 1917

Korniloff advances upon Petrograd with three divisions of soldiers and Artillery in four units. We are in the throes of civil war.

Petrograd, 13th September 1917

   The Korniloff program has broken down completely. After four days of extreme excitement and all sorts of possibilities and rumors Kerensky emerges in
complete command of the situation and the revolt is quelled. At least this is result of all the facts obtainable here in Petrograd. It has been the most interesting and extraordinary four days I have yet experienced. Kerensky has acted
with vigor and real courage. He rises in power and possibility as the result of
these days of conflict and counter-revolution to the supreme command of the
Army and of the State. If he can deliver we have the solution of the complications at hand.[25]

Robins's enthusiasm for the defeat of reaction grew with each day, but
his understanding of the reasons for the failure of Kornilov were developed
only with the help of hindsight. In later years he maintained that responsibility for the defeat of Kornilov rested with "the new power that was growing in Russian life, the Soviet," and that giving credit to Kerensky was "childish" and "contrary to the actual facts." Robins later went even further and
maintained that it was Smolny, headquarters of the Petrograd Soviet,[26] that
sent sailors down from Kronstadt to guard the Winter Palace, replacing the
Kadet Guards who had protected the Provisional Government. "It was from
Smolny and not from the Winter Palace, that the orders went forth that
dug trenches about the environs of Petrograd, setting up machine guns,
placing cannon on unprotected embankments, on the tops of high buildings,
and organized the Red Guard of the Viborg District to meet the advancing
hosts of the counter-revolution, as their proclamation proclaimed the Korniloff movement to be."[27]

These observations were made more than a year after the Bolshevik Revolution and thus placed the Kornilov affair within the context of those later
events. Robins's crediting the Soviets for the failure of the Kornilov revolt
was influenced by Bolshevik interpretations to which it closely adhered. On
the contrary, in the days following its failure, Robins and Thompson credited the power of the Kerensky regime. For both Robins and Thompson,
Kerensky's response to the Kornilov coup attempt renewed their confidence
and mutual efforts in behalf of the regime. At the same time, they were very
critical of the Allied representatives who supported Kornilov. Such Allied
support of a military dictatorship also weakened Kerensky among the ranks
of the revolutionaries who were critical of his cooperation with the Allies.
Robins noted that "he became associated in the popular mind . . . with reaction and counter-revolution."[28]

The uncertain days of the Kornilov revolt were the final test of the two
Red Cross commissioners and their trust for one another. "It was during
these stirring days of the Kornilov adventure," Robins wrote in his *"Statement
on Russia,"*

   that the intelligent mastery of the Russian situation by Colonel William B.
   Thompson was disclosed. Whatever may be thought of my finding my way

around in Russia, thrown out as I was into the actual living situation, with a past inheritance that brought me close to the ground and gave me an understanding, as it were of the language of revolution, that Colonel Thompson, from his position of authority and association with the people of the boulevards, the embassies, the missions, surrounded with the seven per cent, should find his way so surely is little less than a miracle.[29]

In the weeks that followed, Robins carried out one of his old-fashioned speaking campaigns, and even the addition of an interpreter was nothing new; he had used one often in his public addresses during the evangelical Smith-Robins World Tour in 1913. He spoke before soldiers in Petrograd and in the barracks of the Northern Military District on the American democratic experience. Robins was introduced as a representative of American labor. His speech lasted thirty minutes and was always followed by two or more hours of questions and often heated debate. In praising the American experience and linking it with the historical parallels in Russian history, Robins denied the bleak predictions of the nay-sayers, affirming the hope he saw ahead for Russia. An account of one of these speeches appeared in *The Russian Daily News*, an English-language newspaper in Petrograd, just at the beginning of the Kornilov affair. Robins was the main speaker at a reception for the American Red Cross Commission.

> Major Robins laughed all the croakers of gloom to scorn, and boldly preached the doctrine of hope. Briefly sketching the events of the last six months in Russia, he said that the most stupendous thing in history had been crowded into half a year. It was no wonder that the Russian people, who had always been oppressed, should be confused and mentally intoxicated on entering the broadest democracy immediately after the most complete autocracy. For Russia had, at one leap arrived at a position that it took the United States one hundred years to reach.[30]

If the newspaper account is measure of his skill on the platform, his impact was as great in Petrograd as it had been on the evangelist circuit in America. Robins saw the significance of his speaking campaign among the Russian soldiers if not in terms of the influence he had on them, then in terms of the "outdoor" knowledge he gained from "the Russian workman, peasant, and politician inside the ranks."

> I spoke to a number of thousands of Russian soldiers, and got at first-hand contact with them just what they were thinking and what they were planning to do. It was apparent that the desire for bread, land, and peace, with the dogma, "all power to the soviet," made vital by the foundation discontent and misery resulting from hunger, lack of equipment, lack of confidence in their leaders, and the paralysis of the economic arm in Russian national life, was sweeping the army.[31]

Robins attempted to reconcile the mass support for the soviets with his commitment to the Provisional Government by somehow bringing the two together. In effect they were competitive centers of political and military power, each challenging the legitimacy of the other. The overwhelming popularity of the slogan "All power to the soviets" and ultimate Bolshevik control of the soviets were key stages leading to the success of the Bolshevik Revolution. To Robins's perpetual frustration, the "indoor" minds did not understand the significance of the soviets, both before and after the Bolshevik Revolution, as the new "binder" in Russian life.[32]

From the first days in Petrograd, Thompson and Robins put their confidence in the Social-Revolutionary party. The initial money for the propaganda work was distributed through the special "educational" committee, but Robins began to look to the SRs to bring the Soviets and the Provisional Government together.

> I had at this time a number of confidential agents scattered about in the different arms of the public service and in the several barracks in Petrograd. One of these agents was the driver for one of the armored machine guns in the largest tank corps in Petrograd. He reported to me one morning that there had been a conference of that corps and that it was almost equally divided between supporters of the Bolsheviki, of Lenin and Trotsky, and supporters of the Provisional Government, of Kerensky and his associates. "But," said this agent of mine, "the corps is a hundred percent for the Soviet, and there is no man in the corps who will fight against the Soviet." This statement was in agreement with all lines of information I was receiving from day to day.
>
> It was conceived by us at this time that inasmuch as the Soviet was the power in Russia, that if Kerensky would accept the Soviet, we could put it under the Provisional Government, as it were, pushing out of command in the Soviet the more extreme leadership and going forward to a new stabilization for control of the Russian situation. In talking with Kerensky, it was apparent that he understood the situation, but he feared it was impossible to get the Allied representatives in Petrograd to accept his acceptance of the Soviet should he undertake this plan.[33]

Kerensky's fears were certainly justified. Members of the Allied missions were not only wary of the socialist orientation of the Provisional Government, but were active in support of the counterrevolutionary forces of Kornilov and Denikin, as has already been seen in the case of Charles R. Crane. "Subsequent to the liquidation of the Kornilov enterprise," Robins explained,

> Kerensky's government weakened from day to day, more because of misunderstanding by the Allies than because of its inherent qualities. The indoor Allied diplomatic and military mind forced Kerensky to talk Western European liberalism two-thirds of the time for the benefit of the Allies, while he had to talk Russian Slavic socialism one-third of the time for the sake of maintaining his power from day to day. It was this conflict between the patriotic and pious desires of the Allied leadership in Russia and the actual necessities of the outdoor Russian situation that finally destroyed the credit and power of the Provisional Government.[34]

During late September and October Robins continued his public speaking, but most of his time was spent at an endless series of meetings with Russians in the service of the Red Cross Commission, officials of the Provisional Government, and a growing number of Allied representatives. He sustained his support of Kerensky into October and believed "it is now possible to [do] all that I had hoped to do in coming except in the matter of the precious time that has been necessary to get into working order."[35]

Beginning on 27 September and continuing for the next nine days, Robins attended every session of the "All-Russian Democratic Conference," the "first Social-Democratic Conference in which the power of government was represented under socialist leadership in the history of the world."

> The greatest personality of the Conference was Kerensky! He dominated an uncertain audience with skill and made his case. The Statesman of the Conference was Tzerritelli [I. G. Tsereteli], the finest mind and surest leader in the democratic groups of Russia. The most skillful and dangerous leader of the extreme left was Trotsky. He together with Karmeneff [L. B. Kamenev] marshalled the Bolsheviki-immediate-Peace-Social Revolutionary groups with judgement and precision. The meeting lasted twice until after four in the morning. It was a continuous performance of the most exacting nature.
>
> The outcome of the Conference was to leave Kerensky more firmly in the saddle. But it also operated to bring nearer the final conflict between the extreme left—the party of destructionist separate peace tendencies—and the moderates. Many people have left Petrograd believing that the commune and civil war with murder and looting are just a day or two ahead. I am among those that do not believe this will be the outcome and who do believe that the Provisional Government will yet master the situation. I have never been assigned to a task that I felt more ready to undertake, more fitness for its execution nor more eager to achieve than my work here at this time. The fact that we live on the edge of a volcano and that we may be overwhelmed any day simply adds to the zest of the service. If this letter reaches you and the worst happens, I want you to know that I am more grateful for this opportunity than for any work that ever before came to my hand and that no cost is too great for the privilege of this hour. I am satisfied that the Revolution will never turn backward, and that Russia will achieve a great realization of liberty and social progress. Her economic life will be delayed in its fruition and the present organization of her national life may go to pieces but Russia contains a fundamental basis of human, material and cultural nationality and power.[36]

"These are great days!" Robins wrote to Margaret nine days later, this time concerned with the growing confusion and conflict he saw within the ranks of the revolutionary movements—all to the detriment of Russia and the Revolution.

> All the wonder of the greatest human tragedy set to revolution within, and world war without, liberty used to betray freedom, pacifists used to prevent peace, revolutionists used to destroy the revolution, Russians used to betray Russia—a mighty conflict of symbols and war-crises and shibboleths—words

that have become deeds and formulas that drip with blood. Men white with passion over resolutions and proclamations, while famine and murder stalk abroad and one hundred and eighty million people reach the supreme crisis of their national life, and the master moment of western civilization passes—this is the daily sequence in this far away land. Never before in the story of the human race have so great and elemental forces been released in the life of a nation, in so brief a period of time. Yesterday I spoke to 1200 soldiers. For two hours and a half of address, questions, and answers,—a bitter attack met and I think mastered—the play of human emotion seen in strange bearded faces of dark eyes and hungering for the word of Truth, lights dim and the setting so strange and the somber shadows so ominous, and then laughter and kindly cheer and good-will.

My interpreter is an old revolutionist, one of the men that has given all of his youth and manhood to make possible the hour that has now come, and now agitated lest the fatal folly of the extremists make havoc of this supreme moment. He is one [of] the heroic spirits and has worn chains for his faith.

There is no forecasting plans for the duration of our work. We live from day to day. Each morning we have new elements and plans change with the sun. For today it is the best service of my life—for tomorrow all forecast is worthless. Petrograd is not much excited over the advance of the enemy on the Gulf of Riga. Evacuation of some of the business houses and some private homes is in progress, but the main folks follow their old tasks with just a little quickened air of expectant uncertainty.

Remind me to speak of a visit I made yesterday to Krasno Selo. It was a wonderful ride through the late fall world and the coloring of the trees and the simplicity of the village life so unaltered and so good. And then a moment of strain and then the quiet night with the silent stars!

Little Girl—in the world of affairs and the life of the people this is THE GREAT EXPERIENCE! Be thankful let the cost be what it may.[37]

Seven days later, each with "a daily crisis in the affairs of the army and the government" of Kerensky, Robins attended the opening meeting of the Council of the Republic.

It is a sort of Congress of the Revolution and a Committee of Safety on a great scale. 419 members and all the significant men of the Republic are among the delegates.

The opening meeting was futile as a remedy for the need of the hour but wonderfully impressive as a scene in the strange history of the Russian people. . . . The extreme left refused to cheer or stand when a salute was given to the Allies with all the foreign ministers in the Diplomatic Box. Then this same group refused to cheer or stand in salute to the "Russian Republic" and finally under the leadership of Trotsky the whole extreme left rose and left the hall amid the cries of "Traitor" hurled by them at Kerensky and replies by the convention of "German Hirelings" and "liar." A tumult in which you expected bloodshed and then they had left the hall and the meeting was quiet and shortly adjourned.

The whole air is filled with tumult and rumor and secret cabals. Meantime the winter approaches and the cold nights are here. Rumor has it that Moscow will soon declare a closed city, and not allow any more refugees to come into the 20 mile zone. This will doubtless be necessary to save the people of that city from starvation.

Kerensky took the chair and made the opening speech. Young, worn and curiously subdued in manner he told the needs of the hour and made the Call for an All-Russian support of the Provisional Government. It was in the hall of the Marinsky Palace where the old Council of the Empire used to meet. This Council was the heart of the Reaction and the brains of the Autocracy. Now the Czar's picture was covered and the royal standard furled and this young Revolutionist was the leader of the nation. After him came Babushka the old woman in her peasant garb with a shawl over her head and she stood there bent and wrinkled and soft voiced and called upon the men and women as children of the Revolution to save the Freedom of Russia. Madame Breshkovskaya the wonderful old spirit of the Russian Revolution was in the chair as the temporary presiding officer because "of her seniority in service for the Freedom of the Russian people." Then came the address of the permanent chairman Avtsentieff and a [Bolshevik] demonstration that I shall never forget.[38]

His uncertainty and concern over the growing influence of the Bolsheviks led Robins to link the extremist Bolshevik solutions directly to the brutality and dehumanization of the worst phases of industrial capitalism. In the crisis before revolutionary Russia, Robins saw the same problems and social evils beneath the surface that had been his major concern in the slums of Chicago. "Little Girl," he wrote affectionately to Margaret, on 29 October,

> remember that the hardest nut we have to crack here is the industrial injustice and exploitation of our Free America. The wrongs of Colorado and Homestead, and our Sweatshops are the heaviest load in all this tremendous hour. The credit and good faith of America are embarrassed now by these things to the cost of many thousands of human lives and many millions of money for both the Allies and ourselves. Let this burn into your mind and if I fail here and we go down—remember we fail because the long industrial tyranny of our Captains of Industry has come home to roost upon the lives and wealth of our own sons.
>
> > "The Mills of the Gods Grind slowly
> > But they grind exceeding small.
> > In justice stands He waiting
> > With exactness grinds He all."

Robins gave careful consideration to the motives and program of leading Bolsheviks and revolutionary extremists of all stripes. He could not respond to the challenge they posed in Russia or in America unless he could grasp the basis of their ideology and the passion it spawned. In his letter, he referred to the exploited miners and factory workers in America, and also to those exiles and emigrants from the revolutionary ranks who, like Trotsky after the March Revolution, returned to Russia from America and participated in

Bolshevik agitation fiercely directed against the Provisional Government and America and Allied interests. "The despised Russian and Yiddish workmen and women of the mills and the Sweatshops of America are now the greatest bar to the success of the Allies, to the success of ordered Democracy and the Peace of the World. Never let this be forgotten!!!"

Throughout October Robins wrote of the incredible tide of events, of the impossibility of predicting what might happen even the next day. A Bolshevik takeover was only one possibility, and for the first time, in his letter of 29 October, he hinted at the mutual distrust that had developed between the leaders of the Red Cross Commission and their superiors in Washington.

> There is no term that can be put to this task. It will last well into the winter as now planned, and I am deeper in it from day to day. It is now possible in my judgement that it should last beyond the first of next March and it may be concluded in any hour—either by the breakup of the whole enterprise in a bloody civil conflict, the end of the world war, the overthrow of the Provisional Government and a separate peace with the Central Empires, or the recall of ourselves and the substitution of other leadership here that is more intimate and trusted by the administration at Washington.[39]

With this heightened concern about the growing influence of the Bolsheviks, the frustration with the prevailing "indoor" mentality of the Allied representatives, as well as the indifferent cooperation of Washington in his propaganda campaign, Thompson took the unprecedented step of calling a special meeting of the chiefs of the Allied Military Missions in Russia. They were to develop a plan to strengthen the military forces of the Provisional Government on the eastern front. In Thompson's rooms at the Hotel Europe on Friday, 2 November, Thompson, Robins, and the following were present: Maj.-Gen. Alfred Knox, British military attaché at Petrograd, Gen. Henri Niessel, chief of the French Military Mission in Russia, General Judson and, representing the Provisional Government, General Neslouchovsky and Kerensky's private secretary, David Soskice.

Thompson began the meeting by summarizing the critical situation. General Knox spoke next and delivered a scathing attack "on the failures of the Provisional Government, the incompetence, stupidity, or worse of Kerensky." General Niessel then accused the Russian soldiers of being "cowardly dogs." Incensed at these insults, the two Russians left. In Robins's terms, it was a hopeless impasse between the "indoor myths" and the "outdoor realities."

Toward the end of the meeting Robins and General Knox had a duel of words that typified these opposing views on the eve of the Bolshevik seizure of power.

> KNOX: "You are wasting Colonel Thompson's money."
> ROBINS: "If I was, Colonel Thompson knew all about it."
> KNOX: "You ought to have been with Kornilov." I replied that General Knox was with Kornilov, which he knew was only too true, and he flushed at the

statement and said: "Well, that may have been true, but I am not interested in stabilizing Kerensky and the Provisional Government. The only thing worth while in Russia is to establish Kaledine, and a Cossack military dictatorship. These people need a whip over them."

To which I replied that unless I was greatly mistaken he was facing the prospect of a very different kind of dictatorship.

KNOX: "You mean Lenin, Trotsky, and this Bolshevik soapbox stuff."

I said, yes, that was what I meant. To which he replied: "Colonel Robins, you are not a military man. You don't know anything about military affairs. We military men know what to do with that kind of agitation and agitators. We shoot them."

I said: "Yes, if you catch them you shoot them, and while I do not know anything about military affairs, I know something about folks, and I miss my guess if you are not facing a folk's situation in outdoor Russia today."

"On the following Monday, not a week, but the next Monday," Robins recounted,

the Bolsheviki took Peter and Paul Fortress and the arsenal in Petrograd at the point of the bayonet. On Tuesday they took the telegraph and telephone stations and the Nicolayevsky Railroad Station. On Wednesday night they stormed and carried the Winter Palace, making prisoners of those members of the Provisional Government who had not already escaped. Thursday morning, at two A.M., the second all-Russian Soviet convened at Smolney, passed the decree providing for the distribution of all land to the peasants, the decree providing workmen's control of industries, factories, mills and mines, the decree providing all power in the Soviets, and the decree offering a general democratic peace to the world, electing as Commissioners of Peace Lenin, Trotsky and their associates, who have held power throughout European Russia from that hour to this [January 1919]. This reveals just how close the formal diplomatic and military mind in Petrograd was to the actual Russian situation.[40]

Robins's concern regarding the political myopia of the majority of official diplomatic and military representatives in Russia began very soon after his arrival in August. His courageous and, on occasion, desperate efforts in support of the Provisional Government were made more difficult by those, like General Knox, who still hoped that a military dictatorship could bring both order to Russia as well as a renewed and determined Russian effort on the eastern front.

It was the soldiers, particularly General Knox, who "played a major role in the determination of policy towards Russia . . . in the interval between Knox's return from Russia in January and his departure for Siberia in August," wrote historian Richard Ullman. "[H]e [Knox] was the War Office's chief advisor on Russian matters, and his opinions always received a sympathetic hearing in the Cabinet."[41] To individuals like Knox, the failure of the Kornilov affair brought no new insight. Robins gave his all against such misunderstandings of the revolutionary reality and made every effort to sustain Kerensky and the Provisional Government. But unlike his staunch adversaries in official Allied circles whose dogmatism and ideological preconceptions hampered flexibility and realism, when Kerensky fell and the committees of workers', soldiers', and sailors' deputies took power, Robins had the resilience and wisdom to accept his losses and see the new revolutionary reality for what it was, and he continued to serve the national interests of the United States.

12

Robins and Trotsky

. . . your brother never stops work. He doesn't drink. He doesn't smoke. He can go all day without food. He can go all night without sleep—he isn't human.
—Somerset Maugham to Elizabeth Robins, from Moscow, 1918

Wednesday, 25th October 1917 [Russian Calendar]
Wednesday, 7th November
Petrograd—Hotel Europe Room 332
First Day—Bolshevik Commune
The Council of the Republic.
 The boys and the soldiers of the Red Guard. A great day in Russia and the world. The All-Russian Soviet Meets. I can hear the shooting in the Nevsky as I write at 10:26 P.M. War and civil war and the Commune.
 What an hour, o my father. Amen.
 Help America and Russia and the Free peoples of the earth.

ROBINS'S first reaction to the Bolshevik Revolution was written to himself in his pocket diary on the day the Bolsheviks seized power. It reveals a great deal about the events that were yet to unfold from that moment until June 1918, when Robins finally returned to the United States. While fully aware that this second Russian Revolution meant bloodshed, suffering, "war and civil war," he was not frightened by the victory of Red Guard "boys and soldiers." Unlike conventional Allied opinion, Robins's view was that it was a central event in the history of Russia and the world—"a great day."

"We have just passed through the most impossible revolution in the history of the human race," Robins wrote to Margaret.

 On Monday night of last week the Petrograd garrison passed into the control of a group of Anarchist-Socialists and on Tuesday following the city was an armed camp. The pre-parliament or council of the Republic was prorogued at the point of the bayonet and most of the offices of the government were taken by armed men. On Wednesday night following the Winter Palace was shelled and carried by storm and the ministers of government except Kerensky who had fled to the army at the front in an American Automobile under the American flag—were made prisoners and taken to the fortress of Peter and Paul.[1]

 The Palace and seat of the Provisional Government was shelled from gunboats that had come up the Neva from Kronstadt under the command of sailors who sometime since murdered their officers in one of the most terrible mutinies of history. I was on the Neva bank and watched the shells from the cruiser break upon the Palace. It was the most dramatic moment in the life of the Russian Revolution and the most tremendous experience of my life.[2] All day there had been fighting in the streets of the city and barricades were built on all the principal approaches to the centre of the city. The Revolutionary Committee met at the Smolny Institute the centre of the Bolshevik Party and there issued the decrees that meant life or death. It was another commune and the Red Guard were everywhere in the thick of the struggle. The Red Guard are armed working men from the mills and factories and they are a gruesome looking array. Thursday and Friday were days of counter-revolution and for a few hours it seemed as if the Provisional Government would win. Then a battle was fought on the outskirts of the city between the troops of the government under Kerensky and the Bolshevik troops and the latter won decisively. From that hour the cause of the Provisional Government was hopeless and now Kerensky has fled no one knows whither and the Bolsheviks ride Victory throughout the city. In Moscow there has been a terrible three days of fighting and the glorious Kremlin is battered with shells and the centre of the city is in ruins. All over Russia the conflict rages and the end will be sometime in the future. We stand guard by turns every night against looters and up to the present all is well with us. . . .

The meeting of the All Russia Soviet where the land of Russia was distributed by resolution, an armistice decreed on all fronts, and a Ukase passed declaring war on all the capitalist governments of the world by a handful of Russian workingmen, soldiers and peasants was the most impossible body of men in the history of man.

The whole country is rent with a war of factions. There is no peace in sight and yet I have not given up hope of keeping Russia from a separate peace with Germany.

O my darling what an hour it has been! I would not have missed it for worlds and while the rest is more dangerous than what has gone on before I would not leave for any price that could be named. I have had my test Blessed One and the old spirit holds![3]

After three months on the scene, he was convinced that the base of power of the Soviet of Workers' and Soldiers' Deputies was broad and solid. And with Bolshevik control of the Soviets—achieved by ingenious tactics and astute cultivation of the rank and file—Robins, perhaps better than any other Allied observer, understood that the revolution was neither tentative nor an aberration, but a mass movement of free Russian people under skillful leadership. While he strongly opposed the Bolshevik program, and later told Trotsky and Lenin so in numerous face-to-face confrontations, he could not deny their entrenched influence and power.[4] His interaction with Trotsky and Lenin provided a framework for his subsequent importance as an authority on a developing minority view of American-Soviet relations.

Later that week, forces of the Provisional Government offered resistance, but in an engagement outside Petrograd, they were overwhelmed. Any immediate possibility of forceful overthrow of the Bolsheviks had ended.

On the morning of 8 November, the headquarters of the American Red Cross Commission learned that Kerensky was amassing a major anti-Bolshevik army on behalf of the overthrown Provisional Government. Robins, along with the rest of the commission, was stationed at the Hotel Europe on Michaelovsky Street, in Petrograd. The force was being readied for attack against the Bolsheviks at Gatchina. Thompson dispatched Robins to authenticate the report. At midday Robins reached Kerensky's headquarters, where 5,000 soldiers were camped. As Kerensky was giving Robins his assurances that 100,000 more troops loyal to him were on their way, a most extraordinary thing happened. In the words of Herman Hagedorn,

> as he spoke, Robins watching the lines of Bolsheviki troops entrenched within 500 yards of Kerensky's men, saw two hands appear, then a bearded face. With his hand still over the barbed wire, [the bearded man] raised a white flag and then moved across the open space toward the troops of the Provisional Government. Within 20 yards of the trenches, he stopped and began to speak. Robins could not hear what he said, but one after another, men began to climb out of the government trenches. Within 10 minutes half of Kerensky's 5,000 had gone over to the *soviet.*

Similarly, throughout the three months that he had worked on behalf of the Provisional Government, Robins encountered example after example of the growing influence of the workers', soldiers', and peasants' committees— the soviets. No one appreciated the significance of this more than the Bolshevik leadership. Under the banner of the crucial slogans, "All power to the soviets!" and "Peace, land and bread!" Lenin and his comrades managed to achieve supremacy in the soviets. By the summer of 1917, the Bolsheviks had emerged as the most broadly based, effectively led, and militant political organization in Russia.

The bearded old man in the trenches who had encouraged Kerensky's forces to come over to the other side had tapped the war-weariness and frustration of the soldiers fighting for the Provisional Government, still commanded by officers who had been appointed by the Czar's ministers. Following the published appeals of the Bolshevik party, the old man had no doubt argued that the commitment of the Provisional Government to continue Russia's ill-fated role in World War I—a commitment first undertaken by the Czar and then pressed upon Russia by the American, British, and French allies—was a failure. The old man may have also held out the promise of land distribution and soviet assurances of equitable provision of food, following the lines of Lenin's "Decree on Land," issued that very day at the Second All-Russia Congress of Soviets. The soldiers fled to the Bolsheviks, believing that their interests were to be served by joining their brothers. Hagedorn's account continues:

> That evening, muddy from head to foot, exhausted as never before in his life from his journey on foot and by cart from Gatchina, Robins returned to

Thompson's quarters. "Chief, we've got to move pretty fast. Kerensky is as dead as yesterday's 7,000 years. The new folks have the power. There's only two things for us to do: to get in touch with Trotsky and Lenin and work with them, with the possibility of rebuilding the Eastern front; or to pack our grips and get out as fast as we can run."[5]

Thereupon Robins and Thompson, with neither the knowledge nor consent of Francis or of any other official American representative, arranged a meeting with Leon Trotsky.[6]

As commissar for foreign affairs Trotsky had emerged as the Bolshevik leader capable of guaranteeing the safety of the Red Cross Commission and of clarifying the role it would be permitted to play in Russia. He was certainly the man to see about the status of Allied representatives on Russian territory under Bolshevik command.

Just a month before these events, Robins, in a 7 October letter to his wife, had appraised Trotsky as "the most skillful and dangerous leader of the extreme left," and on 21 October, seventeen days before the Bolshevik Revolution—in a note in his pocket diary—he characterized Trotsky as a "curse of false spirit."[7] But quick to appreciate the realities of Bolshevik power, which had obviously created a new situation, Robins soon altered his evaluation. He understood that it was now time to set aside his earlier assessment of the newly installed commissar and to enter into discussions with him.

Many foreigners stationed in Petrograd believed that the Bolsheviks were "German agents, thieves and murderers" and warned against having anything to do with them. But in a speech delivered nine months after he left Russia, Robins remarked, "Suppose they are. In American politics [in Chicago] I have worked with folks . . . and there was . . . [no one] in Smolny any crookeder than some of them."

On 10 November Robins, together with his Russian-American guide and interpreter, Alexander Gumberg, climbed the dozen steps before the grand twenty-foot-high arches at the entrance to the Smolny Institute, "a great stone building in the center of the block, an iron fence all around it, and four big squares on the four sides."[8] It had been one of the most prestigious of Petrograd's girls' schools for the aristocracy before the Bolsheviks seized it and made it their headquarters. Lions' heads on the keystones peered down as guards with heavy machine guns examined the visitors' documents before permitting Robins and Gumberg to proceed.

The elegant halls and passageways, transformed into mess hall, barracks, and arsenal, smelled of soup, bread, bore oil, and gunpowder, and the meals of "the Red Guards and the People's Commissars [were] shared fraternally."[9] Robins and Gumberg passed through the busy corridors and arrived at the sentry post at the door to the little partitioned room that served as Trotsky's office. Robins, one of the first Americans ever to have been admitted, was met by a young captain who had earlier heard Robins denouncing the Bolshevik program to troops in the Petrograd barracks of the Provisional

Government. The Bolshevik captain confronted Robins threateningly, calling out, "Counter-revolutionist, Kerensky! Counter-revolutionist."

"You need be under no illusions regarding me," Robins responded through Gumberg, his interpreter,

"I was for Kerensky. I came here to serve my Government and help the Russian people, and I found Minister-President Kerensky at the head of the Russian Government, and I worked with him day by day, and so far as I had any power, I did my best to give him that power.

". . . I know a corpse when I see one, and . . . the thing to do with a corpse is to bury it and not sit up with it. Tell the Commissioner that I believe the Kerensky government is dead, and I believe he has got all the power there is in Russia today.

"Say to the Commissioner that I want to know whether he wants the American Red Cross to remain in Russia to help the Russian people. If the American Red Cross can remain in Russia without injuring our own national interests, if we can be on that basis, we will stay. If we cannot, we will go.

"Tell the Commissioner that so far as I know his program I am against it, but I am not going to interfere in domestic affairs in Russia. That is not my place.

"Say to the Commissioner that if Kaledin, Kornilov, or the Tsar had the same power he has this morning, I would be talking to Kornilov, Kaledin or the Tsar."[10]

Calmed, the captain admitted Robins to Trotsky's small office. Like the rest of the Smolny Institute, it showed the signs of grandeur of a bygone time.

Robins, 44; Trotsky, 38. A Christian evangelist and a Jewish atheist. Two who considered themselves champions of great causes. For one: complete social justice—the social gospel in the context of the individualistic, free-enterprise system, with labor's voice stronger than that of management. For the other: social, political, and economic equality in a Marxist communist system of proletarian dictatorship and ownership of the means of production. Both were a caricaturist's delight. Trotsky had thick, curly hair, a mustache and small goatee, broad forehead, tiny eyes and pince-nez—suggesting the intellectual. Robins was clean shaven, with short, straight, black hair, clean-cut face, piercing black eyes, and fiercely set jaw—the image of a determined preacher.

Robins stressed the very same issues with Trotsky that he had stressed with the militant captain. While Robins opposed the Bolshevik program on ideological grounds, he was committed to noninterference in the domestic affairs of Russia. What he had done for Kerensky was behind him and now he was convinced that American self-interest dictated negotiation and cooperation with the Bolsheviks. Gauging his impact on Trotsky, Robins rightly concluded that the commissar for foreign affairs found his points honest, realistic, and most importantly, mutually advantageous.[11]

Before he departed, Robins raised some practical problems. Tons of foodstuffs, clothing, medical supplies, blankets, and even ambulances had been sent to Russia by the American Red Cross. The commission had outlined careful strategies to assure that Red Cross supplies would be used at times and places of most urgent need. They had been warehoused and guarded. Later, Robins chose dramatic words to describe his first meeting with Trotsky, but it is doubtful he employed this confrontational tone:

> I want guards around my supplies, to protect the supplies from being stolen. Will you give me the guards, and will they take my orders? Trotsky said, "I will give you the guards and they will take your orders."
> He gave me the guards, and they took my orders.

In the months that followed, 400,000 cans of condensed milk, foodstuffs, blankets, clothing, and medical supplies were kept under armed Bolshevik guard, even through periods of desperate need and food riots. The foodstuffs and milk were being saved for the critical time between March and May, when stores always reached their lowest level and starvation posed the greatest threat.

In another encounter, on the afternoon of 21 December, Robins pressed Trotsky further, seeking to test his trustworthiness on a much more delicate, and politically explosive, matter. Robins urged Trotsky to allow him to send a thirty-two-car train carrying American Red Cross supplies from Petrograd to an American Red Cross post at Jassy, Romania. Robins pointed out that the train had to pass through famine districts; only armed guards could assure safe transit and delivery. Were the Bolsheviks in adequate control of the route? Was Trotsky prepared to supply the "Bolshevik rifles, with Bolshevik guards"?

Robins explained that such an act served America by saving Romania, which was fighting Germany. "I wanted a test," Robins continued emphatically. "If it got through, it would show two things, first, that 32 cars of supplies could be sent from Petrograd, which itself needed those supplies sorely, through a thousand miles of Bolshevik territory, into another land, and it would indicate their willingness to do it. . . . He said he would do it."

Two things demonstrate the importance of this further test. Many of the Allied ambassadors and foreign service officers believed that the Bolsheviks were in the pay of Germany. The suggested evidence was the willingness of the Bolsheviks to begin immediate peace negotiations with Germany. But Romania was still at war with Germany and Austria, and no agent of Germany would have permitted the shipment of supplies that would have been used against Germany. Second, most Allied observers were convinced that Bolshevik power was restricted to specific urban regions of Russia. The safe and swift delivery of the thirty-two cars of supplies through so extensive a stretch of territory would be an incontrovertible demonstration of far broader geographic distribution of Bolshevik power. Robins finished his story: "The train was loaded, packed and went in record time, and I hold the receipt of the commanding colonel of the American Red Cross of Romania, Col. [H. W.] Anderson, saying that every pound taken reached there. We never paid a dollar of graft to anybody. We never had any difficulty with it. It went through on Bolshevik frank, with Bolshevik rifles."[12]

Robins's first visit to Smolny was to shape the entire future course of relations between the Red Cross and the Bolshevik government. His clear purpose—to serve what he considered the best interests of American and Allied forces and, also, the interests of the Russian people—obviously appealed to Trotsky and, later, to Lenin. Acting from political realism and sharp instincts, which had convinced them of Robins's honesty, they welcomed the American Red Cross in Soviet Russia. They also agreed that this step would be mutually beneficial. As leaders of the revolution, Lenin and Trotsky obviously were pleased with Robins's appraisal of their power.

But serious objections emerged among Americans serving in Russia as Robins and his colleagues at the commission sought contact with the new Bolshevik government. A recent study of Robins's role in Russia argues that American decisions were "dictated by the war effort, not ideological concerns."[13] But, in fact, official American policymakers, particularly Secretary of State Robert Lansing, feared that direct contact with the Bolsheviks might be taken as de facto recognition of the new regime. The ambassador and the State Department strongly opposed any communication with the Bolshevik leadership—a policy in sharp contrast with the earlier, normal diplomatic intercourse that had existed between the United States and the czarist regime. What is more, Francis, Lansing, and the president welcomed the fall of the Russian autocracy and the United States quickly recognized the Provisional Government. The United States had not yet entered the war and the hope of a parliamentary democratic Russia was kindled. After the triumph of the Bolsheviks, recognition did not come for more than fifteen years.[14]

Robins quickly concluded that the Bolsheviks were not a fleeting phenomenon of revolutionary chaos. He believed that they could consolidate their power and remain in control—a view that most foreigners in Petrograd did not share. Those, such as Ambassador Francis, who held what Robins called "indoor opinion" awaited the imminent overthrow of the Bolsheviks by a counterrevolutionary czarist general. "I live in the Embassy," Francis wrote to Secretary of State Lansing, "and since the beginning of the revolution have not left it except to attend a meeting of the diplomatic corps and to take an occasional walk after dark." DeWitt Clinton Poole, American consul at Moscow, admitted: "I was not sufficiently sensitive to this driving power back of the Bolsheviks. In this regard, Judson [who shared Robins's thinking] was rather wiser than most of us who shared the belief of the Bolsheviks themselves that this was a flash success and would endure only a short time."[15]

To Robins and Judson, the truth about the revolution could be found only among the Russian masses. Their experience in that "outdoor" reality led them to the accurate evaluation of Bolshevik power and future prospects. Perhaps because Robins understood the staying power of the Bolsheviks, he was received openly and frequently at Smolny in the months that followed. In a speech reported in the Bolshevik party newspaper, *Pravda,* and forwarded by Ambassador Francis to the State Department, Trotsky publicly credited "the chief of the American Red Cross" with an understanding of the power of the Soviet regime. Such praise from Trotsky did not endear Robins to Francis, Poole, or most of the official diplomatic community. Arthur Bullard, a member of the Committee on Public Information in Petrograd, was, for a time, one of the exceptions. "On the whole he [Trotsky] seems fairly well disposed towards Americans," Bullard reported to his superiors in Washington, "and has a real personal regard for Col. Robins, in whom he recognizes a strong fearless, honest man."[16]

Trotsky's acceptance of Robins as a reliable and truthful negotiating partner was matched by a mutual acceptance by Robins, especially following Trotsky's immediate demonstration of good faith. The deliberations of the two men during the eight months following that meeting lent support to that trust.

"Trotsky, 38 years old," Robins recalled, in his most extensive appraisal of the Bolshevik leader, "Russian Hebrew, exile, revolutionist, agitator, writer of very considerable ability; twelve years ago wrote a book in which he worked out his whole program, just what he is trying to do in Russia; has written a number of volumes, and very excellent reading they are, that is, if you care for that kind of reading at all. I do not mean excellent in their programs, but excellent in their structure, excellent in their method of writing." Robins is certainly not alone in this evaluation of Trotsky as writer and political analyst. Isaac Deutscher speaks of *Our Revolution* (one of the books to which Robins referred) as "his chief work of this period . . . the fundamental statement of 'Trotskyism.'" Deutscher, far more familiar with the body of Marx's and Marxist writing than Robins, goes considerably further in his evaluation: "This was the most radical restatement, if not revision, of the prognosis of Socialist revolution undertaken since Marx's *Communist Manifesto,* that is since 1847."[17]

It is clear that Robins never read any of Trotsky's works before he had arrived or during his stay in Russia, unless Alexander Gumberg had taken the time to translate them for him. Given the pace of activity through those bewildering months, that possibility can be ruled out. However, in New York in 1918, acting as Trotsky's literary agent, Gumberg assisted in the publication of an English translation of *Our Revolution.* Gumberg had carried the Russian manuscript with him when he returned to the United States with Robins. In all probability Robins was referring to this book in his speech. And in all likelihood it was Gumberg who had provided Robins with his analysis of the text.[18]

Robins, the man who was a master public speaker for more than twenty-five years, went on to evaluate Trotsky's talents before a mass audience. "Trotsky is the most competent and powerful orator I have ever known. I have known most of the public speakers of my own country and of the Anglo-Saxon world in my generation, and I regard Trotsky as easily the most powerful forensic debater and master of an assembly by public speech that I have ever known. I think he can do more with a mass of people by the spoken word than any man I have ever seen make the attempt."[19]

Most contemporaries agreed with Robins about Trotsky's oratorical skill. The Americans John Reed and Albert Rhys Williams greatly admired Trotsky from the moment of "first hearing him speak and feeling his dynamic quality."[20] In *The Prophet Armed,* Isaac Deutscher explains that after an early traumatic experience at public speaking, Trotsky went on to extraordinary accomplishments as part of his revolutionary work. "This is one of those instances of latent unsuspected talent, bursting forth in exuberant vitality to delight and amaze all who witness it. His speech, even more than his writing, was distinguished by a rare intensity of thought, imagination, emotion, and expression."[21]

Far more complicated than Robins's assessment of Trotsky as political thinker, analyst, writer, and orator is his judgment of Trotsky's mercurial and egocentric behavior, traits Robins shared.

> But Trotsky has the limitation of his gifts. Trotsky . . . loves a crowd, loves the footlights and the bands and the paraphernalia. I think if you would get a large enough crowd together and Trotsky could make a speech to it, he would let you hang him afterwards, he so loves the personal expression to the crowd. He is a sort of prima donna. In the hours of victory he is high-handed and heady and unreasonable and hard to drive. In hours of defeat he is moody and gloomy and irascible and difficult to make pull a load. He lacks that steadiness and patient quality and sureness under strain that is the chief characteristic of Lenin.[22]

Robins could appreciate evaluating Trotsky's oratorical skill and knew his own expertise in that field carried great weight. He may have enjoyed the idea of being compared to Trotsky. But never for a moment, could he have permitted himself to see the parallels in their dispositions and personalities. In every detail of his remarks on Trotsky's personality, Robins could have been providing a perceptive description of himself. Like Trotsky, he fought hard and then soared to joyous heights after victory; in "failure," he plummeted to debilitating depression and, unlike Trotsky, sometimes took months to recuperate from physical and emotional strain.

Louis Fischer, a foreign correspondent and eyewitness to events in Russia after the Revolution, wrote about Trotsky in 1964: "Lenin was as selfless as the human animal can be. Trotsky had a prima donna's sensitivity. It is doubtful whether Lenin could be hurt by hostility. Trotsky suffered. His ego was as great as his gifts. Indeed, while he deferred to Lenin he was also jealous of him."[23]

Robins was a missionary, an evangelist "industrial knight errant" in the cause of the social gospel and social justice in Russia as well as in the United States. He was "above all, a flaming orator of marvelous power, commander of humor, satire, tenderness, emotional appeal in their finest forms." R. H. Bruce Lockhart, Robins's counterpart in the British diplomatic mission, wrote in his memoirs that Robins "was a wonderful orator. His conversation, like Mr. Churchill's, was always a monologue, but it was never dull. With his black hair and aquiline features, he had a most striking appearance. He was an Indian chief with a Bible as tomahawk."[24]

Robins was committed to making a great mark in the world after a childhood of suffering and rejection. Russia, in revolutionary ferment, provided the opportunity to seize an initiative in a just battle against ignorance, myopia, and bureaucratic strictures. In this urgent situation Robins was able to reconcile his Christianity and democratic instincts with the goals of Bolshevism in struggling Russia. His psychological needs could be fulfilled. He could "go the distance" in Russia, in what he called, "his greatest crusade."[25] But Louis Fischer, writing about Robins and his like-minded British and French counterparts, R. H. Bruce Lockhart and Capt. Jacques Sadoul, provides a harsh summation of their roles: "They thought they were writing history. In any event, they wrote themselves into history."[26] While this brevity and wit provide an insight, the complexity of this story is not adequately served by such a dismissal.

In weeks following the Bolshevik seisure of power the Allies worried about what Russia would do about the war. Would the Bolsheviks sign an armistice with the Central Powers? Certainly one issue on which all Allied representatives in Petrograd—including Robins—could agree was that an armistice and a separate peace must be avoided at all cost. But the Allies were seriously divided on how to stop a separate peace. Robins believed that direct confrontation, personal contact, and open exchange would achieve results. In fact, Robins pursued these avenues with independent initiatives, despite his government's reservations, leading to frequent misunderstandings and conflicts with the State Department and other Washington representatives.

Prior to Robins's meeting with Trotsky, members of the Red Cross mission, not knowing what to expect from the Bolsheviks, had stood twenty-four-hour guard protecting their quarters. Trotsky gave assurances of safety to Robins and to General Judson, the American military attaché in Petrograd. Others from the American military mission in Petrograd had also seen Trotsky or Gen. M. A. Muravyev, the Bolshevik military commander of the Petrograd district, and calm was restored. Commission members then formulated plans to meet the new situation.[27] "The plan of Thompson to support the Kerensky Government now left the American Red Cross as a counter-revolutionary influence. The former position had to be changed. Rather than 'save the Revolution of Kerensky by fighting the German imperialists,' it had to be 'save the position of the revolutionary All-Russian Soviet by opposing German imperialists.'"[28]

On their own initiative, Thompson and Robins agreed that the new situation demanded a dramatic, symbolic change at the top of the commission leadership. The American Red Cross had supported Kerensky to keep Russia in the World War. Robins and Thompson had hoped to identify popular revolutionary appeal with the Kerensky government and to depict the "German imperialists" as the major enemy of the revolution. Robins had understood that the Russian masses would fight to save the revolution rather than continue to fight the Germans and Austrians, to acquire territory, or to entrench reactionary policy, which in part had first led the Czar to enter the war on the side of the Allies. The two Red Cross leaders opposed the Bolsheviks primarily because Lenin and Trotsky called for Russian withdrawal from the war. Thompson, the multimillionaire, and Robins, the democratic social reformer, also feared Bolshevik revolutionary Marxist ideology. But with Robins's "outdoor mind," his eyes were open to the realities before him; throughout the months in Russia, he observed and learned.

Robins had played a key role in a propaganda campaign to support Kerensky's Provisional Government. Meanwhile, in their own defense, the Bolsheviks had carried on their own countercampaign, designed to undermine the credibility of the humanitarian purpose of the Red Cross Commission. The Bolsheviks had alleged that the March Revolution, which had toppled the Romanovs, had been supported by Wall Street capital and that Colonel Thompson's true aim was the ultimate domination by American business interests of the postwar Russian economy. One report, published in *Pravda,* repeated the accusation that Thompson had been "trying to get the Trans-Siberian [Railroad] for the Morgans and copper interests for himself."

Shortly after the Bolshevik Revolution, *Pravda* also published a letter, written by Vladimir Badrylov, former secretary to Catherine Breshkovsky, who opposed the Bolsheviks. The letter documented the fact that Thompson had given $1 million of his own funds and had promised enormous additional sums to the SRs. The propaganda campaign in support of the Kerensky government was intended to assure its continued participation in the war.[29] Once the Bolsheviks were in power, though, realism demanded a new strategy. Thompson and Robins still believed that Russia could be kept as a combatant against the common enemy, but this time the appeal had to be made to the Russian masses and Bolshevik leadership in the name of the Bolshevik-controlled "revolutionary All-Russian Soviet," so seriously threatened by the "German imperialists."

Against this background, Thompson became *persona non grata* in Bolshevik Russia. Further undermining his role in Russia and influence in Washington was the swashbuckling image he had cut for himself since his arrival three months earlier. While the wisdom of his cavalier distribution of a million dollars and his call to Washington to keep up the flow of cash to the Kerensky regime was clear to Robins and Judson, others, including the ambassador, were highly critical. Lansing also held Thompson responsible for Robins's unauthorized meetings with Bolshevik leaders. Still, the Red Cross Commission had an essential task to perform—the distribution of the emergency supplies.[30]

Thompson's departure was imperative. No fresh response could have been undertaken in light of Thompson's activities against the Bolsheviks. Robins was formally put in command on 27 November, the day of Thompson's departure. As new head of the commission, Robins could manage the transition in Red Cross policy. Despite the necessity for Thompson's departure, Ambassador Francis alleged that his leaving was really an escape, dictated by fear—a charge Francis repeated more than a year later before the Senate subcommittee investigating Bolshevik propaganda.[31] Robins had already completed his testimony when he learned of these allegations. He demanded the opportunity to testify a second time to assert, unqualifiedly: "That there was no man in Russia during that entire critical period who was less frightened at anything than William B. Thompson, and no man who left in less haste. He left, largely at my earnest request, that he should go out by way of England, and that he would make an effort to get a correct understanding . . . in England."[32]

According to Robins's extensive testimony, nearly all the British representatives in Petrograd were extremely conservative, if not reactionary. Typical was General Knox, their military attaché, who had given support to the abortive "uprising" of the pro-czarist Gen. Lavar G. Kornilov on 3 September 1917. From Robins's and Thompson's point of view, such blindness to Russian realities placed the Allies in grave jeopardy. They feared that Allied support for the Czar's lost cause would speed revolutionary Russia's departure from the war.

Thompson hoped to bring about a change in British policy and personnel in Russia. On his return trip to the United States, he met with his friend and business associate, Thomas W. Lamont, in London. Through Lamont's connections, a luncheon meeting with Prime Minister David Lloyd George was arranged at No. 10 Downing Street. Thompson began their two hours together by presenting the prime minister with a nine-point memorandum summarizing his experience and thinking on Allied policy in Russia during his tenure as head of the Red Cross mission. "The Russian situation is lost and Russia lies entirely open to unopposed German exploitation," Thompson began, "unless a radical reversal of policy is at once undertaken by the Allies."[33]

In his memorandum and reinforced in conversation, Thompson expressed his conviction that Allied cooperation with the Bolsheviks could result in a continued Russian role in the war. Lamont recalled that Thompson affirmed that "the new government was not under German influence," and quoted Thompson specifically:

"At present they are nobody's Bolsheviks. Don't let us let Germany make them her Bolsheviks. Let's make them our Bolsheviks."

Lloyd George liked that idea. "Lets make them our Bolsheviks," he repeated.

It was agreed that an interallied commission be created "to approach the new Russian rulers and seek a basis of cooperation with them."[34]

In response to the Thompson interview, Lloyd George appointed Robert H. Bruce Lockhart as British special commissioner to Russia. Lockhart had earlier spent seven years there, four as acting British consul general in Moscow. He read and spoke Russian well and was young enough and potentially open enough to appreciate the "outdoor" facts and outlook that Robins was to put before him. Lloyd George telegraphed Lockhart and asked that he meet him in London to discuss the important matter. Robins's account of the conversation between the prime minister and Lockhart, who had returned to Scotland from Moscow just the previous September, was given before the Senate subcommittee:

> Mr. Lockhart then told me that the premier had said to him something in substance like this: "I have just had a most surprising talk with an American Red Cross colonel named Thompson, who tells me of the Russian situation. I do not know whether he is right, but I know that our people are wrong. They have missed the situation. You are being sent as special commissioner to Russia, with power. A ship will be ready to take you to Stockholm as soon as you are ready, and you will be able to select your staff and have ample resources. I want you to find a man there named Robins, who was put in command by this man Thompson. Find out what he is doing with this Soviet government. Look it over carefully. If you think what he is doing is sound, do for Britain what he is trying to do for America. That seems on the whole the best outlook on this complex situation; but you are given liberty. Go to it."[35]

Thompson continued on to Washington, where he attempted to win the president and the State Department from their no contact, nonrecognition position. Although he used his considerable influence among his many highly placed contacts, including George Creel, chairman of the Committee on Public Information, nonetheless he failed. He was never allowed to talk directly with Wilson and was granted only a brief opportunity to speak to Lansing. Thompson had been stereotyped, both in the administration and in the press, as a dupe and a potentially dangerous individual.[36]

There is written evidence of only one occasion when President Wilson seriously considered the recognition of the Bolshevik government as a means of countering German influence and possibly keeping Russia in the war. On 20 January 1918 he wrote to Lansing asking, "How shall we deal with the Bolsheviki? This particular suggestion seems to have something in it worth considering." The note was attached to a cable, dated 14 January, Copenhagen, from an American diplomat, suggesting recognition of the Bolsheviks as the most advisable course under the circumstances. Nothing came of this expression of interest, nor from a number of later presidential initiatives that involved the prospect of negotiations with the Bolsheviks.

A year later, in December 1918, Wilson requested that William H. Buckler, American attaché at the London embassy, engage in talks with Maxim Litvinov, the Soviet government's unofficial representative in London, for the purpose of better understanding the Bolshevik leaders. Like Thompson's cold reception in Washington, which foreshadowed the treatment Robins experienced on his return, negotiation toward recognition failed.[37]

With Thompson's departure, Robins was left with five American Red Cross members to assist him. Thomas D. Thacher and James W. Andrews were there from the first, as secretary and treasurer respectively. D. Heywood Hardy was the one member to accompany Robins back to the United States at the time of his recall. Allen Wardwell, a resourceful assistant, undertook many dangerous missions, including two trips in midwinter to the White Sea port of Murmansk. Eventually, Wardwell took command, upon Robins recommendation, when Robins returned to the States. William B. Webster, from Wisconsin, joined the commission after it had been in Petrograd for some time. He had served the American embassy at Petrograd as a representative in central Siberia, working on prisoner of war issues. It was as Robins's representative that Webster investigated Allied and anti-Bolshevik charges that the Bolsheviks were arming prisoners of war in Siberia.[38] Robins's small group was dedicated to a broader appreciation of American-Soviet relations. On 20 November Robins wrote to his wife:

> I will be in command of these five and they will be loyal to me, let come what may. We have all been tried in the fire and are ready for what comes. It has been a curious development by which I have been slowly moved from the position of least consequence to the command of the last stand in Russia. I am more grateful for this than I can say. It is a final vindication for my days work. If we can now serve America and the Democratic purpose of the world to some genuine end—I am wholly content let the final cost, be what it may.[39]

Robins had good reason to believe his first position on the commission to have been of little consequence; his name was even misspelled as "Robbins" on commission stationery.

One of those drawn to Robins during September 1917 was Alexander Gumberg.[40] It was through Gumberg that Robins made his initial contact with the leading Bolsheviks and through Gumberg that Robins maintained his links to the new government.

Born in the Ukraine in 1887, Alexander Gumberg had emigrated to the United States at age fifteen, part of the tide of Jews seeking refuge from czarist oppression. His older brother, Sergei, had visited the United States briefly and returned to Russia in 1917, where he joined the Bolshevik party. Sergei assumed the revolutionary pseudonym Zorin.

As a young man, growing up in New York's Lower East Side, Alexander became involved in socialist politics. For a time, beginning in 1914, he managed the Russian-language American Socialist newspaper *Novy Mir* (The New World). Early in 1917, just prior to the March Revolution, Leon Trotsky had made Gumberg's acquaintance during Trotsky's brief sojourn in New York City. It was then that Trotsky wrote two articles for *Novy Mir*. Soon thereafter, as with his brother and Trotsky, Gumberg returned to Russia. But Alex arrived in Russia as an American citizen and a business representative of an American corporation. That spring, in Petrograd, he was introduced to the various American missions and was engaged to assist them as both translator and guide.[41]

Gumberg first worked for the American Red Cross Commission during its effort to support Kerensky, but after the Bolshevik Revolution, his close and trusting associations with the leaders of the party in power made his services almost indispensable. It was through Gumberg that Robins had arranged his first meeting with Trotsky. Gumberg served as Robins's interpreter, translator, guide, liaison, secretary, and even alter ego. In analyzing the complexities of the first chaotic months of Soviet power, Gumberg had the great advantage of being able to view the revolutionary situation from multiple perspectives. As a democratic socialist, he saw the revolution as the fulfillment of the hopes of the Russian masses who had been ignored for centuries. As a native, he sympathized with Russian suffering. As the younger brother of a devoted Bolshevik, he had access to the views of men making the revolution. But he saw the path to socialism far more flexibly than the disciplined Bolshevik party members did. As a man who reached maturity in New York City, he had gained a critical appreciation of American institutions. While he had indisputably chosen the United States as his homeland, he also carried a Russian passport.

Gumberg was keen of mind and sharp of wit. His insights into the nature of the social and economic fabric of human institutions precluded pat formulas or ideological dogmatism. His insights extended to the nuances of personality of people around him. Albert Rhys Williams, although not a member of the party, stood ideologically with John Reed, a self-proclaimed Bolshevik. Here, writing at the time of the Revolution, Williams captured the essence of Gumberg's personality: "Gumberg . . . baited us, but he baited the Bolsheviks too, and his grinning skepticism was not lost on his employers at the embassy, for that matter. Even when he and Raymond Robins were revealing a growing mutual respect, and Gumberg was of invaluable aid to him, Alex could not resist occasionally poking fun."[42]

Gumberg remained at Robins's side throughout the months following the Bolshevik seizure of power, sharing Robins's uncompromising realism as well as the firm conviction that realism demanded contact, communication, and cooperation between the United States and the new regime. It was with this goal in mind that Robins asked Gumberg to return to the United States with him in May 1918. With his unique experience in both countries, Gumberg grasped the full positive prospect of Soviet-American cooperation and, along with Robins and other allies they could muster, worked toward that end.

Writing decades later, from his firsthand experience and with affection, appreciation, and no small measure of irony, Albert Rhys Williams aptly summed up Gumberg's contribution. "And though Alex and not [John] Reed would wind up on Wall Street, many knowing people would say . . . that, keeping always out of the limelight, this strangely fascinating, provocative, mysterious Gumberg played as important a role in the long effort to obtain recognition of the Soviets as any other one person."[43]

Gumberg worked on Wall Street in the 1920s and 1930s as director of the Amtorg Corporation, a Soviet-American trading company, and with Chase National (now Chase Manhattan) Bank. His connections with Robins and Thompson and their circle of influential friends helped initiate commercial ties between the two countries. Because the United States did not extend diplomatic recognition to the Soviet Union until 1933, Gumberg's financial work played a far more important role in Soviet-American relations during those fifteen years than one might have expected.

So the American Red Cross position in Russia was redefined in terms of Robins's newly acquired leadership and with the mission now safeguarded by Trotsky's assurances. The mission's humanitarian work, the ostensible reason for its being in Russia, could proceed. On the political and military front, Robins saw two priorities: to counter the Bolshevik commitment to withdrawing Russia from the war, and reversing U.S. policy toward the Lenin government.

Action on those commitments began at nightfall on 8 November, after the Bolshevik seizure of power, when 670 delegates to the Second All-Russia Congress of Soviets of Workers' and Soldiers' Deputies met in the Hall of Columns at Smolny. Robins, just back from Gatchina, completed his report on the dissolution of Kerensky's forces and hurried to Smolny to witness the historic congress. Lenin, the mastermind of the Bolshevik Revolution, was to speak, and hundreds in that hall, including Robins, John Reed, and Albert Rhys Williams, were seeing Lenin for the first time.

How extraordinary, the pace and extent of Robins's activities! On that same day, 8 November, he made the arduous journey of sixty miles to and from Gatchina, beginning early in the morning. He returned late in the afternoon, "exhausted as never before in his life," made his report to Thompson, arrived "early" in the evening to witness the Second Congress of Soviets, and remained there until it ended the following morning. Is it any wonder that Somerset Maugham wrote to his friend Elizabeth, Robins's sister, "He can go all day without food. He can go all night without sleep—he isn't human"? But Robins was all too human, and the physical and emotional price he paid for his ceaseless, driven activity was commensurate with his staggering accomplishments.[44]

Lenin's delivery of the "Decree on Peace," one of the most dramatic moments in the history of the Revolution, fulfilled the first rallying cry of "Peace, land and bread," the slogan instrumental in bringing the Bolsheviks to power. Lev Kamenev, a member of the Central Committee of the Bolshevik party, presided and introduced Lenin. With a sheaf of papers in one hand, Lenin quickly walked to the platform. Albert Rhys Williams recorded the excitement and his own riveted attention "on the short stocky figure in the thick worn suit," but took a moment to observe that others were similarly struck, including "Raymond Robins, whom I could see staring at Lenin with those large burning black eyes (he was there early and stuck it out until five in the morning)."[45]

Among other things, Lenin's "Decree on Peace" called for all belligerents to convene armistice negotiations and a peace conference to end the war. It also called for a fair and democratic peace, without territorial seizures and without indemnities. While similar terms were developed further in President Wilson's famous "Fourteen Points" speech, presented exactly two months later (and, to some extent, in answer to Lenin's decree), the Allied leaders were not yet disposed to sue for peace. They were certain they could win, because the full advantage of U.S. entry on the Allied side had just begun to be felt on the western front. They viewed the "Decree on Peace" as Bolshevik propaganda, a ploy to engineer a separate peace. Lenin's appeal surely would be rejected by Russia's wartime allies.

When the Bolsheviks formally communicated the text of the decree to foreign embassies in Petrograd on 21 November, Robins commented in a letter to his wife, "It is the most moving and impossible and tremendous action in the history of man. Only face to face can I tell you all that is involved in this consummation of what the whole world desires in fact, by the proclamation of an irresponsible handful of adventurers."[46]

Robins recognized that the Bolshevik pressure for a separate peace with Germany and Austria was in response to the desperation of Russian soldiers and peasants. Yet Lenin's war policy was clearly opposed to the Allied need to keep the Russian army at the eastern front. For the remainder of his stay in Russia, Robins struggled with this central conflict.

Robins had tried to convince Ambassador Francis and the State Department that it would be in the best interests of the United States to engage in direct negotiations with the Bolshevik leaders. But U.S. policymakers were unwilling to enter into talks with Lenin and Trotsky because the Bolsheviks were committed to an immediate peace. Intelligence reports had also claimed that the Bolsheviks were "in the pay" of Germany. Few foreign policy "experts" believed the new government would stay in power for more than a few weeks. And perhaps worst of all, the Bolsheviks had done the unpardonable—they had published, without consultation or prior notification, secret treaties negotiated between the Allies and the czarist government. What is more, the new regime had renounced responsibility for the hundreds of millions of dollars of the Czar's foreign debts. Finally, their

Marxist, revolutionary, communist rhetoric and ideology were so despised and feared that diplomatic exchange was not considered possible.

In December, Robins wrote to Margaret, "The situation is difficult almost beyond mastery." For Lenin, continuing the war would have undermined the consolidation of embryonic Bolshevik power that was so critically based on fulfillment of the promise of "Peace, land and bread." Concluding a treaty with autocratic, militaristic Germany represented no real ideological compromise for the Bolsheviks. Party leaders expected that, before long, most European governments would collapse anyway as proletarian revolution spread throughout the world. While Robins also anticipated that the Hohenzollern and Habsburg dynasties would soon fall, he and most Western observers believed that some form of constitutional or parliamentary democracy would emerge in Germany and Austria. And yet Robins continued in that December letter to his wife, "I have faith in the outcome for democracy and for the winning of the struggle between the autocratic militaristic forces and the self-governing free men of the world and the conclusion in general peace that will be the defeat of German autocracy without the abiding injury of the German people."[47]

Robins agreed with the conventional wisdom: The old German society would be defeated with soldiers on the battlefield, not with workers in the streets. While excited by the brazenness of Lenin's decree, nonetheless he understood that he could not support it—to do so would have betrayed his mission.

Margaret Dreier Robins was a first-generation German-American, with strong family ties to the Fatherland. She spoke German fluently and had played a minor role in the German-American community in her native New York. The photograph of her that Robins carried with him throughout his Russian experience was taken in her ancestral home in Germany. As he worked to defeat German autocratic militarism, he also appreciated, perhaps more than most Americans, and surely more than most British and French leaders, the need to safeguard the German people from "injury." By 1917 the popular tide of anti-German sentiment in the Allied countries had reached its peak. Margaret and her husband were deeply pained by those who failed to distinguish between the autocratic leadership and the ordinary people of Germany.

"Each hour the situation here grows more grave," Robins wrote to Margaret on 20 December, five days after the signing of the German-Soviet armistice. "Civil War is now added to the troubles of a sick and suffering Russia and starvation may very well claim more than has the Great War from among the Slavic host."[48]

Just one month later, having received no response to the "Decree on Peace" from either Allied or enemy authorities, the Bolshevik leaders wired Gen. Nicholas N. Dukhonin, commander-in-chief of the Russian forces on the eastern front, to make immediate contact with his German counterpart and propose a truce. Dukhonin, a holdover from the czarist army general staff and staunch opponent of the Bolsheviks, stalled for time. Two days later, with the approval of the Council of People's Commissars, Lenin, Stalin, and Ensign Nikolai V. Krylenko, telephoned Dukhonin at his headquarters in Mogilev, 450 miles south of Petrograd and some 300 miles east of Brest-Litovsk, where the Russo-German peace negotiations were to take place. Beginning at 2:00 A.M. and lasting two and a half hours, Dukhonin parried and balked at the demands of the Bolshevik leadership that he initiate armistice talks. According to part of the verbatim record of the conversation published in the Petrograd Soviet newspaper *Rabochy i Soldat* (Worker and Soldier), Dukhonin finally asserted "that the peace Russia needs can be obtained only by a central government," clearly suggesting that the Bolsheviks did not qualify as such. Krylenko, speaking for the three men, then dismissed the general from his command, ordering him to continue at his post and carry out their orders pending arrival of a replacement. The record of the conversation concludes, "Ensign Krylenko is appointed Commander-in-Chief."[49]

On the day that Krylenko finally reached Mogilev to relieve Dukhonin of his command and in contravention of orders to "place them under guard in order to avert acts of summary justice unworthy of a revolutionary army and to prevent these generals from escaping the trial that awaits them," Dukhonin was dragged from his railway car by a group of soldiers and killed. In the same issue of *Rabochy i Soldat,* over the signature of Lenin and Krylenko, Russian soldiers at the front were called upon to "immediately elect representatives to start formal negotiations for an armistice with the enemy." The negotiation process, begun in this way, concluded on 15 December, with the signing of the Russo-German armistice.[50]

What now justified the presence of the American Red Cross Commission in Russia? The food and other aid provided by the commission were support for Russia's military effort. But from the moment of his arrival, Robins saw the urgent need to carry out other—political—activities to strengthen Russia's contribution to the war effort. At that moment, American boys were dying on the western front; many more would die if Russia stopped fighting. The Russo-German armistice talks and the spectre of final Russian withdrawal from the war would mean that the commission had failed. "Our diplomacy is past speaking about," Robins wrote to his wife, in his 20 December letter. At a time when a major American diplomatic initiative should have been carried out, "I, a Red Cross man am the only person in any authority that is permitted by our government to have any direct intercourse with the de facto government that has complete control of over three fourths of Russian territory and more than five sixths of the bayonets of the Russian people." General Judson and members of his staff agreed, as did some others. "I want to hammer this point home," Arthur Bullard declared to his superiors in Washington in his report on conditions in Russia through December. "Instructions should be sent telling the Embassy and the Missions to go the limit in cooperation with the present de facto government—short of formal recognition."[51]

Throughout the twenty-five days of the Brest-Litovsk negotiations, Robins explored alternatives to interrupt or cause the breakdown of those discussions. He was convinced that if the Allies, and particularly the United States, made offers of military and economic assistance to the Leninist government, the Russians would hold out for armistice terms that would be unacceptable to the Germans and lead to the abandonment of negotiations and the resumption of hostilities. But every plan and option necessitated direct communication with the Bolshevik leadership.

13

Robins and Lenin

CURIOUSLY, as the obvious need for deeper contact and communication with the Bolshevik government grew more urgent, Washington persisted with the directive that official representatives were not to interact with the Bolsheviks. Robins's level of frustration intensified. At first, he was among those who were prohibited from having anything to do with the Lenin government. But as crises multiplied, and as the need for contact increased, Robins was permitted to intervene "unofficially." Technically, he headed a private humanitarian organization, funded by public subscription. Like all members of the American Red Cross in Russia, he had been given a military commission before leaving America. At first a major, he was "promoted" to the rank of lieutenant colonel of the U.S. Army, wearing his uniform at all times. This was conveniently overlooked by the State Department when he was given his "unofficial" status.

Had Robins been alone in his conviction that American-Soviet rapprochement was essential to the national interest, his efforts would have been pointless. But tempting his hopes and nurturing his plans were a limited, yet influential, number of men among the Petrograd diplomatic community. Lloyd George sent R. H. Bruce Lockhart to Petrograd to establish "unofficial" contact, much as Robins had done; but even before Lockhart's arrival, Robins could count on the support of a handful of fellow members of the Red Cross Commission. Also committed to Robins's approach was General Judson, who wired his superiors at the War College Staff in Washington of his concern: "The loss of our facilities for written and telegraphic communication or for doing any business here may soon result from the troubles arising from our studied non-intercourse with the Soviet Government on minor matters as to which they possess power."[1]

Another ally in the struggle for official communication with the Lenin government was Arthur Bullard. A capable and perceptive essayist and journalist, Bullard was a personal and unofficial emissary to Russia of President Wilson's close friend and policy advisor Col. Edward M. House. Bullard, of all the American's who witnessed the Bolshevik Revolution, may well have had the closest connection with the president on matters relative to Russia during this period. Bullard's correspondence with Washington was prolific. A newcomer to the official community in Petrograd, Edgar Sisson likewise joined the Robins camp enthusiastically. Sisson, a newspaperman and publicist, headed the Russian department of the Committee on Public Information (COMPUB), which was responsible for propaganda and intelligence operations in Allied countries.

Sisson was dispatched by Washington to evaluate Thompson's "propaganda project" in support of the Provisional Government. However, Sisson did not arrive in Petrograd until 25 November, more than two weeks after the Kerensky government fell. With the ostensible reason for his mission having collapsed, Sisson applied himself to the task of influencing Russia to remain in the war. Bullard, with the strong Washington support of both Colonel House and the chairman of COMPUB, George Creel, who also shared President Wilson's complete support and confidence, joined the Sisson group of COMPUB in Petrograd. Until the first days of February 1918, Sisson, Bullard, and Robins worked toward their common goal—avoiding a separate peace.[2]

"Bullard . . . alone," wrote George Kennan in 1956, "of all the members of the official American community, succeeded in producing written analyses of the situation that achieved independent literary and historical distinction, not lost after the passage of nearly forty years."[3] One of Bullard's reports to Creel, in Washington, on the work of the American Red Cross mission, and on Robins in particular, provides an excellent example of Bullard's thinking. Under a heading marked "CONFIDENTIAL," he wrote one of the most laudatory eyewitness statements on record of Robins's work in Russia:

> There has been a regrettable amount of friction over here between some of the American Missions. Sisson has done a very good job in smoothing a good deal of it down, but some remains and some rumbles of it may reach Washington. Some of their enemies may try to spring a scandal on the Red Cross Mission and it is against that possibility that I make this report.
>
> I suppose that you know Raymond Robbins [sic] personally. I did not till I met him here, although of course I had heard of him before. Among other things I knew that he had followed Roosevelt into the Hughes camp and had done his little utmost to swing the better elements of the Progressive Party with him. From what I see of him here, I judge that when he fights, he does it so wholeheartedly that his opponents do not quickly forget it. And I do not suppose that there is any great cordiality towards him in the camp of the Administration.
>
> But whether or not he has been on the right side before, he has been and is on the right side here. Of all the officials of our Government, whose trail I have encountered here, he has been the most important, the most intelligent, the most most [sic] single minded in his patriotism and the most sympathetic to democracy—in short the best American. In these qualities he has been not only pre-eminent, but—unfortunately—almost unique. The situation here has had too much resemblance to the Mexican Affair. Most of the President's representative[s] have been entirely out of accord with that fine patience towards the mistakes of a struggling Democracy, which has marked Mr. Wilson's policies. Robbins has been as far as I have seen the only man here—at least the

only man of force—who has had, has sought to have, any sympathy for or insight into this tragedy of revolution. It is strange to me how much less democratic some people . . . are abroad then [sic] they are at home. Crane, for instance, whom I like and respect, is one of our best democrats at home. Here, he quit the minute his little group of friends get lost in the appalling shuffle.

Robbins has gone clear through. I have seen a number of reports, which he wrote at intervals of several weeks, and I have been above all impressed by his ability to keep his mind moving with the events. (And believe me that takes some agility here.)

This has been a desperately hard post for everybody. It has been a case of building on the sands—with the foundations washing out every few days. Robbins is the kind, who begin on the building again before the echoes of the crash have died down.

His greatest achievement to my mind has been the way he swung the Red Cross Mission. As it started from America, it was composed of two elements: one, technical men, who had little knowledge of or interest in social or political matters and who did not think it was the "correct thing" for them to consider such problems; two, the business men, led by Col. Thompson—a regular fellow, rough neck, self-made copper king, who had left the semi-respectable job of mining for Wall Street piracy. He believed in "things as they are if it isn't possible to go back to the good old days of Mark Hanna." His satellites were mostly "little brothers of the rich."

Robbins was the only honest to God Democrat in the bunch. He pulled off a missionary stunt which was a wonder. It started when the ship left the dock at home and he delivered the Mission in Petrograd, prepared to [see] that there was something in this talk about world-wide democracy and that perhaps the day of Grand Dukes was passed. I don't suppose that Thompson—a good scout at heart—had ever in all his life talked to a man with such subversive ideas as Kerensky. Out in Butte, they string that kind of undesirable citizens up to a railroad bridge. Robbins did the unbelievable thing of getting the Mission to support the Provisional Government wholeheartedly and kept the Red Cross out of the dirty intrigues of the Kornilov affair, in which almost all the Allied diplomacy got its fingers soiled.

He persuaded Thompson to put up some real money to support the Breshkovsky Committee. I did not know anything about this at the time. If I had been consulted, I would have encouraged the enterprise. It certainly was the best bet. . . .

I write about it at length because I fear that some of those here who dislike Robbins or are jealous of the Red Cross may try to make more out of it than its seriousness warrants. If the matter does not cause any stir at home, keep it quiet. But if a newspaper story breaks on it, it will be well for you to have some idea of what happened.

My own comment on the affair is—Nothing ventured, nothing gained. The Red Cross Mission took a chance. It was their best judgment at the time. It was the best judgment of everybody here who was at the same time trying to keep Russia in the war and at the same time trying to help them in their struggle for democracy. (The Diplomats of some of our allies are very much more deeply involved in the anti-democratic conspiracy of Kornilov.) If Robbins made a false play, it was an error of head not of heart. This victory of the Bolsheviki has been a body blow to all of us. Robbins had recovered his breath and his nerve quicker than any of us and has jumped into the job of building something new on entirely new specifications. We who are here can see the real value of his work. He has done more than any other individual here to win a little respect and trust for our country. I doubt if anywhere in any of the theaters of the war the President's highmindedness and idealism has had a better representative.

My criticism of Robbins' activity is confined to one point. I wish that the work he is doing could be done by someone not in the uniform of the Red Cross. There are a lot of people, of whom I am one, who do not like to see the Red Cross used as camouflage. Robbins is a high class political agent. His activity here has been of the very highest order. I'm sorry that he was done up in a Red Cross uniform.[4]

It is a strange irony, particularly given the unfolding of events that ultimately pitted Arthur Bullard against Robins, that Bullard was a declared Socialist and soon became a fierce anti-Bolshevik, while Robins, a declared anti-Socialist, sought Bolshevik-American friendship and cooperation. "It distressed me," Wilson wrote to Creel of Bullard's socialist publications at the very time of Bullard's appointment to the Russian Bureau of COMPUB, "to think that Mr. Bullard should have written the enclosed. Such articles embarrass the administration." In an article written in 1919, after his return from Russia, Bullard admitted: "I am a Socialist," and then explained away the radical positions he had taken in the articles that had distressed President Wilson. "But first of all I am a democrat. And I am convinced that American democracy—including as it does the Socialists—will in the end, as reliable information reaches them, be just as much opposed [to the Bolsheviks]."[5]

Sisson and Bullard dramatically parted ways with Robins on the issue of U.S. policy and the Bolsheviks after more than six weeks of the most intense joint activity. Sisson's own account, *One Hundred Red Days: A Personal Chronicle of the Bolshevik Revolution*, is a valuable source of information. In *Russia Leaves the War*, George Kennan devotes considerable attention to Sisson, COMPUB, and Sisson's relationship with Robins. Kennan tries to be fair to Sisson, despite some of his misguided activities, but nowhere does Kennan adequately suggest Sisson's vindictiveness toward Robins, the phobic depths regarding the Bolsheviks to which Sisson descended in his memoir, nor the serious misinformation and long-term damage to U.S.-Soviet relations brought about by his work. Writing to President Wilson on the Sisson documents "taken from Smolny institute," George Creel, whose opinion Wilson held in high regard, declared that "they are absolutely conclusive, and contribute the most amazing record of double dealing and corruption."[6]

On 7 January, four days before meeting Lenin, Sisson wrote a letter home: "the Bolsheviks become more angered at being ignored by the world upon which they wage class war. Their general method is that of a suitor who slaps a pretty girl, and then says, 'Kiss me darling!' Yet when it comes to getting permission to have specific things done by their officials, the Bolsheviks are decently human. I have been able to do the things I set out to do." Years later he summed up his changed opinion of Lenin. He writes of "—Lenin, the sly *muzhik* [peasant]! I believe that his realest desire was to destroy the universe. I believe that he hated humanity. He could organize and he could build, but I believe that he meant to destroy even the edifices he reared."[7]

Had these been the remarks of a bitter, deposed aristocrat of the czarist regime, full of rage at his loss of wealth, power, and homeland, they might be understandable. But these are the words of one of the most influential American "experts" on the Soviet Union during the formative period of Soviet-American relations. Loyal to Sisson from the very outset of Sisson's conflict with Robins, Bullard, in the words of Albert Rhys Williams, "like a chameleon . . . had taken on the . . . antipathy for anything Bolshevik."[8] On 17 March, from Moscow, Bullard wrote again to George Creel. "The situation about the Embassy is disgusting," he complained, concerning the lack of trust between the Red Cross Commission and the ambassador. "I wish that I had not written a letter which a couple of months ago I sent to you about Raymond Robins," he continued. "He has been one of the worst personal disappointments of my life. He really did fine work at first. But he got into a row with Sisson and has acted since like a cad. . . . But having written as strongly as I did in his favor, I must give you the tip now that, I have been forced by circumstances to alter my opinion of him entirely. God save us from Sky-Pilots, say I."[9]

Writing just one month earlier, Ralph M. Easley, executive chairman of the National Civic Federation, which launched a vicious campaign against Thompson upon his return to the United States pondered the ironies of the Bullard and Thompson positions. "It is certainly a curious situation when William B. Thompson, the conservative, hard-headed Wall Street devotee, and Arthur Bullard, the radical and one-time friend of Goldman, Berkman and Hillquit, should simultaneously visit Russia, and the Wall Street Thompson come out for Bolshevism and the radical Bullard come out against it."[10]

For thirteen years, between the Russian Revolution and publication of his memoirs, and for decades thereafter, Sisson's approach to Soviet Russia held sway in American foreign policy circles, forming finally the paradigm for McCarthyism and the "evil empire" rhetoric of the early 1980s. Such "red scare" American foreign policy toward the Soviet Union has been the destructive norm, Robins's, the rare exception.

An additional serious complication in Robins's role as U.S.-Bolshevik liaison was an alleged intelligence "leak" in the American embassy. It involved a Madame Matilda de Cram and Ambassador Francis whom de Cram had met and befriended while both were en route to Petrograd in 1916; Francis, to assume his post as American ambassador. Throughout these months, both before and after the Bolshevik Revolution, de Cram was a frequent guest of Francis at the American embassy, but what he did not at first know was that "the police of our allies [were] on his trail" because strong evidence suggested that Madame de Cram was a German agent. "I certainly would have voiced my disgust that the old fool was so indiscreet," Bullard wrote to Creel in Washington. "Imagine the situation, when French and Englishmen will not talk to you unless you promise not to tell your Ambassador. This is what Judson is up against." Dr. Orrin S. Wightman, one of Robins's subordinates on the Red Cross Commission, made a far more damning judgment. "Ambassador Francis was a stuffed shirt, a dumb head who never found out what the whole thing was all about," Wightman confided to Thompson's biographer. "He leaned on everybody, keenly enjoying his authority, while spies slipped in and out under his nose and the diplomats made a monkey of him." Wightman was not among the small circle of Robins confidants, and the record suggests that Wightman played no part in any of the controversial political activities of the commission that would have put him at odds with the ambassador.[11]

By January 1918, Robins's responsibilities as liaison with the Bolshevik government had become virtually institutionalized. He was at the Smolny Institute so often and on so many consequential missions that the American ambassador and the Soviet leadership began to depend on him. Significantly, on 4 January Bolshevik authorities issued Robins pass number 834, permitting him free access to Smolny without prearrangement. A week later, on 11 January he held a most important meeting with Lenin.

Documentary sources are silent regarding the first meeting of Robins and Lenin. Nor do Robins's papers document an earlier encounter; therefore, it is possible that this meeting—held three days after President Wilson's Fourteen Points speech—may have been their first. Edgar Sisson, who together with Gumberg accompanied Robins to that meeting, believes that it was. But William Hard, who bases his text mainly on Robins's own account, suggests that such encounters had begun to take place at least several weeks earlier, well before 21 December 1917. Hard records that Robins was "accustomed to going through Lenin's door into Lenin's room, on a pass, without question." While Robins ultimately may have been offered such freedom, in all likelihood it did not begin before 4 January, the date on which he was issued his free-access pass. The pass itself, numbered, dated, and signed by V. Avanesov, is preserved in the Robins Papers. It is, of course, possible that another pass had been issued prior to this one, or that previous meetings with Lenin, like those with Trotsky and other Bolshevik authorities, had been arranged by Gumberg, without the issuance of a pass. But it is unlike Robins not to have, in some way, recorded such a previous visit.[12]

The weeks prior to that meeting brought a shower of significant developments. On 22 December the first sitting of the peace negotiations between the Soviets and the Quadruple Alliance (Germany, Austro-Hungary, Bulgaria, and Turkey) were held in the German occupied Polish town of Brest-Litovsk, just sixty miles east of Warsaw—territory that had been part of the Russian Empire before the war. The Soviet delegation, at first headed by

Adolf A. Joffe, a long-time Bolshevik, presented at that initial meeting, an "Outline Programme for Peace Negotiations," calling for the principle of "no annexations or indemnities" as the basis of the talks. The German delegation, headed by Foreign Minister Baron Richard von Kuhlman and commander of the forces on the eastern front, Gen. Max Hoffman, "appeared to agree to conduct the talks on these terms," but soon "revealed Germany's annexationist intentions."[13]

The last months of 1917 demonstrated ever more clearly that the action on the western front was a bloody stalemate. The German and Austro-Hungarian military superiority on the Russian front was just as apparent. The Germans had advanced to a line through the Polish cities of Riga south through Dvinsk, Vilna, Pinsk, and Rovno. Given the poor condition of the Russian army, the Central Powers were capable of advancing on Petrograd and Moscow with little fear of significant opposition. The French, under Gen. Robert-Georges Nivelle, attempted yet another breakthrough in the West, but the disastrous failure led to mutiny among French troops. The British fought the battle of Passchendaele, in Flanders, for three months at the end of 1917, gaining five miles at the cost of more than 400,000 men. Their unexpected attack in December, using hundreds of tanks, won them territory deep in enemy lines, but characteristic of the war of attrition, they were forced to give up those gains for lack of reserves. In addition to their demonstrated supremacy on the Russian front at the end of 1917, the Central Powers won a major victory against Italy at the battle of Caporetto. Without British and French reinforcements, much of northern Italy could have been occupied.

During the last weeks of December and the first of the new year in Petrograd, there was a flurry of revolutionary meetings, debates, and rulings. A major focus of attention for Russians and foreigners alike was the imminent meeting of the Constituent Assembly, scheduled to begin on 18 January. This democratically elected body represented a potential challenge to the legitimacy of Bolshevik party rule.[14]

Lenin's work during the days immediately preceeding his first meeting with Robins provides some insight. It may help to understand why he was willing to hold such a meeting in the first place. From 6–9 January, in nearby Finland, while on "vacation" from the extraordinary demands of his office, Lenin took time to write three articles on far-ranging but urgent matters: a four-page article, "Fear of the Collapse of the Old and the Fight for the New," a ten-page essay, "How to Organize Competition," and a two-page "Draft Decree on Consumers' Communes." All were published posthumously in *Pravda* in 1929.[15]

In light of Robins's struggles to impart an open view of the Bolsheviks to his government, Lenin's fierce and confrontational introduction to "Fear of the Collapse of the Old and the Fight for the New," is particularly significant: "The capitalists and their supporters, witting and unwitting, are thinking, saying and writing: 'The Bolsheviks have now been in power for two months, but instead of a socialist paradise we find the hell of chaos, civil war and even greater dislocation.'" Lenin argues,

> They refuse to see that in a few weeks, the lying imperialist foreign policy, which dragged out the war and covered up plunder and seizure through secret treaties, has been replaced by a truly revolutionary-democratic policy working for a really democratic peace, a policy which has already produced such a great practical success as the armistice and has increased the propaganda power of our revolution a hundredfold. They refuse to see that workers' control and the nationalization of the banks are being put into practice, and these are the first steps towards socialism.[16]

In language as strident as any he penned, Lenin pleaded the case for the necessary use of force to achieve the goals of the revolution—the dictatorship of the proletariat—and warns revolutionary leaders against the premature assumption of victory over bourgeois capitalist control, "the grasping, malicious, frenzied filthy avidity of the money-bags."[17] Lenin called for "thousands of practical forms and methods of accounting and controlling the rich, the rogues and the idlers" if socialism had any chance of surviving. His fourth suggestion—"one out of every ten idlers will be shot on the spot"—became, in just a few years after the publication of this essay, the method of Stalin's collectivization.[18] But the economic realities facing Lenin, which suggested such harsh treatment of those who would not cooperate, was the reality upon which the fate of the revolution rested, and that pressed him to seek help from any quarter—even from the "imperialist moneybags."

Lenin's words terrified Western observers, and Robins was no exception, but he believed that the violent extremes of Bolshevism could be avoided by easing the military, political, and, most important, economic crises, which forced such extremes on the revolutionary leadership. Despite the ferocious language—and given the mass base of support—Robins was convinced of the necessity to cooperate with Lenin.

In January 1918, Lenin was forty-seven years old, although he looked considerably older because of baldness and a beard and mustache. To evade the police late in 1917, shortly before the November Revolution, he had assumed the name K. P. Ivanov, a factory worker. He contrived a more youthful appearance by shaving his beard and wearing a wig. He looked like a man in his late thirties. His identity card and photo in the disguise appear in many biographies.[19] His eyes shown prominently because of the continuous expanse of forehead and skull, uninterrupted by hair. His eyes were small and alive, hinting at some Tatar ancestry; his appearance was striking, and suggested extreme intensity.

No photograph of Lenin at work, on the podium, or in his office depicts him other than in shirt, tie, vest, and dark suit, the quintessential image of the businessman or academic. This propriety was capped by his use of a bar passing beneath the knot of his tie, holding the wings of his collar in place. There is truth to the well-known, but possibly apocryphal, comments about Lenin's appearance made by a reporter on the night he delivered his "Decree on Peace," suggesting that if Lenin "were spruced up a bit, you would take him for a bourgeois mayor or banker of a small French city."[20]

The 11 January meeting with Robins, Gumberg, and Sisson, was held in "the deepest back room at Smolny," Lenin's small corner office on the third floor, late in the afternoon. It was arranged to present Lenin with a copy of Wilson's Fourteen Points and to discuss its implications for the Russian-German peace talks at Brest-Litovsk. Wilson's speech covered specific developments in the talks, challenging the German-Austrian shift in position which demanded annexation of territory that its forces then occupied. This positive concern was appreciated by Lenin, particularly because Russia's position in the negotiations with the Central Powers was so vulnerable.

Lenin offered his cooperation to Sisson and his Committee on Public Information, agreeing to disseminate tens of thousands of copies of Wilson's speech to the soldiers on the eastern front, in Russian and German translations. (It appears that it was this activity—COMPUB-Bolshevik dissemination of Wilson's speech—that led to the accusing headlines "Thompson Gives Million Dollars to Bolsheviks.") The Americans and the Soviets hoped that the call for self-determination and a peace free of annexations and indemnities, reminiscent of Lenin's decree, would win over German and Austrian soldiers. If Allied and Soviet aims were seen in such sweeping democratic and just terms, it was hoped that morale among the enemy rank and file could be undermined. Russian forces, uncommitted to the Bolshevik cause, could be won over similarly. The propaganda effort was a rare instance of official Bolshevik-American cooperation.

According to Sisson, Lenin broached the hackneyed libel: "I have been called a German spy." Sisson, who distrusted Lenin, did not grant his apparent honesty in bringing up that sensitive subject. Robins's appreciation of Lenin's forthrightness grew as a result. It was these conflicting impressions of Lenin that led to the break between Robins and Sisson.

Allegations that the Bolsheviks were German agents began even before the outbreak of war in 1914, but Lenin's return to Russia through German-occupied territory on a sealed train confirmed suspicions for many. The "evidence" of German planning, control, and financing of the Bolshevik Revolution continued to emerge years after the Soviet Union was well established. Prior to the conclusion of the Brest-Litovsk peace, these accusations undermined the Bolshevik position, especially among the soldiers, workers, and peasants on whom the new government depended.

Robins was privy to much that went on at Smolny during these anxious days of infighting between different factions of the revolutionary government. They were to decide whether to accept the intolerable annexationist demands of the Central Powers as the price for peace, or raise a new army in the name of the socialist revolution and continue fighting. On one occasion, just after the Soviets received a revised German territorial demand, Robins and Gumberg made their way to Smolny. There they witnessed a mob challenging Lenin and Lenin's response "under fire." Robins recalled, some months after the event, that he had seen a crowd standing beside a wall near a poster proclaiming that "Lenin had absconded to Finland with thirty millions in gold of the State Bank. Russia betrayed by the false leaders. No hope for Russia. Grand Duke Nicholas comes up from the Crimea with a hundred thousand troops, to save Russia."

Robins hurried to Trotsky's office to learn more. There he witnessed Trotsky giving orders, enjoying it like "Horatio on the Bridge." Robins dashed to Lenin's office where, uncannily, Lenin was seated "calmly at his desk, with orderlies coming and going, the master of the show." Moments later, Trotsky entered, hysterically shouting and waving his arms, whereupon Lenin demanded that the leaders of the mob be brought in. Soon some thirty or forty men entered, holding bayoneted rifles, dressed in civilian clothes. "These men come in the room, the leaders of that mob, with the rifles that had lifted Lenin to the power and the rifles that can take him down."

Calmly, with his hands characteristically thrust in his pockets as he rose, Lenin stood some four feet away from them and, according to Robins, Lenin said,

"*Tovarishchi:* I have not run away. I don't blame you for being confused, for mistrusting me, mistrusting your leaders. This is a hard time for Russia. There are many voices in Russia tonight. There are two honest, revolutionary forces, and one of them is wrong and one is right. Tovarish Trotsky, Krylenko—others he named—say to you you should go to the front and meet the German advance. Meet it without economic support. Meet it without an organized army, with your officers really against you, because you are revolutionists and they were long in power, and they will lose their inheritance if you win. They say you should go out there; and it is a fine revolutionary fire that animates you to go out and meet the enemy and conquer, and die, though all you can do is to die. I am not worrying about dying. We all die in the struggle. But let us die for the revolution and not against it, comrades. The Germans advancing will destroy you and the hope of revolutionary Russia, and the bourgeoisie will come back and the Czar will come back, and all the blood will have been spent for nothing.

"No. My word is word. We will make peace with the German robbers. We will make peace with the German Thieves. We will make any kind of peace. They say to you that Tovarish Lenin will make a shameful peace, and I will. They say I will give up the imperial city and your home, and I will. They say I will give up the Holy City, the Kremlin, Moscow, and I will. We will go back to the Ekaterinburg. We will carry the flame of the revolution there. And we will keep it burning, until the comrades revolt against their masters in Berlin and Vienna, by a proletarian revolution."[21]

As Lenin concluded his talk, the rifle-carrying mob leaders were convinced. They left, shouting "Hail to Comrade Nikolai Lenin." For Robins, this was a momentous occasion. He had witnessed the leader of the October Revolution calmly confront death and triumph. Now he dismissed all doubts about Lenin's ability to fulfill Soviet destiny.

Robins did not record his first impressions of Lenin. Sisson, after more than ten years of battling Robins over American policy toward the Soviets, wrote what appears to be an unbiased account of the 11 January meeting. He noted Robins's awe in the presence of Vladimir Ilyich Ulyanov (Lenin), "Some fire in him was lighted."[22] All with whom Robins shared his impressions of Lenin at the time agree with this appraisal. Fifteen months after their meeting, although incorrect on some facts of Lenin's biography, Robins offered this perspective:

> Lenin, 48 years old, Russian gentile, born noble, son of a Starred General of the old regime, born on the ancestral estates at Simbirsk, on the Volga, born in the purple, turned revolutionist by the execution of his younger brother when he was 16 years old for some petty offense; called revolutionist by the autocracy; pledged himself against the autocracy and became a committed revolutionist and, if you will a fanatic soul. He entered the nearby revolutionary circle, took what he could of his patrimony, turned it over to the revolutionary purpose of Russia, was tried and convicted and sent to Siberia; escaped death by a scratch and then became a revolutionist in the capitals of Europe, with headquarters in Switzerland, for quite a while.
>
> A studious, learned and extraordinarily gifted person intellectually is Nicolai [sic] Lenin, if I am any judge. He also speaks and writes English, French, German, Russian, Ukranian, and adds to it Yiddish, and he learned Yiddish so he could talk revolution to Jews. Lenin has written fourteen volumes of abstruse radical economics, and his debates with Plekhanov have been published by learned societies under the old regime in Russia.
>
> Lenin is steadiest under strain, the most committed and certain person to a program in time of blood and death I have ever known, or I ever expect to know. Lenin hates a crowd. He hates the footlights. He never makes a speech when he can avoid it.
>
> Lenin likes the cool quietness of definite executive action, the working out of the program of a movement on his desk.[23]

Robins's portrait of Lenin—as an honorable and self-sacrificing statesman and committed revolutionary—offers a romantic image that Robins never altered. But Robins, the man of action and drama, was not awed by honesty and self-sacrifice alone. Perhaps more than anything, he was impressed by courage in the face of death—a trait he witnessed that day when the mob accused Lenin of betraying the revolution. Similarly, Lenin was intrigued by Robins and found it hard to reconcile Robins's ideology with his fairness to the Bolshevik Revolution. We learn much of Lenin's attitude toward Robins in conversations Lenin had with Arthur Ransome, the British correspondent who covered the Revolution for the *Manchester Guardian*, and who later married Eugenia Petrovna Shalyapina, Trotsky's secretary. "Was Robins really as friendly to the Soviet government as he appeared?" Lenin asked. Ransome replied recalling Robins's words: "Yes, I can't go against a baby I have sat up with for six months. But if there were a Bolshevik movement in America I'd be out with my rifle to fight it every time."

"Now that," Lenin replied, "is an honest man and more farseeing than most. I always liked that man."[24]

There is every reason to accept the truth of this account, and none for Lenin to have felt otherwise. If we compare the anticapitalist rhetoric of Lenin's three essays, written just days before speaking to Robins for the first time, with Robins's anticorruption, prolabor, public ownership, and social service speeches, we find the same critiques of capitalism. Robins made his "labor credentials," as he called them, well known to the Bolshevik leadership, but he also made it clear that his solution to the excesses of capitalism were not those of Marx or Lenin. In his accounts of his meetings with Trotsky, which preceded his first visit to Lenin, Robins explained his experiences as a laborer and union organizer. Robins's background and reputation for fairness in dealings with the Bolsheviks was already known to Lenin.

Of course, neither Trotsky nor Lenin had ever been employed in manual labor to earn their keep. They were bourgeois intellectuals turned professional revolutionaries on behalf of the toiling masses, but had never been in those ranks themselves. Robins had, and Robins knew that the two first leaders of the proletarian revolution had never been workers themselves. The irony was not lost on him and he, a wealthy American, critic of capitalism, and staunch supporter of the Western democratic tradition, played out the hand of "man of the working classes" for all it was worth. But had Robins remained a "worker" or small-town preacher, he would never have been made a member of the Red Cross Commission. Only because of his influential position in reform and philanthropic circles, dominated by the wealthy like himself, was Robins appointed, thereby enabling him to contend for influence.

Lenin appreciated Robins's honesty but must have thought him terribly naive, believing a humane society possible in the bosom of capitalism, and so seriously underestimating the force necessary to overthrow the old order and create the new.

Robins was given to hero worship. He was in awe of Cecil Rhodes and Theodore Roosevelt, and like many who deify others, there was a part of him that wished the same for himself. According to R. H. Bruce Lockhart, Lenin had entered Robins's pantheon, but the relationship was not simple. "Of all foreigners, Robins was the only man whom Lenin was always willing to see and who ever succeeded in imposing his own personality on the unemotional Bolshevik leader."[25] However, it is best to balance the sympathies of Lockhart with the sardonic wit of Gumberg, who remained Robins's life-long, close friend. In testy banter with Albert Rhys Williams about Robins's relationship with Lenin, Gumberg said of Robins:

> "Oh, the Colonel? You know the Colonel doesn't stop halfway. By now he's attributing some of his own best ideas to Lenin. Even puts into Lenin's mouth some remarkable convictions about America. He'll be having Lenin think Theodore Roosevelt is a man of the people next. He believes every word he says, too. He has lots of facts about America—which he selects, of course—and Lenin loves facts. He likes Robins, too. Told me so."[26]

Exactly one week after Robins's meeting with Lenin came the denouement with the Bolsheviks and the Constituent Assembly. Just two weeks after the Bolsheviks seized power, elections for representatives to the Constituent Assembly were held. The elections had been arranged earlier by the Provisional Government, soon after the March Revolution. The results were seriously disappointing to the Bolsheviks. Of the 707 delegates, only 175 Bolsheviks were elected. The Social-Revolutionary party (SRs), which had for more than a generation represented the interests of the peasants—still overwhelmingly the largest constituency in Russia—sent 410 members to the assembly. The Bolsheviks had taken power in the soviets of soldiers, workers, and peasants, the best organized and militant political force in Russia at that time, and with that solid base, and help from other political factions such as the leftwing SRs, had overthrown the Provisional Government. But when the population had the opportunity to vote along party lines in free elections, the Bolsheviks were still a minority.

On 11 December, "the date set for the opening of the Constitutional Assembly which has been so long awaited by the Russian People," Robins was on the scene. He continued, in his prescient letter to his wife:

> It opens under dark clouds. The Bolshevik government does not control this body and seems to fear that it will set up a new government and that it may have to be dissolved by force. The Cadet Party and the Social Revolutionists (minimalists) of the right are eagerly supporting the claims of this assembly to the supreme power. There is today a great demonstration on the streets with masses of men and women with banners and bands marching and all in favor of the supreme power being accorded to the assembly. We understand that here are only about 45 out of 800 members in town and that these have not all their credentials. As I write a great parade is passing in front of the Hotel Europe and shouts and songs float in on the cold winter air. It is the first time that the aristocracy and the business and property classes have shown their heads since the last revolution. Many see in this demonstration the end of the present regime and the return of the reaction. I do not. There are very few soldiers in this demonstration and the rifles are the efficient power in Russia just now. The present government controls these rifles without question or division at this hour.[27]

The Bolsheviks were successful in setting a new date for the opening of the assembly. They had argued that too few representatives had arrived in Petrograd to transact the business of the Constituent Assembly democratically. With a new date—18 January—set for beginning the assembly's deliberations, a barrage of complicated events centering on the armistice and peace negotiations at Brest-Litovsk dominated the next three weeks.

In elections based on universal manhood suffrage, the Constituent Assembly was the only representative body chosen by secret ballot in all of Russian history. Throughout the months between the March and November revolutions, the Constituent Assembly represented the hope for the establishment of democratic institutions in Russia. According to Robins, only the princes, grand dukes, and the supporters of czarist autocracy stood opposed to it and were excluded from participation. Lenin and the Bolshevik party strongly supported it, hoping it might be the instrument to achieve power and fearful that reactionary forces of the old regime would attempt to destroy this bud of Russian democracy. But the Bolshevik Revolution transformed the situation completely.

The Kadet, or Constitutional-Democratic party, modeled on middle-class parliamentary parties of western Europe, placed all their faith in the Constituent Assembly, since it was to function as the first step toward a constitutional convention based on western European or American models. Little distinguished them from the non-Marxist, moderate socialists, akin to British Fabians. Kerensky belonged to this camp. Before and after the Bolshevik Revolution, the right wing of the Social-Revolutionary party joined with the Kadets in support of parliamentary democratic process in the Constituent Assembly. The leftwing SRs, and many Mensheviks,[28] who under Trotsky's leadership had joined forces with the Bolsheviks in July 1917, supported the more "radical" Marxist revolutionary program.

For Robins, as well as for the Allied governments, the Constituent Assembly was the keystone of any form of traditional democracy in Russia, and its fate "under Bolshevik rifles" was watched very carefully. In the street demonstrations that accompanied the first attempt to begin its proceedings, on 11 December, Robins noted the impossible anomaly of elected delegates, empowered to determine the political future of Russia, completely subservient to Bolshevik rifles. During the weeks thereafter, until 18 January, the Bolshevik leadership prepared very carefully for the challenge posed by the assembly. On that day, Lenin composed a declaration of the Bolshevik party delegates to the Constituent Assembly, announcing their withdrawal from participation.

> The Constituent Assembly, as at present constituted, is the result of the balance of forces obtaining before the Great October Revolution. The present counter-revolutionary majority of the Constituent Assembly elected on outdated party lists, is a reflection of an earlier period of the revolution and is trying to throw up a roadblock in the way of the workers' and peasants' movement.

Refusing for a single moment to cover up the crimes of the enemies of the people, we make this announcement of our withdrawal from the Constituent Assembly, leaving it to Soviet power to take the final decision on the attitude to the counter-revolutionary section of the Constituent Assembly.

On the following day, on behalf of the Central Executive Committee of the Soviet government, Lenin composed a decree on the dissolution of the assembly. Arguing that the Bolsheviks had achieved rightful power, without "compromise with the bourgeoisie," Lenin concluded that the rightwing SRs and Mensheviks were engaged in "a most desperate struggle against Soviet Power." Lenin then recited a list of betrayals, noting that the opposition parties were "defending the saboteurs, the servants of capital, and are going as far as undisguised calls to terrorism."

"It is obvious," Lenin remarked, "that under such circumstances the remaining part of the Constituent Assembly could only serve as a screen for the struggle of the counter-revolutionaries to overthrow Soviet power. Accordingly, the Central Executive Committee resolves that the Constituent Assembly is hereby dissolved."[29]

This Bolshevik act confirmed the antipathies of Allied governments and their representatives in Russia. For Robins and his colleagues seeking rapprochement with the Bolsheviks, the dissolution of the Constituent Assembly was just as disappointing, even though it came as no surprise; as early as 11 December Robins knew that Bolshevik power and the assembly were irreconcilable. On the night the dissolution order was issued, two former Kadet members of the Provisional Government, who were elected delegates to the Constituent Assembly, were assassinated while under Bolshevik "guard." The "Bolshevik outlaw" image was growing. "For myself," Consul Poole wired Francis, in response to these developments, "I think that the movement . . . for the reestablishment of a provisional government in Russia . . . under [czarist Gen. Mikhail Vasilévich] Alexeev will have moral and therefore political strength . . . in contrast to the Bolshevik suppression." Arthur Bullard, in Petrograd, wrote to American Consul Maddin Summers in Moscow: "It was a rotten beastly job. Some of the murderers have been caught and are under arrest," but he attempted to calm Summers's fierce anti-Bolshevik anger by adding that "all the other stories of massacre are pure bunk. . . . The Bolsheviki certainly want quiet now and I think they will get it." Nevertheless, the murders made Robins's task all the more difficult.[30]

In later years, Robins was criticized for his open sympathy to the Bolsheviks; but his on-the-spot notes and memoranda show that he commanded a firm understanding of power, politics, and American self-interest. Unfortunately, Robins's unconventional views were compounded by his intensity and sense of the dramatic, traits which encouraged American foreign policy circles to dismiss his recommendations as the ramblings of a misguided zealot—or worse, someone so sympathetic to the Bolshevik cause that he was ready to betray his country.

Robins understood how he was being perceived by officials in Washington throughout his devoted service in Russia, and he painfully reflected on the ironies involved. He wrote to Margaret: "Each hour I am expecting my recall for my services and at the hour that the General commanding the Military Mission of the United States and the sole military attaché of the American Embassy, has to send all communications through me to the Russian government, we are expecting to be reprimanded for the only action between hostile bayonets and our nationals in this country." The list of disappointments, mistakes, and frustrations grew rapidly and nearly overwhelmed Robins. To ease the tension, he confided ruefully to Margaret, "Well, I am almost an anarchist as the result of this experience with the diplomacy of organized government."[31]

On 20 December, the day Robins wrote this letter, the Bolshevik government arrested Andrei Kalpashnikov on suspicion of treason in connection with a planned shipment of ambulances and trucks to Romania for use by "counter-revolutionaries." (This was separate from the shipment requested by Robins, from Trotsky, on 10 November.) Allied diplomats in Petrograd were convinced of Kalpashnikov's innocence and incensed at his arrest, especially since Romania was an Allied country committed to continuing the fight against the Central Powers.[32] Before World War I, Kalpashnikov had been a czarist government attaché in their Washington embassy. Coincidentally, he had set out on the return trip from New York to Russia on the same ship with Leon Trotsky after the March Revolution.

Suspecting Trotsky of being a German spy, British officials in Halifax, Nova Scotia, boarded the *Christianiafjord,* a Norwegian ship. With Kalpashnikov as interpreter, they interrogated Trotsky and then interned him and his family in a camp for German prisoners of war. Obviously Kalpashnikov's role, in league with the British, did not endear him to Trotsky, who also imagined that the spying accusations may have originated with Kalpashnikov himself. Robins was deeply involved in the affair because his relationship with the Bolsheviks hung in the balance. Were Kalpashnikov in any way involved in wrong-doing as an agent of the American Red Cross in Romania, Robins would also have been implicated. Acting as negotiator and liaison between the American embassy and Smolny, after the most convoluted sequence of charges, countercharges, and documentation, Robins finally secured Kalpashnikov's release.[33]

On 13 January, less than three weeks after Kalpashnikov's release and two days after Robins's first meeting with Lenin, another cause célèbre shook the Petrograd diplomatic community—the arrest and imprisonment of Count Constantine Diamandi, Romania's ambassador to Russia. Again the ill-defined jurisdictions of the Romanian-Russian segment of the eastern front where Romanian and Russian forces had fought against the Central Powers had led the Bolsheviks to take so unprecedented and inflammatory a step. The arrest was made to retaliate for, and bring an end to, Romanian attempts to disarm and expel Russian soldiers loyal to the Bolsheviks then deployed in the Romanian province of Moldavia. The Romanians feared that these disorderly soldiers could serve as an army of occupation and would lead to Soviet annexation of the territory. The situation was complex, with justified fears on both sides; but the Bolshevik violation of diplomatic immunity seriously escalated the conflict and led to the unique and most unusual meeting of Lenin, Under Secretary of State Zalkind, Joseph Stalin, and the entire diplomatic corps of Petrograd, who sought out the Russian leaders to protest the arrest and demand the freeing of their colleague Diamandi.

That extraordinary meeting of nineteen diplomats and Lenin, in his office in room 81 at Smolny, was described in detail in the memoirs of the French ambassador, Joseph Noulens. But the record of the twenty-four hours following the meeting, which led to Diamandi's release, is only partially documented. It is clear that Robins and Gumberg engaged in a most frenetic sequence of communications with Lenin and Ambassador Francis. Although the documentation is not available to prove it conclusively, Robins, without authorization, provided Lenin with the assurances that allowed the release of Diamandi while permitting Lenin to save face among his followers.[34] Robins's role in the Kalpashnikov and Diamandi incidents reveals how effective and indispensable he had become in forging desperately needed direct links with the Bolsheviks.

On 16 March 1918 the Congress of Soviets finally ratified the peace treaty with Germany and Austria-Hungary, negotiated at Brest-Litovsk. Russia was no longer in the war—no longer part of the Entente military alliance—leaving only England, France, Italy, and the United States to fight the enemy. Seventeen days earlier, on 27 February, at 2:00 A.M., the American ambassador and his staff, fearing the imminent German occupation of Petrograd, fled the capital for the safety of Vologda, a town some 350 miles to the east. As these dire developments multiplied, Robins's role as chief American liaison with the Bolsheviks grew more important. The charade, that his sole responsibility was the distribution of Red Cross supplies, was abandoned.

14

Brest-Litovsk

> Nobody ever spoke of it as anything but a shameful peace, a robber peace, a peace at the point of the bayonet, but they said, "Because of our broken economic life we will have to accept it, unless we get help from the allies."
> —Robins's speech at the City Club of Chicago, 20 March 1919

THE events of February in Petrograd were, if anything, more bewildering to the foreign community than were those of the three months following the Bolshevik Revolution—"you have to shift from day to day," Robins explained.[1] His work centered on developments in the German-Bolshevik negotiations at Brest-Litovsk. With each demand, response, and counterdemand, Robins and his colleagues in Petrograd made their own moves, communications, and suggestions to their superiors. It was a time of great tension, especially within the ranks of the Bolshevik leadership, which was sharply divided on the question of whether to submit to the harsh German territorial demands or to continue the war. Trotsky led those who maintained that the territory and one-quarter of European Russia's population should not be signed away; Lenin believed that it was terrible, but unavoidable.[2] Lenin's bitter denunciation of those who accused him of making "a shameful peace" while ignoring the possibility of the German destruction of the entire revolution suggests the almost irreconcilable division. "This painful question," wrote George Kennan, "produced the first great crisis within the Soviet leadership—the most serious it was ever to face in Lenin's time. For decades thereafter, the valleys of the Communist Olympus would continue to reverberate, in moments of tension and violence, with bitter arguments and recriminations over the positions taken by individual communist figures at this difficult moment in 1918."[3]

Robins later gave this account of the conflict between Lenin and Trotsky.

> Now at that moment in Russian policy for the first time a cleavage opened between Lenin and Trotsky. Since the revolution of November 7 they had worked absolutely hand in hand until that hour. . . .
> Trotsky said: "We do not have to accept the German terms. If we go back to the Brest conference and say we are not going to fight our German brothers any more, but refuse to make peace with the imperialistic power of Germany, the Germans cannot march an army against non-resistant revolutionary Rus-

sia; they will mutiny and refuse to fight. If they do start across, then the workmen in Berlin and Vienna will revolt and the home line will be shattered and they will be called back."

Lenin, who is an extraordinary realist, no matter what else he may be, said, "That is all humbug. The Germans are so trained that they take orders. The proletariat in Germany is not yet free to revolt effectively. You are too fast with your program."

I heard the debate in the executive committee of the Russian soviet . . . and finally Lenin, as is his custom—he does not like debate—he went back into his office and wrote twenty-one theses, and those theses set out why it is better for revolutionary Russia to accept even the robbers' peace at Brest than to not make peace, that the Germans would advance and then they would have to take a worse peace. . . .

He called a special executive meeting of the All-Russian National Soviet on the 8th of January, 1918, better than four weeks before the actual failure of the Brest peace, and there made his arguments. . . .

Trotsky had all the superficial advantages of the argument. "Why," he said, "if we sign peace with the German thieves and betrayers, our brothers in the Courland and our brothers in Lithuania will say that we have betrayed the revolution, and we should not sign."

Lenin said, "You have got to save the revolution here in Russia, and it is very much better to sign the peace now than at the point of a bayonet."

But the argument was so strong on Trotsky's side and the general revolutionary fervor so strong that Lenin finally said, "Well, I will not press this point. Let Comrade Trotsky go to Brest and try his scheme. I tell you it won't work. I tell you it will cost revolutionary Russia territories and supplies."

. . . Trotsky went back and argued and argued. It will finally be written down—and I speak of this with all the modesty I am able to command—our small part in preventing the Lenin program from going over and in supporting at every point we could those who opposed the immediate separate peace, because we knew that by every week we kept those divisions on the eastern front on whatsoever pretext, we were that much longer holding the western front until American troops might arrive, and we lived in a daily atmosphere of struggle to do that one job.

Trotsky went back. He held the debate as long as he could hold it. It was finally pushed right up to him by the German powers, to the point where they said, "You are either going to sign or you are not. Give us action at once." Those were the words of the German General Command; and Trotsky stood up in that company of men with whom he had been dealing for three months and spoke these words. . . .

"We cannot sanctify outrages. We are leaving the war, but are constrained to refuse to sign the peace treaty."[4]

Robins concluded his account with bluntness and incisiveness;

And he turned around with his Mission and went to his special train and came back to Petrograd and said, "They won't march," and Lenin laughed at him, and within three days the Germans advanced on all fronts, and the rotten Russian army that was not yet wholly demobilized ran pell-mell.[5]

Robins and his "outdoor" camp watched every nuance in the developing negotiations at Brest-Litovsk. And through Gumberg and his own frequent visits to Smolny, Robins was perhaps more aware of the facts of the situation than was any other American. When Trotsky returned to Petrograd on 20 January, after the first series of talks at Brest-Litovsk, which were still far from settlement, Robins found out as much as he could. When satisfied with his grasp of the situation, he sent a telegram to Thompson in New York for "prompt recognition . . . establishment of Modus Vivendi making possible generous and sympathetic cooperation."[6]

Robins's hopes were supported in the last week of January and early February by the successes of Trotsky's supporters. These Bolsheviks saw the salvation of Russia and the revolution in the imminent rising of the workers in Austria and Germany, which would eliminate the great military threat then posed by the German army. They concentrated on propaganda among the soldiers and peoples of the Central Powers, expecting the Russian Revolution to serve as the catalyst for the long-awaited world socialist revolution.

In the propaganda campaign during the previous fall and winter, Robins equated defeat of the Central Powers with the rise of democracy and freedom and the downfall of autocracy and privilege. In February 1918 he began to equate his goals of democracy and freedom with the Bolshevik goals of proletarian democracy and socialism. Given the uniqueness of the Russian experience under the czars, Robins began to see the Bolshevik path as the best taken. The Bolshevik Revolution had to be saved.

After heated debate the Bolshevik leadership finally agreed to meet the German demands. However, the German army was advancing unopposed. Upon receipt of the Soviet government's message of willingness to meet the terms of 10 February, the German negotiators presented extended territorial demands, which further outraged the Bolshevik leadership and caused even greater dissension. In this second round of the conflict between Trotsky and Lenin, the latter finally mustered the necessary support under the pressure of imminent German victory, but not without offering his resignation to the Central Committee of the party if his course was abandoned.

During the critical days following the German resumption of hostilities (18 February), Robins juggled his time and energy to deal with three closely related tasks. Most immediate was the necessity of withdrawing the Allied representatives from Petrograd to a safer point to the east or out of Russia entirely, via Finland or Vladivostok. Ambassador Francis, in consultation with Robins, resolved to keep his mission in Russia, but not to follow the Bolshevik leadership to Moscow. A move of the American and Allied delegations to Moscow was rejected for two reasons: first, that city also stood in danger of German occupation; and second, of particular concern to Francis, such a move would have been construed as a form of recognition of the Bolshevik regime. Robins and Francis suggested to Washington that a temporary embassy be established in Vologda, due east of Petrograd and north of Moscow and equidistant from both. There, American and Allied interests could be looked after with minimal danger to personnel; further, the town had the advantage of good communications facilities and departure possibilities—either north to Murmansk or Archangel or east, via the Trans-Siberian Railroad to Vladivostok. On 24 February, after six days of the renewed German hostilities, the first contingent of Allied representatives left Petrograd for the day-long journey to Vologda. Their transportation and that of the rest of the Allied community was personally arranged by Robins, who consulted directly with Lenin on the matter.[7]

Two days later, after the settlement of embassy business in Petrograd, Ambassador Francis and his entourage arrived at the Nikolaevski Station. At the last moment, when the dignitaries were about to depart, they were informed that for security reasons the train was not to leave. The Bolshevik government had determined that their departure demonstrated a lack of confidence in Soviet control of the situation and might induce panic in the city. Robins went directly to Lenin at the Smolny and convinced him to let the train go. In the bitter early morning cold of the next day, with his No. 447 Red Cross railroad car added at the last moment, Robins set off with the others for Vologda.

Allied missions were soon safely established in the provincial town, but far from the seat of Soviet power. Robins still had two pressing tasks. After fighting desperately against the signing of the peace at Brest-Litovsk, he was determined to avert the ratification of the settlement by the Fourth Special All-Russian Congress of Soviets. The only way to stop its ratification, he was sure, was a fast and generous offer of American military and economic aid to Russia. Such a dramatic demonstration of support, Robins was convinced, would prevent the Congress of Soviets from ratifying the "shameful peace" and would instead unite the Bolsheviks and the Allies in a final struggle against the "German autocracy."

Robins remained in Vologda with his colleagues for three days while keeping in constant communication with Lockhart in Petrograd. And through Gumberg, who had accompanied him to Vologda, he remained in close touch with both Smolny and Brest-Litovsk. After an initial false report of the breakdown of the peace talks and an alarmed telegram to Vologda from Lenin himself, word finally came of the signing of the peace on Sunday, 3 March. Robins immediately arranged to have the Red Cross car attached to the first train heading for Petrograd. As soon as the train arrived in the capital, on the morning of 5 March, Robins went directly to Smolny. He met with Trotsky and they discussed the peace settlement. It was a charged encounter. Trotsky knew all too well that Russia's separate peace with Germany, regardless of the terms, was the object against which Robins had been struggling from the moment of his arrival in Russia. The meeting was one of the most urgent in Robins's negotiations with the Soviet leadership. "And then came the hour," Robins recalled, when the Brest Peace was about to be ratified. Some of us had worked hard to prolong the hour of any sort of settlement between Russia and the Central Powers, and we could have stopped the ratification of the Brest peace by any art in our power. I had instructions from the Ambassador of the United States, with initialed memoranda . . . instructing me what to do, and what representations I was to make to the soviet power, saying he would recommend recognition as a de facto government in certain particular circumstances outlined in the memoranda. . . . And the 5th of March came, and I was in Trotsky's office. . . .

"Do you want to prevent the ratification of the Brest Peace?"

I said, "Yes, that is the one thing I want to do."

He said, "I think you can do it."

I said, "I like to dream."

He said, "Will America help soviet Russia against Germany?"

I said, "Sure."

"Give us military support and economic support?"

I said, "Sure."

He said, "If you will do that, we can defeat the ratification of the Brest Peace."

I said, "Let me be frank with you Commissioner." You see, I was not a diplomat. . . . I did not have to veil anything. . . .

I said, "I don't know anything about these propositions, but let me say this to you: Lenin is for the peace, and Lenin is running the show. I know you are against the peace, absolutely against it, but what about Lenin?"

He said, "If you can assure us from your Government that they will give you military and economic support, we will defeat the ratification of the peace."

I said, "Will Lenin do that?"

"Yes."

"Will you put that in writing?"

He started to say "Yes," almost, and then stopped—"Do you want me to give away my life? We have just signed a paper at Brest, and the Germans are right at the front."

I said, "I don't ask you to sign it. I have not gotten to that yet."

I said, "Commissioner, I have got to have a specific communication, however, on this, because it is so important. You have got to give me a specific proposition so that I can send it direct by cable to the American government, and then I want you to have Lenin and myself and a fourth person present when the statements are made, and I will act on it."

I came back at four o'clock, at Smolny. . . . And I went out of Trotsky's office and he gave me this paper and he walked down to Lenin's office, and we sat down. The paper was interpreted, and the situation developed, and Lenin agreed to the proposition in definite fashion.[8]

The statement orally agreed to but not signed on the afternoon of 5 March was translated by Gumberg as follows:

In case (a) the All Russian Congress of the Soviets will refuse to ratify the peace treaty with Germany, or (b) if the German government, breaking the peace treaty, will renew the offensive in order to continue its robbers' raid, or (c) if the Soviet government will be forced by the actions of Germany to renounce the peace treaty—before or after its ratification—and to renew hostilities—

In all these cases it is very important for the military and political plans of the Soviet power for replies to be given to the following questions:

1. Can the Soviet government rely on the support of the United States of North America, Great Britain, and France in its struggle against Germany?

2. What kind of support could be furnished in the nearest future, and on what conditions—military equipment, transportation supplies, living necessities?

3. What kind of support would be furnished particularly and especially by the United States?

Should Japan—in consequence of an open or tacit understanding with Germany or without such an understanding—attempt to seize Vladivostok and the Eastern-Siberian Railway, which would threaten to cut off Russia from the Pacific Ocean and would greatly impede the concentration of Soviet troops toward the East about the Urals—in such case what steps would be taken by the other allies, particularly and especially by the United States, to prevent a Japanese landing on our Far East, and to insure uninterrupted communications with Russia through the Siberian route?

In the opinion of the Government of the United States, to what extent—under the above-mentioned circumstances—would aid be assured from Great Britain through Murmansk and Archangel? What steps could the Government of Great Britain undertake in order to assure this aid and thereby to undermine the foundation of the rumors of the hostile plans against Russia on the part of Great Britain in the nearest future?

All these questions are conditioned with the self-understood assumption that the internal and foreign policies of the Soviet government will continue to be directed in accord with the principles of international socialism and that the Soviet government retains its complete independence of all non-socialist governments.[9]

In a signed affidavit describing the events surrounding the proposals, Robins asserted, "Commissar Trotsky requested that this statement be transmitted in cipher and stated that this was the first formal statement submitted by his Government seeking cooperation . . . of any of the governments heretofore in alliance with Russia during the present war."[10]

After receiving the proposition, Robins went directly to Lockhart to inform him of its importance. Robins then telegraphed its contents to Ambassador Francis at Vologda and assumed, in light of its extreme importançe, that it was immediately transmitted to Washington. However, at Vologda the message could not be deciphered—the military code was used, and the code books were just then en route to Petrograd with Col. James A. Ruggles, the new head of the American embassy's military mission and military attaché in Petrograd, and his assistant, Capt. E. Francis Riggs. The American consul in Petrograd, Roger C. Tredwell, demanded that Trotsky's message be sent to

Washington immediately through the facilities of the military mission, but Capt. Eugene Prince, in charge at the time, decided to await the return of Ruggles, his superior.

Ruggles reached Petrograd that night and did not send the message until seventeen days later. Speculations about his motives in this situation include an expectation to see Trotsky himself; however, this does not account for not informing Robins or Tredwell that he had not carried out their urgent request. For nine days following the dispatch of the Trotsky questions, Robins anxiously awaited the State Department response, not knowing his message had never been sent. The expected promises of support would result in greatly increased adherence for Trotsky's position in the All-Russian Congress of Soviets and, thus, the defeat of ratification.[11]

By the end of February, another issue began to trouble those who hoped to keep Russia in the war. On 6 March, the day after Trotsky presented Robins with his proposals, Robins telegraphed the following message to Thompson via the offices of the Red Cross in Washington.

> Persistent rumors that Japan encouraged by Allies about to take possession of Vladivostok and advance along Siberian Railroad cutting off all transportation necessary for interior Russia. These rumors said to be credited by Bolshevik government. Such invasion if true and countenanced by Allies will destroy all possibility of Russian resistance to German aggression and will confiscate all American advantages in Russian situation present and prospective. If Allied support is promised to become effective after open breach with Central Powers, substantial resistance to German control possible and important limitation of Russian supplies for Central Powers certain.
>
> You should also see cipher message sent by Ambassador Secstate today. Conditions here more hopeful for effective allied cooperation along lines previously indicated than ever.[12]

On the same day Robins wrote to Colonel Ruggles about the same issues: Japanese intervention and the special communication from Trotsky to the Allied governments. Robins planned to discuss these matters personally with Ruggles and assumed that the communication from Trotsky had already been sent. Robins wrote this letter to confirm that Ruggles had in fact forwarded Trotsky's important message. Robins did not talk directly to him, because Ruggles was en route to Petrograd while Robins was preparing to leave for Vologda. The text reads:

> Yesterday a message in the code of the Military Mission was transmitted to Vologda for the Ambassador addressed to yourself. A copy of this message is in the custody of Captain Prince and I would be grateful if you had it de-coded and gave its contents such consideration as it may seem to deserve. The government at Smolny is greatly exercised over the alleged Japanese invasion in Siberia and the intended control of transportation on the Siberian Railway. I have discussed this matter fully with Commissioners Trotsky and Lenin; and Mr. R. R. Stevens, of the National City Bank, knows my full mind upon the

subject. I am convinced that there is yet considerable salvage in the Russian situation for the benefit of America and the Allied cause.

Because of the difficulty in getting transportation from Petrograd at this time, I feel constrained not to delay my departure, as much as I desire to confer with you. If by any chance, the Ambassador shall have left Vologda, or it be impossible to de-code the message of last night, I hope you will get its contents to him under conditions that will insure secrecy at the earliest possible moment.[13]

The nine days from 5 to 14 March were among the most frantic in all of Robins's ten month stay in Russia. The sleepless nights and desperate efforts proved fruitless.

Robins believed that a positive response from Washington could change the direction of the ratification deliberations, and thus the war and the course of modern history. If the United States and Russia could be reconciled, the Central Powers could be beaten. Shortly after receiving Trotsky's proposals, Robins met with Lenin and pleaded for time to permit the United States to deliberate with France and England. He argued that such a commitment had to be agreed upon by all three Allied powers if they were to have any real meaning.

On the day after his meeting with Lenin, Robins was informed that the Congress of Soviets was to begin in Moscow on the fourteenth, postponing its opening two days from the originally set date of the twelfth. Since this delay was ordered by Lenin himself, Robins assumed that his plea for more time for consideration of the Trotsky proposals had been heeded. Kennan presents considerable and convincing evidence to discount this claim, in opposition to support it has received in Williams's "Raymond Robins" and Wheeler-Bennett's *The Forgotten Peace*. Kennan cites Lenin's unswerving commitment to the ratification to deny Robins's assertion that the proposal on Allied cooperation was taken seriously. Regarding the postponement, Kennan suggests that it was done because of the movement of government offices from Petrograd to Moscow on 10–11 March; the two additional days were required to put things in order before the Congress began.

Kennan concludes that "either he [Robins] was the victim of misinformation that so frequently dogged his path during the months of his activity in Russia, or that his memory failed him, or both." Kennan's analysis presumes that the proposal for Allied cooperation drawn up by Trotsky could not be taken seriously, or worse that it was a mendacious manipulation. Given Trotsky's opposition to the peace, it is this author's opinion that the proposals, if acted upon by the Allies, might have played a role in delaying or altering the terms of the peace. To dismiss their possible or potential importance at a time of such flux and crisis is hasty and incorrect.[14]

Since Robins believed he had done all he could in Petrograd, he left for Vologda to convey the situation personally to Ambassador Francis, whose support had to be enthusiastic if the proposals were to be accepted. Robins and Gumberg arrived in Vologda on the night of 8 March and met with Francis immediately, presenting him with the "original copy" of the proposals. After two days of deliberation on the Japanese threat in Siberia and the possibilities offered by the proposals, Robins and the ambassador reached a consensus. They communicated with Washington by telegraph on several issues, but mistakenly assumed the prior receipt of the proposals. Robins was still awaiting favorable response when he attached his Red Cross car to the regularly scheduled train and set out for Moscow. He arrived there on 11 March, three days prior to the opening of the Congress of Soviets, which he planned to observe. While awaiting the specific response to the proposals, hoping it would arrive soon enough to be properly presented at the Congress, Robins was asked to forward a different message to the Congress of Soviets from President Wilson himself. This telegraphed message of "sincere sympathy which the people of the United States feel for the Russian people" was sent through the office of the American consul general in Moscow, Maddin Summers. On 12 March he passed it on to Robins, who personally delivered it to Lenin.

Wilson's message, like many expressions of goodwill between peoples which ignore the ill will between their governments, was very general and included a three-fold reiteration of the good feelings that Americans have for Russia, her people, and their "attempt to free themselves forever from autocratic government and become masters of their own life." On the matter of American aid to Russia, the pivotal issue that would influence the continuation of Russia in the war, Wilson apologized that "the Government of the United States is unhappily not now in a position to render the direct and effective aid it would wish to render." Robins was disappointed by the inclusion of this passage because it seemed to preclude any possibility of a positive answer to the Trotsky proposals, which he still believed were being studied.[15]

"Then I went down to Vologda and met the American Ambassador," Robins later recounted,

there we were with a united front to deal with the situation as it could be dealt with.

Then I went down to the Fourth All-Russian Soviet and waited, and waited, and I never heard one word. . . . I knew it had reached the military War Department, because it was sent in the military code, but I had not known it had reached the State Department.

When we got in that conference of the Fourth All Russian Soviet, the matter of the Brest peace was in issue. Lenin speaks at the first meeting, carefully, leaving the field free. We adjourned the meeting under conference two days, as will appear from the record. It was called to meet on the 12th. It did not meet until the 14th of March, to give the allied governments time to get together and answer, and then they held up the meeting two whole days and nights before going into a shameful peace. Nobody ever spoke of it as anything but a shameful peace, a robber peace, a peace at the point of the bayonet, but they said, "Because of our broken economic life we will have to accept it, unless we get help from the allies."

And in the last hour of that twenty-four, just before midnight, Lenin was seated on the platform, and I am sitting on a step of the dais that goes up to the platform. I turn and look at him, and he beckons to me and I go up to him.

He said, "Have you heard from your government?"

I said, "No I have not."

He said, "I told you you would not."

I said, "Has Lockhart heard from his government?"

"Not a word."

He said, "The peace will be ratified."

And he went to the platform and spoke one hour and forty minutes, spoke of the revolution, spoke of the situation, spoke of present conditions, and by two and a half or nearly three to one, that meeting voted for the ratification, at the end of his speech.[16]

Not until the investigations of William A. Williams and George Kennan did it become clear that Washington had not been informed of the exact content of the Trotsky proposals until after the ratification by the Congress of Soviets.[17] Decades later Robins remained convinced of the great opportunity that had been lost through what he considered the blundering and poor judgment of American "officials" in Russia and America.

In 1944, twenty-six years after Russia's withdrawal from World War I, Thomas W. Lamont reviewed the vital issues with Robins and asked his "detached" opinion in light of hindsight.

I should like to ask you one question: As you look back over all these years, are you of the impression that, if President Wilson had done something more tangible, sending out not an Edgar Sisson but perhaps naming yourself or someone else to work with Bruce Lockhart, the final result would have been different? Do you really think that the Bolsheviks could have held off from signing and ratifying the Treaty of Brest-Litovsk?

The last time I had any communication with Bruce Lockhart he rather seemed to think that the influences compelling the execution of the Treaty were too strong to have been offset by any efforts that America and Britain might have made.

I rather gather, however from the nature of your own constant communications that you were of the opposite opinion.[18]

Robins's answer to this letter is not in the archives, but the evidence concerning his opinion (correctly stated by Lamont) is conclusive.

In the absence of evidence to the contrary, Robins was convinced that his personal appeals to Lenin (and Lenin's assurances) had caused the two-day postponement of the vote of ratification of the Brest-Litovsk Peace by the All-Russian Soviet from 12 March, its formally scheduled date, to the fourteenth. Robins saw the mistakes of the winter of 1917–18 as a lost opportunity for Soviet-American understanding and cooperation at the critical inauguration of the most important international relationship of the century.

15

Cooperation after Brest-Litovsk

For four months I have been the link between the government of Russia and the government of the United States. I am still apparently trusted by both though we have had awful strains. . . .

—Raymond to Margaret, 14 April 1918

AFTER the ratification by so overwhelming a majority, one might have assumed Robins's final acceptance of defeat. However, Robins telegraphed to Thompson in New York on the day after the vote, and for the first time he raised the prospect and consequences of an Allied armed intervention in Bolshevik Russia:

> Brest Treaty ratified by All-Russian Soviet Congress. Short period until non-compliance with impossible German demands will provoke conflict with Central Powers. Soviet Government still in undisputed control of all effective force of Russian People. For some time to come effective control in Russia possible only three following methods:
> First, cooperation with and support of Soviet government;
> Second, Allied advance in Siberia with sufficient force to overcome opposition which will take form of civil war in every considerable city through which Allied forces advance;
> Third, Russian reactionary control maintained by German bayonets.
> Second method might save Siberia but would permanently lose European Russia. Not to choose either method, in other words a continued policy of inaction, will insure the third method before a great time. I cannot too strongly urge cooperation with Soviet Government.[1]

Robins had not given up. On the contrary, Allied supplies and assistance would strengthen the Soviet position and would inevitably lead to noncompliance with the peace terms and the renewal of hostilities. Robins was also responding to rumors of a Japanese intervention expected in Vladivostok and the possibility of American support for such a move; he predicted dire results and resolved to do all he could to avert armed Allied interference in Russia. His warning, which was ignored, proved accurate.

In spite of his expectation of Russian noncompliance with the German terms, Robins did alter his emphasis and redirect his energies following the ratification. Circumstances and movement on the Soviet scene demanded a change of priorities. Trotsky was no longer minister of foreign affairs. The Council of People's Commissars assigned Georgi Chicherin to the position when Lenin's policy of acquiescence to the German territorial demands had won the day. With Trotsky now as commissar for war, Robins hoped to develop the cooperation that would strengthen Russia's fighting power, a prerequisite for that country's reentry into the war. In addition, given the disastrous condition of the Russian economy and facilities for transportation and distribution of war materiel, Robins turned his attention to renewed plans for economic cooperation.

Long before, Robins had noted the incredible potential of Russia's natural resources and looked ahead to the postwar era—to the mutual benefits of Soviet-American economic cooperation. While he had expressed such ideas soon after the fall of the Czar, even before joining the Red Cross Commission, and had maintained his commitment to the idea under the Provisional Government and through the Bolshevik Revolution, the first formal overtures for such cooperation came from the Bolshevik leadership. As early as the first week of January 1918, Trotsky approached Robins.

> He said, "Have you not got a railroad mission somewhere?"
> I said, "Yes."
> "Where?"
> "Nagasaki."
> "What is it doing there?"
> "Eating its head off."
> "Why does it not come on here?"
> "You know commissioner, we are not sure about this situation here. You know there are a good many sincere men who think this thing is all rotten, and is being directed from Berlin."
> He said, "Do they think that still?"
> I said, "Yes; many of them do."
> He said, "You send in your mission. We will give you control of the Trans-Siberian at all points. We will make any man you designate assistant commissioner of ways and communication, and let him have an office right in with our minister of ways and communication of the Soviet government here in Moscow; [sic] and then we will move the resources in transportation in Russia. . . .
> It was a perfectly selfish proposition. They greatly needed the organization of the transportation, and they did not have the people in the soviet government that could deliver the goods.[2]

On 17 March, two days after the ratification, Trotsky finally arrived in Moscow, having made the journey from Petrograd with Lockhart. On the next day Trotsky met with Robins and renewed his appeal for cooperation. He asked for American army officers to inspect, train, and equip the Soviet army. He also asked for the railroad experts and equipment then stationed in Japan. Robins agreed to these two proposals and convinced Capt. E. Francis Riggs, assistant American military attaché in Petrograd, to suggest formally to Col. James A. Ruggles, his immediate superior, "that the first contingent of railroad men now waiting in the east be ordered by you [Ambassador Francis] to Vologda."

In his telegram to Francis, reporting on the 18 March meeting, Robins raised for the first time the "claims and reports that [German and Austrian] war prisoners are armed in great numbers in Siberia." This reported development (entirely false, according to Trotsky) and the threat to Allied interests that it posed was to dog the rest of Robins's stay in Russia and undercut his plans for Soviet-American cooperation. Trotsky asked Robins to arrange for a "responsible investigator at once to [go to] Irkutsk with [a] Soviet official and under full authority of [the Soviet] government to make [a] report." On his own initiative Robins sent Capt. William B. Webster of the American Red Cross Commission with Capt. W. L. Hicks of the British military mission for this purpose.[3]

Robins, Lockhart, Capt. Jacques Sadoul of the French military mission, and Riggs, along with General Romei, the Italian military attaché, all worked on the question of military advisors and aid. A strong Soviet army, especially one aided and advised by the Allies, would help keep the Germans out of Russia and might help reestablish the eastern front. From all indications, the Bolshevik leadership was anxious to develop these lines of military cooperation. The reorganization of rail transport was equally as vital to the restoration of economic order as it was to the safe and swift movement of the Allied stores still stockpiled at Vladivostok, Archangel, and elsewhere.

The third issue raised in Robins's telegram to Francis, the allegation that the Bolsheviks were arming prisoners of war of the Central Powers in Siberia, was reported to Washington at the same time that Edgar Sisson was forwarding his "documents" that purported to prove that the Bolshevik leadership was in the pay of the German High Command. The Allies were alarmed by these reports on arming prisoners and saw in them a pattern of Bolshevik treachery. Under these suspicions, Washington, London, and Paris saw military and economic cooperation with a jaundiced eye. It was crucial for Robins to do all he could to get at the "outdoor" reality and to demonstrate the Bolshevik willingness to cooperate. "Soviet Government organizing army for defense Russian Socialist Republic," Robins cabled Wardwell on 20 March, "Government asks cooperation American Red Cross units for hospital service. . . . Fear for Japanese invasion forced ratification peace treaty. Continued Japanese menace may force Soviet surrender to pro-German reaction. Skillful German propaganda Siberian war prisoner scare and Petrograd Moscow German control if believed in Washington will finally defeat all plans for American cooperation."[4]

While awaiting a report of POW conditions, Robins pursued the possibilities of cooperation. Within four days of first proposing the use of Allied advisors, Robins reported to Francis that the "French mission here has accepted Trotsky offer and is making assignment of officers for inspection work for

Soviet Army. Specific request by Soviet government," Robins continued, "that I ask you to inquire of American government if Commission for economic and business purposes sent by Economic Commission of Soviet government will be received in United States—It is guaranteed by the Soviet government that this commission will have no political purpose and will not engage in any propaganda work of any description en route or in America."[5]

Although the idea of an economic commission and general long-term trade agreements did not have the same immediacy or urgency as did military organization, railroad supervision, or the supervision of POWs, it was only in this area of Soviet-American cooperation that anything developed. In the six weeks following this first suggestion by Trotsky, specific possibilities of extensive economic cooperation were discussed and formally proposed by the Red Cross mission and Soviet officials. When Robins finally left Russia in May he had great hopes of carrying out these plans, but until then, he focused on the more pressing issues.

Robins rushed about Moscow driving from meeting to meeting in the Red Cross Pierce Arrow car, responding to developments in each case with a barrage of activity. His diary entries for these days, in scrawled cursive symbols, merely hint at the pace of his movement, but they resound with the passionate commitment and spiritual mission that supported his unfailing optimism in the face of grave setbacks.

It was at just this time that Robins and Lenin had one of their most open discussions of basic social, economic, and political issues. Robins's account of the conversation presents Lenin in an informal and frank interchange, a rarity, especially with an American "official." It also suggests the mutual respect shared by the two men. Finally, Robins depicts Lenin, the pedagogue, teaching Marx to an eager, skeptical, and questioning fellow student of history.

> "Along in the latter part of March," Robins began,
> I am in the Kremlin one day, talking to him. He is sitting there in the high court of the Tsar, in the Tsar's chamber, leaning back in the Tsar's special chair, with both hands resting against the Tsar's coronet woven into the fabric of the chair. He turns to me saying,
> "Colonel Robins, do you know the idea in the Russian Revolution?"

There followed a bit of cat and mouse banter—definition and clarification—which, according to Robins, finally provided Lenin the opening to launch into his Marx primer lesson number one.

> "Well there was a religious social control that was valid for a time. There was a feudal social control that was valid for a time. Then there was a middle-class, political bourgeois, capitalist control, and now there is about to be a producers' economic social control. The new social control is economic. The only important task of society today is to feed and clothe and house men, women and children, and that is a great economic task. Every political social control is moribund and outgrown.

"Well," I said, more for the sake of talking than anything else. "That may be true so far as Russia and Germany are concerned, but what about Britain and America? Talk about America being old and moribund? We are only 144 years old. We have all the signs of creative life, inventive genius, etc."

He looked at me rather earnestly and said: "America is entirely corrupt."

I lost my temper for the only time, so far as I could remember.

"Say, Commissioner, that isn't true. I know America fairly well, know its corrupt political conditions, but also know district after district where simple citizens get together and nominate other simple citizens for important public offices, and finally on a certain day these citizens go to the polling places and make a choice of these nominees, uncorrupted and unpaid. No corruption about it."

"I say corrupt. I sometimes use English badly. I mean that your government is lacking in economic integrity. You have a state that is called New York. You have a state that is called Pennsylvania? Ah, Colonel Robins, what is the economic significance of your State of New York in your American Republic? New York's economic significance is fluid capital, capital for investment, capital for the production of new capitalistic enterprises, capital for the reproduction of old capitalistic enterprises. Fluid capital. That is the significance of your State of New York. Who knows most about it? A Mr. Pierpont Morgan, is it?"

"Yes, I suppose so."

"What social use did you make of Mr. Morgan? Did you send him to your Senate, to Congress, so that he could work out his financial system for the benefit of your country? No? Why not? For two reasons. He wouldn't have gone. He won't have wasted his time. Second, you couldn't have sent him. The people would not have elected him. They feared him, suspected him. His very success makes him an object of fear and suspicion. You do not believe in your own system. You do not trust it."

"Your State of Pennsylvania, what is its economic significance?"

I said, "Steel, coal, railroads."

"You have other States that have coal and steel and railroads. It is the State's precedence in the production of steel. That is its economic significance. Who knows most about it? Mr. Gary, Mr. Schwab? What do you do with them? Send them to Congress to advise the government about the production of your basic industry? You do not. And why? For the same two reasons. You do not believe in your own institutions. Your own economic success threatens you as a people. The American system is as an old man, old now, through with his task, has been a great man in his time. The Russian Soviet is a baby in the cradle, maybe, but he has all the capacity for a new creative system."

"What is the economic significance of the Baku to the Russian Soviet Republic? It is oil, light, power. Who will sit from Baku in the Russian Soviet? The producers of oil, hand and brain. Not the parasites, but the producers, hand and brain. From the coal regions will sit the producers, hand and brain. The transportation systems will be represented by the producers of their benefits, hand and brain, in the Russian Soviet. It will be the most intelligent body in the world. We will have the strongest social control in the world."

"Do you know the idea in the French Revolution? There were a number of ideas, but when you understand it there was but one idea. The French Revolution was the emergence of the bourgeois capitalist political social control in contest with the moribund, outgrown feudal social control. The feudal social control united the representatives of this dying control and overthrew the French Revolution, as they supposed, but the idea in the French Revolution destroyed every feudal social control in Europe. Capitalist social control may strangle the Soviet, but the idea of the Soviet will destroy every existing capitalistic control in the world today."

Going back to the Kremlin later, (I had) an opportunity coming to me, I turned to Lenin and said:

"Commissioner, I have been thinking about your producers' economic social control. Do you expect to establish your system in the world through revolutionary propaganda and revolutionary force?"

"Oh," he said, "It is foolishness, external propaganda. Do you not know that all it ever does is to unite and solidify domestic forces, national forces? No propaganda is of any value unless it is domestically created out of domestic conditions. No external force for ideas is ever valuable. You cannot compel ideas by external force. It is not competent. Certainly not at this stage of the world. Our propaganda may be suggestive to your propaganda in America. Our force methods may be the methods adopted by you later, but it must be domestic, it must be native."

"Well, if that is so I feel rather encouraged. I know my country fairly well, and I don't think there is any propaganda for your program."

"Oh, you feel so?" Said Lenin. Then, looking at me rather quizzically amused. "Colonel Robins, why do you not sometimes think? Have you ever considered capitalism? It is selfishness, capitalism is selfishness. Universal selfishness—and then what? You have the paralysis of production, the suicide of capital. The capitalist is always more or less intelligently selfish, getting all he can for himself, producing not for the service of the world, but for his own private pocket, ready to delay or destroy production if he can profit."

"And labor?" I asked.

"Labor has not been selfish in the past. Not wholly so. It has been diverted by religious and national considerations. But labor is becoming selfish, is acquiring the same solidity of selfishness that characterizes capitalism. When labor is wholly selfish and capital is wholly selfish, you have completed the circle. What do they do when each makes such demands upon the common produce as increases the cost of living beyond the reach of the consumers? What do they do? It reduces consumption. It is the paralysis of production. It is the suicide of capitalism. It is taking place throughout the world today as we sit here."[6]

Robins defended the free enterprise system and explained his distinction between individual and social wealth and property, as well as the division of private and public industry and business. But he was impressed with Lenin's thinking and the underlying intent that sought the eradication of selfishness. Robins learned and accepted Lenin's assurances that he (Lenin) was convinced that socialist revolution must be homegrown, that revolutionary propaganda "must be domestic, it must be native." The fear of Bolshevik contagion from Russia was widespread in the west and both Trotsky's economic proposals and Lenin's assurances were intended to ease the suspicions.

In Robins's account of Lenin's analysis of the crisis in capitalism in America —selfish capitalism against selfish labor to the point of economic suicide— much of Lenin's thought can be identified. However, almost as much of Robins's own formulations—his language and critique of uncontrolled capitalism—can be found, put in the mouth of Lenin. These frank exchanges brought Robins closer to Lenin, convincing Robins more than ever of Lenin's sincerity. Robins's respect and admiration for his ideological opponent grew with each encounter.

Robins's optimism about the future of American democracy extended to the "producers democracy" of revolutionary Russia, especially in light of the growing body of positive evidence he found concerning the Bolshevik leadership. In a report of developments wired to Francis at Vologda on 27 March, Robins noted the "almost complete change of the Bolshevik press," which was reporting developments on the western front honestly and expressing opinions favorable to the Allied war effort. After noting the marked cooperation of all the Allied military missions in the planned reorganization of the Soviet army, Robins asked the ambassador if "Washington [would] credit discarded forgeries [the Sisson Documents] of German control?" Robins noted that both England and France favored cooperation in the reorganization of the Russian army. "England has ordered admiral at Murmansk to cooperate fully with Soviet power—France Ditto—," wrote Robins. "Shall we lose our hold throwing away American advantages just when support in London and Paris won?"[7]

The irony underlying this situation, so poignant in light of Robins's open enthusiasm, is seen in a communication from Francis to the State Department wired just one day prior to Robins's report. Francis informed his superiors of his decision to involve the American military mission in assisting in the reorganization of the Soviet army, joining the French and Italians who had already been assigned. However, his reasons for this involvement were not those that Robins gave. Francis explained that such an armed force could "By proper methods be taken from Bolshevik control and used against the Germans and even its creators [the Bolshevik leadership] if [it] prove that [they are] German allies. I anticipate not revealing last reason to Robins and Riggs."[8] Nevertheless, American participation in the plan never materialized because a Department of State directive on the matter forbade such assistance.

In light of this distrust on the part of the ambassador, a formal notice received by Robins and dated 29 March 1918, signed by both Lenin, acting in his official capacity and under the title "Chairman of the Council of Peoples' Commissaries" and Chicherin, "Acting Peoples' Commissaries of Foreign Affairs," was particularly significant. It began with a statement of appreciation for the humanitarian services rendered by the Red Cross and credits Robins's special contribution to its success.[9]

That Robins solicited this statement himself in hopes of strengthening his position with the ambassador and Washington is not beyond possibility. The formulation of the final paragraph suggests the departure of Robins, the mission, or both, and it would seem that Robins believed that the signatures of Lenin and Chicherin would impress American officials of the desirability of retaining both himself and the mission. In letters to Margaret written months before, Robins had expressed concerns about being recalled because of his views. With the expected arrival of Sisson in Washington with his cache of forged documents and his strong opposition to both the Bolsheviks and Robins's plans for cooperation, it could be that Robins decided to provide himself with some additional ammunition for the approaching fight.

Another important problem played a role in Robins's expectations and activities in Moscow. Long before his arrival in the new Soviet capital, he had earned the displeasure of Consul General Maddin Summers, the senior State Department official there. Summers was a career foreign service officer, well-trained and committed to the official lines of communication and command. He hated, distrusted, and feared the Bolshevik leadership from the first. He was convinced that they were in the service of German interests and were without popular support among the Russian people. From this point of view, Summers found Robins dangerously objectionable, a disrupter of the chain of communication and command, and a usurper of authority that had been specifically delegated to others by the State Department; Robins's "flirtations" with the Bolsheviks misrepresented American policy and were in discord with, if not inimical to, American national interest.

Only days after his arrival in Moscow, in mid-March, Robins's reports and suggestions were frequently undermined by those of Summers, whose ideas were formulated under all the disadvantages of "indoor" conditions. Only with the untimely death of Summers and with Robins's recall and humiliation in Washington did this unfortunate struggle finally come to an end.

At the height of the conflict, Robins wrote to Allen Wardwell, who was terminating Red Cross work in Petrograd. He expressed some hope in the situation because of a new British initiative. "Confidentially today (3 April)," Robins wrote, "I was shown a telegram from [Lord Arthur] Balfour [British foreign secretary] to our government asking that I be empowered to cooperate in support of their (British) policy—this policy being the one we have taught Lockhart and that we have fought for now for six months. So wags the world away!" But Robins's hope was restrained. "Between the Ambassador and myself," he continued, "there is perfect good will and no little cooperation, but our relations are a sort of Peace from necessity similar to the German Russian affair at Brest. I am still being used by him for all relations between the two governments and am in receipt daily of confidential communications. Still I know that if he held me over a cliff and could afford to let go he would do so with a sigh of genuine relief."[10]

Two days later, Robins received a wire from Davison, in Washington, inquiring about the work, manpower, and departure plans of the commission. Robins misunderstood its intent, and his curt reply is indicative of the growing tension in his relationship with official Washington. "Murmansk best route for speed Vladivostok for safety. No need now for more Red Cross men here. Unless U.S. supports economic cooperation and constructive program all useful work finished May first. If Administration Red Cross here unsatisfactory kindly recall me."[11] The tension expressed here began weeks and months of extreme bitterness.

On the same day that he received the Lenin-Chicherin document, the first of a series of long-awaited reports arrived from Siberia from Webster and Hicks. The first is interesting not only because of what it conveys of the POW situation but also because it reveals a divergence of opinion on the revolutionary situation that conforms to Robins's "indoor"—"outdoor" dichotomy. The report finds that the only prisoners of the Central Powers who were being armed were approximately one thousand men, primarily Hungarians, who had deserted at the beginning of the war, and most important, all of whom "are social revolutionists . . . thoroughly instilled with Bolshevik ideas." Webster and Hicks concluded that "there is no immediate danger of armed prisoners seizing Siberian Railway." The report discussed the divergent opinion held by Maj. Walter S. Drysdale, American military attaché at Peking, who had also been sent to investigate the POW situation. Drysdale, highly critical of the Bolshevik leadership, was seriously concerned about the danger to Allied interests. To resolve the differences of opinion, Webster and Hicks suggested that a "Small number of American soldiers be attached to the guard of each camp to see the conditions."[12]

Robins quickly embraced the recommendations of Webster and Hicks and, coupled with the unreserved assurances of the Soviet leadership and other corroborating reports, dismissed the tales of danger as misinformed "indoor" opinion. In the weeks that followed, additional reports expressing opposing views were received by Francis, who remained noncommittal on the problem. Unfortunately the reports of danger to Allied interests coincided with the growing weight given to the Sisson documents and caused the interim and final reports of Webster and Hicks to be given little serious consideration. (They have since proven to be quite accurate.) By April Robins's reports and proposals began to be received with similar incredulity.

On 5 April, in response to the murder of three Japanese citizens the previous day, Admiral Kato, commander of the Japanese squadron at Vladivostok, sent 500 Japanese marines ashore, ostensibly to protect the lives and property of Japanese nationals. Two weeks earlier Robins had wired Thompson that "fear of Japanese invasion forced ratification of the peace treaty." On 8 April he wired Francis to the effect that the actual landing would necessarily force the Soviet government to accede to even more disadvantageous demands by Germany. "German menace is much more immediate and if Soviet forced to choose between Japanese bayonets five thousand miles away and German bayonets two hundred miles away the choice is not difficult to guess."[13]

The diplomatic and strategic issues related to the Japanese intervention go beyond the scope of this book. Central, however, is Robins's opposition to the landing and his suggestions to Francis, Thompson, and Davison for American policy vis-à-vis the Japanese. As suggested by Webster and Hicks in their report, Robins proposed an alternative cooperative effort with the Bolsheviks for the maintenance of order and the safeguarding of the Allied interests within Russia. What the "outdoor" community in Moscow was in effect proposing was some form of Allied intervention in Russia by invitation and in cooperation with the Bolshevik leadership. There had been numerous requests and suggestions to this effect on the part of Trotsky relative to military cooperation and army organization. Robins, Sadoul, and Lockhart actively pursued such possibilities, opposed the Japanese landing, and tried to convince their superiors of the advantages of an Allied cooperative intervention with Russian consent.

During April the fulfillment of such plans actually appeared possible.[14] The meetings involving Lockhart, Sadoul, Robins, and either Trotsky or Lenin went on almost daily and, after the Japanese landing, with a marked urgency. Although other matters involved him deeply in his remaining weeks in Russia, Robins gave particular attention to the possibility of an invited intervention.

On the evening of 3 April, the day before the murder of the Japanese, Robins had a special conference with Lenin concerning the vast stockpiles of war materiel that the Allies had at Archangel, Murmansk, and Vladivostok. In his report of the conference to Francis, Robins summarized the issues of Soviet power, the question of German influence, the effect of any Japanese intervention, American trust, and Soviet cooperation.

> Soviet government is evacuating all war materials from Petrograd into the interior and asks who can seriously think that a government whose best soldiers have fought against German control in Ukraine and Finland can now be planning to furnish to Germany the power to enslave their own land. Nothing short of Japanese invasion can change the deep resentment all Russians feel against Germany's robber raid and shameful peace forced upon Russia at the point of the bayonet. Soviet government is eager to satisfy America of good faith and secure economic organization through American supervising skill but if every evil rumor becomes foundation for suspicion cooperation will be impossible. Is not five months of control undisputed by any effective internal force and which has survived armed conflict in the Don, Ukraine, Caucasus, Siberia and Great Russia together with the signing of a shameful peace and

the abandonment of the capital and still maintains control of undisputed power sufficient evidence of the foundation in Russian life and will of the soviet government.[15]

This message, like others Robins sent, was intended to convince the ambassador and those who shared his views of the staying power of the Soviet government. Given its permanence and the American and Allied interests that could be served, Robins had long before concluded the logical necessity of de facto recognition of the Soviet regime. His last chance to win acceptance of his recommendations came during the month of April, and thus his communications in behalf of Allied recognition of the Soviets were urgent.

Five days after filing the report to Francis, yet another series of events corroborated Robins's appraisal of Soviet power and control and disproved reports of German influence and Soviet weakness. Robins relates the events in the staccato language of the telegram.

> April ninth at eleven o:clock morning American Red Cross automobile stolen ten armed anarchists. Placed event before leaders of Soviet Government without resentment demanding final demonstration power government against armed bandits and fortress centers calling themselves anarchists. Yesterday morning at two o'clock soviet forces appeared simultaneously before the twenty six different bandit headquarters demanded surrender all weapons five minutes. Some cases immediate surrender others offered strong resistance machine guns from windows bombs and small cannon. Soviet used four inch cannon where resistance lasted beyond ten minutes. One big house blown pieces. Anarchists fighting from cellar until dislodged by smoke bombs. Five hundred twenty two arrests, forty killed, wounded anarchists. Soviet three killed, fourteen wounded. Large rooms found packed with stolen goods some great value. Some German machine guns new make not elsewhere found in Russia. Number of ex-officers Russian army among prisoners. Soviet government has now destroyed bandit organization.[16]

This telegraphic report to Francis failed to mention Robins's receipt of a warm apologetic and explanatory letter on the situation, written by hand and in English by Georgi Chicherin two days prior to the action taken against the anarchists. Chicherin promised the return of the automobile but explained that the revolution was "going through a period of sudden disappearance of the multisecular system of universal despotism and blind obedience, and the stormy growth of the exuberant and buoyant new proletarian—and peasant—society cannot go on quite smoothly." Robins accepted this explanation, and with the decisive action taken against the anarchists and the return of the automobile, he felt further justification of his trust in the Bolshevik leadership.[17]

To be completely sure that the action taken against the anarchists had brought home the proper point, Robins wired Davison in Paris, through the embassy at Vologda:

Recent events emphasize recommendations for economic constructive program cooperation between Soviet Government and America. Complete wiping out anarchists organized force Moscow final vindication Soviet internal control. Simply repeat cumulative conclusions for five months. Unless such cooperation between Governments useful work ended May 1. Wardwell, Magnuson finishing milk distribution Petrograd. Webster returning from Siberian war prisoner investigation. Well done. Substance reports Secstate Washington complete refutation armed war prisoner scare.[18]

Robins's reiteration of the 1 May date for the end of Red Cross work was not a ploy. As he was not wielding influence on American policymaking from his close proximity to the Bolshevik leaders, he would try to bring his influence to bear in Washington. He had no intention of leaving Russia while the possibility of cooperation could be served by his presence. He rather felt forced to leave by "indoor" men of influence—"the stupidity of the bureaucrats of the allied embassies"—and the inertia that characterized Allied-Soviet relations.[19]

On 14 April, the day he drafted the wire to Davison in Paris, Robins had the first opportunity in many months to write directly to Margaret and Elizabeth. His letters dealt with the problems and expectations of that troubled time, but only in the most general way, for fear of misuse "if opened by the enemy." The letters do not discuss his plans for leaving, but provide the only candid expression of his feelings, anxieties, and hopes (other than his cryptic diary notes) for the period since January. They explain his desire to rush to Washington to try to carry out his program of cooperation there. "At last a chance to send a letter," he began to Margaret,

> I have not written for ages, no chance to get it out—and if it should get out I have hardly dared to send the merest word lest it be subject to misinterpretation if opened by the enemy.
> We have just passed through a local battle with the Anarchists of Moscow and they were cleaned up by the Soviet Government. I am threatened on all sides but you know that I take my chances as of old. I have sent the most important papers and valuable belongings to my private car which is in the yards of the Nikoliefski station where it has been for many weeks stocked with provisions for a month for my command ready to leave at an hours notice. . . .
> When shall this extraordinary hour end! For five months I have been· in command of the American Red Cross mission in Russia and hour by hour almost we have met the surges of revolution and counter revolution and the German advance with crisis after crisis and still the face of the situation is not more stable tonight. We live from day to day and what the hour brings we try to meet with a steady hand.

In letters to both women Robins discussed the forged anti-Bolshevik documents and their exponent, Edgar Sisson. "[He] is pledged to destroy me publicly and politically," Robins wrote to his sister, "and will use a genuine ability and cunning to that end. I expect to beat him in America as I have beaten him here." As a central figure in the vortex of revolutionary events, strange and contradictory rumors surrounded Robins. To Elizabeth, he wrote:

> I am the best hated and the best liked man among the foreign leaders here. But even my enemies respect the fight I have made for the position I support. It is said that I am a German agent, that I have been corrupted by Trotsky and Lenin, that I was an anarchist in America, that I act under the malign influence of a certain Russian Princess, that I am an insane theorist, that I am selling Russia to Wall Street capitalists, that I have betrayed my country and the allies for control of the Siberian Railway, that I have secured vast concessions in the Urals, that I have a monopoly of the platinum resources in Russia, etc, etc.

"The more important things we cannot write of in the public situation," Robins concluded his letter to Margaret. "You will see what the papers carry and from what you now know you can guess the rest. This is certain, it is worth the cost—whatever may betide."[20]

While the accusations made against Robins upon his return home were nowhere as outlandish as these, they were most serious. Suspicion of his Bolshevik leanings and disloyalty to his country pervaded the Wilson administration, and while Robins could laugh away his own list of imaginative indictments, the same cannot be said of his response to the distrust and disrespect he faced at home.

16

Departure:
The Lenin Proposals

It has been my eager desire for over five months to be of some use in interpreting this new democracy to the people of America and I shall hope to continue efforts in this behalf upon my return to my own land.
—Robins to Lenin, 25 April 1918

I personally am not in sympathy with the movement which you represent, but you are in power and we have common interests—particularly as against the Germans—and I assure you that I will act in the utmost good faith.
—DeWitt Clinton Poole to Soviet Foreign Minister
Georgi Chicherin at their first meeting, May 1918

By mid-April, Robins's attitude toward the "indoor opinion" concerning the Bolsheviks and his approach to fulfilling American national interest in Russia were losing support. The fast-changing events, "day by day," and the crises "hour by hour," separated Washington even further from Robins's promotion of Soviet-American cooperation.[1] Robins's metaphor of being held over a cliff by Ambassador Francis, and being dropped if the ambassador could afford it, was becoming a reality. On 13 April Francis reiterated his opposition and perceptively observed that "Robins intense and sincere in everything . . . even saying 'we' when speaking of Soviet. The power of Soviet is weakening daily," the ambassador continued, "making little progress in organizing army. . . . I think time is fast approaching for Allied intervention and Allies should be prepared to act promptly."[2] Robins did not realize the extent of his failure to influence Ambassador Francis against such a course of action. He had devoted countless communications and discussions to convincing Francis of the disastrous repercussions of an Allied intervention and of the need for recognition. Robins had succeeded with other men of prejudicial "indoor" backgrounds such as Thompson, Webster, Wardwell, and Thacher, but he had failed with Sisson and Francis. Washington decided to recall Robins. Fortunately, this coincided almost precisely with his own plans to return to the United States.

Robins's reasons for terminating his work in Russia and his efforts toward Soviet-American cooperation have already been suggested. The reasons that brought Wilson, Lansing, and Davison finally to request Robins's official recall had been gathering force for months.

Throughout the period from Thompson's departure in November to April 1918, Robins's role as intermediary between the U.S. State Department and the Bolshevik leadership was little more than tolerated by Francis, Lansing, and Wilson. At first, unsanctioned contacts with Trotsky and Lenin caused great consternation in Washington, from the president on down. General Judson was punitively recalled for having met with Trotsky. "Referring press reports," Lansing wired Francis at Petrograd on 16 December 1917, "received here last few days concerning communications of Judson with Trotsky relative armistice. President desires American representatives withhold all direct communication with Bolshevik government."

Robins's first secret meeting with Trotsky, and those thereafter, were also viewed with disfavor, but because of the "unofficial" nature of Robins's Red Cross position, such contacts were tolerated and even requested by Francis under the pressures of emergency situations which demanded American-Soviet communication. Finally, on 14 February Lansing wired Francis: "the State Department approves your course and, desires you gradually to keep in somewhat closer and informal touch with Bolshevik authorities using such channels as will avoid any official recognition. The Government is by no means prepared to recognize Bolshevik government officially. Department's previous instructions are modified to this extent."[3]

Throughout the period of Robins's command, his eyewitness reports and those of Gumberg, Webster, Hicks, and others working for the commission were deeply appreciated by Francis and the State Department, to which nearly every scrap was forwarded by the ambassador. But when Robins extended his task beyond the limits of reporter and gatherer of information, officials in both Russia and Washington were upset. Ironically, emergency situations arose that forced Francis to "use" Robins not merely as a conveyor of information, but also to act in Francis's place as a negotiator with the Bolsheviks. This role, developed by both Robins and Francis, is illustrated in this telegram of 30 January 1918, from Francis to Lansing: "Danish and Siamese legations invaded by official armed delegations searching for food but instead of calling diplomatic corps for protest as requested by some colleagues I sent Robins to Smolny. . . . Lenin promised Robins to comply."[4]

From the point of view of Lansing and apparently Wilson, Robins's role was limited to the "humanitarian" work of the Red Cross. The unique position and contacts he developed were barely tolerated as long as they did not interfere with the regular channels of "diplomacy" in the Russian capital. But there were to be no official diplomatic contacts between the United States and the Lenin government. Robins understood his delegated responsibilities differently. "After nearly six months of my administration," he related, "as commander of the American Red Cross Commission in Russia and as unofficial representative of the American Ambassador, David R. Francis, with the soviet government, the American Government and the American Red Cross at Washington relied upon my information and judgement in relation to retention of the mission in Russia, the service it would undertake, and the matter of additional help to carry out its work."[5]

The most pressing reason for dissatisfaction with Robins was his initiation of possible courses of cooperation with the Bolsheviks. At first the plans for military assistance, an economic commission, an advisory role in the organization of the Red Army, a railroad advisory commission, and intervention through Soviet invitation seemed so advantageous to American and Allied interests that Robins's role as initiator and negotiator was tolerated. However, as seen in Francis's telegram of 13 April, such possibilities were being discounted and by the end of the month Francis was calling for immediate Allied intervention, without Soviet consent.

Matters came to a head on 20 April, when Maddin Summers filed a formal request with the State Department for a transfer from his post as consul general at Moscow. He had visited with Francis at Vologda two weeks earlier to plead for Robins's removal because of Robins's interference with the function of his office. Since the ambassador chose not to act on his recommendation, Summers requested a transfer. Enraged by Robins's independent diplomatic initiatives and his own official noncommunication with the Russian government, Summers wired, "there can be no cooperation between Robins and myself."[6] Francis asked Lansing not to remove Summers. He also wired Robins in Moscow of his appreciation for all his valuable help, but "do not feel I should be justified in asking you to remain longer in Moscow to neglect of the prosecution of your Red Cross work."[7]

George Kennan has suggested the following factors that contributed to Robins's decision to leave Russia as well as the State Department and Red Cross decision to recall him. First, the new German ambassador to Soviet Russia, Count Mirbach, arrived three days after Summers's request for transfer, and as Kennan relates, Robins had considered Mirbach's arrival as something of a deadline in the race to begin Allied-Soviet cooperation. Second, Robins's growing role as the Allied representative in relations with the Bolsheviks "may have come as a shock to the Secretary [Lansing] and his advisers, revealing . . . the extent to which Robins was already regarded in Allied circles as the official United States representative to the Soviet government."[8] The third factor related to an urgent message from Sisson received by George Creel, chairman of the Committee on Public Information on or about 25 April. Because of his expectation of the immediate publication of the incriminating (forged) documents at the moment of his arrival in Washington, Sisson warned that all members of his Committee on Public Information (COMPUB) and members of the Red Cross Commission to Russia be ordered home. "On information and advice from Sisson," Lansing telegraphed Bullard, in Petrograd, "who understands aspect of situation of which you are probably ignorant and with indorsement of Creel you and . . . with all possible secrecy to leave . . . all territory controlled by Bolsheviks . . . be out of Bolshevik territory by about May fifth."[9]

Sisson feared reprisal once the revelations that Lenin, Trotsky, and the Bolshevik leadership were in the pay of the German government were made public. It was as a result of the last two points that the Red Cross in Washington finally ordered Robins's return.

"Have discussed situation fully with Davison," Thacher wired Robins from Paris on 26 April, within twenty-four hours of Robins's receipt of the notice of recall. "Have also seen your cables to him and his to you," Thacher continued. "He thoroughly appreciates importance your work and feels you should understand as I do that he cannot make decision until after conferences at home. . . . Davison considers it essential you remain until definite decisions are made unless in your own judgement this appears inexpedient. Sisson in London awaiting advises from Creel. His story stale. Same documents published February in *Petit Parisien* of which I have copies."[10]

Robins did not receive this telegram until days later, by which time he had scheduled his departure. He modified his plans after receiving this cable, but then, on 10 May, he received additional word from Lansing asking that "he return home for consultation."[11]

On that same day, Robins learned that Thomas Thacher, his trusted lieutenant on the mission, had arrived in New York, ready to carry "the outdoor" view about Russia to President Wilson and the foreign policy decisionmakers. Perhaps Thacher would succeed where, five months earlier, Thompson had failed.[12] Two days after his return to his home in New York, Thacher went to Washington to begin his campaign for revision of U.S. policy toward the Lenin regime. As a result of his father's (also named Thomas Thacher) reputation and leadership at the New York Bar, Thacher had access to many powerful men in Washington. Among the first to hear his account of the Red Cross Commission outlook was Secretary of Labor Felix Frankfurter and Supreme Court Justice Louis D. Brandeis, both of whom were impressed by his "persuasive lucidity on the Russian situation. Brandeis and I listened to you," Frankfurter wrote to Thacher, "knowing that your analysis of the facts is correct and your recommendation . . . is wise. Would that one might move those who have the power to see with your eyes and to move in the direction of your thought and move at once."[13]

Thacher also met with his uncle, U.S. Tariff Commissioner William Kent, who promptly wrote to President Wilson, pleading for the opportunity to have his nephew meet with him: "Thomas Thacher, a leader of the New York Bar," Kent began his case,

> is a man of remarkably keen intellect with extraordinary mental discrimination.
> Furthest from sentimental sympathy with wild economics of the Revolution, he believes that the present soviet government is representative of the people and it is the only hope against a reaction manipulated by Germany.[14]

"Secretary of State at President's request desires your presence Tuesday May 28 eleven thirty," Kent telegraphed Thacher on 25 May. However, a 23 May letter from Wilson to Lansing belied the exciting prospects. The president asked: "Would you have time to see Mr. Thacher yourself?" On the same occasion Wilson wrote to Kent: "I am very much afraid that I haven't time to have a real talk with Thomas Thacher just now." The decision to recall Robins had been made; a presidential interview with Thacher would have been seen as yet another equivocation.[15]

Within the next week, Thacher had completed the one course of action for which he had been so well trained professionally. He wrote and privately published, for private distribution, a fourteen-page brief, *Russia and the War*, in which he argued the Robins-Judson-Thompson-Thacher position on the necessity of recognition of and cooperation with the Bolsheviks to fulfill U.S. and Allied war aims. He followed publication with a flurry of letters that accompanied the pamphlet. Lansing, House, Brandeis, Lord Reading (the British ambassador), Senator Calder, Cong. Edward Keating, Kent, Davison, George B. Case, Sen. Hiram Johnson, and William Allen White are just the beginning of the long list of recipients. All the while, Kent had "been pounding the President for an interview," to no avail.[16]

On 26 April, the very day of Robins's first recall notice, the Moscow press carried a story that was to prove seriously embarrassing to Robins, especially at that moment when his departure was imminent. Robins immediately wired an apologetic and conciliatory telegram to Francis explaining that the "Moscow press this morning carries several stupid stories evidently prepared to produce dissension and suspicion among American representatives in Russia." Robins continued, "Confidentially expect your understanding to give you untroubled mastery of the situation. Your proved strength sufficient guarantee against absurd stories both Washington and Russia." Later that day, in a letter to Francis explaining the nature of the news story, Robins continued:

> several stories in unofficial papers to the effect that you had resigned or been recalled and that I was to be appointed in your stead upon some new principle of economic diplomacy. Evidently your management of the situation troubles our enemies and they would have you out of the way or get me out of the way or both if possible.
>
> These small matters I would not bring up at so critical a time were it not for the fact that they are sought to be used to confuse a delicate situation.[17]

Considering that Robins's fondest dreams were contained in the specific details of this false report, his discomfort was undoubtedly hard to bear. He had tried to establish cordial and respectful relations with Francis in spite of their marked differences of opinion. It was certainly no secret, considering Robins's countless initiatives, suggestions, and advice, that he would have very much desired the freer and more powerful hand of an ambassador. But it is just as certain, considering Robins's political expertise, that the leak of such a story could only have the opposite effect from that reported. And Robins wisely included just that judgment in his explanatory letter to Francis. Nevertheless, even after assuring Robins of his continued confidence and trust, Francis fully realized that although the report was false, it reflected what both the Bolsheviks and Robins wanted; it was too close to the truth to be dismissed or forgotten.

In the months and years following these events, part of the acrimonious debate between the "indoor" and "outdoor" forces often included the charge that Robins had tried to replace Francis as American ambassador. The record does show that Robins very much wanted the replacement of "the stuffed shirt" and had worked toward that end along with Judson and Sisson in December 1917, when the ambassador was in close contact with Madame de Cram.[18] However, once it was clear that the Department of State maintained its confidence in Francis and supported his judgments, Robins cooperated fully with him as his subordinate and "unofficial representative."

By the time of the unfortunate newspaper story, Robins had already begun the process of settling Red Cross affairs in Russia. Allen Wardwell was busily overseeing the final distribution of supplies in Petrograd, and Webster had returned from his investigations in Siberia. With his departure possibly only days away, Robins made sure to draft letters of appreciation to both Lenin and Trotsky. The letters are similar but the one to Lenin deserves quotation.

> May I take this opportunity to express my sincere appreciation for your cooperation and courtesies in the prosecution of my work for the American Red Cross Mission in Russia and an abiding hope that the Russian Republic of Soviets will develop into a permanent Democratic Power, and that your ultimate aim to make Russia a fundamental economic democracy will be realized.
>
> Your prophetic insight and genius of leadership has enabled the Soviet Power to become consolidated throughout Russia and I am confident that this new creative organ of the democratic life of mankind will inspire and advance the cause of liberty throughout the world.[19]

Robins chose his words carefully; he rarely used terms of such high praise as "prophetic insight and genius of leadership," especially when addressing the recipient directly. Indeed, Robins never changed his opinion of Lenin. Vladimir Ilyich stood along side Jefferson and Lincoln in his personal pantheon of great men of the modern world. And regarding his promise "to continue efforts" in America "in interpreting this new democracy," Robins devoted a major part of his remaining thirty-five years of life.

In those final days in Russia Robins was torn between his hopes of a change in American policy that would require his remaining and the developing necessity, even beyond his choice, of quickly returning to Washington to try to win adherents to his point of view. This last alternative, so reminiscent of his evangelistic "knight errantry" and crusading campaigns of the past, was to be a struggle far more bitter than he could have imagined.

While still in Russia his hopes continued to soar. His enthusiasm for the new "economic democracy's" growing cooperation with America's did not falter. "The first May Day of the Proletarian Russian-Soviet Power," Robins wrote in his pocket diary on 1 May 1918, in Moscow, "First of the long history of the race. Red Flags, cloudy cool, with a strange quiet over the city. It is ominous of the coming [hour]."

"Yesterday will never be entirely told," he began, in his entry for the following day. "Red Flags banners Discipline of Labor and call for order and New Democratic power. . . . Never a greater hour will come in this old world. Help us our Father! [work] after change in policy. . . . I must fight this through."[20]

On 5 May, after a request from Francis to meet with him personally, Robins left matters in Moscow in the hands of Gumberg and set out for Vologda. Robins had not considered that the ambassador would be coming to Moscow to attend the funeral of Maddin Summers, who had died two days earlier, and Robins had no doubt decided that his discussion with the ambassador would have to take precedence over the funeral.[21] In addition to his plans for departure and the future of the Red Cross mission, Robins went to see Francis armed with a letter from Lockhart written specifically for Robins's last conference with the ambassador, as a final attempt to demonstrate "that a policy of Allied intervention with the cooperation and consent of the Bolshevik Government is feasible and possible."

"I am afraid you will have left for Vologda before I have a chance of seeing you," Lockhart began, in the letter dated 5 May,

> Do let me in support of my view of things here, put before you the following definite instances in which Trotsky has shown his willingness to work with the Allies.
>
> (1) He has invited Allied officers to cooperate in the reorganization of the New Army.
>
> (2) He invited us to send a commission of British Naval officers to save the Black Sea Fleet.
>
> (3) On every occasion when we have asked him for papers and assistance for our naval officers and our evacuation officers at Petrograd he has always given us exactly what we wanted.
>
> (4) He has given every facility so far for Allied cooperation at Murmansk.
>
> (5) He has agreed to send the Czech Corps to Murmansk and Archangel.
>
> (6) Finally, he has today come to a full agreement with us regarding the Allied stores at Archangel whereby we shall be allowed to retain those stores which we require for ourselves.
>
> This information, especially paragraph (5), is for your confidential information only.
>
> You will agree that this does not look like the action of a pro-German agent, and that a policy of Allied intervention with the cooperation and consent of the Bolshevik Government is feasible and possible.
>
> Please destroy this letter when you have finished with it.[22]

Robins, Lockhart, and Sadoul were not the only representatives who were still pleading for Allied intervention with Soviet consent. At this same time, on or about 5 May, an urgent telegram from Ruggles had arrived at the War Department in Washington warning of the "crisis in relations of Allies with Russia rapidly approaching, due to German pressure." Ruggles, who, it will be recalled, was responsible for the long delay in forwarding the Trotsky proposals for Allied cooperation to allay the Brest-Litovsk peace ratification, had changed his mind on American diplomatic recognition of and cooperation with the Bolsheviks. "I believe diplomatic representation in Moscow by Allies important," he continued,

> perhaps by officials there. This [would] offset German diplomacy which cannot be done from here nor from statements by Allied diplomatists for publication. Also we should negotiate with Bolsheviks a modus vivendi by consent to immediate Allied intervention through Siberia and northern ports; maintain military contact, establish commercial contact; have clear understanding of what Allied interests in Russia employed and what our policy is to be.
>
> Unless something is done in the near future I believe that the Bolsheviks through German pressure will compel Allied diplomatic corps to leave Russia. Have sent Bukowski [assistant military attaché] to Petrograd to assist British, French officers in evacuation of material. Pershing informed.[23]

Ironically, at the time this message was received, Francis was in Moscow, but his purpose there did not include carrying out Ruggles's suggestions. On the contrary, he was there to pay homage to Summers, whose illness and death can be attributed to his unstinting service to the causes staunchly opposed to those of Robins, Ruggles, and Lockhart.

Following his return to Moscow from Vologda, events moved swiftly for Robins. On 10 May he received the urgent notification of recall from Davison, which had been sent from Washington on 7 May. On 9 May an about-face: "Reconsidered . . . now considered desirable that you remain in Russia for three weeks longer." This second wire was signed by both Lansing and Davison, but according to Thacher, it was not sent until 27 May. Robins had begun his return journey on 14 May.[24] On 9 May Wardwell arrived in Moscow from Petrograd to serve as Robins's successor as head of the commission.[25] The day was also marked by the usual conference between "L. S. R. G." —Lockhart, Sadoul, Robins, and Gumberg, followed by another with Webster. "Ambassador has secured my recall," Robins scrawled in his pocket diary.[26]

"The tide is ebb now and we are alone in all matters." Robins continued his release of frustration and bitterness the following day, "The start must be made at once. We are leaving for final and tomorrow. Nothing for our gain in serving Russia. Final statement old grim issues. This looks like the face of that 'ancient enemy.' We are finishing the oldest of the long engagements. There is no certainty in the enterprise and no sure outlet for the drive. Still we fight on! Help us our God!"

On the morning of 13 May, after an evening at the Bolshoi Ballet, at which the German ambassador Count Mirbach occupied the box directly below him, Robins's time had come for making his final personal farewells. On that day he saw Chicherin, Karl Radek, and most of the Bolshevik leadership with whom he had contact. Both Trotsky and Lenin presented him with signed "photos" and Trotsky gave him a "fine letter." The latter was in answer to Robins's Russian-language letter to Trotsky of 25 April, doubtless translated for Robins by Gumberg. "Allow me to express to you my sincere gratitude," Trotsky began,

> for those words of greeting with which you were pleased to address me, on the occasion of your, I hope, temporary, departure from Russia. Among the official representatives of foreign countries you were one of the few who wished and could impartially realize the immeasurable difficulties under which the Soviet Government had to labor. All the misfortune, vices, crimes, of the centuries of despotism, deepened by the war, fell upon that revolutionary government which with all its energy is attempting to elevate the life of the Russian people to the height of the principles and demands of the Socialist program. Now, as well as six months ago, in the days of the October revolution, when I had the honor to meet you for the first time, I sincerely believe that the Russian people, led by the working class, will come out with honor from all difficulties, and that the Soviet Republic will not be a slave. Now, as well as six months ago, I have no doubt that the laboring masses of all countries will give us mighty assistance and will help us to establish on our earth, which is impregnated with crimes, a new system, which will bind the humanity of both hemispheres into one brotherly laboring family.[27]

No "farewell" letter from Lenin to Robins has been preserved;[28] however, on the following day, some time before boarding Red Cross car no. 447 to begin the trip back to America, Robins received a remarkable document from Lenin. In light of his gloomy thoughts expressed only days before in his diary, it would appear that Lenin's document, entitled "Russian-American Commercial Relations," came as a surprise.

In essence, Lenin's paper was an analytical summary of the economic conditions in Russia from the time of the Provisional Government. It also included proposals for a privileged position for the United States in Russia's future economic development. Lenin emphasized the international trade situation and Russia's changing trade relationships within that situation, with concern for the impact of the war. Lenin's basic point was obvious: "The fourth year of war greatly exhausted the economic might of Russia. The productive forces of the country being by necessity directed first of all to military needs were far from satisfying the needs of the population."[29] The introductory section concluded with the assertion that the cause of the disastrous economic deterioration, other than the expected effects of a war economy, was the "reduction of imports from foreign countries of tools of production." It was specifically with this point in mind that Lenin drafted the document, hoping, through Soviet-American economic cooperation, to resume heavy industry and factory construction as soon as possible.[30]

The second of the three parts dealt with the growth of the volume of exports from the United States to the world market. Lenin pointed out that American volume became the second largest in the world in 1918, from a position of sixth just prior to the war. He carefully noted the multiplication of exports from the United States to Russia during this period, reaching a peak of 336,454,000 rubles in the year 1917.[31] He then noted the great diminution of Germany's exports to Russia, from a position of first place in 1914 to the discontinuation of exportation during wartime.

After the ratification of the Brest treaty, the avenues for resuming trade with Germany were wide open. However, Lenin explained that "with the present drain on the economic life of Germany there is no reason to expect that she will be in a position to export to Russia merchandise needed by the latter. . . . It will be evident that the prospectus of commerce between America and Russia are very good."[32] Lenin pointed not only to good prospects but to the fact that "Germany will be compelled to surrender her leading place as a source for the economic life of Russia for the next few years to a country which had not been disorganized. . . . Only America can become that country."[33]

Lenin next described the possible financial apparatus to facilitate future transactions. He suggested a number of inviting possibilities for the security of payment that would be provided by the Soviet government, and he promised that "all war materials which were manufactured in England and America for Russia will be transferred to the United States."[34]

In that bleak hour Robins was overjoyed that he could carry such a proposal to Washington, and he saw his personal mission reflected in Lenin's cover letter addressed to him.

> I enclose the preliminary plan of our economic relations with America. This preliminary plan was elaborated in the Council of Export Trade in our highest Council of National Economy.
> I hope this preliminary can be useful for you in your conversation with the American Foreign Office and American Export Specialists.[35]

Robins felt he "had the goods" that would finally convince official Washington of the logic and desirability of entering into such trade arrangements.

Just six weeks later, at the time of his arrival in Washington, Robins explained his views on the questions raised in the Lenin proposal in his "Statement of Recommendations Concerning the Russian Situation: American Economic Cooperation with Russia."[36] Robins's analysis was divided into five parts, the first of which examined Wilson's pronouncement that America was participating in the World War "to make the world safe for democracy." Robins compared it with the ideal that the "Great mass of the Russian People" do not want a forced Allied intervention. He explained that if the ultimate Allied aim was the support of democratic government, then cooperation with the Soviets economically and militarily would accomplish that end and keep Germany out.

Robins then stressed a unified and fundamental bond between Soviet Russia and the Allies. Their goals were mutual—keeping supplies from German hands, nullification of the dishonorable peace settlement, provision for the proper distribution of supplies within Russia, and generally, the establishment of an understanding through close communication and contact.

"The Economic Problem" (part three of the Lenin proposals), Robins held, consisted of the turmoil and disorganization resulting from the conflict between the czarist and socialist economic systems, neither of which fulfilled the needs of the country independently. The hoarding of grain plus the completely inadequate facilities for distribution and the worthlessness of the currency were but two of the problems faced by the Soviet regime. However, one factor was in their favor since "in order to get results they were willing when faced with the practical necessities of the situation, to modify formulas of their economic theory."[37]

Robins pointed out that immediate steps toward the creation of the economic commission proposed by Lenin could be taken without altering the long standing U.S. opposition to recognition of the Soviet regime. "It is apparent from the informality of the suggestion inviting American cooperation that formal recognition of the Soviet Government is not a necessary prerequisite to cooperation. Acting upon this informal invitation, a commission can proceed to Russia and be placed in direct touch with the entire situation without further formality."[38] Robins proposed eleven phases of work that such a commission could undertake: (1) railway control, management, and operation; (2) reorganization of credit and finance, governmental and commercial; (3) commercial distribution of grain and manufactured articles in exchange for grain; (4) food administration and control; (5) shipping and foreign trade, with particular reference to Allied war needs; (6) industrial management and control in cooperation with labor; (7) reorganization of manufacturing and coal-mining industries; (8) development of agriculture; (9) prevention, or utilization, of speculative markets; (10) education; and (11) propaganda. With an Allied voice in these aspects of the Soviet economy and the influence that in time could be brought to bear on Russia, Robins assured Washington that the Soviet government would take action against Germany.

Nowhere in the report does Robins discuss the idea he was to later so eloquently champion, namely that economic cooperation from the Allies would better the living conditions of the Russian masses and therefore "recreate the property interest and the stake in life" which would ultimately replace the most unrealistic socialistic formulas.[39]

A premise of Robins's dealings with Trotsky and Lenin, and essential to his hopes for the future of Soviet-American cooperation, was his trust in both men. Kennan has demonstrated that Lenin's proposals, sent through

Robins to Washington, were motivated by more than the economic well-being of Soviet Russia. Utilizing Lenin's speeches and minutes of the Central Executive Committee of the Bolshevik party, published in Lenin's collected works, along with documents from German ambassador Mirbach to the German foreign office, Kennan has concluded:

> it is only too clear that Lenin's aim, in giving the document to Robins, was to encourage American capitalists to hope that if only the Japanese could be kept out of Siberia there would be serious possibilities for a future preferential economic position of the United States in relation to that area and in the economic reconstruction of Russia generally. The suggested concessions with respect to mineral rights, to participation in electric power plant construction, to a part in the construction of Russian railroads, etc.—all these were conceived by Lenin, in coldest cynicism and contempt, as baits to the American capitalists —irresistible baits, he thought, which would cause them to reject any possible immediate dickers with the "Japanese *bourgeoisie*" and to hold out for future deals with the Soviet government. . . . The attachment to the "sacred right of concessions" was the handle by which, Lenin believed, the behavior of the American capitalists could be manipulated, even by those who themselves despised and abhorred this motivation.[40]

Kennan's analysis is astute, but he fails to give any credence whatever to the desperate economic considerations that were obviously truthfully stated in the document. Regarding Lenin's "coldest cynicism and contempt," one wonders, not in apologia, but in fair confrontation with political realism, whether any other words would better describe the decision to intervene, about which Kennan has written his excellent book?

Robins was unaware of other considerations. His memorandum demonstrates the enthusiasm with which he left Moscow on the evening of 14 May. He saw himself as the bearer of a precious cornucopia that could only be poured out before the secretary of state and the president, who were in the position to implement the proposals. This may explain Robins's behavior when the night train arrived at the station at Vologda the following morning and Robins had his final meeting with Francis. In their conversation, which lasted about twenty minutes, Robins never mentioned the document he had received from Lenin.

Nowhere in the record of the previous months is there any indication of withheld information or evasiveness in Robins's relations with Francis. On the contrary, Robins put his cards on the table in the hope that Francis would see the evidence that was the basis of his own judgments. This was not always the case in Francis's relations with Robins. With the notification of recall, which Robins rightly understood as censure, his trust in Francis ended.

Robins had his last conversation with the ambassador in the train station at Vologda, maintaining a surface cordiality, but his propriety belied his feelings of anger and disgust. Robins's tactical and political judgment were thrown off by his hidden rage and vindictiveness. He not only failed to say a word about Lenin's proposals to Francis, but flaunted the fact that he had such documents with him before other Americans at the station after Francis had left, aware that such revelations would quickly reach the ambassador. This blunt demonstration of mistrust and disrespect caused Francis deep embarrassment. Upon learning indirectly of Lenin's proposals, Francis wired Lansing several times of the entire situation as it developed and expressed his dismay and indignation.

> Robins passed (through) Vologda yesterday in Red Cross car attached to Siberian Express en route Vladivostok thence America, saying departure in compliance with your [telegram] 22 of the 7th. . . .
> Robins construed this cable as definite recall and when asked by me if Davison ordered return, replied no, but said message was from State Department. Robins had intended remaining in the hope that Thompson would influence Department to recognize Soviet government.
> I do not know whether Robins can reach Vladivostok, as Harbin route closed and Amur route reported cut by Semenov, but Robins said latter report untrue, as Soviet government unadvised thereof. Robins was accompanied by Hardy, Gumberg and Brown, representative of *Chicago News.*
> Associated Press representative here and Groves [J. Philip, a clerk in the embassy] after talking to Robins at the station understand that he had definite proposition to the United States from the Soviet government and was hastening to America in expectation of receiving favorable reply and definitely stated expected to return promptly if Soviet government survived, but Robins, with whom I talked fully, made no mention of such mission nor of returning. . . .
> I do not understand Robins' failure to inform me of his plans as he has continuously since (Thompson's departure) expressed friendliness and admiration of my course. . . .
> Of course have no fear of Department's recognizing Soviet government if it should last until Robins' arrival Washington, which I doubt. Bolshevik press states Robins going to America and will return soon, while opposition press claims his recall final.
> May I suggest advising Red Cross and Christian Association to instruct their representatives to confine their activities strictly to the line of their work? Permit me most earnestly to say that if the Department would refuse Russian passports issued to socialist fanatics and sensational newsmongers, it would diminish difficulties and lessen embarrassments of this Embassy.[41]

One week later, after learning more details, Francis wired again. "He [Lenin] commissions Robins to you with what he considers tempting propositions of preferential commercial advantages prejudicial to our Allies, especially to France. Robins while saying nothing to me on the subject told a friend at station that he was going to America 'with the goods.'"[42] Robins's blunders, while not decisive, certainly prejudiced his case in Washington, and the weeks of the long journey passed before he arrived there to argue for the Lenin proposals. Upon arrival, and in enthusiastic expectation of carrying forward his work in behalf of Soviet-American cooperation, all ears were deaf to him and his communications.

17

Return to America
The Fight against Intervention

There is nothing I am free to write regarding the Russian situation. You can surmise the outcome of that stupendous story for the time being by the fact that I shall not return to Russia and that we are sending troops to Vladivostok.
—Raymond to Elizabeth, 27 August 1918

FROM Vologda, Robins had the alternative of continuing north to Archangel or Murmansk, both cities under Soviet control and both Allied ports of call. He chose instead to take the longer route of the Trans-Siberian Railroad and the Pacific Ocean, because, he claimed, it promised to be faster. Robins later gave additional reasons for chosing the Pacific route, and it is of particular interest in light of Francis's warning of Semenov's White counterrevolutionary control in Siberia. "I came out of Russia on the 14th of May, leaving Moscow," Robins explained,

Men said, "How are you going, Robins?" Ambassadors and heads of military missions asked me that question. "Are you going by way of Finland?"
"No, that is full of icebergs and will not soon thaw."
"Why don't you, Robins, try the Archangel?"
"No it is three weeks before the ice is out of the Archangel, and I want to get to Washington as soon as I can. I would rather be here than any other place in the world, but when I am ordered back, I am going back."
"You cannot go out by the Siberian."
"Yes, you can."
"Good God, Robins, don't you know that marauding bands are going up and down and pillaging everything and everybody? Your train will be robbed. Don't you know that Semenov has come down and taken the upper railroad?"
I said, "I don't know that and I didn't care."
They said, "Don't you believe the stuff you hear?"
I said, "I believe part of it." Before I left there I got Nickolai [*sic*] Lenin to write me a letter. This is a photographic copy of it.
"Moscow: 11th day of May, 1918. Workmen's-Soldiers' soviet throughout Russia:" giving me safe conduct, allowing me to move my car from one province to another, allowing me to violate the rules as to carrying arms, allowing me to take along five hundred rifles that I had saved from some time back. I

asked the soviet if I could carry them out on my journey of six thousand miles, and they said if I might need them I could have them.

I made those six thousand miles in only a few hours longer time than it would have taken under the best days of the old regime.

I brought out more documents than had been brought out by anybody [Robins is referring to Sisson and the forgeries] up to that time, since the revolution. I did not fire a shot. I did not hear a shot fired. I did not hear the soviet government questioned throughout the entire 6,000 miles, and that happens to be history, and not hot air.[1]

Robins was deeply impressed with the near-magical power of the two sheets of paper he carried with him: one, Lenin's letter; the second a certificate for the Red Cross car no. 447 for "all possible assistance" in its transit to Vladivostok with "expenses charged to the Commissar of Foreign Affairs" and signed by Chicherin. "Reach Perm and . . . have some trouble about rifles," Robins noted in his diary on 16 May, within twenty-four hours of their departure from Vologda. "Letter of Lenin and Chicherin get us over," he continued, "No permits for arms."[2]

The monotonous days on the Trans-Siberian were a striking and disorienting change for Robins. Such a long period of expectation and waiting were difficult for his temperament, but in light of the manic activity of the preceding ten months, he experienced some relief and enjoyed reading Maxim Gorky's *My Childhood* and Bishop Beary's *Russia*. Once again he took the opportunity to absorb the majestic scenery and daydream. "Mountain gils with flowers from the hills, white, yellow, blue, a towering day. We have made little progress. Going over the Urals is slow stuff. The Urals! How far off they seemed at Rock Hill School. . . . Here in the Urals in the supreme tragedy of the Russian Revolution . . . the wonderful pine forests of the Eastern Urals . . . reminiscence and the call of the Shining Pines and the O.F.C. [Old Firey Cross?] in far Siberian land."[3]

On 22 May, in expectation of their arrival at Irkutsk, the transportation focal point of central Siberia, Robins wired ahead to the People's Commissar of Foreign Affairs for central Siberia, requesting the swift connection of car no. 447 to the "first fast train," proudly informing the local official: "Going to America in interests economic help Russia Siberia. Order for fast travel for us signed Lenin."[4] When Robins and his party arrived at Irkutsk, all was in readiness. "Leaving today expect get through Amur Line," he wired Wardwell in Moscow. "Trip Moscow Irkutsk without incident. Stations clean orderly making good time. Soviet power unquestioned throughout entire distance. All well. Duplicate sent Ambassador."[5]

On 26 May Ambassador Francis received the telegram from Washington which requested that Robins remain in Russia three more weeks. By that time Robins had passed through Chita, three-quarters of the distance from Moscow to Vladivostok. Francis forwarded the request that Robins remain in Vladivostok "without comment," but warned Lansing,

Robins' return to Moscow would indicate American support of Soviet government if not to be considered as recognition thereof. If such is Department's policy, he should be ordered back from Vladivostok, otherwise proceed to America.
    Poole [DeWitt Clinton Poole, American consul at Moscow] has established
cordial relations with Soviet government through Chicherin.[6]

Knowing full well that recognition was entirely out of the question, Francis
was in effect requesting confirmation of Robins's original orders to return to
America. A further renunciation of Robins and the policies toward which he
worked is revealed in Francis's choice of the new liaison with the Bolsheviks.
Rather than using the services of Allen Wardwell, Robins's successor as head
of the Red Cross in Russia, he informed the secretary of state that Poole,
Summers's successor, would perform that function. From Francis's point of
view, and no doubt that of the Department of State, Poole was the more de-
sireable choice, not only in terms of his attitude toward the Soviet government, but because of his position as a foreign service officer within the chain
of command of which Francis was the senior official in Russia.
    The irony in the situation was the fact that in the first days of the No-
vember Revolution, the State Department had forbade any such contact between its officers and the new leadership for fear of suggesting de facto
recognition of the Bolshevik regime. That concern was finally ignored with
the "cordial," yet unofficial, Poole contacts with Chicherin. Had such contacts been approved in November 1917, rather than punished, as in the case
of General Judson, the nature and extent of Robins's negotiations with the
Bolsheviks would have been considerably restricted.
    The contacts and lines of communication with the Bolsheviks through
Poole were maintained for a time, but for ends quite different from those
toward which Robins had worked. In a telegram dated 1 June Francis received
notification that "R.C. has ordered Robins today to continue journey home."[7]
    These developments were unknown to Robins as he continued along the
Amur section of the Trans-Siberian Railway, skirting Russia's northern border with Manchuria. At the city of Khabarovsk, where the Amur line finally completes its circuitous detour around Manchuria's bulge into Siberia,
and turns south, Robins had a memorable experience. Upon presentation of
the letter from Lenin, he was invited to attend a meeting of the Soviet of
the Far Eastern District. During the layover in Khabarovsk he was shown
about the city and had the opportunity to interview some notables. A. M.
Krasnotshorov (Krasnoshchekov), chairman of the Far Eastern Soviet of People's Commissars, also presented him with a warm letter of introduction to
the Vladivostok District Soviet and the Extraordinary Commission, asking
that they "show him all possible assistance and acquaint him with the state
of affairs for the purpose of making possible the establishment of friendly relations," especially since "during his entire stay in Russia he was a friend of
the Soviet Government." Curiously, and with no corroboration or means of

verification, Chairman Krasnotshorov concluded his letter with the further assurance, "Colonel Robins was personally known to me in America."[8]

After a demonstrative farewell, Robins and his party continued south on the last stretch of the journey to Vladivostok. They arrived on the first or second of June and their various letters of introduction put them in touch with Konstantin Sukhanov, chairman of the Soviet Executive Committee of Vladivostok. This Pacific gateway to Siberia on the Gulf of Japan was the scene of the Japanese landing little more than a month before, and the relationship between the local Soviet and the Allied consuls had grown tense, if not hostile. This was the result of continued Allied toleration of the landing, Allied recognition of some remaining officials of the Provisional Government, and Allied unwillingness to adhere to rulings of the local Soviet, which were considered unreasonable. The atmosphere in the city, in which thousands of tons of Allied war supplies were stockpiled, was marked by suspicion and insecurity.

Robins made immediate arrangements for passage to Yokahama and, with the help of Roland Morris, American ambassador to Japan, secured passage on the *Kamo Maru*. At dockside in Vladivostok, just minutes before embarking, Robins had a final conversation with Sukhanov in the company of Albert Rhys Williams and, in all probability, with Gumberg acting as interpreter. Williams, who had been in Petrograd to report on the November Revolution along with John Reed and Bessie Beaty, recorded this conversation in his *Journey into Revolution, Petrograd, 1917–1918*.

> Robins: "If no help comes from the Allies, how long can the Soviet last?"
> Shukanov shook his head and remained tight lipped.
> Robins: "Six weeks?"
> Sukhanov: "Not much longer." Then he flushed and looked Robins in the eyes with the frankness that in the young can be so easily mistaken for innocence. Fortunately Robins would not make that mistake.
> "I assume you mean how long it will be until we are attacked by the Allies, using the Czechoslovaks as their dupes. If it were not for the Allies, and the Czechoslovaks they maneuvered here, we could hold out forever against our own bandit gang, the Whites, Semenov!" He said with contempt. "Where would Semenov be today if he were not being paid by the Japanese? No. We want nothing from the Allies but to be left alone." Then reverting to the manners taught by his father, he bowed formally.
> "As for America, we do not yet know, but we do not count her as the other Allies."
> I saw Robins' face as he climbed the gangplank sad, set, his jaw thrust out grimly. For as long as we could see him he stood at the rail looking back at the city that was so many thousands of miles distant from the "iron batallions" of the new Red Army.[9]

Reflecting further on the tragedy he was witnessing, Williams considered just what the Red Cross chief had done. "Robins was the one American providing actual information to his government from Russia during virtually the entire period after October, having by dint of hard work gained the confidence of Lenin, Trotsky, Radek, and others. All during this time, however, his country, and the other Allies, took the position that this government he dealt with so painstakingly was nonexistent."[10]

Just prior to departure, Robins wired Davison at Washington that he was due in Seattle on 19 June, and with his sense of urgency, he asked that "reservations direct to Washington for seven persons" be ready for his party when they arrived. With a sense of triumph Robins added, "Trip through Siberia record time. Soviet government complete control from Moscow to Vladivostok."[11] Robins's triumph was illusory. By the time of his departure from Japan, the thousands of soldiers of the Czech corps of prisoners of war had staged an uprising and, joining with other anti-Bolshevik forces, had taken over major stretches of the Trans-Siberian Railroad. Characteristic of the tumult and "hour by hour" changes in revolutionary Russia was the fact that had Robins started out only a few days later, he would have encountered an entirely different situation. These facts remained unknown, if not disbelieved, by him long after his return to America.

The official party of three, Robins, D. Heywood Hardy, stenographer of the Red Cross Commission, and Gumberg, along with Louis Edgar Browne, *Chicago Daily News* correspondent in Russia, made the trans-Pacific journey on schedule and without incident. Robins busied himself with Carlyle's *French Revolution,* and he and Hardy looked forward to an arrival just two weeks short of the anniversary of their departure. Robins's "Russian adventure" had been compressed into less than twelve months. How prophetic that at the very beginning he could have written to Margaret: "It is a great moment in the life of every member of this party but bigger for me than for any other member. This is because I mean to go the distance to help Russia to be free and I have an ideal for our work larger than my comrades."[12]

Margaret was at dockside in Seattle on 19 June when Robins walked down the gangplank, finally to share the adventure firsthand. The excitement and joy of their reunion, however, was soon soured by the first of many humiliations. Distrust and suspicion of Robins and Gumberg had been so successfully orchestrated in Washington by those who opposed their views, that instead of the expected diplomatic privileges, the State Department ordered a thorough search and inspection of their baggage by immigration officials. Robins had been informed while in Japan that Alexander Gumberg was looked upon with suspicion, that his reentry into the United States would have to await further State Department consideration, and that he would not be readmitted at the time of Robins's return.

Robins refused to return to the United States unless Gumberg's reentry were assured, and only after receiving such assurances did the group continue on its journey.[13] In Seattle, Robins also received word from the State Department reiterating an order he had received in Vladivostok; under no circumstances was he to make any public statements about the mission. On the train from Seattle, apparently in response to newspaper accounts, Robins learned "that [Miles] Poindexter and T. R. are against us. The fight is hot."[14]

On 4 June, in anticipation of Robins's imminent arrival, Thomas Thacher began distributing *Russia and the War*, his fourteen-page pamphlet. The preparation and dissemination of the document was the culmination of Thacher's month-long effort to get the "Red Cross position on Russia" before the U.S. leadership. From 7 May, the day of his return to the United States, until 19 June, Robins's return, Thacher joined in the effort that had occupied William B. Thompson for months—to alter the course of American relations with the Soviets. During those weeks, Thacher met with presidential friend and advisor Col. E. M. House, Thomas Lamont, Secretary of State Lansing, Vance C. McCormick, Secretary of Labor Felix Frankfurter, Louis D. Brandeis, the British ambassador, Lord Reading, and his uncle William Kent, member of the U.S. Tariff Commission.[15]

By the time the train arrived in Chicago, Robins realized how bitter the fight in Washington would be. "Panther," Thompson confirmed, using the nickname he had given Robins in Russia, "you've got something to learn. There isn't much difference between hero and zero."[16] Nevertheless, Robins knew that he had staunch allies, and they were at the Central Station at Park Row and Eleventh Place to greet him—his old friends and companions in the struggles of the past. In addition to Thompson and Thacher, who traveled with Robins to Washington, there were Graham Taylor, Louis F. Post, Jim Mullenbach of the Municipal Lodging House days, and ten others to welcome him home. Robins stopped off at his tenement flat to pack and, after lunch at the Blackstone Hotel, boarded the Pennsylvania Railroad bound for Washington. He arrived at 4:40 P.M. the next day, forty days after leaving Moscow.

On 26 June Robins finally got to see Secretary of State Lansing to present him with Lenin's economic proposals and to explain his view of the entire situation. At that meeting, Lansing suggested that Robins prepare a written statement. It was that statement, presented to Lansing on 1 July, which has been discussed at length in conjunction with Lenin's proposals of economic cooperation. But far more urgent was Robins's awareness that the gears of Allied military intervention in Russia were grinding forward. In seven terse paragraphs, written specifically to avert such a disaster, Robins attempted to cram all the wisdom of his year of immersion in Russian-American relations.

Washington, July 1, 1918.

Sir: Pursuant to your request I have the honor to present to you herewith a brief printed statement of my recommendations concerning the Russian situation

It seems to me that in all the confusion of statement and conclusion surrounding the Russian situation the following propositions are reasonably clear:

First, that Germany hesitates to employ in Russia armed forces in sufficient number to subjugate the land but desires—as clearly indicated by a consistent course of conduct in Ukrainia, Finland and the Baltic Provinces—to establish so-called governments of law and order which are too weak to support themselves in the great class struggle but which may be maintained and controlled by German force.

Second, that through such governments Germany hopes to control and utilize Russian resources and, if possible, Russian man-power against the Western Allies in this war, and to conclude the war with Russia completely under the economic dominion of Germany.

Third, that forcible Allied intervention opposed by the Soviets would be essentially analogous to what Germany is doing in the Ukraine, in Finland and in the Baltic Provinces.

Fourth, that such intervention unless welcomed by the great mass of the Russian people would be destructive in principle of the entire basis of President Wilson's democratic war policy.

Fifth, that forcible Allied intervention, if uninvited by the Soviet power, will certainly be opposed and will result in civil war.

Sixth, that forcible Allied intervention can not be justified upon grounds of military necessity, and will not prevent but will hasten and make easy the consummation of Germany's war aims in European Russia.

Seventh, that American economic cooperation with Russia will open the way for effective Allied intervention with force and the creation of an actual fighting front opposed to Germany in Russia.

The recommendations enclosed herewith are stated with as much brevity as possible.

Respectfully,

Raymond Robins[17]

On the following night, 2 July 1918, the Supreme War Council of the Allied forces, meeting in Paris, sent a message to President Wilson requesting: "That immediate Allied armed assistance to Russia [uninvited military intervention] is imperatively necessary . . . to assist the Russian nation to throw off their German oppressors . . . in stimulating the national uprising in Russia against German domination . . . to shorten the war by the reconstitution of the Russian front."[18] President Wilson indicated to Secretary of State Lansing that he differed from Robins's statement "only in practical details."

Suggestive of the state of mind of the Wilson administration at the time Robins submitted his 1 July report, was Lansing's recommendation that Robins share his thinking with Henri Bergson and Lord Reading, both ardent proponents of Allied intervention. Robins described the conversation he had with Bergson, whom he met just a few days later.

Bergson's point of view helps explain one of the considerations in the Allied decision to intervene in Russia—the Bolshevik rejection of responsibility for repayment of the Allied loans to the Czar's government. "I saw Henri Bergson," Robins began,

the French philosopher, who had been sent on a secret mission to Washington. . . . He told me all about Russia. He was one of these persons with a single track mind. He had the regulation French point of view of the Russian situation. . . . Then I began to develop the facts . . . and in about five minutes he ceased being a French philosopher, and he stayed two and one-half hours with me—although he had formerly told me he could only spend a few minutes,—and when I finished he said, with tears in his eyes. . . . "Thirty percent of the French peasants have got the savings of a lifetime now invested in the Russian loan. If something is not done to secure their investments, the French government is not safe."[19]

In the following weeks, Robins, Thompson, Thacher, and Gumberg did all they could to rally support for some kind of cooperative policy for America and Soviet Russia. But alarming news reached the west of the uprising of the two divisions of the Czech Legion against Bolshevik control along the route of the Trans-Siberian Railroad. These armed Czech soldiers, staunchly loyal to their national cause against the Austro-Hungarian Empire, had either deserted the ranks of the Central Powers or had been taken prisoner on the eastern front. In the thousands, they were making their way out of Russia to join forces with the armies of England and France on the western front. Their passage was impeded, they rose in opposition, and the Allies were anxious to intervene in Russia in their behalf.

In addition to the plight of the Czech Legion, the Sisson documents, and the array of "indoor" objections to the Bolshevik leadership, there was widespread fear that Allied supplies stockpiled in Russia would fall into the hands of the Central Powers. Through his progressive Republican friends, Robins managed privately to spread the word of his view of the impending intervention in Russia. The State Department ban on his speaking to the press made the task difficult, but with the help of Senators Gifford Pinchot, William Borah, Medill McCormick, Hiram Johnson, and Robert La Follette, Robins managed to stimulate some congressional debate, which brought the beclouded reality of the Russian Revolution before the American people.

Robins's friendship with Hiram Johnson went back nearly ten years of shared stumping in Johnson's successful Progressive party campaigns, first for governor of California, and then for the U.S. Senate. Johnson, while admitting his limited understanding of the complex Russian situation, wrote to Robins of his commitment to the cause:

> Since your wonderful narration of the Russian story, I've been more than ever watching closely the progress of events, and hoping our government would reach a just conclusion. I am not at all clear in the matter and I'm sending you this note to ask if there is any way in which I can assist in having your views and suggestions adopted. The overwhelming propaganda in the country seems to be on the other side, and I fear that the President, because of his ignorance of the situation, may yield to that propaganda. Will you let me know, please, how long you are going to be here, and whether or not you feel that you could talk to another group of Senators, if I could get them together.

Johnson's letter is dated 10 July. Lansing's *aide Memoire* to the Allied ambassadors explaining President Wilson's decision to intervene came just seven days later.

"I have seen all of our Red Cross people in authority," Robins wrote to war correspondent Bessie Beatty. After only three days in Washington, he had also seen

> the Secretary of State, Secretary of War, The British Ambassador, Mr. Hoover, everyone in the State Department [that is] supposed to be familiar with the Russian situation, and many others. . . . I have not seen the president, and have no expectation of being asked to do so. He has up to the present, declined to see either Colonel Thompson or Major Thacher, against whom he has no personal resentment, while in my case as much can not be said.
>   . . . shall probably arrange some way by which we can meet before I return to Russia if I do return, which seems now probable. This statement rests upon a mere supposition and has no authoritative action to warrant it.[20]

The Allied determination to intervene had already been strengthened by Wilson as early as 6 July. Robins's evidence, proposals, and arguments were ignored. His experience and firsthand information on Lenin, Trotsky, Chicherin, and Bolshevik thinking were not only entirely bypassed, but suspected. The most tragic eventualities, against which Robins struggled so for the better part of a year, were coming to pass: a Russian separate peace with the Central Powers and an end to the eastern front in the World War, the resultant threat of an Allied catastrophe in the West at the hands of a strengthened German army, American military intervention in Russia, the ruin of Soviet-American relations, and the apparent complete failure to carry his views on the Russian Revolution to the practice of American foreign policy, and to the hearts and minds of the American public. What the outcome of the first four would have been had Robins's counsel been given deliberate and open consideration is open to speculation. Most students of this period argue the inevitability of Bolshevik withdrawal from the war regardless of any steps the Allies may have taken. Many, this writer included, believe that the mistake of intervention could have been averted. Further, regardless of Lenin's revolutionary rhetoric and manipulative tactics, the economic commission could have been created, establishing a firm and cooperative basis for a developing Soviet-American friendship. The personal tragedy of Robins is palpable. His sister-in-law, fellow social crusader, and friend Mary Dreier wrote of this bitter time. "His convictions came as the result of experience and he thought the President would welcome his information gathered through the months of constant association and work in Russia. But the President was of another mind. He refused to see him and Raymond was shadowed as if he were a criminal and forbidden to speak."[21]

On 2 August, exactly one month after Wilson read Robins's recommendations against intervention, orders to Maj. Gen. William S. Graves began the process of American military intervention in Siberia. Among the explanations for Wilson's decision to intervene were the following: the growing urgency of English and French pressure to intervene, concern for the safety and safe passage of the Czechoslovak legions, so they might quickly join forces with the Allied armies on the western front, fear of the expanding Japanese unilateral intervention, suspicion of Bolshevik complicity with the German army on the basis of the Sisson documents, the reported Bolshevik arming of German, Austrian, and Hungarian enemy prisoners of war, outrage at Bolshevik publication of the secret provisions of the Allied treaties, Bolshevik failure to honor the Czar's treaty and financial obligations, and the confrontational and inflamatory Bolshevik appeals for world revolution.

Robins had evaluated each of these factors and, on the basis of firsthand evidence, had dismissed Bolshevik-German complicity, arming of POWs, interference with the Czechoslovaks, and the danger of Bolshevik propaganda. Committed to reversing the intervention decision, he left Washington, betrayed and humiliated. His conviction that intervention would have the most tragic short- and long-term consequences made his personal failure more grave. Particularly painful for a man of his energy was the continuing State Department ban on public comments on his Russian experience.

Thompson and Thacher had been on the scene in Washington for some months before Robins's return and had already undergone similar experiences. They held out the hope, especially after learning of Lenin's proposals, that Robins might yet carry it off. "I feel as you do, except perhaps more so," Felix Frankfurter wrote to Thacher six days after the decision to intervene in Russia had been made. "My hopes are much paler than they were. If I write in riddles, you will gather that I too, am not a free man. In any event, you and Robins and Thompson did a service of inestimable value. Robins is a peach, he finds himself in a rare manifestation of conscience and disinterestedness."[22]

On 18 August Robins took advantage of yet another private opportunity to tell his story of the Russian Revolution and American diplomacy. Robert La Follette was taking a rest at Hot Springs, Virginia, and Robins joined him there for a day-long talk.

La Follette, like William Jennings Bryan, was a staunch opponent of American entry into the World War. Perhaps more than any other political figure of national stature, La Follette battled the Wilson administration's wartime policies. For this "lack of patriotism" La Follette was pilloried by old enemies, many friends turned against him and his "isolationist extremism," and the press had a field day attacking his "disloyalty." So unpopular had the positions he had taken become that a resolution to oust him from the Senate was fast gaining adherents. In August 1918 La Follette found himself humiliated, distrusted, and suspected for his firmly held convictions.

Robins and La Follette certainly did not see eye to eye on the war, but they judged the Wilson administration policies and mismanagement with equal harshness. La Follette was as eager to hear Robins's tale of Russia as Robins was to win another powerful ally for his cause.

On half-sheets of paper, in pencil, with an urgent cursive script, La Follette took forty-seven pages of notes during his long talk with Robins. While La Follette was never a stalwart in Robins's campaign for diplomatic recognition of Russia, Robins did convince him of the "outdoor view." Furthermore, La Follette's prolific note-taking is a testament to Robins's forceful presentation and his power to win men over to his way of thinking.[23]

After the November elections, followed only days later by the armistice and war's end, La Follette was able to reassume an unobstructed leadership role in the party. The ending of the war removed the resolution of ouster from consideration. In the new Senate lineup, La Follette found that he held the balance of power in the near-evenly divided chamber. It gave encouragement to Robins at a time when all seemed bleak.

Late that August, Thompson suggested to Robins, "Panther, let's go away from the whole damn show for a while and go west. I want to talk about things." They traveled around Wyoming, Colorado, Utah, Arizona, and Montana in a chartered car "and they cruised about, avoiding the hotels, living in cabins, eating simply, talking richly." But Robins could hardly forget what he experienced in Russia, nor could he deny his need to act upon his convictions. The grandeur of the Rocky Mountains and the Grand Canyon were no match for his sense of mission.[24]

On 24 August Robins wrote to Theodore Roosevelt, expressing his indignation and judgments on the poverty of the American "non-policy" toward Russia. "Our policy could not have been more completely muddled and confused than was done in the recent statement of the Assistant Secretary of State, after eight precious months had been wasted in 'Watchful waiting.' Two clear policies were open." Robins explained the alternatives of active and determined intervention or cooperation. But, "the President has adopted neither policy. He stands feebly by the Czechoslovaks, who are alien soldiers at war with the Soviet power, and yet talks of an Economic Commission to the Russian people and says he is against armed intervention. Under these circumstances, his Economic Commission will find little to do, if it ever starts, and the feeble support of the Czechs is simply an encouragement to civil war."[25]

Through the fall of 1918, Robins turned to correspondence long overdue and kept in constant touch with developments in Russia and the war in general. He communicated with those whom he thought might change American policy, but his most powerful asset, his most effective means of influencing people—the podium—was denied him, as was his freedom to give interviews to the press. The conflict of his desire to inform America and the order of his government to maintain silence was excruciating. On 16 September Robins received a telegram from Santeri Nuorteva, the representative in the United

States of the People's Republic of Finland and head of the Finnish Information Bureau, a pro-Soviet propaganda outlet in New York. It reflects the pain of Robins's conflict.

> Papers today contain story issued by Committee of Public Information including Sisson's report of alleged Russian documents. Committee's report officially draws inference that Russian Soviet government now stand proven agents of Germany. You know that Sisson's alleged documents are brazen forgeries. You know how they originated and how Sisson got them. Does not your sense of honor and fair play now at least impel you publicly to reveal the truth. If you are not moved to do so out of respect to truth itself should not your love of the honor to your country impel you to do all in your power to save your country from participation in breaking the seventh commandment, especially when falsity in this connection only will serve to make the misery of the world worse than ever before and to dig a chasm between two nations. Is the wrong already inflicted upon Russia not great enough without these vile falsehoods. I cannot conceive that any other considerations could under the circumstances prevent you from telling the naked truth as you know it.[26]

On the very day he received this telegram, Robins was handed another plea for the truth about Russia. This one came from John Reed, whom Robins had briefly employed in Russia. Although they differed in their fundamental appraisal of Bolshevism, they agreed that recognition and cooperation would best serve both Russia and America and often worked together toward that end.[27] From the Harvard Club in New York, Reed wrote: "Coincident with the publication by Sisson of these letters incriminating Lenin and Trotsky, of which you know the true history, I have been arrested and will be indicted because of a speech defending the Russian Revolution which I made last Friday night. Raymond Robins' testimony on the stand I believe, can do great service for the Russian Revolution. Whether I am to go to prison or not is a minor matter."[28] Robins could not use this or any other opportunity to attack the Sisson documents. He felt that regardless of the consequences, the government-ordered silence had to be honored.

One month later, the New York newspapers headlined the following story: "Raymond Robins in Bolshevist Case," and "Raymond Robins Stars in Comedy." For several days prior to this, U.S. marshals had attempted to serve a subpoena on Robins to appear at the trial of Molly Steimer, "an eighteen year old leader of the New York Bolsheviki, and five men . . . charged with conspiring to violate the espionage law" by demonstrating against President Wilson and American policy toward Russia. The case against the demonstrators rested on the premise that Bolsheviks were in reality German agents and thus their activities were against American national interest, in support of Germany, a nation with which the United States was at war. The government's premise was in turn supported by the Sisson documents, and Harry Weinberger, counsel for the defense, sought Robins's testimony to disprove the authenticity of the documents. Weinberger was quoted as having said, "After Mr. Robins returned to America he was quoted in newspapers in a way that gave the impression that he could tell much about the Sisson exposure if he would."[29]

Robins evaded the subpoena by barricading himself in Mary Dreier's apartment at the northeast corner of Washington Square in New York's Greenwich Village. The foiled ruses of the marshals to gain entry made for the "comedy," a tragic comedy, since Robins would have wanted nothing more than to appear under oath to tell his story. The situation was further complicated by Robins's understanding that the federal court "by collusion with the officers of the federal government" had included all his documents from Russia in the subpoena, "for the purpose of seizing those documents and confiscating them under the claim that [he] was making use of them to aid enemy aliens." Robins prized those documents; they were the evidence that substantiated his claims and interpretation of the Russian Revolution; under no circumstances would he give them up to a hostile lower court.

Robins was finally rescued from Mary's apartment by the intervention of the former United States attorney general, George W. Wickersham, who personally escorted Robins from the self-imposed imprisonment of three days. Mary Dreier characterized the treatment accorded Robins as appropriate for a criminal, with investigators following him and recording his every move.[30]

Robins decided "to make a speedy departure" from the harassment and turn to other war work. The YMCA offered to sponsor him on a speaking tour for soldiers in Canada and England preparing for embarkation to the front. Robins intended to talk on "the war to make the world safe for democracy" and evangelical topics, without touching on the Russian Revolution. Nevertheless, as he later plaintively wrote to a friend, "I was refused a passport by the Wilson Administration and now Margaret is denied a visa by British officials."[31] The U.S. Military Intelligence Section of the General Staff investigated Robins's passport application and rejected it. D. H. Allen, who worked in the office of the secretary of war and was a long-time acquaintance of Robins, characterized the charge of disloyalty as "ridiculous." He tried to soften the impact of the blow, but to no avail.[32] "I will be alright," Robins wrote to Thompson, "when I can forget Russia for a while. Perhaps I can submerge for a time and come up in shape for the final scrap [the presidential election] in 1920."[33]

As winter approached, Robins fell into a state of depression; he suffered from dizziness and pains in his hands and feet. The burden had again grown too heavy.

18

"Free to Speak on Russia"

The U.S. Secret Service have again been shadowing me because of what the officials describe as a Bolshevik speech made by me before the Liberal Club of Harvard. . . . We are in the throes of a nation-wide witch hunt and every voice of dissent from every sort of official ignorance, brutality or neglect is denounced as "dangerous Bolshevik sentiments."
—Raymond to Elizabeth, 21 November 1919

ROBINS'S silence was finally broken on the morning of 3 March 1919, while Robins was in Thompson's office on the twenty-ninth floor of the Metropolitan Tower in New York City. A representative of the Department of Justice in Washington telephoned, asking if Robins would be willing to testify before the Overman Committee on Bolshevik Propaganda without being formally subpoenaed. (Lee Slater Overman, chairman, was a senator from North Carolina.) Robins agreed and on 6 March began his testimony. His enforced silence, which had begun ten months earlier with orders first received at Vladivostok as he prepared to sail for Japan, repeated while in Victoria, British Columbia, "and insisted on again when [he] arrived in Washington," was ended.[1]

The public hearing before which Robins appeared was charged: "to inquire concerning any efforts being made to propagate in this country the principles of any exercising or claiming to exercise authority in Russia, whether such efforts originate in this country or are incited or financed from abroad, and further to inquire into any effort to incite the overthrow of the Government of this country or all governments by force, or by the destruction of life or property, or the general cessation of industry." However, the testimony went far beyond these narrow limits.

While Robins's ten months of silence precipitated a nervous breakdown, when the opportunity finally came to speak his mind, he demonstrated that he had "one or two good fights in [him] yet." His testimony, which lasted about eight hours on three separate days and filled 158 pages in the printed record, was only the beginning of a long and challenging fight.[2] Before the senators of the subcommittee and in the dozens of public addresses on the Russian situation in the months and years that followed, Robins attained heights of eloquence, insight, and prophetic vision that climaxed his career as a public speaker.

"Before the committee," Stanley Frost reported in his account of the Overman hearings for the *New York Times*,

> his force was felt. . . . There was an audience of five, and there was neither applause nor tumult. But in a quiet voice and without oratorical effort, he was no less eloquent and no less compelling, so that the members of the committee, all orators of parts themselves, were fairly spellbound while he talked.
>
> Colonel Robins . . . is a rather small man, dark, nervous, vivacious. His eyes light up as he talks, and he gives the effect of seeing life in deep perspective. He has been a miner, and his hands and shoulders show it in breadth and power, as his mind and sometimes speech show the effect of his years of social settlement work in Chicago.
>
> He was perhaps the only man before the committee who showed no rancor against those on either side in Russia, whose judgements of men were based always on charity.

Toward the end of his first day of testimony, Robins was asked a question that constantly troubled his audiences. Mr. Humes of the subcommittee inquired: "Is it not a fact that the economic strengthening of the Bolshevik government . . . would make it possible for them financially and otherwise, to carry on a stronger propaganda and a stronger agitation and a stronger warfare against our government?" Robins not only justified economic cooperation but also explained the causes of the revolution and the rise of Bolshevism. Robins began by denying the truth of Humes's "fact" in terms that have since been hailed both accurate and prophetic by many, including scholars highly critical of Robins.

> I agree rather with your chief and mine as a citizen of this government that the best answer to Bolshevism is food. I think sir, that economic misery . . . the paralysis of the economic life in Russia and the misery that grew out of it and that whole setting, just as in Germany—Mr. Humes, if the Germans are hungry enough, if there is economic misery enough, the Germans will be Bolsheviki. That is inevitable in my judgement. I believe that the reorganization of Russian life economically, the beginning to give substantial hope here and there, beginning to recreate the property interest and the stake in life, would begin at once to disorganize Bolshevik power and adherence to the formulas. . . . And [when] people began to have a property interest in life, a hope in life, the formula has less power. I believe that the best answer to Bolshevik Russia is economic cooperation, food, friendliness on the part of America. . . . That would help us help Russia, and operate in this country to weaken the authority and power of Bolshevism.[3]

Robins faced a great challenge when explaining Bolshevism to his audiences. He always began by laying the historic, social, political, religious, and economic foundations of Russia, followed by his understanding of the Marxist theoretical framework accepted and applied by the Bolsheviks. He knew the sincerity with which Trotsky and Lenin embraced that ideology and were attempting Russia's salvation through it. But Robins's attempt to understand Bolshevism and its leaders was often mistaken by his audiences as agreement with Bolshevism.

On 20 March 1919, at the very moment Robins was making his second major public address on Russia, before the City Club of Chicago, Gen. A. N. Dobrjansky was addressing the congregation of the Hanson Place Methodist Church in Brooklyn. Dobrjansky, a bitter anti-Bolshevist who had served in the Russian army in World War I under the Czar and the Provisional Government, attacked Robins with a fierceness unequaled by any other published or spoken words in the records of that time. On the previous day, 19 March, Dobrjansky was one of 1,500 people in the audience at the Hotel Commodore, in New York, where Robins began his nationwide speaking tour on his Russian experience. Dobrjansky was so incensed by Robins's sympathy toward the Bolsheviks that he devoted nearly his entire speech at the Hanson Place Church to vilifying Robins.

What Dobrjansky did not know at the time was that for years Robins had played a leading role in the evangelical movement in Brooklyn and had addressed that very congregation on the social gospel on numerous occasions. Dobrjansky wrote to Dr. J. Lane Miller, pastor of the church, asking why Miller had not published the Dobrjansky speech in the *Brooklyn Eagle* as planned. "Frankly," Dr. Miller responded, "while we are in deepest sympathy with you in your fight against Bolshevism we do not enjoy having one of our most honored and respected citizens assailed."

"You call Col. Robins a Bolshevist," Miller's letter continued. "Nothing could be more unfair and untrue. He has repudiated Bolshevism in every public utterance. But he is able to view the subject more dispassionately than the rest of us and is honest enough to give both sides."

"If you have as you say papers which incriminate Col. Robins they should be produced."

Robins gave serious consideration to filing a lawsuit against the general, and consulted Thomas Thacher on the matter. Finally, following Thacher's advice that "you will simply dignify his scurrilous words" by such an action, Robins decided that he would not go to court. In this instance, as in countless others, Robins used the podium to attack the paranoid thinking and misinformation rather than the man.[4]

Such confusion of his motives and aims required that Robins incorporate into his speeches on Russia a careful statement of his political philosophy. It was his way of demonstrating that a loyal American, devoted to the free enterprise system and constitutional democracy, could openly study and search for an understanding of revolutionary Russia. Well laced with humor, and more typical of his public speaking than the sober testimony at the Overman hearings, was his address at the City Club of Chicago, on 13 April 1919.

I, as is well known to some of you, have been more or less active in radical circles for something like twenty years, and have known the I.W.W. [Industrial Workers of the World] program and fought it steadily, have known the socialist program and fought it steadily, and have been what you call a poor and simple radical—mostly simple, according to the Socialists—my friends [Algie M.] Simmons and [John] Spargo, who are now more simple than I ever was, used to say in the old days that if I had sense enough I would be a good socialist, but the only trouble with me was that I did not have enough intelligence to appreciate the wisdom of the program.

I could never get the class struggle as the proper method of society. I could never get the economic interpretation of history, the socialistic conception of society, the iron law of wages. . . . They did not answer the facts of history and experience as I got them but I found in Russia the whole community, or, rather, the honest leaders of the community saying these formulas, with conviction, and when they got the power, deliberately and definitely going out and realizing them.

Why was that so? Nothing just happens in this old world. There is always a reason, just as much as there is for Grape Nuts. If you go deep enough you will find there is always a reason.

Robins discussed the czarist regime, "static in structure, held there by the power of the autocracy, and the Cossack whip and sword." He discussed the inequity of aristocratic privilege and the bankruptcy of the religious institutions that served the autocracy and not the cause of the Galilean.

By the time Robins was freed from the order to be silent about Russia, the frenzy of the red scare in American public opinion was on the rise. Constantly, Robins faced hostile audiences already blinded by hate. In answer to one of many prejudicial questions, Robins responded in typical form, with the full power of his righteous indignation.

If refusing to slander people, refusing to lie about them, refusing to follow the hounds in a day of propaganda, makes you a defender of a people, I am perfectly willing to take the cost in telling the truth. And that is against any individual or group anywhere. The only desirable time in telling the truth is when it costs something to tell it. I dared to fight Bolshevism where you did not get rewarded for it, where you were in danger of getting shot for it. . . . So far as Lenin and Trotsky's program is concerned, I regard it as economically impossible and radically wrong, and said so in Russia, and say so now; but so far as the individuals are concerned, their sincerity and courage in fighting for their program, there is no reason to lie about it and I refuse to do it.[5]

During a speech presented on 22 March in New York, the first question fielded from the audience concerned a most important issue. Robins attempted to distinguish between the Soviet form of government and the ideology and program of the Bolshevik party, which through Lenin's adept leadership had taken majority control of the Soviets. The grass-root councils, or soviets of workers' and soldiers' deputies, in addition to peasants' soviets, had evolved after the 1905 Revolution. With the fall of the Czar in 1917 the councils or soviets took on new significance as a genuine democratic representative force in Russia. The Bolshevik leadership appreciated the mass base of support of the soviets and, when calling for "All power to the soviets," became the champion of the soviets' legitimacy as a governing force. The gap from first champion to leadership within the All-Russian Council of Soviets was quickly and masterfully bridged by Lenin and his party. Specifically, Robins was asked: "Why do you think the soviet form of government is economically impossible and morally wrong?"

> My answer is, I don't think so. . . . [S]o many people in America . . . confusedly conceive the Bolshevik formula and party, which for the moment invests the soviet structure as the same thing as the soviet. It is the Bolshevik formula which I consider economically impossible and morally wrong. I have no capacity to pass upon the machinery of the soviet government. I would say that my criticism of it if I had one would be that it was too narrow in its interpretation of national interest and held it too definitely to the economic life. Secondly, that it was a very high decentralization and might make it impossible to move as a national power. . . . But I have for the soviet form of government only the interest of an experiment, at once tremendously vital in Russia and possibly useful in the history of human progress.[6]

Robins had found the same confusion among the senators of the subcommittee two weeks earlier. He explained: "The Soviet is a form or framework or method of Slavic democratic social control, exactly as the constitution of the United States is a framework or method or form of political democratic Anglo-Saxon control." And after the events of November 1917, he informed the senators, he came to the realization that "the Soviet was the growing heir to the Tsarist power for control and unity in Russia."[7]

The distinction between the soviets and the Bolshevik party, which Robins drew so clearly, was still a reality during his Red Cross service in Russia. It was within this separation that Robins saw the hope to diminish the "Bolshevik formulas" within the genuine democratic framework of the soviet structure and a possibility of a less restrictive socioeconomic system. It was as part of this rationale that Robins worked so tirelessly for a program of economic cooperation—to help Russia move away from the restrictions of the "Bolshevik formulas."

Instead President Wilson chose the course of intervention. Its effects from Robins's point of view were disastrous, especially in light of the above considerations. Robins spoke of three major repercussions of intervention.

> First, it stabilized the present government in its worst form, because it stabilized in the soviet the worst vices that had been then existent. The soviet tell them [the Russian people] that we put our boys and our forces behind the Japanese forces and the Japanese Generals, and that justified the worst things that could be done in Russia. . . .

When the bayonets came, particularly behind the yellow figure, having fought four hundred years against the Tatars and against the Mongols and against the Yellow invasion, they said, "Well, the bourgeoisie invited in those rifles, but we will get the bourgeoisie first," and I believe that was when the period of genuine terror started, after the intervention.

The second thing it did was to justify in the minds of the soviet a reign of terror against the intellectuals and that portion of the people in Russia, because they [the Bolsheviks] said they [their political opposition] were the ones who called for intervention. And third, it brought to the support of the Bolsheviki, people who would not otherwise have supported them, but would support any party who would fight against invaders of the home land. And so far from doing any good, it seems to me it has done nothing but harm.[8]

On this same occasion Robins was asked if he thought Russia would remain a "radical socialist nation." His response, cautious in the dangerous realm of prediction, is perceptive and prophetic.

My thought is that if foreign rifles stay out of Russia, that the soviet social control will stabilize; that it suits the Russian people for the time being. I believe that the Bolshevik Party will either modify their hard formulas, as I said—they probably have already modified them—or they will be thrown out of power and some other party come in. But I believe a sort of socialist state will be tried for a period in Russia, that there is enough of the radical mind and the soviet mind in it. Suppose some time we try, for once, to think of other people than ourselves.[9]

Perhaps Robins was foreseeing Lenin's New Economic Policy or perhaps Stalin's "socialism in one country," when suggesting the necessity of modifying formulas. The observation "that there is enough of the radical mind" to perpetuate socialism for "at least a period, in Russia" was offered before the Overman committee: "But I would never expect to stamp out ideas with bayonets. I would never expect, sirs, to suppress the desire for a better human life for men, women, and children no matter how ill founded in political fact and political experience, with force. The only answer for the desire for a better human life is a better human life."

In nearly all of his speeches on Russia after the Overman hearings, Robins incorporated his suggestions for an immediate revision of American policy toward Soviet Russia. He enumerated five points.

First, lift the embargo at once on all Russian fronts, so that men, women and children do not starve.

Second, enter into direct negotiations for an armistice on all fronts where Allied or Czech forces are engaged.

Third, insist in armistice negotiations upon general political amnesty to be declared and guaranteed by both sides, Allied forces to be retained in Russia solely for the purpose of enforcing such guarantees and to be used after signing of armistice in reorganizing and operating Russian railroads primarily for transport of food supplies throughout Russia.

Fourth, send relief through American Red Cross to Petrograd and Moscow immediately upon signing of armistice.

Fifth, send industrial commission of inquiry with trade experts to Moscow, to ascertain and report on present situation in Soviet Russia and best means of bringing social peace, economic reorganization and relief to all the peoples of Russia.[10]

With these proposals, Robins hoped to return American-Soviet relations to the status that existed at the time of his departure from Moscow, or at least to the state of affairs prior to intervention. Points three and five, he hoped, would save his earlier plans for mutually beneficial economic cooperation, even at that late date.

"Now is the Russian Soviet and its culture a menace to our order and a menace to the world?" Robins often asked his audience rhetorically, and dramatically, without a moment's pause, he answered,

In my judgement, absolutely yes. And more of a menace, because it is in its fundamental plan sincere, because it has come out of centuries of oppression, of ignorance and economic misery, and because it challenges with the stark, bald formulas of Marxian economics, materialistic class control of governments and of institutions of the world.

I believe . . . it is understood and known, that there is only one nation on the earth today competent to meet the challenge, competent to deal with it as it should be dealt with. Bayonets against ideas is an old failure in the history of the human race. Wherever a man or group of men conspire or act against the institutions of this government by force or violence, they should be suppressed by whatever force and violence is necessary to its suppression.

I would deal with it with unhesitating power, but I would beware of the witch hunt, I would beware in this hour of the world's history of libel and slander, of thinking that you can really cover fundamental currents of human effort and human hope by any such means, however unfounded, unsound, however wrong they may be.

The Russian Revolution is understandable in Russia. The soviet government and Bolshevik control are understandable in Russia. The Bolshevik formulas have no place in America; and I have faith enough in my institutions and their merits, to believe that we can meet it on the square and send back the ferine poison to the center from whence it comes. I would not suppress free speech and free press in a panic of childish fear. I would meet the issue as an issue.

I would inform America. I would deal with Russia intelligently, courageously and unfalteringly, but I would not expect to use foreign bayonets to reestablish order.

Robins's faith in the American capacity to meet the challenge of Bolshevik formulas head on, without lies and without curbs on free speech and free exchange of ideas, was not shared by many Americans in 1919 (neither in the 1950s nor in the neoconservatism of the 1980s). Perhaps they were not as well grounded in the fundamentals of the American democratic spirit as Robins and those of the "outdoor" view of revolution.

"Beyond our Christian sanction," Robins continued,

> there is yet a validity in our life. I know the decadence of the Christian posi-
> tion in many great centers, but I also know the little white church on the hill,
> the little red church in the valley. I know that back behind our country there is
> the social power and self-control in the Christian sanction of the life.
>   I believe that we can meet the challenge on the square, in the open, in the
> full light of day, giving truth where truth should go, and giving honor where
> honor should run, not finding it necessary to libel or lie.
>   I believe that we can answer that tide that is stirring in the hearts of men,
> that demands a better human life, in the only way it will ever be answered, by
> providing a better human life. I believe that our institutions provide the best
> human life for the most men, women and children, that the world has yet
> known, and contains the promise of meeting the full need of our time and the
> growing good of the world by obedience to the constitution and the law.[11]

Robins was committed to the American way of life—to the free enterprise system modified by the moral and social responsibilities demanded by
the social gospel of Jesus. He could not separate that ethic from the spiritual
force of Christ which stood behind it and gave it its power. Nor could these
be separated from the essential ideas of the dignity of the individual, which
could best be protected by the Constitution and due process of law.

In Robins's view, Russia had undergone an unfortunate and disturbed
historic development that left the archaic Romanov dynasty in power long
after its "sanction" had disappeared. The heir to that power, he believed,
was the essentially democratic, indigenous institution of the soviet. But most
important, in that time of its infancy under the aegis of the Bolshevik party,
there were possibilities for changing the course of its development toward
the more positive direction that had been taken by the young American republic. Robins saw those possibilities in the vitality of the Russian people
and within the dynamic revolutionary situation; he also saw great benefits
for America and the world in such a movement. With the mixed feelings of
anger over a lost opportunity and the hope that the chance was not lost
forever, Robins came to the close of his speech before the League of Free
Nations Association in New York,

> the American government could have organized the economic power of Rus-
> sia, could have furnished the economic brain of Russia, could have controlled
> the raw materials of Russia, not because they were our friends, but because
> the menace of the German militarist power required of them in violation of
> their formulas the necessities of the outdoor world, cooperation. And after we
> had gotten control, if they had sought then to attack us, we would have made
> it deliberate, so that the whole question in debate would have been removed
> forever from the realm of conjecture and would have been up among the liv-
> ing facts. I make the statement that with immense natural resources and a
> market for manufactured products of America, the chance to stabilize a culture
> that while revolutionary and wrong in its formulas will yield, like all other

formulas, to the light of experience and practical necessity, it may even yet, after all the futility and wrong that was dealt to soviet Russia, be possible to save the values of that situation for America, for the Allied interests, for the economic interests of the Allies, instead of forcing Russia into the hands of Germany. There are only two possible centers for the new economic organization of Russia: either the Central Empires, or America and the Allies. Which shall it be?

Shall soviet Russia continue to be lied about, continue to be denounced? Shall soviet Russia be forced, driven into cooperation with Germany? Shall soviet Russia be stabilized in the opinion that we are an imperialistic capitalism and that we will back Japanese imperialism in Siberia? Has that got to be? Or is it possible to break through this barrage of poisonous gas, of libel, of slander and raise up the living facts? Is it possible that America, great, free America, may find the living truth and not be controlled by propaganda groups who look back upon lost privileges or who suffer from the pique that comes in hours like this, when theoreticians are thrust aside and men of action take the helm?[12]

Robins made about twenty major public addresses on the Russian situation after testifying at the Overman hearings. He recounted the events, gave his appraisals, and expressed his hopes, much as they have been presented here. But he realized that the tide of public opinion in America had already been shaped by the "indoor" mentality. After a month on the speakers' circuit, he wrote to Gumberg in New York of the difficulties of informing the American people and changing America's Russian policy.

My meetings are largely attended and overwhelmingly friendly. . . . There is however in every meeting a small-in-number but powerful-in-influence dissenting minority. The newspapers report my addresses from a biased viewpoint adversely to me and to the truth. I am made the advocate and apologist for Lenin and Trotsky and the Bolshevik program as the result of nearly every write-up in the public press. This, however, is an old story to me; and while, when one talks to two or three hundred or two or three thousand hearers and the newspapers speak to from one hundred thousand to a million readers, one is under a very real disadvantage. I expect to create centers of opinion that will have an influence in finally fashioning a sound American policy in relation to Soviet Russia.[13]

American intervention in the Soviet Union did not end until 1920, and Robins made good his pledge to Gumberg that he would continue his effort to change the mistaken policy. Robins's public addresses and lobbying continued against intervention and in behalf of American diplomatic recognition of the Soviet Union. But no "center of opinion" bore as much irony nor was more unusual than the prestigious group that met at the Waldorf Hotel in New York on 20 September 1919, six months after Robins's letter to Gumberg and seven months after his testimony before the Overman committee. "The personal fortunes of those present aggregated over six hundred millions of dollars," Robins calculated in his letter to Elizabeth. "Thompson was toastmaster," he continued,

To my right sat Will Hayes the Chairman of the Republican National Committee. Presidents of the largest banks and corporations of New York made up the company. Not five would have come out to hear me speak. They came because the copper wizard [Thompson] invited them. I was the only speaker. It was in the Astor Gold Room. The decorations were more splendid than anything I had yet seen. I was overwhelmed. It was too much for me and I spoke badly. The Florida pine forest, Louisville, Alva, the Yukon Trail, San Francisco, Chicago tenements, rose up and merged into the Russian story of red revolution, the night in the barracks at Gatchina, Lenin at Smolny and in the Kremlin, Kerensky in the Winter palace of the Czars![14]

While Robins's charisma may have made an impression on this audience, the "outdoor view" on Russia did not find fertile ground. The moguls of Wall Street and the captains of American industry were not convinced. The magic Robins had worked on Thompson, after weeks of personal contact, could not be carried off in a single afternoon of speech making.

Part Four

The Last Campaigns

19

The Peace Settlement
and Recognition of Russia, 1919–1924

So far as I am presently concerned, I shall give up my entire time to battling against Wilson's administration, Wilson's League and the witch-hunting of Postmaster General Burelson and Attorney General Palmer. I hope to make the infamy and betrayal of Wilson's pseudo-liberalism and secure its overwhelming repudiation at the polls, which is to me the first obligation of our progressive citizenship.

—Robins to Hon. Julius Kespohl, 4 September 1920

THROUGHOUT the 1920s, Robins maintained the pace of his tumultuous ten months in Russia. His meetings, nationwide speech making, political caucusing, and vast personal correspondence were focused on the urgent "campaigns" of the time. Like the zealous young settlement worker in Chicago's Seventeenth Ward in 1901 and the quixotic adventurer in Alaska, the only diminution of activity resulted from actual collapses of a mind and body no longer able to sustain the overload. Medical treatment and rest and quiet in Chinsegut's Florida paradise always brought relief. Often within weeks he was back on the campaign trail.

Like most leaders in the Progressive movement and like the American public in general, until the outbreak of World War I Robins was seldom involved in international political concerns. While in 1908 he had been instrumental in rescuing Christian Rudovitz from extradition to czarist Russia and in 1912–13 Robins had circled the globe in the Smith-Robins evangelical campaign, his speeches, correspondence, and organizational commitments reflected little or no attention to conflict in the international community. The World War changed that for an entire generation, but for Robins in particular the Russian experience permanently altered his life, making American reconciliation with Soviet Russia and world peace the major focus of his energies.

After his release from the State Department ban on public disclosures about his service in Russia and following the Senate Bolshevik Propaganda Hearings, Robins campaigned against the misrepresentations and lies about the Russian Revolution. He campaigned against the Allied and Japanese interventions and the American embargo of Soviet Russia, not lifted until January 1920. Working with Alexander Gumberg, William Thompson, William Hard, and many other veterans of the American Red Cross Commission, and

Senators Hiram Johnson, William Borah, and former governor James P. Goodrich of Indiana, Robins constantly pressed every opportunity to bring about American diplomatic recognition of Soviet Russia. At the same time, he championed critical projects like famine relief in Russia. During the 1920s Robins and his allies explored and successfully inaugurated mutually beneficial Russian-American commercial and trade relations.

In 1919 Robins added "World Disarmament or World Revolution—Which?" as a key subject in his public lectures. Disarmament quickly became one of his most well received talks; it reflected the beginning of his long-term commitment to international peace, which evolved into the movement for the outlawry of war. "There is a greater general sentiment favoring disarmament now in this country, than I have ever known before to be aroused for any one purpose," Robins wrote to Senator Borah in July 1921, congratulating him on the occasion of the senator's successful advocacy of an international disarmament conference. "For some months," Robins continued, "I have been speaking for your resolution as opportunity offered and on all occasions the . . . resolutions have been adopted, in most instances unanimously." And to the aftermath of the World War, the impatience and disgust with war, which so deeply permeated Robins's consciousness, Borah replied: "I am utterly opposed to the old system of diplomats, to wit, to settle everything before you talk about disarmament. I am in favor of disarmament and then adjust these questions afterwards in the court of reason and conscience."[1] It was during this disarmament campaign that Robins made a new, devoted, and life-long friendship with Salmon O. Levinson of Chicago, whose dedication to the cause of peace exceeded even Robins's.

Levinson was the son of Austrian Jewish immigrants. His father worked as a tailor in Noblesville, Indiana, where Sol, as he was called, was born. He "fought up and through Yale University and the Chicago Bar," and he "made Wall Street and railroad presidents give him room and money for his opinions. He is now more than a millionaire." Levinson's reputation and wealth was earned as a corporation lawyer specializing in rescuing failing large enterprises—railroads, meat packers, and rubber combines. "The most important Banker in Chicago will not move in matters of that sort without Levinson as counsel," Robins confided to his sister, "and he is used and feared in Wall Street." With his rimless glasses, salt-and-pepper mustache, kindly soft eyes, and predictable three-piece suit, he had more the appearance of a loving doctor-grandfather than anyone who could inspire fear. After the Robinses finally gave up their "tenement workshop" in the Seventeenth Ward in 1924, Robins was always Sol's houseguest when in Chicago.[2]

Robins and Levinson worked together closely throughout the long struggle for the outlawry of war. They campaigned for the creation of an international treaty with every state as a signatory, not only to renounce war for the settlement of disputes, but to declare all acts of war illegal, outlawed by the community of nations. Like Thompson, Levinson was a man of great wealth and political influence who did not spare either asset to further the cause. Such resources, along with Robins's oratorical power and political skill, made for a campaign to be reckoned with.

Robins viewed American and Allied ostracism of the Soviet Union from the family of nations not only as a serious impediment to normal relations between states, but to peace. He therefore continued to try to bring his understanding of the Russian Revolution and the Bolshevik government before the American public, particularly in light of the credence given to the Sisson documents and the runaway anti-Bolshevism that pervaded the State Department and American public opinion. As Robins's letter to Gumberg of 11 April 1919 demonstrates, it was always a challenging and often a bitter task. He was often misquoted and misrepresented in the press, and on occasion, he was refused permission to speak.

As early as 1918 Robins was convinced that President Wilson was an enemy of peace. Robins's opposition to the United States' participation in Wilson's League of Nations stemmed from his strong objections to the vindictive provisions of the Versailles Treaty. Since Wilson had succeeded "in sewing the League of Nations" into the Versailles Treaty, in the words of historian Allan Nevins, Robins was convinced that the League had to be rejected; otherwise, another Franco-German war would result. Disarmament and the outlawry of war were viable alternatives to the League.

An early critique of the League of Nations came in a speech given in the spring of 1920 in behalf of Hiram Johnson's Republican primary campaign for the presidency. Robins identified the Treaty of Versailles and the provisions for the League of Nations as inseparable, the negative aspects of the treaty mitigating any of the attributes of the League. His view of the postwar world, the treaty, and the League mirrored an important segment of American public opinion. "I am unqualifiedly opposed to both the Treaty and the League," Robins affirmed. "I denounce those instruments as instruments of violence and force, promoting war rather than peace, and I believe that the pledge under the League of Nations would mean to bind the manhood and the money of America to the support of imperialistic purposes and bankrupt nations of Europe, rather than to the service that needs a place in this land."[3]

In Robins's opinion, ratifying the treaty and entering the League were mistakes almost as serious as the belated entry of America into the war. The lines in the war had been clearly drawn between the institutions of democracy and the "larger militaristic autocracy threatening to wipe out the freedom of all lands." Robins was proud of the fact that he had judged the situation correctly and, as early as 1916, had personally committed himself to the Entente by working with Theodore Roosevelt for American entry into the war. In 1916 he had also volunteered for a speaking campaign throughout Canada, urging Canadians to enlist in their armed forces and fight the Central Powers. During the speaking campaigns of the 1920s in behalf of outlawry of war, he was often accused of pacifism, both in the press and by his audiences. He often referred to his militant position of 1916 and his 1917–18 war efforts in Russia to silence such accusations.[4] Robins, the Christian evangelist, one-time minister in Nome, and "World Gospel Crusader," denied any pacifist leanings.

On the other hand, in his religious campaigns for the social gospel, he paid much more heed to the teachings of the Good Shepherd and his Sermon on the Mount. The ultimate end of the outlawry of war movement was pacifist, even though the means and instruments which it used to reach that end were couched in the language of international law. The domestic and international atmosphere against which the movement struggled was, however, dominated by power politics that left little room for pacifism. The tragic experience of Jane Addams, Robins's ally of so many struggles of the settlement years, was vivid in the consciousness of all postwar peace activists. Addams's loss of leadership in the American settlement movement and her nearly universal condemnation in the press was a heavy price to pay for her staunch pacifist position during World War I.

If the only path to success followed the thinking and language of political realism, Robins and Levinson refused to engage in the mediating and compromising "language of imperialism" used by those who sought lasting peace through power politics bargaining. Robins and Levinson, while denying pacifism, struggled for a formal international treaty to outlaw war. All other peace plans and leagues were false, if not dangerous panaceas, and could quickly lead to war since they did not rule out sovereign states' legitimate resort to war—what Robins called "the war system."

Robins judged the Treaty of Versailles imperialistic and condemned it on that basis. The ceding of the German-speaking Saar Valley to the French and the reparations demands were the clear signs of the kind of primeval conquest that goaded suppressed peoples to war. "[T]o take a German people, a German land, and put it under a French government, French language, and French flag will mean but to produce the seed of a bleeding sore in the heart of Europe, and so do in 1920 exactly what Bismark did in 1870, when Bismark took the French men and women and children in Alsace and Lorraine and put them under the German flag and German government, and laid the foundation for the war which has just devastated the world."[5]

Robins agreed with the verdict on the guilt of the kaiser and announced "that he ought to be tried, convicted and executed for high crimes." But he accused the signatories of the treaty of "sham and humbug" in their contrived trial in London and attempt to force Holland to refuse the political asylum which it had granted Kaiser Wilhelm.

The *Italia Irridenta* and *Revanche* movements, in Italy and France, which sought the return of "homeland" territory lost in expansionist peace settlements of the nineteenth century, had played their role in bringing on the Great War in 1914. Robins was convinced that such passionate movements of nationalist redemption would again bring war if they were given just cause.

His own ties with Germany through his wife's family gave him a personal insight into the reception of the Versailles *Dictat* in Germany. He had reason to be concerned about any prospects for a future peace, and based upon this conviction, he had to fight the League, which was being established to sanctify and preserve the evil treaty.

Among the most outrageous injustices Robins believed to be perpetuated by the treaty was the legitimation of Japanese imperialistic control of the Shantung province of China. His bitterness was accentuated by his personal experience with Japanese imperialism in Russia. While in Moscow and Vologda, during the first months of 1918, he had pressed Ambassador Francis to intercede with the State Department to forestall a Japanese landing in Siberia. Francis wired the State Department to warn Japan against the landing, and Japanese imperialism, for the moment, had been thwarted.[6] Robins took special pride in his role in bringing American pressure to bear and boasted that Lenin himself had credited him with averting the Japanese landing.[7]

In light of the foregoing, the Allied acceptance of Japanese aggression in China received Robins's special wrath. "This nation [the USA] had been fair and reasonable and just in its past international relations," he declared.

> We went into Cuba, established order, justice and freedom, and turned Cuba back to the Cubans. We have developed in the Philippines, that ultimate unity of national life that we make them self-governing. In relation to China, we have in the Boxer uprising, dealt with the Chinese in such a fashion as to make them our fast friends. And we have returned the indemnity. Not only so, America has made an international law in relation to the Chinese world. . . .
> [B]ut the Treaty of Versailles violates its fundamental principles. . . . There is no one in the sound of my voice but knows that Japan today is seeking to do in the Orient exactly what the Germans sought to do in the West and that exactly the same methods, the will to power, the idea that might makes right, the development of ruthless force—that has been her method in dealing with Korea, in dealing with Formosa; that has been her method in dealing with Manchuria, and is her method in dealing, tonight as we are gathered here, with Shantung. . . . And now tonight the imperialistic group in Japan can justify their imperialism in the terms of the rich province that has been brought to them by their sword and their demands at the Council of Versailles. I wonder if there are any homes of the men in California, any money in the state which wishes to be expended, under the League of Nations, in enforcing the right of Japan over the thirty million Chinese in Shantung.[8]

While arguing for a true peace through American commitment to a just treaty, Robins evoked the isolationist imagery of 1916 and a hint of the old Populist xenophobia. "[T]hey ask of us that this nation shall commit in the League of Nations to nine men sitting in Geneva, one American, eight other foreigners, the destiny of the manhood and the money of this Republic or the violation of our sacred honor, but if you prefer . . . refuse your moral obligation or that we shall use these resources of our people to enforce the

Saar Valley on the one hand and Shantung on the other."⁹ Robins was part of a widespread and growing international movement that called for the rejection or revision of the treaty. With the exception of France, where the Germanophobia had such deep roots, this movement received a continued and friendly hearing in the United States and in the international community. Robins held that even France would finally drop her vehement support for the treaty "as soon as the impossibility of it becomes clear. Then if America aids in revision and we get a treaty that is just and enforceable and fair and makes for peace, there will be no unwillingness on the part of the American people to aid the people of Europe in coming back to life and hope and order and peace."¹⁰

At no time throughout the 1920s and 1930s, after many revisions had been made in the Versailles Treaty—especially the reparations provisions— did Robins and his outlawry associates accept the treaty, the League, or the League provisions for a World Court. They were all stigmatized by the "Carthaginian" terms of the peace and the opponents felt they should be abandoned in favor of the outlawry of war.

On 27 February 1920, Robins arrived at Leland Stanford Junior College as leader of a YMCA team for recruiting students to the Life Service Campaign of the Interchurch World Movement. It was very much like his college evangelical campaign of 1915–16, except that he was dividing his time between this work and his support for Hiram Johnson's bid for the Republican presidential nomination. In the office of Dr. David Starr Jordan, president of Stanford College, "I was waited upon by a committee of students," Robins wrote, "dressed in the uniform of the U.S.A. and threatened with reprisals if I spoke again upon that campus." These students were reacting to published accusations against Robins made by David Barrows, president of the University of California, Berkeley.¹¹ Barrows had responded to a YMCA request for involvement in the campaign: "that under no circumstances would [he] invite Mr. Robins to speak at the University." He was familiar with Robins's interpretation of the Russian Revolution and had concluded that he was a liar, a "dupe," and supporter of terrorism. "Within the past year he [Robins] has gone on record as thoroughly condemning Bolshevism and the Soviet regime in Russia. He condemns it for its moral degeneracy and for its political futility. This present attitude of his, which I must regard as a pose, taken for purposes of self-exculpation, is inconsistent with his conduct while in Russia." This in response to a letter from Arthur Arlett, who had written Barrows to ask him to reconsider his judgment on Robins—"He is America's greatest spiritual voice to our young men," Arlett pleaded. But Barrows was vehement. "Confession that he was duped by Lenin and Trotsky is the only thing which . . . will ever make his conduct consistent and honorable," Barrows continued.

> There is abundant evidence, some of which is in my possession, which proves that he not merely consorted with Lenin and Trotsky and other Soviet leaders

in Russia . . . but that he gave active support and encouragement to their policy of terrorism. I have this from one of his own associates, himself a Bolshevik propagandist. He worked zealously for American recognition of the Soviet government. . . . How can these actions be reconciled with the moral judgment which he himself has passed upon Bolshevism and upon Trotsky and Lenin? His testimony before the Senate committee, the elaborate account of his performances published by Mr. William Hard, who is another pro-Bolshevik, and his own public utterances leave the whole matter in a perfect maze and befuddlement. . . . [T]he whole constitutes a record which, in my opinion, damns him completely as a moral leader.[12]

Barrows was not alone in these harsh judgments. The "maze and befuddlement" of the social and political forces unleashed by the Russian Revolution continued to confuse many knowledgeable and sophisticated observers for years thereafter. Barrows could not understand how Robins could express moral condemnation for Bolshevism and at the same time express sympathy for the Russian people, its history and socioeconomic reality, which had driven leaders like Lenin and Trotsky to adopt the "Bolshevik formulas." Barrows, like the majority of the Allied diplomatic community in Russia during the time of the revolution, along with generations of Americans since, was not willing or able to imagine that the Lenin leadership had majority mass support. Nor could they understand that American national interest would best be served through communication with the revolutionary leadership and, where mutually beneficial, in cooperation with them. Barrows's "maze and befuddlement" is the very thing that makes Robins's critical and prescient insight of the events of 1917–18 all the more remarkable.[13]

At the very time that Barrows sought Robins's condemnation, Gen. William V. Judson was deep in a personal campaign to convince the Wilson administration that Robins and Thompson should receive the Distinguished Service Medal (DSM) for their role in aiding the Allied cause while in Russia. Judson, it will be remembered, had served as American military attaché in Petrograd until January 1918, when he was recalled. He was among the most objective and appreciative eyewitnesses to Robins's activities, both in Russia and on the campaign trail against U.S. intervention and for U.S. recognition of the soviets. After discussing his role and supporting his own claim to the DSM, Judson concluded that Robins's and Thompson's activities in Russia had significantly helped win the war for the Allies. "The Brest-Litovsk treaty was not approved by the Russians until the middle of March, 1918," Judson explained in a secret memorandum to Secretary of War Newton D. Baker. "If this treaty had been consummated several months earlier," he continued,

the Germans would have had from five to six hundred thousand more men in their spring drive against the channel ports and Paris. . . . It is difficult to believe that this additional force might not have changed the result. Among those most responsible for this result, . . . were Colonels Thompson and Robins, and certain other members of our Red Cross Mission to Russia who have had much obloquy cast upon them by persons who themselves should have done something to prevent the Russian debacle but did not. Justice seems to demand that the services in particular of Colonel William B. Thompson and of Colonel Raymond Robins should be now pointed out by someone who was officially on the ground, who knew the history of those days and who has no motive now to misrepresent their services.[14]

Judson began his campaign soon after Robins completed his testimony before the Senate subcommittee and with renewed vigor after learning that Ambassador Francis had been awarded the medal. Judson felt slighted that he had not been similarly recognized and outraged that Robins and Thompson had been ignored. Beginning with letters to his friend Albert Burelson, U.S. postmaster general, the campaign for the DSM award lasted nearly a year and drew in many veterans of American service in Russia during the revolution.[15] "I quite agree with you in believing Raymond Robbins deserves a D.S.M.," Maj. Monroe C. Kerth wrote to Judson. (Kerth served as assistant military attaché in Petrograd in 1917.) "His value," Kerth continued, "[was] much more than that of our combined Embassy with Mr. Sisson thrown in for good measure." And some months later, in another letter to Judson, added: "If the President really knew his [Robins] fine character, he would use him with great advantage in connection with labor troubles in the U.S."[16]

While the medal was ultimately awarded to Judson, Robins and Thompson had to be satisfied with the belated receipt of the official papers that conferred on each of them their commission as lieutenant colonels, U.S. Army. However, the award of the commissions signified no change in attitude or foreign policy.

Robins's public speaking in 1919 and 1920 was divided between campaigns for recognition and disarmament, and against the treaty and the League of Nations. In addition, he angrily denounced the red scare and the unconstitutional arrest of social reformers, union organizers, and radicals and the suppression of newspapers and organizations of social protest. It was Wilson's complicity in anticommunist paranoia that determined, in part, Robins's strong opposition to the administration and the League. Wilson and Lansing had permitted Robins to be humiliated upon his return from Russia and Robins's resentment never diminished, but was not expressed publicly with the full force that was in his heart. Only in his private correspondence can its depth be gauged. "He has walloped the Great White Father out of his sacrosanct position in the holy of holies," Robins wrote to Elizabeth about Sen. Hiram Johnson's challenge to Wilson's foreign policy, "and that hypocritical wordmonger and traitor to Truth has had to get out and fight for his position like any common hack politician." Robins was hardly the only one who felt such rage toward Wilson. Thompson, Gumberg, Allen Wardwell, and Thomas Thacher, among the veterans of the American Red Cross in Russia, represent only part of a long list. In fact, given Allied intervention in Russia and the witch-hunting hysteria that pervaded the Wilson administration, it is questionable as to whether Robins's response would have been different even if there had been a respectful hearing upon his return to the United States.[17]

Because he had been chairman of the Progressive National Convention in 1916, Robins's position on the League of Nations and support for the candidates in the 1920 presidential race was particularly influential. In 1920 he made a decision that mirrored one he had made in 1916, when he and other prominent leaders of the Progressive party supported Republican Charles Evans Hughes's bid for the presidency, and vowed to remain a progressive in the ranks of the Republican party. Robins now reaffirmed that vow. He believed that he could be more useful as a force for change, for social reform, for the recognition of and cooperation with Soviet Russia and for disarmament and the outlawry of war, by exercising his influence within a Republican administration. Unlike his 1916 decision to support the clear underdog Hughes, Robins knew well enough that the Republican party would win the presidency in the 1920 election; he felt he could use his political following and vote-getting power to counter the conservative forces in the party.

Robins placed himself in a key position as political advisor, campaigner, and "progressive Republican in residence" in the administrations of Harding, Coolidge, and Hoover. With ready access to these presidents, Robins made every effort to advance the causes of Russian-American relations, the outlawry of war, and when possible, the progressive platform of social, labor, and political reform.

Of particular significance was Robins's involvement in the 1924 three-way race between the incumbent Coolidge, Democrat John W. Davis, and progressive third party candidate Robert La Follette. This election, more than any other, demonstrates the splintering of the Progressive movement and Robins's painful role in that process. Added to his never-ending social gospel evangelism, Robins also became a relentless spokesman in the "Allied Campaign" for the enforcement of the prohibition amendment to the Constitution.

California senator Hiram Johnson was a long-time progressive ally of Robins and co-worker on labor, social, and welfare reform. As a progressive governor and senator, Johnson was among the key individuals to whom Robins turned for help to carry out reform policies after the demise of the Progressive party. The relationship between Robins and co-workers like Johnson, who held high political office and power, was always reciprocal. In return for support on reform measures he was championing, Robins lent his oratorical skills, time, and energy to political campaigns. Many expressed their deep thanks and conviction that Robins's charisma and speeches on the campaign trail had made the difference and won elections. In March 1920 Robins began his campaign for Johnson's nomination for president in the California Republican primaries with his own $500 contribution. Johnson won the primary in May, but Harding won the nomination at the Republican National Convention in June.[18]

Johnson's nomination and election would have fulfilled Robins's hopes of continuity of domestic social reform, and Johnson's position against the League was even stronger than Robins's. However, with Harding's nomination, domestic issues had to be shelved; Johnson joined Robins in the ranks of the regular Republican party in the fight against the League and for recognition of Russia and the outlawry of war.

In a letter from Charles McCarthy, of Wisconsin, to Gifford Pinchot, of Pennsylvania, both Robins's Progressive contemporaries, the situation was articulated:

> As far as I can see there isn't anything to be done about it. *Harding is absolutely sure of being elected.* If I were you I would get Leonard Wood, Raymond Robins, and a bunch of men of that kind who are now supporting Harding . . . and absolutely demand certain cabinet positions from him. I feel certain that Hoover will be in the cabinet. If he is, the only way to strengthen the back-bone of the cabinet is to have some good strong men sitting in the cabinet so that that gang will be afraid of him. . . . They will go out through the country in case there is anything going wrong on the inside. This is the only recourse you have and it ought to be done mighty soon. You have enough strong progressives now supporting Harding to control the situation, *provided they are organized into a compact body who will meet occasionally and insist upon their policies being carried out.* Without that compact body you can do nothing and the country will be handed over to Mr. Penrose [Sen. Boies Penrose of Pennsylvania, a leading reactionary Republican].[19]

Robins was not as optimistic as McCarthy. On three occasions during July and August 1920, he met with Senator Harding to sound him out on his domestic and foreign policy views. It was only in the latter field that Robins received any reassurance. On domestic issues he was totally disappointed.[20] He knew that a Harding victory meant definite curtailment of virtually all programs of social reform. Big business, the antilabor open shop, and policies of political bossism, against which Robins had been struggling since before the turn of the century, were indirectly advocated by Harding. But Robins was ready to make the sacrifice to prevent Democratic candidate James M. Cox's election, to keep the United States from membership in Wilson's League of Nations, and to stop Attorney General Palmer's red scare.[21]

Three days after beginning his public campaign in support of Harding, which was covered extensively in Republican newspapers throughout the country, Robins wrote privately:

> In my judgement we have to choose in the impending election between an endorsement of Wilson's administration with its betrayal of America for the Treaty of Versailles, or Senator Harding and the Republican party. I [know] in making my choice for the time being our progressive domestic program will inevitably suffer. But if America is kept free from the Wilson military alliance, by 1924 we can proceed with our rewarded progressive development true to the genius of our own institutions and national inheritance.[22]

Following his election, at least in part in repayment for campaign support, Harding invited Margaret Dreier Robins to a national conference "to inquire into the volume and distribution of unemployment to advise upon emergency measures that can be properly taken by employers and local authorities . . . to give impulse to the recovery of business and commerce to normal." Robins hoped that Thompson would be offered the cabinet post of either secretary of the treasury or commerce. Thompson hoped that Robins would be made secretary of labor. In the end, Margaret could not accept Harding's invitation. "I am sailing September seventeenth for Geneva to convene second international congress of working women," she wrote proudly to Harding. Thompson was offered the ambassadorship to Germany and declined it, but he did accept appointment to the Advisory Council for the American Delegation of the Conference on the Limitation of Armaments. Harding asked for a confidential letter from Robins "telling [him] what service you would be most interested in performing to make a success of this administration." It is unclear whether Robins asked for or was offered a cabinet-level position; Robins took none in the Harding administration, nor any in that of Coolidge or Hoover.[23] He did ask for open consideration of U.S. recognition of Soviet Russia, but following the naming of the cabinet, it was clear that the chances were nil. Republicans Johnson, Borah, and La Follette in the Senate were strongly in favor, while Secretary of Commerce Hoover, Secretary of State Charles Evans Hughes (former attorney for the Standard Oil Company, whose resources in Russia had been expropriated by the Bolsheviks), and staunch conservative Elihu Root were opposed.

Hughes established his formula of preconditions to U.S. recognition of the Soviets very early in his tenure. It required assured safety of life, guarantees of private property, respect for contracts, and the rights of free labor, all rigidly interpreted virtually to preclude recognition. But in the face of famine in Russia in 1921, a federal commission was established to provide relief, and at the same time, individual initiatives were carried out to foster the chances for recognition, most noteworthy, those of former governor James P. Goodrich of Indiana.

Goodrich was appointed to the presidential commission on Russian aid chaired by Hoover, and after his contacts with Gumberg, Robins, Borah, and Johnson, Goodrich became a key figure in the drive for recognition in conjunction with his relief work.

When Goodrich returned from his first famine relief trip to Russia on 20 April 1922, he was particularly optimistic regarding recognition possibilities. Gumberg, who had hoped to serve as translator and aide for the mission, as he had for Robins and the Red Cross Commission, was there to meet Goodrich upon his return and traveled with him to Baltimore and Washington to learn all he could firsthand. Goodrich was planning another trip to Russia within the month, and once again, Gumberg held out hopes of assisting. "I judge from conversation with him that some things he wanted done were not taken care of," Gumberg wrote to Robins. "I am sure that if I was with him the things he mentioned would have been done. I now feel sorry that I did not go with him . . . because I could have been very useful in healing the breach between America and Russia. . . . I hoped that you would come to Washington and put your shoulder to the wheel. 'THIS IS THE HOUR TO STRIKE FOR FREE RUSSIA!'"24

Arrangements for Gumberg to serve as aide and translator for the second trip of the Goodrich relief commission were completed but for the receipt of a British visa. It never came! The suspicion that pervaded the years after the return from Russia of both Robins and Gumberg continued to plague them. For that same reason Robins insisted that his public addresses on Russia throughout the early 1920s (and they numbered in the hundreds) be sponsored by unquestionably mainstream, if not conservative, organizations and church groups. Again, for the same reason, it was of inestimable importance to have national figures of the stature of Hiram Johnson and William Borah press the case for recognition. On 9 June 1921, at Robins's urging and following the recommendations of Gumberg on the basis of Goodrich's optimism, Borah made another major address in behalf of recognition.

Later that month, as Goodrich was involved in "recognition discussions" in Russia, Robins received some encouragement to make recommendations on Russia from Secretary of Commerce Hoover. Robins submitted a plan for an American commission of inquiry into the economic situation in Russia, but unlike other commissions, the personnel that he suggested favored recognition. Allen Wardwell, Thomas Thacher, and Gumberg, all veterans of the Red Cross Commission of 1917–18; in addition, Robins named Goodrich, Dwight Morrow, and George Sutherland. Like so many of the initiatives of Robins and his allies, nothing came of this proposal.

Nevertheless, on a regular basis during Harding's thirty months in office, Robins had the chance to be heard. On 3 June 1923 the specific subject of discussion was American policy toward the Soviet Union. While these private conferences were "in the main at swords points," Robins and Harding remained "friendly enemies," each valuing the real or anticipated help of the other. But in spite of the campaign "promises" of 1920, the relentless efforts of Borah, and those of Johnson, Goodrich, and later that June, the help of Will Hays, Harding took no action on recognition, invoking Hughes's stale formula of preconditions.25

After Harding's death in office on 2 August 1923, Robins attempted to establish a cordial relationship with Coolidge. On 9 November, a few days after a lengthy discussion with Coolidge on the State of the Union Message, which was to be delivered in December, Robins drafted a four-page letter to Coolidge "for the sake of clarity . . . [to] restate some of the observations I made." Robins deftly explored the 1924 election prospects for Coolidge, advising him about the dangers of some mistaken aspects of his public image as an "extreme conservative." Robins reviewed disarmament, treaty revision, prohibition, war outlawry, and Russian recognition. His tone was respectful, and with an election pending, his advice was politically sensible.[26] However, the portion of the message dealing with Russia that Coolidge finally delivered was not quite what Robins had hoped for. "I do not propose to barter away for the privilege of trade any of the cherished rights of humanity," Coolidge began.

I am willing to make very large concessions for the purpose of rescuing the people of Russia. Already encouraging evidences of returning to the ancient ways of society can be detected. But more are needed. Whenever there appears any disposition to compensate our citizens who are despoiled, and to recognize that debt contracted with our Government, not by the Czar but by the newly formed Republic of Russia, whenever the active spirit of enmity to our institutions is abated; . . . our country ought to be the first to go to the economic and moral rescue of Russia. We have every desire to help and no desire to injure. We hope the time is near at hand when we can act.[27]

As a prospective presidential candidate in need of Robins's support, Coolidge had led Robins to believe that he was quite receptive to American diplomatic recognition of the Soviet Union. Coolidge's State of the Union Message also gave reason for hope of recognition. Rather spontaneously, on the morning of 1 December 1923, Coolidge extended an invitation to Robins to come to the White House. "I lunched with the President and Mrs. Coolidge and then talked with the President alone for over an hour on Russia," Robins wrote to Elizabeth. "His [State of the Union] Message is the first step toward sanity that this nation has taken through any responsible executive in more than six years. Poorly and haltingly and with stupid provisos as it is—it is a forward step. Six years of fighting and at last the first streak of Dawn!"

On the very day of the luncheon with Coolidge, Robins wrote a letter to Gumberg in which he outlined the steps necessary to take advantage of the new, although limited, possibilities for recognition. The first step was taken immediately after his luncheon with the president when Robins, seeing an opportunity for the inauguration of direct communication between the U.S. and Soviet governments, composed what he considered to be an appropriate Soviet response to Coolidge's positive remarks on Russia in the State of the Union Message. Robins had his draft response cabled to Moscow in the code of the Russian government. (In all probability this was done by Victor P. Nogin, an agent of the Soviet government who had arrived in the United States only a week earlier to carry out a major cotton purchase.) The very response that Robins had composed, expressing readiness for discussion and the desire of the Soviet Union to do all in its power to develop friendly relations with the United States, arrived in Washington from Moscow on 16 December, from Foreign Minister Chicherin and addressed to Coolidge. No direct answer from Coolidge was forthcoming because it would have represented a form of recognition. Instead, through indirect channels and in the most terse language, Hughes reiterated his formula and concluded that: "This Government can enter into no negotiations until these efforts [propaganda to overthrow the government of the United States] directed from Moscow are abandoned."

Robins spent the week following the meeting with Coolidge with the Executive Committee of the National Republican Committee at the White House. "The New Year promises to open with 'battle and sudden death' in the political field all along the line," he wrote to his sister, "Uncle Hi. [Hiram Johnson] has begun his fight in every Direct Primary State, and Coolidge is doing likewise. I have not yet taken a stand for any candidate. With the promises to free the Politicals [red scare victims] and to recognize Russia and to give aid and comfort to the Outlawry of War program by Coolidge I am in quite a quandary. I am working with Borah and as He Hates Johnson it is a bit of a twist."[28]

Events in January 1924, though far less exciting, proved to be of more lasting importance in the drive for recognition. As early as the previous January 1923, the recognition camp had begun to consider a Senate hearing on recognition of the Soviet Union, an idea first suggested by Gumberg. Such a hearing would be referred to the Senate Foreign Relations Committee and, with Borah's guidance, a parade of friendly witnesses consisting of notables who had recently visited Russia could win the day for recognition. "It may be just what Borah wants to do to bring this to the attention of the people," Gumberg wrote to Robins.[29]

After a year of being batted around in the camp of recognition and the competitive Senate schedule, the hearings were finally held between 21 and 24 January 1924. Although the friendly witnesses were heard in significant numbers, Robins had forecast the outcome well in advance. "It is an adverse committee, unless the Big Chief [Coolidge] gets into the game."[30] The State Department position of nonrecognition won the day in the Senate subcommittee, press, and public opinion. Evan E. Young, chief of the Eastern European Division of the Department of State demonstrated that the Communist party of the Soviet Union dominated the Third International Workingmen's Association and was responsible for its propaganda seeking the overthrow of the government of the United States and world Communist revolution. The Communist ideological commitment to world revolution was presented as an immediate danger to democratic governments worldwide, making the Soviet government an outlaw regime.[31] From that extreme view of the CPSU and the Third International as active forces of violent governmental overthrow, recognition could not move forward. For powerful senators like Borah, the recognition of Russia was the "GREAT immediate contribution in domestic and foreign statesmanship, [for which] . . . he will let every other issue slip if he can win this one."[32] Nevertheless, it was obvious that a change of American understanding and outlook toward Communist ideology, practice, and the Soviet regime needed to precede any chances for recognition.

20

National Politics, Prohibition, and Outlawry of War

IN June 1924, at the Republican Convention in Cleveland, following weeks of negotiations between the conservative and progressive wings of the Republican party over who would be the vice-presidential running mate of Coolidge, Charles G. Dawes was selected. He was a former comptroller of the currency of the U.S. Treasury, never before elected to public office. Robins could express nothing but exasperation and wry resignation when he explained the significance of Dawes's candidacy to Elizabeth:

> The platform and the Ticket have one dominant note and significance, property, *property*, PROPERTY. It is the apotheosis of reaction in American politics. If the voters stand for it they will stand for anything. I regard the ticket as:
> COOLIDGE & DAWES
The Golddust Twins, Address Wall St.

Robins made no commitments, but planned to attend both the Democratic National Convention in New York and Robert La Follette's Conference for Progressive Political Action (CPPA) third-party convention in Cleveland. With "outlawry of war" and U.S. recognition of the Soviet Union as the first considerations, Robins would make a decision and lend his support. But "from this time forward," he concluded his letter to Elizabeth, "the Republican Party will be the Tory, Conservative, Property party of this country. The Roosevelt influence is entirely liquidated."[1]

The issues in the 1924 election were even more complex and confused for the participants in the campaign than they are for later generations. Particularly for veterans of the Progressive movement, and for those, like Robins, who sought recognition and outlawry, the alliances and power struggles at the time were a puzzle. "I must be suffering from political senility," Harold Ickes had written to Robins two months after urging Robins to run for the U.S. Senate on the Republican ticket. Not without a heavy measure of sarcasm, Ickes attempted to dismantle Robins's teetering edifice of political reasoning. Ickes had hoped Robins would join him in support of Hiram Johnson for the Republican nomination for the presidency. Robins felt he could not because "Uncle Hi" was not actively rallying the "true progressives" in the party. Nor was Johnson's campaign being managed by trusted veterans of the progressive struggles of the past. Robins, under these circumstances, felt compelled to support Coolidge. "For the life of me," Ickes continued, in answer to a Robins letter,

> I cannot follow the reasoning of your group. Apparently you don't want either Coolidge or McAdoo; you would be entirely satisfied with La Follette, but there is no chance of La Follette's running or of being elected if he should run and, therefore, you have decided to let both Coolidge and McAdoo be nominated so that you will be sure to have some one for president that you don't want. . . . Coolidge is for God knows what because Coolidge doesn't know. La Follette . . . will support McAdoo as against Coolidge if the two shall be nominated. McAdoo is against governnment ownership of railroads and no one knows where he stands on Russia. Coolidge is ditto on railroads and wrong on Russia. Johnson's attitude on both railroads and Russia is or might be satisfactory. Therefore the group is opposed to Johnson. Johnson more nearly represents what the group is supposed to stand for generally and the group is therefore irresistably driven to support Coolidge for the nomination. You can't persuade Johnson to declare for the one particular matter you are interested in and so you will wait and later choose between Coolidge and McAdoo, both of whom are publicly on record for what you don't believe in.
>
> Old fellow, I am hanging over the ropes panting for breath and the referee is about to count me out. I am too simple minded for the 1924 brand of politics.[2]

With West Virginia representative John W. Davis, an attorney for the J. P. Morgan Company, and noted engineer Charles W. Bryan, the Democratic nominees, and the Coolidge-Dawes combination, Robins found himself in a position of compromise, especially since "Fighting Bob" La Follette, the "Old Man" of the Progressive movement, had entered the race. To complicate matters further, La Follette had invited Robins to run with him as the candidate for the vice presidency. "But I am opposed to many of his domestic planks," Robins explained to Elizabeth, "—government ownership of railroads for an example—and also to his to me absurd proposal for a referendum on peace or war."[3] Robins did manage to win the adoption of an "outlawry of war" plank in the platforms of both the Democratic and La Follette parties but, ironically, not on that of his own, the Republican party.

Harold Ickes, George Record, Jane Addams, Amos Pinchot, and Mary Dreier—all allies of the Progressive struggles of 1912 and 1914—supported La Follette. But for reasons of political realism (the new party had no chance of winning the election), La Follette's Socialist party "wild men" radicalism (in Robins's words), and disillusionment with La Follette's mercurial political egotism, Robins did not support him. Instead he prepared a public statement in the name of progressive Republicans against La Follette and in support of Coolidge and again worked within the Republican administration.

"What Senator La Follette would not do for a sound Progressive movement because he was not the candidate [in 1912], he now does for a destructive radical one because he is the candidate," Robins summed up in the printed statement. It was sent out to more than fifty leading progressives by E. A. Van Valkenberg, editor of Philadelphia's *The North American,* in August 1924.[4] However, many progressives could not accept Robins's rationale and were deeply upset by his apparent betrayal of values. "I thought progressives fought year by year for ideals, and never cared about bandwagons," wrote John Lapp in September 1924,

> In your view, the majority of seven million for Harding must have settled some questions rightly for all time, and if Coolidge would get more votes than La Follette, we must assume that it is the voice of progress! What better illustration of the fact could be given than that the signers of the statement which I deliberately branded as "silly," were not progressives, but now I find you are the author of the statement!
>
> I was a follower of Roosevelt, but I thought I was so for principle's sake, not as a hero worshipper, and have always regretted that I did not see more clearly the nature of the Progressivism of the leaders of thàt time. To parade as progressive now, such men and women as Henry Allen, Lawrence Abbott, Duncan Clarke, A. B. Hart, Elen H. Hooker, James R. Garfield, A. R. Garford, Frances Kellor, and Mrs. Medill McCormick, to mention only a few is to me a confession of the bankruptcy of progressivism of the Republican Party. Scarcely any but hero worshippers of Roosevelt are included in the list.
>
> Hardly a one but would have supported Taft just as heartily if Roosevelt were not running. Age, too, has taken its toll out of the little progressivism that actually existed in 1912. And now these men and women give out a statement primarily intended to help Coolidge, who, by all fair standards, is the most completely reactionary candidate who has been before the people in this generation.[5]

Robins, of course, privately agreed about "Cool Cal," yet publicly he held firm to his distrust of La Follette's ambition. However, Robins would not relinquish his access to the president. Coolidge supported the outlawry of war in his acceptance speech and promised to continue to act in its behalf. Hopeful that he might manage to collect on the president's private and public promises, Robins campaigned for Coolidge. "Deep in my heart," he wrote to Elizabeth, "I have a real regret not to be with brave courageous old Robert Marion La Follette. He is the VETERAN of the progressive movement in American politics." And, two months later, Robins wrote to Elizabeth again: "I am the only nationally known Progressive of the Roosevelt Adventure of 1912 who is leading the battle for Coolidge. I am finding some strange bed-fellows —but such is the brutal game of politics."[6]

As early as 3 September 1920, in Mt. Gilead, Ohio, Harding had made a campaign speech in which he stated: "If I catch the conscience of America, we'll lead the world to outlaw war."[7] At that particular time, under the influence of Levinson, the phrase "outlaw war" began to capture Robins's attention. Harding's embrace of the phrase was a significant encouragement. For Levinson, it was a major breakthrough in his embryonic campaign to present the total outlawry of war as the alternative to the League of Nations and the foundation for the postwar peace. Harding's public advocacy of war's out-lawry was the first made by any candidate for national office. Levinson was encouraged by the use of the phrase and, after Harding's election, hoped to elicit support from the president to fulfill the campaign "promise."

Although Robins entered the Harding campaign with many misgivings, once committed, he worked strenuously. As a result of the strain of that campaign and financial worries and, in part, because of the rending ambivalence of working for so conservative a candidate, Robins had another nervous breakdown in the summer of 1921. Rest at Chinsegut brought recovery, and by winter he was again carrying out a long series of well-remunerated public addresses under the sponsorship of the James B. Pond Lyceum Bureau of New York.[8]

The key speech of the tour was publicized as "World Limitation of Armaments or World Bankruptcy—Which?" or "World Disarmament or World Revolution—Which?" In November 1920 the U.S. Senate rejected the Wilsonian plan for a postwar peace. Robins sensed an enormous upsurge of public interest and support for disarmament as an alternative.

This focus on disarmament came on the eve of Robins's association with Levinson, at which time Levinson's theme of outlawry of war took center stage in Robins's public addresses. He was much-sought-after in the lyceum and Chautauqua circuit where, between 1922 and the end of 1923, he made 214 addresses. He continued under the Pond agency in 1925 and, throughout that period, disarmament and outlawry of war were his most frequent subjects.[9] In Robins's own words, written to publicize the tour, "These talks are pro-Christ and pro-democratic and anti-Marx and anti-Materialist socialism. While progressive and by some considered radical, they stress the achievements of the constitutional republican social control under the melioration of the Christian ideal, and suggest the complete realization of a free and just industrial society within the provisions of the American constitution, plus a vital relationship with the ideal of Jesus."[10]

Robins's disarmament speech began with a dramatic accounting of the costs of the Great War: "Ten million dead—twenty million more crippled and wasted youth. . . . Three hundred and thirty billions of wealth spent. . . . Propagandas of Hatred among the peoples of the earth."[11] He stressed that "we do not half appreciate what the Great War cost," citing the unknowable impact of the war's destruction of the cream of the youth of Europe. Some of the best of an entire generation swept into the grave. In many of his earlier speeches Robins stressed that "economic surplus is the foundation of social progress and industrial liberation." What had the war done to the productive forces of the belligerents and what price would have to be paid in terms of democratic institutions and social welfare in light of lost, war-squandered resources? The destruction of trade throughout the world was obvious, but the invidious effect of wartime censorship and curbing of free speech were still evident three years after the war.

Robins's major concern: *"We do not think of what the next war will cost,"* was both frightening and prophetic. His nightmarish vision, based on contemporary understanding of the potential of military technology pale before the reality of World War II. "Whole nations not armies anymore make war[.] Women as well as men—double draining of the blood," read the notes from which he spoke,

> Whole wealth and economic strength—no limit to the cost of war
> No limit to the machinery of death:
> Lewiston Gas—invisible-heavier than air—odorless—instantaneously deadly—
>   55 times the spread—kills the life of the soil
> The new pneumatic gun—300 miles 500 pound shell
> Fleets of airplanes—controlled by wireless carrying two ton gas bombs—Paris,
>   London Wiped out in a night
> Germ bombs—anthrax
> Lethal rays
> Men and women, aye, children animals and the life of the soil—all involved in
>   the next war.

Arms races were "breeders" of wars. The "swords into plowshares" mandate of Isaiah had many implications: the necessity of using the productive forces of each nation for life-sustenance rather than life destruction; the psychological danger of "studying war" and preparing for war as a self-fulfilling prophecy. "Increasing armaments paralyzes the spirit of brotherhood," he continued. "The world needs brotherhood—increasing armaments means the international spy system and the spread of propagandas of hate and fear."

In his call for American leadership in disarmament, Robins cautioned his audience, "Do not despise public opinion." It was public opinion that he relied on to move statesmen toward disarmament. The underlying assumption was always that if he moved enough people to active participation in the cause, the cause could be realized.

In 1922 it was clear to all the world that the United States was the world's most powerful nation. Robins asked: "Of whom are we afraid—who can disarm if we will not . . . ? America could disarm the world!" The unprecedented position of strength "makes a special charge upon America to lead in the salvation of the world from armaments and war."[12]

"What can you do?" he challenged his audience. The driving force for calling the Washington Disarmament Conference later that year (1922) had come "from the people—common folks. . . . Demand publicity for the decisions of the conference—no other way for public opinion to be effective—demand and keep demanding." A grass-roots taxpayers' revolt could effectively curb the runaway armaments and naval spending. The public outcry could force the politicians to reconsider the assumed wisdom of "military preparedness" and other euphemisms for the arms race—especially if they feared repercussions at the polls. The American people had most to fear apathy and acceptance of political impotence. The strength of American democracy was to be found in the moral and social responsibility of its people and institutions, and the war had demonstrated that responsibility now demanded disarmament. "This is a great hour in the life of the nation and the world," he implored, with evangelical urgency,

> It is the hour of opportunity for America to liberate humanity from the curse of war from the thraldom of the sword.
> Men and women of the Churches, what of the war to end war—act or be disgraced
> Women mothers of the race—for the first time in history you have immediate political power—
> Conservators of life of the race
> Hope the power of conviction—The battlefields—
> These silent lips plead for your sons—
> What will your answer be?[13]

On 9 December 1921 Raymond and Margaret Robins joined Salmon O. Levinson, his sister, Mary Levinson Langworthy, and a number of other treaty revision advocates in the formation of the American Committee for the Outlawry of War. The occasion marked the formal beginning of Robins's campaign for an international agreement for outlawry and his close cooperation with Levinson, at whose Chicago home the meeting of founders was held. Robins warmed to the outlawry idea slowly. His successful speeches in behalf of disarmament and his commitment to that specific cause made him cautious about adopting this new and more ambitious plan. But the Washington Disarmament Conference soon became a reality and the warship limitations that resulted were a demonstration of the practical accomplishments possible through negotiation. The campaign that Robins had waged in the year prior to the Washington conference had been legitimized and his hopes began to be fulfilled. Now was the time for the more comprehensive plan for lasting peace.[14]

"The Outlawry of War—The Next Step in Civilization" took the place of "World Disarmament or World Revolution" as Robins's leading speech. His commitment to United States' recognition of Soviet Russia occasionally took up his time, but only when a particular international or domestic development seemed to improve its chances.

In addition to the remarkable schedule of speeches from 1921 to 1928, Robins used his influence and powers of persuasion to win assistance from his friends and associates in high elective and public office. Idaho's Senator Borah, chairman of the key Senate Foreign Relations Committee, master of debate, and, in Robins's words, "the moral and intellectual leader of the Senate of the United States," was the focus of both Robins's and Levinson's efforts to win Senate approval of an outlawry resolution.[15]

One thoughtful deliberation on outlawry, reflecting thinking then current, was a "Dear Chief" letter to William B. Thompson in which Robins recounted the pressing concerns and impressions of a speaking tour he had taken with Margaret during the summer of 1923. Robins was invited to present his outlawry speech at Hyde Park in London. In narrating his experience of giving that speech, after discussing political, social, and economic developments in Europe, Robins shared his thoughts on the dangerous prevailing mood.

> All over the world there is a widespread sense of disillusion regarding political social control through democratic processes and a corresponding distrust of political officials whose futilities or worse is held responsible for the sufferings of the people. This disillusionment and distrust works a special hardship upon the leaders of the party in power. Witness the declension of Wilson, Clemenceau, Nitti, and George and the rise of Mussolini, Lenin and yesterday Rivera. People in the mass do not make nice distinctions and as Republicans we [have] this burden of the "ins" for the battle of 1924.[16]

Robins pointed out the necessity of the Republican party responding to the sentiment pervading the country and the world. He feared that the conditions that led to impasse in 1914 could be repeated in 1923. Robins then turned to outlawry specifically:

> The fundamental trouble with the international social order is the legality of the war institution and force system for the settlement of international disputes and the absence of an international code based on equality and justice for their peaceful settlement by law; just as the fundamental trouble with our domestic social order in 1850 was the legality of the slave institution and force system of settling labor disputes and the absence of a domestic code based upon equality and justice for their peaceful settlement by law. The right solution then was to outlaw the slave institution and force system and to make slavery a public crime and to substitute mutual consent and law based on equality and right for individual force and violence. This was the method by which the institution of the duello [duel] and of the saloon were likewise abolished, also of the international slave trade and of piracy. . . .
> The Republican Party won the historic ascendancy fighting for the abolition of the domestic slave system, it can retain its leadership of American life by fighting for the abolition of the international war system.
> This idea absorbs, concentrates and directs to useful ends all the vast sentiment against war, all of the peace organizations, and neutralizes the mass of foreign propaganda that has in the past and still continues to flood our country.[17]

While this formulation of the outlawry position rests heavily on idealist and utopian assumptions, its reliance on successful historical precedents of international outlawry of other human institutions or behavior lent credence to it. However, the examples Robins chose from the domestic history of the United States do not apply to the international arena. The abolition of slavery by the Thirteenth Amendment and the legislation that institutionalized collective bargaining involved long and bitter struggles—even war—but they were domestic struggles within a sovereign state. Slavery continued as an institution in dozens of countries long after its abolition in the United States. However, the precedent of the outlawry of the international slave trade and of treaties against piracy was very convincing both to sophisticated as well as to popular audiences. The fact that both the slave trade and piracy are not usually associated with the modern exercise of state sovereignty, whereas the right to carry out "defensive" war is considered one of its cornerstones, was deliberately overlooked by Robins and the outlawry advocates.

Furthermore, they rejected the critical issue of an international outlawry treaty provision for enforcement of the war-fighting ban. In Robins's example of the American outlawry of slavery through the Thirteenth Amendment, the full judicial and policing powers of the government of the United States were brought to bear to enforce the new law. For the international outlawry of war, a most formidable enforcement apparatus, with sizable contingents from every major military power, would have been necessary if the aims of outlawry were to be anything more than a statement of principle.

Robins's passing reference to the outlawry of the saloon is significant. For years, he and Margaret and his circle of reformer friends actively campaigned for prohibition of production and sale of alcoholic beverages and the ratification of the Eighteenth Amendment. Once it became law, Robins traveled the speakers' circuit for the enforcement of prohibition. Since he was active in the Law Observance Campaign for prohibition during the same years that he worked for outlawry of war, he drew a political and moral connection between the two causes.[18] "Frankly," he wrote to Alex Gumberg, "if we get our two planks, outlawry and the maintenance of the Constitution [the Eighteenth Amendment] into the Republican platform, I will support any candidate that is nominated."[19]

Robins believed that the moral forces involved in the "age-long struggle of civilization against primitive appetite" had won a great victory in the Eighteenth Amendment, but the postwar world faced an even greater moral struggle.

> In all the nations that participated in the Great War we find an increase in crime. We are the only one of these to outlaw the liquor traffic. Therefore, the crime and lawlessness of this hour must have another and universal cause. We need not seek far. Here is an aftermath, a backwash, of the Great War. Millions of the youth of great nations, taught to disregard the life and property of the alien, now allow their appetites and greed for gain a free dominion under a wave of force and disregard for law and authority.[20]

"Alcoholic poison" and the poison of war, were terrible sources of pain, according to Robins. The "realists" asked: Aren't they the *result* of human need, greed and fallibility? Even if alcohol and war could be eliminated, would it end these human weaknesses? Shouldn't energy be directed at these basic failings rather than at alcoholism and war, its symptoms?

Robins disagreed. He chose not to accept the view that the underlying problems of the human condition could never be solved. With his faith secure, he set out to make his crusade. He was not alone; his generation was marked by many with the same faith and zeal.

Robins hoped to use the outlawry plan as a major and popular plank in the Republican party platform, but he had to deal with the pragmatism of tough party leaders such as Borah, who asked: "Suppose we make war a crime and a nation like Germany or Japan begins war?"[21] Or Hiram Johnson, who at times responded skeptically to Robins's plan.

> I recognize as you do the hope and aspiration of many of our good people, expressed so hazily and blindly in the familiar phrases of "promoting peace," "prevention of war," "succoring humanity," and "saving civilization." I am sympathetic, just as sympathetic as you are with this hope and aspiration. The only difference between us is whether the plan you so forcefully and eloquently and persuasively present would accomplish what is sought. . . . I do not and will not discard or disregard the plan you suggest. I cannot, for the moment, publicly, conscientiously adopt it.[22]

Robins admitted the difficulty of gaining the support of European governments. Still, even if the United States were alone in its adoption of an outlawry treaty, it would serve a significant purpose. It would win world public opinion to the cause and then perhaps lead to acceptance and ratification.

This recourse was not necessary. Movement in the outlawry cause, although slow, did provide the affirmation that the stalwarts needed to sustain their campaign. The objections of the realists were argued away by the moral imperative and the growing popular commitment for an international agreement. On 13 February 1923, exactly seven months after expressing his skepticism about outlawry to Levinson, Borah introduced Senate Resolution 441, a resolution for the outlawry of war.

Borah's resolution cited the horrors of war and reflects the language of Robins's speech on outlawry as "the next step in civilization." The two key passages, which distinguished the outlawry plan from all other peace plans proposed at the time, were those that rejected the use of force as a means for maintaining peace.

> Whereas all alliances, leagues, or plans which rely upon force as the ultimate power for the enforcement of peace carry the seeds either of their own destruction or of military dominance to the utter subversion of liberty and justice; and
> Whereas we must recognize the fact that resolutions or treaties outlawing certain methods of killing will not be effective so long as war itself remains lawful; and that in international relations we must have, not rules and regulations of war but organic laws against war.

The utopianism of the movement lies in the assumption that once the nations of the world declare all forms of war illegal, they would not resort to war to resolve differences. A further assumption was that the nations of the world could maintain their sovereignty through judicial sanctions rather than through an international police force.

> That a judicial substitute for war should be created . . . in the form or nature of an international court, modeled on our Federal Supreme Court in its jurisdiction over controversies between our sovereign States, such court to possess affirmative jurisdiction to hear and decide all purely international controversies, as defined by the code, or arising under treaties, and to have the same power for the enforcement of its decrees as our Federal Supreme Court, namely the respect of all enlightened nations for judgements resting upon open and fair investigations and impartial decisions and the compelling power of enlightened public opinion.[23]

The United States Supreme Court had never had such machinery, was not designed to, and had functioned admirably for a century and a half. The reason: public respect for its decisions as the law of the land. The alternative: the disruption of the body politic and the entire social and economic system. Why couldn't the international political system operate on those same principles—respect, order, and law?

Robins brought home the imagery and dramatic potential of these themes to audiences throughout the country, winning adherents and fulfilling deeply felt needs for some hope of future security and peace. It was the era in which conservatives were elected to the highest positions in the land with the promise of "normalcy"; outlawry appealed to those same instincts on the international level.

"War has become national and international suicide!" Robins began his speech. War took on ghastly associations—the personification of evil—as well it should, but Robins anthropomorphized it and dissociated it from human beings and their willful actions; in his telling, it lost a dimension of reality.

> The war system is now known to be the arch murderer of the youth of the nations, the poison in the cup of brotherhood between the peoples of the earth, the forerunner of pestilence and famine, the paralysis of industry and the suicide of commerce—the great common oppressor and menace of the human race, crucifying Christ afresh on every battlefield.
>
> What is this Monster War? It is the product of the legal institution, the war system, organized and maintained in every nation of the earth. The war institution is today just as legal as marriage or the home, as the church or the school.[24]

By 1924, after several years on the public platform, Robins had developed cogent and persuasive answers to the objections of opponents. To the criticism raised earlier in connection with prohibition and the outlawry movement regarding the causes of alcoholism and war, Robins made this rebuttal:

> Always the successful method for the liberation of society from the effects of an outgrown legal institution has been to outlaw the institution and to make

its exercise a public crime. Never has the attack been upon causes. There are just as many causes for duels today as there ever were, just as many persons who would like to get human labor without paying for it, just as many thirsts for liquor as ten years ago; but there are no duels, no human slavery and no legal saloon in the United States. Institutions that are outlawed and their operation made a public crime die out of the life of the world. That is the verdict of history.[25]

One serious objection was not directly answered: his examples did not question the ultimate exercise of national sovereignty as did the proposed outlawry of war. The most serious objections to the plan were raised and refuted in the highly respected two-volume work by Frances Kellor, *Security Against War, International Controversies, Arbitration, Disarmament, Outlawry*, published in 1924. Robins often cited the work and its comprehensive analysis of the treaty and peace developments in the six years since the armistice. The thirty-ninth and final chapter, concluding nearly eight hundred pages, deals with the outlawry of war. No contemporary scholarly work provided more foundation, nor more evidence, on behalf of the outlawry cause than *Security Against War*. Robins's role in the preparation of that chapter was significant, although his florid and dramatic podium language is noticeably missing.[26]

Robins had been won over from the position that disarmament should come before any provisions for war outlawry. His later understanding of the "war system" precluded the possibility of effective disarmament. Arms, he argued, must first find a substitute in the alternative security of war outlawry and juridical institutions. Only then could effective disarmament take place.

Some objected to the plan on the ground that "war can be regulated by agreements as to the manner in which it is to be conducted." Robins pointed out that between 1918 and 1923 fourteen international controversies arose that were settled by the use of force. "The preparation for war," he maintained, "the inventions for war, the alliances for war, all prove beyond doubt that the engines of war once let loose cannot be regulated. The idea that men may be legally killed and women and children may not; that one form of bullet is permissible and another is not; that one form of killing is legal and another illegal, because it is caused by different instruments, would be abhorrent if transposed into individual terms and applied to murder or arson."[27]

The stalwarts of the League of Nations believed that all efforts for world peace should be directed through the deliberative, consultative, and judicial institutions of the League. All energies divided between the League and the non-League peace plans merely dissipated peace energies, weakened the League, and caused international disharmony. Kellor cites the Conference of Ambassadors, the Hague Organization, the Little Entente, and the Baltic States Combination as examples of non-League institutions promoting peace on which, in fact, the League itself depended. An international agreement for the outlawry of war would not detract from the work of the League; it would support it.

Finally, Robins stated the proposal of the American Committee for the Outlawry of War.

> (1) A mutual treaty outlawing the war system and making war a crime under the law of nations.
>
> (2) An international code for the legal settlement of all disputes between nations based on the principle of equality in justice and right between all peoples great and small.
>
> (3) A statute providing an international tribunal with affirmative jurisdiction to hear and determine all disputes arising between the nations in accordance with such international code.[28]

Robins concluded his speech in a crescendo—listing the great contemporaries who had joined in the outlawry crusade: the senators, "Professor John Dewey, the philosopher educator of America," court justices, and "the Presbyterian General Assembly, the Methodist General Conference, the Pacific Coast Unitarian Conference, the Canadian Presbyterian, the National Lutheran Assembly, the National League of Women Voters, the National Education Association and the Women's Trade Union League." His thunderous final words were almost always matched by a standing ovation: "Let us unite to outlaw war, and liberate mankind from the age-long thraldom of the sword, thus providing that the countless dead upon the battlefields of the Great War did not die in vain."

The outlawry of war movement, while successful in promulgating a multilateral treaty, was among the most illusory and tragic in the twentieth century. It was ambitious, far-reaching, visionary, and perhaps the least attainable of all the causes toward which Robins ever worked. In its initial phases, Levinson had distinguished between defensive war and aggression, including provisions for international punishment (military force) for the latter. Robins argued that all combatants claimed to be fighting defensively and the problem of definition of aggression would be insurmountable. "The aggressor nation is always that nation against which *we* fight, and every important war has been a 'defensive war' in so far as the people of each nation participating is concerned. The peoples and governments of the earth either want to abandon war as an instrument of national policy or they do not." His belief that "it seemed of little moment to change the *name* of war if we kept the *fact*" eventually prevailed "and force was eliminated from the program."[29]

The movement advanced noticeably with the addition of John Dewey to its ranks, followed soon thereafter by Senators Philander Chase Knox and Borah himself. Florence Allen, justice of the Supreme Court of Ohio, and John Haynes Holmes, of the Community Church of New York, soon joined as well. Charles C. Morrison aided the cause with his book *The Outlawry of War* in 1927, which followed the 1926 Christmas issue of the *Christian Century*, which was devoted entirely to publicizing the movement. The historian James T. Shotwell and Columbia University president Nicholas Murray Butler, while disagreeing with the Levinson-Robins outlawry formula, were also supporters, though they lacked political influence in Washington.[30] The movement—which lobbied, publicized, and won noted adherants—did receive the attention and patronage of candidates for the highest offices in the land. The resolution for the outlawry of war was introduced in the Senate by Borah on three separate occasions, until it was finally approved in the form of the Pact of Paris in 1928.

The outlawrists were ecstatic when Aristide Briand, the French foreign minister, on 9 April 1927, in a statement to the Associated Press, suggested a treaty outlawing war between the United States and France. Briand wrote: "If there were need for those two great democracies to give high testimony to their desire for peace and to furnish other peoples an example more solemn still, France would be willing to subscribe publicly with the United States to any mutual engagement tending 'to outlaw war,' to use an American expression, as between these two countries."[31]

Frank Kellogg, U.S. secretary of state, replied with the suggestion of widening such a pact to all the nations of the world. The cause had finally reached the highest levels of international diplomacy.

The initiative for Briand's statement had not come from any member of the American Committee for the Outlawry of War, but rather from Briand's desire to further amicable relations between France and the United States. However, the origins of the modest statement were not the concern of Robins, Levinson, and their allies. A crack had been opened in the closed doors of international rhetoric and diplomacy and the flurry of activity to get a foot in that door was remarkable.[32]

Robins had for years yearned for the opportunity to bring their plan to that high level of international consideration. With Borah as chairman of the Senate Foreign Relations Committee, along with Secretary of State Frank Kellogg of Minnesota, and with the strong recommendation of President Coolidge, Robins and Levinson pressed for a multilateral treaty. The Pact of Paris—the Treaty for the Renunciation of War—was signed in Paris on 27 August 1928, but the long process of ratification among the signatories was to take many more months. In the United States, the ratification had to await the congressional and presidential elections, only three months away.

Throughout that election campaign, Robins focused on assuring Senate ratification of the Pact of Paris. Enforcement of prohibition—the election of a staunchly "dry" president and candidates to both houses of Congress—was the second priority. The campaign for U.S. recognition of the Soviet Union had shown so little progress during the Coolidge administration, particularly under the strong opposition of Secretary of State Hughes, that Robins had virtually suspended activity in its behalf, focusing all his foreign policy campaigning on the final stretch for outlawry.

After the failure of Hiram Johnson to win the Republican presidential nomination in 1920 and as early as the first years of the Coolidge presidency, Robins envisioned and promoted the Republican presidential candidacy of William Borah. The Idaho senator drew very close to Robins by the midtwenties, and eventually, the two saw eye-to-eye on each of Robins's three central concerns of that period. Furthermore, Robins understood full well the power Borah exercised in both the Republican party and, after the death of Henry Cabot Lodge in November 1924, as his successor in the chairmanship of the Senate Foreign Relations Committee.

In February of 1928, with the Republican National Convention approaching and the possibility of a Borah candidacy, Robins faced the political realities. "While Borah will never be the president of these United States," he confided in a letter to Elizabeth, "no man can now be elected next November on the Republican ticket without his endorsement. And this bitter truth is now known to all the ablest masters of the political game in our America. So far has the drive of a Sober-America [gone] . . . and for the outlawing of the war institution among the nations of the earth."[33]

In the spring of 1928, a disheartened Robins considered Herbert Hoover as the nominee. From the time of Robins's return from Russia and throughout the 1920s, Hoover had been among the most unyielding opponents of recognition of the Soviet Union. Only Hughes mounted a stronger opposition. "If nominated," Robins wrote to Elizabeth in April, "his chances for election will be less than any other Republican prominently mentioned for that honor. He is in my judgment weakest where we need the most strength—with the farmers and in the coal districts of America and in Wall Street."[34] But the results of the Kansas City Republican National Convention in June, in which Robins played an active role, changed his mind, because the Hoover faction finally accepted the complete Borah platform, including war and liquor outlawry, in exchange for Borah's support. When Hoover was confronted by the opposition of the New York State delegates and big money financial and industrial interests, he had no choice but to sue for peace with Borah and create new alliances within the party.[35]

From Kansas City Robins stopped off in New York and was "in a whirlwind en route to Houston and the Democratic Convention," where he hoped to win similarly strong planks for outlawry and prohibition enforcement in the Democratic platform. In a letter to Elizabeth written during the layover in New York, Robins analyzed the changing foundation and social dynamic of the Republican party reflected in the convention.

> There is now a new order and a new control in the Republican Party. The old political minded group gave way to the new economic minded leadership. Political social control yielded to economic social control, the political voodoo doctor to the engineer with a blue print. Abstract shibboleths of ancient political gospel—such as "equal right to all with special privileges to none, etc, etc—gave way to competent economic ideas of markets, credits, organization, standardization, production costs, giant power, etc, etc. The old rural control of individualist farmers and pioneers passed forever to the new urban control of the producers hand and brain in the cities and towns. If the "agrarian revolt" materializes in a militant rebellion in the corn belt, Hoover will be beaten—person-

ally I believe he will WIN. It will be a merry fight and those who say that at this writing Hoover has a "cinch" do not know the forces united behind Al Smith.[36]

The Progressive movement had demonstrated its concern with efficiency, organization, and standardization well before the turn of the century. The settlement house and municipal lodging house social research, which had involved so much of Robins's time, are but two examples. Robins was clearly impressed with Hoover's administrative and engineering credentials and was optimistic that the new "economic social control" would provide the rational basis for social and economic improvement, eventually including the old Progressive reform agenda. Robins had reason for some hope as he and fellow progressive Republicans celebrated a most important Hoover faction concession. After twenty years the party finally included a plank in the Republican platform calling for collective bargaining. The language of this provision validated the regular unions and representatives of organized labor and formally put company unions into the compromised status they always deserved. "Without the women and the 'dry' support," Robins wrote to Elizabeth, "we would not have dared to press this point—with that support in our hands Hoover did not dare to refuse."[37]

The Democratic nomination of governor of New York Alfred E. Smith was a disappointment to Robins's camp because Smith's position on prohibition was compromised and his election meant nonenforcement or even repeal of the Eighteenth Amendment. Nevertheless, the Democratic platform approved in Houston included a strong statement in favor of prohibition enforcement. Robins was also concerned because a Smith victory would almost certainly have led to a redrafting of the terms of the signed outlawry treaty and a delay or failure in Senate ratification. Smith was also far more personable and charismatic than Hoover, which made him the better political campaigner.

Early in July, to help prepare a nomination acceptance speech and the kickoff of the presidential campaign, Robins was invited to Hoover's Washington home for the first time. Robins, as the designated representative of the "dry" coalition, had input on the prohibition portion of the address. In addition, Robins helped plan Hoover's remarks on the Kellogg-Briand Outlawry Treaty being considered at that very moment in Paris. The two men discussed these issues amicably for an hour, and Robins at least was pleased with the exchange. "Hoover has a vigorous mind, capable and alert. He is a great relief after Harding and Coolidge, just in the matter of intellect," Robins confided to his sister. But, he continued, in a letter written a few days after the meeting, cautioning her:

> Do not misinterpret my relations with the Honorable Secretary [of Commerce Hoover]. He needs me for votes and I need him for issues. We are meeting with the "guard up" and after he is elected the less he sees of me the better he will be pleased. But if I beat the Wets, Tammany, the Roman Hierarchy and

establish the Outlawry of War through this election—and this I think a reasonable hope—I can retire to Chinsegut Hill . . . for the remaining few years of my little day.[38]

In August, while taking a week of rest and speech writing at Southwest Harbor, Maine, at Mary Dreier's summer home, Mary, Margaret, and Raymond learned the news of developments in the Kellogg-Briand Pact and telegraphed to Levinson in Maine: "When the treaty to outlaw war is signed tomorrow in Paris by the fifteen great nations, we shall think especially of you and your vast creative idea superb devotion through these ten years . . . to get outlawry and liberate mankind. . . . We know who should receive the praise and gratitude of the entire world."[39]

The next three months found Robins on the campaign trail at his usual relentless pace. As the campaign progressed, he was concerned that the big money of America was divided in the campaign for the first time since the Civil War. To his surprise, Arthur Curtiss James, one of the leading owners of railroad stocks in America, supported Smith, as did General Motors' John J. Raskob and Standard Oil's Harry Payne Whitney. But for Robins, while the big money was divided, the alignment of the forces of good and evil were obvious: "The old Distillery Kings and Brewery Barons are lined up behind Smith to a man," he wrote to Elizabeth. "The power of the ancient church is behind Smith. . . . The organized liquor traffic of the world knows that Smith's election is crucial for their dominion to continue outside of the U.S. and to return to power in this country. If the women did not vote we would be beaten to a standstill."[40]

Two minor confrontations between Robins and Hoover were both amicably resolved and led to Robins's improved opinion of Hoover. Of greater consequence was a reconcilliation between William B. Thompson and Hoover, who had been bitter opponents for more than seven years. Though both Hoover and Thompson were Republicans of long standing, Thompson, the multimillionaire copper magnate, had come very close to making major contributions to the Smith campaign and bringing his influence to bear in the Democratic camp. Hoover sent a letter of rapprochement to Thompson written entirely by Robins, and Thompson, Robins's close friend, sent a letter of reply to Hoover, every word, again, written by Robins. In the end Thompson made a major contribution to the Hoover campaign.[41]

On 4 December 1928, just one month after the election, President Coolidge submitted the General Treaty for Renunciation of War to the Senate for ratification and finally, under Borah's pressure, the vote was taken, eighty-five in favor to one opposed, on 15 January 1929. It formally went into effect on 24 July 1929, after the ratification by the last of the original signatories, Japan. The substantive section of the treaty consisted of two short articles.

Article I

The High Contracting Parties solemnly declare in the names of their respective peoples that they condemn recourse to war for the solution of international controversies, and renounce it as an instrument of national policy in their relations with one another.

Article II

The High Contracting Parties agree that the settlement or solution of all disputes or conflicts of whatever nature or of whatever origin they may be, which may arise among them, shall never be sought except by pacific means.[42]

The words "outlaw war" did not appear in the treaty, nor was there reference to any law, legal system, or assertion of war's criminality. Instead there was condemnation and renunciation of war. The pact was therefore a moral declaration. It lacked the sanction, power, and instruments of binding law. It was only an expression of principle, but on it Robins and his allies built their hopes. They believed that the expression of such principle was only a step away from its realization. They ignored the suppression of nationalist aspirations by competing expansionist and colonial powers. The realities of impoverishment among most of the human race and the adversarial nature of the international political arena were viewed by Robins as the primary challenges of the civilized world, which would assume the highest priorities of skilled statesmanship to solve. Robins did not adequately credit the depth of American isolationism, or of British and French war-weariness. Nor could he clearly foresee the pathological drive of expansionist Nazism, although in his speeches against the Versailles Treaty and the League of Nations, he cautioned against sowing the seeds of German vengeance and Japanese and French imperialism. He emphasized the perfidy and power of the "war system" and yet, because of the passionate desire to end that system and assure lasting peace, he extolled the two weak articles of the pact and saw in them salvation for mankind. In retrospect, Robins's crusader zeal for this particular solution to world peace was naive—a moral-religious pilgrimage and self-sacrifice. As with many of his campaigns or crusades, although the goal was deeply deserving, his passion and involvement were far more evident than was the efficacy of the project.

The treaty ceremonies, at which President Hoover officially received the deposit of the Japanese ratification documents and declared the Pact of Paris in effect, were the symbolic climax of years of campaigning. Among the official delegations attending those ceremonies in the east room of the White House, was one private citizen, Salmon O. Levinson, the guest of the secretary of state and the president. "It is splendid and fitting that you should be a member of the group proclaiming the international renunciation of war," Robins telegraphed to his friend. "At last all our work finds full fruition. I am in a rapture of prayer and thanksgiving. . . . O captain General, it is great!"[43] Robins and his contemporaries were traumatized by World War I, but they had not relinquished the prewar ideal that human and social salvation could be achieved.

21

The Inner World

After weeks of searching by every means and method, nothing more is known now than was known when he walked away from the City Club at 55 West 44th Street, the afternoon of September 3, at about four o'clock.
—Fred B. Smith, "About Raymond Robins," 27 October 1932

THE afternoon of 3 September 1932 was no different from countless others while Robins was on the speaker's circuit, except on that afternoon, he disappeared.[1] He was scheduled to take the train to Washington, D.C., to keep one of a long series of meetings with President Hoover, to plan prohibition enforcement strategy and the presidential reelection campaign. Banner headlines screamed out the first fears after the disappearance—that Robins had been kidnapped or murdered by the liquor interests. Within days, as many as 185 special agents of the Prohibition Bureau, under Attorney General William D. Mitchell, had been ordered into the hunt. Within a week, investigators were studying reports that he had been seen on the streets of Chicago on several occasions by old acquaintances who said he had acted strangely. These reports led to the further speculation that Robins had amnesia and was lost.

Ten weeks later, on 18 November, Robins was discovered in Whittier, North Carolina, suffering a complete loss of memory but using the name Reynolds H. Rogers. Robins arrived in the small western North Carolina mountain town a week after his disappearance, identifying himself as a Kentucky miner. He took a room in a boarding house and spent his time prospecting, making trails in the forest, and very quickly finding a niche in the community by telling stories and even giving speeches in honor of Theodore Roosevelt's birthday, world peace, and the reelection of Hoover. Carl Fisher, a twelve-year-old Whittier boy, recognized Robins from a photograph, even though the stranger had a full beard. In response to advertised offers of a reward, the boy wrote a letter to Salmon Levinson in Chicago explaining the resemblance and Rogers's activities, and U.S. Prohibition Bureau agents were immediately dispatched to the scene. John C. Dreier, of New York, Robins's nephew, also arrived to make the positive identification; but Robins did not recognize his nephew, nor could Dreier manage to win back his uncle's memory.

Margaret arrived at her husband's side from Brooksville, Florida, the next day, 19 November, and took Robins to the Appalachian Hall Sanatorium in nearby Asheville. On Monday, 21 November, while under the care of Dr. Mark A. Griffin, he finally regained his memory, in the presence of Margaret and Dr. Griffin. Robins experienced an enormous physical strain and weakness upon regaining his identity and was kept quiet and completely isolated from any public contact. Elizabeth, who had journeyed to America as soon as she learned of the disappearance, was there in Asheville to see him. Two days later, in the company of Margaret, John Dreier, Mary Dreier, and Margaret's personal secretary, Lisa von Borowsky, Robins returned to the seclusion of Chinsegut Hill.[2]

Robins began writing two weeks later, in an attempt to record his limited recollections of the lost weeks.

> I have come through a terrible experience. Here in my home surrounded by my family and the friends, and associations I have loved since I was a boy, I am being fully restored. Those who are wise in matters of this sort assure me that the darkness that overtook me in the midst of my days work was a provision of nature to save me from a serious collapse. Those who have known my life in the past will not believe that I have been a quitter. For the generous and tender helpfulness of many dear friends in these hours of suffering for my wife and family I am grateful beyond words. . . . in the main truthful and fair treatment—accorded me by the public press, I cherish abiding gratitude. All that I ask for the future is judgment upon the facts of my way and work from day to day.
>
> I do not assume to understand the cause nor to feel a certainty of the facts of the shadowed conditions and events through which I have passed for some eleven weeks. My last clear recollection is leaving the City Club of New York to get a ticket and berth for Washington City where I was to see President Hoover. . . . From then on for what seems to me now a considerable period there is a jumbled sense of pain in the head, danger, darkness, pursuit and escape. Then follows a sense of lessening pain and freedom from danger and trying to get well from an illness. This getting well after the escape from danger seems the chief thought and purpose of many days. There is also the hazy memory of a conflict between this inside reality of an old prospector getting well, and the outside pressure now and again of some other person and events, that bring periods of returning pain in the head, confusion and darkness. The mountain trails, sunlight and silence bring me relief and these periods of pain and confusion diminish in frequency and force. I seem to feel more clear, secure and well. I begin to plan to live there and start prospecting for minerals. I want the people around me to like me and to want me to stay. I am surprised and happy that they are so generous and friendly. Clearest as I write is a little town, a river—two rivers—mountains, trails and forest; a house, dear and kindly folks that understand, comfort and good food, shelter, kindness, sunshine, and the silence of the forest trails in the mountains increase daily the sense of health and well-being. In this last phase I was found.[3]

Available evidence suggests that Robins had experienced a postictal fugue condition "in which the patient suddenly leaves his previous activity and begins to wander or goes on a journey which has no apparent relation to what he has just been doing, and for which he has amnesia afterwards." Indeed, it is not uncommon in fugues of long duration for the patient to "appear completely normal to the observer." While a causal connection between Robins's childhood history of psychic epilepsy and his adult amnesia cannot be ruled out, the connection is unlikely: epileptic fugues generally are "disorderly," characterized by very obvious abnormal behavior. Rather, in "a psychogenic reaction, they [the patients] appear often to be precipitated by a need to escape an intolerable situation; such fugues are typically 'orderly.'" This attribute of orderliness, combined with Robins's preceding painful dilemma of having to fulfill his promise to campaign for Hoover for a second term in the presidency (not to mention his three- to four-year worsening depression), supports a fugue diagnosis for Robins's adult condition.[4]

Serious emotional problems had always hung as a specter over Robins's life. His amnesia of 1932 may be seen as a culmination of a lifetime of strain and emotional crisis, beginning as early as his family breakup and his childhood epilepsy.

Often cited as the underlying cause of Robins's problems was the fact that his father and mother, Charles and Hannah, were first cousins. In addition, even before he was born, financial ruin had undermined family cohesion, and emotional catastrophe had struck with the death of Charles Robins's most beloved child, Eugene, Raymond's half-brother. Charles Robins remained pathologically inconsolable. But the nervous breakdown of Robins's mother, Hannah, six weeks after his birth and her chronic schizophrenia were the most intense sources of suffering and a life-long reminder of his psychological vulnerability. In his fifty-year correspondence with Elizabeth, "little brother" Raymond reflected over and over again the pain of his childhood and his salvation through the love of "big sister" "Bessie." But at the age of five, when he and his two brothers (Vernon, six, and Saxton, eight) were sent to live in Louisville, Elizabeth, fifteen, was sent off to boarding school. Nevertheless, and perhaps more so because of their separation from that point for nearly all their lives, Elizabeth was and always remained his emotional focus. This intense connection between Elizabeth and Raymond was due to their perception of themselves as the two extraordinary Robinses who transcended the destructive family spell. At the same time, the family lineage served, in part, to explain to each the remarkable attributes of the other. Raymond was convinced that the same mysteries of biological inheritance that had caused the "break in [the Robins] line" was responsible for Elizabeth's creative genius, and Elizabeth was similarly sure: "At the end of our line there is a genius."

From 1878 to 1883 Hannah functioned well enough to look after her three boys, and with the financial help of her absent husband and medical attention from her brother-in-law, Dr. James Morrison Bodine, she and her boys were often together. It was while they were living in a boarding house on Second and Chestnut Streets in Louisville, between 1882 and 1883 that Raymond passed through the hell of terrible seizures.

The first signs of illness appeared in January 1882 and came as a shock to everyone. "You can have no idea of the piercing resonant sound of his screams," his grandmother wrote to Elizabeth, "or of the strength of his muscular contortions—his strange idiotic looks—." "He passes his first night in Louisville at our boarding house," Hannah related in a detailed letter to Elizabeth,

> had a paroxysm the moment his head touched the pillow. Saxton and I worked with him for nearly one hour having a sheet tied around his waist and the other end fastened about mine. His struggles were fearful[;] fortunately he didn't scream or make much disturbance lowed like a cow meowed imitated a cat rubbing and purring barked and scratched with his hands like a dog said rat and shook his mouth as though he had caught one. Kicked and bit hung his tongue out of his mouth eyes rolled back in his head while foam or froth came from his lips recited the poem about the racoon and the ditty about old Uncle Sam and twice the strange chant in an unknown tongue. It took both Saxton and myself with all our strength to keep him from doing himself injury. . . . Another night the Dr. was telephoned for at 12 o'clock had to give him morphine. Dr. says he never beheld anything like it.[5]

Charles was hopeful that he would emerge "from the hysterical zone through which he has been passing for two months," but that was not the case. Matters grew worse, and his mother was concerned about yet another symptom, which she had first noticed nearly a year before. He "romances fearfully insists . . . upon occurrences which exist only in his imagination. I am sometimes puzzled he tells things in such a straightforward honest earnest manner." The weeks from late March into April were particularly bad, with three attacks in the first ten days of April alone. "His pugnacity is always predominant," Hannah reported further to Elizabeth, often apologizing in her letters for having to share such painful news, "fighting biting scratching kicking imitating animals. Sometimes his eyes are wide open but vacant and expressionless. God alone knows how this will end. Dr. Bodine fears these attacks are tied to mental alienation. WE KNOW THERE IS A FATAL INFIRMITY IN THE ROBINS FAMILY AND MUCH ECCENTRICITY AMONG THE HUSSEYS."[6]

Charles and Dr. Bodine ruled out "the strain of schooling" for Raymond and decided that "some discipline of occupation . . . errand boy or whatever" would help him turn his mind to other matters. From April 1882 through the fall of 1883 Raymond worked, first as a "cash boy" and then as "assistant soda water boy . . . 8 A.M. to 3 including Sundays." The paroxysms, of changing severity and frequency, seemed to trail off by the summer of 1883. Dr. Bodine had predicted that "R. will outgrow his somnambulistic tendency," but by late November his "light recurrences of former troubles" convinced Bodine and Charles that a change was necessary. "Hannah's mental illness grows worse," Bodine wrote to Charles, early in December. "R. R. can't stand strain of cash boy in a busy store," Charles wrote to his mother, "he needs outdoor life. . . . He must be away from Hannah and . . . it is better that he be away from Saxton." It was under these dire circumstances that Raymond was sent along with his cousin Lizzie "Mother" McKay, her husband Zack, and their daughter Mary to make a life at Bodine Grove, Florida.[7]

After leaving his mother and the boarding house in Louisville, Raymond's seizures never recurred. From the first days in Florida, he was the picture of good health and contentment, happy in the company of his new family and Fielder Harris. But Raymond never forgot those two agonizing years and there is the distinct possibility that his later amnesia was somehow connected to his childhood paroxysms.

During his visit to Louisville as an adult, only months away from his first serious depression and nervous breakdown, Raymond wrote to Elizabeth explaining the roots of his emotional problems:

> When I thought of Vernon and Saxton and myself living there with our poor mother and what the whole tragedy meant to so many lives, I seemed to feel again that curious sense of need to flee from some unseen terror—of need to be so close to the ground that when it came I could just lie down and die without injury to others. Always this impending doom, certain failure, utter loss and defeat, has been just a little ways behind. Standing there on that corner looking up at the one room where we lived I felt a sudden coldness and shivered and turned away. The day was quite warm.[8]

As an adult Robins was subject to severe depression. His first encounter with such a debilitating crisis came at the age of twenty-seven, after months of struggle on the Yukon River, Big Chimney Camp, and the Alaska winter trail. In Nome, Robins began the pattern of work and behavior that continued for the rest of his active life—unrelenting commitment of time and energy, seven times to the point of physical and mental breakdown. Elizabeth was witness to the compulsive and destructive lengths to which Robins drove himself. During her visit to Raymond in Nome in 1900, she warned him against the brutal pace of his labor and, finally, got him to leave Alaska; but she was never able to convince him to lead a normal work life.

In Alaska he found a way to evade the pervasive pain and terror of his existence and build a life of meaning and valuable social contribution. He also learned to direct the powerful life-sustaining forces within him—including his passion for his sister Elizabeth—to the service of others, a form of personal sacrifice, like that of Father Barnum of the Holy Cross Mission. But the dream and the failure, once again, of plans to make a life with Elizabeth kept him on the emotional brink.

During his first years in Chicago (1901-5), he fought the old agony and doubts and desperate yearning to be with "Bessie," and he submerged himself in fourteen to sixteen hours of work each day. In 1902 he came close to physical collapse and managed a reprieve, but in August 1903, under the multiple strains of his work, a decision to make a marriage proposal to Anita McCormick Blaine, and the additional blow of her rejection, he entered a deep depression. Recovery was slow, but a trip to Florida and rest at his boyhood home in Bodine Grove finally brought back his strength. Elizabeth once more consumed his thoughts and plans, leading to the saga of Chinsegut—the purchase of Snow Hill and the creation of a Robins estate there.

However, six months after that tumultuous time Raymond met and within six weeks married Margaret Dreier. He fantasized living together at Chinsegut with Elizabeth and Margaret—leaping from his former life of painful loneliness to one of abundant love and camaraderie. But Chinsegut was to be the home of Raymond and Margaret; Elizabeth, who had been Raymond's inspiration for creating such a haven and with whose $5,000 the house was purchased, was only an occasional visitor. The marriage led to a change in his responsiveness to Elizabeth when they were together, and although he tried to compensate for the change, going so far as to have Margaret invite Elizabeth along to Florida for their honeymoon, jealousy—of both wife and sister—soon won out.

In addition, bitter disagreements arose over building and financial arrangements for Chinsegut, masking the real issues of Raymond's betrayal of his promises never to marry and remain true to his covenant with Elizabeth. Conflict between Margaret and Elizabeth, both strong-willed and each accustomed to getting her way, was expressed through Raymond as intermediary and, within only a year or two, resulted in the essential estrangement of the sisters-in-law for the rest of their lives. The ten-year conflict over Chinsegut and the finances (read as feelings of betrayal and jealousy) grew so charged on occasion that brother and sister nearly had to settle their differences in court. However, during the forty years of his married life and until Elizabeth's death in 1952, they maintained their intimate, prolific, and extraordinary correspondence. Raymond's vital and deeply needed connection to Elizabeth never abated, nor hers to him.

The marriage of Raymond and Margaret was a godsend for both of them. Margaret, at thirty-seven, had long since given up on the chance for a marriage and, in painful jest, often signed her letters to her nephews, "your spinster aunt Gretchen." And Raymond's elation challenged his skill with the written word. Even Elizabeth, writing in bewilderment two days before the wedding, appreciated how "wonderful that these two people have found each other. She is quite amazingly *the* person for him, so far as even the jealous human eye can see."[9]

Elizabeth's intuition and the high hopes of Margaret and Raymond were fulfilled in a joyous marriage devoted to one another and their long list of social and political causes. But the "shadow" in Raymond's life was always there, even in times of bliss. "We roved in the woods back of the farm,"

Raymond wrote to Elizabeth in the spring of 1907, as always sharing the joys and sorrows of his life,

> and built a great fire of fagots and played like children and came back to the big house at sunset she with a glorious joy in her dark eyes and the pure red blood flaming in her cheeks and I with a great peace in my heart.
>
> Over all these later months there has brooded only one shadow. Margaret greatly wants to bear me a child. This sorrow I do not share personally. I have too sure an appreciation of the break in our line to be over anxious for another generation to share the costs of the Robins blood. If a child had come I should have met the little life gladly and hopefully because of its blessed mother with her sound red German blood, but I find her barrenness no sorrow and the prospect of its permanence no personal regret.[10]

The Robinses learned from medical specialists that Margaret would never be able to have a child, which removed the single possible obstacle to their complete dedication to a life of public service. However, Raymond's "personal" relief that he would not father a child is a poignant testament to his unshakable conviction that the mental illness which took his mother and her sister, Mary Bodine, undermined his father's capacity to succeed at anything, brought his brother Saxton to suicide, and plagued him was all connected, congenital, and irreversible. This conviction lent a terrible urgency, if not desperation to his entire life.

Robins's marriage did not alter his near-manic behavior. The pace of ceaseless work did not abate. On the contrary, his aim was to do more— more than last year, more than the year before that. With Margaret's presidency of the National Women's Trade Union League and the countless demands upon her time and resources, her schedule of work was often the match of Raymond's. The only difference was that her administrative duties did not usually demand the travel that Raymond's nationwide speaking campaigns required. She also did not drive herself, as Raymond did, beyond the clearly marked points where her health was put in jeopardy.

Raymond worked compulsively to overcome the pall of failure that had dominated his father's life and constantly pained Raymond as a boy and adolescent. The similarity of activities that Raymond undertook to those of his father establishes that either consciously or unconsciously Raymond tried to emulate his father and succeed where he had failed. Both were involved in the urban business world and ventured off to mine for gold. Charles studied and did practice assaying, while Raymond, in Alaska, applied for permission to examine records for the purpose of opening an assayer's office. Both became involved in social reform, although only Raymond took direct action. And finally, both made building an agricultural paradise in Florida a major drive in their lives.

Chinsegut was far more than an estate to Robins. It was the fulfillment of a dream at which his father had failed. It was the affirmation of Raymond's success as an adult, to counter the treatment he received as a boy at the

Chinsegut in all its glory. (Courtesy of the Elizabeth Robins Papers, Fales Library, New York University.)

hands of Frank Bodine, who regarded Raymond as a charity case—a barely tolerated poor relation. But his father's anguish at having failed at his orange grove—Nama—had an overwhelming impact on the fragile psyche of young Raymond. "He had been fighting for and loosing homes all his life," Raymond wrote to Elizabeth about their father, while Raymond was recovering from a nervous breakdown in 1914.

> It must have been this battle in my pre-natal and early youth that so im-
> pressed me with the fear of a home. It seemed to me for thirty years the one
> thing to avoid and instead of wanting to build one I have fled from the idea of
> one—until just now. Is this a manifestation of the enemy? . . . I am a nomad and
> with all my love for Chinsegut as a home I am half afraid of it all the time, in
> that curious way that is a part doubtless of the—enemy—in my consciousness.[11]

Margaret very quickly fell in love with Chinsegut and, over the years, invested her heart and money in making it a beautiful and comfortable haven from the fourth floor of 1437 West Ohio Street and the seething issues of Chicago labor and politics. For Raymond, the more important haven was Margaret. "She is the most generous, gentle, wise, courageous, faithful, simple, single hearted soul I have ever known," Raymond wrote to Elizabeth, two months after their fifth wedding anniversary.

Think of it—NOT FIVE MINUTES OF TEMPER—between us in five years! Physically, mentally, spiritually in an abiding accord. In matters of money, in matters of religion . . . politics . . . labor . . . family and friends, in matters of home and table and clothes, in substantial and happy and effortless agreement for five years. And yet men say that the age of miracles is passed! In some ways I am the hardest headed, meanest, most stubborn, most opinionated man I know. Margaret has never found it out. She thinks I have Sunny Jim [their well-behaved horse] beat a mile for gentleness and good temper and patience. Its a queer world.[12]

The sunshine and joy of their married life did not diminish. There are dozens of letters like this one, written by Raymond over the next twenty years to Elizabeth and to Mary Dreier. However, the strained periods of convalescence and the months of Raymond's disappearance during his bout with amnesia bore heavily on Margaret. It weakened her and, for the first time, soon thereafter a change in her mild disposition became noticeable. For Raymond, the episodes of mental strain and depression came regularly, and predictably, they accompanied periods of driven activity.

Between February and August 1913 he was involved in the ambitious Smith-Robins World Evangelical Tour. Immediately upon his return, the Illinois Progressive party pressed him into service to resolve conflicts between factions in the party and to plan the 1914 campaign. He was elected chairman of the State Central Committee and immediately began the organizational meetings and rallies for all 102 counties in the state. In October 1913, while on a speaking tour, Robins passed through Louisville and visited the house where he had lived with his brothers and mother, later writing Elizabeth of "doom, certain failure, utter loss and defeat." His depression was slowly taking control.

A month later, in November, his schedule day-by-day filled with commitments for the next four months, he wrote to Elizabeth:

I have defied the "terror" and am holding large responsibilities for the people and the Cause. Daily these responsibilities increase. Behind me grins the old pursuing "Demon" and now and again I feel that I am being cornered by the "Shadow" and will break under the strain. It is a curious sense of seeing something that no one else sees. All is fair and calm and yet I shiver with the sense of impending failure and the closing in of doom. This "thing" has been with me ever since I can remember. It bid me not to marry, never to hold important office, always to work through others, to flee from fixed duties and responsibilities; always to know that large achievement and abiding success could never be mine. Now that I am doing exceptional work and hearing the most extravagant praise and begin to feel that great issues are being molded by my personality, committed to my leadership—at times I could cry out and flee from the battle line forever.[13]

The pace of work did not ease. County by county, the speeches were made and the meetings were held and the praise for his work continued. By the end of January, physical symptoms began to be added to the terror and "knowledge" of failure—growing nervousness, lack of sleep. At the end of March, he broke.

As soon as possible, Margaret brought him to Chinsegut to mend. He slowly recovered, although his derangement continued to be reflected in his correspondence with Elizabeth for many months. By late summer, when he was much improved, the demand that he head the Illinois Progressive party ticket as candidate for the U.S. Senate could no longer be ignored. Resigned to sure defeat, Robins accepted the nomination and the responsibility to make a vigorous campaign for the three months before election day. For the next eighteen months he continued to suffer from serious sleeplessness and the fear that under so weakened a condition he would suffer a relapse. But he was fortunate, and by the spring of 1916, he was again able to sleep and return to normal health and the usual pace of activity. It was in this sound condition that Robins set off on the mission to Russia.

Nowhere in his personal papers is there the slightest hint that his emotional problems caused him any difficulty during the tension-filled months in Russia. And if we are to believe Somerset Maugham's amazed testimony, Robins's incredible pace of activity there was "not human." Between the time of his return to the United States in June 1918 and his testimony before the Senate subcommittee in March 1919, he fell into a depression. The disparity between his efforts and hopes for what he considered a responsible U.S. policy toward Russia and the policy actually adopted was so great that his sense of defeat was overwhelming. This, coupled with his enforced silence and humiliation, was too much for his proud spirit. But he did not break under the strain. He continued the struggle to bring his understanding of the Russian Revolution to the American people.

Although Robins worked so often at a feverish pace, he cannot be clinically diagnosed as "manic depressive," because none of the specific symptoms of mania were present in his behavior. On the basis of a study of more than thirty of his letters, written over the course of as many years, in which he described his profound depression experiences, a tentative diagnosis of "unipolar depression" is suggested. Current studies (1988–91) may determine the relationship of genetic factors in the incidence of both uni- and bipolar depression, particularly in families of creative individuals. The fearful suppositions that Raymond had inherited his "terror," a belief that was shared by Hannah, Elizabeth, and Raymond, indeed might be plausible.[14]

It was not until February 1921, well after the completion of his strenuous and compromising campaign to defeat the policies of Wilson and the Democrats by electing Harding, that Robins had his most serious depression and nervous breakdown. "You see he got very little to eat in Russia," Margaret explained to Elizabeth, breaking the news to her of Raymond's breakdown,

> and since his return home he was on too great a tension to eat much and his body has finally rebelled. These last four years have been difficult years for

him, but the joy to be serving in Russia so far overshadowed the difficulties that he was not conscious of the strain he was under. Then came these hideous years at home. He had felt so confident that our government would play fair and be ready to help those struggling millions, especially the children and when instead the government played its contemptible hand Raymond felt that the people must be told and that America could be trusted to answer the President and his Cabinet and so he fought on. The answer [Harding's election] was made on November second [election day, 1920] and for the first time in four years Raymond had no immediate call made upon him, and the pause gave his body its chance of rebellion.[15]

Five months before his collapse, in the home stretch of the election campaign, with symptoms appearing and past experience clearly signaling the danger, Robins carried on. "It will have been my heaviest campaign and I shall be thankful if I get through without blowing up," he wrote to Elizabeth. "My eyes are beginning to fail a little and I am getting occasional pains in the head and along the neck down the right arm. I need the land of the Shining Pines and I expect to go there when this final battle is over."[16]

And that he did, soon after the election. "I went to work as is my custom and had a blessed time at hard labor," he explained to Elizabeth in an extraordinary letter chronicling the entire course of his breakdown.

> I probably did a little more than was wise forgetting that I was nearing the half century mark and had done little physical labor for nearly two years. The first symptoms of trouble were loss of appetite and a heaviness and disinclination to read or see people even my neighbors. Then I began to lose sleep. . . . Then quite suddenly I was plunged into the most terrible depression I have ever known. . . . A very rapid depletion of my physical powers set in, I lost flesh daily, heavy night sweats wasted me, my mind ran an unceasing gamut of miserable and cowardly anticipations of loss and suffering. I began to think upon suicide and to wish for death . . . fighting with imaginary evils chasing troops of Bluedevils I would sit up in the bed in the dark with such a sense of misery. . . . [I] hated to see anyone[,] would want to run from my best friends and the simplest talk of Bishop or Fulton would make me want to cry out as if in real pain.

Following the medical practice of the time, Robins received two "electric treatments." These low-voltage homeopathic treatments were administered in mid-March to break the depression, and they appear to have helped. For the first time in six weeks Robins had a night of sound sleep. His physical suffering eased and he seemed to be on the mend.

> Then the most extraordinary thing happened. CHINSEGUT BECAME THE ENEMY! For a time I hated the old hill-top. It was too much of a load and would break both Margaret and myself. . . . The house was leaking and it could not be recovered so that it would not leak, the house would surely burn down . . . snakes were getting more plentiful and would someday soon bite and kill Margaret, I would

always have malaria while I lived in Florida. I should never have gone to Florida for a home, I should never have tried to make a home for anybody anywhere. . . . The very beauty of the forest seemed to mock me and to be a sort of false brilliance trying to hide the inevitable terror suffering and doom! . . . Such was my dogs life for nearly two months on the hill-top. . . .

There came upon me an utter lack of the power of fixed decision. One day I wanted to leave the hill-top and the next I would refuse to go. . . . The next I wished . . . to sell Chinsegut and leave Florida forever.

Under the pressure of this wrenching ambivalence surrounding Chinsegut and the anguish his father imparted to him from his own failure in Florida, Margaret and Raymond escaped to the North. He went from doctor to doctor, from one drug therapy and sanitarium to another, "from pillar to post living in a profound depression of body and mind."

And then I went to Muldoon's! . . . One of the most extraordinary men I have ever known. Retired champion wrestler of the world, never beaten during 20 years . . . now president of Muldoon's Hygienic Institute, White Plains New York. He is the most tyrannical, brutal and ruthless mortal I have ever known, seventy six years young, light as a cat on his feet quick as a panther, rides his eight miles daily and takes the fastest work in the gymnasium with athletes under thirty. . . . In three weeks he did more good than I would have believed possible this side of a miracle. Weak and flabby as I was he drove me savagely, was insulting and brutal, threw away all medicines of every description, put up an absolute bar on all stimulants and narcotics of every character including tea and coffee. . . . Now I am almost normal. Should I slip downward again I will go at once to Muldoon's. . . . I have now been a week out of prison, have addressed the Ohio Congregational Conference with nearly all of my oldtime power, and shared in three important conferences without so far any evidence of slipping backward.

Throughout the ordeal, Margaret was steadfast in responding with patience and courage to the wild mood changes and impossible behavior. "Only one anchor held," Raymond shared with Elizabeth, "my love for Margaret and her faultless devotion to me."[17]

By midsummer 1921 Robins was back in harness in Chicago, focusing on the battle to force Harding to call for a conference on disarmament and beginning his work with Levinson on the outlawry of war. A crash in the securities market seriously cut Margaret's income. Sleeplessness remained a continuing problem in his struggle for recovery, and deeply undermining his spirit, Harding was reneging on making policy changes in U.S.-Soviet relations. "What a devil this is," he wrote to Elizabeth. "It is now all mind—night after night ringing the changes on the Russian situation, the broken promises at Washington, and the financial loss at home." In the throes of the real adversities and his lingering depression, Raymond also thought he saw a change in Margaret—an aging from the strain of the months of his illness. That she was to pay a permanent price for his madness was hard for him to bear. Life seemed futile. He wanted to escape. He chose to dream of the sweetest time of his life. "Sister Bessie lets forget it all—all the heat and hurry of long years—, let us go out and swing in the hammock under the tulip tree. Let's sit on the stone steps of the terrace near the catalpas, and after a while we will gather some lilacs for your room. Grandmother looks out of the window and calls 'Bessie Bessie' and you are gone!"[18]

Following the La Follete–Davis–Coolidge presidential race of 1924, the Robinses finally closed down their Chicago workshop in the Seventeenth Ward and made Chinsegut their permanent home. In that process, the question of Elizabeth's joint ownership and the future of the estate exploded into a bitter fight that lasted many months and nearly landed the brother and sister in court. The settlement, which left Raymond and Margaret as sole owners, was based on Elizabeth's initial loan to Raymond.

It called for the secured payment of fifty $500 payments to Elizabeth, one every six months, for twenty-five years or until her death. Securities at more than $25,000 in market value were held by a bank to secure the payments. While the financial concerns and emotional attachments to Chinsegut after nearly twenty years of building, planting, and making a home were intense, the underlying pain, anguish, jealousy, and resentment sprang from Raymond's betrayal of the old "Roadhouse" dream and promises made before the turn of the century. Communication between brother and sister, masters of correspondence for more than thirty years, broke down completely. Simple thoughts were misread or misinterpreted on both sides and the level of hurt and frustration mounted.

Elizabeth projected her emotional victimization into the dollars lent and owed. Raymond's desperate attempt to find "sound financial solutions" to compensate her for her share in Chinsegut was never adequate or represented yet another betrayal. The impasse was tragic, and even at the height of misunderstanding and vindictiveness, Raymond clung to "the deepest and oldest devotion of my human heart." In each of the final letters ending the crisis, he tried to ease Elizabeth's hurt by quoting sage advice: "THIS TOO SHALL PASS AWAY," using capitals, to assure her.[19]

Robins was elated both at Hoover's election in November 1928 and at the outlawry victory in July 1929. This satisfaction was undercut by the Wall Street crash three months later and was soon replaced by a long, intensifying depression. In the following three years, much of Margaret's stock holdings was lost, her income was drastically cut, and a time of long-term financial crisis for the Robinses and Chinsegut began.

Since their permanent move from Chicago to Florida in 1924, Robins had become financially involved in the First National Bank of Brooksville. He often received expert advice from Thompson, Levinson, and, ironically, from "Bolshevik" Alexander Gumberg's "Wall Street" investment firm, the Atlas Corporation. These business-wise friends were a constant source of financial advice for Robins's personal finances as well as those of the Brooksville bank. Robins was perhaps the only nationally known celebrity in that small, west coast Florida community and Chinsegut was certainly one of the grandest estates for miles around.

After the crash, the bank was reorganized and Raymond became chairman of the board. His sense of responsibility and pride as a "leading citizen" of Brooksville drew him into the financially disastrous enterprise of saving the bank from going under, along with securing the life savings of many of his friends and neighbors. The struggle to save the bank, which lasted more than three years, required the steady commitment of more and more of the already depleted Dreier-Robins assets. Once they began pouring money into the bank, their own financial future was more seriously jeopardized and began to depended on their success at saving the bank. Were it not for the expertise of Levinson, Gumberg, Thompson, and Thompson's colleague, Charles F. Ayer, a "copper king" and expert in the investment banking field, they would have failed. But the emotional burden on Robins of the steady depletion of Margaret's inheritance and impending loss of everything began to weigh too heavily. It was for Robins the reenactment of his father's loss of his mother's fortune; it meant the very failure that had filled his heart with dread since he was a small boy.[20]

From 1929 until 1932, Robins received a frequent but unpredictable sequence of telegrams and letters of alarm from the First National Bank of Brooksville, his financial advisors, and his brokers. These were followed by his instructions for stock sales (rarely purchases) and the transfer of funds to the Brooksville bank. These communications provide an extraordinary counterpoint to the annual Robins financial reports and their totals, each year diminishing by tens and hundreds of thousands of dollars, while in Sisyphean desperation, Robins's annual income from his public speaking for the Allied Campaign rose by mere hundreds of dollars, reaching a peak in 1932 of $3,165.

The symptoms of emotional trouble began in the winter of 1930, during the demanding but well-paid ($300 per lecture) tour that Robins undertook through the Pond Lyceum Bureau. He had explained only to Elizabeth, during her visit to Chinsegut, his fears that another breakdown was coming. She responded, in one of the longest letters of their correspondence, with a detailed plan for the reorganization of his life to ease his work commitments and at the same time to reduce his financial obligations to avert the impending disaster.

She suggested that he reject the quest for money, include manual labor in his life, and turn to a simple life-style without relinquishing his important work. Was Reynolds Rogers, his amnesiac persona, acting on Elizabeth's good advice? Predictably, Raymond Robins would not. "At the moment, the obligations under which I labor do not seem to open any probability of my being able to follow any of your suggestions," he wrote in response to Elizabeth. "[O]ne has obligations that may ruin one to carry, but to refuse to *try* to carry them is to be ruined at once. My earnings are essential to keep the ship from sinking NOW and while it is most probable that she will sink in any event, to abandon the ship is to sink it and myself and others in what would seem a dishonorable surrender."21

For nearly two years Robins remained on this precarious emotional perch, sharing his fears only with Elizabeth, protecting Margaret, and at the same time, giving to his relationship with Elizabeth the trust of his life. He carried out his campaigns for the enforcement of prohibition, advised and carried out missions for President Hoover with astuteness and skill, and developed a level of intimacy, if not friendship with the president far exceeding that of his relationship with either Harding or Coolidge.

It was not unusual at this time for him to dine frequently with Hoover, and he occasionally spent the night at the White House.22 At the same time, he felt he had to continue his paid speaking engagements, as he witnessed the continuing decline of Margaret's holdings. In self-destructive resignation, he made no effort to avert the coming disaster. "When one is caught in dangerous rapids, to go forward may be to embrace Death, but to hesitate or attempt to turn back is at once–Fatal," he wrote proudly to Elizabeth in language reminiscent of the dangers of Alaska and Russia.

> If I know myself I have never cared greatly for LIFE as such, defeat comes in some measure to most humans, and death to all, but to be a conscious QUITTER— that is incomparably worse to me than defeat or death, or both. It is for this reason that I want YOU to believe that if this cloud thickens and I stumble into Eternity, that I fell only AFTER the mind gave way. It was that I was in the rapids, that all that I had was called upon for each days survival, that made your presence here so terrible so terrible a diversion. YOU mean to me something apart from all others, YOU have been the longest LIGHT in my pathway, the *hidden treasure* in my heart for the most years . . . and surviving I shall swing into the circle of your Flame again.23

By the spring of 1931, as much a result of his emotional as his financial state, Robins was convinced that the realities of the Great Depression made the loss of Chinsegut inevitable and he began preparations for its sale. His initial negotiations with nearby Rollins College fell through, but with the help of his political connections in the Hoover administration, he managed to deed the 2,000-acre estate to the federal government and have Chinsegut declared a national sanctuary for wildlife and agricultural study. The house and the hilltop were to remain in the hands of Margaret and himself until their death.

Through this time, Robins was obsessed by quotations from Scripture, what he called the "texts of TERROR."

> In the morning thou shalt say Would God it were even! and at even thou shalt say, Would God it were morning! [Deut. 28:67]

> And thy heaven that is over thy head shall be brass, and the earth that is un-
> der thee shall be iron, and thy life shall hang in doubt before thee, and thou shalt
> fear day and night, and shall have none assurance of thy life [Deut. 28:23].[24]

Yet another image of terror compounded the anguish and consumed him in-
cessantly, "of one lying in bed and the four walls moving together until you
are crushed? I am in that bed and four granite walls so high you can just see
the light above them are moving in irresistibly to crush me to death. You
see them coming but there is no escape." He pleaded with Elizabeth, in depression, defeat, and guilt, to be loving and understanding of Margaret.

> I took her from a beautiful home into a tenement. I took her from security
> and a comfortable social position, into storm and stress and bitter struggle. I
> have wasted her comfortable inheritance, I leave her divorced from her old as-
> sociations, old, broken, and penniless. She was and is your Little Brother's
> wife. For his sake, where mention of her cannot be generous, by the love of
> long years between thee and me and in answer to the supreme request of my
> heart of yours—BE SILENT!
>
> With love for and faith in THEE, MY BIG SISTER,
Little Brother[25]

Six months later, there was no change in his psychological condition. His
work for the Allied Citizens Campaign for Law Enforcement (of prohibition), by November 1931, included "73 cities, nineteen state capitals and 31
states. Over 76,000 voters have enrolled. . . . Day by day Sunday and Monday rain and shine we are on the march, and the platform." But "the terror
of sleepless nights" continued and the exhaustion followed. "Twice recently I
have faltered on the platform," he confided to Elizabeth, "things have gone
black before my eyes and it has been a few minutes before I really knew
what I was saying. But the old machine rights itself and runs on. I say nothing to my associates, just line up and march—day by day." The tragic hero:
courageous and undaunted in the face of sure destruction, crushed by the
enemy and risen to continue the struggle. Through all the real suffering, he
was proud of his sacrifice, particularly in the eyes of his big sister. By 6 June
1932 the number of cities had grown to 261, "every capital city and every
major city in every state in the union."[26]

Robins remained as politically astute and as tactically sharp as ever, in spite
of these years of emotional and financial depression, on both the national and
personal levels. Within months after the Hoover landslide victory of 1928,
the greatest to that date in American history, Robins was predicting a Hoover
defeat in 1932 of even greater proportions. "Hoover has lost more of dominion and prestige in one short year—than I have before known to overtake
any leader in American politics," he wrote to Elizabeth in confidence.[27] But
Robins's political bed was made, and there he stayed, in the Republican party,
until well into the first years of Franklin Roosevelt's administration. Publicly,
Robins remained loyal to his party and kept to his limited agenda of U.S.

recognition of Russia, world peace through outlawry, and maintenance of prohibition in spite of the economic disaster destroying his life and the lives of millions of Americans. The only change in the commitment of his time and energy was the complete reversal of priorities of the threefold mission. Prohibition, with only questionable connection to the social and economic well-being of the American people, had swept to center stage.

In 1920, when Hiram Johnson's progressivism had been pushed aside by Harding's reaction, Robins was reluctantly drawn into the support of Harding's candidacy, with its focus on alcohol prohibition and the abandonment of labor, and social, economic, urban, and political reform. Robins had consciously allowed prohibition, the impractical "church-uplifters" pseudo-reform, to replace the real reforms for which he had worked so hard. This sacrifice was the price Robins was willing to pay for recognition of Russia and defeat of the treaty and the League, to assure world peace through outlawry of war.

Ten years later, after Coolidge and Hoover, Russia still a pariah, and the American economy wrecked as badly as his personal life, Robins chose to give all his time to prohibition.[28] Like so many of his desperate and disillusioned contemporaries, he embraced a delusion. He could find no solution to the economic disaster enveloping America, no reform campaign that promised economic recovery to which he could lend his support. But Robins was not alone in such hopelessness. Indeed, most of his companions in the Progressive movement had to struggle with the same personal and collective experience of failure. "As I look back over the struggle of our generation," Harold Ickes wrote to Robins after a bitter defeat for progressive forces in the Chicago elections of 1929,

> I sometimes wonder whether it has been worth while. We certainly haven't succeeded in planting the standard that we carried in advance of the line that we occupied at the beginning of the war. I think it can be demonstrated that, politically speaking, Chicago and Illinois are much worse off than they were when we volunteered for the fight. . . .
>
> I have realized for a number of years, how futile my contribution to the common cause has been and yet I haven't had sense enough to admit defeat and make the most of my remaining years for myself and my family. I suppose I always will be like that. I imagine that one has to be at least 90% damn fool to plunge headlong into every hopeless fight that calls for volunteers.
>
> And the tragedy of it is that we have been working to improve the social and political conditions of people who don't want any improvement. . . . I never felt so much alone as I did during this last fight.[29]

Robins, like Ickes, was incapable of idle resignation, so he "kept on marching" for prohibition. However, the depression and terror were compounded by his growing experience of failure: on Russia, the progressive agenda, the loss of Margaret's inheritance, and his painful commitment to support Hoover. In a letter to Levinson captioned "FOR 'CONFIDENTIAL DESTRUCTION,'" Robins showed no sign of charity for Hoover, whom a year earlier he had grown to respect. With uncharacteristic bitterness, Robins opened his heart on the subject of Hoover. "Let us be frank with each other however much we must veil our thoughts with others," Robins began his litany of woe.

> Hoover is a complete wash out as a political leader, he has failed utterly as the BIG WISDOM in the worst economic crisis I think I have ever known this country to suffer, he has been a lap or six behind on all relief and done nothing vital or creative after his first effort to prevent cuts in wages and employment. He has lost control in both houses of the Congress even before the last election. He has alienated Labor, the Negroes, Women, all the Social Justice folks, and the most effective hard-boiled organization leaders along with Borah, Cutting, Vandenberg and many others of liberal minds. . . . A man who worshipped at his shrine for years before he was President, and who gave one of the largest contributions for his primary campaign, said to me last week, "Hoover is a dead mackerel on the political shore shining and stinking in the pale moonlight that precedes his complete eclipse, leaving simply a memory of a bad smell."

Sixteen months later Robins confided to Elizabeth: "I would risk anything I have on the certainty of the defeat of Hoover in November."[30]

By the first week in August 1932, the Allied Campaign for Law Enforcement had already prepared a schedule of speeches for Robins that began on 28 August and continued, without a free day, until 7 November. On 15 August Robins telegraphed Roy Breg, director of the Allied Campaign, that he could accept no commitments until after the presidential election, since he had been "drafted" to help Herbert Hoover. Walter Newton, secretary to Hoover, was in regular correspondence with Robins at this time for help on Hoover's speeches, particularly on how to treat the prohibition plank. On the nineteenth of August Robins received a letter from C. W. Ramseyer, director of the Speakers Bureau of the Republican National Committee, asking Robins's advice on campaign strategy and whether he would be available to participate in the presidential campaign that was about to begin.

"I will be glad to be used as fully as may be helpful," began Robins's lengthy reply, staking out all the essentials for the Republican cause. "I will answer to your call any time, any where," Robins concluded his letter, "asking two things: that I be not sent to unimportant meetings and that there be arranged a tolerable publicity synopsis. . . . You are fully advised that I am most effective among Progressives, Labor folks and Drys."[31]

Ten days later, on 3 September, on his way to a meeting with the president and before beginning the campaign "to walk and speak and write and work for the election of Herbert Hoover—to the hidden music of a dead march to an open political grave," Robins disappeared, and the terrible ordeal of amnesia began.[32]

22

A Dream Fulfilled, a Final Challenge

I have been on the final lap of a sixteen year finished struggle in re Russian American relations. The end was last Friday night in the grand ballroom of the Waldorf-Astoria with seventeen hundred diners at a banquet to Commissar Litvinov, in which "Wall Street" by its most weighty members stood at attention while the band played the INTERNATIONALE. The stars and stripes were crossed with the hammer and sickle on its red field.
—Raymond to Elizabeth, 26 November 1933

I witnessed this NEW ORDER being born in the land of the Czars, and knew the MAN OF CREATIVE MIND AND VISION, whose dauntless WILL and COURAGE brought it to birth . . . for the Promise of that "more abundant life" for which the Great Galilean peasant and carpenter, lived, labored, suffered and died. LENIN did not know that the source of his POWER was this Galilean JEW, despite the fact that his Followers "had all things in common" as the record runs.
—Raymond to Elizabeth, 10 June 1945

ROBINS'S recovery of strength and well-being was surprisingly rapid. Unlike the agonizing three-year intensification of depression that led to the amnesia, or the drawn out fight for healing following his 1921 depression and breakdown, he felt none of the nagging "terror" after regaining his memory.[1] His illnesses of the past, however, had been private matters. He had withdrawn from public life, recuperated, and when ready, returned to the battle. Only family and friends had been aware of the nature of his illness. The ten weeks of his disappearance, on the other hand, drew as much national publicity as he had ever garnered for his campaigns. When news of his "discovery" reached the media, reporters descended on Asheville, and while Raymond was safe from their predations, Margaret was caught "running down the fire escape in the hospital to escape about twenty reporters only to find two photographers at the other end."[2]

Margaret had always feared that publicity of Raymond's mental illnesses would dangerously undermine his work. On Raymond's fifty-ninth birthday, 17 September 1932, two weeks after his disappearance, Margaret wrote a note thanking Alex Gumberg for his concern and understanding "during these days of terrible strain," and explaining that she was repelled by any suggestion of amnesia.

I have no patience with the theory of amnesia and I do not like his friends to use that term, for should he return such uncertainty as amnesia any minute, would destroy the usefulness of his work. And the country will rally to Raymond and his work if they fear foul play. I feel that he is well, but kidnapped,—I do not believe they will harm him unless they did so at once. And I believe we are in for a long winter,—we must dig in as at Valley Forge, and pray and hope and believe.[3]

These fears proved well founded. Long after Robins's complete recovery, his booking agents received harsh rejections when carrying out the usual solicitations; many were cruel. "While I should like to have Col. Robins come, I don't know what our committee will say about his wandering tendencies," wrote one group to the Pond Lyceum Bureau, which planned his lecture tour for the summer of 1933. "He was and I am afraid still is considered a joke in these parts; while it shouldn't interfere with his knowledge of the Russian question, it has injured his prestige." The press sensation of the amnesia story was a serious blow to Robins's popular image and credibility, and although after a few years it was no longer mentioned in the press, the psychological and public damage had been done. Even with many of his allies, a new caution pervaded their relationship.[4]

All the currents of my work narrow down. The calls for me to go there and do this and help yonder that were incessant for so many years have ceased. I try to keep a good front, and in some measure succeed, but the bread is bitter, for the body is strong and the mind still keen. The connections are broken and I who never cared for any game in which I did not play—am looking on in Venice. If it were only an interim it would not cut so deep—if I could retire decently that would be something else again. As it is I hang on the outer edges and keep alive.[5]

Robins's regimen for convalescence at Chinsegut was strict, involving exercise, work, and an emphasis on rest. By the turn of the new year, his sixtieth, his recovery was accelerated by an old dream that began to charge his imagination and occupy his thoughts—a return to Russia. As early as 1927, the Soviet government had extended an invitation to Robins to be an honored guest at the tenth anniversary of the Bolshevik Revolution. But during October and the same first week in November, when the festivities were to be held in Moscow, he was deeply involved in the last of his Chicago-wide political campaigns—the effort to reelect incumbent reform mayor William E. Dever. The reformers lost the fierce struggle and five tempestuous years were to pass before the dream of returning to Russia could again be explored.[6]

Robins's idea for the trip was encouraged by the open consideration of recognition of the Soviets in Franklin Roosevelt's incoming administration. Back on 25 July 1932 Gumberg had helped to arrange a discussion and interview between candidate Roosevelt and Walter Duranty, the *New York Times* Moscow correspondent. The meeting, widely covered in the press, indicated both Roosevelt's interest in increasing trade with the Soviet Union and suggested study of the prospect of recognition. Later, after Roosevelt's election, the cause was advanced by William C. Bullitt, Henry Morganthau, and the cabinet appointments of Harold Ickes as secretary of the interior, Frances Perkins for labor, and Henry Wallace for agriculture, all of whom favored recognition.

Robins first shared the idea of the Russian trip with Alex Gumberg, who was immediately supportive and helpful. Gumberg raised the idea with Peter Bogdanov, the Russian government trade agent in the United States, and Bogdanov was enthusiastic. Frances Kellor thought "it would be a swell idea." Robins's trip plans came quick on the heels of a new surge of activity for recognition among the directors of the American-Russian Chamber of Commerce, who, during their meeting of 12 December 1932, did not discuss whether recognition was possible, but rather whether recognition should be conditional or unconditional. Gumberg suggested that Robins quietly go to the Soviet Union under the auspices of a major American newspaper or news service and, while on the scene, submit a series of stories that would advance the cause.[7]

The plan for the trip coincided with the final stages of his recovery, both very encouraging. In mid-February, Robins headed north from Chinsegut to Boston, where he gave his first major public address, "Should the U.S. Now Recognize the Soviet Union?" In Boston, before the Foreign Policy Association, and then in Princeton, at the DeWitt Clinton Poole School of International Affairs, Robins argued his strong affirmative. (It was no small irony in the latter case, since DeWitt Clinton Poole was the American consul in Moscow in 1918 who succeeded Maddin Summers and strongly opposed Robins's efforts toward American recognition at that time.)[8]

Throughout March and early April, Robins was back in political harness in Washington and New York preparing the way for his trip. Of particular importance to him personally and for the cause of Russian recognition was the resumption of his strong ties to old progressives in the Roosevelt administration with whom he had fought side-by-side in reform battles in Chicago and the Progressive party campaigns of 1912 and 1914. His close friendships with Ickes and Perkins had never waned and had withstood the test of time and even Robins's support of Harding, Coolidge, and Hoover. William Hard was a close personal friend of Secretary of State Cordell Hull, and through Hard, Robins found a receptive hearing, unlike his experience with Wilson's secretary of state, Robert Lansing. Hard, it will be remembered, was a veteran of the American Red Cross Commission, the author of *Raymond Robins' Own Story* (New York, 1920), and among the most dedicated in the long struggle for recognition.

"The friends of Russian Recognition in Washington have sent me a 'hurry up' call, and in view of our plans for the Russian visit, I have thought it best to respond," Robins reported to Levinson, in the middle of his flurry of activity.

I am leaving at noon tomorrow for Washington. . . . It is believed that this Administration believes in Recognition but the way to do it is confused with conflicting counsel. They have asked that I remain here for some weeks, say until the 10th of April hoping for action by that date, and failing this I am to go on to Moscow and do what I can there along the line we have discussed. All of this is of course CONFIDENTIAL.

Borah seems without special influence among those with whom I have talked in this Administration. There is a distinct mistrust of him and a tendency to leave him alone and take whatever comes from his cooperation or opposition as all in the days work.

Robins saw Senator Borah frequently, but concluded that although the new administration had virtually neutralized the influence of the once powerful "Lion of Idaho," "the hour will come when BORAH will be an important element in the success or failure of Roosevelt in the international field."[9]

Robins feared that while Roosevelt and Hull had "all the best intentions" on recognition, "there is a fatal tendency to take the step at a time method . . . which spells defeat." In another report to Levinson, Robins suggested the necessary course:

The same bold and direct action that Roosevelt has taken in the other [domestic] matters is demanded here. To get this I am now and have been since my arrival here seeking to secure. If we win the job is done after fifteen years of futility and witch-hunting in our diplomacy, and I will go to Russia fairly hopeful of results. . . . If we fail I shall go none the less and seek to make the approach to this goal from that end.

In this same letter Robins reflects (for the first time in his correspondence) on the rising tide of Nazism and anti-Semitism in Germany. He also demonstrates his perceptive understanding of the relationship between anti-Semitism in czarist Russia and the role of Jews in the Russian Revolution. "Anti-Semitism seems to me the supreme savagery of this age. It was the liberation from this immemorial threat over the lives and homes of the Jews in Russia that helped in my understanding and sympathy with the Soviet 'thieves murderers and German agents' amid the flaming fires of the Bolshevik revolt— which I knew was a fundamental REVOLUTION in the Russian land."[10]

On 9 April, four days before Robins sailed for Southampton, as fate would have it, on the *President Harding,* he shared with Elizabeth his innermost thoughts and expectations about what he would find in Stalin's Russia. In her last letter to him, dated 30 March, she had written about a published interview with a British engineer who had just returned from the Soviet Union and reported on brutal treatment of Russian workers. Robins was aware of such reports, and for more than three years, through Alex Gumberg, he had first-hand information on the purges that were shaking the Soviet state.

Gumberg's brother, Venjamin, had been a prominent member of the Bolshevik party well before the revolution and, until his arrest and exile to Siberia, had been vice-president of the Chemical Syndicate of the USSR.

His brother's exile was a bitter experience for Alex Gumberg, because he believed that his emigration to the United States and involvement in the highest circles of American capitalism was in part responsible for the suspicion cast on his brother. Robins and Alex Gumberg knew the complete innocence of Venjamin and the arbitrariness of Stalin's justice. Nevertheless, Alex remained a staunch advocate of American recognition of the Soviet Union while making every effort to exonerate his brother. It is not known whether or not Alex's efforts were effective, but some years later, Venjamin was "rehabilitated" and resumed a significant place in the Soviet government.[11]

On the eve of his trip to Russia, Robins was ill-informed about the hardships facing the Russian masses whose cause he had always championed. But his fifteen years of experience with misrepresentation and outright lies concerning the Russian Revolution and Bolshevik leadership made him skeptical of all negative reports on the Soviet Union. Only two years earlier, in 1931, Edgar Sisson's memoir of the Russian Revolution, *One Hundred Red Days,* was published along with the documents purporting to prove that Lenin and Trotsky "were thieves, murderers and German agents."[12] When Elizabeth wrote to him, giving credence to the engineer's account of hardship for Russian workers, Robins responded defensively, providing telling testimony to his outlook on the Soviet Union. "I would question if there was more force in the Russian labor situation than in Italy, Poland, and shortly or now is in Germany," he wrote, avoiding the harsher terms "oppression," or "slave labor."

> It is the hour of ruthlessness and FORCE in not a little of our world, and there may be quite as much incentive to individual excellence there [in the Soviet Union] as in considerable other areas where dictatorships of capitalists and hereditary privilege are not too gentle in their method of dominion. But always that sort of dictation will be better "pressed" in our capitalist prints tha[n] the Soviet brand. If we are to have dictatorships and suppression of all the guarantees of individual freedom we have in the past held so dear, I would be glad that one at least was so much in behalf of the group of toil that it held for twelve years the hatred and fear of all capitalist governments in all lands. This at least is true. I saw its birth and eight months of being closer possibly than any other Allied officer, I have tried to keep in fair touch with it ever since, and I now return to Moscow with more eager desire than I have ever returned to any land other than my native soil.[13]

Robins reached Moscow in time for the celebration of May Day. He had also been there on May Day in 1918. In 1933 the United States had still not recognized the Soviet Union, but the signs were more encouraging than at any other in the fifteen-year struggle. "These days are filled to overflowing,— All that can be done for me is being done," he wrote to Margaret of hopes of the moment and the honor being bestowed upon him. The portent of his return to Russia, May Day, emotions running high, recognition imminent—

they swept him off his feet. "A gorgeous morning and the whole city in gala dress, with the ancient land of the Muscovites robed in Red and the folks of the Soviet faith dreaming the Grand Dream," he wrote to Margaret in evangelical ecstasy, from Moscow.

> Ever since I boarded the S.S. Dzerjinsky I have been back again in the Russian land. That eager childlike faith,—and was it not as "little children" that another disturber of the people said folks should enter into the Kingdom—I found again on that ship, and in Leningrad and here in the shadow of the Kremlin, and Lenin's Tomb I find it yet again. The belief in *tomorrow*, in the day of Liberation, in the Good Time coming out of all the struggle and suffering of this present time and dark past,—this is the fundamental quality of the Soviet Mind! A vast Hope, however long delayed may be its realization, a Hope in which is the daring and the dreaming of a million years!

In his long letters to Margaret Robins chronicled with almost equal enthusiasm dozens of accomplishments of the Soviets. Education, culture, science, technology, agriculture, industry, military power, and political organization— from the Pioneer Youth and Communist Youth League to the Communist party, social and economic system, and national cohesion—all were areas in which advances could be seen. Of particular importance was the contrast Robins reported between the ideological foundation of the 1918 May Day and that of 1933. "Fundamental, underlying all the symbols in these two extraordinary demonstrations,—the first May Day and the fifteenth in the Soviet Union,—was a dominant note or motiv," he wrote to Margaret.

> In 1918 it was the Call to World Revolution to the proletariat of every nation, a sort of Macedonian Cry to all the working people of the earth to rise up in answer to and in support of the Russian Revolution. In 1933 it was a Call to the People of the Soviet Union to maintain and develop their industrial and cultural life, and a promise to defend their right to maintain and develop the Workers Republic, the Socialist State in their own land. In the first May Day the motiv was *international*, in the fifteenth it was *domestic*. The fundamental motiv in each celebration was cumulative and overwhelming. When the last banner passed the Reviewing Stand today the whole great pageant ended in a final cumulative note—Defend and Develop the Soviet Union. Stalin's pithy sentence was everywhere: "We want no foot of any other land, we will yield no inch of our own." All the bayonets and the banners, all the cavalry and the factory workers, all the tanks and the machines, all the guns and the shibboleths,—had a single final unity,—*Our Soviet Socialist Republic*, For It We Will Work, For It We Will Fight! It was the death of Trotskyism and the apotheosis of Stalinism.[14]

The spirit of jubilation that accompanied the grand celebrations at Red Square pervaded both his letters to Margaret and Elizabeth, as well as his many accounts of the trip that he presented upon his return to the United States. Robins was swept up by the dramatic personal importance of his return visit and by the possible impact it could have in finally realizing U.S. recognition. Given his personal and diplomatic agenda, there was no place in his approach to what he saw for a critical or analytical detachment and objective appraisal. He was therefore perfectly suited to convey to the West all of the essential messages that Stalin and the Politbureau wished to project there.

The litany of Soviet great achievements is quite predictable, but Robins's evaluation of the different "motivs" of the 1918 and 1933 May Days reveals just how carefully he was drawn into the service of very specific Soviet propaganda requirements. Never before in his life had Robins written the word "motiv" or "leitmotiv," a German word that had found its way into both English and Russian languages. Robins's three interpreters, Isaac Luknitsky, Tatiana Krasnoschokoba, and George Andreichin, in their highly sensitive political role, gave him "every advantage of skilled knowledge of people and places and able interpretations for conversations," which projected Stalin's "socialism in one country" principles and relegated Trotsky's international revolutionism to a place in history past.

During the two weeks he was in Moscow, Robins met with Spencer Williams of the American-Russian Chamber of Commerce, Anna Louise Strong of the *Moscow Daily News,* and many "gentlemen of the Foreign Press" representing the *Chicago Daily News,* the *New York Times,* the *Herald Tribune* and the Associated Press. He toured the city and, of course, went to Lenin's Tomb. "I have seen Lenin!" he proclaimed in his second long letter to Margaret, "Utterly lifelike, as if sleeping, face and features and hand as I saw him again and again in the great hours of the Year of the Revolution in Smolny and the Kremlin." It was an "unforgettable moment" before "the greatest revolutionary."

Robins was able to meet with a number of Soviet officials with whom he had worked fifteen years earlier ("Mr. Serebreakov and Mr. Yazikov, both in the department of roads construction and both old friends.") On 13 May, the day before setting off on his trip to the Soviet interior, Robins "spent over an hour with Commissair STALIN in the Kremlin. This is a record," he wrote to Elizabeth late that night, proud that he was deemed important enough to be granted such a rare and lengthy interview. He continued with this brief appraisal of Stalin: "There is an able man at the helm of the Soviet Union. Direct, quiet, unassuming, a master of detail, knowing his country and its people and the present outdoor facts better than anyone it seems to me that I have yet met. Commissair Litvinov and his assistant Karahan (the latter a close friend of the old Revolutionary period) have given me unhurried conferences."

Robins detailed meeting after meeting for Elizabeth, including his warm encounter with Karl Radek, whom he called the "Tom Paine of the Russian Revolution."

> Peters who was second in the Cheka when I was here in 1917–18 . . . has been a generous and informing friend.
> I have met with the correspondents of the foreign press some of them very hostile to the regime here, and Americans[,] workers and engineers and some

other foreigners with whom I have eaten and talked in freedom. Some of them are bitter against the Soviet and all its works. I go where I please day and night, with folks whom I choose. While it takes a pass to get into the more important factories, when I get in I go as I please with my own interpreter. I have been checked not once so far. . . . I wrote to you of my trip on which I start tomorrow. Sverdlovsk, Chelyabinsk, Magnitogorsk, Samara, Stalingrad, Rostov, Dnieperstroy, Kharkov back to Moscow.[15]

Upon his return to Moscow on 8 June, Robins found a letter from Elizabeth dated May 31 and added his amazement at the speed of the mails to his long list of "colossal" accomplishments of Soviet society since the revolution. Amid the same deluge of praise and enthusiasm with which he wrote to Levinson in Chicago, Elizabeth in London, and Margaret at Chinsegut, Robins in passing hinted at Stalin's repression, but, unperturbed, surged on with his tribute. "[A] peasant world turned upside down, a NEW ORDER OF THINGS visible, vibrant, clashing ruthlessly with the old order—YOUTH in the saddle and riding hard, ever at hand the RED soldier with his bayoneted gun fighting sabotage within and counter-revolution without." Again, in awe rather than with critical judgment, Robins described the Communist party's omnipotent and omnipresent role in terms both accurate and astute:

It is a confused, strange, wild, impossible thrilling scene. At the top two million COMMUNIST PARTY members, then four million Komsomols, then four million Young Pioneers. In every shop and factory they lead the Red Corner, on every State Farm and Collective they are the cutting edge of the workers, in every barracks they spur the laggards—shouting texts from the gospel of Marx and his prophet LENIN.[16]

Robins, like thousands of liberals and progressives of his generation who sought reconciliation with the Soviet Union in the face of red scare hysteria, for the moment brushed aside the nagging questions: Who were the saboteurs, counterrevolutionaries, and laggards? What were their specific crimes? How were they found out? How were they punished? The focus of Robins's concern was winning recognition.

He returned to the United States via England, with only the "briefest visit" with Elizabeth at Backsettown, her country home in Surrey, "to tell [her] . . . the Russian tale as it has been unfolded to me." The transatlantic voyage was again made on the *President Harding*, but this time while on board, Robins received a radio message concerning the successful negotiations of Raymond Moley, the American assistant secretary of state and representative at the London Economic Conference (along with William Bullitt) with Maxim Litvinov, the Soviet commissar for foreign affairs. An agreement had been reached between the Soviet Union and the United States on the sale of wheat on the world market. In his excitement, Robins had somehow misinterpreted part of the radio message and wrote to Levinson: "the recognition

of the Soviet Union was definitely determined upon by the Administration."[17]
While developments were moving ahead quickly, no such decision had yet
been made.

Within a day or two of his landing in New York, Robins was off and running in behalf of recognition, first to Baltimore to see Senator Borah, who
was recuperating from surgery, and then to Washington. On 13 July Robins
met twice, privately, with Secretary of Agriculture Henry A. Wallace. He
spoke with Commerce Secretary Daniel Roper, then with his old friend of
the Chicago days, Harold Ickes, secretary of the interior and, finally, with
Frances Perkins, secretary of labor. "The hearing was in the main ample," he
wrote confidentially to Gumberg, "but there is no assurance that the information reaches the centre [the president] or that I shall have direct communication there. . . . All are in favor of our position, but none ready to
DO anything about it."

Two days later, Robins had lunch with Ickes who was to be in conference
with Roosevelt, Rexford Tugwell, and the rest of the "braintrusters" later in
the day. Robins calculated that "six out of ten in the top circle" are with us.[18]
On 17 July, after receiving a second letter from Robins, Gumberg met with
Secretary of Labor Perkins and Philip La Follette in the hope that they could
arrange a meeting between Robins and President Roosevelt. Perkins managed
the appointment but at the last moment other matters prevailed in FDR's
schedule. Robins offered his thanks to Perkins and reiterated his commitment
to having such a meeting in a letter to Perkins, and went on to explain the
critical commercial and economic role of closer Soviet-American ties. He also
alluded to the Japanese threat and ambitions in the Far East at Russia's expense (without mentioning Japan by name), which he argued would be
thwarted by U.S. recognition. Finally, and particularly in light of Hitler having come to power in Germany the previous January, Robins suggested that
normalization of Soviet-American relations could not but help the cause of
world peace and reduce international tensions and the arms race.[19]

At 9:15 P.M., E.D.S.T., on 26 July, for the first time in his long public speaking career, Robins was given a nationwide radio audience. In light of his recent visit and meeting with Stalin (William Bullitt, who had been in Russia
at the same time, was not accorded the honor), the National Broadcasting
Company invited Robins to their Fifth Avenue studios in New York to speak
on Russia. Many passages of his speech were taken verbatim from his letters to Margaret and, like the letters, enthusiastically recounted the amazing
accomplishments in every aspect of Soviet society over the previous fifteen
years. Unlike his letters, he chose to defend Soviet socialism on a number of
important points. He wanted to believe that the "iron disciplined law and
order, and the first planned economy among the nations of the earth" were
positive developments. We can assume that the data and explanations carefully provided by his Intourist interpreters and guides were the basis of his
challenge to Western notions of a tyrannical Stalin dictatorship.

And this planned economy is not handed down from above by a committee of supermen as has been supposed, but comes up from individual factories, mines, farms and economic units, through communities, districts, states; and when it reaches Moscow more than a million minds have worked upon the details of this plan. And those who have submitted the plan have to share in carrying it out. With power goes responsibility throughout the Soviet Union.

In fifteen years the revolutionary Bolshevik power has become the oldest executive without substantial change among the governments of the world, and I could find nowhere anyone who knew or said he believed in any organized resistance against the Soviet Government throughout the Russian land.

The penal system of the Soviets has abolished all punitive elements. The whole method of their detention is educational and correctional. No one is treated as a sinner nor an outcast. They are dealt with as comrades who have been ill or unfortunate. They assume that the basis of all anti-socialist conduct is either ignorance, economic need or physical or mental defect.

Robins was prophetic in 1917, and to sustain the validity of that vision of the Bolshevik Revolution, he found himself obliged to defend Stalin. U.S.-Soviet rapprochement—recognition—demanded it. "There is a bitterness here among the anti-recognitionists that would stop at nothing to discredit any pro-recognitionist, and we must keep our powder dry and take no unnecessary chances," he had written to Gumberg ten days before the radio address. Robins did not witness the worst excesses already prevalent in the Soviet Union in 1933, nor the graver extremes that came in the years to follow, but he did tell his listeners about some of the price that had been paid by the Russian masses since 1917.

There has been terrible cost in freedom and life to the Russian people during these fifteen years. There have been hunger, bitter suffering, starvation and death to pay for the New Order of Things—that is rising out of the old Russia. Everywhere there is the presence of armed force, and propaganda is around the citizen from the cradle to the grave. Are the gains worth these colossal costs? That is a matter of personal opinion. Certain I am that no western nation (would) [struck out] could [in Robins handwriting] have paid the price the Russians have had to pay. Certain I am that we would not tolerate the Soviet system twenty-four hours in our America.

Reiterating the same advantages to be won by U.S. recognition of the Soviet Union that he presented in his letter to Secretary of Labor Perkins a week earlier, Robins concluded his radio address with a resounding: "Of course, we should recognize Russia!"[20]

By mid-August, the wheels were again set in motion for Robins to meet with Roosevelt on recognition, but the meeting did not take place until Friday, 13 October. On 9 October, arriving in New York after a series of speaking engagements, Robins received a telephone call from Secretary of State Hull, asking if he could come to Washington to discuss recognition. Robins left for the capital the following night and, on Wednesday, the eleventh he "had a full conference with the Secretary and was able to give him light . . . on several points in re the Soviet Union." More specifically, Hull, like every secretary of state since Lansing, was concerned about Soviet propaganda and revolutionary agitation and sought Robins's "light" on those dangers.

On Tuesday, 10 October, three days prior to Robins's meeting with Roosevelt, the president used the established indirect lines of communication to extend an invitation to Michael Kalinin, president of the All-Russian Central Executive Committee to send a Soviet representative to the United States for the purpose of holding discussions leading toward the exchange of U.S.-Soviet diplomatic representatives. Given the conference with Hull the following day and the close connection to Hull, through William Hard, Gumberg and Robins were doubtless aware, on 13 October, that this invitation had been made and that movement toward recognition was in high gear.

"On Friday . . . I had three quarters of an hour with the President, on the Russian issue," Robins wrote excitedly to Elizabeth, from their hometown, Louisville, a week later.

> Friendly and co-operative I found his mind, and toward me personally cordial and apparently confidential, with a trusting attitude. He gave over to me two propositions that seemed of first importance to get him the desired information. Leaving the White House I went at once to New York City, got Gumberg and the head of Amtorg Trading Company, [Peter] Bogdanov, and the head of the Russian press service in the U.S. my old friend Durant and we worked that night and the next day. . . . We cabled Stalin direct (")) 9% 5&8# ?9:%8$3:58") [sic] which should read, (ALL OF THIS CONFIDENTIAL) and I was able to mail to the President before I left for Chicago the information and assurance desired. The end of the interview with the President spelled VICTORY for the fifteen years struggle on the Russian question. However I did not dare to wire you then, lest it occasion trouble.[21]

Robins does not mention the specific nature of the "information and assurance," but given Hull's concerns at the meeting on the eleventh, propaganda and revolutionary agitation appear to be the probable issues.

On 20 October headlines nationwide announced the breaking story that Roosevelt had invited the Soviets to send a representative for discussions on establishing diplomatic relations. "How I hope and pray that we shall have recognized the Soviet Union before the next war begins," Robins wrote to Senator Borah on the eve of the arrival of Soviet Foreign Commissar Maxim Litvinov, who was to serve as the Soviet negotiator. "As the Europeans' contradictions stand, a next war seems inevitable." The Soviet-American talks began in Washington on 8 November. On 11 November Robins was in the capital, and while not participating directly in the formal discussions, he did meet "with some of the officials of our government" and privately with Litvinov. "It was a happy meeting," he wrote to Elizabeth. "Litvinov was very sceptical when we talked in Moscow—he admitted generously that I was right and he wrong when we talked of the prospects of RECOGNITION by the U.S. . . . I was able I think to help iron out one or two little snarls."

On 16 November the United States and the Soviet Union exchanged notes of agreement, which formally initiated diplomatic relations, with William C. Bullitt and Alexander Troyanovsky named the U.S. and Soviet ambassadors respectively. "At last—VICTORY!" Robins began a letter to Elizabeth the following day. "Sixteen years of struggle abuse and defeat ending in TRIUMPH! Roosevelt has been weather wise in his method, has parried all the blows of the opposition, and acts at last with the support of the country. He is as Harold Ickes declared 'a superb politician.'" While Borah, Gumberg, Ickes, Levinson, and others among the veteran "recognitionists" (including Robins, in his heart of hearts) had quietly hoped that Robins might be appointed the first U.S. ambassador to the Soviet Union, Robins was convinced that Bullitt was "a good selection . . . I am glad Roosevelt sent him." In fact, six months earlier, while in Moscow, with no apparent authoritative information other than his own political instincts, Robins had assured Charles H. Smith of the Associated Press that Bullitt would be given the post.[22]

On 24 November, eight days after recognition was a fact, the Russian-American Chamber of Commerce sponsored a banquet in the grand ballroom of the Waldorf-Astoria Hotel in honor of Litvinov, who was to leave for the Soviet Union the following day. The 1,700 people in attendance heard the band play the national anthem and the "Internationale," and Litvinov and Robins spoke; in the background, "the stars and stripes were crossed with the hammer and sickle on its red field."

What led to the decision by President Roosevelt finally to recognize the Soviet Union? It is far too simple to attribute it to the meetings that had been held earlier that year at the London Economic Conference between Raymond Moley and Litvinov on the question of wheat sales, as has been suggested by a number of authors.[23] We have seen that six out of ten of the Roosevelt cabinet and "brain trust," as well as Roosevelt himself, favored recognition from the first. Their reasons coincide significantly with those pressed upon them by the "recognitionists," most notably, reasons of U.S. security. Also among the important considerations, especially if one judges from the press, was the depression and the hope that economic recovery would be aided through increased trade with the Soviet Union.

Robins's report on the dynamism of the Soviet economy could only have lent support to the already strong lobbying for recognition from a number of American business interests, particularly the machine-tool and agricultural implement industries. The rising tide of fascism in Europe had long since drawn the concern of all but the most fanatic anticommunists in both the business and political arenas in the United States, and with Hitler's appointment to the chancellorship just ten months earlier, the Roosevelt administration demonstrated a new urgency for involving the Soviet Union in securing the peace. Similarly, the growing threat of an expanding Japanese empire in Asia necessitated the inclusion of the Soviet Union in the international community of legitimate states, in part as a warning against Japanese aggression against Soviet Pacific maritime provinces. While this latter consideration was uppermost in the minds of Soviet leaders and was put forward specifically in Litvinov's note of diplomatic exchange on 16 November, U.S. policy in Asia also demanded a curb on further Japanese expansion.[24]

The Democratic administration had let a year pass after taking office; it had not rushed blindly into recognition, but by the fall, the time was ripe.

"I cannot now tell the tale of the END in GLORIOUS TRIUMPH of a long trail," Robins wrote to Elizabeth, after describing the grandeur of the banquet celebration for Litvinov. "I suppose that it [recognition] was noticed in all the capitals of the world, but how much I cannot guess—not TOO much surely—," he reflected wistfully, "except in Moscow. Well it is DONE. Amen." And soon thereafter he asked: "Is there anything of *real* value in my tale?"

"Regarding the effect upon my personal career of this Russian incident and its happy termination, there will not be much of any effect I judge," he confided in the 17 November letter to his sister, the day after the recognition agreement, the excitement still pervasive. "If it does not help my lecture work, it will pass with very little effect at all. In my own consciousness it is very helpful, as it has proved my continuing usefulness in important affairs. Beyond that—NAUGHT!"

The serious financial problems that began with the 1929 crash had not abated and his only recourse was the lecture circuit. "Russia—After Fifteen Years," his subject since his return, had put him before record-breaking audiences from coast to coast, but the engagements were few in number and had little impact on easing the money problems. "From now on it is all a toss, either there will be more interest in the Soviet Union, or as the matter is settled *less*, and the public mind move to the next unsolved problem. . . . I am doing my best and Pond [Lyceum Bureau] is doing his—with poor results."[25]

Robins's gloomy words may be seen as a reflection of his old problems with depression, but at sixty years of age, in financial trouble, the campaign for recognition of the Soviet Union finally accomplished, his popularity as a public speaker sullied by the sensationalized press reports of his amnesia and the frequent accusation that he was a communist apologist, Robins had good reason to take stock of his life and question its *"real"* value." Even more painful was the full realization that the sacrifices Margaret had made in their marriage and reform partnership had cost her a terrible price. "She endured my absence around the world for seven months," he wrote to Levinson,

> my absence on war work in Russia for thirteen months, my absence for four months on the return to Russia in 1933—not only without protest, but with hearty support and steady good cheer. I have long known that my illness and silent absence for two and a half months in 1932, was a strain from which she has never recovered. . . . In our thirty years of loving loyalty and common

work together, I have not before known Margaret under such stress of body, mind and spirit as holds her now.

Margaret was sixty-six years old when this was written and Robins hoped, finally, to fulfill the vow he had made after recuperating from amnesia, "that the rest of my life should have one first obligation—unfailing tenderness and daily support of the welfare and happiness of Margaret Dreier Robins." Disregarding the financial difficulties, still troubling in 1935, he cancelled all speaking engagements through the Pond Lyceum Bureau; he would not accept Levinson's earnest offer that he lead the Chicago Anti-Nazi Executive Committee delegation to the London Nonsectarian Anti-Nazi Conference, "to put every ounce of pressure we can upon Hitler" through a program of educational, political, and economic action.

Levinson hoped that Robins would travel the well-established lecture circuit with a powerful antifascist, anti-Nazi message. "Once you get turned loose over there, particularly among the trade unions and church people . . . you will have a wide range of policies and objectives and you will be able to make not only a reputation for yourself but the rendition of service beyond price." Robins resisted the challenge and remained with Margaret at Chinsegut to care for her and work the land.[26]

Throughout his life, Robins loved to immerse himself in farm labor: planting, weeding, and tending animals and trees. It was a glorious release of the physical energy that he had in abundance but seldom had opportunity to use; his speaking and political work taxed only his intellectual and nervous energy. In 1921, after the Harding presidential election campaign, he had returned to the manual labor on the hilltop, but had overdone it and that, in part, brought on his most serious breakdown. In 1933, as part of his regimen of recuperation from amnesia, he exercised and did farm work. "I like it immensely," he wrote to Elizabeth at the time, "only I am not so strong nor clearheaded when high up a ladder as in the old days. But it is very good for me, as I see things in a tree that our father saw . . . and these trees now belong to this Sanctuary—FOREVER."[27]

At 2:30 in the afternoon on 21 September 1935, while on a ladder pruning one of those trees, Robins fell and broke three vertebrae in his back, which left him paralyzed from the pelvis down. He spent three months flat on his back in the Tampa Municipal Hospital, and for at least four years thereafter, he struggled with agonizing pain and one medical treatment and therapy after another in the effort to beat the paralysis. No improvement ever came. During the search for a cure and for the rest of his life, Robins fought for the physical mobility that his legs would not provide. With the zealous determination that characterized the social and political campaigns of his youth, in old age he fiercely struggled to move about the house, grounds, and countryside of Brooksville. Using crutches, a wheelchair, ramps, a Chevrolet pickup truck, a "walker," a hand-propelled tricycle, and with his feet strapped into the stirrups of "Sunny Jim," he won the fight round by round.

Robins standing proud in his walker four years after the "smashup" which left him paralyzed from the waist down. This snapshot, taken at Chinsegut, was attached to a letter Robins wrote to Elizabeth on 1 March 1939. (Courtesy of the Elizabeth Robins Papers, Fales Library, New York University.)

Robins's first letter to Elizabeth after the accident was written "on the ceiling as it were," two months after the fall, while still on his back in a hospital bed. He explained many of the details of his condition, showing fortitude and good humor, but he could not resist sharing his observations on the forthcoming presidential elections. "The political pot boils furiously. Borah will *not* be nominated. Nor I think will Hoover. Vandenberg [Arthur H.] of Michigan (Senator) has a real chance but were I to wager at this time I would split my money between Frank Knox and Landon." Writing on 22

November 1935, eight full months before the Republican convention, Robins won double the bet. Alfred M. Landon was the Republican presidential candidate and Knox was his running mate.[28]

The scenario never changed for the rest of Robins's life. He disregarded his handicap as much as he could, worked diligently to be informed on national and international developments, and remained a knowledgeable and deeply involved observer and advisor on every issue on which he had been an active participant. Books (more than 8,000 volumes filled the shelves of Chinsegut by the time of his death in 1954), newspapers (*New York Times*, the *Chicago Sun*, and numerous others daily), and journals of politics and opinion (*Time*, *The Nation*, *New Republic*, *Atlantic*, *Saturday Review of Literature*) filled his days. From the hilltop flowed a formidable correspondence with all the friends and fellow crusaders of the past, and Robins initiated many new relationships. One of the most notable was that with the junior senator from Florida, Claude Pepper. Robins struck up a correspondence in 1937, which soon led to a close friendship. Robins had hopes that Pepper would be "a dark horse . . . to take his place in time among the great presidents."[29]

The most important political decision Robins had to make after his "smash-up," as he called it, was who to support and vote for in the 1936 election. He had been a Democrat in Chicago before 1912 and had stumped for William Jennings Bryan in California in 1896. His involvement in Teddy Roosevelt's bid for the presidency in 1912 drew him into alliance with Democrats and liberal Republicans who had left conservative Taft behind. Twenty-four years later, after identifying himself as the prolabor, proreform "recognitionist" advisor to three Republican administrations, Raymond was joined by Margaret Dreier Robins in support of FDR and the New Deal, and returned to the Democratic fold.[30]

Margaret and Raymond were disillusioned at the failure of their reform agenda during the World War and for the twelve long years of the Harding, Coolidge, and Hoover administrations. The Robinses had campaigned for the three Republicans with all their might, although with painful ambivalence and little heart. The inauguration of the reform era of the New Deal found the Robinses excluded by their history of support for "normalcy" Republicans for so long. Nevertheless, many of their closest friends and allies of the Chicago Progressive years entered New Deal administrations, most notably Secretary of the Interior Harold Ickes and Secretary of Labor Frances Perkins, and through them, the Robinses, during their years of retirement at Chinsegut, managed to bring their reform thinking to the New Deal policymakers. While some particular appointments and policies of Franklin Roosevelt did not receive their support, by the end of Roosevelt's first term they embraced the New Deal and celebrated its fulfillment of countless policies and programs they had fought for as progressives. "As the record now stands, I would vote for Roosevelt," Robins wrote to his most trusted political alter ego Gumberg, less than a year after the accident.

I would do this more on account of Russia than for any other one reason. All the witch hunters will be for Landon. Hearst I regard as insane from the property mind fear. I do not regard Landon as either controlled by Wall Street, or the natural servant of Privilege. I regard him as a distinct gain over the last three Republican presidents. Roosevelt is wholly politically minded, knows nothing of economics and less of finance. There is a quality in his nature of seeming insincerity that troubles me, but he seems to have committed his fortunes to a sentimental sympathy with Labor, Farmers and the underdog, and he has more courage when it comes to the taboo of Big Business and Bankers, than any man who has been President in my day. And he did recognize Russia![31]

Because Robins knew many of the leading Bolsheviks personally in 1917–18 and renewed that sympathetic relationship during his three-month visit in 1933, he was frequently queried about the puzzles and incomprehensibility of the purges, "show trials," and extraordinary, if not unbelievable, confessions of dedicated Communists who had sacrificed their lives for the cause of the Russian Revolution. In 1936 the purges undermined not only the Communist Party of the Soviet Union (CPSU) and the Soviet state, but the international Communist movement. Robins responded to such questions from John Dewey, in May 1937. In addition to insights on Trotsky's personality, Dewey wanted clarification on the whys and wherefores of the show trials. Robins, like so many noncommunist sympathizers of the Soviet Union, would only admit his own bewilderment to his most likeminded friends, Gumberg and Mary Dreier. Robins walked a tightrope between justification of Stalin's acts and trying to present an objective analysis. The Russian demand for solidarity in the face of the imminent threat of Nazi and Japanese aggression remained a nagging obstacle to such objectivity.

> What I know of these men [Zinoviev, Kamenev, Radek, Pyatakov, Serebryakov] personally, and what their confessions seem to me to portray is that their attitude towards Stalin changed with the seeming success or failures of Stalin's leadership. . . . Opposing Stalin during his struggle for power, they are banished so soon as he is victorious. Then after some months, when it appeared that Stalin's policy was successful, these men recanted, returned to Moscow and accepted important political offices under the Stalin government. Then when the stress of agricultural industrialization and the campaign against the Kulaks seemed to threaten Stalin's success, they again secretly joined in the opposition. In 1936 Stalin's success and the failure of their own plans brought them to confessions of error once again,—but this time too late.
>
> Perhaps the controlling fact in this whole matter to me is that Stalin and the Soviet Government alone face with *power* the threat of Fascist and Nazi dominion throughout Europe. . . . [T]he one effective barrier to the triumphant march of military imperialism over Europe and the Orient is Stalin and the Soviet Government. Trotsky and the Trotskyites weaken the Soviets and aid the Nazi and fascist dictators.[32]

Four months earlier, in January, when Robins wrote to Gumberg, whose sympathy for Russia and the revolution was unshakable, he expressed thoughts and feelings he would not share with Dewey. "The bringing of Radek and Serebryakov to trial under such charges makes me sick at heart." And, about his friend Radek, he wrote: "If they put out the light of that rare international intelligence, it would seem that the ancient Hebrew should run against the masters of these proceedings. . . . It is this sort of persecution that was the curse of the Inquisition and of all the other theological proscriptions of human history."[33]

One month later, again writing to Gumberg and full of joy in expectation of the visit of Alex and his wife, Frances Adams, Robins expressed his political credo based on faith in human freedom. "And because of this Faith, I oppose all regimentations of man by his fellows—and regard all force systems, fascism, Nazisms, and communisms BY FORCE, as an old failure in the age long struggle for 'a more abundant life.'"[34] A few days later, Robins wrote again to Gumberg, explaining the central fact that shaped his thinking on the Soviet Union for the rest of his life.

> I have steadily believed that something of great moment to the advance of human civilization, something that would result in the creative release of the power and beauty in the individual human spirit was potential in THE NEW ORDER, building in the Russian world. If this has ceased to be true in the Russia of Stalin NOW, then I must suffer the greatest personal disappointment of my life, and the SUPREME PROMISE of this generation will be unfulfilled, dissipated and betrayed.[35]

In April 1937, the Soviet ambassador to the United States arrived for a visit at Chinsegut. Because travel for Robins was a hardship, the guest book quickly filled with the names of many notables who wanted a personal word with Robins. "Yesterday Alexander Troyanovsky and his secretary Mr. Haskel were here for dinner," Robins wrote to Mary Dreier. "We had a fine talk, and the more I see of this quiet clearheaded Ambassador of the Soviet Union the better I like him. Margaret and he were snapped under the LENIN oak. So has the representative of the Peasants and Workers of the Russian land found his way to Chinsegut Hill in the U.S.A. It's a far cry from the Red Guard—he served in it—and the wind swept steppes of the Siberian plain, to this land of the Shining Pines."[36]

However, only two months earlier, Robins had pleaded with Gumberg to use "any influence with Troyanovsky" to have him "use all the grip he has to prevent more of the type of 'Moscow Trials,'" since they were "very helpful to the fascists and imperialists in all lands." Troyanovsky had no such influence and, later, was himself removed from his position.[37]

On 29 November 1937, through Robins's and Gumberg's introduction, Salmon Levinson had a two-hour private conference with Troyanovsky. Levinson came prepared with documentation and a novel solution to the liquidation of the $192 million Russian debt to the United States. One of the major stumbling blocks to the full resumption of diplomatic and commercial relations between the United States and the Soviet Union from 1917 on was the outstanding debt, which the leaders of the Bolshevik Revolution had declared void. They would not fulfill the fiscal obligations of either the czarist or Provisional governments.

To further the cause of peace and to bring the United States and Soviet Union closer together in the face of the growing threat of Nazi aggression, Levinson devised a symbolic plan of compromise that would permit a portion of the debt to be paid and clean the slate for future Soviet loans and trading partnerships. Troyanovsky's initial response to the proposal was open and interested, and Levinson's expectation for achieving the long-sought solution was keen, particularly since the ambassador had been friendly, outgoing, and had given two full hours to hearing the plan. But Levinson's efforts to get another appointment with the ambassador failed, as did his efforts to elicit any response to the proposal. Facing a dead end, Levinson wrote a six-page report for Robins and asked for his advice and help.

Nothing ever came of Levinson's initiative. However, this episode and others like it allowed Robins to remain an active and involved participant in many important developments during his years of retirement at Chinsegut. His access to Troyanovsky through his well-established record of knowledgeable and competent service in the cause of Soviet-American friendship, and his personal relationship with the ambassador, gave great weight to his advice and influence.[38]

Throughout the late 1930s and 1940s, Robins's typewriter was seldom silent. Except for his three serious bouts with influenza and a close-call appendectomy, he was forever busy hammering out letters to Elizabeth, Mary, Gumberg, and Levinson. Robins ignored the constant suggestions that he write a book—an autobiography—or work with a biographer.[39] As situations warranted, the circle of correspondents grew larger and developments in the international arena drew his attention, critical analysis, and occasionally his prophetic vision.

He followed the painful stages of the Spanish civil war, condemning the "ostrich" neutrality of the United States, Britain, and France with almost as much venom as the "phoney" neutrality of Nazi Germany and Fascist Italy, which poured assistance into the cause of Francisco Franco. Every appeasement of nazism and fascism drew his wrath, from the remilitarization of the Rhineland to the "deliberate sellout and betrayal of democratic principles and individual freedom" of the Munich Agreement.[40]

Of course, the Soviet Union always preoccupied Robins. "I have the Anniversary Issue of the *Moscow News*—the paper that Anna Louise Strong founded. To read it turns my stomach," he wrote to Mary in disgust.

> It is seeking to vitalize the Stalin lie, that he and not Trotsky was the leading Comrade of LENIN in the Great October Revolution. Thank God there are enough records of those SUPREME DAYS to insure that the *fact* and not this *lie* shall live outside of Russia. How terrible when the machinery of a great people's government is devoted to the *falsification* of HISTORY, and the record of the Great

Adventure of a thousand years is sought to be written in LIES! I wonder what Anna Louise Strong would say if we could see and talk with her—outside of Russia? I do not say this out loud, as despite this LIE, Stalin and the Soviet Government and its people ALONE—face with effective FORCE the Fascist Tide in Europe and the Orient. On this record the leadership of Stalin will perish and that of Trotsky will live forever. YOU know how hard it is for me to write this—but on the record now before me it is the TRUTH.[41]

In May of 1939, as the disastrous and inevitable logic of the Munich Agreement gave Hitler more and more of what he demanded, Robins received news that Alex Gumberg had suddenly died of a heart attack. "So passes my Comrade of the Great Adventure," Robins wrote to Mary of the loss of his closest male friend.

Wise, courageous with a patient ardor for the economic liberation of the Group of Toil, Gumberg was the ablest of all my associates in those MIGHTY DAYS that shook the world. . . . He nearly broke up my Mission, when I took him on as my private secretary. Those who denounced him and threatened mutiny, learned to trust him quite as much as I did, and perhaps more. He knew LENIN well, and Trotsky like a book. He did more to save the Revolution in its hours of greatest need than any man outside the inner circle at Smolney and the Kremlin. One of the hopes that now passes unfulfilled into the infinite yesterdays, was to visit Russia with Alexander Gumberg, and compare the Russia of the Revolution with the Russia of today.[42]

Several days later, Robins acknowledged receipt of the telegram from Floyd Odlum, president of Atlas Corporation, informing him of Gumberg's death. Robins's letter to Odlum is a tribute to Gumberg and a fitting obituary.

Alexander Gumberg was the best informed, and most luminous, loyal and courageous intelligence in all the Allied embassies and missions in Petrograd during the most critical months of the Russian Soviet Revolution. On intimate personal terms with Lenin, Trotsky, Djerjinsky and Chicherin he knew every member of the First Council of the Peoples Commissars. Loving his native land, yet wholly loyal to his adopted country, he worked valiantly for understanding and economic cooperation between the struggling Russian Soviets and these United States. He returned with me to his adopted country seeking to help in the true interpretation of the significance then and in the near future of the people, resources and government of Russia under the Soviets for America and the world. In the long struggle to secure formal recognition of the Soviet government by our government his was the ablest and most continuous effort.

Coming to these United States a poor emigrant lad, Alexander Gumberg won the trust and admiration of men and women of the first rank in business, finance, journalism, politics, literature and the drama; and quickened every circle in which he appeared by his intelligent appreciation and mordant humour. He was rarely gifted for enduring friendship and those who share the sorrow for his loss are legion. When Alexander Gumberg passed over the Great Divide the clearest light on Soviet Russia went out, and a brave, wise, resourceful and generous personality passed into the Great Silence.[43]

Robins's anticipation of a visit from Gumberg two years earlier barely suggests the importance of their relationship to Robins. "Almost twenty years I have known and trusted and loved Alexander Gumberg," Robins wrote to Alex shyly, using the full proper name to avoid the too intimate "you," "sharing as we have in the Hope of this Supreme Revolution of all time, having known LENIN and his matchless mind and daring in the service of the liberation of the Group of Toil—we thank our lucky stars and go forward without fear to the end of our journey on this third planet from the Sun."[44]

Not only did Robins lose a dear friend, but "Since the death of Alexander Gumberg I have felt isolated from vital contacts with the realities in progress in the Russian land." With Gumberg's extraordinary direct and indirect contacts with Soviet decisionmakers, Robins had available information unique for an American-born private citizen. With Gumberg's death the "clearest light on Soviet Russia" did indeed go out, and Robins was pushed yet further to the sidelines of Soviet-American relations.[45]

Gumberg's death, at fifty-two years of age and in good health, was a shock and a great blow to Robins. Struggling against paralysis for nearly four years, Robins's suffering, vulnerability, life, and death had been the focus of the two friends. Gumberg, fourteen years younger, had been a safe haven, a secure mooring during the many times of trouble from as early as Petrograd in 1917 to the years following the "smashup," when poor health and age took their toll on Robins.

In 1941 Margaret suffered a stroke and a serious heart attack. She had had a bad leg injury, a dangerous infection, and years of debilitation following Robins's "smashup." Margaret was bedridden in her room on the second floor of the house at Chinsegut and Lisa von Borowsky, Margaret's secretary and sanctuary horticulturist for nearly twenty years, cared for her as would a daughter. Each day, "by the strength of his giant arms," Robins slowly made his way up the stairs to spend some hours with his ailing wife, who many times was unable to acknowledge his presence.

Margaret was well enough through the last years of her life to struggle with Raymond through the complexities and implications of the Nazi-Soviet Pact and the U.S. role in the war and rejoice with him, particularly with the Russian success at Stalingrad, over the Allied victory against the Axis powers. Like so many progressives, the feat accomplished by the Red Armies at Stalingrad went far in changing Robins's appraisal of Stalin. Soviet sympathizers in the West and former Communist party members, who either broke with the Communist party or condemned Stalin's purges or the Nazi-Soviet pact, carried out a similar reappraisal in the aftermath of that notorious battle.

Upon greeting the headlines: "STALINGRAD SIEGE ENDS," on 25 November 1942, Robins dispatched an emotional letter to Elizabeth reveling in the implications and historic significance.

If true—then Hitler has lost the second Russian Campaign, and Stalin has won the War, *his part of it.* . . . One of the most curious and interesting events has also happened in this connection: *a lie has been transformed into the truth!* The one sign all over Russia when I returned in 1933 that angered me beyond telling was this—Lenin-Stalin *Lenin-Stalin* LENIN-STALIN. It was everywhere and the inference and spoken meaning given it was that they were the TWO MEN who made the Soviet Revolution, which was an unmitigated LIE. . . . And now this lie has been made historic truth for all the future story of the Soviets—history will say "'Lenin-Stalin,' Lenin the creator and Stalin the preserver—Lenin the Washington, Stalin the Lincoln of the Soviet State."[46]

During those difficult years, Margaret's condition and the Allied war effort were Robins's preoccupations. He often reported proudly to Elizabeth, who had returned to the United States soon after the outbreak of the war, on his struggles and victories against immobility. Only occasionally did he fall into self-pity or fantasize a life free of his condition. "Raymond broken in his early boyhood growing up in the back woods of Florida uneducated," he wrote to "BELOVED BIG SISTER," in 1942,

having a flare for action and adventure, just missing high success several times, broken in body and pocket book at 69 living on at the cost of others incapable by physical disability of action in the Supreme struggle of a thousand years [the Allied cause]—Were I well I would have been either Ambassador or President's special agent to Russia and sharing importantly in mighty days just before his threescore and ten—finishing in the back woods of Florida a burden to himself and others.[47]

On 21 February 1945, just a few months before their fortieth wedding anniversary, Margaret died "without pain and passed from mortal sleep over the GREAT DIVIDE," Raymond wrote to Elizabeth.

She was buried this morning at Sunrise under the Altar Oak [on the hilltop, near the house], Rev. Fletcher Weston with a simple and genuine religious service. Only this household, white and black. . . . She rested in her coffin all night in the Kentucky Room, and this morning at 7:15 we all, white and black, filed by and took a last look over the mortal remains of Margaret Dreier Robins. A prayer, a song, some verses of scripture, a few words from me, then a song, Margaret's body lowered into its final resting place, just as the SUN came over the horizon—and the household covered . . . her coffin with blossoming branches—and the mortal tale of MY MARGARET was ENDED.[48]

Robins lived for nine more years after Margaret's death, finally joining her beneath the Altar Oak and over the Great Divide on 26 September 1954, a week after his eighty-first birthday. Elizabeth died in England at ninety years of age on 8 May 1952.

Epilogue

DURING those last years at Chinsegut, Robins railed against the growing Cold War and anticommunist hysteria that prevailed over reasoned resolution of American-Soviet differences and the flagrant violation of civil liberties nationwide. Between 1945 and 1954 the American ambassador in Moscow and the ambassador of the Soviet Union in Washington actually met and communicated directly with the governments to which they were assigned. But in countless other respects, in Robins's view, U.S. foreign policy toward the Soviet Union following World War II was no different from Woodrow Wilson's misguided, aggressive, interventionist policy following World War I.

Even on the domestic scene, Wilson's "red scare" attorney general, A. Mitchell Palmer, was more than matched by Sen. Joseph McCarthy. However, unlike 1918–20, the years after World War II demonstrated that the Soviet-American relationship has become the central concern of global survival. "To prevent the THIRD WORLD WAR and the use of the ATOMIC BOMB for the death and destruction of Mankind and all his works, is the most important task before all thoughtful and informed men and women in all lands," Robins wrote in 1946.[1] Repetition of the anti-Soviet World War I mistakes would not have such limited repercussions if repeated after World War II.

Jerome Davis, the noted journalist who covered the Soviet Union in the 1930s and 1940s and Robins's friend and correspondent, wrote of his teaching experience at Hiram College in 1947. He had his history class read the stenographic notes of Robins's 22 March 1919 address to the League of Free Nations Association on Russia. "It is a fact that considering the hysteria of the present hour," Davis wrote to Robins, "your remarks are strangely apropos of the crisis which Truman has thrust on us. The boys saw the parallel between our going in and fighting the Bolsheviks in 1918 and our Greek and Turkey program. We have the opportunity today to give Russia a loan and be friends or fight them around the world and we have chosen the latter."[2]

The Soviet-American "friendship" of World War II began souring well before the war had ended. Sharing a common enemy was no basis for a lasting friendship. Robins constantly weighed the American and Soviet contributions to the origins of the Cold War and, in his correspondence and conversation, tried to untie the dangerous knot of confrontation. Hadn't Stalin signed the nonaggression pact with Hitler that provided the "green light" for starting the war? Hadn't the appeasement policy been directed, at least in part, at fulfilling Hitler's expansionist ambitions to the east at the expense of the Soviets? Had the American and British Allies delayed the initiation of the second front in the west to force Russia to bear the brunt of destroying the Nazi armies? Were the Communists determined to overthrow all Western democracies at all costs? Was the West committed to destroying the Communist threat?

These questions were central to the growing fears that developed after the war and culminated in McCarthyism's powerful grip on American domestic politics. In spite of his old age and infirmity, Robins joined another crusade, another campaign—to stem the postwar tide of red-baiting, to bring the truth about the Soviet Union to the American people, and to stop the Cold War and find a mutually beneficial and cooperative basis for American-Soviet relations. Robins kept his typewriter in high gear, searching for and finding new, young, capable allies to add to the ranks of the veterans like himself. He sorely missed and mourned his dead friends, particularly Gumberg, but determined, he continued his personal campaign for social justice, racial understanding, and peace. When he found kindred spirits, he wrote and enlisted in their cause, or used all his powers of language to add new recruits to his own cause.

"I am reading with immense satisfaction and no little surprise, your VERY GREAT BOOK 'SOVIET POLITICS at Home and Abroad,'" he began a four-page, single-spaced letter in large typeface to Frederick Schuman, in October 1946. (Robins reserved this typewriter for only the most important correspondence.) "It is a masterpiece of historic accuracy," Robins continued, "comprehensive understanding and profound sense of the meaning of obscure FACTS, that affect the WORLD PEACE and the future welfare of mankind." He wrote to offer his help for the book's "largest possible circulation," and to invite Schuman to visit Chinsegut so that "we can talk over some of the persons and events in which my knowledge was personal and direct."[3]

Robins wanted to befriend Schuman and help him in his attack on Cold War policy and interpretations of history. Robins also raised the possibility that Schuman might consider writing a biography of either or both Margaret and himself. Only three months earlier, Sherwood Eddy had added his plea to the growing list of those who were anxious to write a Raymond Robins's biography, but Schuman's achievements as a well-respected and widely read "progressive" (in the 1940s, read pro-Soviet) scholar, drew Robins to him as a prospective biographer, although to no avail.

In 1946 appeared yet another book that drew an even more excited response from Robins. Michael Sayers and Albert E. Kahn's *The Great Conspiracy Against Russia* had been in preparation for more than three years, and from the first, during the rising wartime tide of Soviet-American friendship and cooperation, the authors had consulted and been in correspondence with Robins. As the title suggests, the book was intended as a vindication and defense of Soviet domestic and foreign policy and as an indictment of American, British, and French policy toward the Soviet Union. In November 1943, as the Allied victory in Europe drew near, they asked Robins about his judgment of the mass support of the Bolsheviks in 1917; his explanation for the "deliberate campaign following your return to the U.S. in 1918 to prevent your message from reaching the American people"; whether the Russians want peace; and "What forces in the world were primarily responsible for the continually inciting antagonism against the Soviet Union since November, 1917?"

Robins's answer to the first question had not changed at all over the years, but his answer to the second had taken on an anticapitalist and anti-Catholic dimension that had not been present in the 1920s.

> 1st. British and French Intelligence Services, which steadily held to the Czarist Russian views on the Soviet Revolution and greatly influenced our State and War departments.
>
> 2nd. The Roman Catholic Hierarchy, which saw in LENIN'S Marxian Program the most powerful anti-authoritarian-church influence and possible power since the Germanic Reformation.
>
> 3rd. The fear of Capitalism in all lands that Communism and the success of the Producers Republic, would destroy its power for the exploitation of labor and raw materials for PRIVATE PROFIT; and thus gave color and tone to the Capitalist press throughout the world.[4]

In the 1930s, Robins made every effort to counter the predictable misrepresentation of the Soviet Union. Like many Progressive movement veterans and noncommunist sympathizers of the Soviets, he felt compelled to keep his doubts and fears of Stalin's totalitarianism to himself and to only one or two trusted friends. But in the aftermath of World War II, in the context of the extraordinary Soviet sacrifice made in the defeat of Nazism, Robins's pro-Soviet perspective became more dogmatic. Like many in the camp of noncommunist Soviet sympathizers, well-represented by those who endorsed *The Great Conspiracy,* Robins became a thorough apologist of Stalin's Russia and accepted almost all of the Communist party line. Particularly unsettling is Robins's final acceptance of the Stalinist explanation of the purges and the extraordinary, paranoid accusations against Trotsky, which fill one-third of the book. The Cold War had so polarized positions that Robins, now nearing seventy-five, found no room for a critical approach to Soviet policy.

While the thesis of a conspiracy against Russia can be supported on the basis of evidence and Robins's eyewitness experience, Sayers and Kahn produced many seriously flawed chapters, full of unsubstantiated accusations and anti-Trotskyite diatribe, completely in harmony with the contemporary Communist party line.

The Great Conspiracy was first published in a $3.50 edition, which was followed only a few months later by a $1.00 newsprint edition to stimulate a wider circulation. Among its notable endorsers was the former ambassador to the Soviet Union, Joseph E. Davies, who was quoted on the cover of the newsprint edition:

> Nothing is more important to Peace than that the public . . . should know the facts which, in the past, have justified Soviet suspicions of the Western Powers. . . . It is a very valuable contribution as the background for an understanding of one of the most serious situations which probably has ever confronted us, namely, the preservation of good relations with the Soviet Union.[5]

Sen. Claude Pepper of Florida wrote a glowing introduction to the book, reflecting in both substance and language Robins's influence. Henry A. Wallace was quoted on the back cover: "Everyone who is interested in the present and future welfare of the world should read *The Great Conspiracy Against Russia*."[6]

"In the midsummer of the fateful year of 1917," read the first words of *The Great Conspiracy*, "as the Russian revolutionary volcano seethed and rumbled, an American named Major Raymond Robins arrived in Petrograd on a secret mission of the utmost importance . . . to help keep Russia in the war against Germany."[7] The following eighteen pages trace Robins's Russian experience and the U.S. decision to intervene in Soviet Russia. "The testimony you gave before the congressional committee shortly after your return from Soviet Russia has proven to be one of our richest sources of information on that period," Arthur Kahn wrote to Robins in 1944, as the book neared completion, quickly adding, "—no, that shouldn't be qualified; it has been our richest source. For understanding, wisdom and eloquence, what you had to say is matchless."[8]

Robins was charged with excitement with the publication of the book. Given the growing American-Soviet distrust in 1946, he wanted to put *The Great Conspiracy* into the hands of every friend and acquaintance in a position to take up the challenge of improving U.S. foreign policy toward the Soviets. In so many ways, it was a reenactment of his crusade of 1918–19. Instead of stumping the speakers circuit, he compiled lists of friends and correspondents and sent them copies of the book at his own expense. After all, it spoke his very words. But, just as in 1919, the opposition was fierce. "The reviews of *THE GREAT CONSPIRACY* are all hostile, and some bitter to an extreme," he wrote plaintively to Mary Dreier. "I have checked the facts in this book in so far as I can from my own notes, experiences and observations in 1917–18 and again in 1933," he continued, quite surprised that so much of the account had come under fire. "All I have read and heard in between those dates and since. [*sic*] They seem sound in so far as I can tell."

The serious inaccuracies, particularly concerning the "Trotskyite conspiracy," were unfortunate, especially in a time of growing American-Soviet tension; but scholarly responsibility was not the point at issue for Robins, and particularly for the period after 1934, of which he had little firsthand knowledge. The essential issue for the rest of his life was the grave danger, once again, of Soviet-American estrangement and the Cold War. As in 1918–20, he lay the major blame on U.S. policymakers and, in the face of the greater dangers of nuclear weapons, hoped to avert the threat of war.[9]

In December 1951, at the height of the Cold War, *Labour Monthly*, "A Magazine of International Labour, published in London under the distinguished editorship of R. Palme Dutt," issued "A Conversation with Colonel Raymond Robins." One year later, the New York-based *National Guardian, The Progressive Newsweekly*, republished the interview as "Guardian Pamphlet 3," under the title *An American Prophet Speaks, A Historic Interview with Premier Stalin on the Eve of U.S. Recognition of the U.S.S.R. by President Roosevelt in 1933*, by Col. Raymond Robins, "with a foreword by Cedric Belfarge," an editor of the *Guardian*. According to the pamphlet, "It had first been published [in Russian] in Moscow in the latest volume of Stalin's collected writings and statements." The avowed purpose of publishing the interview at that time was to serve as example and rebuttal to the Cold War writings of Maj. Gen. Robert W. Grow, who was until January 1952 U.S. military attaché in Moscow. Sadly, Robins's "interview" with Stalin was a none-too-subtle example of Soviet "cult of personality" propaganda in which Robins plays more the role of sycophant than interviewer. The pamphlet, if written at all by Robins, was, in all probability, freely based on Robins's recollections, but written some time around 1950. The tenor of the pamphlet can be seen from this quotation attributed to Robins in the foreword:

> As a private citizen [as he told Stalin] he took his outdoor mind all over the U.S.S.R. and saw for himself that the three most widespread notions about the socialist state were nonsense. The Russian worker was just as capable as any other of learning to use machines. The vast majority of the peasantry were sold on farm collectivization, and it was "producing." And far from being "terrorized by secret police," as John Dewey was telling America, Soviet children were better cared for than any others in the world. At Magnitogorsk, where on his previous visit there had been nothing, Robins tells of his remark to a Soviet worker: "Lenin ought to be here." The worker replied: "He is."[10]

Stalin died in 1953, Robins, the following year. The Russian revelation of the horrors of the Stalin dictatorship did not begin until 1956, when, at the Twentieth Congress of the CPSU, Nikita Khrushchev made his famous speech of condemnation. But Soviet-American relations have remained dangerously confrontational through the subsequent decades. The rapprochement and cooperation for which Robins worked is only now being realized through the extraordinary initiatives of Mikhail Gorbachev. The Bush administration and the last years of the Reagan administration provide hope. Robins would have been ecstatic with the American-Soviet Intermediate Nuclear Forces agreement and the disintegration of "Bolshevik formulas" in eastern Europe and the USSR. Soviet multiparty democracy, which he championed in 1917–18, is finally being realized. Were he alive today, he would rightfully lay claim to his prophetic vision of 1918, when he carried the Lenin economic proposals to Washington. At every step of Soviet democratization, arms limitation, military disengagement, growing Soviet-American trade, and scientific and technical cooperation, Robins's vision of American-Soviet friendship and peace is vindicated.

Appendix A

City of Chicago Special Park Commission Report on Conditions, Seventeenth Ward, May 24, 1902

THIS densely populated river ward contains about 60,000 people, mostly of the artisan class. The only breathing space is Bickerdike Square, a 1–3/10 acre front yard strip in the west end, containing a few trees and weedy grass. Twelve thousand children attend the public and parochial schools of this ward. It is the most populous school district in Chicago except one. The great number of children shows that this is a ward of homes. These children have no proper place to play and develop their bodies equally with their minds. Swarms of boys and girls can be found after school hours in the unpaved, muddy or dust laden streets. There are few yards of any size in the ward, the lots being mostly covered with the modern three and four-story brick tenement, the old frame dwelling of village times or the "Double decker."

There are in some parts a conglomerate mass of old-style tenements, with many rooms damp and sunless. A narrow strip along the river and adjoining the North-Western Railroad on the south is devoted to commercial purposes. A careful investigation proves that the resident population is increasing much faster than the manufacturing interests and that by far the larger part of this ward will be increasingly a district of homes for generations to come. The population in parts of the ward reaches 250 persons to the acre, is steadily rising in density as the modern many-storied flat building displaces the small frame tenements.

This ward has the smallest number of transients of any of the city's populous districts.

The Health Department records show that in proportion to population, for every child who dies in the 7th Ward four children perish in the 17th. The comparison is almost as startling when the figures as to the deaths of adults are considered, the proportion in those wards being 3 to 1. The 7th ward has the largest park area of any district in Chicago, the 17th has practically none.

An examination of the Juvenile Court records shows that of the 2,900 delinquents in Chicago since the Court was established, 700 lived in the two districts of which the 17th Ward is a part. These two north-western districts of the Juvenile Court have contributed about one-fourth of the city's total delinquency among children.

A small playground is maintained by Chicago Commons Social Settlement at Grand Avenue and Morgan Street. This is the only play space for the multitude of children in the populous river end of the ward.

[ED. This report is in the Raymond Robins Papers, State Historical Society of Wisconsin, Madison.]

Appendix B
The Platform of the Progressive Party
of the State of Illinois in the Election of 1914

(AFTER a list of candidates headed by Raymond Robins for United States senator from Illinois, there appear the following platform statements:)

These men stand for the following principles, as embodied in the Progressive Party for social and industrial justice.

We pledge ourselves to work unceasingly in state and nation for:

Effective legislation looking to the prevention of industrial accidents, occupational diseases, overwork, involuntary unemployment and other injurious effects incident to modern industry;

The fixing of minimum safety and health standards for various occupations, and the exercise of the public authority of state and nation, including federal control over interstate commerce and the taxing power, to maintain such standards;

The prohibition of child labor;

Minimum wage standards enabling women to provide a living scale in all industrial occupations;

The prohibition of night work for women and the establishment of an eight-hour day for women and young persons;

One day's rest in seven for all wage-workers;

The eight-hour day in continuous twenty-four-hour industries;

The abolition of the convict contract labor system; substituting a system of prison production for governmental consumption only, and the application of prisoners' earnings to the support of their dependent families;

Publicity as to wages hours and conditions of labor; full reports upon industrial accidents and diseases, and the opening to public inspection of all tallies, weights measures and check systems on labor products;

Standards of compensation for death by industrial accident and injury and trade diseases, which will transfer the burden of lost earnings from the families of working people to the industry, and thus to the community;

The development of the creative labor power of America by lifting the last load of illiteracy from American youth and establishing continuation schools for industrial education under public control and encouraging agricultural education and demonstration in rural schools;

The establishment of industrial research laboratories to put the methods and discoveries of science at the service of American producers.

We favor the organization of the workers, men and women, as a means of protecting their interests and of promoting their progress.

The Progressive Party also favors:
A Constitutional Convention to revise the State Constitution.
Complete suffrage for women.
Initiative, Referendum and Recall.
Short Ballot.
Non-partisan city elections.
Corrupt Practices Act.
Abolishing the Spoils System.
Voting at primaries without disclosing party to which voter belongs.
State Supervision of private banks.
Women's 54-hour week labor law.

[Source: *Kewanee Call*, Kewanee, Ill., 9 October 1914]

Appendix C
Excerpts from letters on the Bolshevik Revolution, Raymond to Margaret

Petrograd, 20th November, 1917

Darling Blessed One:

It is now Fourteen Days since the Bolshevik Commune took control of the government of this city and in so far as there is any, the government of Russia. The outlook is extremely uncertain but I have still hope for the people and the land of the Slavs. We have in Lenin a practical dictatorship of the extreme socialist type and it is marching toward a genuine control of the masses of the people. The rifles and the peasants are behind his leadership at this moment.

It is a tremendous drama! Each day we face a new contingency and the interest of the play is breathless and the element of danger adds to its power and absorption. I am wondering now if it can ever be told so that we in America can reap some benefit from this sweeping tragedy. How I wish that some master spirit for writing a living story were here.

I wonder if you know how I love and thank you in this great Hour! The three pictures are very dear. The one I love best is of you riding Jim on the old hill-top, and it is before me on my desk all the time. The little girl on the way home from school quickens my heart and the dear steady face that looks out to me from the one I carry in my Bible blesses each day. Little Girl Little Girl keep the fires burning and the trees growing on the crown of Chinsegut in the land of the shining pines.

So the women have won [suffrage] in New York. How glad I am for them and especially glad for Mary and this consummation of her fine work with the working women of her State. This victory should make the National Amendment certain within the near future. . . .

What is the probable term of my stay in this troubled land? There is not even a guess possible just now. Tomorrow we send out the last contingent and of the 29 who came only five will remain. I will be in command of these five and they will be loyal to me let come what may. We have all been tried in the fire and are ready for what comes. The final stand of the American Red Cross in Russia will be made by Robins, Thacher, Andrews, Pirnie and Hardy. Wardwell is now in Roumania and may stay there, come here or go out later as may then be determined. . . . It has been a curious development by which I have been slowly moved from the position of least consequence to the command of the last stand in Russia. I am more grateful for this than I can say. It is a final vindication for my days work. If we can now serve America and the Democratic purpose of the world to some genuine end—I am wholly content let the final cost be what it may.

I have seen that the employees of the Federal Government have been permitted to organize by Wilson under the lead of Gompers. Things of this nature I want kept for me so that I can get them quickly when I return. It is not in Russia only that the social movement shows great agitation and progress—it is world wide.

This is the most interesting and vital hour in the history of the human race. Nothing like it has before existed and the nearest approaches are the birth of Christ and the Dawn of the Germanic Reformation. It is a wonderful privilege to live in such an hour. God bless and keep you Little Girl!

[signed] Your Raymond

Petrograd, 21st November, 1917

Dearest Blessed One,
Sweetheart Mizpah Margaret,
Beloved Glory Robins with
the Golden Shoes:

This letter is not going out with Colonel Thompson after all! It is going with Captain Pirnie who is not to be one of the final group but sails for the U.S. tomorrow from Arkangel [sic]. So the turn of the wheel has brought changes. Blessed one we hear rumors of Peace from all over the world but as the Bolsheviks control the telegraph and all lines of communication we know nothing of the outside world with certainty.

Think of it, the most extreme socialist peace semi-anarchist government in the world maintaining its control by the bayonet, proscribing all publications except those that favor their program, arresting persons without warrant and holding them for weeks without trial and without charge, searching houses and persons indiscriminately and making Catherine Breshkovsky a fugitive as a reactionary! It is a crazy world. . . .

Tell my old Negro what it all means and let his old mind be quickened with the thought that "Mr. Raymond" "my boy" as he likes to call me when he thinks it will not be disrespectful is now Colonel Robins Commander of the American Red Cross in Russia and helping in the most difficult and dangerous spot of the world war.

Let him know that ministers of government, ambassadors and heads of Military Missions are asking for the advice and judgment of his "boy."

For the rest—Keep your Spirit Free and bring to others the power and beauty of your unconquerable soul! If we meet again in this world it will be with added wisdom, steadfastness and power. If the Master Calls we will go to meet Him with an untroubled heart, grateful beyond all words for this—GREAT HOUR!

Today the Bolshevik government has offered peace to all the world by a formal order to the Commander in chief of the Russian Armies and the several Embassies in Petrograd. It is the most moving and impossible and tremendous action in the history of man. Only face to face can I tell you all that is involved in this consummation of what the whole world desires in fact, by the proclamation of an irresponsible handful of adventurers.

Love, Love, Love.
Your, [signed] Raymond

[Source: Raymond Robins Papers, State Historical Society of Wisconsin, Madison.]

Appendix D
Letter of Brig. Gen. William V. Judson
and Lt. Col. Monroe C. Kerth
to David R. Francis, American Ambassador, Petrograd

December 26, 1917

Sir:—

The Bolsheviks are in control of Great Russia.

The American Government has its Embassy here in Petrograd and has no communication with the *de facto* Bolshevik government. As a result all American aid to the Russian people is at a standstill while the German emissaries are everywhere, working day and night in the interests of the enemy. The terrible responsibility for this deplorable condition, fraught with untold dangers not only to the Russian Democracy but to the Democracies of the world, rests primarily upon the Ambassador and the Chief of the Military Mission, upon each of whom is imposed the duty of informing the American Government as to conditions here and of suggesting appropriate action.

It is necessary that the United States adopt at once a broad Russian policy.

In our opinion this policy should be based upon the following general principles:—

1: In view of the fact that the Bolshevik Government is the most important and extensive in Russia today, enter into helpful, sympathetic and friendly relations with it.

2: Pour oil on troubled waters. Try to discourage civil war by all possible friendly intercessions, representations and advice. Seek to convince all elements that a fair constitutional convention is necessary.

3: Recognize the almost insuperable difficulties confronting Russia today, which well might incline even the most conscientious and patriotic Russian to believe that his country is not justified in seeking further to conduct war if reasonable and honorable peace terms can be secured. Self-preservation knows no law. If Russia feels thus constrained to seek peace and can secure reasonable terms, let us assist her to make them as favorable to herself (and as disadvantageous to her enemies and ours) as possible. If on the other hand Russia finds her enemies refuse to consider terms which are acceptable to the Russian people and consistent with their honor, then offer her the material assistance of her Allies on a far larger scale and of a more practical character than has heretofore been considered necessary or advisable; offer also to immediately assist her in the reorganization of all the elements of military strength still present in Russia, in order that she may be better prepared to continue her defence in case the present peace negotiations fail.

384

4: Do not stand on dignity. Such conduct might be in order if we were dealing with an established power experienced in protocol; and etiquette. In fact what we are dealing with is for the most part an aggregation of simple but honest persons, unacquainted with the ways of government, not experienced in the conduct of it, threatened with anarchy as the result of their inexperience, who find themselves in their present situation largely because we have encouraged their democratic aspirations by our words and by our example, and because they have fought for three years, without the facilities for modern war possessed by the industrial nations of the west, thus rendering vital assistance to the cause of victory over autocratic Germany whatever may be their future course.

5: Act on the theory that Russia is entitled to sympathy not condemnation. She is passing through a dreadful experience in many ways unequalled in history. Under similar conditions no other nation might be expected to act otherwise.

If such a policy is not speedily adopted there will be no competition with Germany possible for the friendship of the Russian nation and the Russian people.

Russia will become practically a German colony and will be organized by Germany, long before this war is over, to render vitally needed assistance to the Central Powers, which will more than likely enable them to win the war. The probable cost to our country of a failure to adopt such a policy is then defeat; the death of hundreds of thousands of young Americans; tons of billions of debt [*sic*]; and a burden that will set us back a hundred years.

As Colonel Kerth, the second in rank of the Military Mission, is in agreement with its chief as to the contents of this communication, it has seemed reasonable that both should sign it.

Very respectfully,

[signed] W. V. Judson
      Brigadier General, U.S.N. Army,
      American Military Attaché,
      Chief of the American Military
      Mission to Russia
[signed] M. C. Kerth
      Lieutenant Colonel, G.S.C.
      United States Army,
      Assistant Military Attaché.

[Source: William V. Judson Papers, Newberry Library, Chicago. Copy in the Raymond Robins Papers, State Historical Society of Wisconsin, Madison, with the handwritten notation, "Copy for Col. Robins, *Confidential*," in the upper margin.]

Notes

1. Childhood

1. C. E. Robins to S. S. D. Thompson, 21 March 1872, Elizabeth Robins Papers, Fales Library, New York University (hereafter cited as ERP). The Elizabeth Robins Papers are the most important source for family genealogy and Raymond Robins's childhood. Through the efforts of Prof. Leon Edel, professor of English at New York University and noted biographer of Henry James, the papers were purchased from the Elizabeth Robins estate. Prior to their sale, Leonard Woolf and the Hon. Mable Smith, coexecutor of the estate, separated the papers from other personal belongings. In 1984, with the help of a grant from the National Endowment for the Humanities, work was begun on the cataloging and preparation of the Elizabeth Robins Papers for use by researchers. An excellent key to the collection has also been prepared, and the entire collection is now open to the scholarly community. Epigraph, letterpress book of Charles E. Robins, ERP.

2. Thomas Robbins to Raymond Robins, 15 March 1917, Raymond Robins Papers, State Historical Society of Wisconsin, Madison (hereafter cited as RP). The Raymond Robins Papers collection, including diaries, correspondence, and manuscripts, has been the single most important source for this book. Other Robins papers are housed at the University of Florida at Gainesville (cited as RPG) and at the former Robins estate, Chinsegut (cited as RPC). See the bibliographical note concerning the RPC papers for more information.

3. Charles Robins presented his professional resumé, including the loss of $30,000, in a letter of application for a job. However, Elizabeth, who held all the family papers and letters, had penciled in the margin that the money was her mother's (ERP; Elizabeth Robins, *Both Sides of the Curtain*, pp. 54–57; also in another of her books, *Raymond and I*, pp. 13-14).

4. Robins, *Both Sides of the Curtain*, pp. 54–55.

5. C. E. Robins to J. M. Bodine, 17 November 1872, letterpress book, ERP; Robins, *Both Sides of the Curtain*, p. 54. Elizabeth was born in Louisville, Kentucky, on 6 August 1862.

6. Lisa von Borowsky, interview with the author at Seal Cove, Maine, 6 August 1971. Ms. von Borowsky joined the Robins household at Chinsegut, Brooksville, Florida, in 1924, as a young woman in her early twenties. While she came as an assistant and companion of Margaret Dreier Robins, Raymond's wife, Lisa became their ward, surrogate daughter, and heir. She worked on the estate as a knowledgeable horticulturist and naturalist and tended the extensive plantings and wildlife. She has been both a valued source of information and a warm and generous host to me.

7. Robins, *Both Sides of the Curtain*, p. 54.

8. Robins, *Raymond and I*, pp. 15–16.

9. Hannah M. Robins to Elizabeth Robins, 28 May 1881, ERP. Elizabeth wrote: "At the end of the line we have a genius in our family. At an early age and ever after, he left us and others in no doubt of the fact" (*Both Sides of the Curtain*, p. 53).

10. Jane Robins to Elizabeth Robins, 18 February 1882; Raymond Robins to Elizabeth Robins, 14 October 1913, ERP. After a careful analysis of the contemporary letters of eyewitnesses to Raymond's seizures and in close consultation with Dr. Lawrence Sharpe, assistant professor of clinical psychiatry at the College of Physicians and Surgeons of Columbia University, and New

York State Psychiatric Institute, it is possible to suggest that Raymond was suffering from a form of psychic epilepsy with a probable focus for the problem in the temporal frontal area of the brain. It may well have been a result of a problem with myelinization, or nerve cell development, a hypothesis that fits his age in particular. This form of psychic epilepsy, in which the widest range of unusual behaviors are seen, would have left him with no recollection of the fit episode. Dr. Sharpe has virtually ruled out Charles Robins's conviction that his son's trouble was *"pure* neurosis." See also chapter 21, note 14.

11. Charles E. Robins to Jane Hussey Robins, 13 March 1882, ERP.

12. Hannah M. Robins to Elizabeth Robins, 6 June 1883, ERP.

13. Charles Robins to Jane Robins, 13 June 1883, ERP; Unpublished typescript of an incomplete biography of Raymond Robins entitled "The Goldseeker: The Life and Times of Raymond Robins," by Sherwood Eddy. This typescript, along with the collection of the Eddy Papers (hereafter cited as SEP), are in the private possession of Louise Gates Eddy of Jacksonville, Illinois, who kindly allowed the author to study the notes and partial draft. Most of the work on the draft was done in the years 1947 and 1948. The partial draft in the Eddy Papers consists of portions of several chapters, totaling approximately fifty pages. However, there are an even greater number of handwritten pages of notes, obviously the record of Eddy's interviews with Robins, and these have been of even greater value here. Most significant are Eddy's notes taken from Robins's "butcher-paper diary," which Raymond gave to Elizabeth to help her in the writing of *Come and Find Me* and *The Magnetic North.* This diary recorded Robins's most exciting and dangerous experiences in Alaska. The Eddy notes were taken from the diary in 1947, while Eddy was visiting Elizabeth in England. The "butcher-paper diary" is not in the papers of Elizabeth Robins in the Fales Library of New York University. Elizabeth's detailed diary of her visit to Raymond in Alaska is in the Elizabeth Robins Papers and has been masterfully edited and annotated for publication by Joanne Elizabeth Gates and Victoria Joan Moessner. Elizabeth's notes, correspondence, and manuscript of *Raymond and I* are also in the collection. See Robins, *Raymond and I,* pp. 13–14; and scattered entries in Raymond's diary of 1909, RP.

14. Charles Robins to Jane Hussey Robins, 21 November 1883, 27 February, 1 March, and 12 March 1884, quoting letters to him, from Lizzie B. McKay to "uncle Charlie," ERP; Robins, *Both Sides of the Curtain,* p. 63; Progressive State Committee of Illinois, "Raymond Robins—Progressive Nominee for U.S. Senator from Illinois," 1914 campaign pamphlet, p. 3, RP.

15. Quoted in Robins, *Both Sides of the Curtain,* p. 64. The physical description of Charles Robins is from a letter, Raymond Robins to Elizabeth Robins, 30 November 1894; Nama failure, in Raymond Robins to Elizabeth Robins, from Chinsegut, Florida, 15 November 1938, ERP. Robins concluded: "YOU [Elizabeth] were the only one in all those yesterdays of my early youth in the family home, who was not touched with the *doom,* and always VICTORY seemed to sit eagle-winged on your crest."

16. Raymond to Elizabeth, 15 November 1938, ERP. Nineteenth-century American poet Arabella Eugenia Smith is the author of "If I Should Die Tonight."

17. William Appleman Williams, "Raymond Robins and Russian-American Relations, 1917–1938" (Ph.D. diss.), p. 4 (hereafter cited as Williams, "Raymond Robins"). Between 28 July and 11 August 1949, Professor Williams held extensive interviews with Robins regarding the story of his life. Special attention was focused on the subject of Williams's dissertation, Russian-American relations and the ten months of Robins's role in Russia during the Russian Revolution.

18. Joanne Elizabeth Gates, "'Sometimes Suppressed and Sometimes Embroidered': The Life and Writing of Elizabeth Robins, 1862–1952" (Ph.D. diss.), p. 3 (hereafter cited as Gates, "Life of E.R.").

19. Gates, "Life of E.R.," p. 3. George Parkes's suicide note is preserved in the ERP.

20. Robins, *Raymond and I,* pp. 15–16.

21. His hurt is reflected in Robins's feelings for his father in later years, as he related them to his friend Sherwood Eddy. In a letter to Robins, written from England after having interviewed Elizabeth, Eddy wrote, "She has a higher opinion of your father than you ever gave me" (Sherwood Eddy to Raymond Robins, 15 June 1947, RP).

22. Raymond Robins to Salmon Levinson, 31 December 1924, RP. When Raymond and Margaret Dreier Robins built their Florida estate, Chinsegut, Fielder Harris became their foreman and remained at the job to the end of his life. It was most unusual for a black man to hold such a position, especially because some whites worked under his supervision.

23. See Ethel Armes, "On the Trail of Roosevelt, the Most Venerated Horseshoe in the World," *The Grand Rapids Press*, 5 August 1924. This story, in which Robins was quoted, related the meeting between Fielder Harris and Theodore Roosevelt. The meeting was arranged by Robins, and at Oyster Bay, Fielder was given "the shoe cast by the horse that the Colonel had ridden under fire in the Spanish American War." After making a name for himself, Robins returned in triumph to his old Florida home and bought the most impressive piece of land available. He renewed his friendship with Harris and became the philanthropist of the "Blue Sink colored community" where Harris was a preacher. Robins's new role as patron and master of an estate did not hinder the close relationship with his old friend.

24. Fielder Harris to Raymond Robins, 24 June 1912. This paragraph appears after a lengthy discussion of a land sale and purchase made by Harris in Robins's name. The letter indicates the great financial trust shared by the two men, giving Harris virtual power of attorney over Robins's estate.

25. Robins to Levinson, 31 December 1924, RP.

26. Raymond Robins to James H. Shaw, 17 July 1915, RP.

27. Charles E. Robins to Elizabeth Robins, 19 July 1887, ERP.

28. "Colonel Raymond Robins Arrived in Hernando County Fifty Years Ago Today," *Brooksville Florida Sun*, 8 December 1933.

29. Raymond Robins to Elizabeth Robins, 14 May 1893, RP.

2. "Success," 1890-1897

1. Carbon copy of a letter from Raymond Robins to Dr. and Mrs. Alfred Jackson Hanna, circa 1949, RP. Robins's thoughts on his ancestry are revealed in a letter to Anita McCormick Blaine, 3 April 1904, Anita McCormick Blaine Papers, State Historical Society of Wisconsin, Madison (hereafter cited as MBP). Epigraph, RP.

2. Williams, "Raymond Robins," p. 5.

3. The accounts of his work at Coal Creek, Tennessee, and Leadville, Colorado, for the period between 1891 and 1892 are based entirely on Robins's recollections after 1905. There is, uncharacteristically, no extant contemporary correspondence nor documentation of these experiences in any of the three Robins archives.

Robins's narratives of the Coal Creek and Leadville experiences are numerous. They appear in the following sources: Progressive State Committee of Illinois, *The Story of Raymond Robins' Life*, 1914 campaign pamphlet (hereafter cited as Progressive Committee, *Story*); Robins's own statement in "Why I Believe in Organized Labor," RP, an undated typescript based on many speeches on the same subject that he gave in the period between 1905 and 1910. The notes for "The Goldseeker" in the SEP and Williams, "Raymond Robins," also detail his experiences at Coal Creek and Leadville, based on interviews with Robins.

4. Robins, "Why I Believe in Organized Labor," p. 1.

5. Philip S. Foner, *History of the Labor Movement in the United States*, 2: 118-29.

6. Robins, "Why I Believe in Organized Labor," pp. 2-3. There are no corroborating sources for this account.

7. Ibid. In Williams, "Raymond Robins," the account of this episode, based on an interview with Robins on 27 July 1949, is on p. 6: "Meanwhile the company reopened the mine with a trainload of scabs and militia. In a few days, however, the scabs began to join the union." The scabs referred to here could not have been contracted convicts.

8. Robins, "Why I Believe in Organized Labor," pp. 2-3.

9. Foner, *History of the Labor Movement*, 2: 118-29.

10. Throughout his correspondence with his wife, Margaret, from 1905 to 1908, Robins referred to himself in this manner; see RP.

11. Ten years later, as a settlement worker in Chicago, Robins headed the Chicago Municipal Lodging House (MLH) for men and boys without money or jobs. Robins personally worked with the vagrants, providing medical help when needed along with food and board while searching for jobs through the house's placement facilities.

12. Robins, "Why I Believe in Organized Labor," p. 6.

13. Quoted in Robins, *Raymond and I*, p. 18; Raymond to Elizabeth, 14 May 1893, RP. This same letter is quoted in chapter 1, note 29, in which Robins refers to his finally becoming *"somebody."*

14. Progressive Committee, *Story*, p. 5.

15. Raymond Robins to Elizabeth Robins, 2 July 1894, ERP.

16. Ibid.; Williams, "Raymond Robins," p. 8, based on his interview with Robins on 1 August 1949.

17. Raymond Robins to Elizabeth Robins, 7 April 1894, from Burnett, Texas, and 30 November 1894, under the letterhead of O. T. Green, attorney at law, Ocala, Florida, ERP; the latter excerpts are also found in Robins, *Raymond and I*, pp. 21–22. Other portions of this grandiose and self-righteous letter, which Elizabeth does not quote in full, include Raymond's vows "to take care of father" and to save $500 for Elizabeth, to pay for her care if her illness persisted. Only after his father died in 1893 and his sister was well did Raymond devote himself to the full-time study of law.

18. Robins, *Raymond and I*, p. 23–24; Raymond Robins to Elizabeth Robins, 27 December 1896, under the heading "Raymond Robins, Attorney at Law, 318 Golden Gate Avenue, San Francisco, California"—this fourteen-page letter reporting every important detail in his studies and career development, in addition to the plight of Saxton discussed later in this chapter, is in the ERP; Williams, "Raymond Robins," pp. 8–9. LL.B. diploma granted to Robins from the Columbian University, dated 7 June 1896, RP; Progressive Committee, *Story*, p. 5.

19. Raymond to Elizabeth, 27 December 1896, ERP.

20. Ibid.

21. According to one account, based on an interview with Robins when he was seventy-six, his train connections to Denver and San Francisco were poor, and he had a long layover in Chicago in July 1896. "To pass the time of day he walked over to the Democratic National Convention, where he heard William Jennings Bryan's Cross of Gold speech. Robins was 'won completely' and decided to support Bryan in the presidential campaign that followed" (Williams, "Raymond Robins," p. 5). Robins did become a devoted worker in the election campaign of Bryan; however, we can conclude that Robins wanted to strengthen his connection to Bryan by inventing that he was on the scene at Bryan's most dramatic public address. For the sake of audience impact and to enhance his image before the public, Robins did "embellish" accounts of his exploits. But in all other respects, documentary and eyewitness evidence substantiate his accounts of events.

22. Raymond to Elizabeth, 27 December 1896, ERP; Robins, *Raymond and I*, pp. 24–25.

23. Ibid.

24. Raymond Robins to Elizabeth Robins, 25 October 1902, ERP.

25. Doris Muscatine, *Old San Francisco: The Biography of a City, from Early Days to the Earthquake*, pp. 406, 411–27.

26. Robins was quickly admitted to the California bar on the motion of Joseph Leggett, law partner of Judge James G. McGuire, whom Robins had met in Washington when McGuire was a congressman. Leggett was also responsible for getting Robins the chairmanship of the city and county organization committee of the Democratic party; see Louis F. Post, *Raymond Robins, A Biographical Sketch: With Newspaper Accounts of and Comments on Mr. Robins' Work*, p. 2 (hereafter cited as Post, *Biographical Sketch*). This pamphlet was published to stimulate the demand for Robins as a public speaker in behalf of the *Public* magazine.

27. Williams, "Raymond Robins," p. 10; Progressive Committee, *Story,* p. 6; Robins, *Raymond and I,* pp. 26–27.

28. The laws were passed in Sacramento on 3 and 8 March 1897. See Williams, "Raymond Robins," pp. 10–12; San Francisco *Chronicle,* 14 November 1896, 31 March 1897, 1 and 2 April 1897, and 5 February 1899, as cited in Williams, p. 10n.3; *Popper vs. Broderick,* 123 California 456, or 56 Pacific 53 (Supreme Court of California, 2 February 1899); *The Pacific Reporter* (1899), p. 54, as cited in Williams, p. 11n.14; Progressive Committee, *Story,* p. 6; Robins, *Raymond and I,* pp. 26–28; and Raymond Robins to Elizabeth Robins, 5 April 1897, under the heading "Law Offices, Raymond Robins, Room 11 and 12, fourth floor, Mills Building," RP.

29. Robins, *Raymond and I,* pp. 26–28.

30. Ibid., p. 28; Raymond Robins to Elizabeth Robins, 24 April 1897, ERP.

31. Raymond to Elizabeth, 24 April 1897, ERP.

32. Robins, *Raymond and I,* pp. 29–30.

3. Alaska, 1897–1900

1. Raymond Robins to Elizabeth Robins, 25 July 1897, ERP, also quoted in Robins, *Raymond and I,* pp. 30–31. F. B. Smith wrote to Raymond from Taylorsville, Kentucky, that "it had not occurred to me that 'filthy gold' would draw you away, even temporarily, from a pursuit in which you were achieving conspicuous success" (3 September 1897, RP). Joanne E. Gates, in her *Life of E.R.,* maintains that "It was Saxton who first caught the craze for Alaskan gold" (p. 232). Epigraph, Raymond to Elizabeth, 25 July 1897, ERP.

2. Raymond to Elizabeth, 24 April 1897, ERP.

3. Raymond to Elizabeth, 25 July 1897, ERP, also quoted in Robins, *Raymond and I,* pp. 30–31.

4. Robins, *Raymond and I,* p. 31.

5. Progressive Committee, *Story,* p. 6; Williams, "Raymond Robins," pp. 11–12; Sherwood Eddy, notes, SEP. The Eddy Papers are especially useful in reconstructing this period of Robins's life. Because of Eddy's involvement in Christian evangelical work overseas for much of his life, he was very interested in Robins's conversion to Christian service, which took place in Alaska.

6. Eddy, notes, SEP; the notes were taken by Eddy from the Robins diary, often referred to as the "butcher-paper diary." Elizabeth made extensive use of the diary in writing her successful novel *The Magnetic North* (1904). It is a relatively accurate account of Robins's adventures along the Yukon River, with only the names of the participants changed. Raymond's pseudonym was Morris Burnett and Saxton was Harry Earle. However, during the whole adventure Saxton actually used this alias. In Saxton's handwritten will, dated 2 August 1897, he wrote: "I Saxton Robins—otherwise known as Harry Earle." The will is in the Raymond Robins Papers, Library of the University of Florida, Gainesville (hereafter cited as RPG), which have been microfilmed as part of the papers of Margaret Dreier Robins, Library of the University of Florida, Gainesville (hereafter cited as MRP), and have been included in the microfilm *Papers of the Women's Trade Union League and its Principal Leaders,* reel 2974. The original documents were consulted at Gainesville and the microfilm was used in the Tamiment Library of New York University. In the marginal notes in Elizabeth's draft of *The Magnetic North* (included in ERP), the use of the alias is explained. Joanne E. Gates and Victoria J. Moessner have edited a transcription of Elizabeth's Alaskan diary of 1900, which is available along with the holograph in the ERP in the Fales Library (the transcription is hereafter cited as Elizabeth's Alaskan diary, ERP).

The Alaskan adventure provided Elizabeth with material for at least two other fictional works. "Monica's Village," a short story published in *The Century Magazine* in 1905 deals with the dangerous trek of Robins and his partner, Albert F. Shulte. *Come and Find Me* (1908), a novel dealing with Robins's Nome experience, is far less biographical but still valuable for information on Robins.

7. Robins, diary excerpts in the SEP are further confirmation of Saxton's use of the pseudonym and his insecurity.

8. Eddy, notes, direct quotation from the "butcher-paper diary" entries for 8, 10, and 11 August 1897, SEP.

9. Ibid. Photographs of these four and the Robins brothers, taken aboard the *National City* by Shulte, were later presented by Raymond to Elizabeth, along with his diary of those months. These were essential sources for Elizabeth's writing on Alaska, both fiction and nonfiction (see note 6 above). The photographs as well as the diary are in the ERP.

10. Robins, diary excerpts, SEP, p. 34.

11. Ibid., p. 37.

12. One year earlier he had described himself as: "an Individualist, an Equal-Rights-Single-Tax-Democrat and A Deist or Liberal Unitarian. For each position I entertain the clearest reasons for the faith that is within me" (Raymond to Elizabeth, 27 December 1896, ERP). See also, Robins, diary excerpts, SEP, p. 51.

13. Robins, diary excerpts, SEP, p. 6.

14. There are several marked and interesting similarities between Robins and the writer Jack London. Not only did they share the great adventure of the North, but they were both deeply interested in and sympathetic to Russia and its future. London reported the Russo-Japanese War as a correspondent and later, as a socialist, was deeply involved in American reform and the movement for American-Soviet cooperation.

15. This is the thought of "the boy" Morris Burnett, Elizabeth's pseudonym for Raymond, taken from Burnett, Texas, where he first wrote her of his "worship of Mammon"—his search for wealth (Elizabeth Robins, *The Magnetic North*, p. 175).

16. Robins, *Magnetic North*, p. 179.

17. Elizabeth Robins, "Monica's Village," *The Century Magazine* 70, no. 1 (May, 1905): 19–30. In a letter to Margaret Dreier Robins, Robins wrote: "Elizabeth has a story in the May *Century*. It is really true" (22 May 1905, RP). See also Robins, diary excerpts, SEP; Progressive Committee, *Story*, p. 8; Robins, *Magnetic North*, throughout.

18. Raymond Robins to Elizabeth Robins, 31 August 1899, quoted in Robins, *Raymond and I*, pp. 41–42.

19. Ibid.

20. Ibid.

21. Robins, *Raymond and I*, pp. 80–81. In January 1972 I was the guest of Lisa von Borowsky at her home near Chinsegut, the Robins family estate in Florida. While visiting the main house at Chinsegut (now attached to the University of South Florida as a conference center), Harold Thornton, the superintendent, suggested that Ms. von Borowsky and I examine a box of old papers slated for the trash heap. These papers and diaries, which had been found behind the walls of the old Sunshine cottage in the course of its demolition, were early Robins letters and diaries especially relevant to this period of the Alaska adventure. They were found in a state of some deterioration but not beyond hope of restoration in hands of a skilled archivist. These papers were forwarded to the State Historical Society of Wisconsin where the bulk of the Raymond Robins Papers are kept. It was hoped that these papers would shed more light on Robins's activities between the spring of 1898 and the late summer of 1899. Unfortunately, during the processing of these papers at the State Historical Society of Wisconsin, they were mistakenly destroyed sometime between February and May 1973.

22. Leonard Woolf, Foreword to Robins, *Raymond and I*.

23. Quoted in Robins, *Raymond and I*, pp. 33–34. According to Elizabeth's interview with Wirt in Boston on her way to Alaska, Raymond once said to Wirt: "My sister is my patron Saint." See also Elizabeth's Alaskan diary, p. 20, ERP.

24. Elizabeth's Alaskan diary, pp. 263–64, 269. Lisa von Borowsky recounted Saxton's death at the hands of Indians; she appeared not to know of his suicide (interview with the author at Seal Cove, Maine, 6 August 1971). Elizabeth learned of Saxton's death only a few days after she received word of the death of her mother in June 1901. Hannah Maria Crow Robins had

recovered significantly from her nervous breakdown and was taken out of the Oaklawn Sanitarium by Elizabeth in 1899. She spent the last two years of her life happily in a "Church home" in her native Louisville.

Saxton's diary, which may have thrown light on his suicide and other questions, was among the documents accidentally destroyed at the State Historical Society of Wisconsin (see note 21 above). Much of this account of Raymond's activities after the first winter in Alaska is drawn from Elizabeth's interview with Loyal Lincoln Wirt (she calls him Silbert in *Raymond and I*). *Raymond and I* follows Elizabeth's Alaskan diary account of the interview closely, although the diary is considerably more detailed.

25. The inside back cover of a notebook has the following entry: "Juneau Alaska, April 23, 1899. Dedication of First Congregational Church, Douglas Island" (notebook of 1899–1906, RP).

26. This is Elizabeth's account of her conversation with Wirt in *Raymond and I*, p. 80. It is taken from p. 21 of Elizabeth's Alaskan diary, ERP.

27. Robins, *Raymond and I*, p. 34.

28. Entry "begun on Dec. 20, 1898," notebook of 1897–98, RP.

29. Robins, *Raymond and I*, p. 80; based on Raymond Robins to Elizabeth Robins, 31 August 1899, ERP.

30. Robins, *Raymond and I*, p. 80; based on Elizabeth's Alaskan diary, pp. 21–22.

31. Raymond Robins to Elizabeth Robins, 2 March 1928, ERP. See also Raymond Robins to Elizabeth Robins, 4 January 1928, ERP.

32. John C. Dreier, ed., *Road to Chinsegut: Stories of the Early Life of Raymond Robins as Told by Him to Lisa von Borowsky* (Washington, D.C.: Private distribution, 1978), p. 40.

33. Ibid., pp. 57–58; notebook of 1899–1906, RP.

34. Robins, *Raymond and I*, p. 36.

35. Authorizations as a preacher are in letters from J. J. Walter, superintendent of Alaska missions to Raymond Robins and from J. J. Walter and J. B. Denny, secretary of the Quarterly Conference of Juneau Alaska Missions, RP.

36. Robins, *Raymond and I*, p. 43; Raymond to Elizabeth, 31 August 1899, ERP.

37. Robins, *Raymond and I*, p. 43; Raymond to Elizabeth, 31 August 1899, ERP; Williams, "Raymond Robins," pp. 14–15, 123; Elizabeth's Alaskan diary, p. 77, ERP; Robins, *Come and Find Me*, throughout.

38. William M. Cannon, San Francisco, to Raymond Robins, at Nome, 10 July 1900, RP.

39. Robins, *Raymond and I*, pp. 45, 58; Raymond Robins to Elizabeth Robins, 2 November 1899, ERP. Elizabeth wrote, "Through the days that followed, that cry of the heart sounded louder than the Jesuit alarm" (*Raymond and I*, p. 58).

40. This document (in the RP) is under the letterhead of the "Hospice of St. Bernard, an Institution under the Auspices of the Congregational Churches of America, which aims to reach the Arctic Miner with that Threefold Ministry which once made its Alpine Prototype a Center of Beneficent Life. Physical Healing, St. Bernard Hospital; Intellectual Culture, St. Bernard Library; Spiritual Life, St. Bernard Congregational Church." Under the third heading appears, "Raymond Robins, Pastor."

41. Robins, *Raymond and I*, p. 83.

42. An extensive account of the claim jumping and corruption at Nome appear in fictional form in Rex Beach's *The Spoilers* (1906). His series of articles, "The Looting of Alaska, or the True Story of Robbery by Law," in 1906 in Appleton's *Booklovers Magazine*, presents a factual exposé of the situation. Alaska's senator Ernest Gruening's *An Alaskan Reader, 1867–1967*, presents an analysis and excerpts from the account, pp. 141–46.

43. Gruening, *Alaskan Reader*, pp. 135–36.

44. Ibid., pp. 206–7; Williams, "Raymond Robins," p. 15.

45. Elizabeth's Alaskan diary, p. 280, ERP; also see Progressive Committee, *Story*, p. 9; Robins, *Raymond and I*, p. 206; Post, *Biographical Sketch*, p. 17; Claus Naske and Herman E. Slotnick, *Alaska: A History of the Forty-ninth State*, pp. 73–75, including excellent contemporary photos of Nome's beach claims and streets in 1900; Gruening, *Alaskan Reader*, p. 145.

46. Bernard Schwarz to Raymond Robins, 10 October 1916, RP.

47. Gruening, *Alaskan Reader*, pp. 141–46.

48. The full story of the evolution of Nome's governing institutions goes well beyond the scope of this biography and still remains to be written. The minutes of the mass meetings, which are in the Margaret Dreier Robins Papers (MRP) at the University of Florida, Gainesville and on microfilm, in addition to the extensive collection of contemporary photographs of Nome, many taken by Elizabeth Robins and in her papers in the Fales collection (ERP), will be among the essential sources for such a study.

49. Robins, *Raymond and I*, sec. 3, throughout.

50. Elizabeth's Alaskan diary, Nome chapter, ERP.

51. Ibid., pp. 63–65; see also Robins, *Raymond and I*, pp. 107–8.

52. Robins, *Raymond and I*, pp. 141, 155–56, based on Elizabeth's Alaskan diary, ERP.

53. Robins, *Raymond and I*, p. 144; Elizabeth's Alaskan diary, p. 87, ERP.

54. Handwritten statement in Robins's hand and signed by Loyal L. Wirt, 20 July 1900, RP.

55. Robins, *Raymond and I*, pp. 189–91.

56. Ibid., p. 145.

57. Ibid., pp. 145, 246–47; Elizabeth's Alaskan diary, pp. 87–90, with her fears recorded on p. 139, ERP.

58. Ibid., p. 265.

59. Williams, "Raymond Robins," p. 16. The figure $250,000 is found many times in the accounts of Robins's Alaskan adventure as well as in the notes in the SEP. Until the Elizabeth Robins Papers were made available to researchers, there was no documentary evidence to clear up the claim that Robins struck it rich in Alaska. All published and unpublished accounts of his finding gold—and there are more than two dozen of the first and an innumerable quantity of the second—accept the tale that he "cleared over a quarter of a million." This would have to have been accomplished between the time of Elizabeth's departure and his attack of typhoid, less than four weeks later.

60. In a letter to Elizabeth dated 13 May 1901, Raymond wrote: "The help I want from you is not money and if you need the money you have previously loaned me I will borrow this amount and forward at once." In a letter dated 10 November 1904, Raymond acknowledged Elizabeth's offer to let him "use bonds for security"; and in a letter of 27 December 1904, he wrote to her: "dearest do not send me any more money. I have not used your checks for $80. Numbers 4 and 5, nor the November interest of $100 on the bonds." These letters are in series 4A, box 1, folders 2, 5, and 6, respectively, ERP.

61. Robins, *Raymond and I*, p. 341.

4. The Settlement Worker

1. Robins, *Both Sides of the Curtain*, p. 65; H. W. C. Davis and J. R. H. Weaver, *Dictionary of National Biography*, s.v. "James Keir Hardie (1856–1915)." Epigraph, Margaret Dreier Robins to Elizabeth Robins, September 1905, ERP.

2. Hugh D. Camitta, "Raymond Robins: Study of a Progressive, 1901–1917" (honors thesis), pp. 28–29. Camitta cites the Sherwood Eddy Papers, and since he worked on the papers in their repository in the home of Louise Gates Eddy, in Jacksonville, Illinois, he has uncovered some significant additional material. I was afforded the opportunity of having the Robins material in the Eddy papers mailed to me, a courtesy rarely afforded a researcher, and a reflection of Mrs. Eddy's trust, kindness, and consideration. See Allen F. Davis, *American Heroine: The Life and Legend of Jane Addams*, p. 49, for an account of the impact of Toynbee Hall on America's most notable settlement personality.

3. Raymond Robins to Elizabeth Robins, 5 April 1901, ERP.

4. Lincoln Steffens chose the title "An Example of Reform" for his chapter on the Windy

City in his *Autobiography*, pp. 422–29. See appendix A, "City of Chicago Special Park Commission Report on Conditions, Seventeenth Ward, 24 May 1902," for a contemporary description of the physical conditions in the Seventeenth Ward.

5. Eddy, notes, SEP; see Allen F. Davis, "Raymond Robins: The Settlement Worker as Municipal Reformer," *Social Service Review* 33 (June 1959): 131–41; Raymond to Elizabeth, 5 April 1901, ERP.

6. Chicago and national settlement data from Robert A. Woods and Albert J. Kennedy, eds., *Handbook of Settlements*. See Davis's discussion of the variety of settlement worker motivation in *American Heroine*, pp. ix–x. He compares the writing of Richard Hofstadter, in *The Age of Reform, from Bryan to F.D.R.*, Staughton Lynd, in "Jane Addams and the Radical Impulse," pp. 54–59, and Christopher Lasch, in *The New Radicalism in America, 1889–1963*, and rejects sweeping generalization in favor of careful analysis of the individual settlement worker under analysis, an approach which I have used here.

7. All quotes are from Charles R. Henderson, *Social Settlements*. Canon Barnett is quoted on p. 164. These notes are in the "1897 Ledger," but were written in 1901, RP. See Allen F. Davis, "Raymond Robins: The Settlement Worker as Municipal Reformer."

8. Robert Hunter to Raymond Robins, 31 December 1901, RP.

9. Raymond Robins to Elizabeth Robins, 22 February 1902, ERP.

10. Ticket found in RP. Raymond Robins, "The Tramp Problem and Municipal Correction," *The Commons* 7, no. 74 (September 1902): 1–9, and Robins, "Chicago's Municipal Lodging House: How the Human Flotsam-and-Jetsam of a Great American City is Scientifically Cared for and Returned to the Ranks of Industry," *Merchants Association Review* (San Francisco, August 1902): 5–6 are major sources for information on Robins's MLH activity.

11. The letterhead of the MLH reads: "City of Chicago, Department of Police, Municipal Lodging House, 12 North Union Street."

12. Raymond Robins, "Report to the Conference on the Tramp Problem," RP; *Report of the General Superintendent of Police of the City of Chicago to the City Council, The Chicago Municipal Lodging House,* (31 December 1903), pp. 117–19, and (31 December 1904), pp. 125–27, in the Chicago Historical Society. Robins and Assistant Superintendent James Mullenbach kept extensive statistics on the men served by the MLH. For the report of 1905, for instance, 18,872 lodgings were given to 17,006 single men and 1,866 married men, of whom 10,548 were American born, 1,681 Irish, 2,279 German, 1,387 English and Scotch, and "all other nations," 2,977. Age groupings, time in Chicago, level of employment skill, medical condition and treatment, and disposition of each case were carefully noted and tallied, RPG.

13. On the evolution of the MLH, see Thomas Lee Philpott, *The Slum and the Ghetto: Neighborhood Deterioration and Middle Class Reform, Chicago 1880–1930*, p. 108. Notes and itineraries for Robins's MLH tours are in the RP.

14. Raymond Robins to Elizabeth Robins, 14 April 1904, ERP.

15. Wescott's daily two- to three-page typewritten reports to Robins are a valuable record of the problems and functioning of the MLH. The police department order allowing Wescott to take command is undated but new letterheads bearing his name began to be used in January 1903. The order as well as the reports are in the RP.

16. Letter of agreement, W. A. Hamilton to Raymond Robins, 25 July 1903, RP: "Mr. Robins at his own suggestion is to receive no salary from the Settlement Association but in lieu is to receive a secretary paid by the council."

17. Letter of introduction from the City Homes Association, 28 December 1903, RP. A detailed analysis of the campaign is found in letters from Raymond Robins to Elizabeth Robins, 12 and 21 April 1904, ERP.

18. Clarence Darrow served as chairman of the executive committee and Robins was one of the nine members; William E. Burns to Raymond Robins, 17 October 1902, RP.

19. Winston Salisbury to Raymond Robins, 26 February 1916, RP.

20. Notes in Robins's hand, circa 1902–4, RP.

21. M. D. Hull to Raymond Robins, 16 March 1907, and Victor Elting (President of the City Club of Chicago) to Raymond Robins, 30 October 1906, RP, thanking him for his contribution of $1,500. This sum came from the fund for such contributions set aside by Robins and his wife Margaret Dreier, from the earnings of her endowment.

22. Robins was invited by Dr. W. T. Belfield to discuss "the sexual and venereal problem" with members of the Physician's Club. He also appeared before the Chicago Society of Social Hygiene (letter of invitation, 15 October 1906, RP). His paper, "Sexual Vice and Venereal Disease Among the Homeless," was published in the *Proceedings* of the society's 1906 meeting, RPG.

23. News clipping from an unidentified Chicago newspaper, circa 1904, in which Robins is quoted, RP.

24. Raymond Robins to Elizabeth Robins, 27 January 1902, ERP.

25. Raymond Robins to Elizabeth Robins, circa 6 February 1902, ERP.

26. Raymond Robins to Elizabeth Robins, 22 November 1902, ERP.

27. Raymond Robins to Elizabeth Robins, 14 January 1903, ERP.

28. Raymond Robins to Elizabeth Robins, 25 February 1904, ERP.

29. Raymond to Elizabeth, 27 January 1902, ERP.

30. Raymond Robins to Elizabeth Robins, 6 December 1903, ERP, written on the letterhead of the NUS.

31. Raymond to Elizabeth, 25 February 1904, and undated [1903], on the letterhead of the Chicago Commons, ERP.

32. Raymond Robins to Anita McCormick Blaine, 1 April 1904, MBP.

33. Fragment of a letter to Raymond Robins, 3 March 1905, R.P.

34. Raymond Robins to Elizabeth Robins, 19 July 1904, ERP, on the letterhead of the MLH.

35. Raymond Robins to Elizabeth Robins, 5 October 1904, ERP.

36. Raymond Robins to Elizabeth Robins, 11 December 1904, ERP.

37. Ibid.

38. Ibid.

39. Raymond Robins to Elizabeth Robins, 10 February 1905, ERP.

40. Raymond Robins to Anita McCormick Blaine, 3 March 1905, MBP.

41. News clipping from the German-language newspaper *Revue,* New York, 2 July 1905, of an article entitled "Liebe und Socialreform—Wie sich frl. Margarethe Drier und Herr Raymond Robins sennen und lieben lernten," RP. The article discusses their mutual commitment to reform and relates their experiences in the settlement movement. See also Edward T. James, ed., "Margaret Dreier Robins," *Papers of the Women's Trade Union League and Its Principal Leaders: Guide to the Microfilm Edition,* pp. 61–63; Elizabeth Payne, *Reform, Labor and Feminism: Margaret Dreier Robins and the National Women's Trade Union League.*

42. Raymond Robins to Margaret Dreier, 8 May 1905, RP. The letter is on the stationary of the NUS. Her response is not in the Robins Papers, but in his next letter, her name is spelled correctly.

43. Raymond Robins to Margaret Dreier, 29 May 1905, RP.

44. Ibid. Robins wrote Margaret daily during the month of May and sometimes more than once a day. He wrote poems and quoted appropriate psalms and composed lengthy dedications. He often signed these letters, "Raymond of Hernando, Knight of Alaska." He did this as a flourishing jest, but he took very seriously the self-image of knight errant in the cause of social justice.

45. Mary E. Dreier, *Margaret Dreier Robins: Her Life Letters and Work,* p. 24 (hereafter cited as Dreier, *Margaret Dreier Robins*).

46. News clipping from the *Interocean,* Chicago, Ill., 10 June 1905, RP.

47. The first published accounts of Robins's striking it rich appear in 1907, two years after his marriage. As to the $5,000 loan, see Raymond Robins to Elizabeth Robins, 8 October 1907, indicating the repayment plan, at five percent interest and referring to December 1905 as the time of the loan. The loan, the ownership of Chinsegut, the plans for the building of the house and its landscaping—these were all points of bitter contention between Elizabeth and Raymond,

involving legal intermediaries and nearly ending up in court. The underlying issue appears to have been Raymond's choice of Margaret as his life's companion, not money or the house.

48. Raymond to Elizabeth, 8 October 1907, ERP. In a letter from Margaret to Elizabeth written at the same time, Margaret prepared a detailed floor plan of the entire flat to share in some way their home with her "Dear Sister" (circa September 1905, ERP).

49. Allen F. Davis, *Spearheads for Reform: The Social Settlements and the Progressive Movement, 1890–1914*, p. 146 (hereafter cited as Davis, *Spearheads for Reform*).

5. Organized Labor

1. Philip Taft, *Organized Labor in American History*, p. 162 (hereafter cited as Taft, *Organized Labor*). Section 10 of the act, which made this nondiscriminatory provision, was held unconstitutional by the U.S. Supreme Court in *Adair v. United States*, 208 U.S. 161 (1908); see Taft, *Organized Labor*, pp. 246, 297. First epigraph, Raymond Robins to Elizabeth Robins, 5 August 1909, ERP; second extract, quoted in Post, *Biographical Sketch*, p. 23.

2. His seven-page biographical statement, entitled "Why I Believe in Organized Labor," deals with those experiences and served as a major source for this study (typescript of statement, n.d., RP).

3. George E. Mowry, *The Era of Theodore Roosevelt and the Birth of Modern America, 1900–1912*, p. 134 (hereafter cited as Mowry, *The Era of T.R.*).

4. Williams, "Raymond Robins," p. 114.

5. Mowry, *The Era of T.R.*, p. 139.

6. In the Robins Papers (RP), there are several fleeting allusions to Robins's role in the appeal for arbitration by the United Mine Workers Union, but there is no detailed account. Williams's interviews with Robins are the primary source here; see "Raymond Robins," p. 20.

7. *Proceedings of the National Conference of Charities and Correction* (1907), p. 326. See also Davis, *Spearheads for Reform*, p. 46; this source is especially valuable for Robins's early Chicago years. With the coming of the insurmountable problems of the depression, both Raymond, Margaret, and many others in the settlement, reform, and labor movements saw the need for and supported the active intervention of the federal government as the only available solution. Discussion of the paper "The One Main Thing" appears in Robert Hamlett Bremner, *From the Depths: The Discovery of Poverty in America*, pp. 246–47.

8. Taft, *Organized Labor*, p. xv.

9. Post, *Biographical Sketch*, p. 23; Earl E. Beckner, *A History of Labor Legislation in Illinois*, p. 162 (hereafter cited as Beckner, *Labor Legislation*). Also cited in this connection is Camitta, "Study of a Progressive." The quote about Jane Addams is from a letter written by Raymond to Elizabeth, 3 March 1903, ERP.

10. Raymond Robins to Elizabeth Robins, 2 November 1904, ERP. Robins's speech was entitled "Three Opposing Forces in Industrialism," headline and account of speech, *Chicago Herald*, 10 October 1904.

11. This information was recounted in an address by Anton Johansen, *Bulletin of the Women's Trade Union League of Chicago* 37, no. 3 (March 1945).

12. This four-page speech, with many corrections and emendations in Robins's handwriting, was probably written in 1907. The evidence for this is the allusions to events in that year as well as the identical format, typewriter, and paper of other speeches dated 1907 in the Robins collection. His references to "we" may mean the trade union movement as a whole, which would be far too sweeping a generalization of its position, or it could simply refer to himself and Margaret, who shared these convictions regarding socialism. The speech is in box 2, folder 4 of the RP. In another folder, No. 5, in the same box, there is a typescript of another speech containing much of the above-quoted paragraphs, incorporating the corrections in Robins's handwriting. However, this typescript represents pages ten and eleven of a speech delivered by Margaret with

further corrections in her handwriting. The conclusion I would draw is that their ideas on socialism were first formulated and written down by Raymond. This was also the opinion of Lisa
von Borowsky (conversation with the author, 12 August 1971).

13. See my discussion on Robins's reading of Trotsky in chap. 12, especially note 18.

14. Post, *Biographical Sketch*, p. 15; this biographical sketch, prepared in 1908 with Robins's
cooperation, reflects his continued adherence to the single tax idea. See also Henry George,
"The Single Tax, What it is and Why We Urge It," pamphlet widely distributed by the Joseph
Fels Single Tax Fund, 1913, attached to a letter from the fund to Raymond Robins, 30 January
1913, RP. Additional discussion is presented in Chester McArthur Destler, *American Radicalism,
1865–1901*, pp. 12–13; Robert H. Wiebe, *The Search For Order, 1877–1920*, p. 137.

15. A. M. Simons to Raymond Robins, 15 January 1910, RP.

16. H. H. Jacobs to Raymond Robins, 4 May 1912, RP, on the letterhead of the University
Settlement, 861 First Avenue, Milwaukee, Wis.

17. Robins's telling reversed the sequence of events. Debs's brief meeting with Harding
came after his release (Eddy, typescript of biography, p. 319, SEP); H. Wayne Morgan, *Eugene V.
Debs, Socialist for President*, p. 192.

18. One very effective cartoon depicts a fat representative of the "Beef Trust" knocked to
the ground by a puny beef boycotter and alludes to possible damages based on the *Loewe v.
Lawler* precedent, RP.

19. Raymond Robins to Margaret Dreier Robins, 19 April 1908, RP.

20. *Address by Raymond Robins at the National Protest Meeting of the Chicago Federation of Labor, April 19,
1908*, p. 6 (authorized edition of 5,000 copies, RP).

21. Ibid., p. 8.

22. Ibid., p. 12.

23. Ibid., p. 15.

24. Raymond to Margaret, 19 April 1908, RP.

25. Post, *Biographical Sketch*, p. 8. In a letter to Robins from John Fitzpatrick, president of the
Chicago Federation of Labor, dated 4 May 1908, the same tribute was expressed: "The address
of Raymond Robins was never surpassed in a plea for the cause of labor."

26. Raymond Robins to Margaret Dreier Robins, 13 November 1908, RP.

27. Raymond Robins to Margaret Dreier Robins, 15 November 1908, RP. His sense of self-
importance and the dramatic did not blind him to some objectivity, and he did have a sense of
humor. At the end of this letter he added, "Don't show or tell this Child's letter's contents to
anyone. R."

28. Undated news clipping from a Chicago newspaper, circa January 1910: "Ten Hour Law
Starts Dispute—Davies Says He's not to Blame for Late Filing of Brief," RP.

29. Ibid. In a letter to his sister-in-law Mary, dated 9 February 1910, RP, Robins discussed
this situation. He wrote, "This is the result of a conspiracy of which I shall tell you when we
meet again." In this same letter he cautions her and Margaret "to make an absolute transfer of
all your personal property to protect you against suits for personal damages in those strikes
where you are active in the ordinary course of your work." Robins thought these precautions
necessary because of the precedent of the damages award in the Danbury Hatters case, but
warned her to "not speak of this aspect of the matter as it will unduly frighten some of our
good goo-goo friends."

30. Robins, *Raymond and I*, p. 225.

31. *Report on Conditions of Employment in the Iron and Steel Industry*, vol. 3, p. 131, as quoted in Taft,
Organized Labor, p. 198.

32. Raymond to Elizabeth, 5 August 1909, ERP, written on the letterhead of "Hotel Kramer,
Leo J. Kramer, Prop., Elwood, Ind." See also Dreier, *Margaret Dreier Robins*, p. 62; this is from a
letter written by Margaret to her sister, August 1909.

33. William R. Edwards and Robert Edwards to Raymond Robins, 23 October 1914, RP,
with heading, "The Man I Know." This was a testimonial to Robins in connection with his Progressive party campaign for the U.S. Senate from Illinois in 1914.

34. Dreier, *Margaret Dreier Robins,* p. 63.

35. Raymond Robins to Mary Dreier, 4 November 1909, RP; Samuel Yellin, *American Labor Struggles,* pp. 251–52.

36. Raymond Robins to Elizabeth Robins, 21 August 1910, ERP.

37. Raymond Robins to Mary Dreier, 20 November 1909, RP.

38. Raymond Robins to Margaret Dreier Robins, 19 May 1910, RP.

39. Raymond to Elizabeth, 21 August 1910, ERP.

40. Raymond Robins to Margaret Dreier Robins, 25 October and 4 November 1910, RP. See also undated front-page news clipping from an unidentified Philadelphia newspaper with the headline: "Nothing Conceded, Says P.R.T. (Philla. Rapid Transit); Wold Now Vice President.— Company sees No Change in Swing Run Policy. STRIKE NEEDLESS—Agreement Belittled in Statement by the Corporation—$25,000 to LOYAL MEN" RP; *The Philadelphia Record,* 9 November 1910, report of the complete arbitration agreement, signed John G. Vogler and Raymond Robins, with full discussion of the proceedings and a statement by Robins.

41. Raymond to Margaret, 4 November 1910, RP. There is no newspaper report of C. O. Pratt's abduction. It appears to have been kept from the press to avoid inflaming already exasperated passions.

42. For four years all went well, until the ownership of the P.R.T. Company changed hands, at which time there was an attempt to renege on the arbitration agreement. On 10 March 1914, H. B. Barron, who had been the secretary of the grievance committee and cosigner of the arbitration agreement for the union, wrote to Robins asking for his help once again. Fortunately the dispute was settled quickly, since at that moment Robins was far too busy to help. He was involved in the U.S. Senate race on the Progressive party ticket in Illinois, the one bid for a major elective political office that he ever attempted (H. B. Barron to Raymond Robins, 19 March 1914; preliminary arbitration agreement dated 17 October 1910, RP).

43. Dreier, *Margaret Dreier Robins,* p. 25. This passage was written by Mary Dreier, Robins's sister-in-law. Shortly after his marriage to Margaret, Robins had established with Mary a very close and deep relationship, filled with intense respect, love, and mutual commitment to the causes of social reform, brotherhood, and world peace.

44. The Rudovitz case involved the arrest and extradition proceedings brought against a Russian alien who sought political asylum in the United States. Robins's efforts in his behalf are discussed in chapter 7. Buck refers to the Buck Stove and Range Company boycott, discussed above. It seems that Robins considered these the two most noteworthy accomplishments of the year (Robins's diary, 1908–13, entry for 31 December 1908, RP).

6. The Mission of the Social Gospel

1. Robins, *Both Sides of the Curtain,* p. 53. According to the *Guide to Manuscripts in the Wisconsin State Historical Society, Supplement 2,* the text of a sermon dated 17 June 1888 in the RP was "delivered at a prison chapel at the age of 15" (p. 165). Epigraph RP.

2. See Robins's speech, "The Association and the Forces That Tend to Disintegrate Faith and Character," delivered at the YMCA Cleveland Conference on 13 May 1916, stenographic typescript in the RP.

3. "Politics and Labor" was a series of reports on a number of current developments in brief reportorial style: praise for Theodore Roosevelt for his support of the "wageworker" and criticism for Roosevelt's attack on philosophical anarchists; the annual convention of the American Federation of Labor, then meeting at Scranton, Pennsylvania; a proposal for an "anti-strike conference" of big business and labor and even a section entitled, "Labor Conditions in Japan." See Louise C. Wade, *Graham Taylor: Pioneer for Social Justice, 1851–1938,* p. 155 (hereafter cited as Wade, *Graham Taylor*); "Politics and Labor," *The Commons* 6, no. 66 (January 1902): 10–13. A major source of information on the Chicago years, including many articles written by or about Robins, are *The Commons* and *The Public. The Commons* was published from 1905 to 1909, after

which it merged with other New York social service and reform publications under a new name, *The Survey*, which continued to publish until 1952.

4. Also see Walter Rauschenbusch's *Christianizing the Social Order* (1913). Sherwood Eddy, Robins's friend and fellow evangelist, wrote: "It was from Robins' lips that I first heard 'the social gospel' as it was then called, before I ever heard Walter Rauschenbusch or Washington Gladden." This is from an incomplete draft of an untitled book by Eddy dealing with his experiences and meetings with many great men who were his contemporaries. He began his account of Robins with: "The life that was the most dramatic and romantic of any of my friends was that of Raymond Robins," SEP.

5. Dickey, as Robins's agent, entered into an agreement with the publisher in which "Raymond Robins is to take the platform visiting various cities, the chief object of his work being to increase the circulation of *The Public* and to solicit subscriptions to the capital stock of the Public Publishing Company." Raymond and Margaret, as well as members of Margaret's family (following Raymond and Margaret's pleas) had all subscribed to save *The Public* from going out of business. Memorandum of Agreement of 10 September 1907 between Dickey and the Company; also a statement of Robins's accomplishments on the tour and a record of all monies received by contribution and otherwise up to 20 June 1908, RP.

6. Following the tour, Dickey solicited letters of appreciation from the sponsors of the groups before which Robins spoke. Some of the most complimentary, and those from well-known national figures, eventually appeared as an addendum to Post's *Raymond Robins, A Biographical Sketch*.

7. Printed flyer, RP.

8. Raymond Robins to Mark M. Fagan, n.d. (circa October 1907), RP. A letter from James Mullenbach to Raymond Robins reads in part: "Although the fight is a local one, I think as a matter of fact it is the beginning of your national work. From Chicago as a center, I believe that henceforth you will be called more and more into the big fight that is nation-wide. It was a good place to begin in Jersey City [with its] hostile layer of predatory monsters of all kinds" (15 October 1907, RP).

9. The report on Robins's work in 1908 was prepared by Dickey, cited in note 5.

10. Subjects included: Tales of Alaska; Practical Politics; Industrial Freedom; Crime and Criminals; The New Censorship; Trades Unions and the Home; The Ultimate Sanctions for Life; Men's Clubs and Civic Patriotism; Civic Corruption and the Way Out; Sidelights on Graft and Grafters; The Social Consciousness of Christ; 'Except the Lord Build the House'; Woman Suffrage and Civic Progress; Social Settlements and Social Justice; Henry George, Prophet of Social Justice; 'And this is the Victory that Overcometh'; Homeless Men or Industrial Human Waste; Women in Industry and the Social Conscience; Abraham Lincoln the Incarnation of Democracy; Public Education and the Children of the Workers; Joseph Mazzini and the Heroes of Young Italy; the Endless Chain in Graft or the Ruin of Citizenship; Thomas Jefferson and the Democratic Theory in Government (Post, *Biographical Sketch*, p. 80).

11. See the 31 December 1908 entry from the 1908–13 diary, RP.

12. E. G. Ray to Luther S. Dickey, 4 November 1907, RP.

13. See chap. 4.

14. Raymond Robins to S. Wirt Wiley, General Secretary of the YMCA, 17 May 1912, RP.

15. Raymond Robins to Mary Dreier, 6 January 1912, from Worchester, Mass., RP.

16. Raymond Robins, "Sermons on Social Service, Being Stenographic Reports of Parts of the Addresses Delivered Each Week for Twenty-Six Weeks by Mr. Robins as Social Service Member of Team No. 3 of the Men and Religion Forward Movement," *The Survey* 28, no. 1 (6 April 1912): 35–64. This is the most important published source of Robins's social gospel thought and work.

17. Daniel Kiefer to Raymond Robins, 19 April 1912, RP, on the letterhead of the Joseph Fels Fund.

18. C. H. Ingersoll to Raymond Robins, 15 May 1912, RP.

19. Unsigned note to Raymond Robins, September 1912, Paris, Illinois, among other papers dated 1912 in the RP.

Interesting in this light is an article that appeared in *The Public* at the beginning of the MRFM, "A Business Movement in Religion," vol. 14, no. 704 (29 September 1911): 1003. It discusses J. P. Morgan's sponsoring of the MRFM with more than a hint of sarcasm. Considering the constant praise of Robins as activist and social reformer throughout the long publishing history of *The Public*, this article certainly reflects distrust for Robins's evangelical work. *The Survey*, because of its charitable and religious orientation, in contrast to the more political position of *The Public*, actively supported the MRFM; see Fred B. Smith, "The 'Forward Movement,'" *The Survey* 28, no. 1 (6 April 1912): 33; and "Men and Religion Movement to Circle Globe," *The Survey* 29, no. 3 (19 October 1912): 86.

20. Note about Carnegie, dated only 1907; Henry Clay Frick to Raymond Robins, 22 October 1911, RP.

21. Raymond Robins to Elizabeth Robins, 23 November 1912, ERP.

22. Raymond Robins to Elizabeth Robins, 16 August 1911, ERP.

23. Fred B. Smith, "About Raymond Robins," *The Congregationalist and Herald of Gospel Liberty* 117, no. 43 (27 October 1932): 1391.

24. Raymond Robins to Harry N. Holmes, of the World Alliance of Churches, n.d., carbon copy, RP.

25. Raymond Robins to Elizabeth Robins, 24 April 1905, ERP. Immediate results from Robins's speeches were not uncommon. "Your address to the City Club had one practical result—," Carroll M. Davis wrote to Robins after a speech delivered at Christ Church Cathedral, "the wages of the waiters have been raised to the union scale" (22 December 1911, ERP).

26. Raymond Robins to Margaret Dreier Robins, 28 and 30 January 1912, RP.

27. "Preliminary Statement Concerning the World Tour of Fred B. Smith and Raymond Robins," printed brochure, RP; "Men and Religion Forward Movement to Circle Globe," p. 86.

28. Raymond Robins to Frieda Maynard, 22 February 1913, RP.

29. Raymond Robins to William Fulton, 20 August 1913, RP.

30. Raymond Robins, "Why I have Given a Year to Evangelistic Effort with Students," a three-page typescript, undated, but probably written in 1916, RP.

31. Printed decision card, RP.

32. Raymond Robins to John Childs, 17 December 1915, RP. The conflict grew quite heated in the case of the opposition of the local campus organizers at Princeton University. Thom Evans opposed compulsory attendance and the distribution of decision cards and sought autonomy for the local campus organizers. Finally, Robins ran the program, but without the distribution of decision cards (Thom Evans to J. L. Childs, 12 November 1915, RP).

33. C. H. Ingersoll to L. S. Dickey, 27 January 1908, published in Post, *Biographical Sketch*, p. 69.

34. The author of an unsigned letter to Robins sympathetically advises him on this subject: "I would also suggest that you make clear at the outset of your talks that you are bound to draw from your own personal experience for illustration. Certain critical, undiscriminating souls are likely to claim that the speaker unduly stresses the ego" (18 December 1915, RP).

35. Raymond Robins to Mary Dreier, 16 and 17 June 1915, RP.

36. Undated typed list entitled "Campaigns," with additions in Robins's handwriting, RP. Information in brackets has been added by the author.

7. Chicago Politics

1. Robins addressed this question in "A Settlement in City Politics," *The Commons* 8, no. 82 (May 1903): 1–3.

2. An excellent work that focuses on the role of the settlement worker in political activity

to achieve reform is Davis, *Spearheads for Reform.* Some of the same questions are dealt with in Wade, *Graham Taylor.*

3. Steffens, *The Shame of the Cities,* p. 173. Taylor was chosen by George E. ("King") Cole, a respected, self-described "second-class business man," who in turn was chosen as one of the "Nine." The idea for the "Nine," who would then seek out the "One Hundred" to join them, had come at a meeting of the conservative, very respectable, "but inefficient universal reforming association," the Chicago Civic Federation.

4. Wade, *Graham Taylor,* p. 132.

5. Davis, *Spearheads for Reform,* p. 166.

6. Steffens, *The Shame of the Cities,* pp. 173, 181. According to Robins, the margin of Republican victory in 1901 was 1,257 and William Dever's Democratic-Reform plurality of 1902 was 1,819 (Raymond Robins to Elizabeth Robins, 5 April 1902, ERP).

7. Robins's account of the "Anarchist excitement" was written on 5 September 1914, in response to the request for more information on the subject from Medill McCormick, then chairman of the Progressive Party State Central Committee. At that time Robins was heading the state ticket of the Progressive party in his bid for the United States Senate from Illinois. Robins was clarifying his role in a situation that was controversial and, in the minds of some, politically embarrassing. His account was attached to a letter to McCormick with the above date, both in the RP.

8. Ibid., p. 2.

9. The Isaacs case can be compared to Robins's defense of the church lands against the claim jumpers in Nome just a year before and his later fight against the extradition of political refugee Christian Rudovitz.

10. Robins, "Politics and Labor," p. 11.

11. Robins to McCormick, 5 September 1914, RP.

12. Ibid., p. 4.

13. Raymond Robins to Elizabeth Robins, 11 September 1901, ERP.

14. Raymond to Elizabeth, 5 April 1902, ERP; Steffens, *The Shame of the Cities,* pp. 173, 181; Davis, *Spearheads for Reform,* p. 167.

15. Henry Barrett Chamberlain to Professor Graham Taylor, 16 December 1902, RP. In addition to his own support for Robins, Chamberlain refers to assurances he had received from Alderman John Smulski and William E. Dever in support of Robins's candidacy. Four days later, 20 December 1902, Robins received a letter from Graham Taylor suggesting that he run on the Democratic ticket. Taylor also cites support from Walter L. Fisher, RP.

16. Typescript of a speech beginning, "Gentlemen of the 21st Senatorial District," with notations in Robins's handwriting, pp. 2 and 3, RP.

17. Ibid.; Raymond Robins to Elizabeth Robins, 25 October 1902, ERP. See also *The Record Herald,* Chicago, 19 November 1902; clipping from another Chicago newspaper of the same date, headline: "Brisk Fight on 'Ben,'" ERP; Davis, *Spearheads for Reform,* p. 168.

18. Davis, *Spearheads for Reform,* pp. 163, 168.

19. Raymond Robins to Anita McCormick Blaine, 8 October and 1 November 1904, along with attached circulars, MBP; Allen Davis appears to cite this correspondence in his account of the campaign. He speaks of Robins's "forlorn hope" (*Spearheads for Reform,* pp. 168–69). See also Raymond Robins to Elizabeth Robins, 12 April 1904, ERP.

20. Among the most dramatic conversions to an unpopular radical position was that of multimillionaire conservative William Boyce Thompson, in Russia at the time of the Bolshevik Revolution. In the 1920s and 1930s, Robins supported Harding, Coolidge, and Hoover in their successful bids for the presidency.

21. Raymond to Elizabeth, 10 February 1905, ERP.

22. S. T. Hammersmark to Raymond Robins, 3 March 1905, RP. The writer's disbelief and concern led him to say that "if the statement is to be corrected, no one would be more pleased to hear so than I."

23. William Bransford to Raymond Robins, 15 March 1905, RP.

24. Article in the *Chicago Daily News*, circa 15 March 1905, clipping, RP.

25. In 1912 Robins broke with Harlan because of Harlan's opposition to the Progressive party.

26. Raymond Robins to Mayor Edward F. Dunne, 8 May 1905, carbon copy, and Dunne to Robins, 9 May 1905, RP. This letter was published under the title "Open Letter to Mayor Dunne," in *The Public* 8, no. 371 (13 May 1905): 89.

27. Margaret Haley, quoted in Post, *Biographical Sketch*, p. 49.

28. Raymond Robins to Elizabeth Robins, 6 October 1906, ERP; Margaret Dreier Robins to Mary Dreier, 6 November 1906, cited in Dreier, *Margaret Dreier Robins*, p. 31.

29. *Chicago Tribune*, 19 October 1906.

30. Margaret Dreier Robins to Lincoln Steffens, 6 November 1906, cited in Dreier, *Margaret Dreier Robins*, p. 29. This letter provides a detailed examination of the Board of Education situation. In response to this attack, Robins led the Board of Education in passing a resolution to file suit against the *Chicago Tribune* and referring all the facts to the State's Attorney General. The resolution was written by Robins and published in *The Public* 9, no. 446 (20 September 1906): 677.

31. Margaret to Mary Dreier, 6 November 1906, cited in Dreier, *Margaret Dreier Robins*, p. 31.

32. Ibid., p. 29; Margaret to Lincoln Steffens, 6 November 1906, cited in ibid., p. 31; Margaret Dreier Robins to Jane Addams, November 1906, RP.

33. News clipping, *Chicago Tribune*, 19 February 1907, RP. The *Chicago Record Herald* covered the arrest of John Kane, Frank Kersine, and W. Flannery in articles on 25 and 26 February, and the discharge of their indictments on 14 and 27 March. An untitled article, without a byline, also appeared in *The Public* 8, no. 412 (24 February 1907): 778, expressing outrage regarding the attack on Robins. For Madden's philosophy, see Stephen Longstreet, *Chicago, 1860–1919*, pp. 414–15.

34. Sworn typewritten statement by Raymond Robins, dated 3 August 1910, RP.

35. Raymond Robins to Elizabeth Robins, 23 September 1910, ERP. Publicity on the threats to Robins's life was widespread and if anything had happened to him, all those he had attacked for corruption would have been suspected of the murder.

36. See chap. 5.

37. Raymond to Elizabeth, 6 October 1906, ERP.

38. Dreier, *Margaret Dreier Robins*, p. 28.

39. Receipt from the Board of Election Commissions of Chicago, dated 31 December 1907, RP.

40. "Insiders and a City—Extracts from Raymond Robins' Talk on 'Franchise Grabbers and Plain Citizens,'" in the *Kansas City Times Star*, 13 July 1909, RP. Robins made this speech before the City Club of Kansas City during its consideration of municipal ownership of its street railways.

41. Ibid. This is an excerpt from the speech that was frequently interrupted by the audiences cheers of approval, especially after Robins's proclamation that: "whenever there is an effort to exploit a community, you hear on every side the argument, 'widows and orphans.'" The reference to "widows and orphans" concerns the stockholders who argued that reduction in profits would harm the fixed incomes of widows and orphans who depended on stock holdings.

42. Subcommittee Report to Committee on Utilities of the Chicago Charter Convention for Municipal Ownership, 1906, typescript, RP.

43. Post, *Biographical Sketch*, p. 20.

44. Elizabeth's novel, *My Little Sister* (the American version of *Where Are You Going To?*, published in London), dealing with prostitution and women's rights, was similarly radical and widely discussed after its publication in 1913.

45. Raymond Robins to Elizabeth Robins, 13 October 1911, ERP.

46. Raymond Robins to Mrs. Grace Wilbur Trout, president of the Illinois Free Suffrage Association, 5 September 1914, RP. This carbon copy of a long letter on his women's suffrage position was one of many. He wrote it on the occasion of his race for the U.S. Senate on the Progressive party ticket for Illinois in 1914; the suffrage issue was considered an important one. This is described in his letter to Antionette Funk, 19 July 1915, in which he also pledged the last weeks in October 1915 to work for the New York Suffrage Campaign, RP.

47. News clipping, no byline, the *Minneapolis Tribune,* Tues., 24 March 1908, R.P. Adjoining the article is an excellent cartoon caricature of Robins in the posture of an adamant speaker. On such stereotypes, see Aileen S. Kraditor, *The Ideas of the Woman Suffrage Movement: 1890–1920,* chaps. 3 and 5.

48. Raymond Robins to Margaret Dreier Robins, 8 June 1911, RP.

49. Catherine Waugh McCulloch to Raymond Robins, 8 January 1907, and reply, 14 January 1907, RP.

50. Raymond Robins to Elizabeth Robins, 18 October 1907; Post, *Biographical Sketch,* p. 20; Progressive Committee, *Story,* p. 11.

51. Copy of bill of particulars in a suit dated 21 March 1907, *Raymond Robins, et al. v. Fred Busse, the Board of Education,* MBP.

52. Post, *Biographical Sketch,* p. 19.

53. See chap. 6

54. "Bryan at New Haven," *The Public* 10, no. 505 (7 December 1907): 850–51.

55. L. J. Quinby, "Raymond Robins in Omaha," *The Public* 10, no. 520 (21 March 1908): 1209–10.

56. Raymond Robins to Margaret Dreier Robins, 6 March 1908, RPG. No explanation is extant.

57. "Raymond Robins at the Denver Convention—Address of Raymond Robins of Illinois, Before the National Democratic Convention at Denver, July 9, as reported by the Associated Press," *The Public* 11, no. 542 (21 August 1908): 497–98; "Raymond Robins and the Campaign Issue," *The Public* 11, no. 552 (24 April 1908): 73–74; Margaret E. Chase, "Raymond Robins in Boston," *The Public* 11, no. 525 (24 April 1908): 82; "Labor Federation of Illinois," *The Public* 11, no. 552 (30 September 1908): 731–32.

58. See chap. 5 for a full discussion of the National Protest speech.

59. Pamphlet entitled "The Right of Asylum, The Attempt of Russia to Extradite Christian Rudovitz for a Political Offense—The Rudovitz Case: A Statement," "Issued by the Political Refugee Defense League, Raymond Robins, Secretary, 372 W. Ohio St., Chicago, Illinois," n.d., p. 3. The address of the Political Refugee Defense League was the same as Robins's residence. Although undocumented, I assume that Robins wrote the pamphlet and also paid for its publication and distribution. The pamphlet, in poor condition, is in the RP.

60. Ibid.

61. *Chicago Tribune,* 30 November 1908; "Russian Extradition," *The Public* 11, no. 557 (4 December 1908): 843–44.

62. Williams, "Raymond Robins," p. 26. Williams cites his conversation with Robins on 9 August 1949 for Robins's account of his meeting with Theodore Roosevelt in connection with the Rudovitz case.

8. The Progressive Party

1. Richard Hofstadter abridged his identification of the "distinguishing qualities" of progressivism in *The Progressive Movement, 1900–1915,* pp. 4–9; Hofstadter, *The Age of Reform, From Bryan to F.D.R.* Gabriel Kolko, *The Triumph of Conservatism: A Reinterpretation of American History, 1900–1916.*

The Progressive Era and the very meaning of the terms *Progressive* and *Progressivism* have spawned one of the most wide-ranging and interesting historiographical debates and revisionisms in American history. Daniel T. Rodgers, "In Search of Progressivism," *Reviews in American History* 10, no. 4 (1982): 113–32, is an enlightening guide through the labyrinth of definition, categorization, and debate in this extensive literature. Epigraphs, letters from ERP.

2. Raymond Robins to Elizabeth Robins, 10 August and 30 September 1910, ERP; Mowry,

The Era of Theodore Roosevelt, pp. 273–74; George E. Mowry, *Theodore Roosevelt and the Progressive Movement,* pp. 128–32 (hereafter cited as Mowry, *T.R. and the Progressive Movement*).

3. Telegram, Robert M. La Follette to Raymond Robins, 22 April 1912, RP; copy in ERP. The balance of power was retained by the Republican party regulars, entrenched and under the patronage of the incumbent Taft.

4. The personal motives of and conflicts between Roosevelt and Taft, which were very important factors in Roosevelt's championing the third-party cause, are not directly pertinent here. One important point, considering Robins's many anti-Wilson speeches during the campaign, is Roosevelt's essentially positive opinion of Woodrow Wilson before 1912. After the Democratic convention at Baltimore, "Roosevelt wrote a friend that had Wilson been nominated before the Chicago convention, he would not have remained in the fight" (Mowry, *T.R. and the Progressive Movement,* p. 256). Robins's evaluation of Taft's nomination appeared in a letter to Elizabeth, 4 July 1912, ERP.

5. Raymond to Elizabeth, 4 July 1912, ERP.

6. Paul Kellogg to Raymond Robins, and Owen Lovejoy to Raymond Robins, 15 July 1912, ERP.

7. Raymond Robins to Elizabeth Robins, 20 July 1912, ERP.

8. Raymond Robins to Margaret Dreier Robins, 20 July 1912, Robins's emphasis, RPG. One letter corroborates the meeting: "out to Oyster Bay and for three hours . . . with Roosevelt. . . . Roosevelt gave me special consideration all through the talk and I sat at his right at luncheon" (Raymond to Margaret, 20 July 1912, RPG).

9. Raymond to Elizabeth, 20 July 1912, ERP.

10. Hagedorn's account and letter in RP.

11. Raymond Robins to Clarence A. Barbour, 16 September 1912, RP.

12. Clarence A. Barbour to Raymond Robins, 12 September 1912, RP.

13. Robins to Barbour, 16 September 1912, RP.

14. Ibid.

15. Ibid.

16. Paul Kellogg to Raymond Robins, 10 July 1912, RP.

17. Benjamin C. March to Raymond Robins, 12, 15, and 26 July 1912, RP. While Robins had been an active single taxer, speaking widely in its behalf, he did not press for this more radical cause in the adoption of the Progressive party platform in 1912.

18. According to George Mowry, George Perkins "surprisingly enough . . . approved of the speech" (*T.R. and the Progressive Movement,* p. 266). The "Confession of Faith" speech had reiterated the points made in his earlier Osawatomie speech, which was "probably . . . the most radical speech ever given by an ex-president" (Ibid., p. 144). Mowry does not cite any evidence to demonstrate Perkins's approval, although he does cite correspondence with Frank A. Munsey, another conservative, who politely approved of the speech.

19. *New York Times,* 7 August 1912, cited in Mowry, *T.R. and the Progressive Movement,* p. 265. The *New York Times* observer was commenting on the zeal with which the delegates received Roosevelt, and of his utter dismay. The reporter was perceptively implying that Roosevelt could not understand his reception because he could not share their passions and aspirations for the future era of reform.

20. Medill McCormick to Raymond Robins, 4 August 1912, RP. Reference is made to the speakers bureau of the Progressive party.

21. J. Y. Chisholm, chairman of the Speakers' Bureau of the Progressive Party to an unknown recipient, 5 October 1912, RP: "I had 25 calls for him in my mail this morning, 24 of which I turned down and you know what the other one was. As Chicago is 2/5ths of the state and there are nearly a million working men to be reached here and as Raymond Robins is the only man to do it, we must absolutely refuse to send him out after that date and must use him here. "

22. H. Wayne Morgan, "Eugene Debs and the Socialist Campaign of 1912," *Mid-America* 39 (1957): 210–25.

23. Raymond Robins to Elizabeth Robins, 23 November 1912, ERP.

24. Ibid.

25. W. A. Hamman to Raymond Robins, 13 October 1912, RP.

26. Raymond Robins to Frieda Maynard, 19 January and 1 July 1913, RP; these letters were written while he was on the World Tour. Frieda was the teenage daughter of an old friend and a devoted follower of Wilson, and Robins's kind words may, in part, be attributable to this fact.

27. Raymond Robins to Frances A. Kellor, 14 October 1913, and to J. F. Schureman, 8 November 1913, RP.

28. Raymond Robins to Elizabeth Robins, 14 October 1913, ERP.

29. Raymond Robins to Horace F. Morse, 3 December 1913, and William Allen White to Raymond Robins, 26 February 1914, RP, and 7 March 1914, ERP. In this 7 March letter, White wrote: "I believe that with six years in the senate you would emerge in 1920 as the undisputed leader of the Progressive movement in America, and that as its leader you would find yourself in the White House."

30. Raymond Robins to Elizabeth Robins, 1 February 1914, ERP. On that same day, Raymond also wrote to Mary Dreier: "If I run it will be just to help the party for 1916, as the outcome is inevitable defeat. If I think it will be of sufficient service, I will run, otherwise, not" (RP). In this letter to Mary, Robins complained: "I am still suffering from lack of sleep, I have never been as nervous as I am now. I am sure this is due simply to a lack of rest before taking on another hard task. I have to have a long rest after this campaign."

31. Raymond Robins to Montaville Flowers, director of the Progressive National Lyceum Service, New York City, 22 October 1913, RP. Robins included similar messages to numerous correspondents as an excuse for refusing invitations to speak. He had constantly to remind people across the nation that "I should remain close to my task here in Illinois."

32. Raymond Robins to T. H. Hollister, member of the Illinois State Central Committee, 22 October 1913, RP. Robins unremittingly faced the warning that "a three cornered fight means the election of a Democrat," because the major source of Progressive strength was the reform wing of the Republican party. Robins maintained that the Progressive party welcomed and sought support from the reform-minded of both old parties, and he saw no reason not to expect a widespread bipartisan move in the direction of the new party. This sentiment is expressed in a letter from Frank Suite to Robins, 13 November 1913, RP.

33. William A. White to Raymond Robins, 14 February 1914, RP; Raymond Robins to Harold Ickes, 17 February 1914, Harold Ickes Papers, Library of Congress, Washington, D.C. (hereafter cited as HIP).

34. Raymond Robins to Geo. Perkins, 9 and 10 March 1913, RP.

35. David Thelen, *Robert M. La Follette and the Insurgent Spirit*, p. 17.

36. Harold Ickes to Raymond Robins, 24 April and 12 May 1914, RP.

37. See chap. 3, esp. p. 58.

38. Theodore Roosevelt to Raymond Robins, 21 May 1914, RP, and 12 August 1914, eleven pages, Theodore Roosevelt Papers, Library of Congress, Washington, D.C. (hereafter cited as TRP); Raymond Robins to Elizabeth Robins, 29 June 1914, ERP, discussing Noyes's telegram. Two days before receiving Roosevelt's 21 May letter, Robins fell and dislocated his right knee. He recovered swiftly, although at first there was concern about whether or not he could carry out an arduous campaign.

39. Raymond Robins to Mary Dreier, 3 and 5 July 1914, RP.

40. Ibid.

41. Raymond Robins to Elizabeth Robins, 3 and 5 July 1914, ERP. In his 3 July letter, in the same paragraph, Robins wrote these suggestive and contradictory sentences: "Keep in mind that I have done my utmost to avoid a situation that shall bring to light all the shadow land of my own life and that of the Robins clan. . . . Steady yourself for the slime. There is no true word regarding me that need cause you to tremble." Robins was concerned about his personal and family problems of mental illness, not moral or political scandal or corruption.

42. Raymond to Elizabeth, 5 July 1914, ERP; Robins to Mary Dreier, 5 July 1914, RP.

43. Raymond Robins to Mary Dreier, 22 August 1914, RP.

9. Campaign for the U.S. Senate

1 "Keynote Speech by Raymond Robins, Nominee for United States Senator, Delivered at the Progressive State Convention, in Urbana, Illinois, September 18, 1914," Progressive State Committee, Chicago, Ill., p. 7, RP. The platform of the Illinois Progressive party in the 1914 campaign is printed in full in appendix B.

2. "Keynote Speech." See also Hugh Reid, Secretary, Democratic Raymond Robins League of Cook Co., to Margaret Haley, 2 October 1914, Chicago Teachers Federation Papers, Chicago Historical Society (hereafter cited as CTP).

3. *Chicago Tribune*, 12 October 1914, as quoted in *The Geneseo News*, 27 October 1914, in the "Robins Supplement," RP.

4. *The Commoner*, August 1914, quoted "Robins Supplement," RP.

5. *The Geneseo News*, 27 October 1914, in the "Robins Supplement" RP. Roosevelt went on to do some campaigning for Robins. On 24 and 25 September Roosevelt spoke at Rock Island and at Centralia: "flash-lighted, dug coal with Raymond Robins, the Bull Moose candidate for Senator"; untitled news clipping (TRP). See also Wm. B. McKinley to Chas. D. Hilles, 28 September 1914, in the William E. Borah Papers, Library of Congress (hereafter cited as WBP).

6. *New York Times*, 6 October 1914. Owen, Norris, Clapp, Crosser, and Manahan were members of the National Popular Government League, which sent its endorsement in a telegram from Washington dated 5 October 1914, published later that week in *The Public* 17, no. 862 (9 September 1914): 975–76. *The Public* had published an article entitled: "Raymond Robins Deserving of Democratic Support," 17, no. 852, p. 762, as early as 31 July 1914, and continued to seek Democratic support for his election. One article by Samuel Danziger, with the self-explanatory title: "Robins' Election Means Approval of Wilson," 17, no. 836 (16 September 1914): 985, attempted to place Robins in Wilson's camp and thereby win Wilson votes.

7. W. F. McCombs, chairman of the National Democratic Committee and Postmaster General Albert Burelson were two of the high-ranking Democrats who were selected to counterbalance the support being given Robins by other prominent Democrats; *Chicago Tribune*, 2 October 1914, quoted in Williams, "Raymond Robins," p. 30.

8. "Robins' Popularity," *The Commercial News*, Chicago, 20 October 1914.

9. C. D. Thomas to Raymond Robins, 21 October 1914, and W. W. Wright to Robins, n.d., RP. To help answer this charge, Samuel Danziger, the new editor of *The Public*, published an article entitled: "Senator Sherman and the Single Tax," 17, no. 861 (2 September 1914): 941–42, denying its truth and, further, attacking the reasoning that the single tax would destroy the farmer and small householder. *The Public* stood firmly in support of Robins on nearly every issue.

10. C. S. Raymond, "Raymond Robins," *Chicago Tribune*, 29 October 1914, clipping, RP.

11. *The Public* 17, no. 870 (4 December 1914): 1165; also cited in Williams, "Raymond Robins," p. 31. In Marion County, Illinois, Robins received 38 more votes (2,137 to 2,099) than Roosevelt had in 1912. He received 500 more votes than any other Progressive candidate in Piatt County, which "is considered the strongest Republican county in the state," and came within 111 votes of beating out Sullivan for second place. See Vern E. Joy, publisher of the *Egypt Daily*, to Raymond Robins, 7 November 1914, and Evan J. Horbacker to Robins, 5 November 1914, RP.

12. Raymond Robins to Elizabeth Robins, 15 November 1914, from Chinsegut, Florida, ERP.

13. Raymond Robins to J. J. Lansing, 11 November 1914, RP.

14. Raymond Robins to Frank H. Bode, 9 November 1914, RP.

15. Harold Ickes to Raymond Robins, 3 December 1914, RP.

16. Raymond to Elizabeth, 15 November 1914, ERP.

17. Telegram, "George Plimpton, Mrs. William H. Baldwin, Charles C. Burlingham have

chosen you. Answer, 44 Cedar Street, N.Y.C." RP. See Davis, *American Heroine*, chap. 12 for an explanation of the evolution of these organizational names.

18. George Porter to Raymond Robins, 12 January 1915; Jane Addams to Robins, 13 January 1915; Larou Louges to Robins, 11 January 1915, RP. Jane Addams indicated that the $10,000 referred to in the initial telegram had come from the Carnegie Foundation and that the league had been organized in New York only about two weeks before the offer to Robins. Addams did not specify the turncoat leaders.

19. Margaret Dreier Robins to Raymond Robins, 23 August 1914, with the first mention of the war in their correspondence, RP.

20. Raymond Robins to Elizabeth Robins, 12 February 1915, ERP. In the same vein, Robins wrote a letter to Charles Crane, thanking him for his support in the Illinois race and concluding: "It will now be possible to rally all the genuine progressives to the Wilson standard in 1916 if he keeps the faith." 7 January 1915, Charles R. Crane Papers, Bakhmeteff Archive, Butler Library, Columbia University (hereafter cited as CRCP).

21. Raymond Robins to James Andrews, 17 May 1915, RP.

22. Raymond Robins to Theodore Roosevelt, 3 May 1915, RP.

23. Theodore Roosevelt to Raymond Robins, 3 June 1915, RP.

24. Raymond Robins to Gifford Pinchot, 19 July 1915, RP.

25. Raymond Robins to George Record, 19 July 1915, RP. Here, Robins was specifically referring to Medill McCormick.

26. Raymond Robins to Elizabeth Robins, 14 February 1916, RP.

27. George Perkins to Raymond Robins, 26 January 1916, RP; Minutes of the Progressive National Committee, 11 January 1916; Roosevelt MSS as cited in Mowry, *T.R. and the Progressive Movement*, pp. 330–31.

28. *New York Times*, 8 June 1916. The account of the speech and the first day of the convention presented here are based on the extensive coverage in this issue of the *Times*. Excerpts from Robins's speech and some interesting analysis are also to be found in "The Progressive Convention," *The Public* 19, no. 950 (16 June 1916): 562–63. Robins role as keynote speaker and temporary chairman are analyzed by him in a letter to Elizabeth: "It was against my better judgment that I have taken this task. I preferred to wait for the real task when I have to lead an endorsement or a bolt as the case may be. But . . . it will not be without its advantages" (16 May 1916, ERP).

29. *New York Times*, 8 June 1916.

30. Ibid.

31. *New York Times*, 11 June 1916; *Chicago Tribune*, 11 June 1916.

32. Typewritten memorandum, Roosevelt MSS, as cited by Mowry in *T.R. and the Progressive Movement*, p. 354, n. 17.

33. "Progressives Become Obsolete," 13 June 1916, clipping, RP.

34. Raymond Robins to Mary McDowel, 21 June 1916, RP.

35. Ibid. Robins wrote to G. E. Allen, "The National Committee will not favor a National Progressive ticket if Col. Roosevelt does finally decline the nomination. My action personally will be to some degree determined by the recommendation of the National Committee" (21 June 1916, RP).

36. Raymond Robins to Frank P. Walsh, 27 July 1916, RP.

37. Untitled news clipping quoting Robins, among papers and letters, July 1916, RP.

38. Raymond Robins to George Perkins, 13 July 1916, RP.

39. William A. Fulton to Raymond Robins, 19 July 1916, and Robins to Fulton, 26 July 1916, RP.

40. Raymond Robins to H. H. Baker, 20 July 1916, RP. In a draft fragment of his autobiography, Harold Ickes, whose son Raymond was Robins's godchild, claimed: "Only great persuasiveness on my part made a progressive out of Robins in 1912 . . . and in the end I had the personal gratification of hearing Raymond say that I had convinced him and that he would support Hughes," HIP. Ickes and Robins were close friends and long-time veterans of many reform

struggles, and while certainly an influence, no one man's opinion could have been so definitive, given Robins's powerful personality.

41. Raymond Robins to Frank P. Walsh, 27 July 1916, RP, emphasis added.

42. "Statement of Raymond Robins (Chairman of the Progressive National Convention) to the Progressives of the Country. Released for publication, noon central time, Aug. 5th, 1916," printed press release, nine pages, RP. A letter, highly critical of Robins's decision to support Hughes, asked for an explanation of his about-face. It concludes with the question: "Did you or did you not, join with the other Progresives at Chicago, when they repeatedly chanted, in no uncertain voice: 'We don't want Hughes. We won't have Hughes!'?" J. A. H. Hopkins to Raymond Robins, 22 October 1916, RP.

43. Raymond Robins to Harold Ickes, 20 August 1916, HIP.

44. Raymond Robins to R. Davant, 10 August 1916, RP.

45. Raymond Robins to George E. Lee, 10 August 1916, RP, emphasis added.

46. Raymond Robins to Hiram Johnson, 11 August 1916, RP.

47. Raymond Robins to Elizabeth Robins, 30 September 1916, ERP.

48. Chester H. Rowell to George Perkins, 27 September 1916, HIP.

49. See L. G. Livesay to Raymond Robins, 29 September 1916; and J. J. Pettyjohn to Robins, 29 August 1916, RP. This second letter, eleven pages long, examined every point of the statement and, in my opinion, argued by far the better case for enlistment in the ranks of the Democratic party. James M. Tadlock of Monroe, Washington, wrote to Robins on the very day the statement was made public and is quoted here.

50. The following are the pertinent articles in the debate as they appeared in *The Public*, all in volume 19: Staughton Cooley, "Choosing Sides," no. 956 (11 August 1916): 747–48; "Raymond Robins for Hughes," no. 956 (11 August 1916): 748; Hugh Reid, "The Passing of Raymond Robins" (letter to the editor), no. 958 (11 August 1916): 752; Peter Vanderwende, "The 'Old Guard' Still Alive" (letter to the editor), no. 960 (25 August 1916): 801; "Raymond Robins Challenged," no. 946 (2 September 1916): 899; A. J. Huie, "Open Letter to Raymond Robins," no. 967 (13 September 1916): 976–77; Frank H. Bode, "Justice to an Opponent," no. 967 (13 September 1916): 977–78.

51. An example of this almost desperate struggle to maintain his righteousness and fervor can be seen in a speech for Hughes that he delivered at Foot Guard Hall, at Hartford, Conn., on 2 October 1916. A printed text of the speech is in the RP.

52. Raymond Robins to Fielder Harris, 9 October 1916, RP.

53. Telegram, Margaret Dreier Robins to Raymond Robins, 20 October 1916, RP.

54. Raymond Robins to George E. Lee, 24 June 1916, RP. A perceptive and well-documented examination of the impact of World War I on the decline of domestic reform in Europe, and to a lesser degree in the United States, is Arno J. Mayer, *Political Origins of the New Diplomacy, 1917–1918*. Its interest here lies primarily in the applicability of his analysis of the European situation to Robins's understanding of the decline of domestic reform in America.

10. Origins of the Mission

1. For this discussion of Robins's Russian adventure I have relied on George Kennan's excellent two-volume *Soviet American Relations, 1917–1920*, vol. 1, *Russia Leaves the War* (1956), and vol. 2, *The Decision to Intervene* (1958); and William Appleman Williams's 1950 doctoral dissertation, "Raymond Robins and Russian-American Relations, 1917–1938." These are the best sources on this period of Robins's life. Epigraph Robins's speech, 20 September 1916, RP.

2. Raymond Robins to J. Davant, 9 November 1916, RP. Three years later, the conflict over the Treaty of Versailles and the League of Nations was to justify his concern of 1916.

3. From Raymond Robins's speech before the National Association of Life Underwriters, 20 September 1916, Chicago, transcript, RP.

4. Robins was very impressed with Japanese industry and organization while on the Smith-Robins World Tour in 1912–13. This was the only apparent basis of his judgment, other than the outcome of the Russo-Japanese War, that indicated the important future role of Japan in world affairs and economic development. His attitude toward Russia was not based on any travels there, but rather on his early studies of Russian history (see chap. 3) and his efforts in behalf of Christian Rudovitz (see chap. 5). Robins made these same points in his letter to Theodore Roosevelt while trying to convince Roosevelt to accept the nomination for president in 1916.

5. Raymond Robins to Elizabeth Robins, 30 May 1915, ERP.

6. Raymond Robins to Elizabeth Robins, 19 July 1915, ERP; interview with Lisa von Borowsky, Seal Cove, Maine, 16 August 1972.

7. Raymond Robins to Elizabeth Robins, 29 April and 25 May 1917, ERP.

8. Raymond Robins to A. C. Vinal, American Telephone and Telegraph Company, 16 May 1917, RP.

9. Raymond Robins to Mrs. Victor Morowitz, 16 May 1917, to Dr. William Irvine, 16 May 1917, and to Mary Dreier, 2 March 1917, RP.

10. Raymond Robins to Elizabeth Robins, 16 May 1917, ERP.

11. Raymond to Elizabeth, 25 May 1917, ERP. "Not being able to fight, I shall farm or talk. As I can talk better than I can farm and most non-combatants can farm better than they can talk, I shall probably talk" (quoted in Mowry, *T.R. and the Progressive Movement*, pp. 370–71).

12. Telegram, Theodore Roosevelt to Raymond Robins, 10 June 1917, RP. It was not Roosevelt himself who thought of Robins for the commission. In a letter to Robins dated 28 June (RP), Roosevelt explained: "I wrote to Miss [Francis] Kellor, who you may remember I told you, had suggested your name to me, when I asked her whom I should suggest to Davison. I told her I should never cease being ashamed of myself for having failed to think of you myself. My dear fellow, you will do a great work. I cannot say how glad I am that you are going over."

13. "Address of Raymond Robins at the Meeting in Honor of the French High Commission at Dexter Pavilion, Chicago," press release for Sunday morning newspapers, Sunday, 6 May 1917, RP.

14. For example, in June 1917 Robins was a speaker in a very successful U.S. Marine Corps recruiting program (M. Brackett to Raymond Robins, 12 June 1917, RP).

15. T. K. "Daddy" Webster to Raymond Robins, 25 June 1917, RP, in which Robins's ambitions for his work in Russia are discussed. Webster reported his conversation with William Hard, who had discussed this idea with Robins previously (Herman Hagedorn, *The Magnate: William Boyce Thompson and His Time, 1869–1930*, p. 181; hereafter cited as Hagedorn, *The Magnate*).

16. Raymond Robins to Theodore Roosevelt, 30 June 1917, RP. Sherwood Eddy related two additional points regarding the organization and instructions to the mission to Russia: "Major, later Colonel Raymond Robins had been suggested as a member of the American Red Cross Division by ex-president Theodore Roosevelt *who had declined the leadership of the Mission, and unofficially Robins was in the service of the Intelligence Division of the United States Army, reporting to the Secretary of War, Newton D. Baker*" ("The Goldseeker," p. 132, SEP, emphasis added). Robins's role in this capacity cannot be documented since it was unofficial. Kennan never mentions this as a possibility (see n. 1 above). Eddy's source for this information was apparently Robins himself. See Williams, "Raymond Robins," p. 57, citing "Baker to Wilson, Aug. 13, 1917, Wilson MSS; 52/f2; Baker to Lansing, Sept. 6, 1917, Judson MSS, B5."

17. Raymond Robins to Margaret Dreier Robins, 4 July 1917, RP.

18. Edward Nockles and John Fitzpatrick of the Chicago Federation of Labor, to "Brothers, the members of the Russian Trade Unions and Friends of Organized Labor," 27 June 1917, RP; Louis F. Post, writing in behalf of the United States Department of Labor, 27 June 1917, RP.

19. Cablegrams sent 19 June 1917, RP.

20. Hagedorn, *The Magnate*, p. 181. The western or Gregorian calendar is used here. The Julian calendar, thirteen days earlier than the Gregorian, was used in Russia until 14 February 1918. Russian sources often use the Julian calendar for dates prior to the conversion to the Gregorian.

21. Entry of 9 August 1917, diary of George Gibbs, in the George Gibbs Papers (hereafter cited as GGP), State Historical Society of Wisconsin, Madison; also cited in Kennan, *Russia Leaves the War*, pp. 55–56.

22. Thompson, aboard the *Empress of Asia* while en route to Russia, received the following telegram from H. P. Davison, following a meeting of the Red Cross War Council: "Your desire to pay expenses of Commission to Russia is very much appreciated and from our point of view very important. . . . We would like to arrange that all expenses of Commission of course within reason be paid by say Neil Bliss [Cornelius N. Bliss, deputy director of the American Red Cross in Washington] representing you, funds to be transferred to him from your office as required." Minutes of the Red Cross War Council, May–September 1917. On 8 October 1917 at the Hotel Europe, Petrograd, Thompson received from "Morgan," in New York, the following telegram: "Your cable second received we have paid National City Bank one million dollars as instructed" (William Boyce Thompson–Herman Hagedorn Papers, Library of Congress, hereafter cited as WTP).

23. Hagedorn, *The Magnate*, p. 181. Arthur Bullard to George Creel, 20 December 1917, Arthur Bullard Papers, Library of Princeton University (hereafter cited as ABP). Robins's letter to Roosevelt used exactly the same language: "any work which was necessary or advisable in the effort to prevent the disintegration of the Russian forces" (see n. 16 above).

24. Hagedorn, *The Magnate*, p. 184. See also Hagedorn's notes from an interview with Raymond Robins, 31 January 1931, WTP. The uncharitable remarks of both Robins and Thompson about one another were made on the train platform in Chicago, as the roll was called before departure for Vancouver. In the RPG are two lists of members of the commission, one prepared to allot stateroom assignments (with Robins's name misspelled "Robbins"), the second an addendum to the list, prepared by Robins on his own stationery. The combined total of the lists is thirty men, but they are definitely incomplete.

25. Hagedorn, *The Magnate*, p. 185. Typed draft of manuscript in the SEP chap. 12, "The Drama of Soviet Russia," p. 133.

26. Raymond Robins to Margaret Dreier Robins, 18 July 1917, from the Imperial Hotel, Tokyo, RP.

27. William B. Thompson to Gertrude Thompson, from Yokahama, 16 July 1917, WTP. Hagedorn qualifies this appraisal of Robins: "But Thompson's capitulation was only intellectual. In the realm of the emotions, the magnate's aversion to the reformer remained" (*The Magnate*, p. 186). It was only after the strain of the Kornilov Affair, in September, that the two finally became fast friends.

28. Raymond Robins to Margaret Dreier Robins, 26 July 1917, RP.

29. Raymond Robins to Margaret Dreier Robins, 2 August 1917, RP. Typescript draft narrative by Henry S. Brown, entitled "Red Cross Mission Background—September–October 1917," and dated October 1917, WTP. This dramatic incident was related by Robins to William A. Williams and confirmed in the Archives of the American National Red Cross. Robins's letters to Margaret only hint at the "recent trouble" with the radical "pacifists," because of its "sensitivity." Williams, "Raymond Robins," p. 2, n. 1, cites H. S. Brown and Frank Billings to Henry P. Davison, 7 August 1917, Archives of the American National Red Cross, Washington, D.C., file 948.08.

30. Robins, pocket diary, 1917–18; Raymond Robins to Margaret Dreier Robins, 3 and 4 August 1917, RP.

31. Robins, pocket diary, 1917–18.

11. The Provisional Government

1. In his letter to Elizabeth (1 October 1919, ERP), Robins waxed far more poetic on the coincidence of the dates: "on the 7th of August 1897 at the sunset hour I sailed out through the Golden Gate for the Far North. On the 7th of August 1917 at the sunset hour—just twenty

years later—on the Imperial Train I rolled into the Nicoliafski railroad station in the imperial city of the Czars. The first was some adventure, but the last was THE GREAT ADVENTURE!" First epigraph, Raymond Robins to Margaret Dreier Robins, 7 August 1917, RP; second epigraph, Raymond Robins to Elizabeth Robins, 1 October 1919, ERP.

2. Raymond to Margaret, 7 and 8 August 1917, RP. The judgment of Root and Thompson was made by Alexander Gumberg, who in September 1917 became interpreter and advisor to the Red Cross Commission. He is more fully introduced in chapter 12. In Gumberg's interview with Herman Hagedorn on 20 February 1931, Gumberg further suggested that "His [Thompson's] fortune was founded upon his ability to grasp the new thing in finance. So he was ready to understand the revolution in Russia" (typescript of interview, WTP).

3. Raymond Robins to Margaret Dreier Robins, 18 August 1917, RP.

4. Entry of 10 August 1917, pocket diary, 1917–18, RP; "Record of Events by Dates Since August 7th, 1917," ERP; George F. Kennan, *Russia Leaves the War*, p. 176. In Kennan's discussion of the role of Crane, he cites Paul V. Harper, ed., *Memoirs of Samuel N. Harper*, p. 6. Samuel Harper was a University of Chicago professor of history whose primary interest was Russian affairs and whose field and department were well endowed by Crane. On the same date of his meeting with Crane, Robins attended a "Dinner at Harper's with [N. V.] Shedlowsky [Shidlovsky, a leader of the centrist-liberal Octobrist party] of Duma Block."

Ataman General Kaledin was a commander of Cossack forces that joined the counterrevolutionary White armies, which fought the Bolsheviks from 1918 to 1920 in a bitter civil war. On 11 February 1918, after failing to raise a large enough voluntary force of his own, and learning that White General Kornilov could no longer lend military support, Kaledin committed suicide.

5. David R. Francis to Charles R. Crane, 28 February 1916, Charles R. Crane Papers, Bakhmeteff Archive, Butler Library, Columbia University, New York (hereafter cited as CRCP). In a letter to Woodrow Wilson that followed the offer to Francis, but was written before Crane had learned of the offer, Crane had recommended George Rublee as the new American ambassador to Russia.

6. In a letter to Margaret on 25 August, RP, Robins wrote of his meeting Judson: "Last night I had dinner with Colonel Judson. He is the biggest American I have met in Russia. He was left here by the Root Commission and will be the most important man here not excepting the Ambassador himself in so far as the policy of America in Russia is concerned. We seem to see eye to eye and I like him very much. . . . After the other guests left I remained at Judson's request and had a fine conference with him over the whole Russian situation. I think that we shall be good friends."

7. The official pamphlet describing the work of the American Red Cross during World War I, entitled "Work of the American Red Cross, Statement of Accomplishment," published in 1920, devotes several pages to Red Cross work in Russia. Beginning on page 82, it describes only this distribution function and no mention whatever is made of the political or diplomatic activities undertaken. A copy of the booklet was presented to Robins after his return to the United States; it is in the RP.

8. The typescript of these "Observations" is in the RP. It was written prior to Sunday, 16 August 1917.

9. Ibid.

10. Robins to Theodore Roosevelt, 18 September 1917, RP. Williams, in "Raymond Robins," refers to "Some Observations . . . September 10, 1917, in the T. R. MSS. Incoming box, Ro-1917," in p. 63 n. 29.

11. Typescript of statement on Russia, written by Robins circa January 1919, RP (hereafter cited as Robins, "*Statement* on Russia"). This is not to be confused with the "Observations," which were written soon after his arrival in Petrograd.

12. Ibid., pp. 11–18; Gen. William V. Judson to Raymond Robins, 19 June 1919, RP; paraphrase of Telegram No. 8, Gen. William V. Judson to Warcolstaff (War College Staff), 6 October 1917, William V. Judson Papers, Newberry Library, Chicago (hereafter cited as WJP).

13. Raymond Robins to Margaret Dreier Robins, 15 August 1917, RP.

14. Ibid.

15. Raymond Robins to Margaret Dreier Robins, 22 August 1917, RP.

16. Raymond Robins to Margaret Dreier Robins, 25 August 1917, RP.

17. Robins, *"Statement* on Russia," p. 6.

18. Ibid.; Raymond Robins to Margaret Dreier Robins, 1 September 1917, RP.

19. Ibid. Robins arrived in Moscow on 30 August and spent his first day in "conference with the men of the Russian Army and Russian Red Cross and the Zemstvo-Union." They met in the palace of Count Zoboff and "arranged the cooperation of the American Red Cross with the agencies of the Russian people." The next day, 1 September, Robins attended the above-mentioned conference of the "All-Russian opinion" and left that night for Ekaterinaslov. This information is found in "Extracts from Letters of Raymond Robins, Member of the American Red Cross Commission to Russia, prepared by Margaret Dreier Robins" (hereafter cited as "Extracts of Letters from Russia"). These extracts were among the papers found at Chinsegut Hill Sanctuary, Brooksville, Florida (hereafter cited as RPC).

Alexis I. Illovaisky, who had been "an officer in a Cossack regiment under the old regime," was interpreter for the commission in these early days; see his notes on service in Russia, in the Allen Wardwell Papers, Bakhmeteff Archive, Butler Library, Columbia University, New York (hereafter cited as AWP).

20. *Bolshevik Propaganda Hearings before a Subcommittee of the Committee on the Judiciary, United States Senate, 65th Congress Third Session,* p. 799 (hereafter cited as *Bolshevik Propaganda Hearings*). Robins testified on his qualifications to judge the revolutionary situation: "I had credentials from the labor groups of this country, which permitted me to be introduced properly and to make the appeal as a representative labor man—for I had been a coal miner in my youth—and I spoke the language of labor. I had been active in labor debate and controversy in America, always anti-socialist, as I then was and am yet, progressive if you please, in mind, but a step at a time progressive—a very poor sort of progressive from the point of view of some people."

This source has been one of the major means of determining Robins's opinions and actions regarding his Russian experience. At these hearings many individuals who figured prominently in Russian-American relations in 1917–18, presented their views. The hearings and Robins's involvement will be discussed at length in chapter 18.

21. "Report of General William V. Judson, American Military Attaché, Petrograd, Oct. 10, 1917," p. 12, considered this a "reasonable estimate," WJP; Robins, *"Statement* on Russia," RP.

22. Raymond Robins to Margaret Dreier Robins, 14 September 1917, from Petrograd, RP.

23. Charles Edward Russell to Woodrow Wilson, 7 November 1917, George B. Creel Papers, Library of Congress (hereafter cited as GCP). Robins, *"Statement* on Russia," RP.

24. In this same letter, Margaret was informed that Col. Billings and several members of the commission were returning to the United States immediately and that "I will remain for some weeks at least and quite possibly for some months" (Raymond Robins to Margaret Dreier Robins, 9 September 1917, RP).

25. These letters are all in the RP. Robins also wrote to Elizabeth during his service in Russia, although not as frequently as he had before or after the mission. Mail service to England was not reliable in wartime and Robins did not chose to use British diplomatic mail. However, I am convinced that a significant number of letters from Robins in Russia to Elizabeth in England have been misplaced or lost.

26. The Smolny Institute was a school for the daughters of the czarist aristocracy until the revolutionary days of 1917. In the summer of 1917 it became the headquarters of the Petrograd Soviet and, with the November Revolution, housed the offices of Lenin and the Bolshevik party. It was, therefore, for a time the seat of the revolutionary government of Russia.

27. Robins *"Statement* on Russia," RP.

28. Typed transcript of Herman Hagedorn's interview with Raymond Robins, 31 January 1931, WTP.

29. Robins, *"Statement* on Russia," RP.

30. *Russian Daily News,* Monday, 10 September news clipping in the RP. Robins prepared a typed outline for this speech, entitled "Russian American Fellowship," and in it he included all of his underlying assumptions regarding the war and the historic relationship between Russia and America.

31. Robins, *"Statement* on Russia," p. 12.

32. "Extracts of Letters from Russia," 21 September 1917, RPC.

33. Robins, *"Statement* on Russia," p. 19.

34. Ibid., p. 11. In an interview with Herman Hagedorn on 3 January 1931, Robins reaffirmed this analysis, maintaining further that: "Instead of endeavoring to bring Kerensky and the people closer together . . . the Allied representatives did everything they could to widen the breach, driving Kerensky to the conservative right" (typescript of notes, WTP).

35. Raymond Robins to Margaret Dreier Robins, 28 September 1917, RP.

36. Raymond Robins to Margaret Dreier Robins, 7 October 1917, RP. I. G. Tsereteli was a leader of the Russian Social Democratic party and supporter of the Zimmerwald Program of European Socialists, which maintained unswerving neutrality in the World War.

37. Raymond Robins to Margaret Dreier Robins, 16 October 1917, RP. In a twenty-page report on the availability of food in Russia dated 22 October 1917, in the WTP, Dr. Frank Billings, formal head of the Red Cross Commission, confirmed many of Robins's concerns, especially regarding desperation for food, on the eve of the Bolshevik Revolution.

38. Raymond Robins to Margaret Dreier Robins, 23 October 1917, RP.

39. Raymond Robins to Margaret Dreier Robins, 29 October 1917, RP. Robins noted in this letter that the censorship restrictions were being increased and that some of his personal correspondence had been intercepted and misused. He warned her that his correspondence from then on would diminish in frequency as well as in substance. This is very unfortunate, since his letters to her are the best source of his analysis of the situation week by week, if not day by day, up until that time. After 29 October researchers must rely on the short, cryptic, and often indecipherable entries that he made in his small pocket diaries, the official communications and telegrams which have survived, and the numerous written and oral accounts of the events made after Robins's return to the United States in June 1918.

40. Robins, *"Statement* on Russia," pp. 20–21; Robins, diary entry for Friday, 2 November 1917, RP, the date the meeting was held in Thompson's suite at the Hotel Europe. In his testimony and many speeches on the coming of the Bolshevik Revolution given during and after the Senate Hearings on Bolshevik Propaganda (Bolshevik Propaganda Hearings), Robins often related the story of the meeting with the military attachés, the conversation with Knox, and the Bolshevik seizure of power five days later. Although the sequence of events makes one wonder about the shortsightedness of the Allied representatives in positions of responsibility, it is important to remember that the events of November 7–9, were nearly as much a surprise for Thompson and Robins as for the other foreign observers in Petrograd.

41. Richard H. Ullman, *Intervention and the War,* vol. 1 of *Anglo-Soviet Relations, 1917–1921,* p. 131. On p. 132, Ullman quotes from a paper in the manuscripts of Viscount Lord Milner, member without portfolio in the War Cabinet, written by Knox, "The Delay in the East," which was circulated to the British War Cabinet. Here the general provides his candid opinion of Robins: "a fanatic with the temperament of a hero-worshipping schoolgirl, and while without the mental equipment or the experience to enable him to advise on policy . . . a dangerous companion for anyone."

12. Robins and Trotsky

1. Raymond Robins to Margaret Dreier Robins, 16 November 1917, RP. In a letter to Lansing, 20 November 1917, Ambassador Francis referred to "Kerensky's escape in a comman-

deered (Mr. Whitehouse) auto with American flag," Robert Lansing Papers, Library of Congress (hereafter cited as RLP). For a detailed account of Kerensky's escape from Petrograd, see Kennan, *Russia Leaves the War*, pp. 71–73. Michael Kettle, in *The Road to Intervention*, explains that Kerensky fled Russia on a Serbian passport given to him by Robert Bruce Lockhart (p. 220); see also Robert H. Bruce Lockhart, *Memoirs of a British Agent*, p. 278. First epigraph, W. Somerset Maugham to Elizabeth Robins, 4 January 1918, ERP. On 8 October 1917 Robins had a "conference with Maugham on secret service," and again on 18 and 29 October; these are the basis of Maugham's characterization. From Robins's carbon copy "Record of Events by Dates Since August 7th, 1917," ERP. Second epigraph, Robins, pocket diary, 1917–18, RP.

2. "The bitter fruit of oppression," Robins brooded in his diary. "Let this scene sink deep." On 14 November, as a witness to the same events, General Judson telegraphed his prescient observations to the War College Staff and, "that he may show to the President should he see fit," to his friend Postmaster General Albert Burleson.

"Russia may be put into anarchy and out of the war as a result of the shock of the present crisis on top of her past experiences. Under conditions requiring for life itself some order . . . there exist in Russia 180,000,000 people mostly ignorant as plantation negroes, scattered over one sixth of the land surface of the earth. All order and system are departing. Conditions make possible a cataclysm which may dwarf the great war and be a tremendous blow to democracy. The resulting world-shock is apt to lead everywhere to an accentuated struggle between extreme socialism and severe reaction with a general setback to civilization and democratic system" (Telegraph No. 78, WJP).

3. Raymond Robins to Margaret Dreier Robins, 16 November 1917, RP.

4. Lansing had received substantiated reports of the extent of Soviet control long before the Bolshevik Revolution. "Soldiers in this camp," Ira N. Morris, U.S. minister to Sweden, cabled Lansing on 11 September 1917, of a Russian camp of 50,000 troops, "decline to recognize any order given by commanders unless approved by the executive committee of Workmens and Soldiers Council" (National Archives, Dept. of State, Record Group 59, 861.00/502).

Robins carried with him back to the United States proposals from Lenin to President Wilson and the State Department entitled: "Russian-American Commercial Relations." This will be discussed at length in chapter 16.

For Robins' account of the events of the Bolshevik Revolution, see appendix C, the texts of two of his letters to Margaret: 20 and 21 November 1917. These letters were personally delivered to her by Captain Pirnie, a member of the Red Cross Commission who left for America via Archangel on 22 November 1917.

5. See "Decree on Peace," and "Report on Land," 8 November, V. I. Lenin, *Collected Works*, vol. 26, pp. 249–61 (hereafter cited as Lenin, *Collected Works*). Hagedorn, *The Magnate*, pp. 241–42; stenographic typescript of "An Account by Raymond Robins Before the City Club of Chicago, 20 March 1919," typescript in the RP (hereafter cited as Robins speech, 20 March 1919).

6. The only hint of his first visit appears in a diary entry for 10 November, Robins, pocket diary, 1917–18, RP.

7. Robins, pocket diary, 1917–18, RP.

8. Robins speech, 20 March 1919, pp. 70–73. This transcript is the basis for most of the details on this encounter with Trotsky.

9. Joseph Noulens, *Mon Ambassade en Ruisse Sovietique, 1917–1919*, vol. 1, p. 185 (hereafter cited as Noulens, *Mon Ambassade*).

10. Robins's first address to soldiers in their barracks was on 18 September; there were at least ten other such occasions, the last, on 6 November, the day before the Bolshevik Revolution, was at the Orenbaum barracks. Robins noted, "Return to find Baltic station armed camp. Bridges open," "Record of Events by Dates Since August 7th, 1917," ERP. In the first of several speeches delivered before the City Club of Chicago, sixteen months after his first meeting with Trotsky, Robins explained, in arresting detail, exactly what happened and what was said. Robins gave this account of his response to the captain's charges; but he used the opportunity before his audience

in Chicago to explain even more, stressing the pragmatic, realistic, and mutually beneficial results he had hoped to achieve through Soviet-American rapprochement. This passage is what Robins recalled having told the soldier guarding Trotsky's door. It is from Robins speech, 20 March 1919.

11. Robins speech, 20 March 1919; Isaac Deutscher, *The Prophet Armed: Trotsky, 1879–1921,* p. 348 (hereafter cited as Deutscher, *The Prophet Armed*); James K. Libbey, *Alexander Gumberg and Soviet-American Relations, 1917–1933,* p. 28 (hereafter cited as Libbey, *Alexander Gumberg*).

12. Robins speech, 20 March 1919. In his Telegram No. 213, sent to the Warcolstaff (War College Staff-Washington) on 28 December 1917, Judson wrote: "Until prohibited yesterday Robins maintained valuable relations and he was able yesterday to get off a train of supplies for Roumania only by personal negotiations" ("Paraphrase of Message," WJP).

13. Joan Doverspike Davison, "Raymond Robins and United States Foreign Policy Toward Revolutionary Russia," Ph.D. diss., p. 1. Betty Miller Unterberger, in "Woodrow Wilson and the Russian Revolution," in Arthur S. Link, ed., *Woodrow Wilson and a Revolutionary World, 1913–1921,* demonstrated that Wilson was committed to a policy of noninterference and self-determination for revolutionary Russia. However, she argued that the pressures toward intervention from the British and French allies, and fear of Japanese domination of Asiatic Russia, forced him into anti-Bolshevik and interventionist policies, which he regretted from their very inception.

14. On 20 March 1917, after receiving Ambassador Francis's 18 March request that the Provisional Government be recognized, Lansing telegraphed the following instructions to Francis: "Please call on Miliukoff, Foreign Minister of the new Government, and ask for an appointment with the head of the Provisional Government to acquaint him with the desire of this Government to open relations with the new Government of Russia." The simple and immediate response stands in stark contrast to the convoluted path leading to the U.S. recognition of the Soviet Union in 1933 (Lansing telegram to American Embassy, Petrograd, National Archives, Dept. of State, 861.00/284).

15. David Francis to Robert Lansing, 20 November 1917, RLP. In this same letter Francis expressed for the first time: "I have strong suspicion that Lenin and Trotsky are working in the interest of Germany." Poole's statement in DeWitt Clinton Poole, Oral History Research Office, transcript of recorded reminiscences, Butler Library, Columbia University, New York (hereafter cited as DPO), pp. 126, 271; Poole's oral history interview was made between January and March 1952.

16. Jane Degras, ed., *Soviet Documents on Foreign Policy,* vol. 1, p. 13 (hereafter cited as Degras, *Soviet Documents on Foreign Policy*); U.S. Department of State, *Papers Relating to the Foreign Relations of the United States: 1918, Russia,* vol. 1, p. 301 (hereafter cited as *Foreign Relations, Russia, 1918*); Telegram No. 2091, 12 December 1917, David Francis to Dept. of State; Arthur Bullard "Memorandum on the Bolshevik Movement in Russia," January 1918, p. 30, ABP.

17. With all his fiery power at the podium, Robins spoke before the standing-room-only house at the City Club of Chicago on 13 April 1919. His previous speech on his mission in Russia, in the same hall just three weeks earlier, had resulted in banner headlines in the Chicago papers. On the evening of 13 April, the crowd was charged with excitement even before Robins said his first word, Robins speech, 13 April 1919, pp. 14–17, RP. Deutscher, *The Prophet Armed,* pp. 150, 527; Libbey, *Alexander Gumberg,* p. 51, and p. 187, n. 25; Trotsky to Alexander Gumberg, 13 May 1917, Alexander Gumberg Papers, State Historical Society of Wisconsin, Madison (hereafter cited as AGP).

18. Stenographic typescript of a speech before the City Club of Chicago, delivered by Robins on 13 April 1919, pp. 14–17, RP; Robins could have been alluding to one of three works of Trotsky written between 1904 and 1906. *Our Political Tasks* appeared in Russian in Geneva in August 1904; it was a 200-page booklet that he dedicated to "My dear teacher Paul B. Axelrod," one of the early Russian Marxist theorists. It was "the most strident bill of impeachment that any Socialist had ever drawn up against Lenin" (Deutscher, *The Prophet Armed,* p. 89). *History of the Soviet,* a joint project edited by Trotsky, was published in Russian in 1906. It was a careful analysis of the first soviet in Russian history, which lasted only fifty days following the Revolution of

1905. Betraying the promises of the Czar's October Manifesto, the Czar's ministers had the members of this soviet arrested and imprisoned. It was there, in prison, that Trotsky edited this book.

19. Robins speech, 13 April 1919. General Judson, after six weeks of contact with Trotsky, conveyed his measure of the man to the War College Staff in Washington. "To understand Trotsky is very important. All the evidence has been studied by myself and Robins, the latter since the days of Kerensky. Apparently Trotsky is a pacifist, idealist, and internationalist, possessing his own controlling motives and apparently has never been under German direction. His pacifist activities suited the Germans and their propaganda was parallel until two months ago. He risked failure during the armistice negotiations in order to hold the enemy on this front and the fault is largely due to his Russian officer technical advisers" (telegram, Judson to Warcolstaff, 28 December 1917, WJP).

20. Albert Rhys Williams, *Journey into Revolution: Petrograd, 1917–1918*, p. 51 (hereafter cited as Williams, *Journey into Revolution*). Frances Adams Gumberg, the wife of Alexander Gumberg, assisted Lucita (Mrs. A. R.) Williams in the preparation of this volume for publication. It is dedicated to the memory of Mary Dreier, Robins's sister-in-law and lifelong friend of the widowed Mrs. Williams. With the exception only of his wife and sister Elizabeth, Robins was closer to Mary than to any other individual.

21. Deutscher, *The Prophet Armed*, pp. 69–70, and quoting V. Medem, *Von Mein Leben* (in Yiddish), vols. 1–2, pp. 7–9.

22. Robins speech, 13 April 1919.

23. Louis Fischer, *The Life of Lenin*, p. 182 (hereafter cited as Fischer, *Lenin*).

24. Charles E. Merriam, letter, *The Congregationalist*, 27 October 1932; Robert H. Bruce Lockhart, *Memoirs of a British Agent*, p. 220. In the second volume of Lockhart's diaries (p. 756), he recounts a discussion with Arthur Ransome, who had just finished reading George F. Kennan's *Russia Leaves the War*. Ransome was indignant because, in the aftermath of the Bolshevik Revolution, based on Robins's sources, Kennan stated that "it was Robins who persuaded us [Ransome and Lockhart] to stay on with the Bolsheviks, whereas it was exactly the opposite." While Ransome and Lockhart were convinced of the wisdom of recognition and cooperation with the Bolsheviks, the record demonstrates that Robins had reached those conclusions well before the arrival of Lockhart, and certainly was not brought to that position by the advice of his two British colleagues (Kenneth Young, ed. *The Diaries of Sir Robert Bruce Lockhart: 1915–1938, 1939–1965*).

25. Robins used these phrases often in his letters to Margaret while in Russia and in his accounts of his experiences afterward, see his letters of 20 and 21 November in appendix C.

26. Fischer, *Lenin*, p. 165.

27. George Kennan, *Russia Leaves the War*, p. 81, cites General Judson's diary for 14–16 November 1917. See appendix D for General Judson's important letter to Francis pleading for American de facto recognition of and cooperation with the Bolshevik regime. Judson's Telegram No. 133–110, to the War College Staff, sent on 1 December 1917, WJP, reports his further discussions with Trotsky. "I had a long interview with Trotsky this morning on military features of Lenin-Trotsky programme especially relating to armistice negotiations beginning tomorrow. I emphasized unofficial character and had Ambassador's consent. I pointed out the parallel features, in many ways, of Russia's and Allies' interests."

28. *Bolshevik Propaganda Hearings*, p. 799.

29. The account of the *Pravda* article appears in *Foreign Relations, 1918, Russia*, pp. 291–92; Telegram, Francis to Lansing, 18 December 1917.

30. Raymond to Margaret, 16 November 1917, RP.

31. Kennan, *Russia Leaves the War*, p. 61 n. 41, cites a letter from Francis to Lansing, 20 November 1917, RLP.

32. *Bolshevik Propaganda Hearings*, p. 1024.

33. Memorandum, William B. Thompson to Lloyd George, 3 pages, WTP.

34. Thomas W. Lamont to Herman Hagedorn, 4 June 1932, copy, WTP.

35. *Bolshevik Propaganda Hearings*, p. 1024.

36. Lamont and Thompson first saw Creel and then went on to plead their case with William G. McAdoo, secretary of the treasury; Frank L. Polk, counselor of the Department of State; and Supreme Court Justice Louis D. Brandeis. "All realized the importance of Thompson's plan," Lamont explained in a letter to Herman Hagedorn. "All felt that it might clear the Russian situation and bring about a basis on which the conservative western nations could deal with the radical government of Russia; all went to see Wilson and urged him at least to hear what Thompson had to say; but all failed" (Lamont to Hagedorn, 4 June 1932, WTP). Henry S. Brown, journalist, writing to Thompson confirmed that Lamont had an hour's talk with Creel on 18 February 1918, in which Creel promised that he "was going to leave absolutely nothing unturned to bring you [Thompson] and the President together; because he believed that if you could have a talk with Mr. Wilson you would have no difficulty in making him see the light and getting him permanently on the right side. . . . [T]he trouble with Wilson was that he had imbibed Lansing's prejudice." George Creel to Woodrow Wilson, requesting an interview for Thompson, 31 December 1917, GCP. The misrepresentation in the press is exemplified by the *New York Tribune* article of 31 January 1918, "Thompson Gives Bolsheviki Million to Sway Teutons." During the month of January, in a futile attempt to win public opinion to his side, Thompson published articles (many, it would appear, at his own expense) on Russia in nearly every New York newspaper. In many cases, to counter the "accepted wisdom," he made mistakes of fact and interpretation concerning Lenin and Trotsky. "Bolsheviki as Seen by An American," appeared in the *New York Evening Post*, 24 January; "Russia as a Democracy: Why and How We should Help," appeared in the *New York World*, 10 January, p. 1, and 13 January, p. 3. It appeared in *The Wall Street Journal*, 18 January, p. 12, and the *New York Times*, on 27 January, p. 32. His letter, "The Misunderstood Bolsheviki," appeared in the *New York Tribune* on 20 February.

37. Fischer, *Lenin*, pp. 179–80 n. 48. On 16 January 1919 the Prinkipo Plan emerged. It called for representation of both the Red and White forces in the Russian civil war to meet at a conference sponsored by the Allies. Wilson also supported the mission to Russia of William C. Bullitt, the purpose of which was not quite clear even to the principles—an initial step toward recognition or merely a fact-finding enterprise. Like those that preceded it, no move toward recognition resulted. For extensive discussion of these Wilson initiatives, see Edward M. Bennett, *Recognition of Russia: An American Foreign Policy Dilemma*, chap. 1, "The Origins of Nonrecognition"; William A. Williams, *American-Russian Relations, 1781–1947*, pp. 160–67 (hereafter cited as Williams, *American-Russian Relations*).

38. Webster's report dated 29 March 1918, in RP.

39. Raymond Robins to Margaret Dreier Robins, 20 November 1917, RP. Both Wardwell and Thacher had law degrees and had practiced in New York City. During the 1920s and early 1930s they went on to notable success and often worked with Robins in his efforts to bring about American diplomatic recognition of the Soviet Union.

40. The papers of Alexander Gumberg are at the State Historical Society of Wisconsin (AGP), along with those of Robins. They were placed there through the efforts of William Appleman Williams whose "A Note on the Papers of Alexander Gumberg" in the bibliographical file on Gumberg at the society has been of help in this brief sketch of Gumberg's background. Libbey's *Alexander Gumberg* is the only monograph devoted to Gumberg. Fortunately, it is thorough and authoritative. Gumberg had served as interpreter and "guide" to the Root Mission and the American Advisory Commission of Railway Experts. John F. Stevens, a Railway Commission member, had recommended Gumberg to the Red Cross.

41. Libbey, *Alexander Gumberg*, p. 17.

42. Williams, *Journey into Revolution*, pp. 50 and 210. Gumberg was not employed by the embassy, nor did he receive a salary from the American Red Cross. He was salaried by Sisson's Committee on Public Information and by funds made available by William B. Thompson. All compensation was deposited directly in his New York bank account. He had no intention of remaining in Russia. See Libbey, *Alexander Gumberg*, p. 17 n. 8.

43. Williams, *Journey into Revolution*, p. 232.

44. Ibid., p. 126; while he managed to maintain his health during the ten months in Russia, Robins suffered four months of depression, dizziness, and pains in his hands and feet after he returned home. "I am a sort of a crippled has-been who belongs in the hospital corps," he wrote to Thompson in February 1919. "Oh I've got one or two good fights in me yet, but I'm over-strained just now" (Robins to Thompson, circa 28 February 1919, written in answer to Thompson's request, in a letter of 25 February, that Robins assume the secretaryship of the Theodore Roosevelt Memorial Committee. Roosevelt had died on 6 January, and the movement for such a committee began immediately. Prior to his friendship with Robins, Thompson, a Republican stalwart, had been a political enemy of Roosevelt, especially after Roosevelt engineered the formation of the Progressive party and split the ranks of the Republicans.

45. Williams, *Journey into Revolution*, p. 126.

46. Raymond Robins to Margaret Dreier Robins, 21 November 1917, RP. For the full text of the "Decree on Peace," see Degras, *Soviet Documents on Foreign Policy*, vol. 1, p. 1.

47. Raymond Robins to Margaret Dreier Robins, 11 December 1917, RP.

48. Raymond Robins to Margaret Dreier Robins, 20 December 1917, RP.

49. Lenin, *Collected Works*, vol. 26, pp. 309–10.

50. In Kennan's account of this murder, in *Russia Leaves the War*, p. 210, he quotes a telegram of Ambassador Francis to Secretary of State Lansing in which Francis indicates that Krylenko "looked on" as Dukhonin was beaten to death. In *Journey into Revolution*, p. 171, Williams indicates that it was a group of drunken soldiers who, learning of Dukhonin's release of counterrevolutionary Generals Kornilov and Denikin, carried out the murder, without Krylenko's assent.

51. Arthur Bullard, "Memorandum on the Bolshevik Movement in Russia," January 1918, p. 30, ABP. On 1 January 1918, Robins composed a telegram on the basis of "confidential information [that] has come to me from Professor Procovsky, historian, political leader and the ablest member of the Russian Peace Commission." This is Robins's most astute statement of the wisdom of and necessity for American recognition of the Bolshevik government to forestall the signing of a separate peace and minimize German advantage in the negotiations (dated "January 1st, 18" in Robins's handwriting, ERP).

13. Robins and Lenin

1. Telegram, General Judson to War College Staff, 23 December 1917, WJP.

2. Wilson's executive order creating COMPUB was signed on 14 April 1917. A "Preliminary Statement to the President" on the scope of COMPUB responsibilities was prepared by Creel and submitted to Wilson on 17 May 1917. Numerous letters were exchanged between Wilson and Creel on the creation of COMPUB between April and June 1917, GCP.

3. Kennan, *Russia Leaves the War*, p. 49.

4. Arthur Bullard, "Confidential" report, ABP.

5. Woodrow Wilson to George Creel, 14 June 1917, GCP; draft of article entitled "Russia," dated 31 March 1919. Bullard, like Robins, had been a settlement worker. At the University Settlement House on New York's Lower East Side, Bullard had served in a number of capacities, including probation officer. After his trip to Russia, following the Revolution of 1905, he was the press representative of the Friends of Russian Freedom in America and was an active member of the Socialist party. In 1914 he wrote a number of radical pieces for the militant socialist monthly, *The Masses*, and one of his radical articles in the *International Socialist Review*, "The Only Possibilism" (October 1907, p. 3), concludes with: "To make Socialism a fact in this land, we must stir up an immense awakening of the Social Conscience. We must preach a deeper and more stirring gospel. To inspire the whole nation to an effective enthusiasm, we must advocate nothing less than 'The Social Revolution.' This is the only Possibilism" (ABP).

6. George Creel to Woodrow Wilson, 9 May 1918, GCP.

7. Edgar Sisson, *One Hundred Red Days: A Personal Chronicle of the Bolshevik Revolution*, 7 January

letter, pp. 202–3; on Lenin, p. 42. His account of the meeting between Lenin, Robins, Gumberg, and himself, on pp. 207–9 (hereafter cited as Sisson, *One Hundred Red Days*). Sisson published the forged documents in October 1918, as No. 20 of the War Information Series under the title *The German-Bolshevik Conspiracy*, issued by George Creel's Committee on Public Information. The introduction states that: "The documents show that the present heads of the Bolshevik Government—Lenin and Trotsky and their associates—are German agents. They show that the Bolshevik revolution was arranged for by the German Great General Staff, and financed by the German Imperial Bank and other German financial institutions." The sixty-eight "documents" and the "Report of the Special Committee on the Genuineness of the Documents," are printed in facsimile at the end of *One Hundred Red Days*.

8. Williams, *Journey into Revolution*, pp. 204–5.

9. Arthur Bullard to George Creel, 17 March 1918, ABP.

10. Typescript copy of portions of article by Ralph M. Easley, "Bolshevism, IWW'ism and Anarchism," 14 February 1918, WTP.

11. Arthur Bullard to George Creel, 20 December 1917, ABP; typescript of notes of interview of Wightman by Herman Hagedorn, 8 May 1931, WTP. The de Cram Affair, as it has come to be known, is chronicled in Kennan's *Russia Leaves the War*, pp. 38–41, where he rightly warns against the harshest judgments and points to the "injustice" of having stationed a person of Francis's age and experience at so difficult a post. An eight-page, thirty-eight-point "Report of certain events in Russia, 1917–1918," to Secretary of War Newton D. Baker, also deals with the de Cram Affair. It is in the WJP, dated 18 June 1919. In point 25, Judson explained: "I personally appealed to the Ambassador to see Madame de C. no more and I showed him the dossier relative to her which Captain Riggs borrowed from the Interallied Passport Bureau. Thus I was the only one who personally approached the Ambassador on the subject of Madame de C. Doubtless for a month or more thereafter he erroneously attributed to me the submission to Washington of some report on Madame de Cram."

12. Sisson, *One Hundred Red Days*, p. 207; William Hard, *Raymond Robins' Own Story*, p. 115; Williams, *Journey into Revolution*, p. 177, agrees with Sisson, that "It was Robins' first such interview (and I believe Sisson's only one), although Robins had seen Trotsky, also through Gumberg's maneuverings, within a few days after the October Revolution."

13. Lenin, *Collected Works*, vol. 26, p. 349, and p. 563 n. 130.

14. For a complete discussion of this subject and American concerns surrounding the Assembly, see chap. 17, "The Constituent Assembly," in Kennan's *Russia Leaves the War*.

15. Lenin, *Collected Works*, vol. 26, pp. 400–403. *Pravda*, No. 18, 22 January 1929, No. 17, 20 January and No. 18, 22 January respectively. The first two are signed "Lenin," and all are "published according to the manuscript."

16. Lenin, *Collected Works*, vol. 26, p. 400.

17. Ibid., p. 403.

18. Ibid., pp. 404–14.

19. See Fischer, *Lenin*, p. 181; Robert Payne, *The Life and Death of Lenin*, pp. 253–68.

20. Williams, *Journey into Revolution*, p. 130, as quoted by the author.

21. Robins speech, 20 March 1919, pp. 70–73.

22. Sisson, *One Hundred Red Days*, p. 213.

23. Robins speech, 13 April 1919, pp. 14–17. The following mistakes of biographical fact in the speech should be noted: (1) Lenin's father was a school inspector and a member of the minor nobility. He was not a general, and while Vladimir Ilyich Ulyanov Lenin did not suffer the disadvantages of the Russian peasantry, Robins is seriously overstating the status and prestige of the Ulyanov family; (2) Lenin's older brother, Alexander, was arrested in Petersburg on 1 (13) March 1887, as an accomplice in an attempt on the life of Czar Alexander III. He was found guilty and was hung on 8 (20) May 1887; (3) Lenin began his law studies at the University of Kazan in August 1887 and participated in a revolutionary student group until his arrest, expulsion from the university, and exile to his grandfather's estate in Kazan. There was no "patri-

mony" to speak of to be turned over to the revolutionary cause. He studied law independently and passed examinations at the University of Petersburg. He did not "escape death by a scratch in Siberia"; and (4) Lenin's "knowledge of Yiddish" was at best an adaptation of his fluency in German. There is no evidence that suggests he had command of or even studied it for the purpose suggested.

24. Arthur Ransome, *Russia in 1919*, p. 165. Ransome, who also covered the revolution and the Soviet scene for the *Daily News* of London, was, like John Reed, ideologically committed to the Bolshevik cause.

25. Lockhart, *Memoirs of a British Agent*, p. 220.

26. Williams, *Journey into Revolution*, p. 211.

27. Raymond to Margaret, 11 December 1917, RP. Robins concludes this letter with yet another affirmation of his role in the revolutionary turmoil and the significance of that role in his life's purpose: the "Cause of the People."

"I feel that all your Great Spirit is using me and that I am more worthy of your love at this hour than at any other in the great yesterdays. I have at last that relationship to life and the Cause of the People that I have desired and I am free to meet a great situation with great responsibilities and power. Be glad for me—let come what may—I HAVE HAD MY DESIRE!!!"

28. The Menshevik-Bolshevik division occurred at the Russian Social Democratic party second congress in London in 1903. Julius O. Martov and Pavel B. Axelrod, with Trotsky's support, called for broadly based party membership, to include the intelligentsia. Lenin's group demanded very tight party membership, consisting of only those involved in underground activity. This division lasted until after the Bolshevik Revolution because Trotsky brought only the Left Wing Menshevik faction with him when he joined the Bolsheviks.

29. Lenin, *Collected Works*, vol. 26, pp. 429–36. The first document published in *Pravda*, no. 5 (evening ed.) 19 January 1918; the second, in *Izvestia*, no. 5, 20 January 1918.

30. DeWitt Clinton Poole, quoting his own telegram no. 14, 4 pp., in DPO, p. 148; Arthur Bullard to Maddin Summers, 24 January 1918, ABP.

31. Raymond Robins to Margaret Dreier Robins, 20 December 1917, RP.

32. Sisson, *One Hundred Red Days*, pp. 144–66; Libbey, *Alexander Gumberg*, p. 32; Kennan, *Russia Leaves the War*, pp. 191–94.

33. Leon Trotsky, *My Life*, pp. 268–75; William Hard, *Raymond Robins' Own Story*, pp. 115–18; Kennan, *Russia Leaves the War*, pp. 191–218, is the best single source on the complexities of this affair.

34. Noulens, *Mon Ambassade*, vol. I, pp. 185–89; Sisson, *One Hundred Red Days*, pp. 222–23; Kennan, *Russia Leaves the War*, pp. 330–41.

14. Brest-Litovsk

1. *Bolshevik Propaganda Hearings*, p. 801. Among the most carefully detailed accounts of the Red Cross role in the Brest-Litovsk negotiations can be found in a 10 July 1918, eight-page, documented letter written by Thomas Thacher to Elizabeth Beatty, two months after his return to the United States from Russia. The letter corroborates the narrative of this chapter in all essential details; it is in the Thomas D. Thacher Papers, Butler Library, Columbia University, New York (hereafter cited as TPC).

2. Thomas Thacher to Elizabeth Beatty, 10 July 1918, TPC.

3. Kennan, *Russia Leaves the War*, p. 367. Kennan devotes the better part of four chapters in his study to the negotiations at Brest-Litovsk and American responses, involving extensive analysis of Robins's activities. On the question of the negotiations themselves, Sir John W. Wheeler-Bennett's *The Forgotten Peace, Brest-Litovsk, March 1918*, is the authoritative source (hereafter cited as Wheeler-Bennett, *The Forgotten Peace*).

4. At this point in his spellbinding testimony before the Bolshevik Propaganda Subcommittee of the U.S. Senate, Robins read most of the verbatim text of Trotsky's speech, and ended with this paraphrase of Trotsky's declaration.

At some point after Trotsky gave the speech, which was originally presented to the negotiators on 10 February, Robins made a handwritten copy in his diary, taken down with great care, unlike most of the scrawled entries. It is the last written passage in the 1917–18 diary, written down apart from the day-to-day entries to distinguish it because of its importance, Robins, pocket diary, 1917–18, RP.

5. Robins speech, 13 April 1919, pp. 36–42.

6. Copy of telegram, Raymond Robins to William B. Thompson, 23 January 1918, RP.

7. *Bolshevik Propaganda Hearings*, pp. 799–800.

8. Robins speech, 20 March 1919, pp. 70–73.

9. Handwritten draft of translation in Gumberg's hand, in the AGP; several photostatic copies of this same translation in typewritten form in the RP.

10. Typed copy of affidavit signed by Raymond Robins and Alexander Gumberg and dated 10 March 1918, RP; photostatic copy of original in TPC. The affidavit begins: "This document was handed to Raymond Robins and Alexander Gumberg in the office of the Peoples' Commissaries" and was clearly prepared as an explanatory statement of introduction to the Trotsky proposals for cooperation. It was doubtless attached to a copy of the proposals that were telegraphed in cipher to the State Department.

11. Kennan, in *Russia Leaves the War*, presumes that Ruggles withheld the message because he "was resentful of the free-wheeling negotiations of Robins and Lockhart." He indicates (p. 500) that Ruggles did not send the message to Washington until 22 March, a full week after the final ratification of the Peace of Brest-Litovsk by the Congress of Soviets. Kennan's chapter dealing with this period is entitled "Robins and Ratification." It deals thoroughly with the events in Vologda and Petrograd as well as the response to ratification in Washington and the complicating issue of imminent Japanese intervention in Siberia.

12. Copy of telegraphic message with "O.K. R.R." in Robins's handwriting on the heading. It was sent to "Major Thomas Thacher, American Red Cross, Care British Consul, Murmansk" on 6 March and contained the message Robins had sent to Thompson, in RP. On the issue of the Japanese intervention, Robins found almost complete consensus against the move among his fellow Americans in Russia. Not least among those warning against such action was Francis himself, who had telegraphed Secretary of State Lansing to this same effect three days later, after meeting with Robins in Vologda. A paraphrase of this message from Francis is in the Robins Papers as well as in C. K. Cumming, and Walter W. Petit, eds., *Russian-American Relations, March 1917–March 1920: Documents and Papers*, pp. 84–85 (hereafter cited as Cumming and Petit, *Russian-American Relations*). This document is also quoted extensively in Kennan, *Russia Leaves the War*, pp. 505–6.

13. Carbon copy, Raymond Robins to Col. James A. Ruggles, "Wednesday, March 6, 1918, Hotel d'Europe, Petrograd," RP.

14. Kennan, *Russia Leaves the War*, pp. 501–5; Williams, "Raymond Robins," p. 135; Wheeler-Bennett, *The Forgotten Peace*, p. 297.

15. *Foreign Relations, 1918, Russia*, vol. 1, p. 395; also cited in full in Kennan, *Russia Leaves the War*, pp. 510–11. Kennan examines developments in Washington that led to the drafting and sending of this message as well as the reception and response it received before the Congress of Soviets, to which it was read on 15 March.

16. Robins speech, 20 March 1919, pp. 62–63.

17. In the affidavit cited in note 10 above, the following passage appears: "this statement [Trotsky's proposals] in cipher as above was transmitted direct to the War Department of the United States at Washington, U.S.A." Robins's use of the word "direct" certainly meant immediately upon request, which was the sixth of March, 1918. He was mistaken; Ruggles did not send it on that date.

18. Thomas W. Lamont to Raymond Robins, 16 May 1944, RP.

15. Cooperation after Brest-Litovsk

1. Repeated in Telegram No. 7, 16 March 1918, Raymond Robins to Thomas D. Thacher "Care British Consul or American Lieutenant Martin, Murmansk," RP. Epigraph, Raymond Robins to Margaret Dreier Robins, 14 April 1918, RP.

2. *Bolshevik Propaganda Hearings,* pp. 787–88. Robins is anticipating matters, because at the time of this conversation the seat of this office remained at Petrograd. It moved to Moscow only after 11 March 1918.

3. Telegram, Robins to Francis, 19 March 1918, RP; also cited in Cumming and Petit, p. 104.

4. Copy, telegram, Raymond Robins to William B. Thompson, 20 March 1918, RP; on the same day Robins sent a separate cable to Wardwell, in Murmansk, in which he quoted the cables he had sent to both Henry P. Davison, head of the American Red Cross, and Thompson, Allen Wardwell Papers, Butler Library, Columbia University, New York (hereafter cited as AWP).

5. Copy, telegram, Raymond Robins to David Francis, 22 March 1918, typed and annotated in Robins's hand, RP. Robins included this same message as a quotation in a telegram to Thompson in New York. His aim was to secure Thompson's support for a Soviet economic commission by the administration in Washington. He also informed Thompson that "after departure Creel's agent [Sisson] all financial resources for our work from funds under his control ceased. Now using your personal funds. Work continues same character should not be charged your personal account. Can you arrange for me to draw on publicity fund or secure special fund and advise me."

6. Untitled typescript of stenographic record of an interview of Robins dated 4 December 1920, beginning with the question: "What is your judgement of Kerensky's personal character," box 17, folder 1, RP.

7. Copy, telegram, Raymond Robins to David Francis, 27 March 1918, RP.

8. *Foreign Relations, 1918, Russia,* vol. 1, David Francis to Robert Lansing, 26 March 1918, p. 487. Also cited in Kennan, *The Decision to Intervene,* p. 117. Indeed, Francis did not inform Robins or Riggs.

9. V. I. Lenin and Georgi Chicherin to Raymond Robins, 29 March 1918, RP.

10. Raymond Robins to Allen Wardwell, 3 April 1918, AWP, copy in the RP. "He [Sisson] has been the most disastrous element in the combination so far," Robins wrote ruefully in this same letter.

11. Copy, telegram, Raymond Robins to Henry Davison, 5 April 1918, RP. On 10 April Davison wired Robins the following message: "Distressed you should have misconstrued cable regarding assistance," and went on to praise Robins's work during his command of the commission. Robins later presented this telegram under the heading of "Robins Document #13" before the Senate subcommittee in an attempt to counter the direct and implied slurs that had been made against him at the hearings.

12. Copy, telegram, Capt. William B. Webster and Capt. W. L. Hicks to Raymond Robins, 29 March 1918, RP.

13. Copy, telegram, Raymond Robins to David Francis at Vologda, 8 April 1918, RP.

14. Kennan denies this possibility. He has examined Lenin's statements and writings on the question of Allied military cooperation with the Soviets with great care and concludes that "It is difficult to understand from a distance of nearly forty years how it was possible . . . in the light of Lenin's statements, to believe that there was a serious possibility that the Soviet government might invite the Allies in" (*The Decision to Intervene,* p. 134). In this discussion Kennan is assuming an intervention beyond any Soviet control and publicly announced—such a public invitation would have flown in the face of all Bolshevik anti-imperialist pronouncements and commitments. Kennan ignores the possibility of a secret Bolshevik invitation for an Allied intervention, which Robins considered one of several serious possibilities. Further, Kennan uses statements made by Lenin two months after the ratification of the Brest peace, at a time when Soviet leaders had finally begun to believe in the German adherence to the terms of the

settlement. In early April much insecurity regarding the German intent still existed and the possibility of Allied support remained a real alternative for many weeks.

15. Copy, telegram, Raymond Robins to David Francis, 4 April 1918, RP.

16. Copy, telegram, Raymond Robins to David Francis, 13 April 1918, RP.

17. Georgi Chicherin to Raymond Robins, 10 April 1918, AGP. Kennan, *The Decision to Intervene*, reproduces the entire letter and a facsimile plate, but indicates its source as the Robins rather than the Gumberg papers.

18. Copy, telegram, Raymond Robins to Henry Davison, 15 April 1918, RP.

19. Raymond Robins to Margaret Dreier Robins, 21 January 1918, RP.

20. Raymond Robins to Margaret, 14 April 1918, RP; to Elizabeth Robins, 14 April 1918, ERP.

16. Departure: The Lenin Proposal

1. De Witt Clinton Poole, Oral History Research Office, transcript of recorded reminiscences, Butler Library, Columbia University, New York, p. 189 (hereafter cited as DPO). First epigraph, Raymond Robins to V. Lenin (copy), 25 April 1918, RP. Second epigraph, De Witt Clinton Poole to Georgi Chicherin, in Poole's recorded reminiscences, p. 189, DPO.

2. *Foreign Relations, 1918, Russia*, vol. 2, pp. 123–24. In his discussion of Francis's position on "Allied intervention without Soviet consent," Kennan appears to have overlooked this early inclination for such a move on Francis's part. On pages 211–12 of *The Decision to Intervene*, he asserts that it was only at the end of April that "Francis reversed his opinion and despatched [*sic*] to Washington a telegram in the opposite sense" (in favor of intervention without Soviet consent).

3. *Foreign Relations, 1918, Russia*, vol. 1, pp. 289 and 381.

4. Ibid., p. 369. The references to Robins in Francis's telegrams became so numerous that Francis found it convenient to refer to him simply as "R."

5. *Bolshevik Propaganda Hearings*, p. 103.

6. Kennan, *The Decision to Intervene*, p. 181 n. 27. Kennan cites the State Department file 123 Su 61/120 in the National Archives for this communication from Summers.

7. Copy of telegram from David Francis to Raymond Robins, undated but probably 20 April 1918, RP. Also appearing in Cumming and Petit, *Russian-American Relations*, p. 156; and cited from this latter source in Kennan, *The Decision to Intervene*, p. 182.

8. This discussion, piecing together the disconnected yet relevant parts of the puzzle of Robins's recall, is to be found on pp. 181–86 of Kennan, *The Decision to Intervene*.

9. "Cipher Telegram, April 26, 1918, #248, from Lansing, Caldwell to Bullard from Irwin Compub," ABP.

10. Telegram, Thomas D. Thacher to Raymond Robins, 26 April 1918, RP.

11. Copy of telegram, Robert Lansing to Raymond Robins, 7 May 1918, reprinted in *Foreign Relations, 1918, Russia*, vol. 1, p. 523. It was received by Robins in Moscow on 10 May as indicated in another telegram from Francis to Lansing dated 16 May from Vologda (ibid., p. 530). The text of the Lansing notice of recall was submitted by Robins as "Robins Document No. 14" at the Senate Bolshevik Propaganda Hearings and appears on page 1023 of its record: "Under all circumstances consider desirable that you come home for consultation we are very reluctant however to withdraw entire Red Cross Commission anticipating that there will be many opportunities to help distribution food and other Red Cross relief measures next two months must leave decision in your hands for you alone can judge possibilities of personal welfare members Commission also likelihood continuing service but all here feel that Red Cross will find much valuable relief work to do and hope you before leaving will find possible arrange for sufficient personnel to remain and if you desire we will endeavor send other Red Cross representatives to help in maintaining Red Cross efforts position in Russia founded on the fine basis established cable promptly care Davison."

12. Thomas D. Thacher to Sen. Hiram Johnson, 21 January 1919, indicated that Thacher left Russia for Paris on 22 March 1918; telegram, Thacher (New York) to Robins (Moscow), 10

May 1918, indicating Thacher's arrival in New York on 7 May, Thomas Thacher Papers, New York Public Library (hereafter cited as TPN).

13. Felix Frankfurter to Thomas Thacher, 15 May 1918, TPN.

14. William Kent to Woodrow Wilson, 22 May 1918, TPN.

15. Telegram, William Kent to Thomas Thacher, 25 May 1918, TPN; Woodrow Wilson to Robert Lansing, 23 May 1917, RLP; copy of letter, Woodrow Wilson to William Kent, 23 May 1918, TPN.

16. Thomas Thacher to William B. Thompson, 11 June 1918, in which he repeated what had been in the letter to each recipient: "these pamphlets will be used privately and will not be published or quoted publicly." Section 4 is entitled "The policy of doing nothing in Russia . . . does not commend itself to anyone," while section 5 warns, "Allied intervention by force . . . will arouse the antagonism of the Soviet forces throughout Russia." Section 6 asserts that "German effort must be opposed through the Soviet Government, which is the strongest internal force available for this purpose." Section 7 concludes, "A Commission . . . through cooperation with the Soviet Government should be sent to Russia at once" (Thomas Thacher, *Russia and the War*). Letter on continued effort to get an appointment with Wilson, William Kent to Thomas Thacher, 11 June 1918, TPN.

17. Carbon copy, Raymond Robins to David Francis, 26 April 1918, RP, including the text of the wire sent earlier that day.

18. Robins referred to Francis in this way in the privacy of his pocket diary on 4 December. The entire de Cram Affair is treated at length in Kennan, *Russia Leaves the War*, pp. 124–28. See also chap. 13, note 11 above.

19. Carbon copies of both letters dated 25 April 1918, RP.

20. Robins's pocket diary, 1917–18, RP. On 1 May, and apparently unknown to Robins, Margaret was sharing with him the same sense of momentous historical importance of that particular May Day. Near their Florida home at Chinsegut, Margaret planted a Live Oak sapling to commemorate the occasion. In future years the tree was christened the "Lenin Oak." Fifteen years later, in 1933, it was the scene of many ceremonious meetings between Robins and the first representatives of the newly recognized Soviet Union.

In 1959, five years after Robins's death, Lisa von Borowsky fulfilled Robins's wish to mark the spot with a commemorative plaque. It read: "Placed by Margaret Dreier Robins, 1st of May 1918—In memory of the Leader of the Russian Revolution Nikolai Lenin," and concluded with the biblical quotation: "The Kingdom of Heaven suffereth violence and the violent take it by force." Two years after its installation the bronze plaque was torn up and destroyed by the administrators of the estate in the wake of a local furor over "the only known monument to the founder of world communism on federal land." The Live Oak dedicated to Lenin still stands at Chinsegut Hill, Florida (interview with Lisa von Borowsky, at Seal Cove, Maine, 24 August 1971).

21. Robins wrote the following note to Chicherin: "Important matters have demanded my leaving for Vologda for conference with Ambassador Francis. . . . During my absence any matter that would be brought to my attention should be sent to me in care of Alexander Gumberg Esq. my personal secretary. If discussion is necessary you will feel free to speak with him as you would with me" (carbon copy in the RP).

22. Robert H. Bruce Lockhart to David Francis, 5 May 1918, RP, copy in TPC. The letter was also presented in evidence in Robins's *Bolshevik Propaganda Hearings* testimony, p. 1020. Also cited in Cumming and Petit, *Russian-American Relations*, pp. 202–3, and in *The Decision to Intervene*, p. 201.

23. *Foreign Relations, 1918, Russia*, vol. 1, pp. 516–17.

24. Ibid., p. 525. Thomas Thacher to George B. Case, War Council of the American Red Cross, Washington, D.C., 7 June 1918, copy in TPC. Thacher suggested an intentional delay.

25. Robins assured the ambassador that "Wardwell fully informed admirably fitted command situation" and further that "more men unnecessary now." Robins did not want the entry of any new Red Cross personnel for fear that they might be sent specifically to recast the role of the

commission according to "indoor" State Department guidelines and thereby undermine his carefully cultivated connections with the Bolshevik leaders, so necessary to carry out his plans for cooperation. He trusted Wardwell and hoped for at least the maintenance of the status quo under his command of the mission; copy of telegram, Raymond Robins to David Francis, 13 May 1918, RP.

26. Entry for 10 and 12 May 1918, Robins, pocket diary, 1917–18, RP.

27. Leon Trotsky to Raymond Robins, 13 May 1918; Robins, pocket diary, 1917–18, RP.

28. Robins's diary entry for 13 May relative to his meeting with Lenin reads: "Then Lenin and farewell letter and photo signed and place made." The RP contain no "farewell letter" from Lenin. The photos referred to in Robins's diary were recently discovered (January 1972) in the attic of the main house at Chinsegut. They are actually lithograph portraits of Lenin and Trotsky, each signed and framed. They were deposited, along with the RPC, in the State Historical Society of Wisconsin at Madison.

29. Cumming and Petit, *Russian-American Relations*, pp. 204–12.

30. Ibid., p. 205.

31. Ibid., p. 207.

32. Ibid., p. 208.

33. Ibid., p. 210.

34. Ibid., p. 211.

35. Photostatic copy of covering letter, in Lenin's hand, in English and dated 14 May 1918, RP. Also cited in full in Kennan, *The Decision to Intervene*, p. 217.

36. This statement was prepared by Robins at the request of Lansing, whom Robins had seen on 26 June 1918, at which time Lenin's proposals were handed to Lansing. Robins's written statement is dated 1 July. A more thorough discussion of Robins's return and reception in America will be found below. The text of his statement appears in U.S. Department of State, *Papers Relating to the Foreign Relations of the United States: The Lansing Papers, 1914–1920*, vol. 2, pp. 365–72 (hereafter cited as *The Lansing Papers*); also in Cumming and Petit, *Russian-American Relations*, pp. 212–19; and in Kennan, *The Decision to Intervene*, pp. 475–85, as an appendix.

37. *The Lansing Papers*, vol. 2, p. 370.

38. Ibid., p. 371.

39. *Bolshevik Propaganda Hearings*, p. 855.

40. Kennan, *The Decision to Intervene*, p. 223.

41. *Foreign Relations, 1918, Russia*, vol. 1, pp. 530–31, telegram, David Francis to Robert Lansing, 16 May 1918, 9 P.M.

42. Ibid., pp. 538–39, telegram, David Francis to Robert Lansing, 23 May 1918.

17. Return to America: The Fight against Intervention

1. On other occasions Robins testified under oath that he had "five rifles and 150 rounds of ammunition" (stenographic typescript of a "Deposition of Raymond Robins before the Department of Education of the City of New York," 3 April 1919, p. 74, RP). The 500 rifles referred to in the stenographic record of the speech is a mistake. The same figure, "five rifles" is cited in Robins's speech before the Free Nations Association, "One View of the Russian Situation," 22 March 1919, stenographic typescript, RP; see also Robins speech, 20 March 1919, pp. 74–76. Epigraph, Raymond Robins to Elizabeth Robins, 27 August 1918, ERP.

2. Certificate signed by Chicherin and dated 13 May 1918; letter, in Russian and dated 11 May 1918, signed by Lenin in RP.

3. Entry for 17 May 1918 in Robins, pocket diary, 1917–18, RP.

4. Copy, telegram dated 22 May, in the RP.

5. Copy, telegram, Raymond Robins to Allen Wardwell, 22 May 1918, RP.

6. *Foreign Relations, 1918, Russia*, vol. 1, p. 543, telegram, David Francis to Robert Lansing, 27 May 1918.

7. Ibid., p. 549, Robert Lansing to David Francis, 1 June 1918.

8. Translated copy of the certificate, indicating that it was "signed and with the seal of the Far Eastern Soviet," 29 May 1918, No. 1226, RP.

9. Williams, *Journey into Revolution*, pp. 306–7.

10. Ibid., p. 262. Williams was unable to leave Vladivostok. He had been ordered to remain there by the State Department and was suspected of treasonous conduct. His return to the United States was finally effected through the efforts of friends at home; Raymond Robins to Bessie Beatty, 27 June 1918, RP.

11. Copy, telegram, Raymond Robins to Henry Davison, 5 June 1918, RP.

12. Raymond Robins to Margaret Dreier Robins, 4 July 1917, RP.

13. William A. Williams found that "Basil Miles [Russian Desk officer in the State Department], unrelieved that Robins had been recalled, asked Lansing for permission to search Robins' luggage when he arrived in Seattle. The Secretary thought it an excellent idea, and told Miles 'to make it thorough'" ("Raymond Robins," p. 155). Account from Lisa von Borowsky, who had discussed the attempt to deny Gumberg entry with Robins on many occasions; interview with Lisa von Borowsky, Seal Cove, Maine, 12 August 1971.

14. Robins, pocket diary 23 June 1918, RP. Miles Poindexter was a prominent Republican congressman.

15. Felix Frankfurter to Thomas Thacher, 15 May 1918; Thomas Thacher to Col. E. M. House, 31 May 1918, TPC. Telegram, William Kent to Thomas Thacher, 25 May 1918; William Kent to Thomas Thacher, 24 May 1918, 11 June 1918; Woodrow Wilson to William Kent, 23 May 1918, TPC.

16. Carbon typescript of Hagedorn interview with William Boyce Thompson. Prepared by Herman Hagedorn, WTP.

17. *Lansing Papers*, vol. 2, pp. 365–66.

18. *Foreign Relations, 1918, Russia*, vol. 2, p. 245.

19. Robins speech, 13 April 1919.

20. Carbon copy of a letter, Raymond Robins to Bessie Beatty, 27 June 1918, RP. Hiram Johnson to Raymond Robins, 10 July 1918, RP.

21. Dreier, *Margaret Dreier Robins*, pp. 137–38. Wilson had not been endeared to Robins in 1916, at the time of the dissolution of the Progressive party. After interviews with Wilson and long deliberation, Robins supported and campaigned for Hughes. This old wound may not have played a part in the events of 1918 but, as revealed in his letter to Miss Beatty, Robins believed it did, and that embittered him all the more.

22. Felix Frankfurter to Thomas Thacher, 8 August 1918, TPC.

23. "Office Scratch Book, No. 4060," in the hand of Fola La Follette (Robert M. La Follette's daughter): "Notes in pencil by R. M. La Follette, heading 'R.R. Reached Russia in July 1917. . . . These notes were made by R. M. L. when Raymond Robins came to see him at Hot Springs, Virginia in August, 1918," Robert M. La Follette Papers, Library of Congress (hereafter cited as BLP).

24. Hagedorn, *The Magnate*, p. 276.

25. Carbon copy of letter, Raymond Robins to Theodore Roosevelt, 24 August 1918, RP.

26. Telegram, Santeri Nuorteva to Raymond Robins, 16 September 1918, RP.

27. Robins worked successfully against Chicherin's appointment of Reed as "Consul of the Russian Republic in New York." This appointment was cancelled by Chicherin after Lenin's intervention in January 1918. Robins agreed with the ambassador that Reed could only cause embarrassment for both America and Russia by serving in this position. See Kennan, *Russia Leaves the War*, pp. 405–10, for a full discussion of this question.

28. John Reed to Raymond Robins, 15 September 1918, RP.

29. News clipping, *New York Times*, 15 October 1918, RPC.

30. "I've been dogged by Secret Service, Naval Intelligence, War Intelligence, special Bolsheviki Squads and other minions of my government," he complained to Elizabeth in a letter, 1 October 1919, ERP.

31. Copy of letter, Raymond Robins to D. H. Allen, in the Office of the Secretary of War, 27 October 1918; copy of letter, Raymond Robins to Medill McCormick, 14 September 1921, RP.

32. D. H. Allen to Robins, 27 October 1918, RP.

33. Copy of letter, Robins to Thompson, circa 28 February 1919, RP, written in answer to Thompson's request of 25 February that Robins assume the position of secretary of the Theodore Roosevelt Memorial Committee (Roosevelt died on 6 January 1919).

18. "Free to Speak on Russia"

1. Copy of stenographic typescript of "Deposition of Raymond Robins before the Department of Education of the City of New York, April 3, 1919." Immediately after the phone call, Robins prepared a statement, undated, describing the circumstances of this notification, RP. Epigraph, Raymond Robins to Elizabeth Robins, 21 November 1919, ERP.

2. The full charge of the Subcommittee of the Committee on the Judiciary, under the chairmanship of Senator Overman, appears on p. 6 of the record in *Bolshevik Propaganda Hearings;* Robins's testimony appears on pp. 763–896 and pp. 1007–32.

3. Ibid., pp. 855–56. Writing in 1958, in *The Decision to Intervene* (pp. 237–43), Kennan lauds Robins's prescient and determined effort to know and understand the Bolsheviks and their program without prejudice, but finds Robins dangerously naive when he advocates food as the solution to entrenched "Bolshevik formulas." Do we lend greater credence to Robins's view in the era of *glasnost* and *perestroika* in the Soviet Union and "incentive economics" in China?

4. Copy, text of Dobrjansky speech, 12 pages; carbon copies, A. N. Dobrjansky to Dr. J. Lane Miller, 26 March 1919; Dr. J. Lane Miller to A. N. Dobrjansky, 2 April 1919; Thomas Thacher to Raymond Robins, 14 April 1919, TPC.

5. Robins had spoken before the City Club of Chicago on 20 March, one of the first public addresses after his appearance before the Senate subcommittee. On that first occasion he began by asking that the title of his talk be changed from "The Truth about Russia," to "One View of the Russian Situation," a title which he retained for many of his public addresses on Russia. On 20 March Robins warned his audience that "I am going to talk as long as there is anybody here. Feel free to go. This is apt to be quite a considerable performance." He went on, keeping up the humor, to describe "just one statement on the Russian Situation that has pleased me wholly since I came out of Russia, and that was a cartoon in *The New York Tribune:*

"It pictured a man being carried down the street, that is, taken by force of arms. His clothes were torn and his eyes were black, and his collar was unfastened, but the people who were there showed a little wear also. An innocent bystander broke in and said, 'Good gracious alive, why are you so violent and brutal with this man?' And the others reply. 'Now you stay out of this thing, we know exactly what we are doing. This man is a lunatic, he is incurably insane, and we are taking him to the asylum.' 'Oh,' said the bystander, 'what is the matter with the poor fellow?' 'Why, he thinks he knows all about the Russian situation.' (Laughter)." Also see text quotations from stenographic typescript, Robins speech, 13 April 1919, pp. 18–19 and 57, RP.

6. Typescript of stenographic record of address before the League of Free Nations Association, "One View of the Russian Situation," 22 March 1919, RP (hereafter cited as Robins speech, 22 March 1919).

7. *Bolshevik Propaganda Hearings,* pp. 857–65.

8. Robins speech, 13 April 1919, p. 86.

9. Ibid., p. 66.

10. Ibid.

11. Robins speech, 20 March 1919.

12. Robins speech, 22 March 1919. Robins did not read from a prepared text, at most only an outline, and although several speeches were given with the same title, the stenographic record reveals major differences between their sequence and content.

13. Carbon copy of letter, Raymond Robins to Alexander Gumberg, 11 April 1919, RP.

14. Raymond Robins to Elizabeth Robins, 1 October 1919, ERP.

19. The Peace Settlement and Recognition of Russia, 1919–1924

1. Raymond Robins to William Borah, 19 July 1921; William Borah to Raymond Robins (carbon copy), 22 July 1921, WBP. Epigraph, Raymond Robins to Julius Kespohl, 4 September 1920, RP.

2. Raymond Robins to Elizabeth Robins, 9 April 1927; Robins wrote by way of introduction to Elizabeth in London in anticipation of a visit from the entire Levinson clan to her adopted city, ERP; John E. Stoner, *Salmon O. Levinson and the Pact of Paris: A Study in the Techniques of Influence*, pp. 2–8 (hereafter cited as Stoner, *S. O. Levinson and the Pact of Paris*). Stoner's reading of the relationship between Levinson and Robins places his protagonist, Levinson, in the dominant position, orchestrating the years of work in behalf of outlawing war. William A. Williams, in "Raymond Robins," challenges Stoner and argues that it was Robins's political expertise and connections in Washington that gave the indispensible impetus to the Levinson dream. On the basis of the archival sources, I must agree with Williams.

3. The speech was given in California one week prior to the California primaries. It is preserved in the RP in a carbon copy of the stenographic notes of the speech, 51 pages, with notes and corrections in Robins's hand, pp. 5–6.

4. Ibid., p. 6.

5. Ibid., pp. 11–12.

6. Telegram, David Francis to Robert Lansing, Vologda, 9 March 1918, Department of State files, 861.00/1262.

7. Raymond Robins to Mary Van Kleek, 25 July 1939, RP.

8. Address in behalf of Hiram Johnson, May 1920, RP.

9. Ibid., p. 16.

10. Ibid., p. 17.

11. Raymond Robins to David P. Barrows, 29 March 1920, RP. Robins's letter demanded a "written disclaimer" from Barrows or he would take him to court, but Robins's handwritten note added to the copy of the letter indicates: "The original of this was never mailed and no action of any sort to date—Signed (Robins)."

12. Arthur Arlett to David P. Barrows, 24 February 1920; David Barrows to Arthur Arlett, 26 February 1920, RP.

13. Barrows's was by no means representative of the most frenzied examples of the popular hysteria. The following anonymous letter, to Rev. J. M. Moor, of Brooklyn, New York, dated 26 March 1919, RP, is an instructive example: "Being one of the attendants at the services at the Marcy Avenue Baptist Church last Sunday evening, permit me to express my deep indignation and disgust that a person of Raymond Robin's [*sic*] calibre should have been permitted to exploit himself and defile the fair name of your Church and the community with his subtle, insidious and abominable propaganda.

"His frank advocacy and ardent appeal for recognition of the 'Red Regime' of Trotzky, Lenine & the Soviet, by the U.S. Government was a flagrant insult to the intelligence of the members of your church and congregation.

"It was manifestly evident that he is absolutely under the *influence and control* of that red-handed band of murderers and selfprofessed wreckers of our civilization, who seek by all the foul means possible to foist upon the world at large their damnable doctrine of wholesale slaughter of their betters and the denationalization of women.

"Had this address been delivered in any edifice other than a place of worship Mr. Robins would never have been allowed to continue his nefarious and seditious utterances, unless I misjudged the temper of his audience."

14. Memorandum, 18 June 1919, WJP. Only days after Robins testified before the Senate subcommittee, Judson wrote to him "that you, (almost entirely *you*) with a little bit of sympathy rather than assistance from a few others, were able to delay the signing of the Brest-Litovsk Treaty . . . so long—and stir up so much ill-feeling between Bolsheviks and Germans—that the German spring drives lacked man-power, and failed by just the margin you created to win the war for the Hun" (William V. Judson to Raymond Robins, 12 March 1919, AWP). On 6 December 1921, Maj. Gen. J. G. Harbord, deputy chief of staff, submitted a memo to the secretary of war, reiterating in Judson's own language the arguments that Judson had presented in behalf of Thompson and Robins in his 18 June 1919 memo, suggesting the award of the DSM; copy of memo, WTP.

15. William V. Judson to Albert Burelson, 10 April 1919, WJP.

16. Kerth and Judson coauthored the 26 December 1917 letter to Ambassador Francis regarding the realities of Bolshevik power in Russia. The letter can be found in appendix D. Monroe C. Kerth to William V. Judson, 4 August 1919, and 23 November 1919, WJP.

17. Raymond to Elizabeth, 1 October 1919, ERP. Kennan, in *The Decision to Intervene* (p. 361 and note 41), wrote of "the curious aversion Wilson appears to have had to receiving anyone who had come [back to the United States] from Russia." Kennan lists Thompson, Judson, Thacher, Robins, Sisson, Crane, Samuel Harper, and Ambassador Francis, who received "no more than a single reception."

18. Receipt for $500, "Contribution to Hiram W. Johnson for President, March 2, 1920," RP.

19. Charles McCarthy to Gifford Pinchot, 20 October 1920, Charles McCarthy Papers, State Historical Society of Wisconsin, Madison (hereafter cited as CMP), McCarthy's italics. These issues had been with Robins from the moment he learned of Theodore Roosevelt's death, on 6 January 1919, and in a long letter to Robins written four days after T. R.'s death, Harold Ickes had spelled out all these nuances from his point of view; Ickes to Raymond Robins, 10 January 1919, HIP.

20. These meetings were reported in the *New York Times* on 13, 16, and 24 July and 2 August. On 19 August 1920, Margaret wrote one of her infrequent letters to Elizabeth, explaining their ambivalence: "You will understand how difficult it was for us to receive the Harding nomination. Senator Harding was one of Theodore Roosevelt's bitterest opponents, and further, has really no record of achievement along the lines which are of especial interest to us."

In an interview with Herman Hagedorn on 1 February 1931, Robins explained that at a luncheon meeting between himself, Thompson, Fred Upham, the Republican party national treasurer, and Will Hays, chairman of the Republican National Committee, Thompson pledged $300,000 to the Harding campaign. Robins was suggesting that he was influential in winning Thompson's support; typescript of notes of interview, WTP.

21. Hiram Johnson to Raymond Robins, 26 July 1920, RP.

22. Raymond Robins to Julius Kespohl, 4 September 1920, RP. In the Robins Papers is the "News Release Morning Papers, Wednesday, September 1, 1920" entitled "WHY VOTE FOR HARDING?" by Raymond Robins, "Chairman Progressive National Convention, 1916," 12 pages. Unfortunately for Robins and the progressive Republicans, Calvin Coolidge's administration proved to be as inhospitable to the ideals of social, labor, and economic reform as had Harding's.

23. Warren G. Harding to Raymond Robins, 26 February and to Margaret Dreier Robins, 9 September 1921, RP; Margaret Dreier Robins to Warren G. Harding, 9 September 1921; on Thompson's offer of German ambassadorship: Raymond Robins to Elizabeth Robins, 18 October 1921, ERP; Hagedorn, *The Magnate*, pp. 286–87. Johnson, like Charles McCarthy, was interested in Robins's getting a position in Harding's cabinet as secretary of labor. Nothing came of these suggestions, even though supported by many Republican notables. In a letter to S. S. Anderson on 17 November 1920, RP, Robins wrote: "With reference to a position in Mr. Harding's cabinet, I have always regarded any mention of my name in such connection as simply 'honorable mention.'"

24. Alexander Gumberg to Raymond Robins, 21 April 1922, RP; Sister Anne Vincent Meiburger, in *Efforts of Raymond Robins Toward the Recognition of Soviet Russia and the Outlawry of War*,

1917–1933, relies extensively on the correspondence between Robins and Gumberg and also quotes significant portions of this letter (pp. 77–79). Meiburger is sympathetic in her treatment of Robins, but presumes that he was entirely confused in his understanding and judgment of the Bolshevik leadership and their motives. She accepted the "conventional wisdom" of the State Department that the Marxist ideology of world revolution necessitated an aggressive and violent global confrontation on the part of the Soviets in their spread of communism. Therefore the underlying policies of the Bolshevik leadership precluded the kind of friendly and cooperative relationship toward which Robins worked (hereafter cited as Meiburger, *Efforts of Raymond Robins*).

25. Raymond Robins to Elizabeth Robins, 4 June 1923, ERP. On 9 December 1922 Robins wrote a letter of introduction for Gumberg, addressed to Senator Borah (in WBP): "I want you to know him," Robins wrote to the champion of recognition, "to have his help in your splendid battle for an intelligent policy of relationship between our government and that of the Soviet Republic of Russia. I am ready to assume full responsibility for his ability, his integrity, his courage and his common sense. He may be of real use to you in the development of American-Russian relations."

26. Draft of letter, Raymond Robins to Calvin Coolidge, written from Cleveland, Ohio, 9 November 1923, RP; it appears not to have been sent. Raymond Robins to Elizabeth Robins, 8 December 1923, ERP.

27. Arthur M. Schlesinger and Fred L. Israel, eds., *The State of the Union Messages of the Presidents, 1790–1966*, vol. 3, p. 2643.

28. Raymond to Elizabeth, 8 December 1923, ERP. In a letter to Levinson dated 1 December 1923, Robins recounted the same effort to inaugurate communication: "cabled to Moscow in the cipher of that government" a Soviet response to the State of the Union Message, in the Salmon O. Levinson Papers, Libraries of the University of Chicago (hereafter cited as SLP).

29. In Gumberg's letter to Robins, 12 January 1923, RP, he suggests: "There are people like the Governor [Goodrich], Allen [Wardwell], Frank Walsh, Burns, Graham, Mason Day and Philip Chadbourn of the Barnsdall Corp. who got the oil concession in Baku, Roy Anderson and a score more of people. . . . There are also people here like Dr. Sherman who bought 10 millions dollars [*sic*] worth of supplies in this country in less than a year for Russia. In general conditions now are extremely favorable for such a hearing."

At this same time, Robins, Thacher, Gumberg, and the recognitionist camp produced a fifty-page brief of statements on recognition and trade with the Soviets from American, English, and French notables in various fields.

30. Raymond Robins to Salmon O. Levinson, 12 January 1924, SLP.

31. In response to the barrage of State Department documentation of Soviet propaganda, Borah asked for Robins's assistance in framing a rebuttal. "I would like to have . . . your views and your information with reference to the Soviet government being responsible for any propaganda in this country during the last three years. I want also . . . to have you within call so that you may be permitted to make a statement before the Committee. I am convinced there is nothing in this charge so far as the last three years are concerned" (William Borah to Raymond Robins, carbon copy, 20 December 1923, WBP).

32. Robins to Levinson, 12 January 1924, SLP.

20. National Politics, Prohibition, and Outlawry of War

1. Raymond Robins to Elizabeth Robins, 13 June 1924, ERP.

2. Harold Ickes to Raymond Robins, 29 January 1924, and carbon copy, Raymond Robins to Harold Ickes, 24 January and 1 February 1924, HIP. In November 1923 Ickes wrote: "I am more than ever convinced that you can be nominated . . . and that you ought to make the race. . . . It seems to me that you could do more for your cause from the floor of the Senate than you can do otherwise" (quoted in Raymond Robins to Salmon Levinson, 13 November 1923,

SLP). Ickes was not alone in his total bewilderment with Robins's support of Coolidge. Amos Pinchot, with brilliant wit, sharp analysis, and extensive quotation from key passages in Roosevelt's Osawatomie speech, destroyed all rationale of progressive support for Coolidge in 1924. After announcing his support for La Follette, maintaining that "Fighting Bob's" program was essentially the same as that of Roosevelt in 1912, Pinchot was denounced in E. A. Van Valkenburg's Philadelphia *North American*. Pinchot's brilliant letter of rebuttle to Van Valkenberg, written on 25 October, could just as well have been written to Robins; see Amos Pinchot to E. A. Van Valkenburg (carbon copy), Amos Pinchot Papers, Library of Congress (hereafter cited as APP).

3. Raymond Robins to Elizabeth Robins, 19 July 1924, ERP.

4. Raymond Robins, in a letter to Elizabeth, 6 August 1924, ERP, wrote: "This is the same Van Valkenburg that suppressed my interviews on the Russian situation after my return in 1918—after having paid a round figure for the privilege of printing them. He turned against me and became a fierce witch-hunter—but he purred like any old pussycat for some two hours in our conference."

5. Printed statement, lists of names of progressives, "Signers" and "Declined" attached to letter, E. A. Van Valkenberg to Raymond Robins, 27 August 1924; John A. Lapp to Raymond Robins, 17 September 1924, RP.

6. Raymond Robins to Elizabeth Robins, 19 August, and 11 October 1924, ERP.

7. On 1 September 1920 Robins kicked off his campaign for Harding's election with the widely distributed press release: "Why Vote for Harding?" Significant portions of the release attacked the Versailles Treaty, the League of Nations, and called for disarmament and a just peace. In a note in the RP, Lloyd George is also quoted as follows: "Above all to insure that war shall be declared a crime under the law of nations and made punishable under the code."

8. Robins received from $250–350 for each engagement, which lessened some of the financial worries that had been troubling him.

9. Typewritten note on Robins's old Chicago Commons stationery, RP. See also the text of the publicity flyer that was used by the Pond agency in connection with Robins's third tour in 1924–25.

10. Robins to the Affiliated Lyceum and Chautauqua Society, 27 June 1921, RP.

11. Outline of speech, "World Disarmament or World Revolution—Which?" Written on the stationery of the National Women's Trade Union League, no date, but obviously written and used during the spring of 1922 before outlawry became the central theme of his lectures, RP.

12. Ibid., emphasis in original.

13. Ibid. This is Robins's conclusion of the disarmament speech. He later added to these same lecture notes in handwriting the new demand: "Declarations that war should be outlawed and made a crime against the law of nations."

14. Meiburger, *Efforts of Raymond Robins*, pp. 106–9.

15. Ibid., and Stoner, *S. O. Levinson and the Pact of Paris*. The essence of Robins's thinking on outlawry can be found in various kinds of evidence: the record of his public addresses, his notes and critiques of alternative peace plans (which were numerous in the period from 1920–36), and his personal letters, many written to enlist friends in the cause. The voluminous correspondence with Senator Borah is particularly informative; e.g., Robins's letters of 14 May 1927, 26 March, 16 June, 15 July, and 13 August 1928. Also see the resolutions that Borah introduced in the Senate and House. The following are the early resolutions: 67th Cong., 1st sess., S.J. Res. 17 [Joint Resolution], 13 April 1921; 67th Cong., 1st sess., S.J. 18, 13 April 1921; 67th Cong., 1st sess., H.R. 4803, 4 May 1921, Amendment.

16. Raymond Robins to William Boyce Thompson, no date, carbon, written from 3 University Place, NYC, RP. This was Mary Dreier's home, where Robins stayed while on business in New York. It was also the address of Frances Kellor, with whom he collaborated on the final chapter of her *Security Against War, International Controversies, Arbitration, Disarmament, Outlawry* (hereafter cited as Kellor, *Security Against War*).

17. Robins to Thompson, no date, RP.

18. In 1932, when outlawry had become secondary to considerations of the World Court in Robins's international concern, he undertook one of the most grueling speaking schedules in behalf of the Allied Campaign in support of prohibition. Beginning on 8 September in Columbus, Ohio, and ending in Poughkeepsie, New York, on 16 October, he spoke in a different major city every day for thirty-nine days in succession, traveling from coast to coast and back again.

19. Raymond Robins to Alexander Gumberg, 30 March 1928, AGP.

20. Pamphlet, "Prohibition, Why? How? Whither?" by Raymond Robins, was printed in the thousands during the 1920s and sold at cost in behalf of the Law Observance Campaign, copy in RP.

21. William Borah to Salmon O. Levinson, 13 July 1922, SLP, as cited in Meiberger, *Efforts of Raymond Robins*, p. 110.

22. Hiram Johnson to Raymond Robins, 5 October 1923, RP.

23. Senate Resolution 441 (67th Cong., 4th sess.).

24. The speech "The Outlawry of War—The Next Step in Civilization," was published as part of *American Policy and International Security, The Annals of the American Academy of Political and Social Sciences,* Philadelphia, 1925, vol. 120 (hereafter cited as *American Policy and International Security*).

25. Ibid.

26. Notes of a draft chapter, which demonstrate this collaboration, RP.

27. Kellor, *Security Against War,* pp. 795–96; Kellor included significant sections of Robins's speech in her section on the process of achieving outlawry, see vol. 2, p. 788.

28. *American Policy and International Security.*

29. Raymond Robins to Elizabeth Robins, 30 January, and 3 September 1928, ERP. This second letter provides Robins's own history of the outlawry movement, and it is corroborated in its essentials by both the Stoner and Meiburger studies. Quotations from "The Outlawry of War—The Next Step in Civilization," in *American Policy and International Security.*

30. Raymond Robins to Elizabeth Robins, 30 January and 3 September 1928, ERP. The issue of the definition of an "aggressor nation" and the necessity of a punitive response from the international community constantly challenged Robins, Levinson, and the outlawry campaigners. They saw the perpetuation of the "war system" in such thinking and as an evasion of the essential outlawry position. Shotwell was one of the advocates of what Robins called "the aggressor nation humbug"; see Raymond Robins to Salmon O. Levinson, 7 December 1927 and again on the eve of Senate ratification, 27 December 1928, SLP.

31. David Hunter Miller, *The Peace Pact of Paris,* Doc. 1, p. 155.

32. In addition to Meiburger and Stoner, see Robert H. Ferrell, *Peace in Their Time: The Origins of the Kellogg-Briand Pact,* and John C. Vinson, *William E. Borah and the Outlawry of War.*

33. Raymond Robins to Elizabeth Robins, 4 February 1928, ERP.

34. Raymond Robins to Elizabeth Robins, 18 April 1928, ERP.

35. Raymond Robins to Elizabeth Robins, 4 February, and 18 April 1928, ERP.

36. Raymond Robins to Elizabeth Robins, 22 June 1928, ERP.

37. Ibid.

38. Raymond Robins to Elizabeth Robins, 14 July 1928, ERP.

39. Telegram, Mary Dreier, Margaret Dreier Robins, and Raymond Robins, to Salmon O. Levinson, 26 August 1928, SLP.

40. Raymond Robins to Elizabeth Robins, 3 September 1928, ERP.

41. Transcript of notes taken by Herman Hagedorn of two interviews, one with Robins and another with Cornelius Kelleher, Thompson's personal secretary, the latter interview on 17 October 1931, in which Kelleher confirms the account of Robins's writing both letters, WTP.

42. General Treaty for Renunciation of War, in Stoner, *S. O. Levinson and the Pact of Paris,* in Appendix F, p. 355.

43. Telegram, Raymond Robins to Salmon O. Levinson, 18 July 1929, SLP, as quoted in Meiburger, *Efforts of Raymond Robins,* p. 142.

21. The Inner World

1. Coverage in *The Congregationalist and Herald of Gospel Liberty,* 27 October 1932, pp. 1391-93, during Robins's disappearance. Epigraph, ibid.

2. Telegram, Washington, D.C., 9 September 1932, Associated Press dispatch by Clarence M. Wright, RP. Carl Fisher's letter to Levinson, dated 11 November, SLP, rules out the possibility that Robins was conspiratorially hiding his identity: "He has a good education and is a world wide traveler," the boy wrote to Levinson. "When he came here he was slick shaven and now he has beard, and wears a overall jacket suit. He says he was a personal friend of Teddy Roosevelt, and is a personal friend of Mr. Herbert C. Hoover. He gives his name as Mr. R. H. Rogers. . . . If there is any rewards out for finding him please give it to me if he is the right man."

See also typewritten account "of the facts of the recent finding and return of Colonel Raymond Robins, prepared in consultation with Mrs. Robins, by John C. Dreier. . . . Issued for publication to the Brooksville *Journal and Sun,* Hernando County, Florida," November 1932, RP; *New York Times,* 9 and 11 September and 21 November 1932; *Chicago Daily News,* 23 November 1932; James Mullenbach to Elizabeth Robins, 11 October 1932, ERP; *New York Herald,* Paris ed., 20 November 1932, ERP; "The Gold Seeker," MSS in the SEP, p. 304.

3. Typewritten statement in the RP, circa December 1932.

4. Leland E. Hinsie and Robert J. Campbell, *Psychiatric Dictionary,* s.v. "fugue."

5. Hannah Robins to Elizabeth Robins, 12 March 1882, ERP.

6. Charles Robins to Jane Robins, 7 March 1882; Hannah to Elizabeth, 12 March 1882, ERP.

7. Charles Robins to Jane Robins, 13 March 1882, 22 June 1883, 21 November 1883, 5 December 1883, and 1 and 12 March 1884 (attesting to Raymond's remarkable good health and happiness); Charles Robins to Dr. James Morrison Bodine, 20 May 1882; Hannah Robins to Elizabeth Robins, 8 December 1883, on Raymond's departure for Florida, ERP.

8. Raymond Robins to Elizabeth Robins, 14 October 1913, ERP. I am "completing my round and the summing up [of] . . . life at this my fortieth year," Robins wrote to Elizabeth, about his visit to Bayside, Staten Island, earlier that October to visit the place of his birth. But he could only remember details of the place from previous visits as an adult.

9. Elizabeth Robins to Florence Bell, 19 June 1905, ERP, as quoted in Gates, "'Sometimes Suppressed and Sometimes Embroidered.'"

10. Raymond Robins to Elizabeth Robins, 18 April 1907, ERP.

11. Raymond Robins to Elizabeth Robins, 14 June 1914, ERP.

12. Raymond Robins to Elizabeth Robins, 21 August 1910, ERP.

13. Raymond Robins to Elizabeth Robins, 27 November 1913, ERP.

14. This conclusion is based on my discussion of diagnostic possibilities on the basis of the available evidence with Dr. Lawrence Sharpe, 26 October 1988. The genetic research is being carried out by Nancy C. Andreasen, John Rise, Jean Endicott, et al., "Familial Rates of Affective Disorder: A Report from the National Institute of Mental Health Collaborative Study," *Archives of General Psychiatry* 44, no. 5 (May 1987): 461-69. Also see Nancy C. Andreasen, *The Broken Brain: The Biological Revolution in Psychiatry;* see above, chap. 1, n. 10.

15. Margaret Dreier Robins to Elizabeth Robins, 12 March 1921, ERP.

16. Raymond Robins to Elizabeth Robins, 5 September 1920, ERP.

17. Raymond Robins to Elizabeth Robins, 12 May 1921, ERP.

18. Raymond Robins to Elizabeth Robins, 17 July 1921, ERP.

19. Raymond Robins to Elizabeth Robins, 7 and 29 June, 24 October 1925, ERP. The volume of correspondence, documents, and financial records surrounding Chinsegut and this conflict in particular is enormous in both the ERP, RPG and especially in the RP.

20. As early as 16 and 17 July 1929 Robins was asked if he could make deposits of first $25,000, and then $100,000, to avert runs on the bank's funds. After the crash and the bank reorganization, Robins was named chairman of the board. Thereafter a steady flow of liquidated Robins assets sustained the bank; see telegrams, F. B. Coogler (Robins's Brooksville attorney) to Raymond Robins, 16 and 17 July 1929, RP.

21. Elizabeth's twelve-page letter was written to Raymond on her homeward voyage on the Cunard's *R.M.S. Scythia,* dated January–February 1931. His response, written from Mary Dreier's home, is dated 19 February 1931, ERP.

22. One such occasion, 20 June 1930, was portentous, since on that night William B. Thompson died. Reflecting on the coincidence, Robins wrote to Gumberg: "Curious that I should be sleeping in T. R.'s [Theodore Roosevelt's] room when W. B. goes over the great divide. One my closest political the other my closest business friend" (Raymond Robins to Alexander Gumberg, 20 June 1930, AGP).

23. Raymond Robins to Elizabeth Robins, 22 February 1931, ERP.

24. His first quotation of the text was in a letter to Elizabeth on 22 December 1930 and, forgetting that he had already shared it with her, repeated on 21 August 1931, ERP. From the same chapter of Deuteronomy (28:33), he recorded the following: "and you will be oppressed and cursed at all times without surcease, until you are driven mad by what your eyes must look upon." And Deut. 28:30: "Though you build a house you will not live in it. Though you plant a vineyard, you will not enjoy its fruit." With the exception of Elizabeth, he told no one of his worsening depression.

25. Raymond Robins to Elizabeth Robins, 22 May 1931, ERP. Throughout May and June, Robins carried out his speaking tour of the west and spoke on the following topics: "The Constitution, Shall We Scrap It?" "The Briand Peace Pact and Next Steps for Peace," "Is Civilization Essential to Democratic Civilization?" "Theodore Roosevelt: The Man and his Message," and "Russia: Menace or Hope," see notes in RP.

26. Raymond Robins to Elizabeth Robins, 21 November 1931, ERP; Raymond Robins to George F. Cahill, 15 August 1932, RP.

27. Raymond Robins to Elizabeth Robins, 8 May 1930, ERP.

28. Raymond Robins to Elizabeth Robins, 6 June 1932, ERP.

29. Harold Ickes to Raymond Robins (carbon copies), 28 July and 17 November 1930, HIP. In the latter, Ickes is once again reporting his activities on the progressive firing line, in spite of his disillusionment.

30. Raymond Robins to Salmon O. Levinson, 3 March 1931, SLP; Raymond Robins to Elizabeth Robins, 17 July 1932, ERP. On the same day, Robins also wrote to Mr. and Mrs. E. A. Van Valkenberg, old-time Republicans who claimed the progressive mantle, but unwilling to share "the hidden depths of [his] heart, knowing the unwelcome *truth,*" he wrote to them in a melodramatic spirit of hope and devotion to the Hoover cause which we know was entirely insincere: "Not long ago I was lunching with the "CHIEF" on that balcony . . . of the White House—it was an hour of stress on the Hill, and the hosts of the fake 'heroes' of Booze and the Bonus whipped up by Hearst were marching and countermarching on capitol plaza—southward rose the simple and glorious shining shaft dominating and serene of the Father of this America of ours, and the quiet strong kindly man seated there HIS TRUE SUCCESSOR Herbert Hoover calm in the midst of a world cataclysm, by wild waves driven and great winds blown—yet was he also, steadfast and serene pointing as the needle to the pole the right course for our Ship of State" (letter in RP).

31. Raymond Robins to C. W. Ramseyer, 19 August 1932, RP.

32. Raymond to Elizabeth, 17 July 1932, ERP. Robins was taken with this phrase: "dead march to an open political grave" and in his correspondence in later years chose it often, finally using only the abbreviation "D. M. T. O. P. G."

22. A Dream Fulfilled, a Final Challenge

1. Raymond Robins to Elizabeth Robins, 26 November 1933, ERP. Epigraphs, Raymond to Elizabeth, 26 November 1933 and 10 June 1945, ERP.

2. Telegram (mailed "To avoid further publicity"), Margaret Dreier Robins to Alexander Gumberg, 30 November 1932, AGP.

3. Margaret Dreier Robins to Alexander Gumberg, 17 September 1932, AGP. Margaret's signature, written at the end of this note in the most uncharacteristic shaky handwriting, tells a different tale than Margaret's brave words. She paid a heavy price through these ten weeks of worry and uncertainty.

4. Pond Lyceum Bureau to Raymond Robins, 10 August 1933, RP.

5. Raymond Robins to Elizabeth Robins, 8 October 1934, ERP. These words should be reconsidered in light of the aftermath of his accident, just one year later.

6. Raymond Robins to Elizabeth Robins, 2 October 1927, ERP.

7. Alexander Gumberg to Raymond Robins, 19 December 1932 and 5 January 1933, RP. The William E. Borah Papers in the Library of Congress contain a voluminous body of material, consisting of correspondence, organizational reports, and printed media on the question of trade with the Soviet Union as a remedy for the depression. Exemplary of the correspondence is a letter from J. D. Mooney, president of the General Motors Export Company, to Borah, 29 December 1930, congratulating and encouraging Borah to press on with recognition in expectation that the Soviets will "buy some of our own goods and contribute thereby to our own prosperity." Hugh L. Cooper and Allen Wardwell, president and vice-president, respectively, of the American-Russian Chamber of Commerce, maintained a steady flow of reports and telegrams in support of recognition. The "Memorandum on American-Russian Trade, June 24, 1932," written after a year of significant decline in the volume of trade, was "prepared to assist . . . movement to remove the obstacles now blocking the way to recovery of this valuable outlet for American products."

8. Notes in Robins's handwriting in the RP.

9. Raymond Robins to Salmon O. Levinson, 13 and 17 March 1933, RP.

10. "Your appreciation of Einstein is extraordinarily fitting and beautiful," Robins continued in his letter to Levinson. "There is something strangely moving to me in the fact that the first MIND of the age is an expatriate JEW. At the hour when the modern Prophets of his race are about to establish international peace and end the age long thraldom of the Sword, and are lifting the wide horizons of human thought about and understanding of the Universe—a savage persecution of his suffering people is begun in the land of his birth!" (Robins to Levinson, 17 March 1933, RP).

11. In *Pravda* on 7 April 1930 Alex Gumberg managed to defend his brother in the letters-to-the-editor column. See "A Note on the Papers of Alexander Gumberg," by William Appleman Williams (unpublished) in the AGP. James Libbey, in *Alexander Gumberg*, p. 177, suggests that Alex's brothers Venjamin and Sergei were purged, like so many others, because of their past connection with Trotsky and Zinoviev, rather than because of Alex's activities.

12. Writing to Gumberg on 26 April 1931, RP, shortly after publication of Sisson's book, Robins stated: "It is all directed to the thesis that 'the leaders of the Bolshevik revolution in Russia were thieves, murderers and German agents.' If that thesis can *now* be maintained then the human race is hopeless. A controversy between that poor fish and myself would give him a publicity after all these years of obscurity that he does not deserve."

13. Raymond Robins to Elizabeth Robins, dated 7, 9, and 19 April 1933, ERP, written in part en route: "Tomorrow if all goes well I shall see YOU [Elizabeth] once again!" Robins wrote of going "to many points of strain in the Soviet Union," and of the chance that he might "come upon disaster in the Russian land . . . to serve the TRUTH in a world of conflict, propaganda and confusion." It is not clear what dangers he had in mind, but as with all his adventures, he wanted to convey his courage and self-sacrifice to Elizabeth.

14. "Excerpts from Letters of Colonel Raymond Robins Written from Moscow, to Margaret Dreier Robins, Hotel National, Moscow, May Day 1918, May Day 1933, Copy," RP and ERP (hereafter referred to as "Excerpts, May Day, 1933"). See Raymond Robins to Elizabeth Robins, 13 May, Moscow; 22 May, "Samara on the Volga"; 8 June, Moscow, 1933, ERP, for further details of the trip.

15. Robins identified the following newsmen and news organizations: "Stoneman of the *Chicago Daily News*, Kinkaid of the *New York Times* (Duranty being away for some weeks), Barnes

of the *Herald Tribune* and Richardson of the Associated Press" ("Excerpts, May Day, 1933," pp. 5–6); Raymond to Elizabeth, 13 May 1933, ERP.

16. Raymond Robins to Elizabeth Robins, Salmon O. Levinson, and Margaret Dreier Robins, 8 June 1933, in the ERP, SLP, and RP, respectively.

17. Raymond Robins to Salmon O. Levinson, on board the *President Harding,* 30 June 1933, SLP; also cited in Meiburger, *Efforts of Raymond Robins,* p. 174. A 7 July letter to Levinson repeats the same information and continues: "Also the message said that the R.F.C. had agreed to give credits for Russian purchases in the U.S. None of this has been confirmed."

18. Raymond Robins to Alexander Gumberg, 14 and 16 July 1933, AGP.

19. Raymond Robins to Frances Perkins, 20 July 1933, RP.

20. Robins added one additional item to his list of reasons for recognition in his radio address: "to truly stabilize international price levels," RP.

21. Raymond Robins to Elizabeth Robins, 19 October 1933, ERP.

22. Raymond Robins to William E. Borah, 31 October 1933, WBP; Raymond Robins to Elizabeth Robins, 17 November 1933, ERP. Among the letters of congratulations to Robins on the achievement of recognition is that of Smith, who wrote from Paris four days after the announcement and expressed his wonder at how Robins could have made such a prediction (Charles H. Smith to Raymond Robins, 20 November 1933, RP). "The situation . . . would be perfect now if your good self could represent us when recognition takes place," Borah wrote to Robins from Boise on 8 November. "I can hardly hope that that can be possible yet it would be eternally the right thing to do" (Borah to Robins [carbon copy], WBP).

23. Meiburger, *Efforts of Raymond Robins,* p. 183; and Marian C. McKenna, *Borah,* p. 304.

24. Williams, *American Russian Relations, 1781–1947,* pp. 235–37; Bennett, in *Recognition of Russia,* chap. 3, "The American View: Peace Prosperity and Recognition," examines the complex crosscurrents faced by FDR in the year preceding the decision to recognize the Soviet Union. In *Recognition of Russia* and in his *Franklin D. Roosevelt and the Search For Security: American-Soviet Relations, 1933–1939,* Edward M. Bennett concludes that U.S. security remained the first concern: "He [FDR] . . . was far more worried about the prospect of another world war that would disrupt economic recovery, spread obnoxious doctrines by conquest, and destroy democracy in the process" (p. xiii in the latter book); Thomas Maddux, in *Years of Estrangement: American Relations with the Soviet Union, 1933–1941,* concurs in this judgment; Robert Paul Browder's *The Origins of Soviet-American Diplomacy,* and, Beatrice Bishop Berle and Travis Beal Jacobs, eds., *Navigating the Rapids, 1918–1971,* are also valuable sources in the study of the domestic and international considerations that finally led to recognition.

Typical of the barrage of articles and cartoons calling for recognition and trade with the Soviets are those found in the *New York World-Telegram* of 30 July and 16 August 1932: "Another Hunger Striker," depicts the ragged United States rejecting "Billions in Trade" offered by "Russia." "Tear Down the Barrier!" depicts Uncle Sam's pushcart of "Made in U.S.A." goods stopped at the border crossing marked "Failure to Trade with Russia," both in the WBP.

25. Raymond to Elizabeth, 17 and 26 November 1933, ERP.

26. Raymond Robins to Salmon O. Levinson, 19 February 1935, RP.

27. Raymond Robins to Elizabeth Robins, 4 January 1933, ERP.

28. Raymond Robins to Elizabeth Robins, 22 November 1935, ERP.

29. "The Gold-Seeker," pp. 311 and 316, SEP. Robins was quoted in the Tampa *Morning Tribune,* 18 July 1949, predicting that Pepper would rise to national prominence and be president. However, some years later, Pepper, always following Robins's advice to support a conciliatory U.S. policy toward the Soviets, found himself at odds with the rising tide of Cold War red-baiting. In 1946, at Robins's suggestion, Pepper had written the introduction to *The Great Soviet Conspiracy,* an extreme pro-Soviet book. Soon thereafter he was labeled "a communist sympathizer," and in 1947 this led to the loss of his seat on the Senate Foreign Relations Committee (Claude Pepper to Raymond Robins, 9 January 1947, RP). Robins and Pepper remained close friends until 1950, when they parted political and personal company over their disagreement on the Korean War. Robins was highly critical of the U.S. role.

30. Payne, in *Reform, Labor and Feminism,* presents a lengthy and eloquent discussion on the antagonistic "collision between Progressive ideology and New Deal practices." Reflecting the contemporary revisionist interpretation of the New Deal, Payne argues that the New Deal was a betrayal of the voluntaristic American reform tradition that had culminated in the Progressive movement. Payne cites Margaret Dreier Robins as a prototypical example of the progressive disillusioned by Roosevelt's coercive big government and states that Margaret considered the New Deal "a bureaucratic, 'Prussianized' state, driven by an urge to control and supervise, intent on regulation and regimentation, dedicated to planning and paternalism, yet itself essentially devoid of moral intent and traditional virtue" (p. 165). Payne's erroneous portrayal is not limited to Margaret Dreier Robins as a bitter opponent of the New Deal. "It is, however, equally true," Payne goes on to assert, without supporting evidence, "that most Progressives lamented that the New Deal highway necessarily led to an intellectual and moral dead end" (p. 176). Payne has chosen to give inadequate attention to the three causes of Margaret's profound and general disillusionment in her last ten declining years: her deteriorating physical and mental health brought on, in part, by Raymond's depressions, the strain of his long disappearance due to amnesia, and his accident and paralysis; the Robinses financial ruin; and the exclusion of the Robinses from positions in the Roosevelt administration because of their Republicanism.

31. Raymond Robins to Alexander Gumberg, 16 August 1936, RP.

32. Raymond Robins to John Dewey, 21 May 1937, RP.

33. Raymond Robins to Alexander Gumberg, 22 January 1937, RP.

34. Raymond Robins to Alexander Gumberg, 22 February 1937, AGP.

35. Raymond Robins to Alexander Gumberg, 25 February 1937, AGP.

36. Raymond Robins to Mary Dreier, 14 April 1937, RP.

37. Raymond Robins to Alexander Gumberg, 25 February 1937, AGP.

38. Salmon O. Levinson to Raymond Robins, 6 December 1937, RP.

39. Louis Adamic and Ellery Sedgwick were often suggested in the years immediately after the "smashup." Later, in the 1940s, drafts of a biography were prepared by Sherwood Eddy, followed by William Appleman Williams's, but no effort was made to complete and publish these drafts.

40. Raymond Robins to Alexander Gumberg, 28 March 1939, AGP. This is one of Robins's last letters to Gumberg before Gumberg's death on 31 May 1939.

41. Raymond Robins to Mary Dreier, 1 September 1938, RP.

42. Raymond Robins to Mary Dreier, 31 May 1939, RP.

43. Raymond Robins to Floyd Odlum, 31 May 1939, RP.

44. Raymond Robins to Alexander Gumberg, 22 February 1937, AGP.

45. In a letter to Miss Mary Van Kleek, 25 July 1939, RP, Robins asked Van Kleek ("with your permission I have chosen you") to take Gumberg's place "as the medium of a continuing line of intelligent understanding regarding the happenings in Russia." A correspondence was begun, but it was not sustained beyond the year.

46. Raymond Robins to Elizabeth Robins, 25 November 1942, ERP.

47. Raymond Robins to Elizabeth Robins, 29 June 1942, ERP.

48. Raymond Robins to Elizabeth Robins, 22 February 1945, ERP.

Epilogue

1. Raymond Robins to Prof. Frederick Lewis Schuman, Woodrow Wilson Professor of History at Williams College, 11 October 1946, RP. Robins had just read Schuman's book, *Soviet Politics at Home and Abroad,* and was moved to write the author of his appreciation of its historic accuracy.

2. Jerome Davis to Raymond Robins, 18 April 1947, RP.

3. Robins to Schuman, 11 October 1946, RP.

4. Raymond Robins to Albert Kahn and Michael Sayers, 29 November 1943, RP.

5. Michael Sayers and Albert Kahn, *The Great Conspiracy Against Russia,* front cover.

6. Ibid., back cover.

7. Ibid., p. 1.

8. Albert Kahn to Raymond Robins, 2 February 1944, RP.

9. "The battle against the Soviets is at crescendo for the whole 28 years NOW," he wrote to Mary. "I have no sort of doubt of the Soviets riding this cyclone. They are founded on the rock of the People's welfare—on their liberation and enlightenment. Churchill and the Pope the land Lords and the Imperialists are all in action now. If the Soviets ride this storm, they can ride all that may come" (Raymond Robins to Mary Dreier, 8 March 1946, RP).

10. *Labour Monthly* 33 (December 1951): 574-82.

Bibliography

Published Writings by Raymond Robins, Arranged Chronologically

Letter, *The National Single Taxer*, January 1899.

"Politics and Labor." *The Commons* 6, no. 66 (January 1902): 10-13.

"Chicago's Municipal Lodging House: How the Human Flotsam-and-Jetsam of a Great American City is Scientifically Cared for and Returned to the Ranks of Industry." *Merchant's Association Review*, San Francisco (August 1902): 5-6.

"The Tramp Problem and Municipal Correction." *The Commons* 7, no. 74 (September 1902): 1-9.

"A Settlement in City Politics." *The Commons* 8, no. 82 (May 1903): 1-3.

"Chicago Municipal Lodging House." *The New Jersey Review of Charities and Corrections* 2, no. 7 (August-September 1903).

"Vagrancy and its Relations to the Problem of Crime in this Community." Co-authored with Francis O'Neill, Chief of Police of the City of Chicago. *The City Club of Chicago Yearbook, 1904*. Chicago, 1904.

"What Constitutes A Model Municipal Lodging House." *Proceedings of the National Conference of Charities and Correction*, 22 June 1904.

"How a Union Inspired a Working Woman." *The Commons* 9, no. 6 (June 1904): 260.

"Who Shall Be Mayor? To the Independent Voters of Chicago." *Chicago Daily News*, 20 March 1905.

"Open Letter to Mayor Dunne." *The Public* 8, no. 371 (13 May 1905): 89.

"Sexual Vice and Venereal Disease Among the Homeless." *Proceedings of the Chicago Society of Social Hygiene*, December 1906.

"The One Main Thing." *Proceedings of the National Conference of Charities and Correction* (1907): 326-34.

"The Charter Situation. What Next?" *The City Club Bulletin* 1, no. 19 (23 October 1907): 217-20.

"Side Lights on Graft and Grafters." *The Public* 494 (21 September 1907).

Address by Raymond Robins at the National Protest Meeting of the Chicago Federation of Labor, April 19, 1908. Chicago, 1908.

"Raymond Robins at the Denver Convention, Address of Raymond Robins of Illinois, Before the National Democratic Convention at Denver, July 9, as reported by the Associated Press." *The Public* 11, no. 542 (21 August 1908): 497-98.

"The Political and Legal Policies of the American Federation of Labor." *The City Club Bulletin* 2, no. 24 (17 February 1909): 279-92.

"The Moral Value of Labor—From a Speech by Raymond Robins before the City Club of Chicago, February 17, 1909." *The Public* 12, no. 570 (5 March 1909): 228-29.

"Sermons on Social Service, Being Stenographic Reports of Parts of the Addresses Delivered Each Week for Twenty-Six Weeks by Mr. Robins as Social Service Member of Team No. 3 of the Men and Religion Forward Movement." *The Survey* 28, no. 1 (6 April 1912): 35–64.

Address of Raymond Robins as Temporary Chairman, Progressive National Convention, June 7, 1916. Chicago, 1916.

"Social Control in Russia Today." *The Annals of the American Academy of Political and Social Sciences* 84, no. 3 (July 1919): 127–44.

"The Outlawry of War—The Next Step in Civilization." *American Policy and International Security, The Annals of the American Academy of Political and Social Sciences* 120 (Philadelphia, 1925).

"United States Recognition of Soviet Russia Essential to World Peace and Stabilization." *Annals of the American Academy of Political and Social Sciences* 126, no. 215 (July 1926): 100–104, 110–16.

"Universal Peace—A World Challenge." *Annals of the American Academy of Political and Social Sciences* 126, no. 215 (July 1926): 158–59.

"Prohibition, Why? How? Whither?" Law Observance Campaign pamphlet (ca. 1926).

"Soviet Russia After Fifteen Years." Address Delivered Over the National Broadcasting Company Network, 26 July 1933. *The Congressional Record,* appendix (2 June 1943).

An American Prophet Speaks: A Historic Interview with Premier Stalin on the Eve of U.S. Recognition of the U.S.S.R. by President Roosevelt in 1933, foreword and edited by Cedric Belfarge. New York: Boni and Gaer, 1952.

Road to Chinsegut: Stories of the Early Life of Raymond Robins As Told By Him to Lisa von Borowsky, edited by John C. Dreier. Washington, D.C.: Private distribution, 1978.

Manuscripts

State Historical Society of Wisconsin, Madison

Anita McCormick Blaine Papers (MBP)
George Gibbs Papers (GGP)
Alexander Gumberg Papers (AGP)
Charles McCarthy Papers (CMP)
DeWitt Clinton Poole Papers (DPP)
Edward A. Ross Papers (ARP)

Raymond Robins Papers (RP)

The Raymond Robins collection of forty-six archival boxes includes twenty-one bound volumes (four notebooks, nine diaries, and nine short published pamphlets). The collection contains thirty stenographic typescripts of speeches, testimony, and depositions, the latter two relevant to hearings on his activities in Russia. Many of the speeches deal with the Russian experience, but every aspect of his activity is represented in these collected typescripts. Equally important is his enormous correspondence, which comprises more than three-quarters of the collection. Robins made carbon copies of many of his letters. The originals of those sent to his wife, Margaret, and his sister-in-law, Mary Dreier, have been included in the collection. The full list of his correspondents numbers in the hundreds and includes many notable figures in twentieth-century America. *The Guide to Manuscripts in the State Historical So-*

ciety of Wisconsin, Supplement, No. 2 (1966) provides a partial list, as well as a general biographical sketch and description of the collection.

Library of the University of Florida, Gainesville

Margaret Dreier Robins Papers (MRP)
This collection of more than 110 archival boxes includes: correspondence, speeches, reports, and memoranda concerning Chinsegut, the Robinses' Florida estate. A significant part of the collection is concerned with Margaret Robins's organizational affiliations, especially the Illinois, National, and International Women's Trade Union Leagues. This includes notes and minutes of meetings. In addition to materials on all phases of reform work paralleling those of her husband, there are important sources pertinent to all phases of the women's movement during the first three decades of the twentieth century—suffrage, education, discrimination, legal status, and working conditions. This segment of the collection should be used in conjuction with the official archives of the National Women's Trade Union League in the Library of Congress, Washington, D.C. See also Edward T. James, ed., *Papers of the Women's Trade Union League and Its Principal Leaders, Guide to the Microfilm Edition* (Woodbridge, Conn.: Research Publishers, 1981).

Raymond Robins Papers (RPG)
There are fourteen archival boxes of letters written by Raymond to Margaret Robins, beginning in 1905 and ending in the early 1940s. None of these letters were written during the period he was in Russia (July 1917 to June 1918); these all seem to have found their way into the collection at the State Historical Society of Wisconsin, Madison, and the Elizabeth Robins Papers in the Fales Library of New York University. There are several letters from Margaret to Raymond during that period, but they are of little value relative to the developments in Russia. The letters in these fourteen boxes are especially valuable in the study of several of Robins's campaigns, notably his efforts in behalf of George Record, reform candidate for mayor of Jersey City, New Jersey, in 1908, and the organization of the Progressive party between 1912 and 1916.

Fales Library, New York University, New York

Elizabeth Robins Papers (ERP)
The papers of Raymond's sister, Elizabeth Robins—novelist, playwright, actress, and suffragist—contain the entire Robins family archives, extensive written and photographic material documenting Raymond's Alaskan experience, and indispensable correspondence. Although New York University acquired the papers in 1964, they were not made available to the scholarly community until 1984, when work on their organization was begun. That work was completed in 1986, resulting in a carefully arranged and most useful collection.

Library of Congress, Washington, D.C.

William E. Borah Papers (WBP)
George B. Creel Papers (GCP)

Harold Ickes Papers (HIP)
Robert M. La Follette Papers (BLP)
Robert Lansing Papers (RLP)
Records of the National Women's Trade Union League (WTUP)
Amos Pinchot Papers (APP)
Gifford Pinchot Papers (GPP)
Theodore Roosevelt Papers (TRP)
William Boyce Thompson-Herman Hagedorn Papers (WTP)
William A. White Papers (WAWP)
Woodrow Wilson Papers (WPC)

New York Public Library, New York

Thomas D. Thacher Papers (TPN)
Lillian D. Wald Papers (LWP)

Butler Library, Columbia University, New York

George W. Perkins Papers (GWPP)
Oral History Research Office, transcript of recorded reminiscences of DeWitt Clinton
    Poole (DPO) and Allen Wardwell (AWO)
Bakhmeteff Archive: Charles R. Crane Papers (CRCP); Lincoln Steffens Papers (LSP);
    Thomas D. Thacher Papers (TPC); Allen Wardwell Papers (AWP)

Newberry Library, Chicago

William V. Judson Papers (WJP)
Graham Taylor Papers (GTP)

Libraries of the University of Chicago, Chicago

Samuel Harper Papers (SHP)
Salmon O. Levinson Papers (SLP)
Charles E. Merriam Papers (CEMP)

Chicago Historical Society, Chicago

Chicago Teachers Federation Papers (CTP)
Chicago Commons Papers (CCP)
City Club of Chicago Papers (CCCP)

Library of Princeton University, Princeton, New Jersey

Arthur Bullard Papers (ABP)

YMCA National Headquarters, New York

Biographical file on Raymond Robins

A ten-page biographical report on Robins written by his friend and co-worker Gale Seaman, it deals particularly with Robins's evangelical work while in association with the Y. It is a lauditory appreciation.

Private Collections

Sherwood Eddy Papers (SEP), Louise Gates Eddy, Jacksonville, Illinois

Within the Eddy Papers is a file of materials on Robins, consisting of approximately 150 pages. Among these is an unpublished typescript of an incomplete biography of Robins entitled "The Goldseeker: The Life and Times of Raymond Robins," by Sherwood Eddy. The partial draft consists of portions of several chapters, totaling approximately fifty pages. However, there are an even greater number of handwritten pages, obviously the record of Eddy's interviews with Robins, and these have been of great value here. Most significant are Eddy's notes taken from Robins's "yellow butcher-paper diary," which recorded the Alaskan experience. Eddy took these from the diary in 1947 while visiting Elizabeth Robins in England. This diary is no longer in the papers of Elizabeth Robins in the Fales Library of New York University; its whereabouts is unknown. Although not examined by the present author, it is clear that in addition to the Robins file, the Eddy papers also contain an extensive correspondence between Robins and Eddy. They were friends and associates during much of their adult lives, as both were involved in evangelistic work and deeply concerned about international relations.

Assorted papers, correspondence, diaries, and printed matter of Margaret Dreier Robins, Mary E. Dreier, and Raymond Robins taken from the Sunrise Cottage, Chinsegut Hill Sanctuary, Brooksville, Florida, while being razed (RPC)

These documents were brought to light in January 1972 by Lisa von Borowsky and, in cooperation with the author, were to be deposited with the Raymond Robins Papers at the State Historical Society of Wisconsin, Madison. They have since been mislaid and may have been destroyed. However, the following inventory of these materials was made by the author before they were sent to Wisconsin:

1. Diary of Saxton Robins, 1891
2. Packet of "letters of Saxton Robins filled this 19th November, 1950," notation in Raymond Robins's hand
3. Packet of letters labeled "R.R. to M.D.R. filed 1946" in Raymond Robins's hand
4. Packet of letters to Raymond Robins, 1896 to 1901, from addresses in Washington, D.C., several cities in Alaska, and the Chicago Commons
5. Packet of letters from Vernon Robins
6. Letters from Raymond to Margaret Robins from 1919 to 1929
7. A box of assorted photos dealing with the year in Russia, Robins's associates in the Men and Religion Forward Movement, activities and facilities of the Municipal Lodging House, portraits, and many in and around Chinsegut
8. Business correspondence and periodicals of Mary Dreier
9. Materials used by Mary Dreier in writing her biography of Margaret Dreier Robins
10. Assortment of printed matter and periodicals including valuable news clippings as well as popular publications of doubtful value

Additional photographs and two signed portrait engravings of Lenin and Trotsky were also found in January 1972 in the attic of the main house at Chinsegut and are among the materials now lost.

Published Sources

Addams, Jane. *Twenty Years at Hull-House.* New York: Macmillan, 1957.

Adney, Tappan A. *The Klondike Stampede of 1897–1898.* New York: Harper and Bros., 1900.

Andreasen, Nancy C. *The Broken Brain: The Biological Revolution in Psychiatry.* New York: Harper and Row, 1985.

Andreasen, Nancy C., John Rise, Jean Endicott, et al. "Familial Rates of Affective Disorder: A Report from the National Institute of Mental Health Collaborative Study." *Archives of General Psychiatry* 44, no. 5 (May 1987): 461–469.

Andrews, Wayne. *Battle for Chicago.* New York: Harcourt Brace, 1946.

Armes, Ethel. "On the Trail of Roosevelt, the Most Venerated Horseshoe in the World." *The Grand Rapids Press,* 5 August 1924.

Bailey, Thomas A. *America Faces Russia: Russian American Relations From Early Times to Our Day.* Ithaca, N.Y.: Cornell Univ. Press, 1950.

Baker, Ray Stannard. *Woodrow Wilson: Life and Letters.* 8 vols. New York: Doubleday Doran, 1939.

Beach, Rex. *The Spoilers.* New York: Harper and Bros., 1906.

———. "Nome Claim Jumping," and "The Looting of Alaska, or the True Story of Robbery by Law." Appleton's *Booklover's Magazine* 7, nos. 1–6 (June–November 1906): 1–606.

Beatty, Bessie. "The Fall of the Winter Palace." *The Century Magazine* 96 (August 1918): 523–32.

———. *The Red Heart of Russia.* New York: Century Co., 1919.

———. "Gold and Fool's Gold, Col. Thompson Stakes His Faith on the Russian People." *Asia* (August 1918): 665–66.

Beckner, Earl E. *A History of Labor Legislation in Illinois.* Chicago: Univ. of Chicago Press, 1929.

Bennett, Edward M. *Recognition of Russia: An American Foreign Policy Dilemma.* Waltham, Mass.: Blaisdell, 1970.

———. *Franklin D. Roosevelt and the Search for Security, American-Soviet Relations, 1933–1939.* Wilmington, Del.: Scholarly Resources, 1985.

Berle, Beatrice Bishop, and Travis Beal Jacobs, eds. *Navigating the Rapids, 1918–1971: From the Papers of Adolf A. Berle.* New York: Harcourt Brace, 1973.

Berton, Pierre. *The Klondike Fever: The Life and Death of the Last Great Gold Rush.* New York: Caroll and Graf, 1985.

Bode, Frank H. "Justice to An Opponent." *The Public* 19, no. 967 (13 September 1916): 977–78.

Bolshevik Propaganda, Hearings before a Subcommittee of the Committee on the Judiciary, United States Senate, 65th Congress, Third Session. Washington, D.C.: U.S. Senate, 1919.

Boone, Gladys. *The Women's Trade Union Leagues in Great Britain and the United States of America.* New York: Columbia Univ. Press, 1942.

Borah, William E. "The Threat of Bolshevism in America—How to Meet It." *Current Opinion* 66 (March 1919): 152–53.

———. "Senator Borah Pleads for Recognition of Soviet Russia." *Current Opinion* 74 (February 1923): 215–16.

———. "Shall We Abandon Russia" *New York Times Magazine,* 2 December 1917.

Bradley, John. *Allied Intervention in Russia.* Latham, Md.: University Press of America, 1984.

Breckinridge, Sophonsiba, and Edith Abbott. "Chicago's Housing Conditions." *American Journal of Sociology* 4, no. 17 (July 1911).

Bremner, Robert Hamlett. *From the Depths: The Discovery of Poverty in the United States.* New York: New York Univ. Press, 1964.

Browder, Robert. *The Origins of Soviet-American Diplomacy.* Princeton, N.J.: Princeton Univ. Press, 1953.

"Bryan at New Haven." *The Public* 10, no. 505 (7 December 1907): 850–51.

Bryant, Louise. *Six Red Months in Russia: An Observers Account of Russia Before and During the Proletarian Dictatorship.* New York: George H. Doran, 1918.

Buder, Stanley. *Pullman, An Experiment in Industrial Order and Community Planning, 1880–1930.* New York: Oxford Univ. Press, 1967.

Bullard, Arthur. *The Russian Pendulum: Autocracy—Democracy—Bolshevism.* New York: Macmillan, 1919.

Bullitt, William C. *The Bullitt Mission To Russia: Testimony Before the Committee on Foreign Relations, United States Senate, of William C. Bullitt.* New York: B. W. Huebsch, 1919.

Bunyan, James, ed. *Intervention, Civil War and Communism in Russia, April–December, 1918, Documents and Materials.* Baltimore: Johns Hopkins Univ. Press, 1936.

Bunyan, James, and H. H. Fisher, eds. *The Bolshevik Revolution, 1917–1918, Documents and Materials.* Stanford, Calif.: Stanford Univ. Press, 1934.

"A Business Movement in Religion." *The Public* 14, no. 704 (29 September 1911): 1003.

Calhoun, Frederick S. *Power and Principle: Armed Intervention in Wilsonian Foreign Policy.* Kent, Ohio: Kent State Univ. Press, 1986.

Camitta, Hugh D. "Raymond Robins: Study of a Progressive, 1901–1917." Honors thesis, Williams College, 1965.

Carr, Edward Hallett. *A History of Soviet Russia: The Bolshevik Revolution, 1917–1923.* 3 vols. New York: Macmillan, 1950–54.

Carter, Paul A. *The Decline and Revival of the Social Gospel.* Ithaca, N.Y.: Cornell Univ. Press, 1954.

Chambers, Clarke A. *Seedtime of Reform: American Social Service and Social Action, 1918–1933.* Minneapolis: Univ. of Minnesota Press, 1965.

Chambers, John Whiteclay, III. *The Tyranny of Change: America in the Progressive Era, 1900–1917.* New York: St. Martin's, 1980.

Chase, Margaret E. "Raymond Robins in Boston." *The Public* 11, no. 525 (24 April 1908): 82.

The Chicago Municipal Lodging House, Report of the General Superintendent of Police of the City of Chicago to the City Council. Annual reports: 31 December 1903; 31 December 1904.

Chicherin, George. *Two Years of Foreign Policy: The Relations of the R.S.F.S.R. with Foreign Nations, From November 7, 1917 to November 7, 1919.* New York: Russian Government Bureau, 1920.

A Chronicler (John Cudahy). *Archangel: The American War With Russia.* Chicago: A. C. McClurg, 1924.

Coates, William Peyton, and Zelda Kahan. *Allied Intervention in Russia, 1918–1922.* London: Victor Gollancz, 1935.

Coletta, Paolo E. *William Jennings Bryan.* Lincoln, Neb.: Univ. of Nebraska Press, 1969.

"Colonel Raymond Robins Arrived in Hernando County Fifty Years Ago Today." *Brooksville Florida Sun,* 8 December 1933.

Conn, Sandra. "Three Talents: Robins, Nestor and Anderson of the Chicago Women's Trade Union League." *Chicago History* 9, no. 4 (Winter 1980–81).

Cooley, Staughton. "Robins and Roosevelt." *The Public* 17, no. 864 (23 September 1914): 1009–10.

———. "Choosing Sides." *The Public* 19, no. 956 (11 August 1916): 747–48.

Cooper, John Milton. *The Warrior and the Priest: Woodrow Wilson and Theodore Roosevelt.* Cambridge, Mass.: Harvard Univ. Press, 1983.

Cornell, Robert J. *The Anthracite Coal Strike of 1902.* Washington, D.C.: Catholic Univ. of America, 1957.

Cumming, C. K., and Walter W. Petit, eds. *Russian-American Relations, March, 1917–March, 1920: Documents and Papers.* New York: Harcourt Brace and Howe, 1920.

Danziger, Samuel. "Robins' Election Means Approval of Wilson." *The Public* 17, no. 863 (16 September 1914): 985.

———. "Robins' Endorsement of Wilson's Peace Policy." *The Public* 17, no. 865 (30 September 1914): 1035.

Davis, Allen F. *American Heroine: The Life and Legend of Jane Addams.* New York: Oxford Univ. Press, 1973.

———. "Raymond Robins: The Settlement Worker as Municipal Reformer." *The Social Service Review* 30 (June 1959): 131–41.

———. *Spearheads for Reform: The Social Settlement and the Progressive Movement, 1890–1914.* New York: Oxford Univ. Press, 1967.

Davison, Henry P. *The Work of the American Red Cross During the War.* Washington, D.C.: American Red Cross, 1919.

———. *The American Red Cross in the Great War.* New York: Macmillan, 1920.

Davison, Joan Doverspike. "Raymond Robins and United States Foreign Policy Toward Revolutionary Russia." Ph.D. diss., Notre Dame Univ., 1984.

Degras, Jane, ed. *Soviet Documents on Foreign Policy.* Vol. 1, 1917–1924. Oxford: Oxford Univ. Press, for Royal Institute of International Affairs, 1951.

Destler, Chester McArthur. *American Radicalism, 1865–1901.* New York: Octagon, 1972.

Deutscher, Isaac. *The Prophet Armed: Trotsky, 1879–1921.* Oxford: Oxford Univ. Press, 1954.

Dobrjansky, A. N. "The Tragedy of Russia," pamphlet. New York: Private distribution, 1919.

———. "Vital Reasons for the Recognition of the Omsk Government," pamphlet. New York: Private distribution, 1919.

Dreier, John C., ed. *Road to Chinsegut: Stories of the Early Life of Raymond Robins as Told by Him to Lisa von Borowsky.* Washington, D.C.: Private distribution, 1978.

Dreier, Mary E. *Margaret Dreier Robins: Her Life Letters and Work.* New York: Island Press Cooperative, 1950.

Drummond, Henry. *Natural Law in the Spiritual World.* Philadelphia: James Pott, 1892.

Estes, Barbara Ann. "Margaret Dreier Robins, Social Reformer and Labor Organizer." Ph. D. diss., Ball State Univ., 1977.

Ferrell, Robert H. *Peace in Their Time: The Origins of the Kellogg-Briand Pact.* New Haven, Conn.: Yale Univ. Press, 1952.

———. *Woodrow Wilson and World War I, 1917–1921.* New York: Harper and Row, 1985.

Fischer, Louis. *The Life of Lenin.* New York: Harper and Row, 1964.

Foner, Philip S. *History of the Labor Movement in the United States.* New York: International Publishers, 1955.

Francis, David R. *Russia From the American Embassy: April, 1916–November, 1918.* New York: Scribner's, 1921.

Frost, Stanley. "Raymond Robins, Practical Reformer." *The New York Tribune,* 19 April 1919.

Garraty, John A. *Right Hand Man: The Life of George W. Perkins.* New York: Harper and Bros., 1960.

Gates, Joanne Elizabeth. "'Sometimes Suppressed and Sometimes Embroidered': The Life and Writing of Elizabeth Robins, 1862–1952." Ph.D. diss., Univ. of Massachusetts-Amherst, 1987.

Gates, Joanne Elizabeth, and Victoria Joan Moessner, eds. "Elizabeth Robins' Alaska Diary, 1900." Fales Library, New York University.

Gelb, Barbara. *So Short a Time: A Biography of John Reed and Louise Bryant.* New York: Norton, 1973.

George, Henry. *Progress and Poverty.* New York: Random House, 1929.

The German-Bolshevik Conspiracy. War Information Series, No. 20. Washington, D.C.: Committee on Public Information, October 1918.

Gladden, Washington. *Social Salvation.* Boston and New York: Houghton Mifflin, 1902.

Goldman, Eric F. *Rendezvous with Destiny: A History of Modern American Reform.* New York: Alfred A. Knopf, 1952.

"Good Men in Office." *The Public* 13, no. 643 (29 July 1910): 699.

Graham, Otis L., Jr. *An Encore for Reform: The Old Progressives and the New Deal.* New York: Oxford Univ. Press, 1967.

Graves, William S. *America's Siberian Adventure, 1918–1920.* New York: Jonathan Cape and Harrison Smith, 1931.

Gruening, Ernest. *An Alaskan Reader, 1867–1967.* New York: Meredith Press, 1966.

Hagedorn, Herman. *The Magnate: William Boyce Thompson and His Time, 1869–1930.* New York: John Day Co., 1935.

Hard, William. *Raymond Robins' Own Story.* First serialized in the *Chicago Daily News,* July 1919. New York: Harper and Bros., 1920.

———. "Anti-Bolsheviks: Mr. Lansing." *The New Republic* 19, no. 243 (2 July 1919).

———. "The Testimony of Raymond Robins." *The New Republic* 18, no. 230 (29 March 1919): 261–63.

Harper, Paul V., ed. *The Russia I Believe In: The Memoirs of Samuel N. Harper, 1902–1941.* Chicago: Univ. of Chicago Press, 1945.

Henderson, Charles R. *Social Settlements.* New York: Lentilhon, 1899.

Hicks, Granville. *John Reed: The Making of a Revolutionary.* New York: Macmillan, 1936.

Hinsie, Leland E., and Robert J. Campbell. *Psychiatric Dictionary.* New York and London: Oxford Univ. Press, 1981.

Hofstadter, Richard. *The Age of Reform, From Bryan to F.D.R.* New York: Random, 1955.

———. *The Progressive Movement, 1900–1915.* Englewood Cliffs, N.J.: Prentice Hall, 1963.

Hopkins, Charles Howard. *The Rise of the Social Gospel in American Protestantism, 1865–1915.* New Haven, Conn.: Yale Univ. Press, 1940.

Huie, A. J. "Open Letter to Raymond Robins." *The Public* 19, no. 967 (13 September 1916): 976–77.

Hunter, Robert. *Tenement Conditions in Chicago, 1901, Report by the Investigating Committee of the City Homes Association.* Chicago: City Homes Assn., 1901.

Ickes, Harold. *Autobiography of a Curmudgeon.* New York: Reynal and Hitchcock, 1943.

———. "Who Killed the Progressive Party." *American Historical Review* 46, no. 2 (January 1941): 306.

James, Edward T. *Papers of the Women's Trade Union League and its Principal Leaders: Guide to the Microfilm Edition.* Woodbridge, Conn.: Research Publishers, 1981.

Jordan, Philip. "Letters from Russia, 1917–1919." *Missouri Historical Society Bulletin* 14 (January 1958): 139–66.

Kellor, Frances. *Security Against War, International Controversies, Arbitration, Disarmament, Outlawry.* New York: Macmillan, 1924.

Kennan, George F. *Russia and the West Under Lenin and Stalin.* London: Hutchinson, 1961.

———. *Soviet-American Relations, 1917–1920.* Vol. 1, *Russia Leaves the War.* Vol. 2, *The Decision to Intervene.* Princeton, N.J.: Princeton Univ. Press, 1956–58.

———. "Soviet Historiography and America's Role in the Intervention." *The American Historical Review* 64 (January 1960): 302.

Kerensky, Alexander. *The Prelude to Bolshevism: The Kornilov Rising.* New York: Haskell House, 1927.

———. *The Catastrophy: Kerensky's Own Story of the Russian Revolution.* New York: D. Appleton, 1927.

———. *The Crucifiction of Liberty.* New York: John Day Co., 1934.

Kettle, Michael. *Russia and the Allies 1917–1920.* 2 vols. New York: Routledge, Chapman and Hall, 1986–88.

King, David. *Trotsky, A Photographic Biography.* New York: B. Blackwell, 1986.

Knox, Alfred. *With the Russian Army, 1914–1917: Being Chiefly Extracts from the Diary of a Militrary Attaché.* 2 vols. London: Hutchinson, 1921.

Kolko, Gabriel. *The Triumph of Conservatism: A Reinterpretation of American History, 1900–1916.* New York: Free Press, 1963.

Kraditor, Aileen S. *The Ideas of the Woman Suffrage Movement: 1890–1920.* New York: Norton, 1981.

Kraut, Alan M. *The Huddled Masses: The Immigrant in American Society, 1880–1921.* Arlington Hts., Ill.: Harlan Davidson, 1982.

"Labor Federation of Illinois." *The Public* 11, no. 552 (30 September 1908): 731–32.

La Follette, Robert M. *Autobiography.* 3d ed. Madison, Wisc.: Robert M. La Follette Co., 1939.

Lasch, Christopher. *The American Liberals and The Russian Revolution.* New York and London: Columbia Univ. Press, 1962.

———. *The New Radicalism in America, 1889–1963.* New York: Alfred A. Knopf, 1965.

———. *The Agony of the American Left.* New York and London: Alfred A. Knopf, 1969.

Lenin, V. I. *Collected Works.* 36 vols. London and Moscow: Lawrence and Wishart and Progress Publishers, 1965.

Leuchtenberg, William E. "Progressivism and Imperialism: The Progressive Movement and American Foreign Policy, 1898–1916." *Mississippi Valley Historical Review* 39, no. 3 (December 1952): 483–503.

Levin, N. Gordon. *Woodrow Wilson and World Politics.* New York: Oxford Univ. Press, 1968.

Levine, Lawrence W. *Defender of the Faith, William Jennings Bryan: The Last Decade, 1915-1925.* New York: Oxford Univ. Press, 1965.

Levinson, Salmon O. *Outlawry of War.* Senate Document No. 115, Washington, D.C.: 1922.

Lewis, O. R. "A National Committee on Vagrants." *Charities and the Commons* 28 (29 June 1907): 342-44.

Libbey, James K. *Alexander Gumberg and Soviet-American Relations, 1917-1933.* Lexington: Univ. of Kentucky Press, 1977.

Link, Arthur S. *Woodrow Wilson and the Progressive Era, 1910-1917.* New York: Harper and Bros., 1954.

_____, ed. *Woodrow Wilson and a Revolutionary World, 1913-1921.* Chapel Hill: Univ. of North Carolina Press, 1982.

Link, Arthur S., and William M. Leary, Jr. *The Progressive Era and the Great War, 1896-1920.* New York: Appleton Century-Crofts, 1969.

Link, Arthur S., and Richard McCormick. *Progressivism.* Arlington Hts., Ill.: Harlan Davidson, 1983.

Lockhart, Robert H. Bruce. "L. D. Trotsky: A Pen Portrait." *The Fortnightly Review* 239 (April 1923): 295-311.

_____. "Lenin: The Man and His Achievement." *The Edinburgh Review* 239 (April 1923): 295-311.

_____. *Memoirs of A British Agent: Being An Account of the Author's Early Life in Many Lands and of His Official Mission to Moscow in 1918.* London: Putnam, 1932.

_____. *Retreat From Glory.* London: Putnam, 1934.

_____. *The Two Revolutions: An Eye-Witness Study of Russia, 1917.* London: Phoenix House, 1957.

Longstreet, Stephen. *Chicago, 1860-1919.* New York: McKay, 1973.

Lynd, Staughton. "Jane Addams and the Radical Impulse." *Commentary* 32 (July 1961): 54-59.

Maddux, Thomas R. *Years of Estrangement: American Relations with the Soviet Union, 1933-1941.* Gainesville: Univ. Presses of Florida, 1980.

Manning, Clarence Augustus. *The Siberian Fiasco.* New York: Library Publishers, 1952.

Martin, James Arnold. "Raymond Robins and the Progressive Movement: The Study of a Progressive Reformer." D.S.W. diss., Tulane University, 1975.

Maxwell, Robert S. *La Follette and the Rise of the Progressives in Wisconsin.* Madison: State Historical Society of Wisconsin, 1956.

Mayer, Arno J. *Political Origins of the New Diplomacy.* New Haven, Conn.: Yale Univ. Press, 1959.

McCloskey, Robert G. *American Conservatism in the Age of Enterprise.* Cambridge, Mass.: Harvard Univ. Press, 1951.

McKenna, Marian C. *Borah.* Ann Arbor: Univ. of Michigan Press, 1961.

Meiburger, Sister Anne Vincent. *Efforts of Raymond Robins Toward the Recognition of Soviet Russia and the Outlawry of War, 1917-1933.* Washington, D.C.: Catholic Univ. of America Press, 1958.

"Men and Religion Movement to Circle Globe." *The Survey* 29, no. 3 (19 October 1912): 86.

Merriam, Charles E. Letter, *The Congregationalist,* 27 October 1932.

_____. *Chicago, A More Intimate View of Urban Politics.* New York: Macmillan, 1929.

Miller, David Hunter. *The Peace Pact of Paris.* New York: Putnam's, 1928.

Miller, Joan S. "The Politics of Municipal Reform in Chicago During the Progressive Era, The Municipal Voters League as a Test Case, 1896–1920." Master's thesis, Roosevelt University, 1966.

Mock, James R., and Cedric Larson. *Words That Won the War: The Story of the Committee on Public Information, 1917–1919*. Princeton, N.J.: Princeton Univ. Press, 1939.

Morgan, H. Wayne. *Eugene V. Debs, Socialist for President*. Syracuse, N.Y.: Syracuse Univ. Press, 1962.

———. "Eugene Debs and the Socialist Campaign of 1912." *Mid-America* 39 (1957): 210–25.

Morrison, Charles Clayton. *Outlawry of War: A Constructive Policy for World Peace*. Chicago: Willett, Clark and Colby, 1927.

Mowry, George E. *Theodore Roosevelt and the Progressive Movement*. Madison: Univ. of Wisconsin Press, 1947.

———. *The Era of Theodore Roosevelt and the Birth of Modern America, 1900–1912*. New York: Harper, 1958.

Muscatine, Doris. *Old San Francisco: The Biography of a City, from Early Days to the Earthquake*. New York: Putnam's, 1975.

Myers, Phillip Van Ness. *A General History for Colleges and High Schools*. Boston: Ginn, 1895.

Naske, Claus M. *An Interpretative History of Alaskan Statehood*. Anchorage, Ala.: Northwest, 1973.

Naske, Claus M., and Herman E. Slotnick. *Alaska: A History of the Forty-ninth State*. Grand Rapids, Mich.: Eerdmans, 1979.

"National Popular Government League Indorses [sic] Robins." *The Public* 17, no. 863 (9 September 1914): 975–76.

Nestor, Agnes. *Woman's Labor Leader: Autobiography of Agnes Nestor*. Rockford, Ill.: Bellevue Books, 1954.

Noble, David W. *The Progressive Mind, 1890–1917*. Chicago: Rand McNally, 1970.

Nock, Albert J. "Raymond Robins." *American Magazine* 7 (November 1910): 41.

Noulens, Joseph. *Mon Ambassade en Ruisse Sovietique, 1917–1919*. 2 vols. Paris: Librarie Plon, 1933.

O'Connor, Richard, and Dale L. Walker. *The Lost Revolutionary: A Biography of John Reed*. New York: Harcourt Brace, 1967.

Payne, Elizabeth A. *Reform, Labor and Feminism: Margaret Dreier Robins and the National Women's Trade Union League*. Urbana: Univ. of Illinois Press, 1988.

Payne, Robert. *The Life and Death of Lenin*. New York: Simon and Schuster, 1964.

Philpott, Thomas Lee. *The Slum and the Ghetto: Neighborhood Deterioration and Middle Class Reform, Chicago 1880–1930*. New York: Oxford Univ. Press, 1978.

Pinchot, Amos. *History of the Progressive Party 1912–1916*. New York: New York Univ. Press, 1958.

Post, Louis F. *Raymond Robins, A Biographical Sketch: With Newspaper Accounts of and Comments on Mr. Robins' Work*. Chicago: 1908.

Proceedings of the Brest-Litovsk Peace Conference: The Peace Negotiations Between Russia and the Central Powers, 21 November 1917–3 March 1918, Washington, D.C.: 1918.

Proceedings of the National Conference of Charities and Correction. N.p., 1907.

"The Progressive Convention." *The Public* 19, no. 950 (16 June 1916): 562–63.

Progressive State Committee of Illinois. *Raymond Robins—Progressive Nominee for U.S. Senator from Illinois*. Chicago: 1914.

———. *The Story of Raymond Robins' Life*. Chicago, 1914.

Prussing, Eugene. *Municipal Ownership and Municipal Operation of the Street Railways.* Chicago: City Club, 1906.

Pusey, Merlo J. *Charles Evans Hughes.* 2 vols. New York: Macmillan, 1907.

Quinby, L. J. "Raymond Robins in Omaha." *The Public* 10, no. 520 (21 March 1908): 1209–10.

Ransome, Arthur. *Russia in 1919.* New York: B. W. Huebsch, 1919.

Rauschenbusch, Walter. *Christianity and the Social Crisis.* New York: Hodder and Staughton, 1911.

_____. *Christianizing the Social Order.* New York: Macmillan, 1913.

Raymond, C. S. "Raymond Robins." *Chicago Tribune,* 29 October 1914.

"Raymond Robins as an Evangelist." *The Public* 19, no. 931 (4 February 1916): 105.

"Raymond Robins Challenged." *The Public* 19, no. 964 (2 September 1916): 899.

"Raymond Robins Deserving of Democratic Support." *The Public* 17, no. 852 (31 July 1914): 726.

"Raymond Robins for Hughes." *The Public* 19, no. 956 (11 August 1916): 748.

"Raymond Robins Visits Pittsburgh." *The Survey* 29, no. 12 (12 December 1912): 367.

Recognition of Russia, Hearings before a Subcommittee of the Committee on Foreign Relations. 65th Cong., 3d sess. Washington, D.C., 1919.

Reed, John. *Ten Days That Shook The World.* New York: Boni and Liveright, 1919.

Reid, Hugh. "The Passing of Raymond Robins." Letter to the editor. *The Public* 19, no. 958 (11 August 1916): 752.

Relations with Russia, Hearings before the Committee on Foreign Relations. 66th Cong., 3d sess. Washington, D.C., 1921.

Roberts, Sidney I. "The Municipal Voters League and Chicago Boodlers." *Journal of the Illinois State Historical Society* 53, no. 2 (Summer 1960): 117–48.

Robins, Elizabeth (C. E. Raimond, pseud.). *The Open Question: A Tale of Two Temperaments.* London: William Heineman, 1898.

_____. *The Magnetic North.* New York: William Heineman, 1904.

_____. "Monica's Village." *The Century Magazine* 70, no. 1 (May 1905): 19–30.

_____. *Come and Find Me.* New York: William Heineman, 1908.

_____. *My Little Sister.* New York: Dodd Mead, 1913.

_____. *Both Sides of the Curtain.* London: William Heineman, 1940.

_____. *Raymond and I.* New York: Macmillan, 1956.

Robins, Margaret Dreier. Review of *The Long Day,* by Dorothy Richardson. *Charities and the Commons* 17 (1906): 484–85.

"Robins on Russia." *The Survey* 41, no. 26 (29 March 1919): 962.

"Robins' Popularity." *The Commercial News,* Chicago, 20 October 1914.

Rodgers, Daniel. "In Search of Progressivism." *Reviews in American History.* 10, no. 4 (1982): 113–32.

Rosenstone, Robert A. *Romantic Revolutionary: A Biography of John Reed.* New York: Alfred A. Knopf, 1975.

Ross, Edward A. *The Russian Bolshevik Revolution.* New York: Century Co., 1921.

_____. *The Russian Soviet Republic.* New York: Century Co., 1923.

Ruddy, T. Michael. *The Cautious Diplomat: Charles E. Bohlen and the Soviet Union, 1919–1969.* Kent, Ohio: Kent State Univ. Press, 1986.

"Russian Extradition." *The Public* 11, no. 557 (4 December 1908): 843–44.

Sadoul, Jacques. *The Socialist Soviet Republic of Russia, Its Rise and Organization.* London: People's Russian Information Bureau, 1918.

_____. *Notes sur la Revolution Bolchevique.* Paris: Editions de la Sirene, 1920.

———. *Quarante Lettres de Jacques Sadoul.* Paris: Editions de la Librarie Humanité, 1922.

———. *Naissance de l'U.R.S.S.* Vol. 1. Paris: Charlot, 1946.

Salvatore, Nick. *Eugene V. Debs, Citizen and Socialist.* Urbana: Univ. of Illinois Press, 1982.

Sayers, Michael, and Albert E. Kahn. *The Great Conspiracy Against Russia.* New York: Boni and Gaer, 1946.

Schlesinger, Arthur M., and Fred L. Israel, eds. *The State of the Union Messages of the Presidents, 1790–1966.* New York: Chelsea House, 1966.

Schmidt, John R. *"The Mayor Who Cleaned Up Chicago," A Political Biography of William E. Dever.* DeKalb: Northern Illinois Univ. Press, 1989.

Schuman, Frederick Lewis. *American Policy Toward Russia Since 1917.* New York: International Publishers, 1928.

"Senator Sherman and the Single Tax." *The Public* 17, no. 861 (2 September 1914): 941–42.

Seymour, Charles. *The Intimate Papers of Colonel House.* Vol. 3. *Into the World War, April 1917–June 1918.* New York: Houghton Mifflin, 1928.

Shelton, Brenda K. *President Wilson and the Russian Revolution.* Buffalo Studies, vol. 23, no. 3. Monographs in History, no. 7. Buffalo: State Univ. of New York, 1957.

Sikes, George C. "For the Honor of Illinois—Why Sullivan and Sherman Should be Defeated and Raymond Robins Elected U.S. Senator." Chicago: Raymond Robins Democratic League, 1914.

Silverlight, John. *The Victors Dilemma: Allied Intervention in the Russian Civil War.* London: Barrie and Jenkins, 1970.

Sisson, Edgar. *One Hundred Red Days: A Personal Chronicle of the Bolshevik Revolution.* New Haven, Conn.: Yale Univ. Press, 1931.

Smith, Fred B. "About Raymond Robins." *The Congregationalist* (27 October 1932): 1391–93.

———. "The 'Forward Movement.'" *The Survey* 28, no. 1 (6 April 1912): 33.

Soskice, Victor. "The Red Guard Takes a Hand." *Metropolitan Magazine* (August 1918): 21–22.

———. "A Message to Kerensky." *Metropolitan Magazine* (September 1918): 29–31.

Steffens, Lincoln. *Autobiography.* New York: Harcourt Brace, 1931.

———. *The Shame of the Cities.* 1905. Reprint. New York: Hill and Wang, 1957.

Stoner, John Edgar. *Salmon O. Levinson and the Pact of Paris: A Study in the Technique of Influence.* Chicago: Univ. of Chicago Press, 1943.

Strakhovsky, Leonid Ivan. *Intervention at Archangel: The Story of Allied Intervention and Russian Counter-Revolution in North Russia, 1918–1920.* Princeton, N.J.: Princeton Univ. Press, 1944.

———. *The Origins of American Intervention in North Russia, 1918.* Princeton, N.J.: Princeton Univ. Press, 1937.

Taft, Philip. *Organized Labor in American History.* New York: Harper and Row, 1964.

Taylor, Graham. *Pioneering on Social Frontiers.* Chicago: Univ. of Chicago Press, 1930.

———. *Chicago Commons Through Forty Years.* Chicago: Chicago Commons Assn., 1936.

Thacher, Thomas D. "Economic Force and the Russian Problem." *The Annals of the American Academy of Political and Social Science* 84 (July 1919).

———. "Russia and the War." New York: Privately printed pamphlet, 1918.

Thelen, David. *Robert M. La Follette and the Insurgent Spirit.* Boston: Little, Brown, 1976.

Trotsky, Leon. *From October to Brest-Litovsk.* London: Allen and Unwin, 1919.

————. *Lenin*. London: Minton Balch, 1925.

————. *My Life*. New York: Scribner's, 1930.

————. *The History of the Russian Revolution*. 3 vols. New York: Simon and Schuster, 1932.

Ullman, Richard H. *Anglo-Soviet Relations, 1917–1921*. Vol. 1. *Intervention and the War*. Princeton, N.J.: Princeton Univ. Press, 1971.

Unterberger, Betty Miller. *American Intervention in the Russian Civil War*. Lexington, Mass.: D. C. Heath, 1969.

U.S. Department of State. *Papers Relating to the Foreign Relations of the United States: The Lansing Papers, 1914–1920*. 2 vols. Washington, D.C.: 1939–40.

————. *Papers Relating to the Foreign Relations of the United States: 1918, Russia*. 3 vols. Washington, D.C.: 1931–32.

————. *Papers Relating to the Foreign Relations of the United States: 1919, Russia*. Washington, D.C.: 1937.

————. *Records of the Department of State Relating to Internal Affairs of Russia and the Soviet Union: 1910–1929*. General Records of the Department of State, Record Group 59, National Archives, National Archives Microfilm Publication, M 316. 177 rolls. Washington, D.C.: 1971.

Vanderwende, Peter. "The 'Old Guard' Still Alive." Letter to the editor. *The Public* 19, no. 960 (25 August 1916): 801.

Van Tassel, David D., and John J. Grabowski, eds. *Cleveland: A Tradition of Reform*. Kent, Ohio: Kent State Univ. Press, 1986.

Varneck, E., and Harold H. Fisher, eds. *The Testimony of Kolchak and Other Siberia Materials*. Stanford, Calif.: Stanford Univ. Press, 1935.

Vinson, John C. *William E. Borah and the Outlawry of War*. Athens: Univ. of Georgia Press, 1957.

Wade, Louise C. *Graham Taylor: Pioneer for Social Justice, 1851–1938*. Chicago: Univ. of Chicago Press, 1964.

Walforth, Arthur. "The President's Mind." Review of *Too Proud to Fight: Woodrow Wilson's Neutrality*, by Patrick Devlin. *Yale Review* (Spring 1975): 443–50.

Ward, John. *With the "Die-Hards" in Siberia*. New York: George H. Doran, 1920.

Warth, Robert D. *The Allies and the Russian Revolution*. Durham, N.C.: Duke Univ. Press, 1954.

Wheeler-Bennett, John W. *The Forgotten Peace: Brest-Litovsk, March, 1918*. New York: William Morrow, 1939.

Whelpley, J. D. "Russia's Soviet Government." *Fortnightly Review*, October 1925.

White, John Albert. *The Siberian Intervention*. Princeton, N.J.: Princeton Univ. Press, 1950.

Wiebe, Robert H. *The Search for Order, 1877–1920*. New York: Hill and Wang, 1967.

Wilde, Arthur H. *Northwest University: A History, 1855–1905*. New York: University Publishing, 1905.

Williams, Albert Rhys. *Lenin: The Man and His Work and the Impressions of Colonel Raymond Robins and Arthur Ransome*. New York: Scott and Seltzer, 1919.

————. *Through the Russian Revolution*. New York: Boni and Liveright, 1921.

————. *The Soviets*. New York: Harcourt Brace, 1937.

————. *Journey Into Revolution: Petrograd, 1917–1918*. Chicago: Quadrangle Books, 1969.

Williams, William Appleman. *American-Russian Relations, 1781–1947*. New York: Rinehart, 1952.

————. "The Outdoor Mind." *The Nation* 179 (30 October 1954): 384–85.

————. "Raymond Robins and Russian-American Relations, 1917–1938," Ph.D. diss., Univ. of Wisconsin-Madison, 1950.

Woods, Robert A., and Albert J. Kennedy, eds. *Handbook of Settlements.* Charities Publication Committee, Russell Sage Foundation, 1911. Reprint. New York: Arno Press, 1970.

Yellin, Samuel. *American Labor Struggles.* New York: Harcourt Brace, 1936.

Young, Kenneth, ed. *The Diaries of Sir Robert Bruce Lockhart: 1915–1938, 1939–1965.* 2 vols. London: St. Martin's, 1973–80.

Index

Seawell, Emmet, 31
Security Against War (1924). *See* Kellor, Frances
Semenov, Gregory M., 276
Senate Foreign Relations Committee, 314, 327
Separate peace, 204. *See also* Brest-Litovsk, Treaty of
Serebreakov, 356, 366
Settlement house, 2, 66–67, 86, 119, 395n. 6; and Toynebee Hall, 65; and research role, 73–74; reform limitations of, 139
Seventeenth Ward (of Chicago): and political corruption, 2; Robins's home, 66, 111; and political reform work, 119–20. *See also Appendix A*
Shalyapina, Eugenia Petrovna (Mrs. Arthur Ransome), 234
The Shame of the Cities (1905). *See* Steffens, Lincoln
Sharpe, Lawrence, 387–88n. 10, 434n. 14
Shaw, George Bernard, 46
Sherman Anti-Trust Act, 147
Sherman, Lawrence F., 154
Shotwell, James T., 326
"Show trials," 366
Shulte, Albert F., 35, 391n. 6
Silbert, 44
Simons, Algie M., 94, 292
Single tax, 107, 112, 398n. 14, 407n. 9; and MRFM, 109; and Roosevelt, 141, 405n. 17; and 1914 campaign, 155–57
Sisson, Edgar, 249, 252, 266, 430n. 17; and COMPUB, 223–24, 265; and Bolsheviks, 226–27; and Lenin, 227, 228, 231, 420n. 7; *One Hundred Red Days,* 354
Slavery, 321
Smith, Alfred E., 329
Smith, Charles H., 361
Smith, Fred B., 111; and MRFM, 109, 113, 146, 195
Smoke Abatement Committee, 74
Smolny Institute, 204, 206–8, 413n. 26
Smulsky, John, 124, 402n. 15
Snow Hill, Florida, 16, 78–79, 103
"Snow-white cross," 40–41, 44, 48
Social gospel, 2, 79, 105, 400n. 16; and Socialist party, 95; and Progressive movement, 138; and social justice in Russia, 212; vs. bolshevism, 296
Socialism: criticized, 94, 101, 111, 397n. 12,

413n. 20; origin of Robins's opinions, 398n. 12; and Free Floor Forum, 120; and WWI, 414n. 36
"Socialism in one country," 294, 356
Socialist party, 95, 144
Socialist-Revolutionaries (SRs), 185, 235
Social Salvation (1902). *See* Gladden, Washington
Social Security and guaranteed pensions, 74
Social service, 88, 161
Social Settlements (1899). *See* Henderson, C. R.
"Some Observations on the Present Conditions in Russia," 185
Sophia T., 35
Soskice, David, 188–89, 200
Southerland, George, 312
Southern Pacific Railroad, 32
Soviet Politics at Home and Abroad (1946), 374
Soviet Union: government as of May 1918, 280, 314, 353
Soviet of Workers' and Soldiers' Deputies, 179, 218, 247, 293, 416n. 18; at All-Russian conference, 191, 205; and Kornilov Uprising, 194; and mass support, 195–96, 205; and Provisional Government, 196; and Brest-Litovsk treaty, 239, 243–49; and Bolshevik party, 292
Spanish civil war, 368
Spargo, John, 292
Speeches, Robins's: "Why I Believe in Organized Labor," 25–26; "Three Opposing Forces in Industrialism," 397n. 10; National Protest Meeting speech in Danbury Hatters case, 91–92, 95–98; "The Association and the Forces That Tend to Disintegrate Faith and Character" (1916), 399n. 2; list of (1908), 135–36, 400n. 10, 401n. 30, 403n. 40; 404n. 57; and impact, 401n. 25; as battles, 112; and methods used, 116; while in Russia, 414n. 30; at Orenbaum barracks, 415n. 10; about Soviet Russia, 289, 296–98, 416nn. 10, 17, 428n. 5; about disarmament, 302, 318; on international law, 303, 318, 320; and recognition, 320, 352; subjects (1931), 435n. 25
Spreckeles, Rudolph, 30
Springer, Margaret, 71
Stalin, Josif Dzhugashvili, 356–57, 360, 367, 371; and Dukhonin, 221; and collectivization, 230; and Diamandi, 239; and "show trials," 366; and Trotsky, 368–69; and

REFORM AND REVOLUTION

was composed in 10/12 Palatino on a Varityper system
by Professional Book Compositors, Inc.;
printed by sheet-fed offset on 50-pound, acid free,
Glatfelter B-16 paper stock,
Smyth sewn and bound over .088″ binders' boards
in Holliston Kingston Natural cloth,
and wrapped with dust jackets printed in three colors
on 80-pound enamel stock and film laminated
by BookCrafters, Inc.;
designed by Will Underwood;
and published by

THE KENT STATE UNIVERSITY PRESS
Kent, Ohio 44242